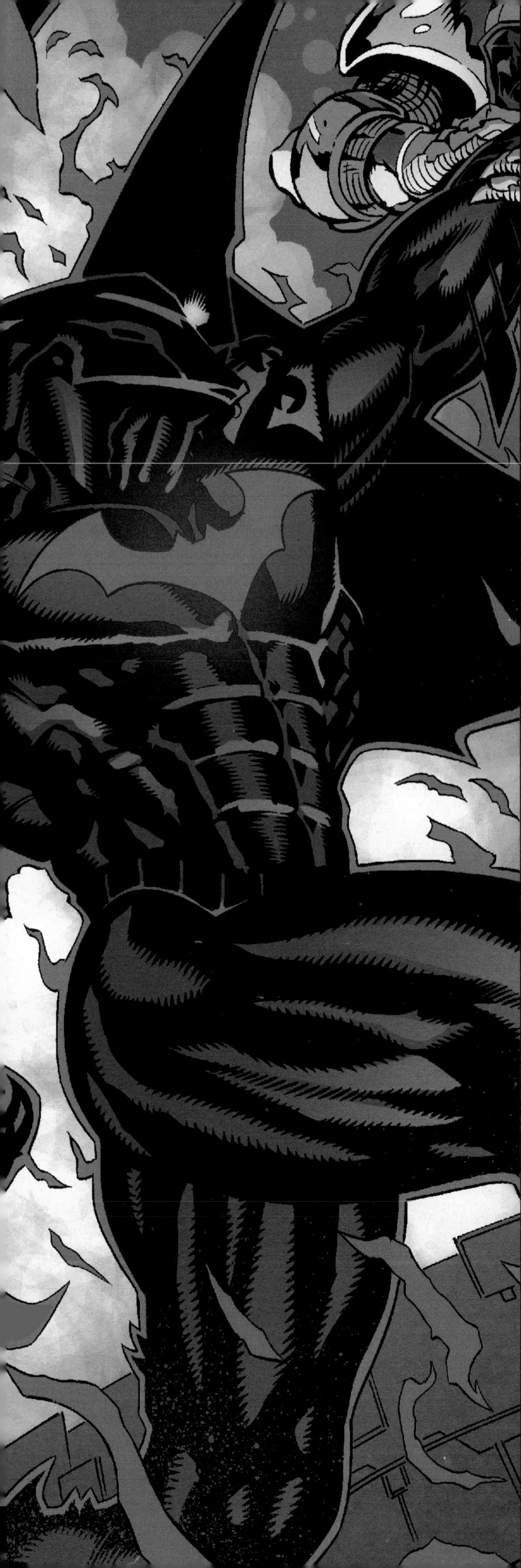

BATMAN AND ROBIN

VOLUME 7
ROBIN

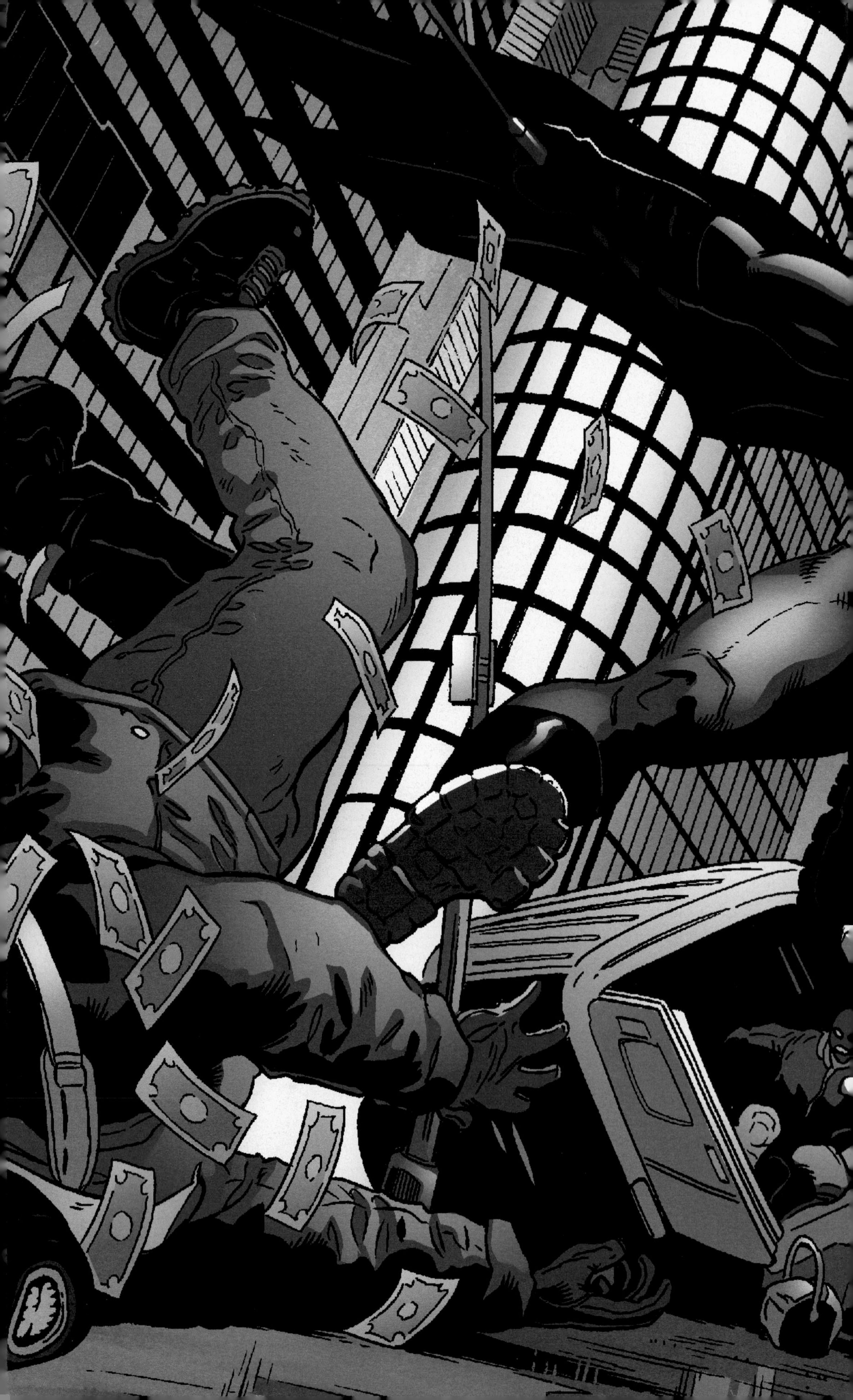

VOLUME 7
ROBIN
RISES

WRITER
PETER J. TOMASI

PENCILLERS
**PATRICK GLEASON
ANDY KUBERT
JUAN JOSÉ RYP
IAN BERTRAM**

INKERS
**MICK GRAY
JONATHAN GLAPION
ANDY KUBERT
JUAN JOSÉ RYP
JORDI TARRAGONA
JUAN ALBARRAN**

COLORISTS
**JOHN KALISZ
BRAD ANDERSON
SONIA OBACK
DAVE STEWART**

LETTERERS
**CARLOS M. MANGUAL
DEZI SIENTY
TOM NAPOLITANO
STEVE WANDS**

COLLECTION COVER ARTISTS
**PATRICK GLEASON, MICK GRAY
AND JOHN KALISZ**

BATMAN CREATED BY BOB KANE

SUPERMAN CREATED BY
JERRY SIEGEL & JOE SHUSTER.
BY SPECIAL ARRANGEMENT WITH
THE JERRY SIEGEL FAMILY.

BATMAN AND ROBIN

RACHEL GLUCKSTERN Editor – Original Series
DAVE WIELGOSZ, MATT HUMPHREYS Assistant Editors – Original Series
JEB WOODARD Group Editor – Collected Editions
STEVE COOK Design Director – Books
DAMIAN RYLAND Publication Design

BOB HARRAS Senior VP – Editor-in-Chief, DC Comics

DIANE NELSON President
DAN DIDIO and JIM LEE Co-Publishers
GEOFF JOHNS Chief Creative Officer
AMIT DESAI Senior VP – Marketing & Global Franchise Management
NAIRI GARDINER Senior VP – Finance
SAM ADES VP – Digital Marketing
BOBBIE CHASE VP – Talent Development
MARK CHIARELLO Senior VP – Art, Design & Collected Editions
JOHN CUNNINGHAM VP – Content Strategy
ANNE DEPIES VP – Strategy Planning & Reporting
DON FALLETTI VP – Manufacturing Operations
LAWRENCE GANEM VP – Editorial Administration & Talent Relations
ALISON GILL Senior VP – Manufacturing & Operations
HANK KANALZ Senior VP – Editorial Strategy & Administration
JAY KOGAN VP – Legal Affairs
DEREK MADDALENA Senior VP – Sales & Business Development
JACK MAHAN VP – Business Affairs
DAN MIRON VP – Sales Planning & Trade Development
NICK NAPOLITANO VP – Manufacturing Administration
CAROL ROEDER VP – Marketing
EDDIE SCANNELL VP – Mass Account & Digital Sales
COURTNEY SIMMONS Senior VP – Publicity & Communications
JIM (SKI) SOKOLOWSKI VP – Comic Book Specialty & Newsstand Sales
SANDY YI Senior VP – Global Franchise Management

BATMAN AND ROBIN VOLUME 7: ROBIN RISES

DC Comics, 2900 West Alameda Ave., Burbank, CA 91505
Printed by RR Donnelley, Salem, VA, USA. 4/1/16. First Printing.
ISBN: 978-1-4012-6114-6

Library of Congress Cataloging-in-Publication Data

Tomasi, Peter.
Batman and Robin. Volume 7, Robin rises / Peter Tomasi, Patrick Gleason, Andy Kubert.
pages cm. — (The New 52!)
ISBN 978-1-4012-6114-6
1. Graphic novels. I. Gleason, Patrick, illustrator. II. Kubert, Andy, illustrator. III. Title. IV. Title: Robin rises.
PN6728.B36T649 2015
741.5'973--dc23
2015028075

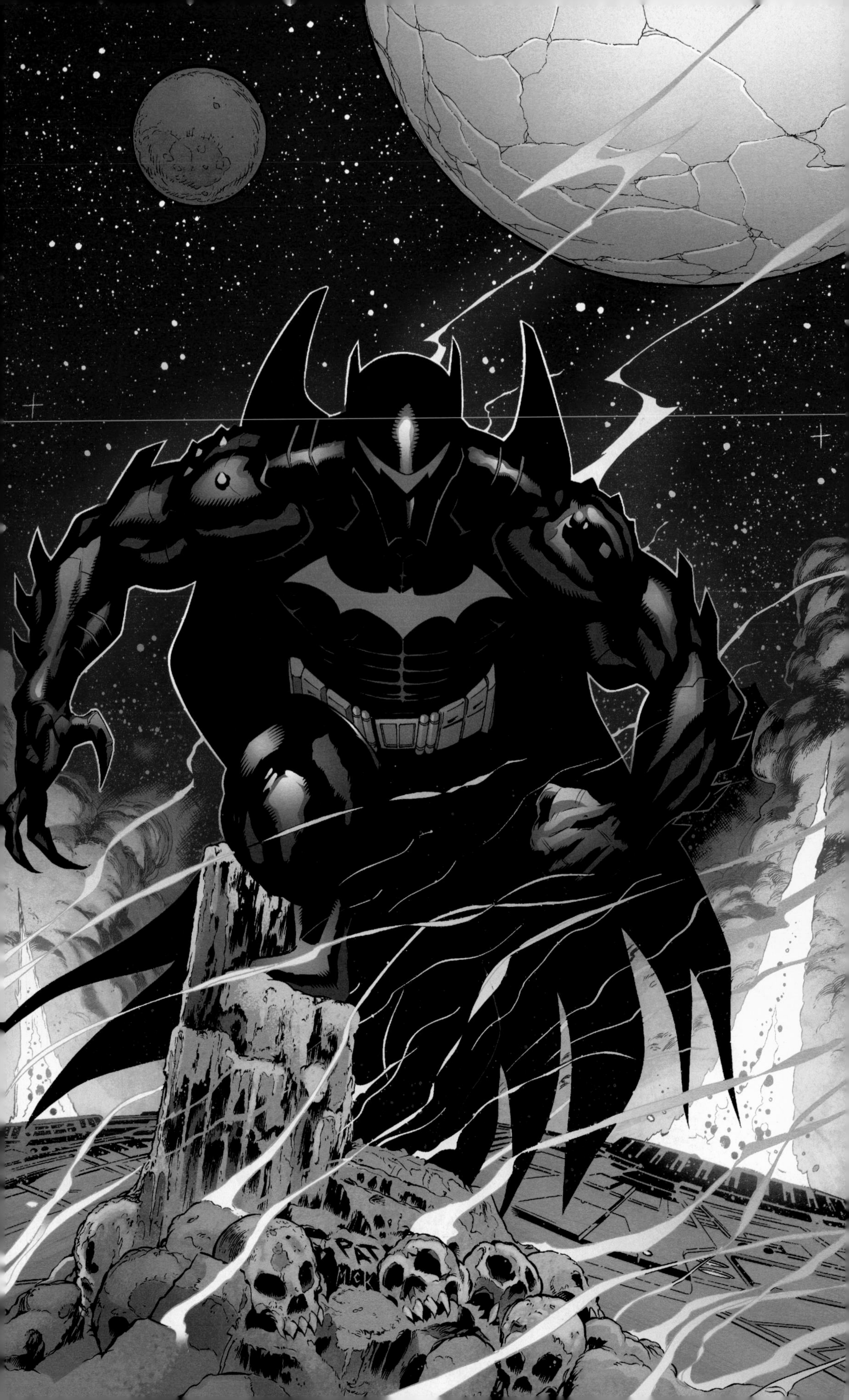

PATRICK GLEASON penciller MICK GRAY inker JOHN KALISZ colorist CARLOS M. MANGUAL letterer cover art by GLEASON, GRAY & KALISZ

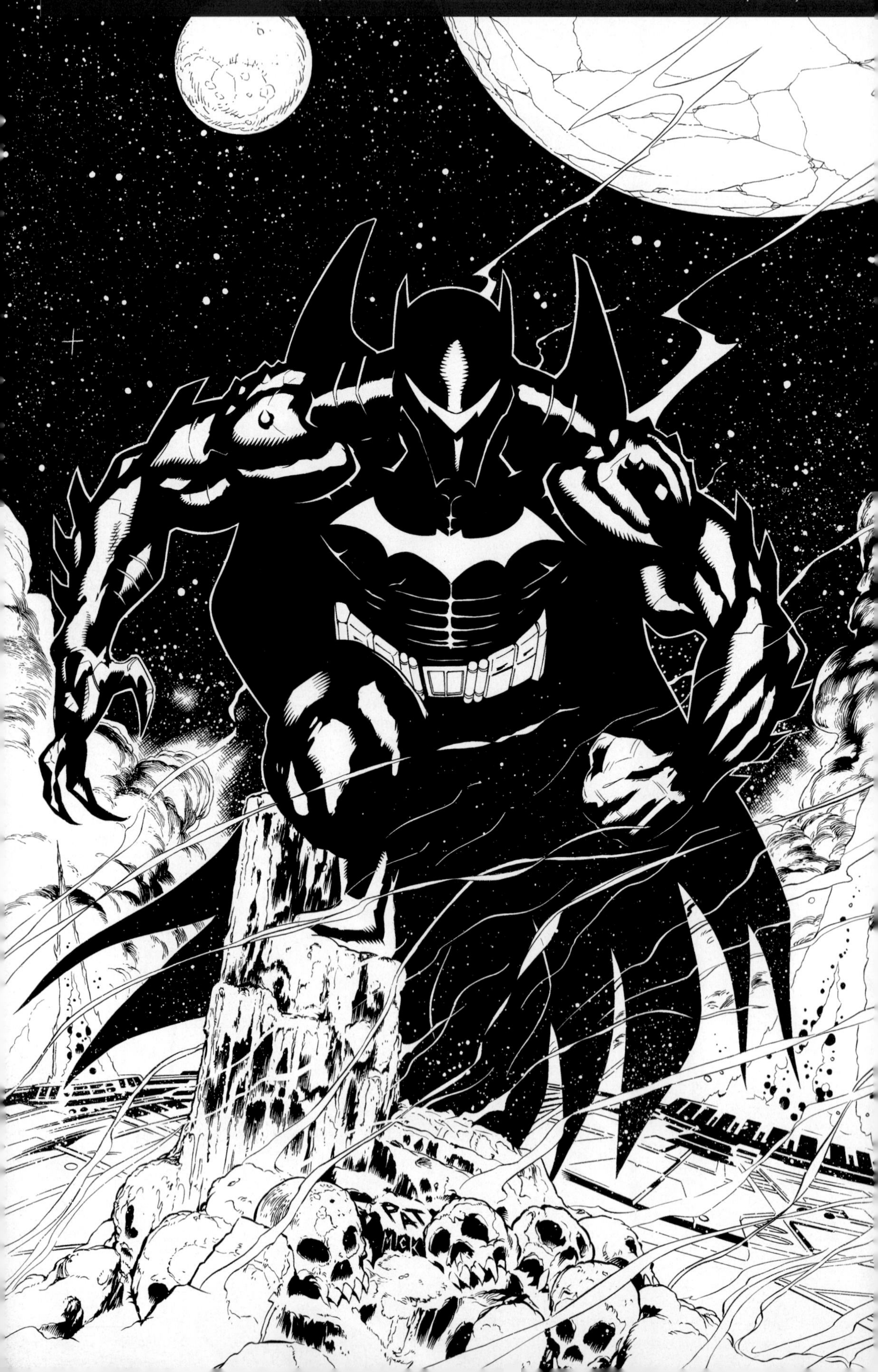

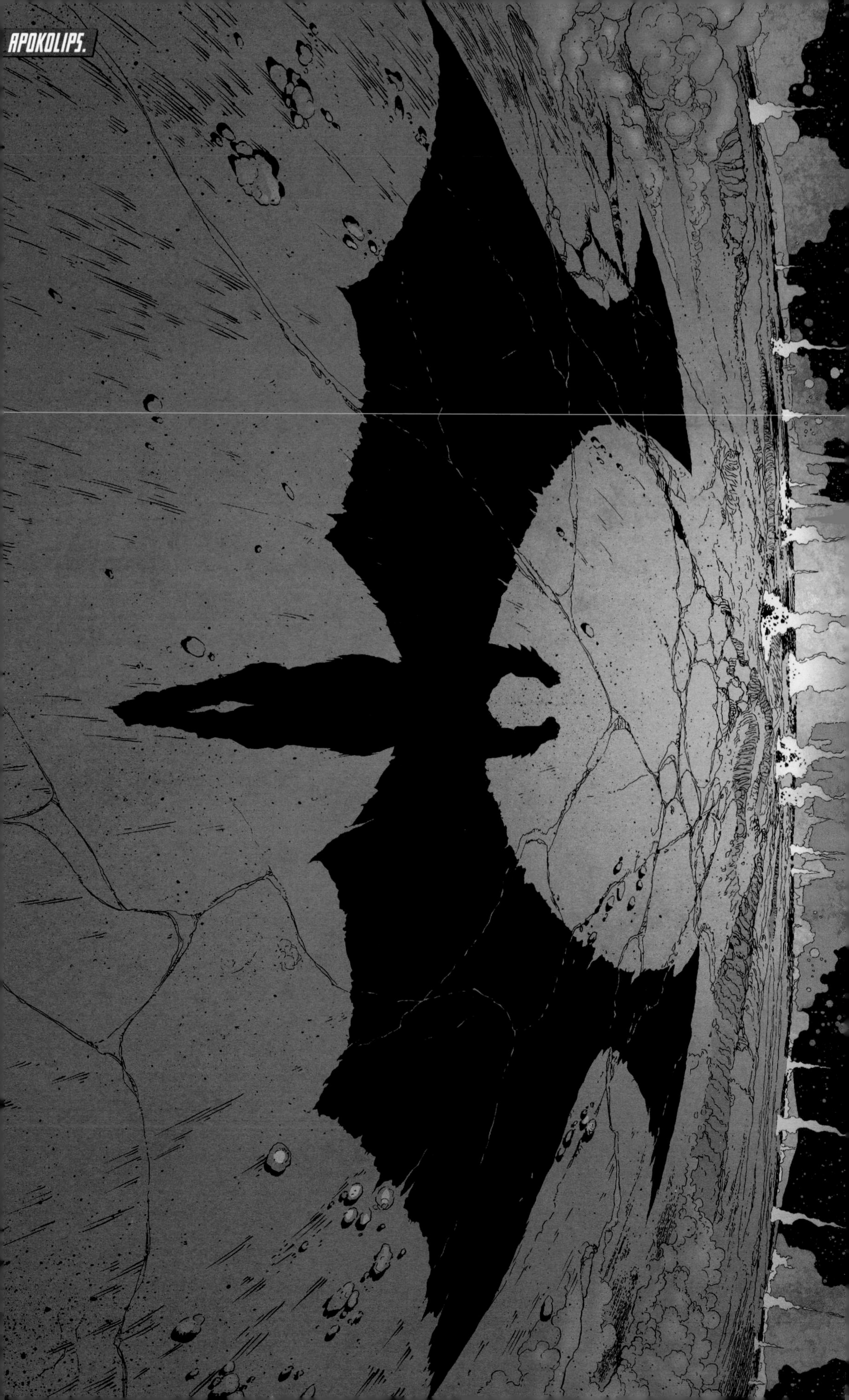
APOKOLIPS.

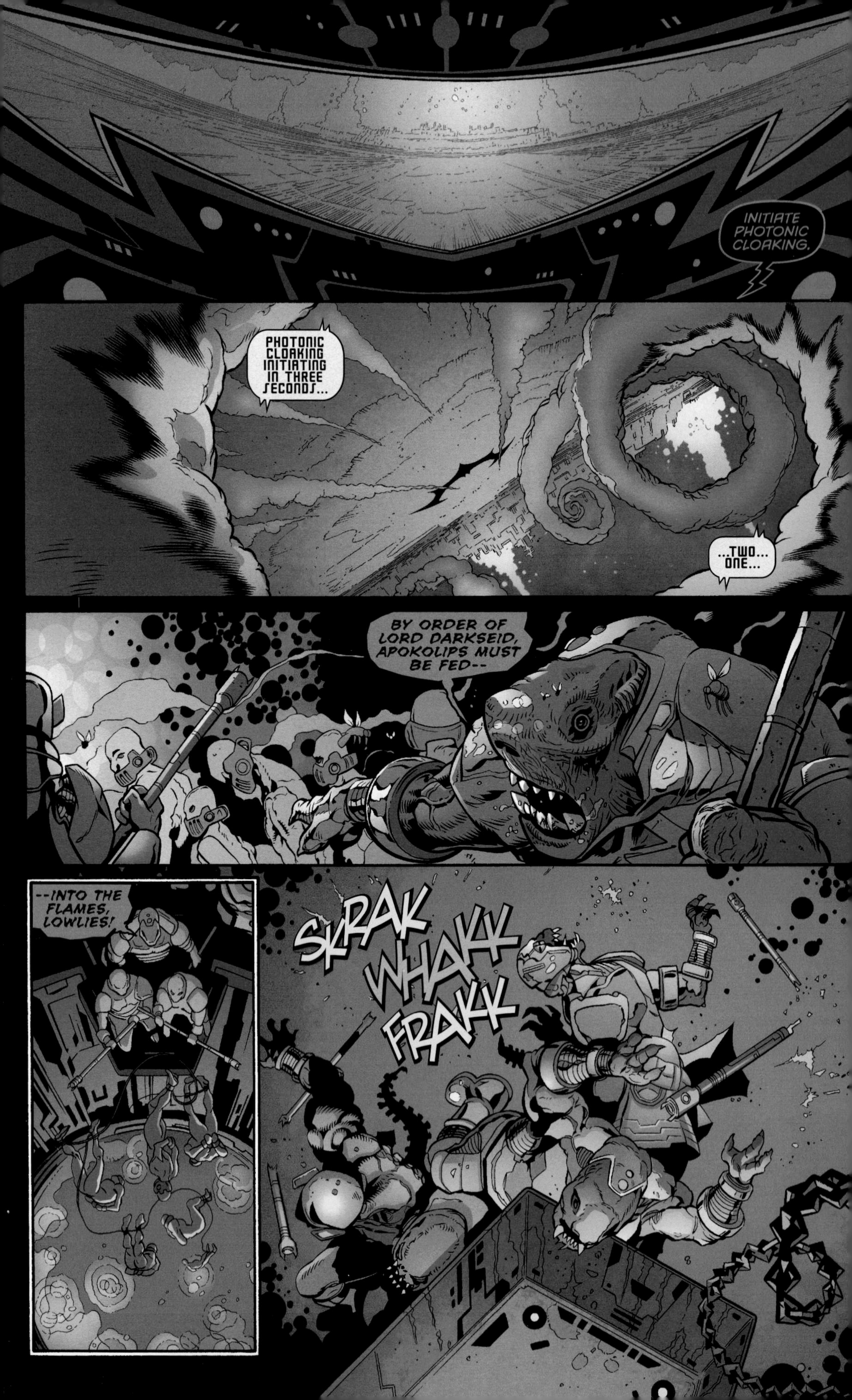
INITIATE PHOTONIC CLOAKING.
PHOTONIC CLOAKING INITIATING IN THREE SECONDS...
...TWO... ONE...
BY ORDER OF LORD DARKSEID, APOKOLIPS MUST BE FED--
--INTO THE FLAMES, LOWLIES!
SKRAK
WHAKK
FRAKK

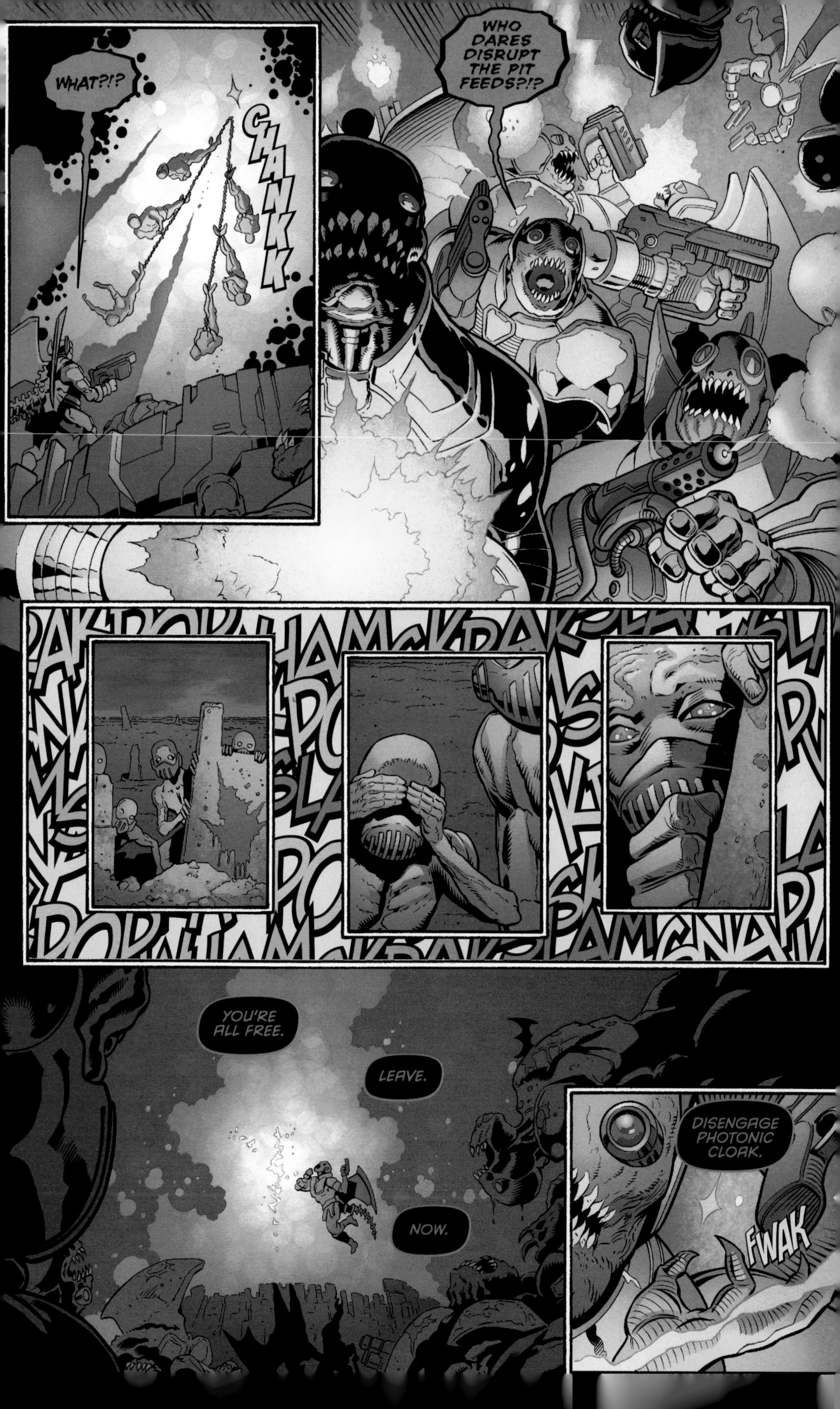
WHAT?!?
CHANKK
WHO DARES DISRUPT THE PIT FEEDS?!?
YOU'RE ALL FREE.
LEAVE.
NOW.
DISENGAGE PHOTONIC CLOAK.
FWAK

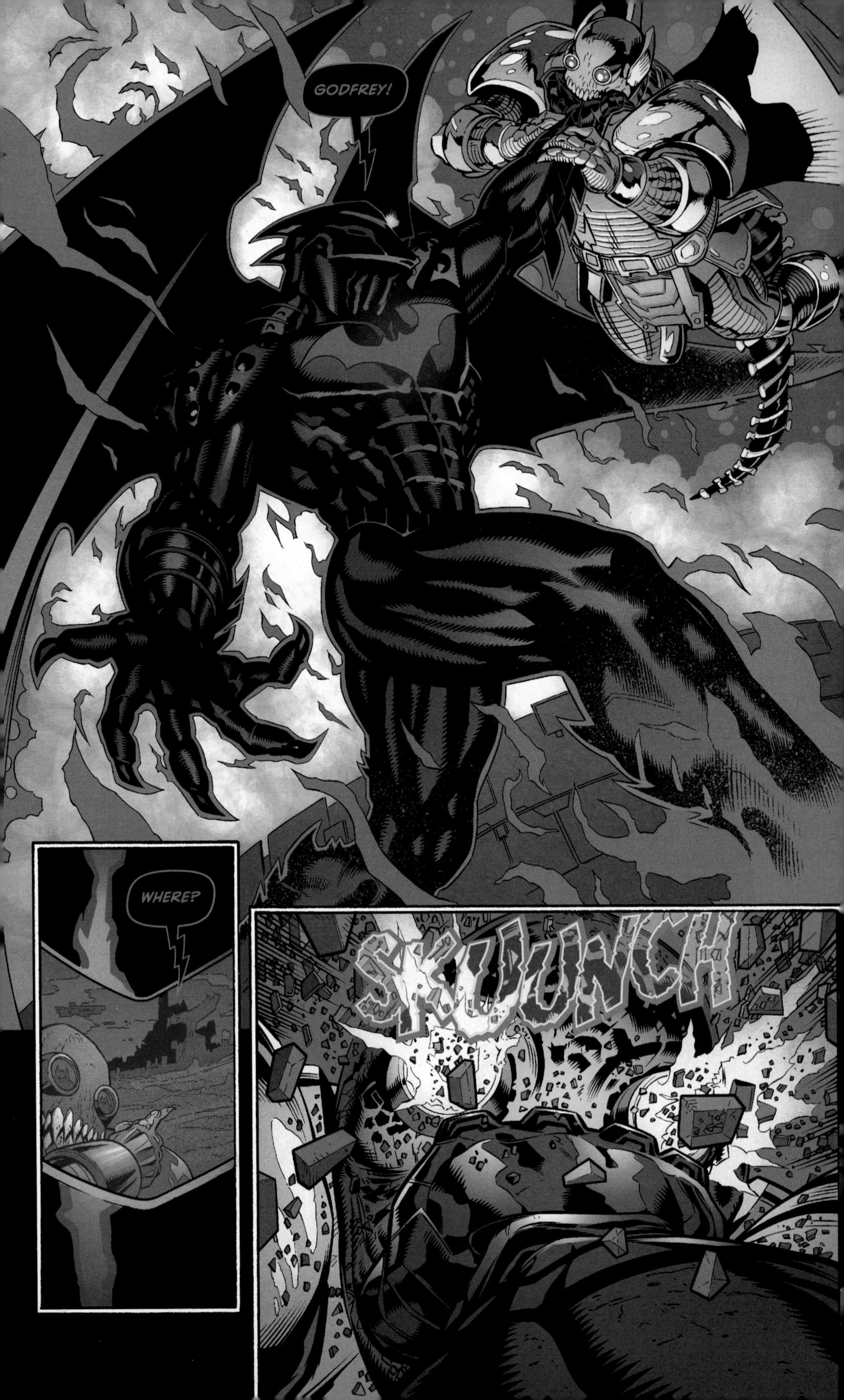
GODFREY!
WHERE?
SKUUNCH

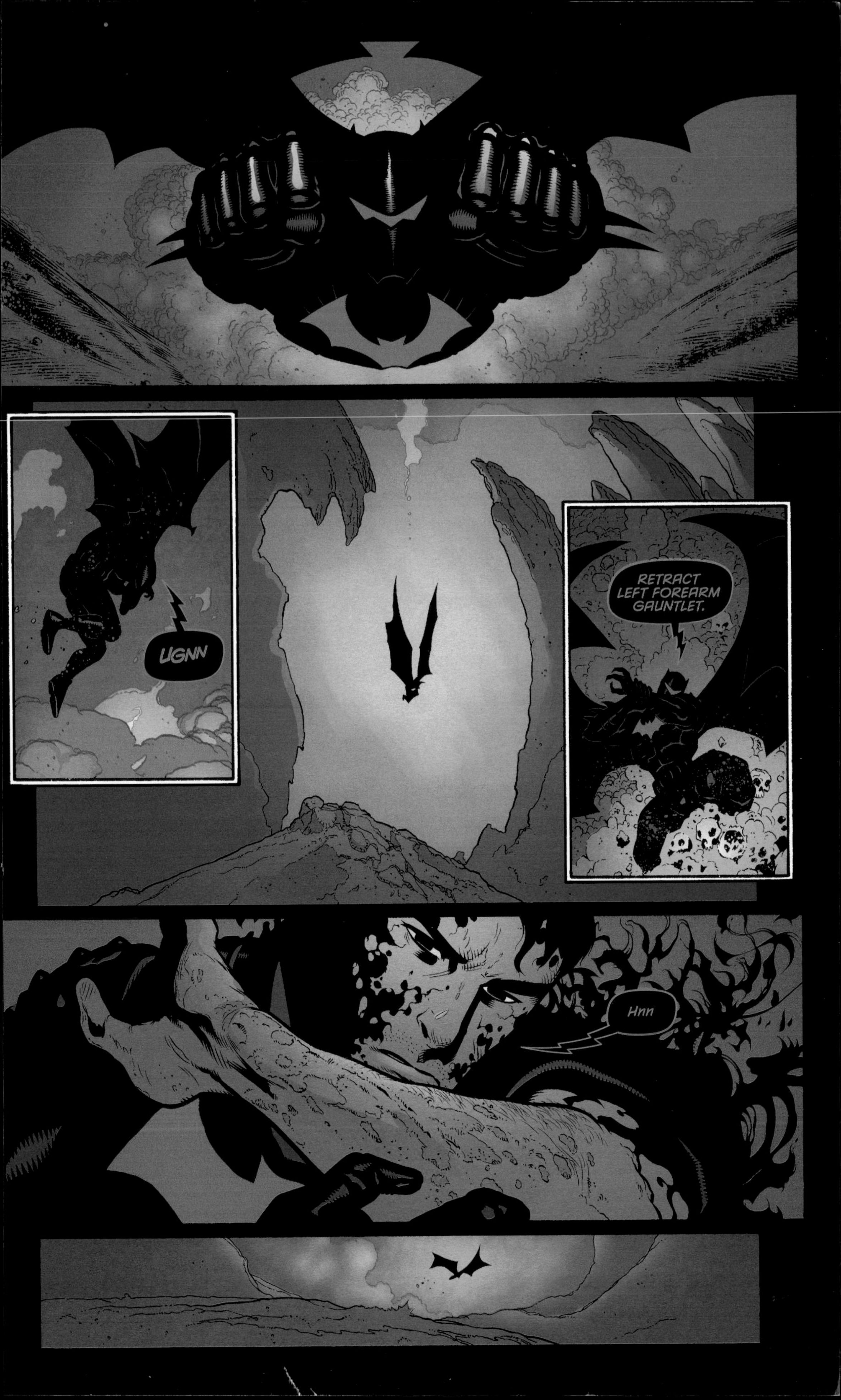
UGNN
RETRACT LEFT FOREARM GAUNTLET.
Hnn

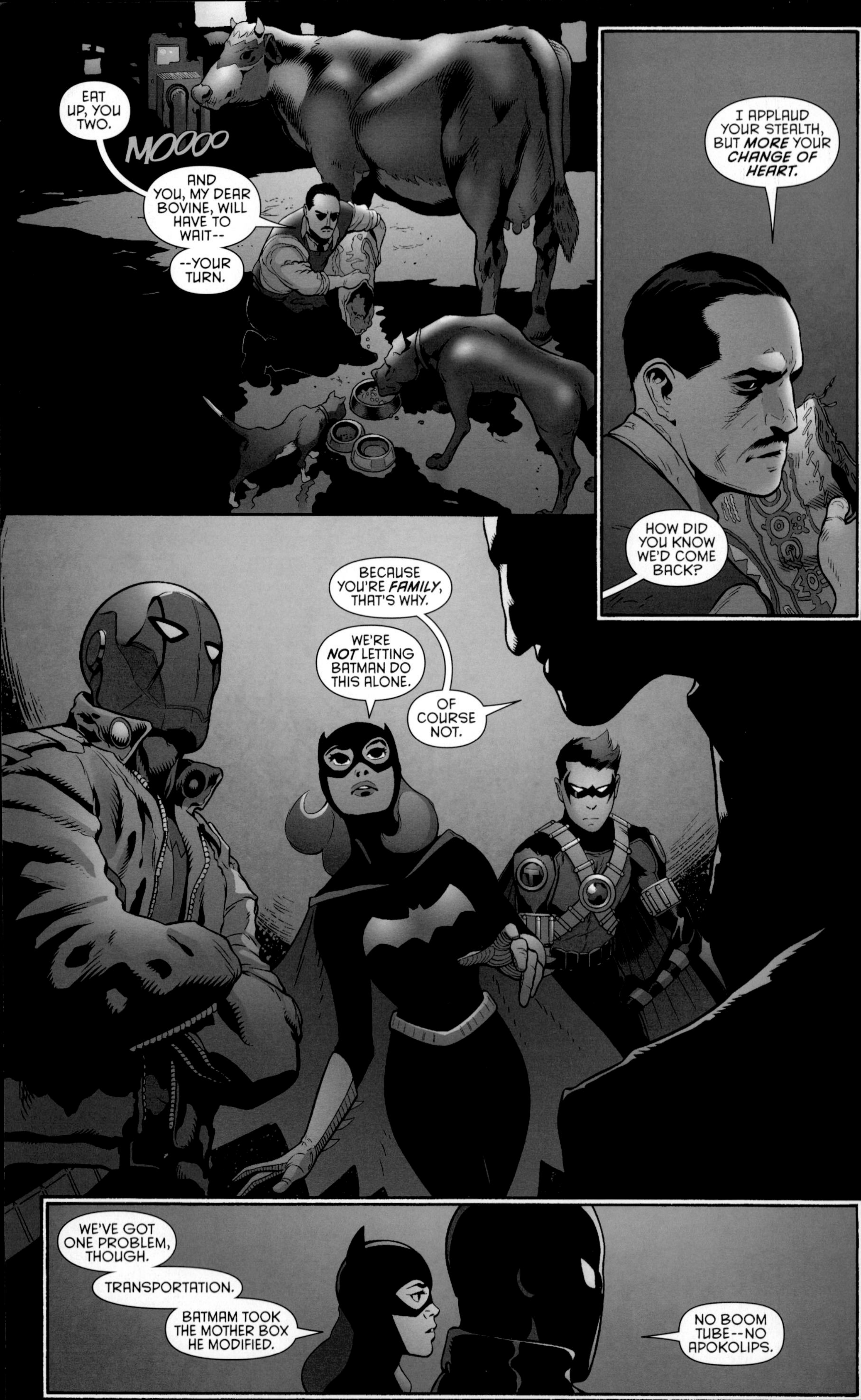
EAT UP, YOU TWO.
MOOOO
AND YOU, MY DEAR BOVINE, WILL HAVE TO WAIT--
--YOUR TURN.
I APPLAUD YOUR STEALTH, BUT MORE YOUR CHANGE OF HEART.
HOW DID YOU KNOW WE'D COME BACK?
BECAUSE YOU'RE FAMILY, THAT'S WHY.
WE'RE NOT LETTING BATMAN DO THIS ALONE.
OF COURSE NOT.
WE'VE GOT ONE PROBLEM, THOUGH.
TRANSPORTATION.
BATMAM TOOK THE MOTHER BOX HE MODIFIED.
NO BOOM TUBE--NO APOKOLIPS.

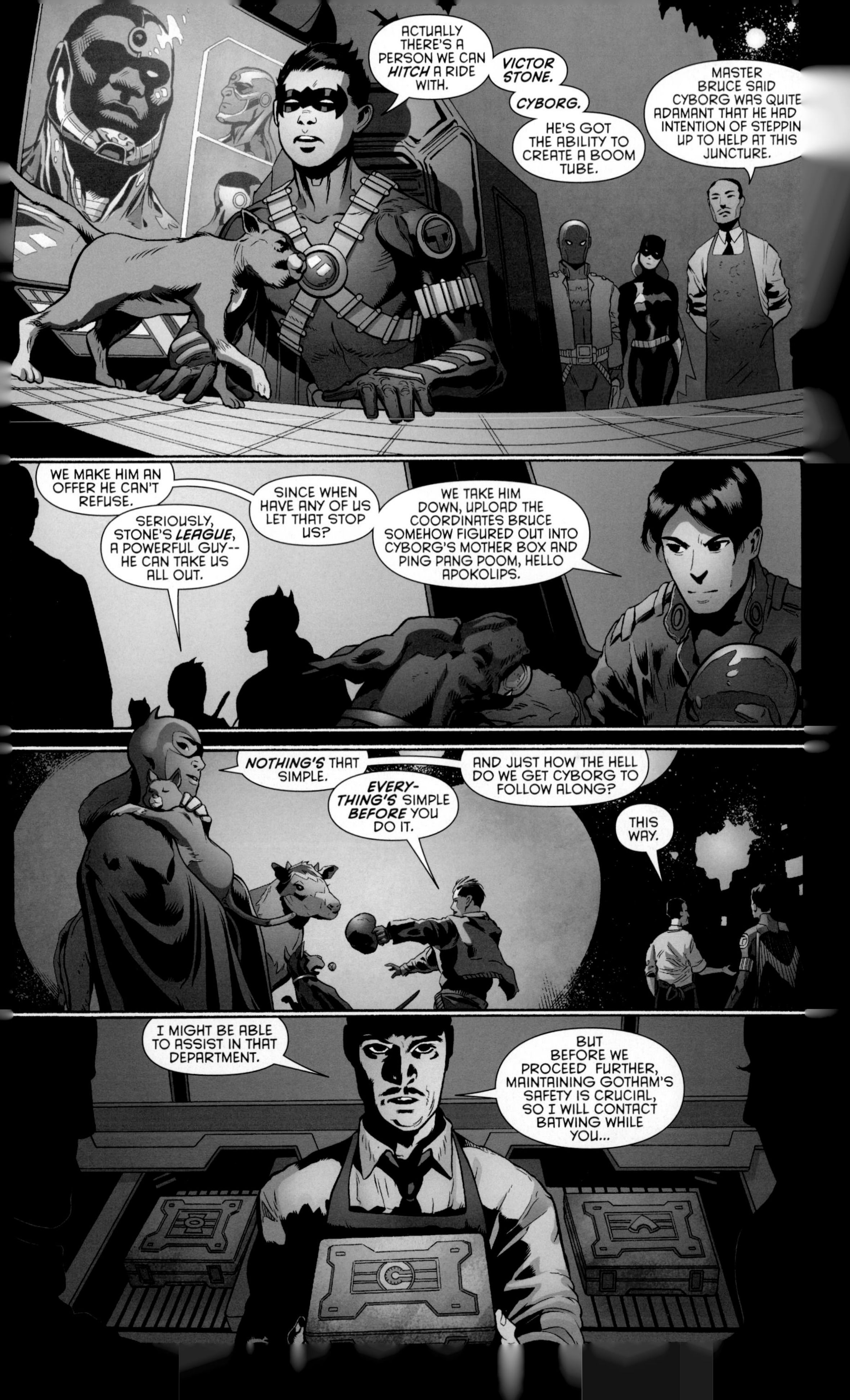
ACTUALLY THERE'S A PERSON WE CAN HITCH A RIDE WITH.
VICTOR STONE.
CYBORG.
HE'S GOT THE ABILITY TO CREATE A BOOM TUBE.
MASTER BRUCE SAID CYBORG WAS QUITE ADAMANT THAT HE HAD INTENTION OF STEPPIN UP TO HELP AT THIS JUNCTURE.
WE MAKE HIM AN OFFER HE CAN'T REFUSE.
SERIOUSLY, STONE'S LEAGUE, A POWERFUL GUY-- HE CAN TAKE US ALL OUT.
SINCE WHEN HAVE ANY OF US LET THAT STOP US?
WE TAKE HIM DOWN, UPLOAD THE COORDINATES BRUCE SOMEHOW FIGURED OUT INTO CYBORG'S MOTHER BOX AND PING PANG POOM, HELLO APOKOLIPS.
NOTHING'S THAT SIMPLE.
EVERY-THING'S SIMPLE BEFORE YOU DO IT.
AND JUST HOW THE HELL DO WE GET CYBORG TO FOLLOW ALONG?
THIS WAY.
I MIGHT BE ABLE TO ASSIST IN THAT DEPARTMENT.
BUT BEFORE WE PROCEED FURTHER, MAINTAINING GOTHAM'S SAFETY IS CRUCIAL, SO I WILL CONTACT BATWING WHILE YOU...

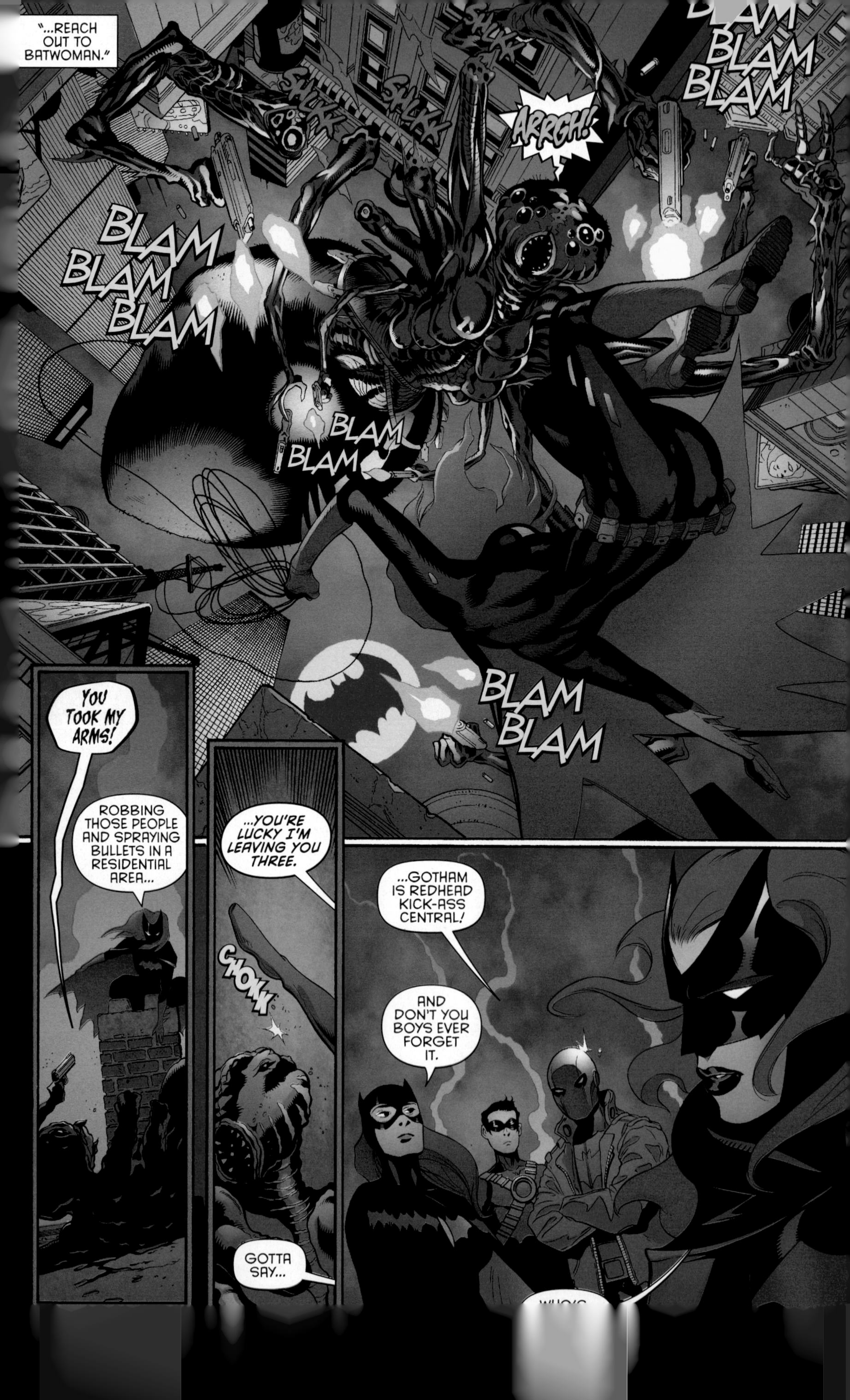
"...REACH OUT TO BATWOMAN."
SHLKK
SHLKK
SHLKK
ARRGH!
BLAM BLAM BLAM
BLAM BLAM BLAM
BLAM BLAM
BLAM BLAM
YOU TOOK MY ARMS!
ROBBING THOSE PEOPLE AND SPRAYING BULLETS IN A RESIDENTIAL AREA...
...YOU'RE LUCKY I'M LEAVING YOU THREE.
CHOKK
GOTTA SAY...
...GOTHAM IS REDHEAD KICK-ASS CENTRAL!
AND DON'T YOU BOYS EVER FORGET IT.

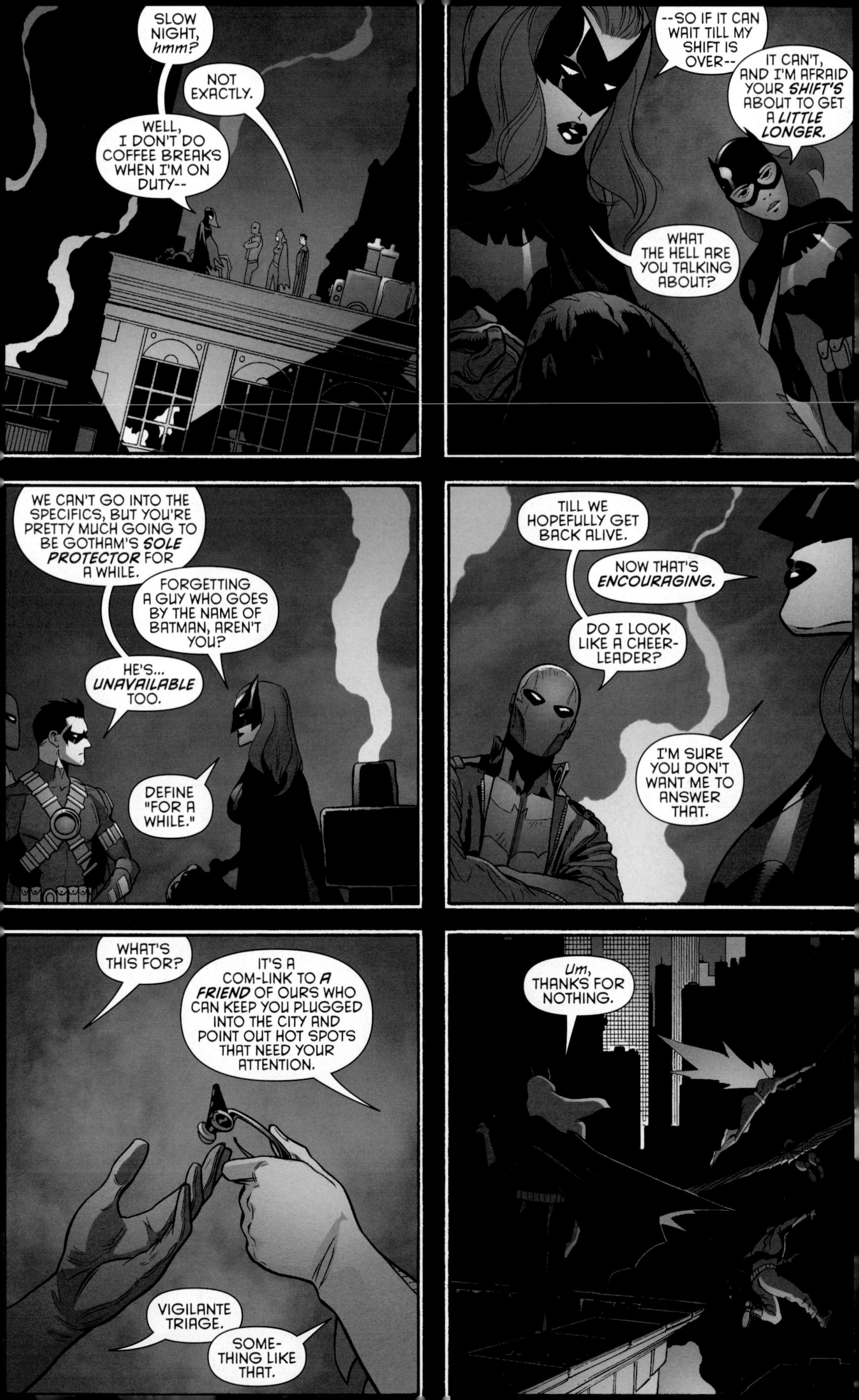

SLOW NIGHT, *hmm?*
NOT EXACTLY.
WELL, I DON'T DO COFFEE BREAKS WHEN I'M ON DUTY--
--SO IF IT CAN WAIT TILL MY SHIFT IS OVER--
IT CAN'T, AND I'M AFRAID YOUR ***SHIFT'S*** ABOUT TO GET A ***LITTLE LONGER.***
WHAT THE HELL ARE YOU TALKING ABOUT?
WE CAN'T GO INTO THE SPECIFICS, BUT YOU'RE PRETTY MUCH GOING TO BE GOTHAM'S ***SOLE PROTECTOR*** FOR A WHILE.
FORGETTING A GUY WHO GOES BY THE NAME OF BATMAN, AREN'T YOU?
HE'S... ***UNAVAILABLE*** TOO.
DEFINE "FOR A WHILE."
TILL WE HOPEFULLY GET BACK ALIVE.
NOW THAT'S ***ENCOURAGING.***
DO I LOOK LIKE A CHEER-LEADER?
I'M SURE YOU DON'T WANT ME TO ANSWER THAT.
WHAT'S THIS FOR?
IT'S A COM-LINK TO ***A FRIEND*** OF OURS WHO CAN KEEP YOU PLUGGED INTO THE CITY AND POINT OUT HOT SPOTS THAT NEED YOUR ATTENTION.
VIGILANTE TRIAGE.
SOME-THING LIKE THAT.
Um, THANKS FOR NOTHING.

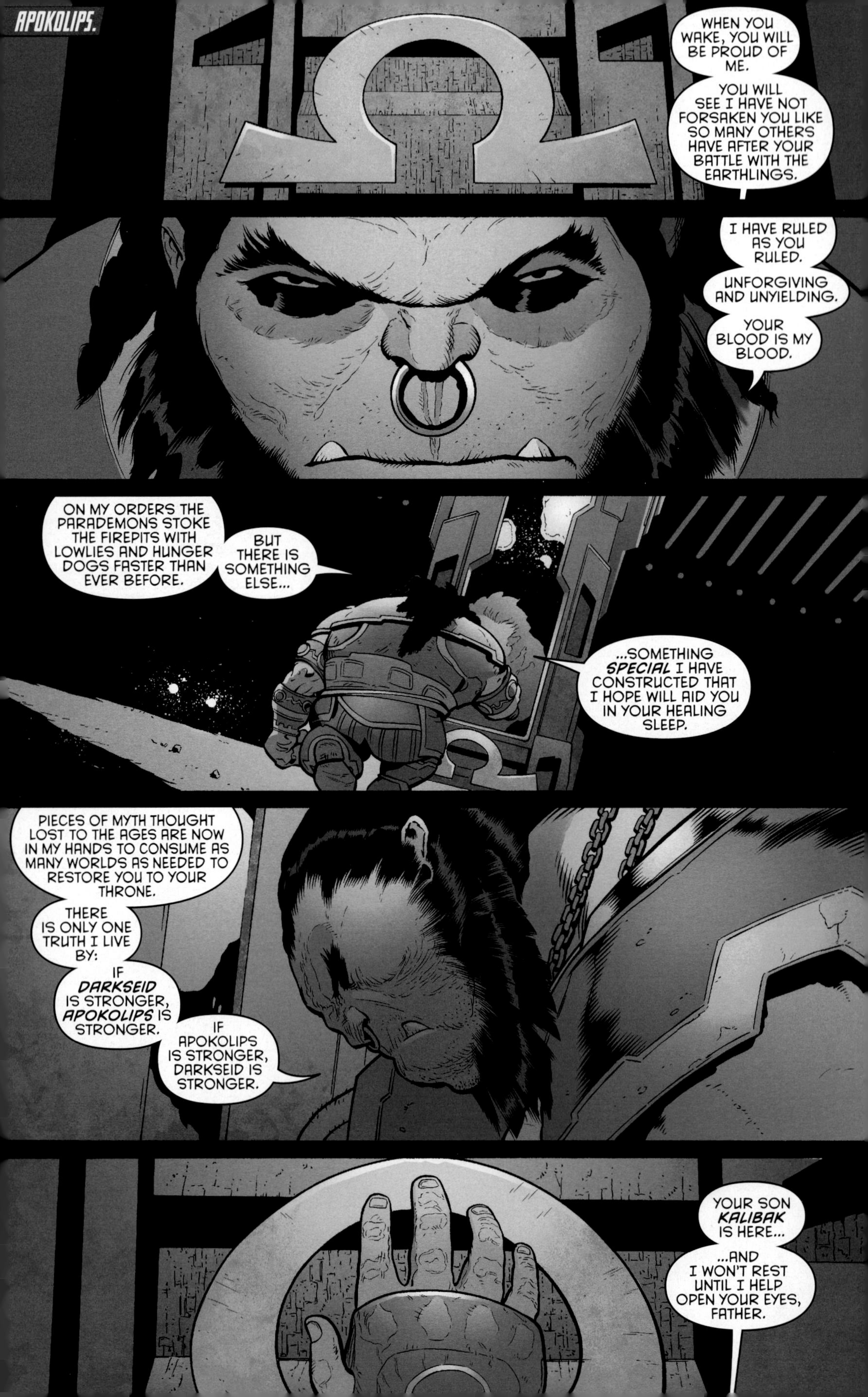
APOKOLIPS.
WHEN YOU WAKE, YOU WILL BE PROUD OF ME.
YOU WILL SEE I HAVE NOT FORSAKEN YOU LIKE SO MANY OTHERS HAVE AFTER YOUR BATTLE WITH THE EARTHLINGS.
I HAVE RULED AS YOU RULED.
UNFORGIVING AND UNYIELDING.
YOUR BLOOD IS MY BLOOD.
ON MY ORDERS THE PARADEMONS STOKE THE FIREPITS WITH LOWLIES AND HUNGER DOGS FASTER THAN EVER BEFORE.
BUT THERE IS SOMETHING ELSE...
...SOMETHING *SPECIAL* I HAVE CONSTRUCTED THAT I HOPE WILL AID YOU IN YOUR HEALING SLEEP.
PIECES OF MYTH THOUGHT LOST TO THE AGES ARE NOW IN MY HANDS TO CONSUME AS MANY WORLDS AS NEEDED TO RESTORE YOU TO YOUR THRONE.
THERE IS ONLY ONE TRUTH I LIVE BY:
IF *DARKSEID* IS STRONGER, *APOKOLIPS* IS STRONGER.
IF APOKOLIPS IS STRONGER, DARKSEID IS STRONGER.
YOUR SON *KALIBAK* IS HERE...
...AND I WON'T REST UNTIL I HELP OPEN YOUR EYES, FATHER.

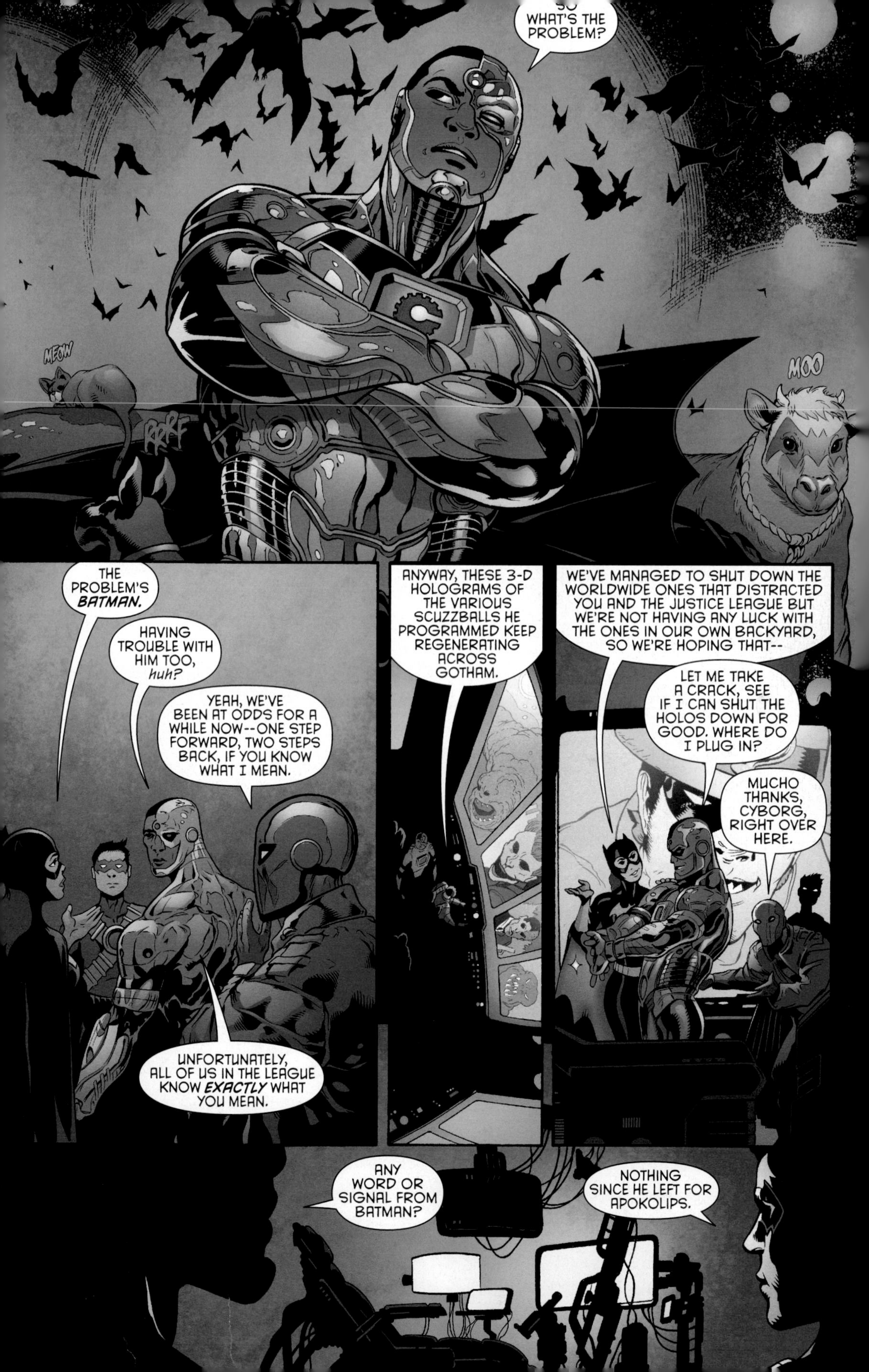
SO WHAT'S THE PROBLEM?
MEOW
RRRF
MOO
THE PROBLEM'S *BATMAN.*
HAVING TROUBLE WITH HIM TOO, *huh?*
YEAH, WE'VE BEEN AT ODDS FOR A WHILE NOW--ONE STEP FORWARD, TWO STEPS BACK, IF YOU KNOW WHAT I MEAN.
UNFORTUNATELY, ALL OF US IN THE LEAGUE KNOW *EXACTLY* WHAT YOU MEAN.
ANYWAY, THESE 3-D HOLOGRAMS OF THE VARIOUS SCUZZBALLS HE PROGRAMMED KEEP REGENERATING ACROSS GOTHAM.
WE'VE MANAGED TO SHUT DOWN THE WORLDWIDE ONES THAT DISTRACTED YOU AND THE JUSTICE LEAGUE BUT WE'RE NOT HAVING ANY LUCK WITH THE ONES IN OUR OWN BACKYARD, SO WE'RE HOPING THAT--
LET ME TAKE A CRACK, SEE IF I CAN SHUT THE HOLOS DOWN FOR GOOD. WHERE DO I PLUG IN?
MUCHO THANKS, CYBORG, RIGHT OVER HERE.
ANY WORD OR SIGNAL FROM BATMAN?
NOTHING SINCE HE LEFT FOR APOKOLIPS.

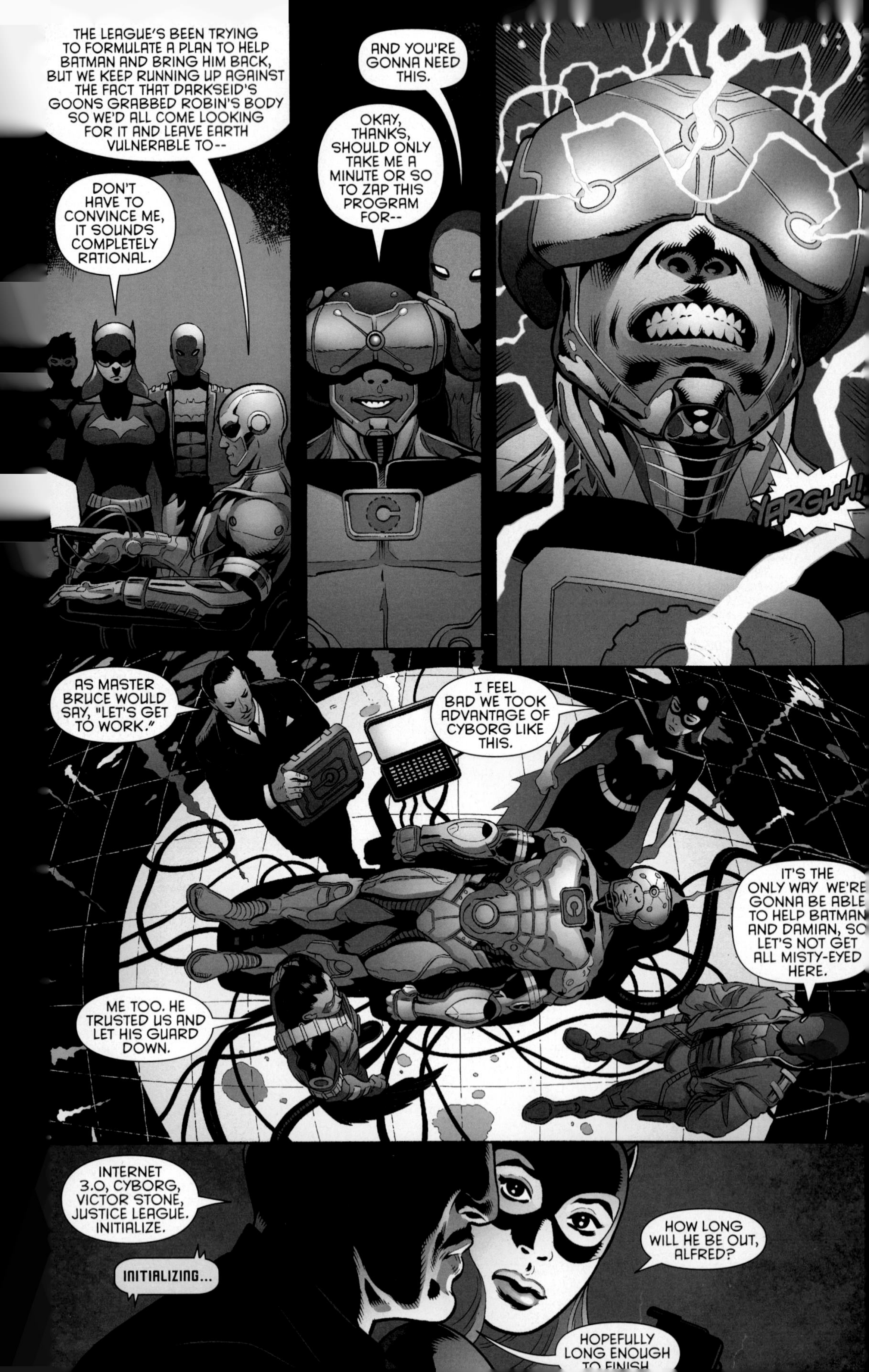
THE LEAGUE'S BEEN TRYING TO FORMULATE A PLAN TO HELP BATMAN AND BRING HIM BACK, BUT WE KEEP RUNNING UP AGAINST THE FACT THAT DARKSEID'S GOONS GRABBED ROBIN'S BODY SO WE'D ALL COME LOOKING FOR IT AND LEAVE EARTH VULNERABLE TO--
DON'T HAVE TO CONVINCE ME, IT SOUNDS COMPLETELY RATIONAL.
AND YOU'RE GONNA NEED THIS.
OKAY, THANKS, SHOULD ONLY TAKE ME A MINUTE OR SO TO ZAP THIS PROGRAM FOR--
YARGHH!
AS MASTER BRUCE WOULD SAY, "LET'S GET TO WORK."
I FEEL BAD WE TOOK ADVANTAGE OF CYBORG LIKE THIS.
ME TOO. HE TRUSTED US AND LET HIS GUARD DOWN.
IT'S THE ONLY WAY WE'RE GONNA BE ABLE TO HELP BATMAN AND DAMIAN, SO LET'S NOT GET ALL MISTY-EYED HERE.
INTERNET 3.0, CYBORG, VICTOR STONE, JUSTICE LEAGUE. INITIALIZE.
INITIALIZING...
HOW LONG WILL HE BE OUT, ALFRED?
HOPEFULLY LONG ENOUGH TO FINISH

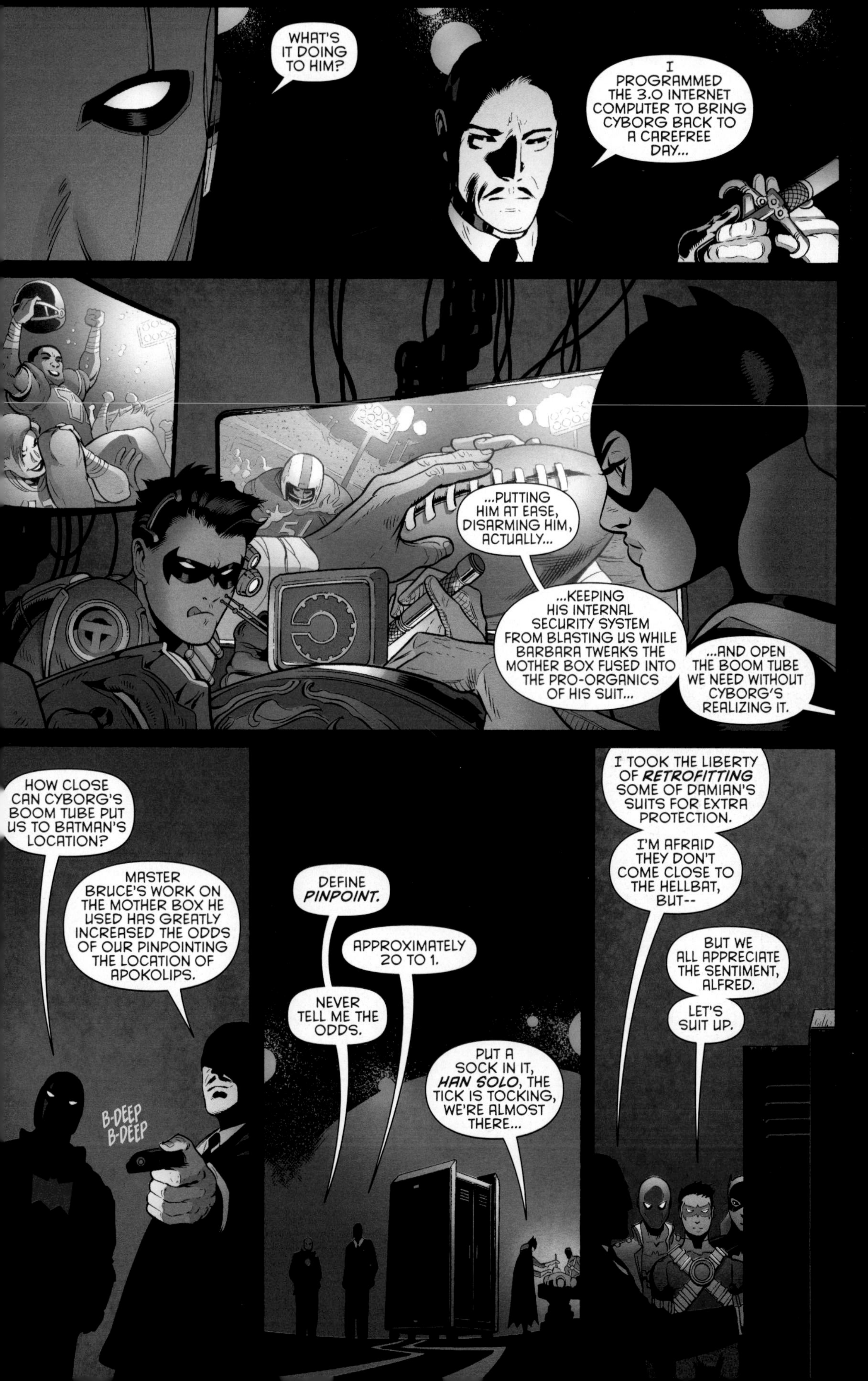
WHAT'S IT DOING TO HIM?
I PROGRAMMED THE 3.0 INTERNET COMPUTER TO BRING CYBORG BACK TO A CAREFREE DAY...
...PUTTING HIM AT EASE, DISARMING HIM, ACTUALLY...
...KEEPING HIS INTERNAL SECURITY SYSTEM FROM BLASTING US WHILE BARBARA TWEAKS THE MOTHER BOX FUSED INTO THE PRO-ORGANICS OF HIS SUIT...
...AND OPEN THE BOOM TUBE WE NEED WITHOUT CYBORG'S REALIZING IT.
HOW CLOSE CAN CYBORG'S BOOM TUBE PUT US TO BATMAN'S LOCATION?
MASTER BRUCE'S WORK ON THE MOTHER BOX HE USED HAS GREATLY INCREASED THE ODDS OF OUR PINPOINTING THE LOCATION OF APOKOLIPS.
B-DEEP B-DEEP
DEFINE *PINPOINT.*
APPROXIMATELY 20 TO 1.
NEVER TELL ME THE ODDS.
PUT A SOCK IN IT, ***HAN SOLO***, THE TICK IS TOCKING, WE'RE ALMOST THERE...
I TOOK THE LIBERTY OF ***RETROFITTING*** SOME OF DAMIAN'S SUITS FOR EXTRA PROTECTION.
I'M AFRAID THEY DON'T COME CLOSE TO THE HELLBAT, BUT--
BUT WE ALL APPRECIATE THE SENTIMENT, ALFRED.
LET'S SUIT UP.

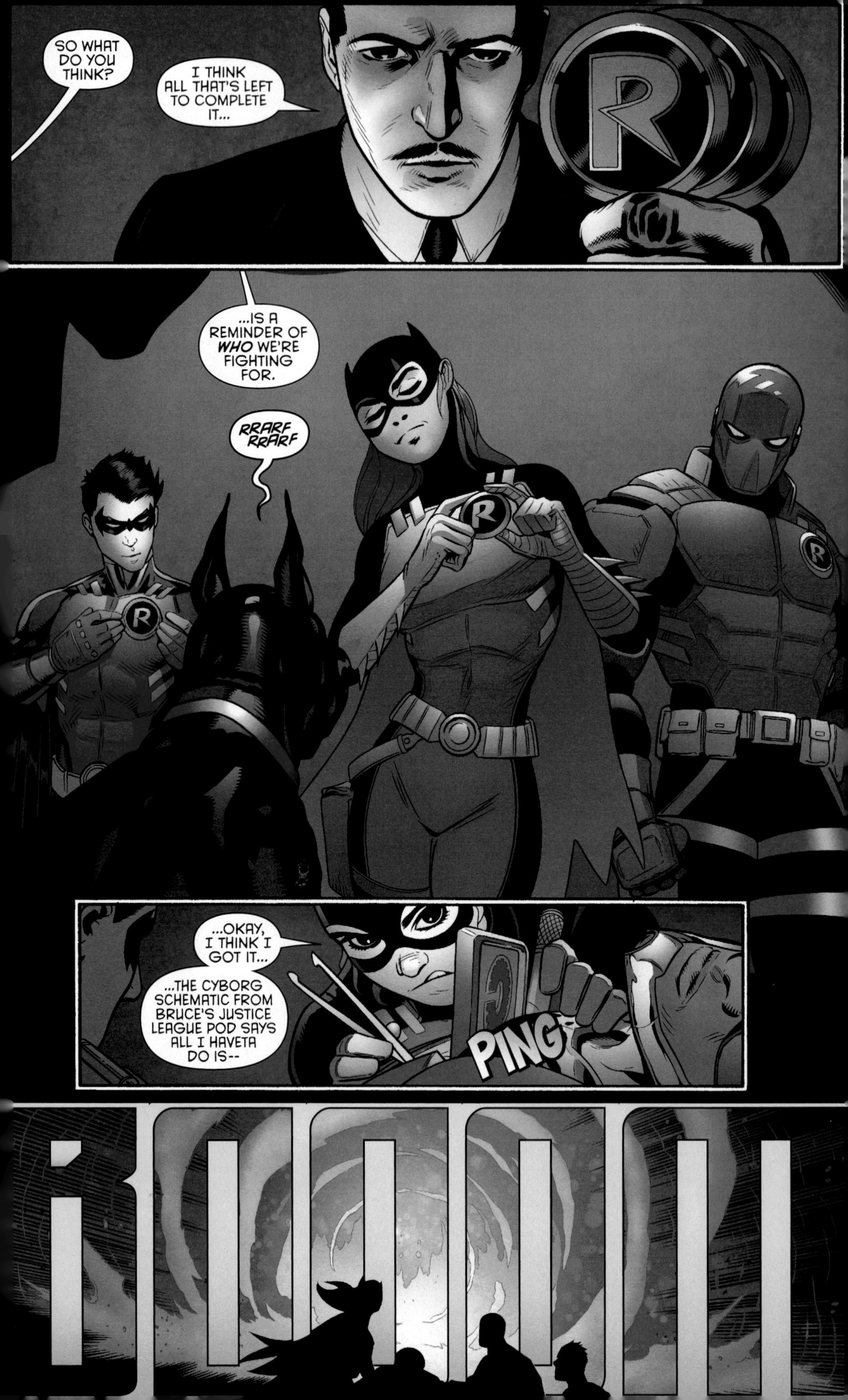
SO WHAT DO YOU THINK?
I THINK ALL THAT'S LEFT TO COMPLETE IT...
...IS A REMINDER OF WHO WE'RE FIGHTING FOR.
RRARF RRARF
...OKAY, I THINK I GOT IT...
...THE CYBORG SCHEMATIC FROM BRUCE'S JUSTICE LEAGUE POD SAYS ALL I HAVETA DO IS--
PING

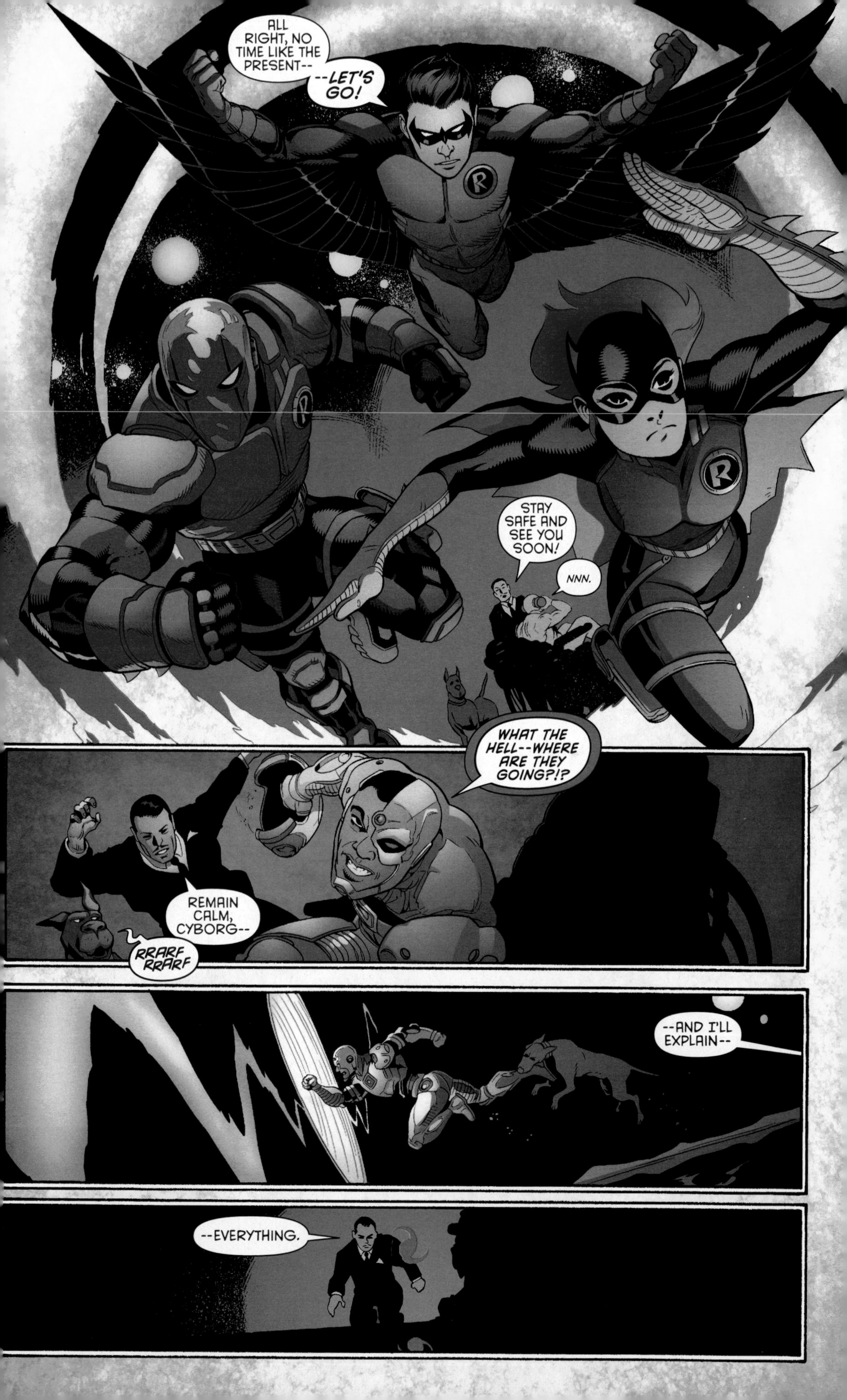
ALL RIGHT, NO TIME LIKE THE PRESENT--
--LET'S GO!
STAY SAFE AND SEE YOU SOON!
NNN.
WHAT THE HELL--WHERE ARE THEY GOING?!?
REMAIN CALM, CYBORG--
RRARF RRARF
--AND I'LL EXPLAIN--
--EVERYTHING.

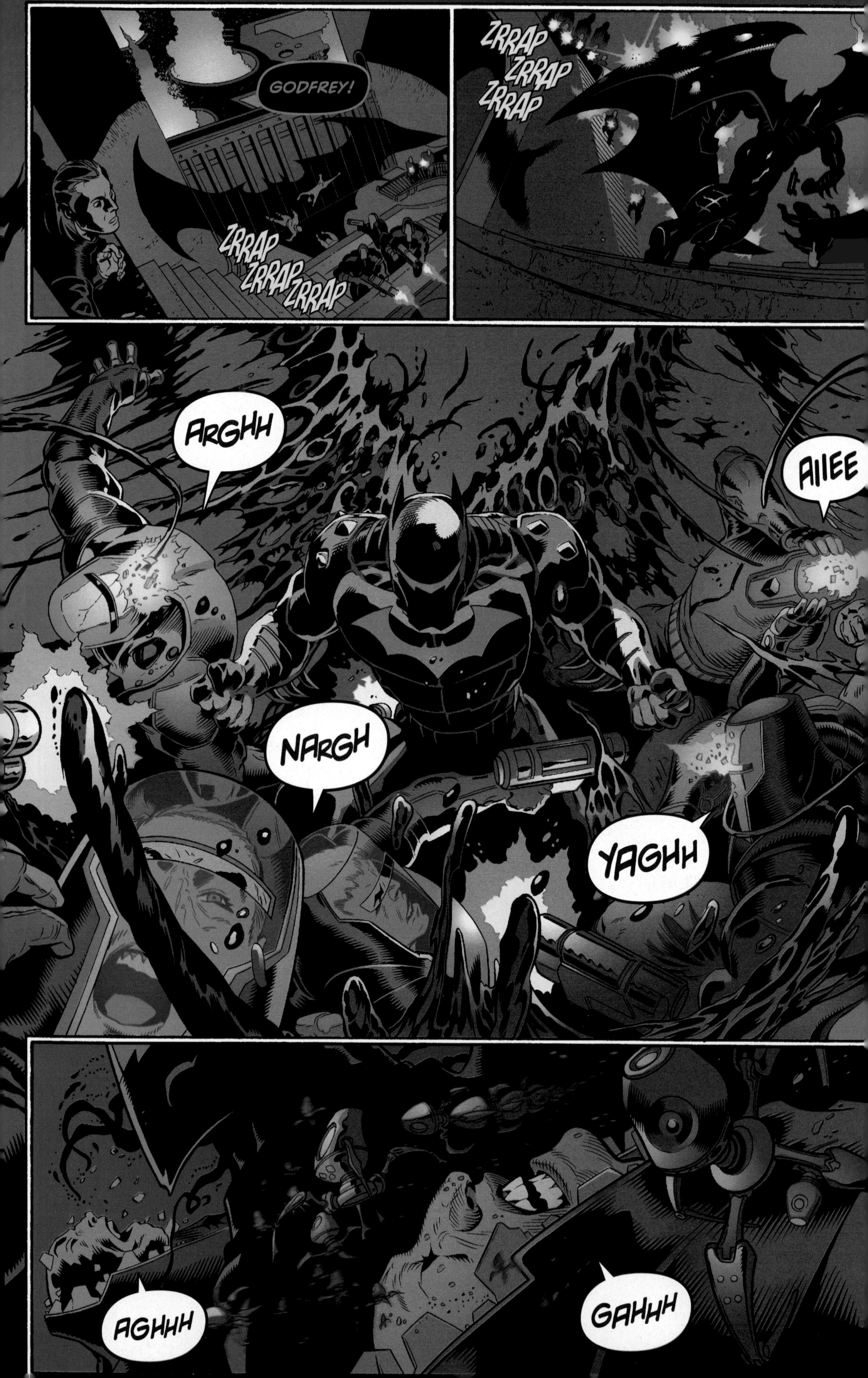
GODFREY!
ZRRAP ZRRAP ZRRAP
ZRRAP ZRRAP ZRRAP
ARGHH
AIIEE
NARGH
YAGHH
AGHHH
GAHHH

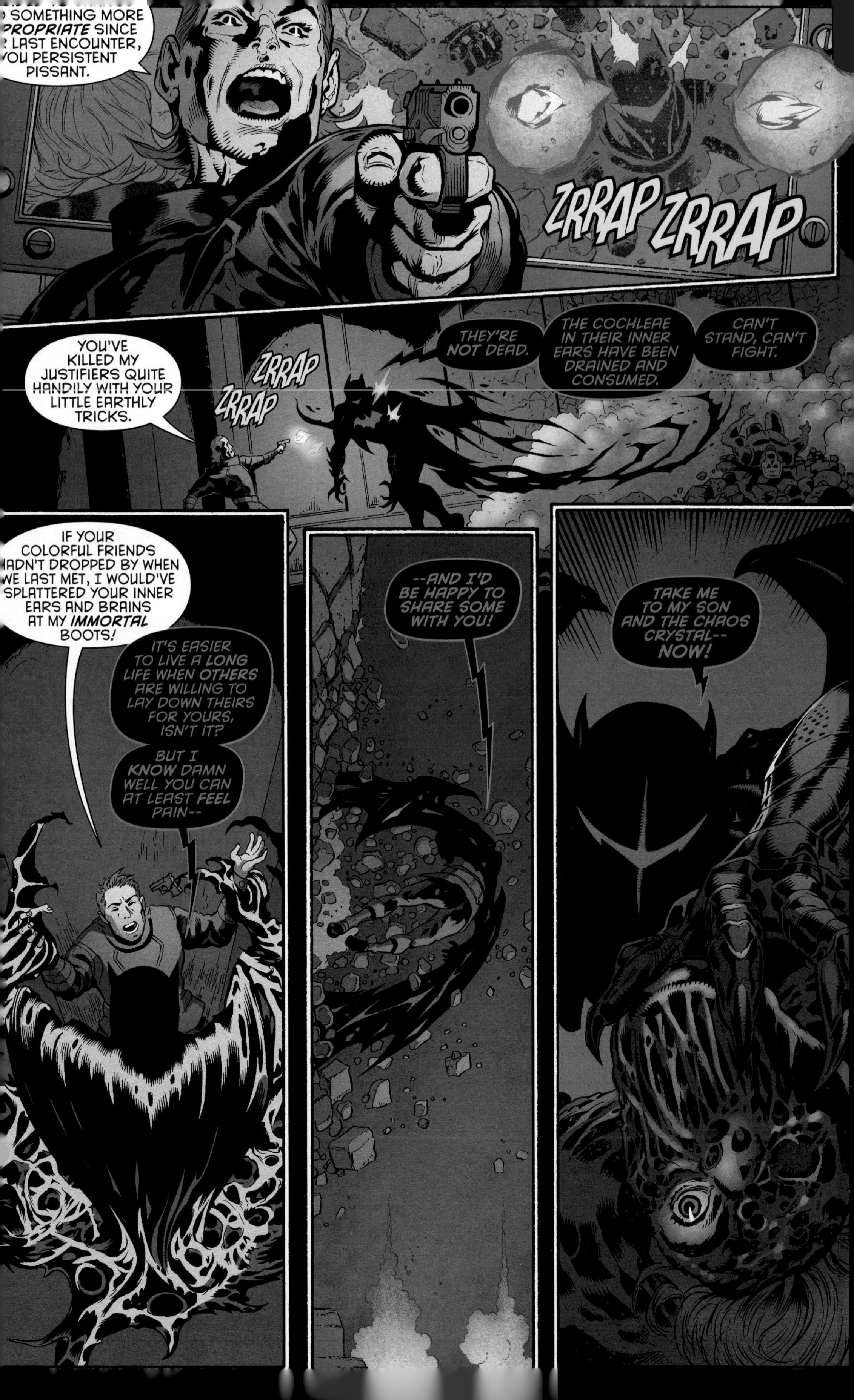

SOMETHING MORE PROPRIATE SINCE LAST ENCOUNTER, OU PERSISTENT PISSANT.
ZRRAP ZRRAP
YOU'VE KILLED MY JUSTIFIERS QUITE HANDILY WITH YOUR LITTLE EARTHLY TRICKS.
ZRRAP
ZRRAP
THEY'RE NOT DEAD.
THE COCHLEAE IN THEIR INNER EARS HAVE BEEN DRAINED AND CONSUMED.
CAN'T STAND, CAN'T FIGHT.
IF YOUR COLORFUL FRIENDS ADN'T DROPPED BY WHEN E LAST MET, I WOULD'VE SPLATTERED YOUR INNER EARS AND BRAINS AT MY IMMORTAL BOOTS!
IT'S EASIER TO LIVE A LONG LIFE WHEN OTHERS ARE WILLING TO LAY DOWN THEIRS FOR YOURS, ISN'T IT?
BUT I KNOW DAMN WELL YOU CAN AT LEAST FEEL PAIN--
--AND I'D BE HAPPY TO SHARE SOME WITH YOU!
TAKE ME TO MY SON AND THE CHAOS CRYSTAL-- NOW!

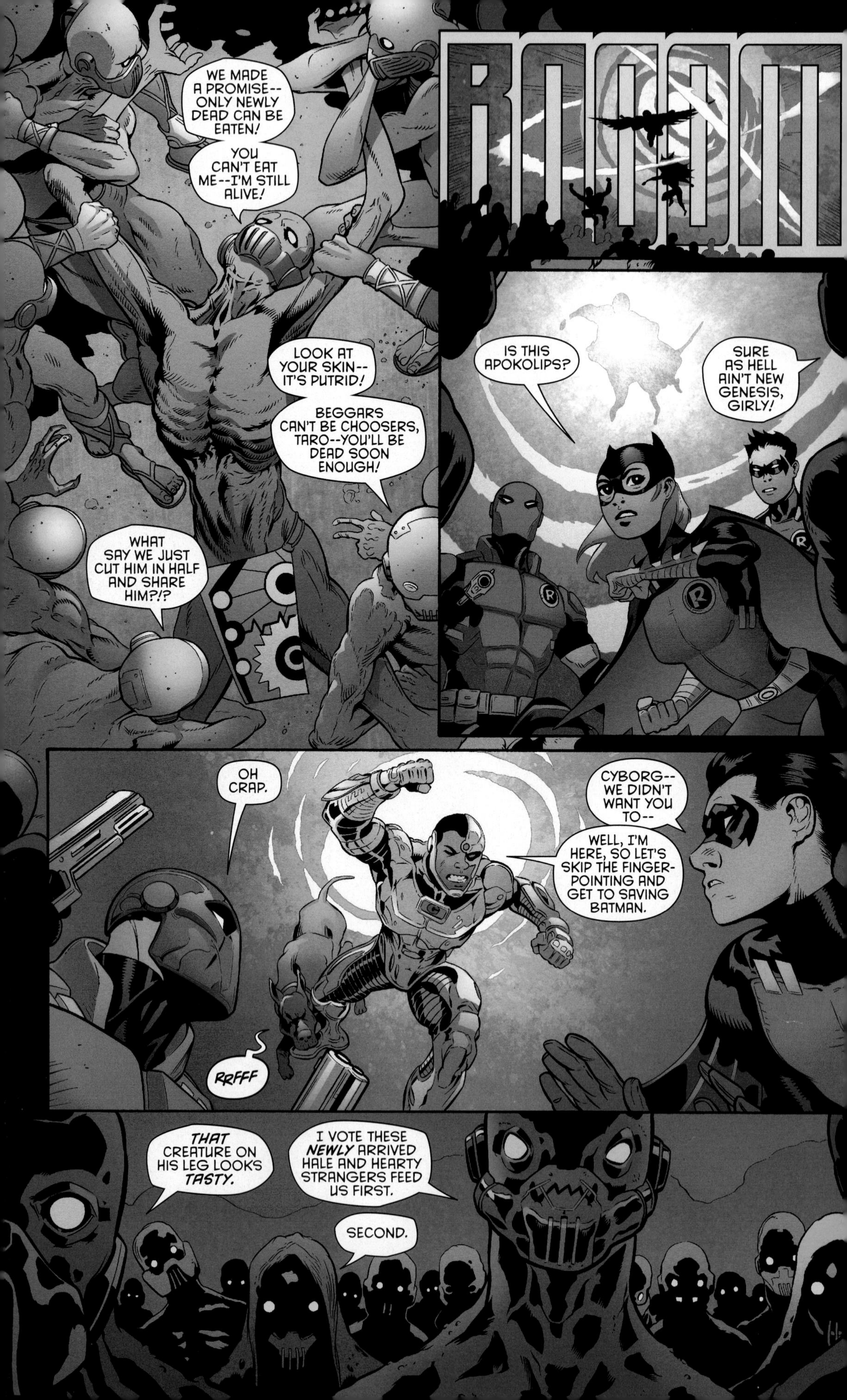
WE MADE A PROMISE-- ONLY NEWLY DEAD CAN BE EATEN!
YOU CAN'T EAT ME--I'M STILL ALIVE!
LOOK AT YOUR SKIN-- IT'S PUTRID!
BEGGARS CAN'T BE CHOOSERS, TARO--YOU'LL BE DEAD SOON ENOUGH!
WHAT SAY WE JUST CUT HIM IN HALF AND SHARE HIM?!?
BOOOM
IS THIS APOKOLIPS?
SURE AS HELL AIN'T NEW GENESIS, GIRLY!
OH CRAP.
CYBORG-- WE DIDN'T WANT YOU TO--
WELL, I'M HERE, SO LET'S SKIP THE FINGER-POINTING AND GET TO SAVING BATMAN.
RRFFF
THAT CREATURE ON HIS LEG LOOKS TASTY.
I VOTE THESE NEWLY ARRIVED HALE AND HEARTY STRANGERS FEED US FIRST.
SECOND.

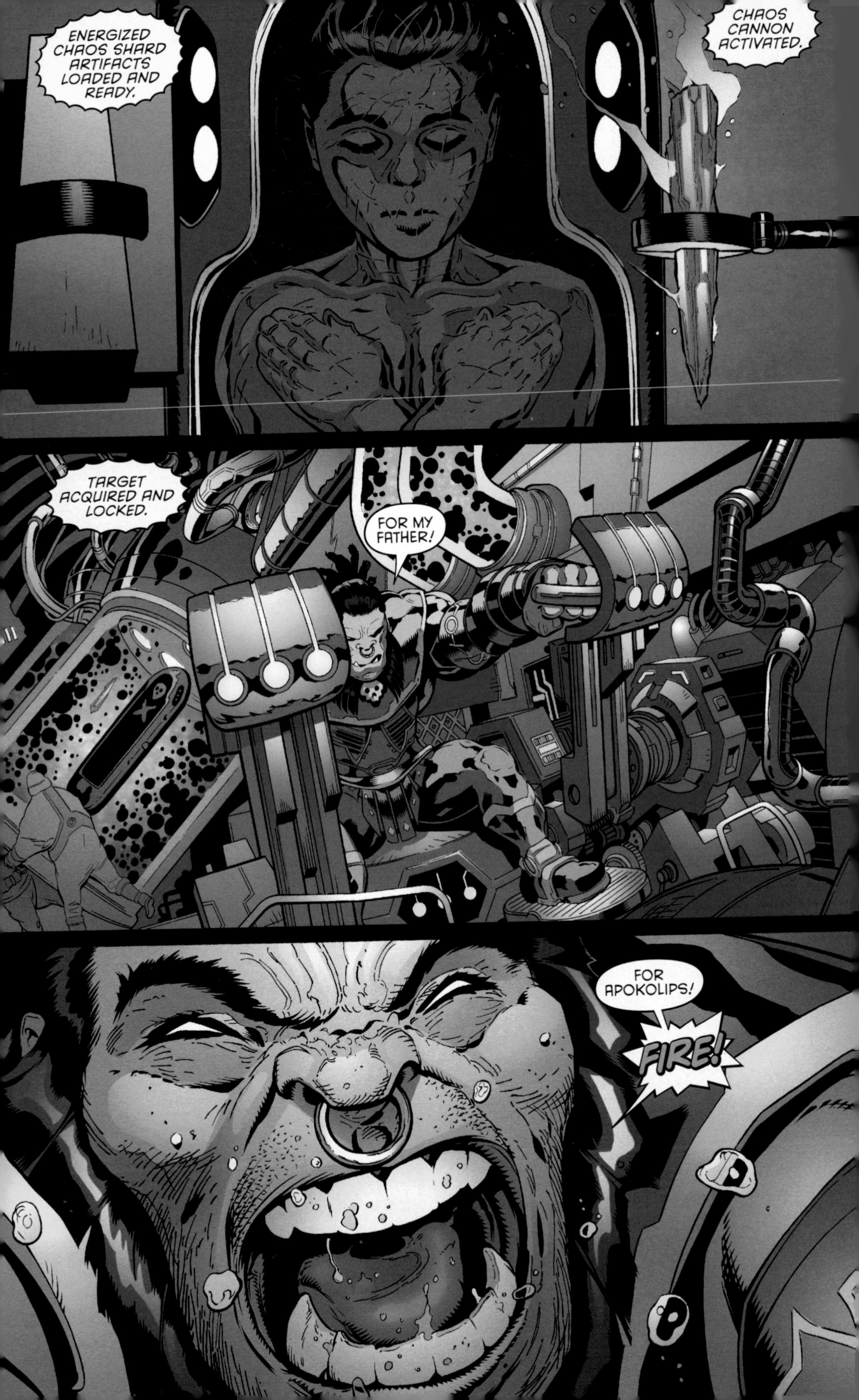
ENERGIZED CHAOS SHARD ARTIFACTS LOADED AND READY.
CHAOS CANNON ACTIVATED.
TARGET ACQUIRED AND LOCKED.
FOR MY FATHER!
FOR APOKOLIPS!
FIRE!

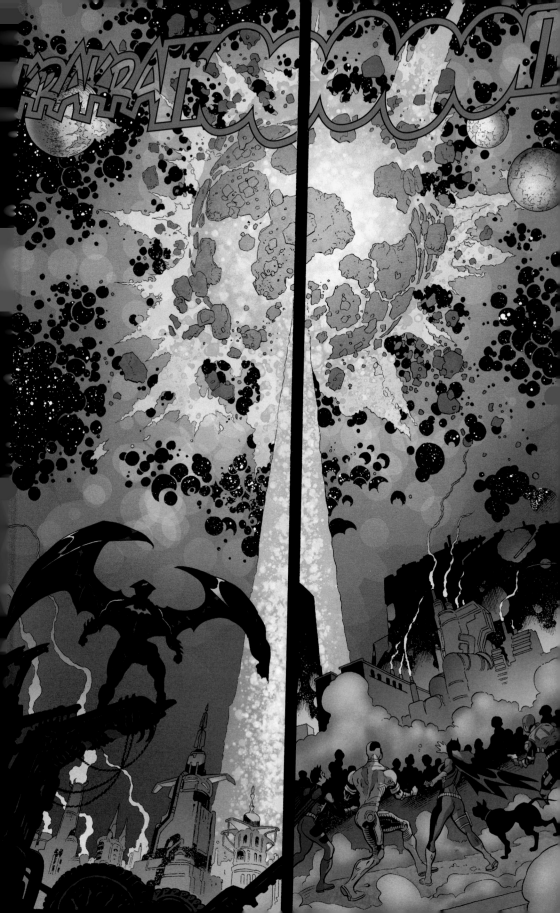

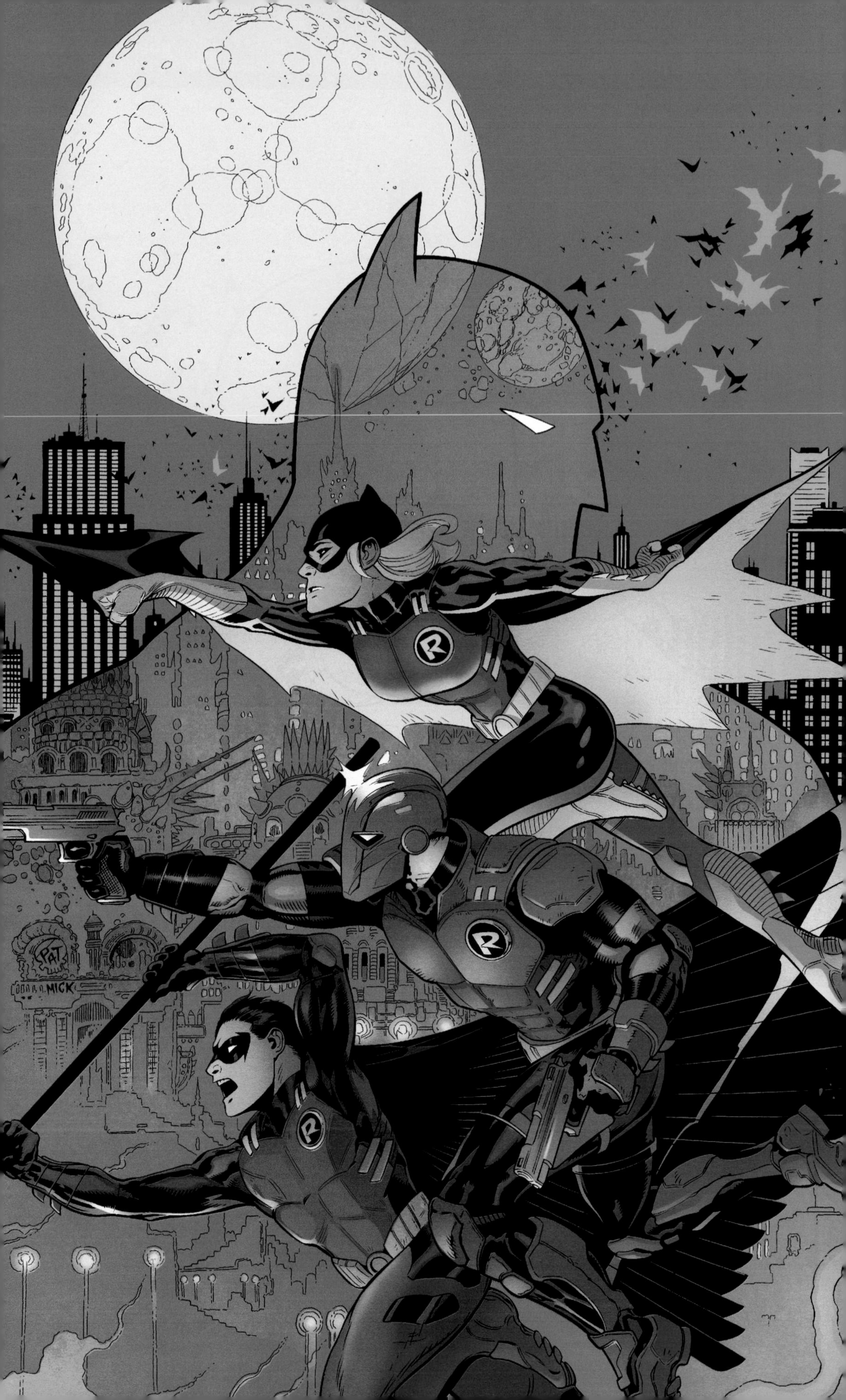
PAT
MICK

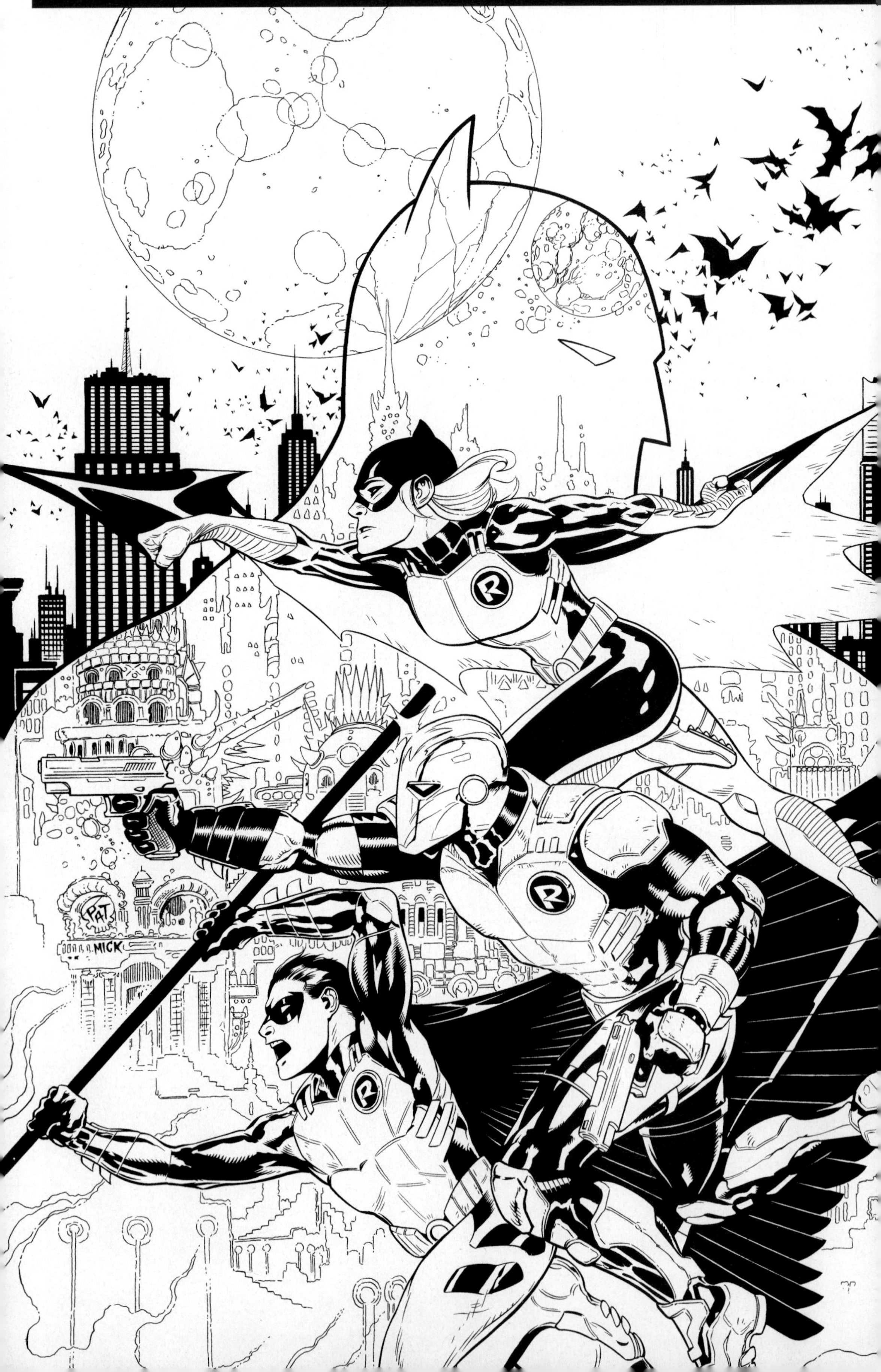
PAT
MICK

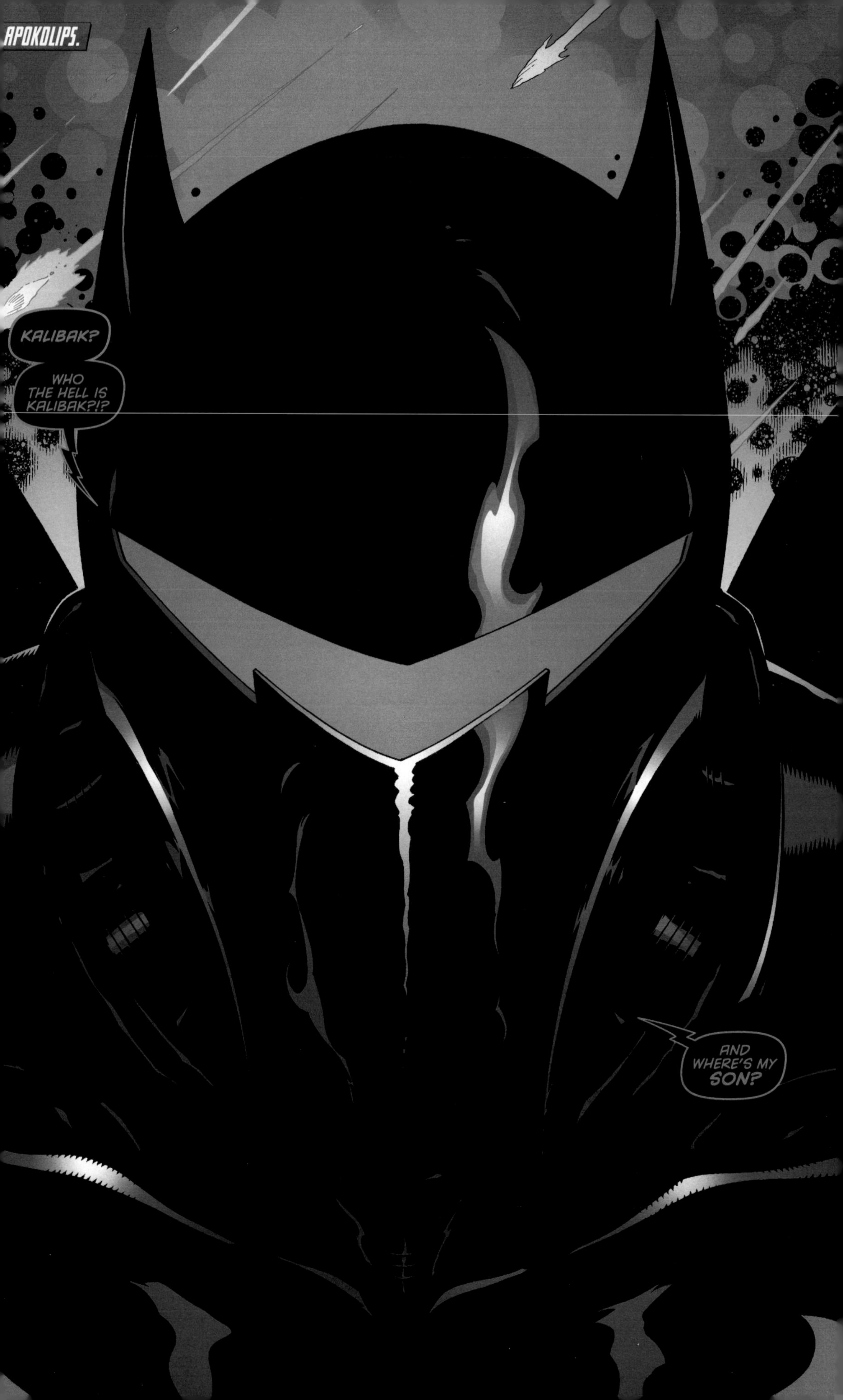
APOKOLIPS.
KALIBAK?
WHO THE HELL IS KALIBAK?!?
AND WHERE'S MY SON?

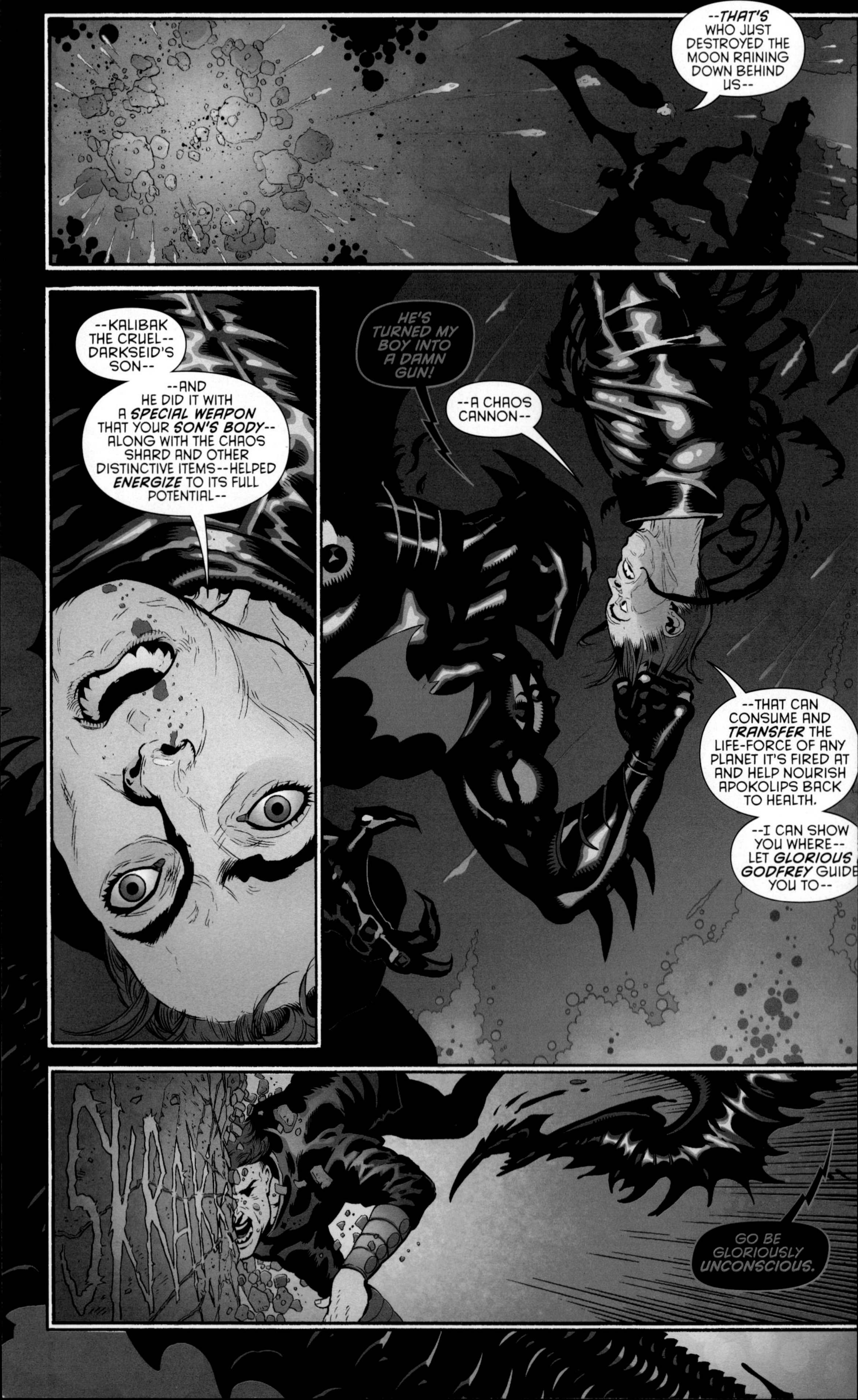
--THAT'S WHO JUST DESTROYED THE MOON RAINING DOWN BEHIND US--
--KALIBAK THE CRUEL-- DARKSEID'S SON--
--AND HE DID IT WITH A SPECIAL WEAPON THAT YOUR SON'S BODY-- ALONG WITH THE CHAOS SHARD AND OTHER DISTINCTIVE ITEMS--HELPED ENERGIZE TO ITS FULL POTENTIAL--
HE'S TURNED MY BOY INTO A DAMN GUN!
--A CHAOS CANNON--
--THAT CAN CONSUME AND TRANSFER THE LIFE-FORCE OF ANY PLANET IT'S FIRED AT AND HELP NOURISH APOKOLIPS BACK TO HEALTH.
--I CAN SHOW YOU WHERE-- LET GLORIOUS GODFREY GUIDE YOU TO--
SKRAKA
GO BE GLORIOUSLY UNCONSCIOUS.

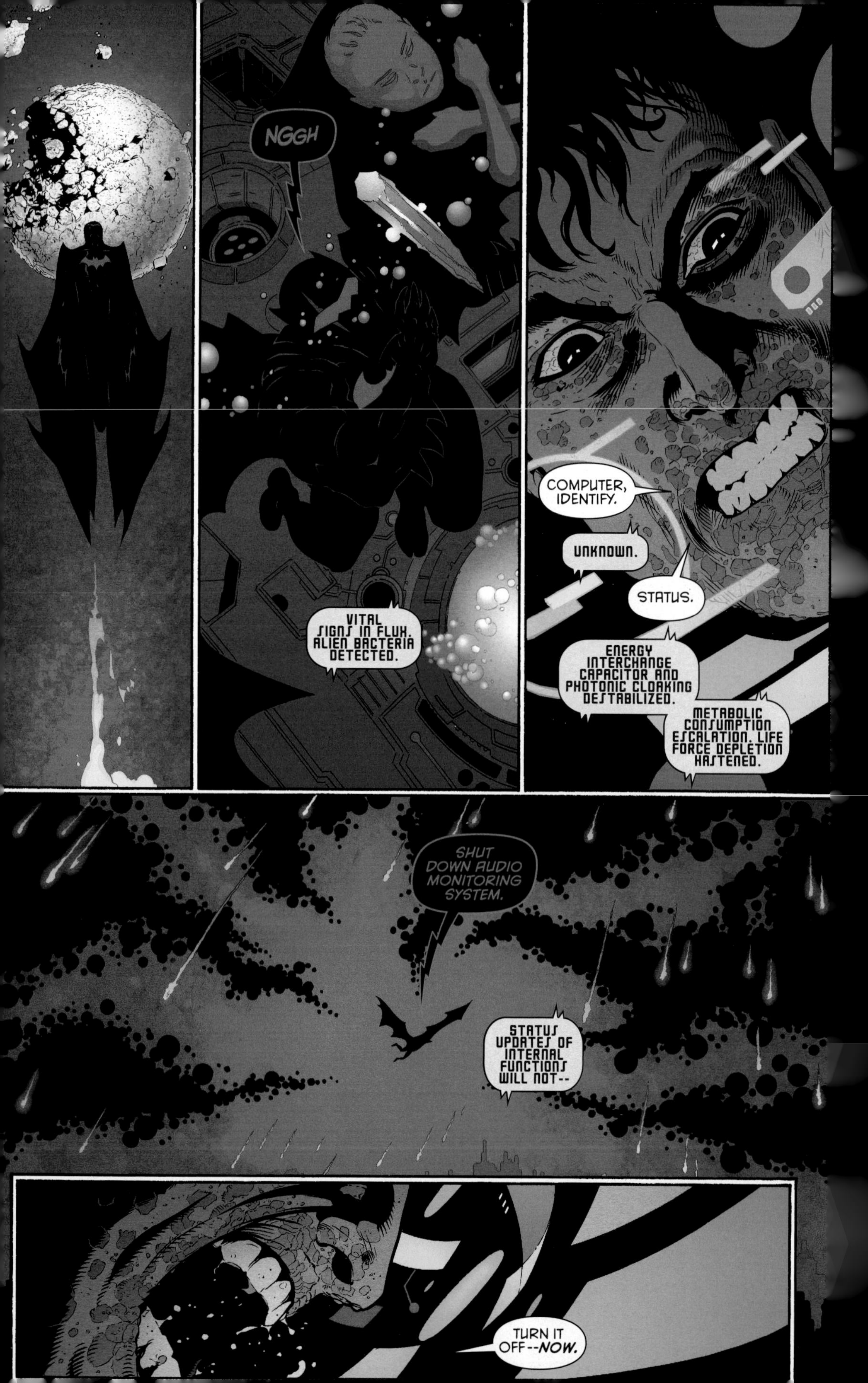
NGGH
VITAL SIGNS IN FLUX. ALIEN BACTERIA DETECTED.
COMPUTER, IDENTIFY.
UNKNOWN.
STATUS.
ENERGY INTERCHANGE CAPACITOR AND PHOTONIC CLOAKING DESTABILIZED.
METABOLIC CONSUMPTION ESCALATION. LIFE FORCE DEPLETION HASTENED.
SHUT DOWN AUDIO MONITORING SYSTEM.
STATUS UPDATES OF INTERNAL FUNCTIONS WILL NOT--
TURN IT OFF--NOW.

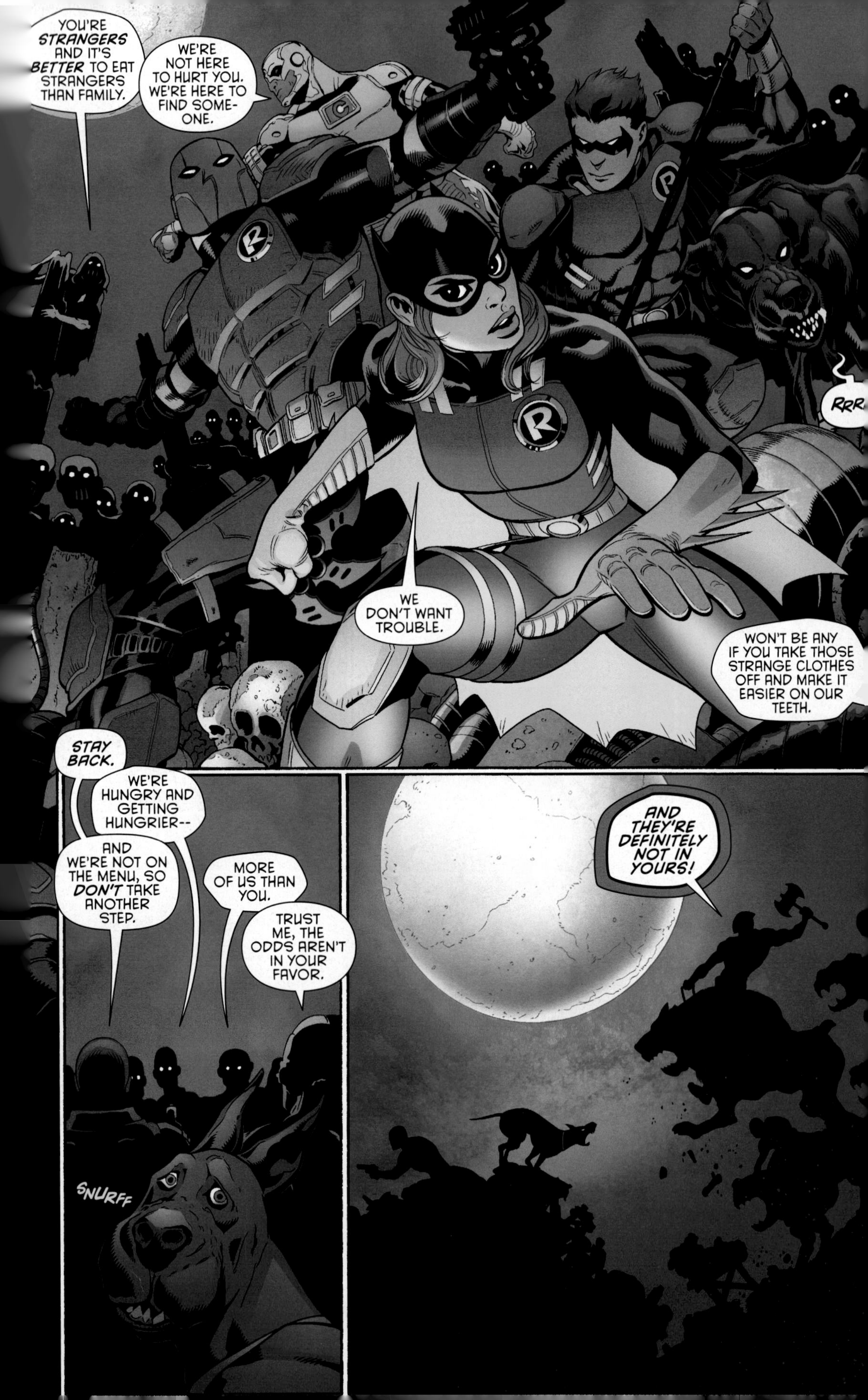
YOU'RE STRANGERS AND IT'S BETTER TO EAT STRANGERS THAN FAMILY.
WE'RE NOT HERE TO HURT YOU. WE'RE HERE TO FIND SOME-ONE.
RRR
WE DON'T WANT TROUBLE.
WON'T BE ANY IF YOU TAKE THOSE STRANGE CLOTHES OFF AND MAKE IT EASIER ON OUR TEETH.
STAY BACK.
WE'RE HUNGRY AND GETTING HUNGRIER--
AND WE'RE NOT ON THE MENU, SO DON'T TAKE ANOTHER STEP.
MORE OF US THAN YOU.
TRUST ME, THE ODDS AREN'T IN YOUR FAVOR.
SNURFF
AND THEY'RE DEFINITELY NOT IN YOURS!

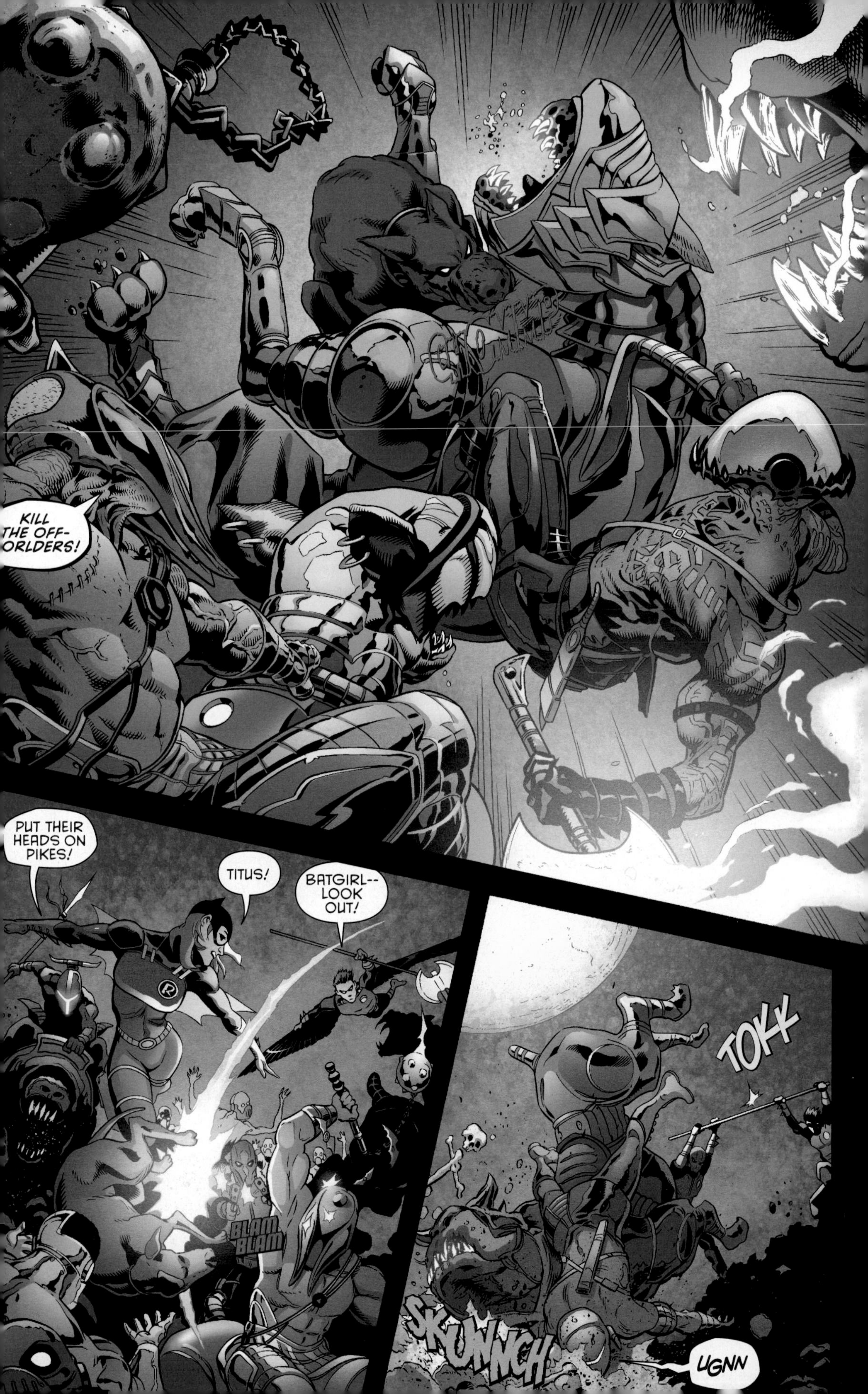
KILL THE OFF-WORLDERS!
PUT THEIR HEADS ON PIKES!
TITUS!
BATGIRL-- LOOK OUT!
BLAM BLAM
TOKK
SKUNNCH
UGNN

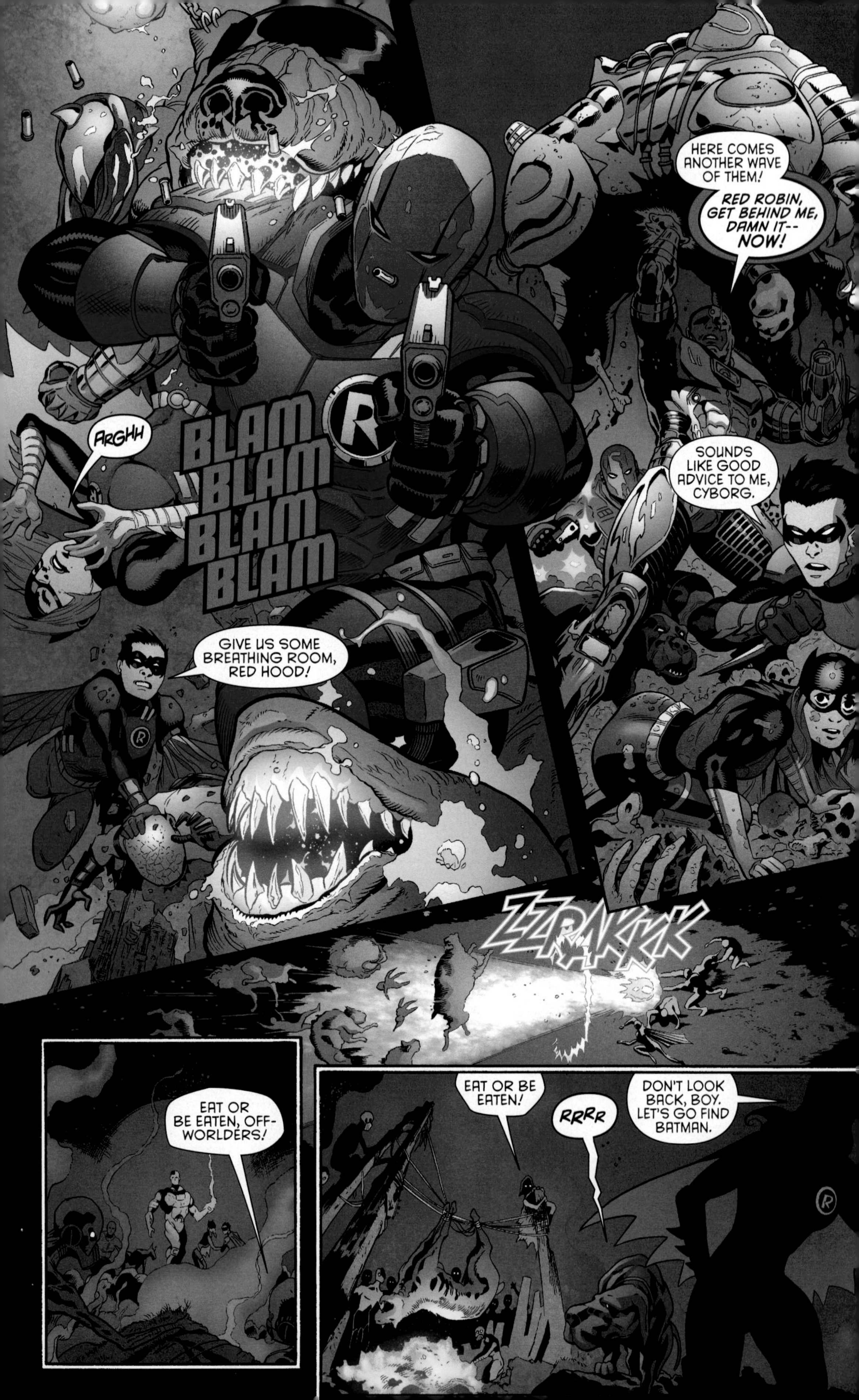
HERE COMES ANOTHER WAVE OF THEM!
RED ROBIN, GET BEHIND ME, DAMN IT-- NOW!
ARGHH
BLAM BLAM BLAM BLAM BLAM
SOUNDS LIKE GOOD ADVICE TO ME, CYBORG.
GIVE US SOME BREATHING ROOM, RED HOOD!
ZZRAKKK
EAT OR BE EATEN, OFF-WORLDERS!
EAT OR BE EATEN!
RRRR
DON'T LOOK BACK, BOY. LET'S GO FIND BATMAN.

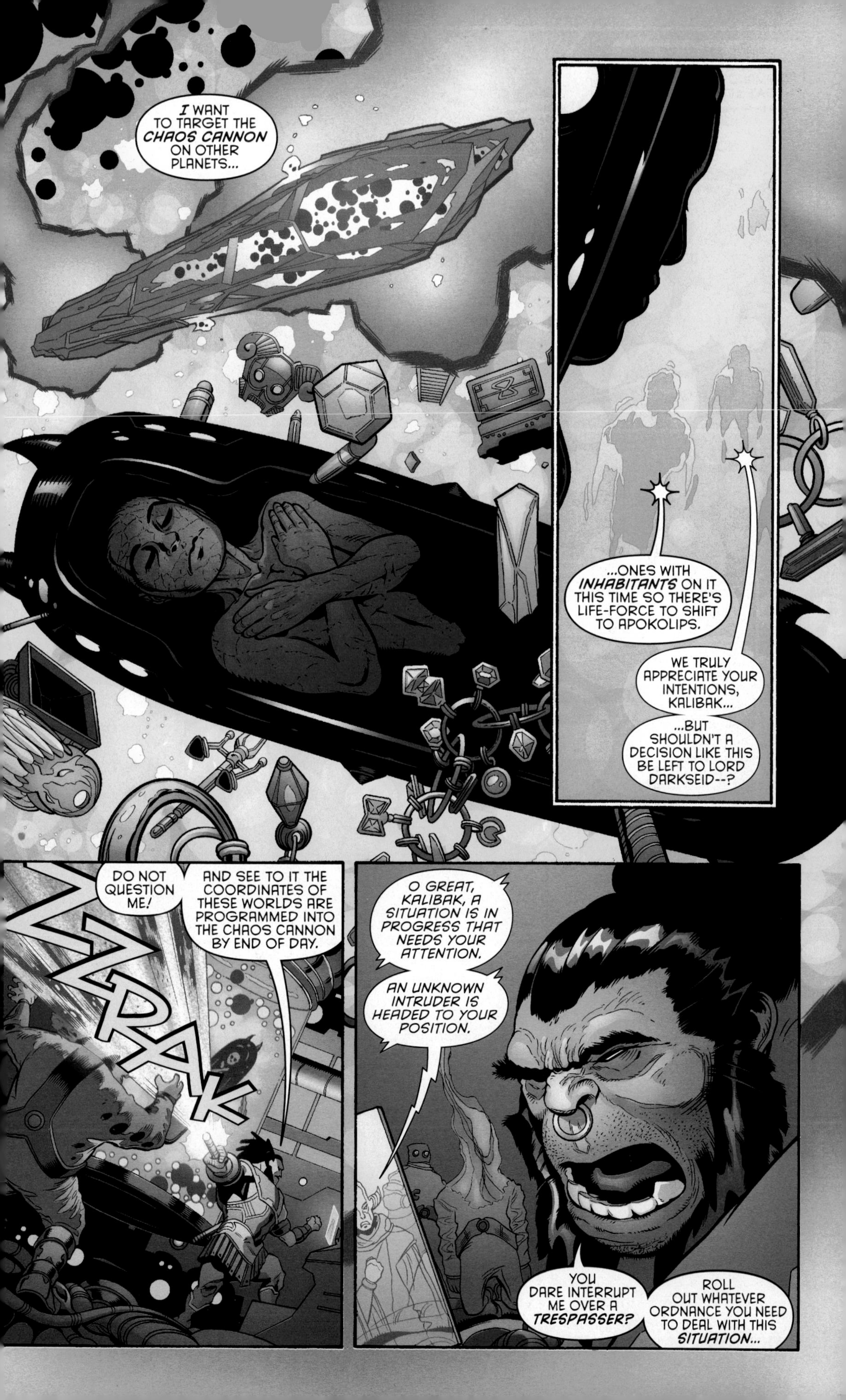
I WANT TO TARGET THE CHAOS CANNON ON OTHER PLANETS...
...ONES WITH INHABITANTS ON IT THIS TIME SO THERE'S LIFE-FORCE TO SHIFT TO APOKOLIPS.
WE TRULY APPRECIATE YOUR INTENTIONS, KALIBAK...
...BUT SHOULDN'T A DECISION LIKE THIS BE LEFT TO LORD DARKSEID--?
ZZRAK
DO NOT QUESTION ME!
AND SEE TO IT THE COORDINATES OF THESE WORLDS ARE PROGRAMMED INTO THE CHAOS CANNON BY END OF DAY.
O GREAT, KALIBAK, A SITUATION IS IN PROGRESS THAT NEEDS YOUR ATTENTION.
AN UNKNOWN INTRUDER IS HEADED TO YOUR POSITION.
YOU DARE INTERRUPT ME OVER A TRESPASSER?
ROLL OUT WHATEVER ORDNANCE YOU NEED TO DEAL WITH THIS SITUATION...

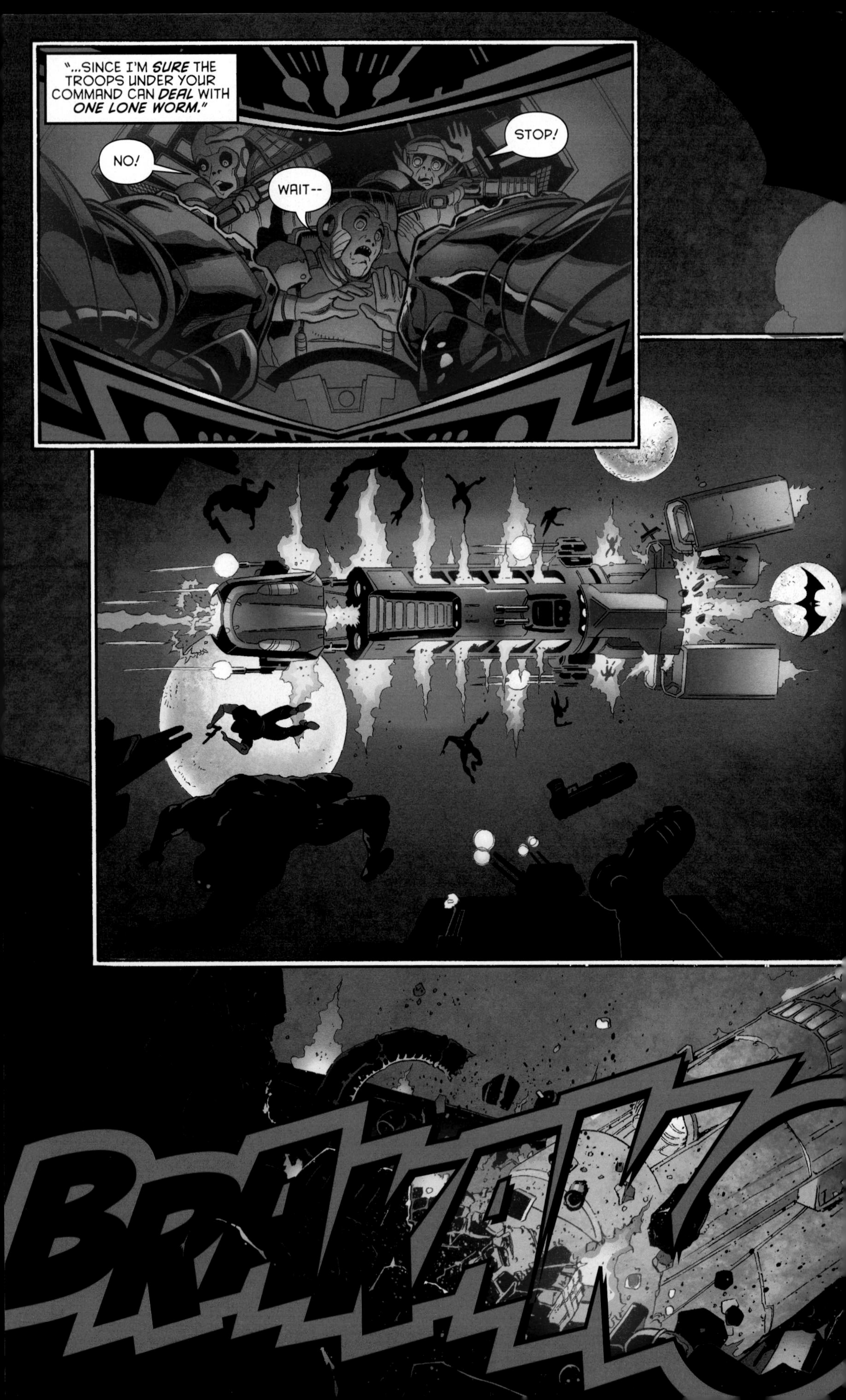
"...SINCE I'M SURE THE TROOPS UNDER YOUR COMMAND CAN DEAL WITH ONE LONE WORM."
NO!
WAIT--
STOP!
BRAKA-KOOM!

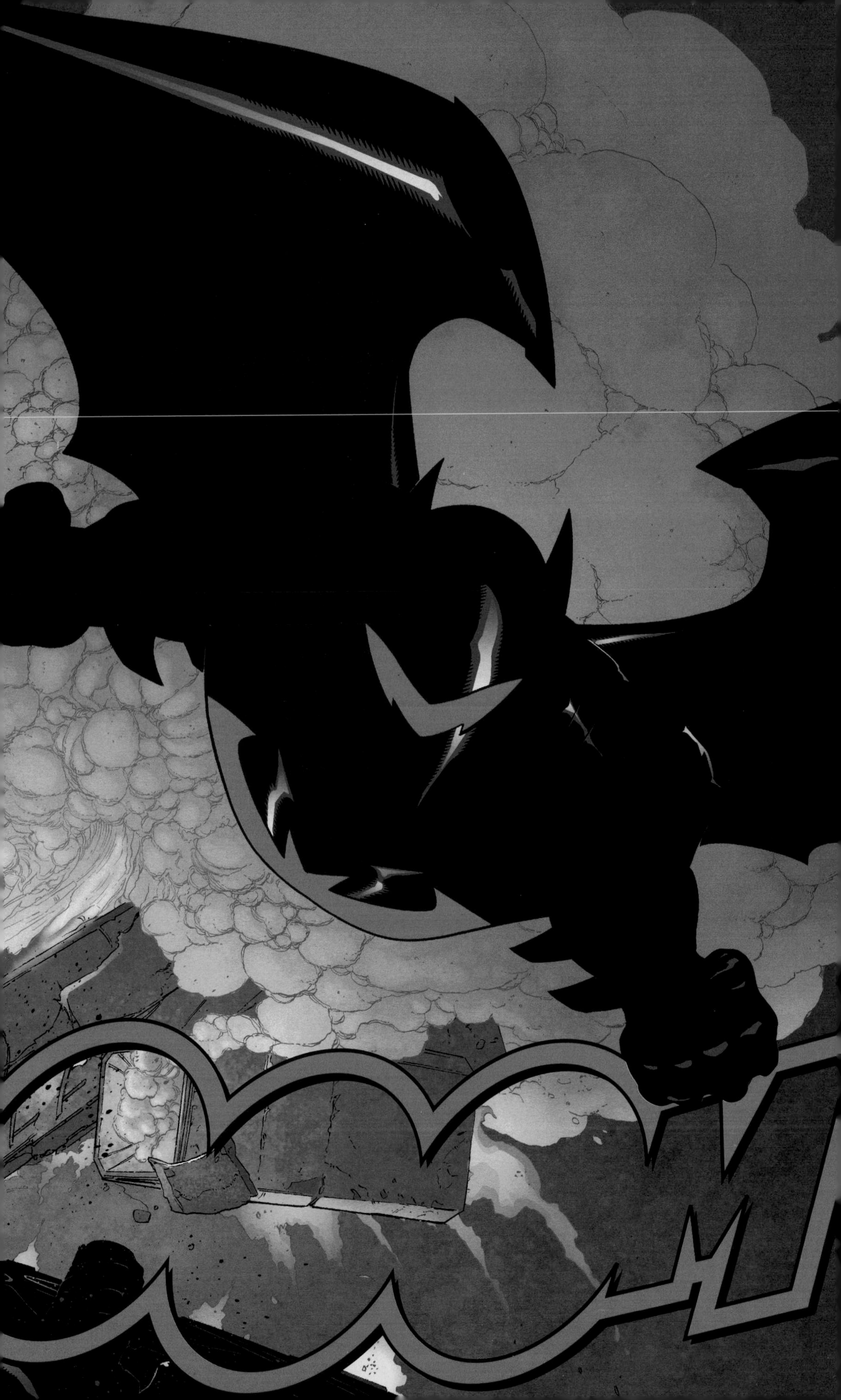

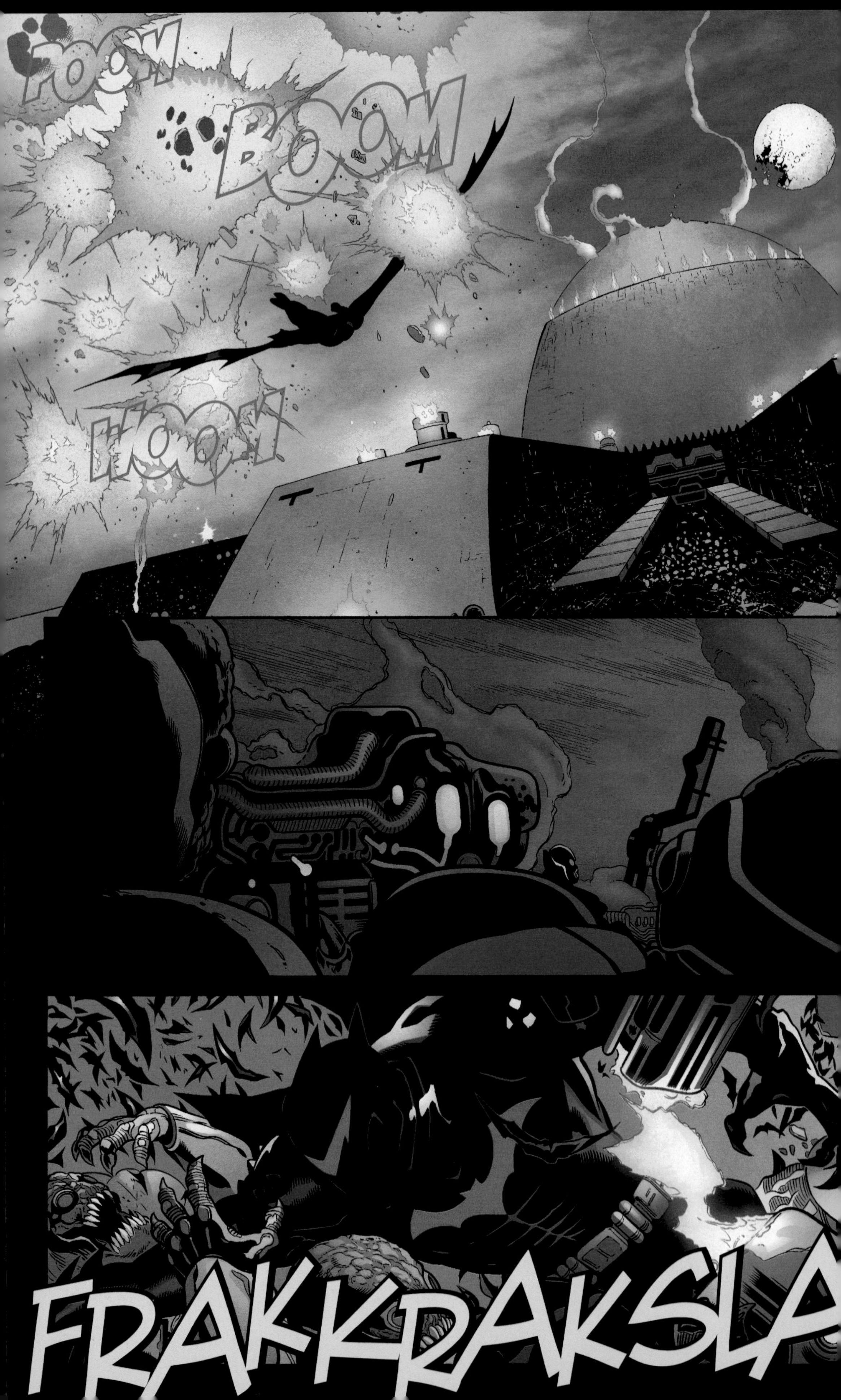
FOOM
BOOM
WOOM
FRAKKRAKSLA

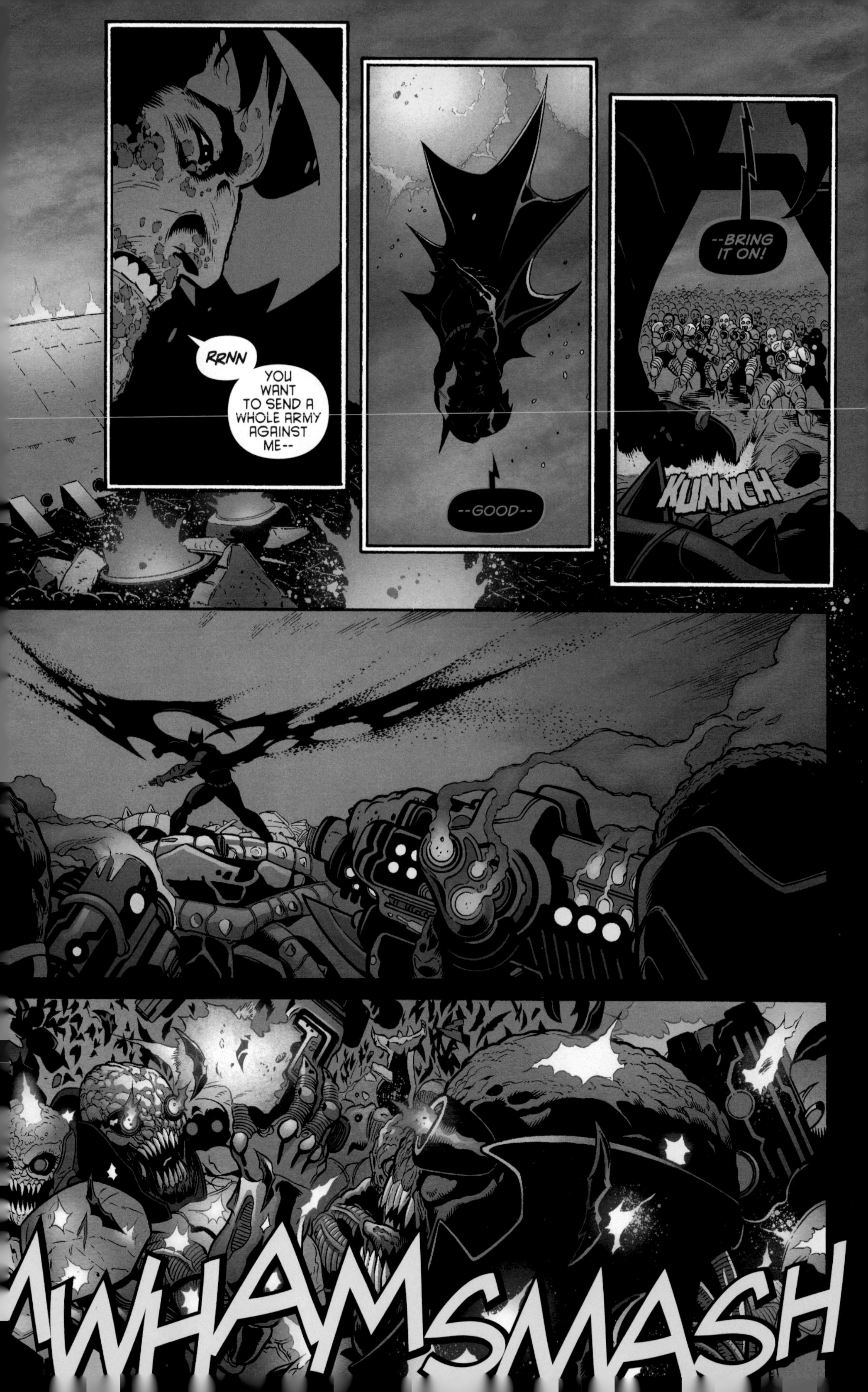
RRNN
YOU WANT TO SEND A WHOLE ARMY AGAINST ME--
--GOOD--
--BRING IT ON!
KUNNCH
WHAMSMASH

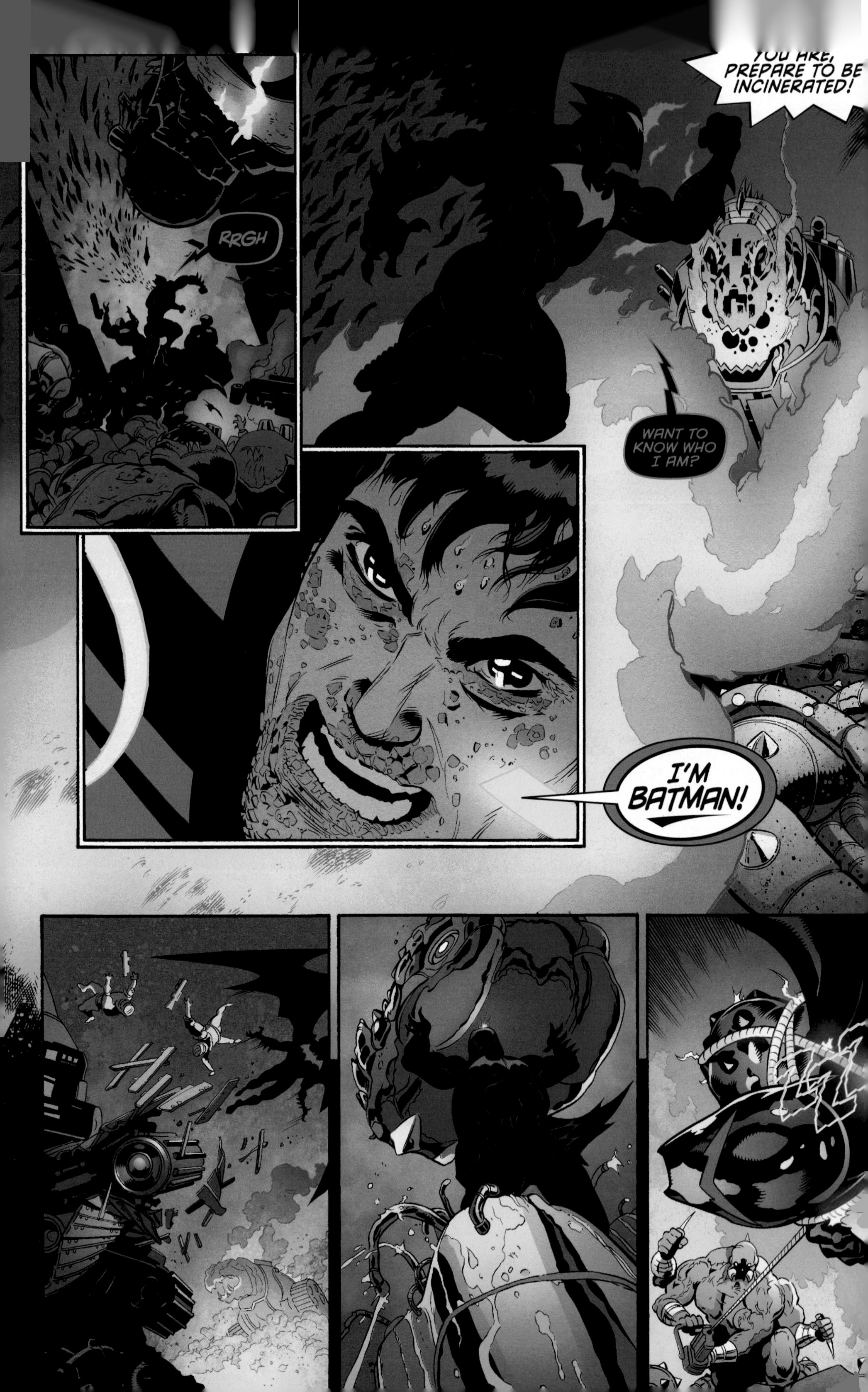
YOU ARE, PREPARE TO BE INCINERATED!
RRGH
WANT TO KNOW WHO I AM?
I'M BATMAN!

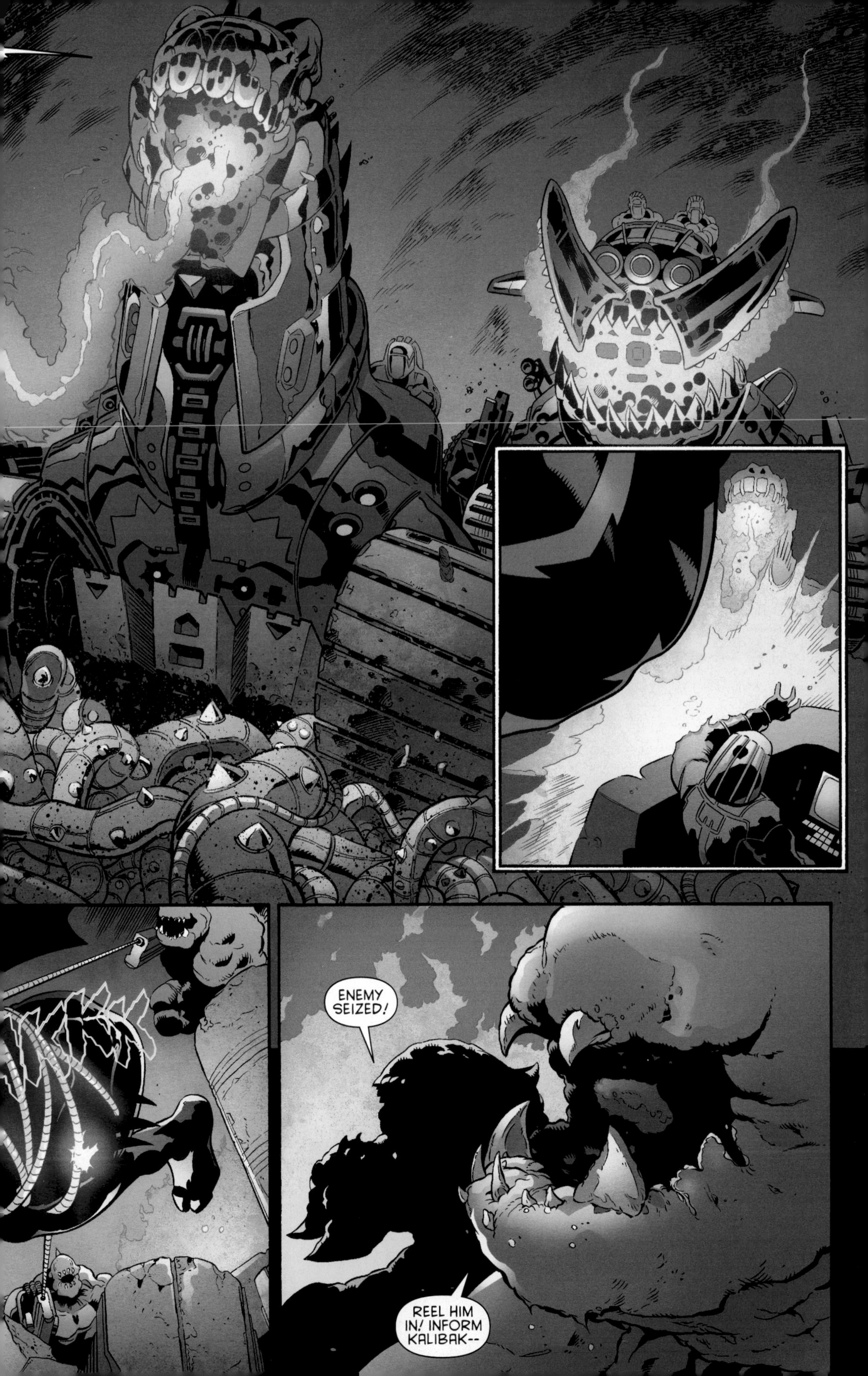
ENEMY SEIZED!
REEL HIM IN! INFORM KALIBAK--

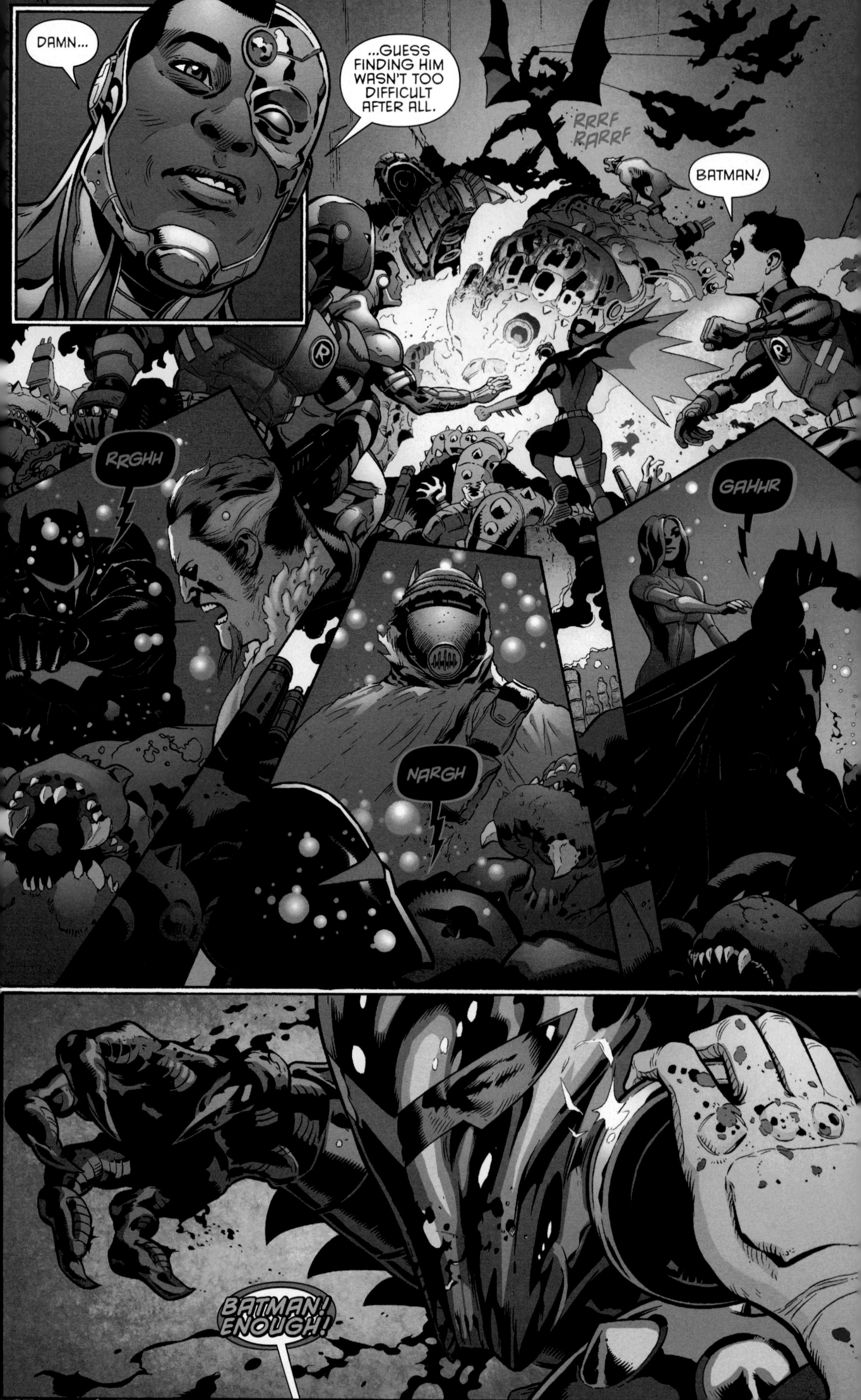
DAMN...
...GUESS FINDING HIM WASN'T TOO DIFFICULT AFTER ALL.
RRRF RARRF
BATMAN!
RRGHH
NARGH
GAHHR
BATMAN! ENOUGH!

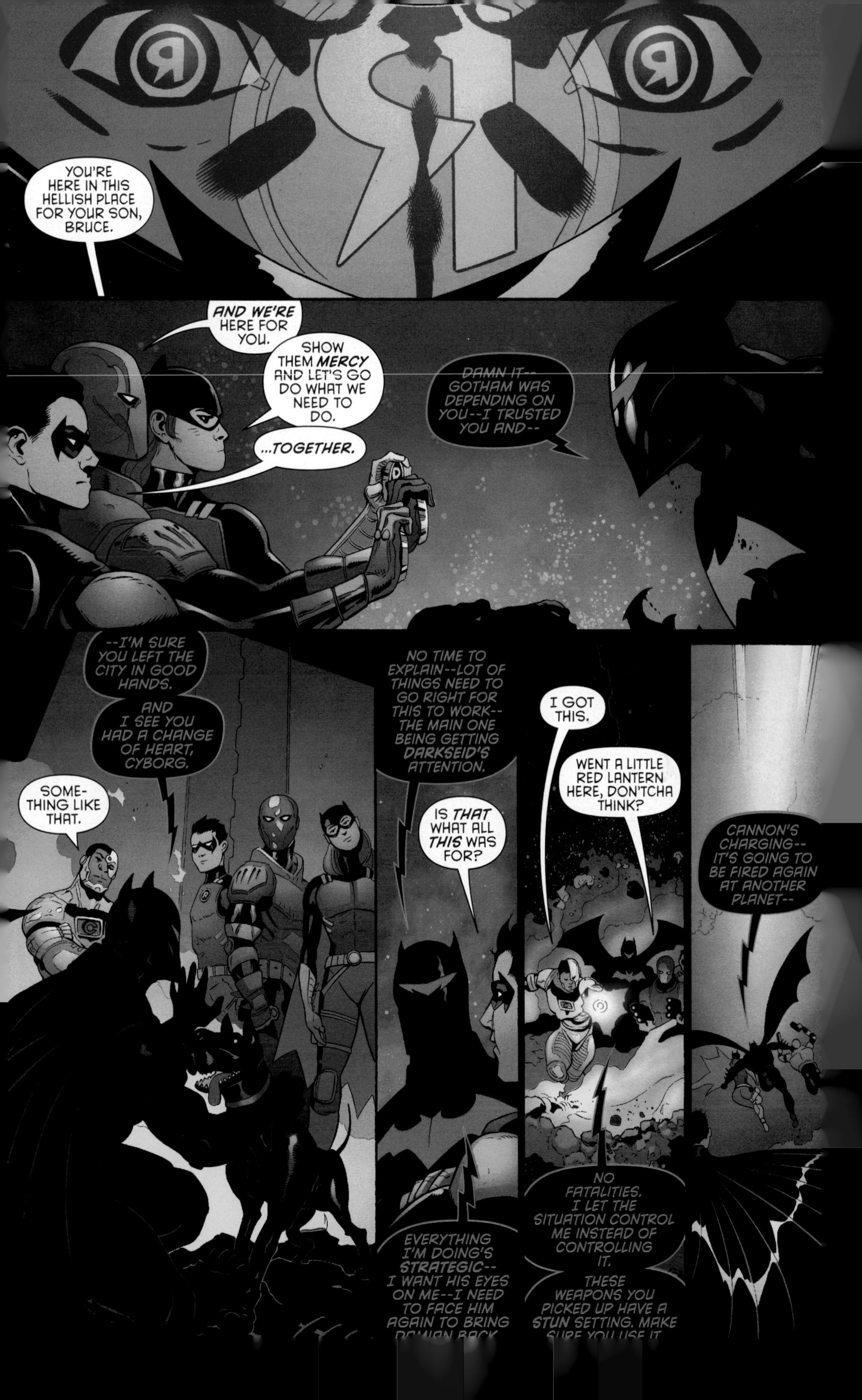
YOU'RE HERE IN THIS HELLISH PLACE FOR YOUR SON, BRUCE.
AND WE'RE HERE FOR YOU.
SHOW THEM MERCY AND LET'S GO DO WHAT WE NEED TO DO.
...TOGETHER.
DAMN IT-- GOTHAM WAS DEPENDING ON YOU--I TRUSTED YOU AND--
--I'M SURE YOU LEFT THE CITY IN GOOD HANDS.
AND I SEE YOU HAD A CHANGE OF HEART, CYBORG.
SOME-THING LIKE THAT.
NO TIME TO EXPLAIN--LOT OF THINGS NEED TO GO RIGHT FOR THIS TO WORK-- THE MAIN ONE BEING GETTING DARKSEID'S ATTENTION.
IS THAT WHAT ALL THIS WAS FOR?
EVERYTHING I'M DOING'S STRATEGIC-- I WANT HIS EYES ON ME--I NEED TO FACE HIM AGAIN TO BRING
I GOT THIS.
WENT A LITTLE RED LANTERN HERE, DON'TCHA THINK?
NO FATALITIES. I LET THE SITUATION CONTROL ME INSTEAD OF CONTROLLING IT.
THESE WEAPONS YOU PICKED UP HAVE A STUN SETTING. MAKE
CANNON'S CHARGING-- IT'S GOING TO BE FIRED AGAIN AT ANOTHER PLANET--

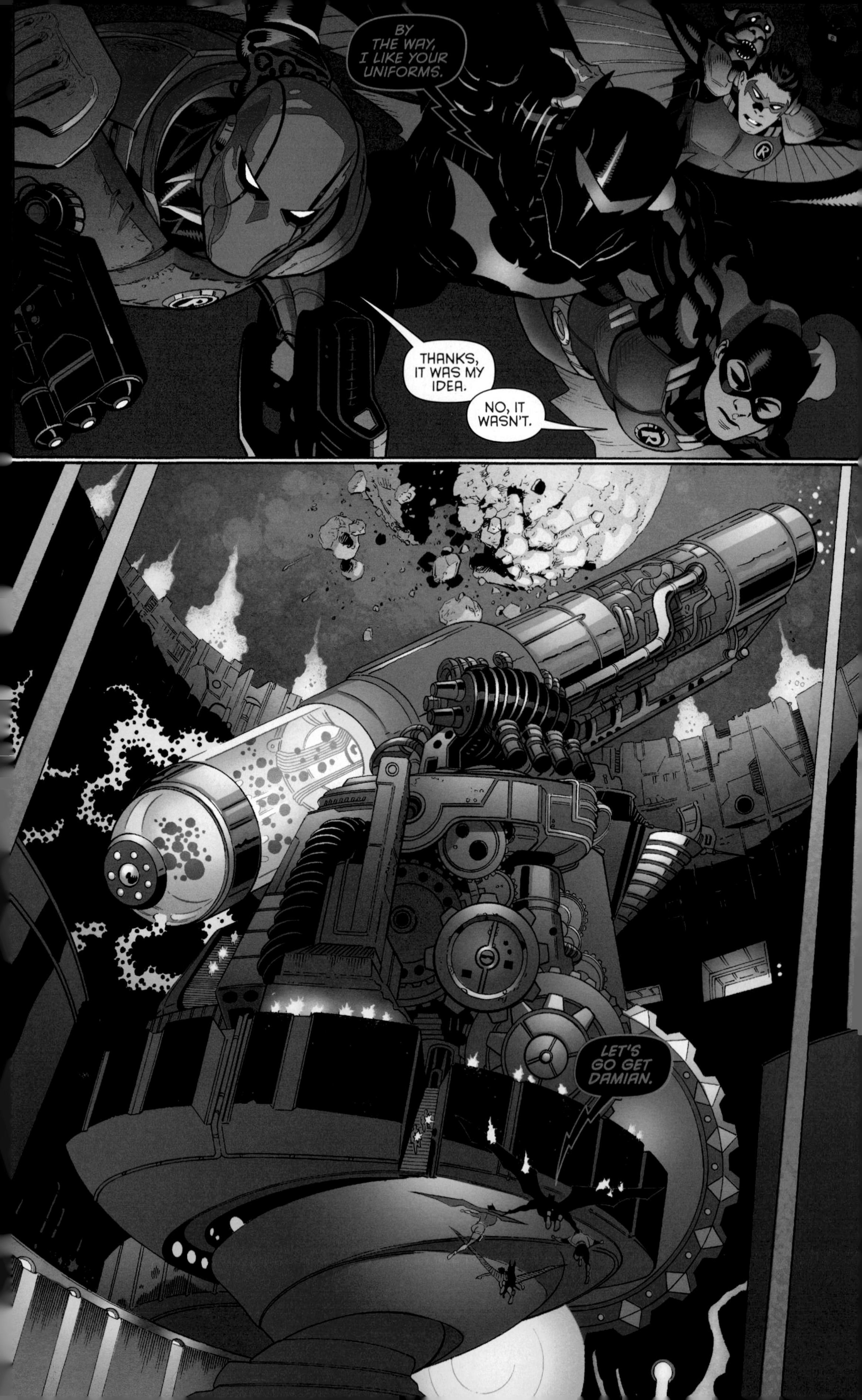
BY THE WAY, I LIKE YOUR UNIFORMS.
THANKS, IT WAS MY IDEA.
NO, IT WASN'T.
LET'S GO GET DAMIAN.

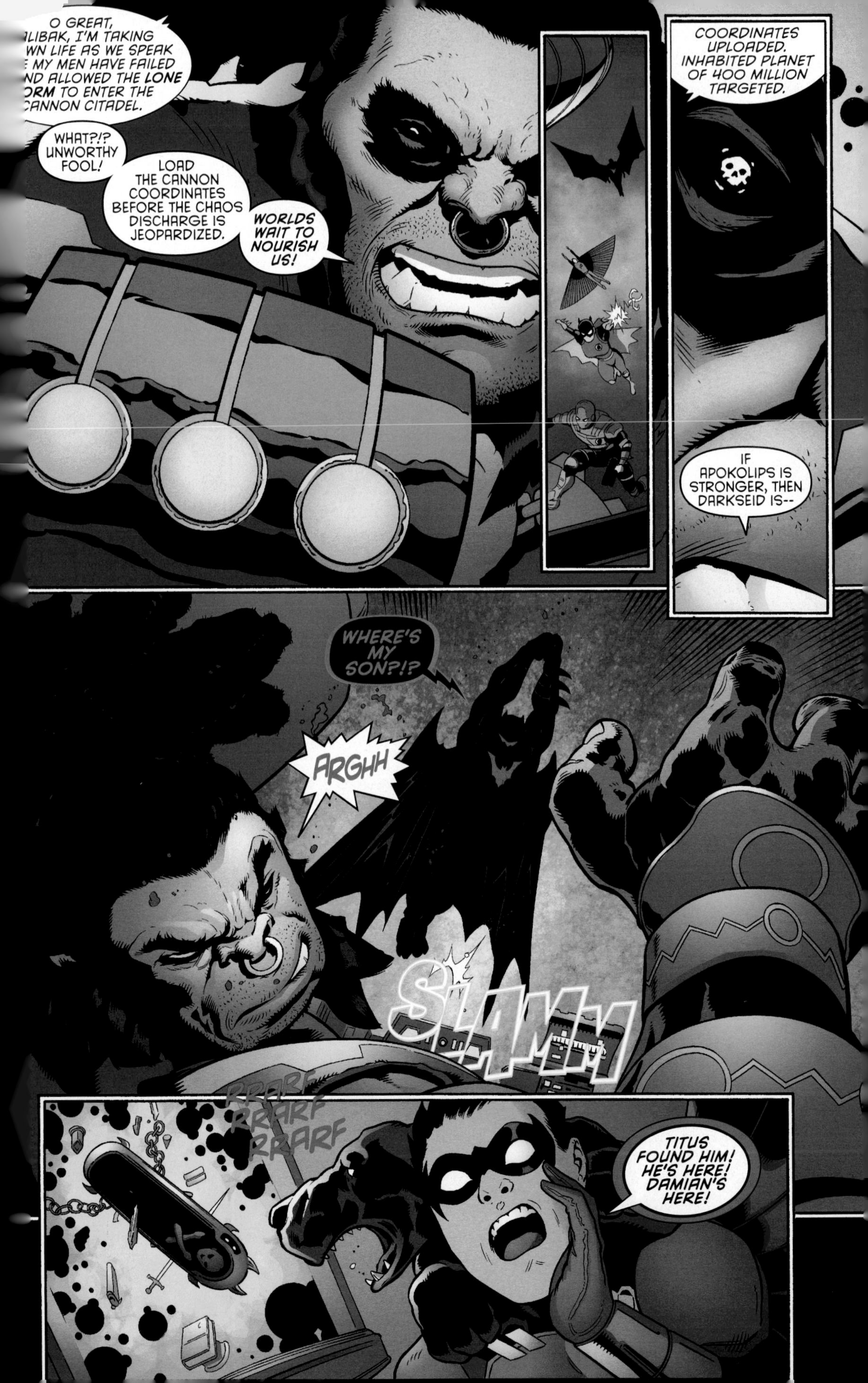

O GREAT, ...ALIBAK, I'M TAKING ...WN LIFE AS WE SPEAK ...E MY MEN HAVE FAILED ...ND ALLOWED THE LONE ...ORM TO ENTER THE CANNON CITADEL.
WHAT?!? UNWORTHY FOOL!
LOAD THE CANNON COORDINATES BEFORE THE CHAOS DISCHARGE IS JEOPARDIZED.
WORLDS WAIT TO NOURISH US!
COORDINATES UPLOADED. INHABITED PLANET OF 400 MILLION TARGETED.
IF APOKOLIPS IS STRONGER, THEN DARKSEID IS--
WHERE'S MY SON?!?
ARGHH
SLAMM
RRARF RRARF RRARF
TITUS FOUND HIM! HE'S HERE! DAMIAN'S HERE!

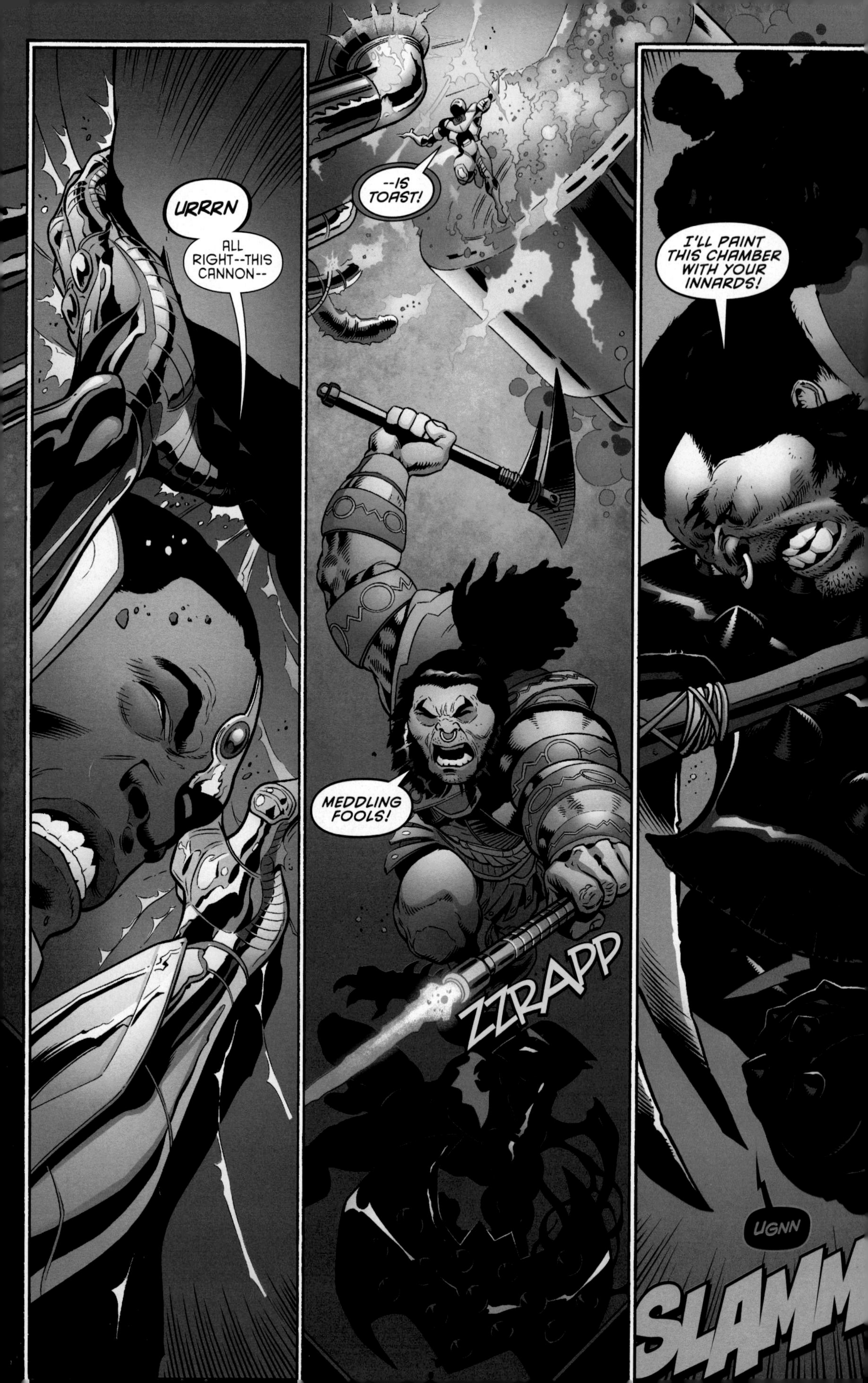
URRRN
ALL RIGHT--THIS CANNON--
--IS TOAST!
MEDDLING FOOLS!
ZZRAPP
I'LL PAINT THIS CHAMBER WITH YOUR INNARDS!
UGNN
SLAMM

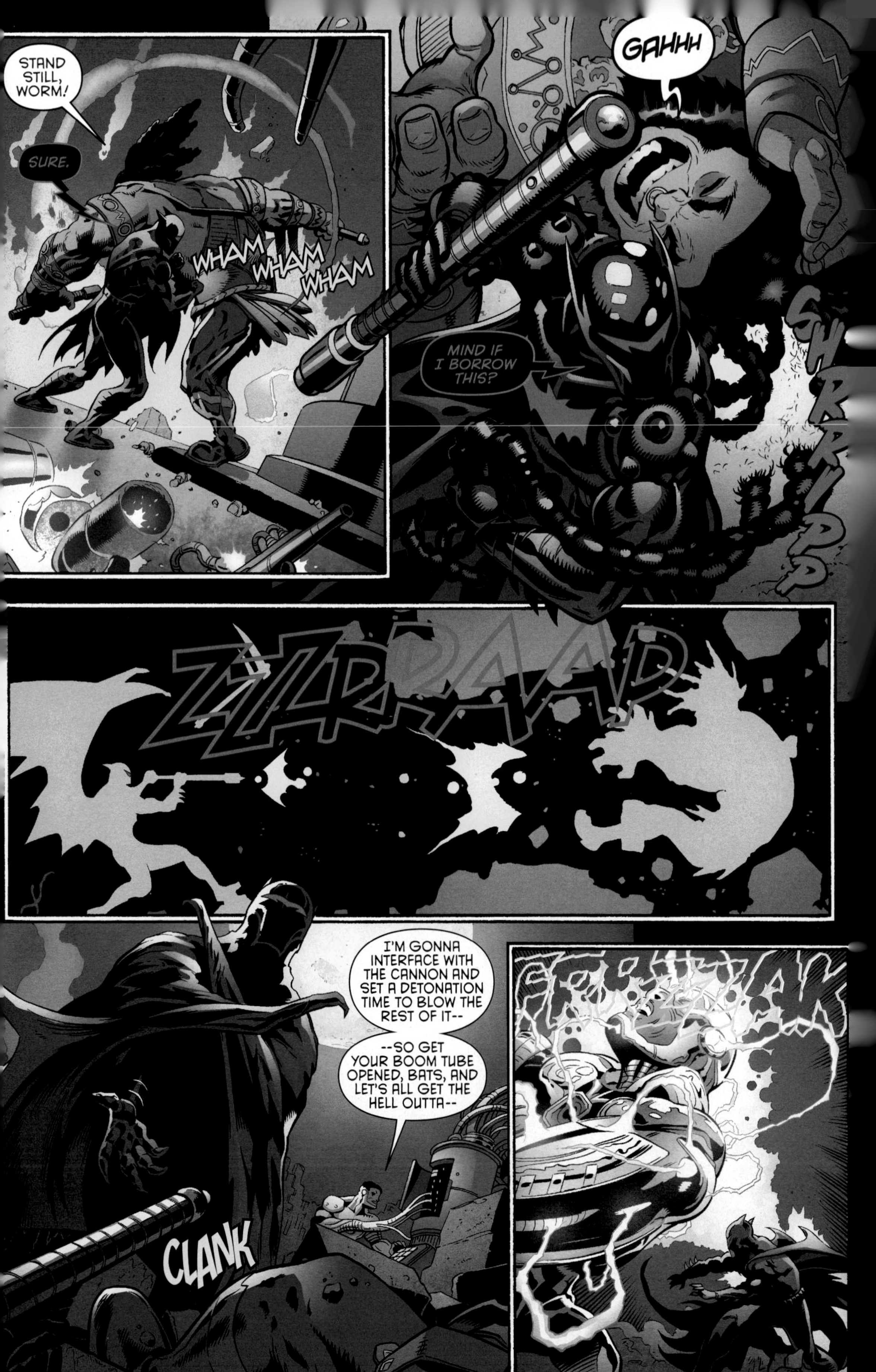
STAND STILL, WORM!
SURE.
WHAM WHAM WHAM
GAHHH
MIND IF I BORROW THIS?
ZZZRAAAP
I'M GONNA INTERFACE WITH THE CANNON AND SET A DETONATION TIME TO BLOW THE REST OF IT--
--SO GET YOUR BOOM TUBE OPENED, BATS, AND LET'S ALL GET THE HELL OUTTA--
CLANK

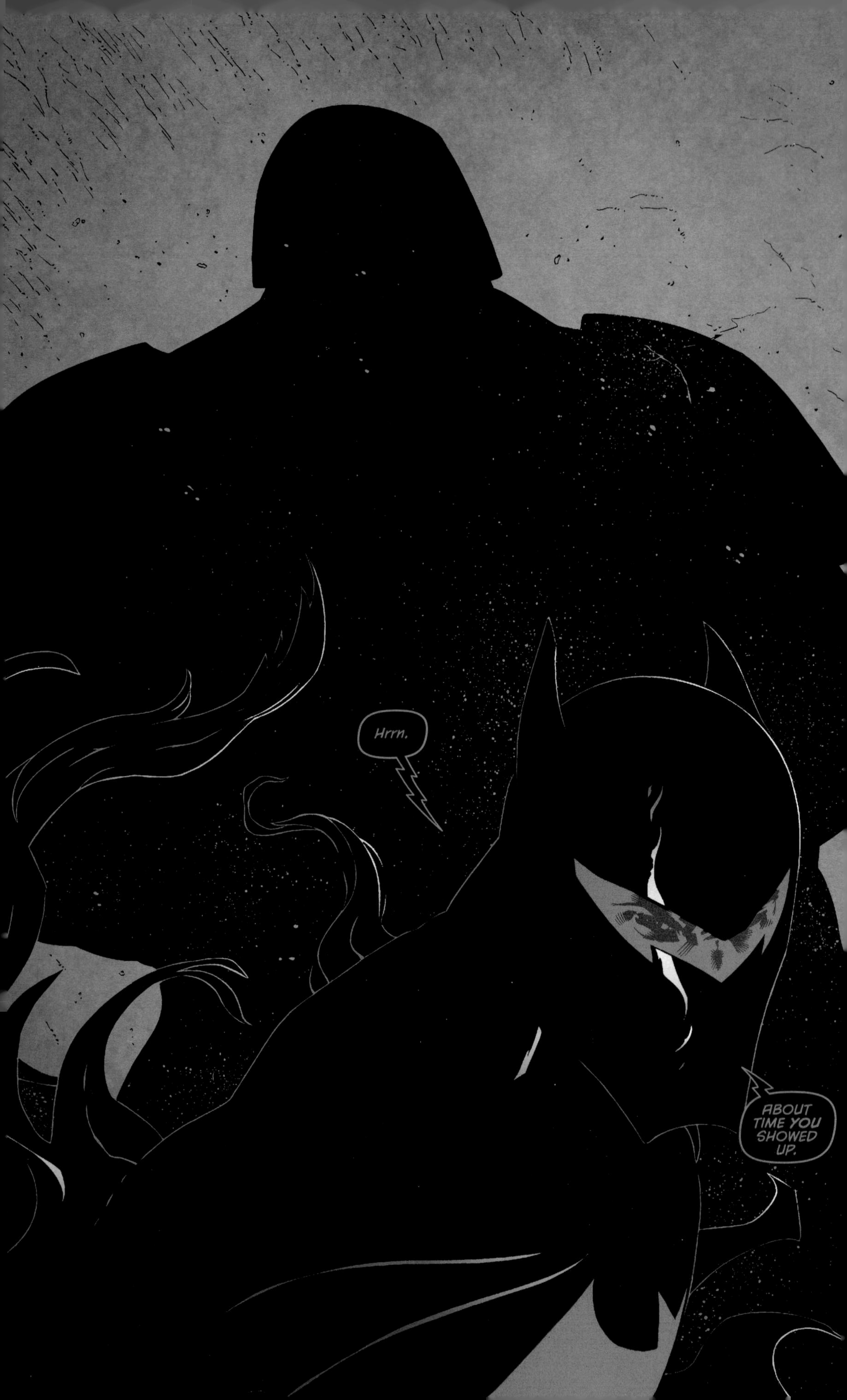
Hrrn.
ABOUT TIME YOU SHOWED UP.

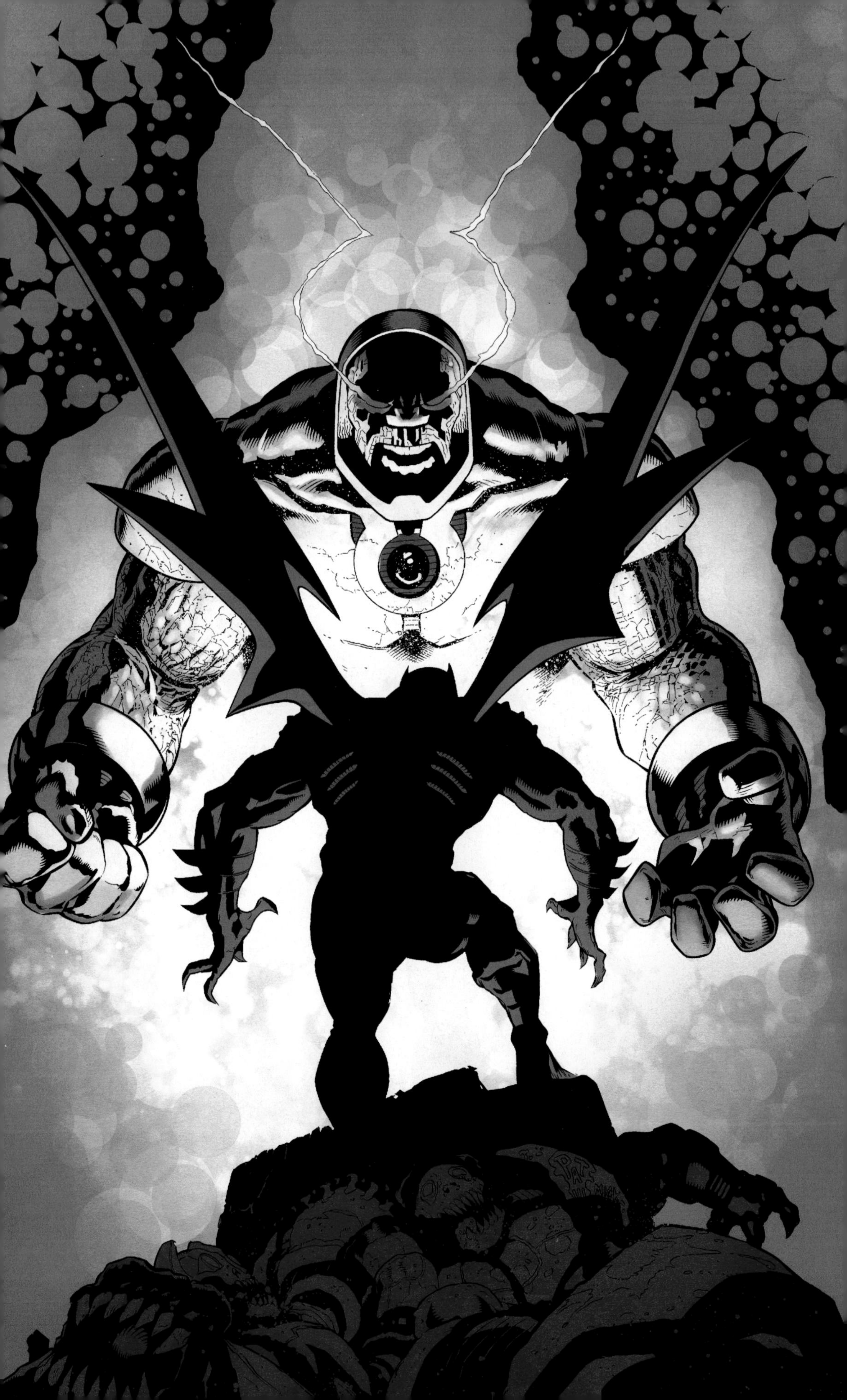

PATRICK GLEASON penciller MICK GRAY inker JOHN KALISZ colorist CARLOS M. MANGUAL letterer cover art by GLEASON, GRAY & KALISZ

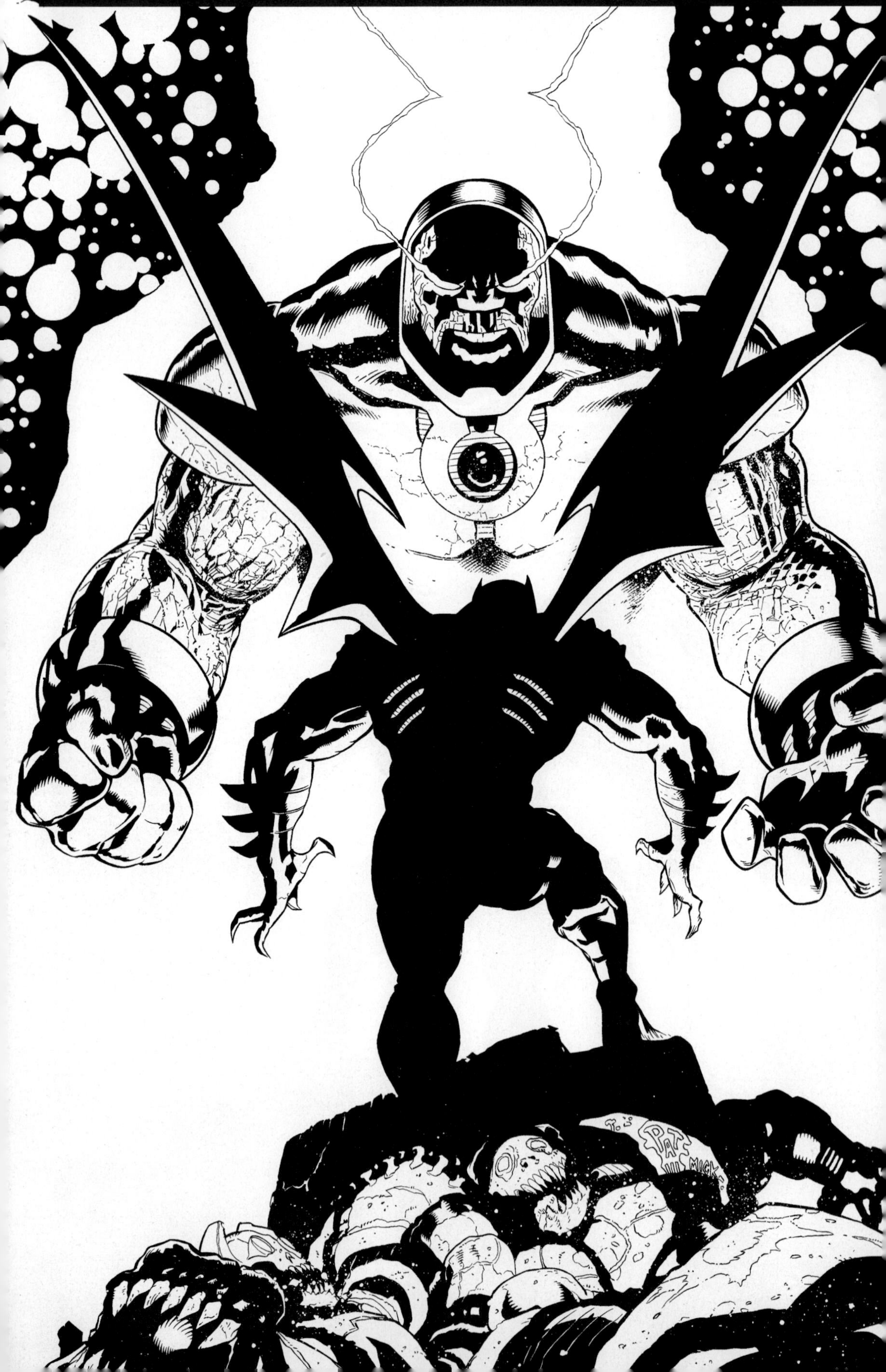
PAT
MICK

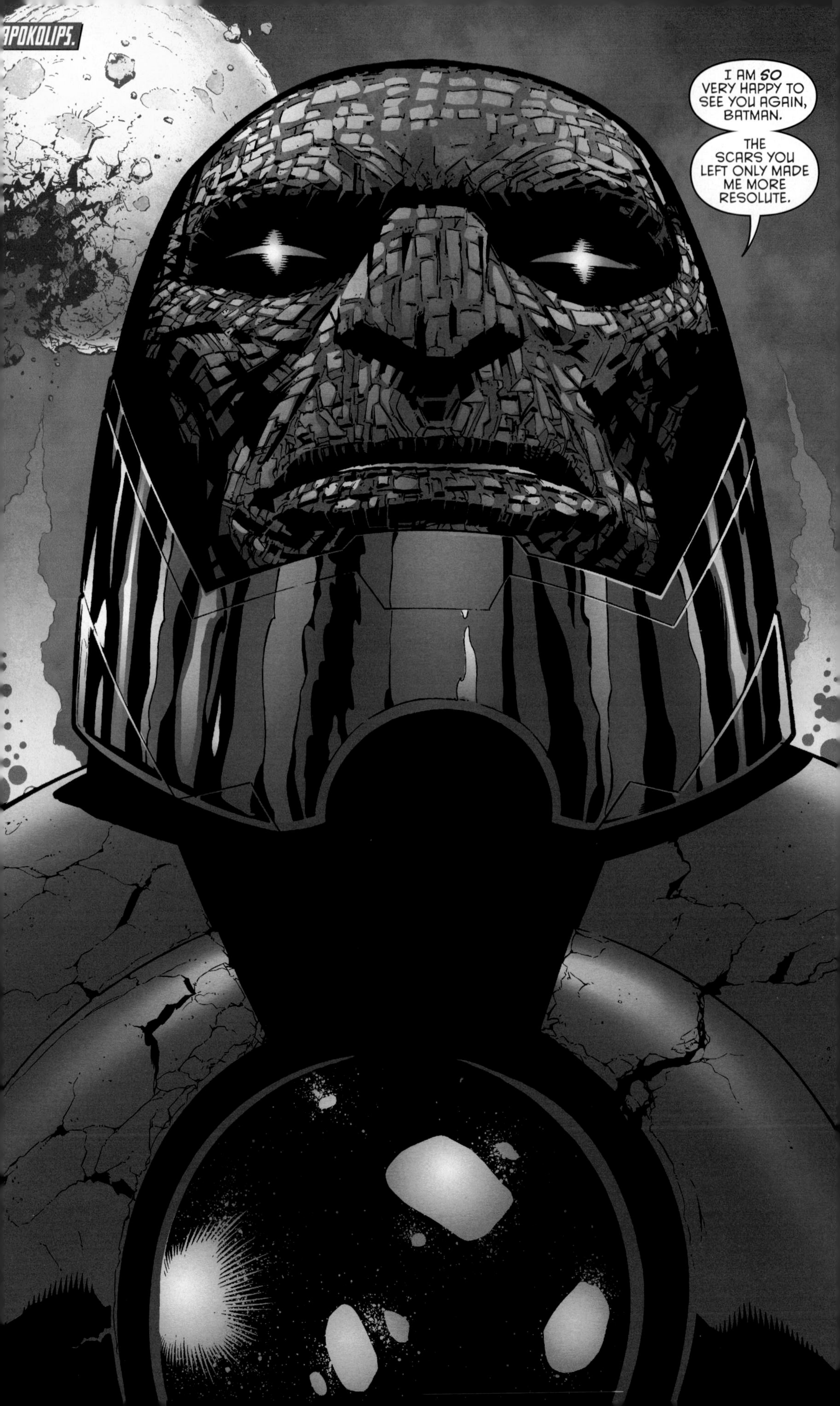
APOKOLIPS.
I AM *SO* VERY HAPPY TO SEE YOU AGAIN, BATMAN.
THE SCARS YOU LEFT ONLY MADE ME MORE RESOLUTE.

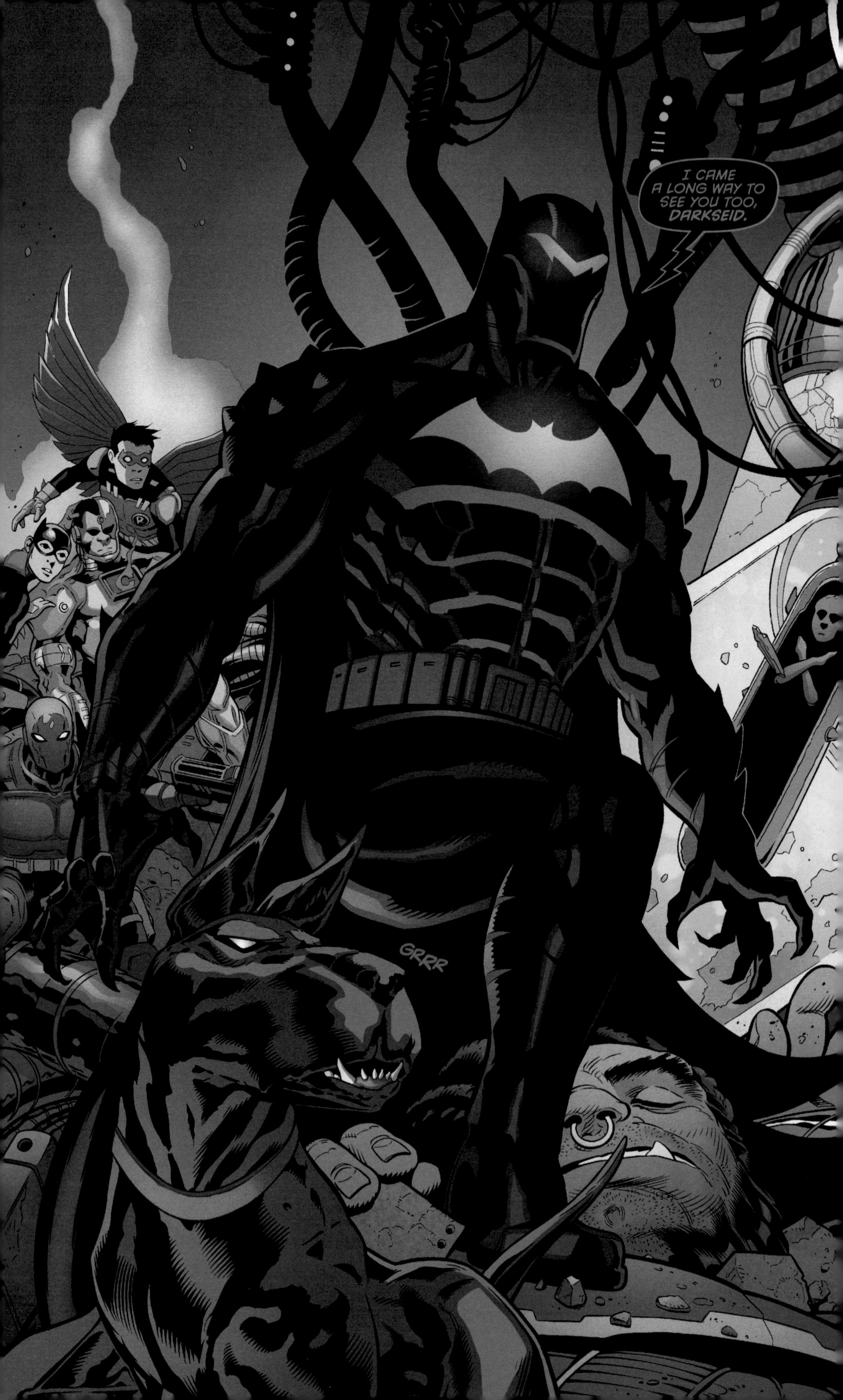
I CAME A LONG WAY TO SEE YOU TOO, DARKSEID.
GRRR

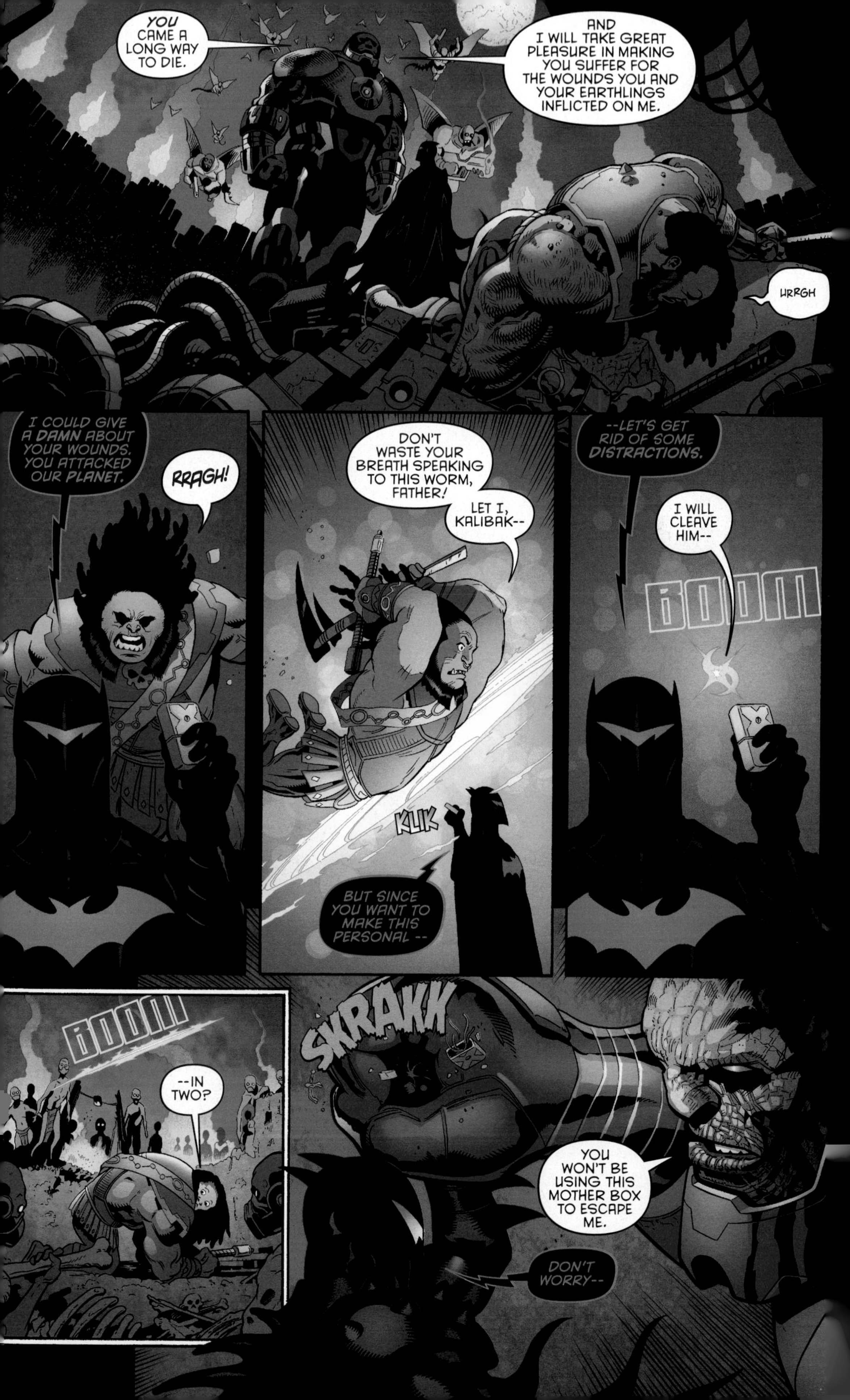
YOU CAME A LONG WAY TO DIE.
AND I WILL TAKE GREAT PLEASURE IN MAKING YOU SUFFER FOR THE WOUNDS YOU AND YOUR EARTHLINGS INFLICTED ON ME.
URRGH
I COULD GIVE A DAMN ABOUT YOUR WOUNDS. YOU ATTACKED OUR PLANET.
RRAGH!
DON'T WASTE YOUR BREATH SPEAKING TO THIS WORM, FATHER!
LET I, KALIBAK--
KLIK
BUT SINCE YOU WANT TO MAKE THIS PERSONAL --
--LET'S GET RID OF SOME DISTRACTIONS.
I WILL CLEAVE HIM--
BOOM
BOOM
--IN TWO?
SKRAKK
YOU WON'T BE USING THIS MOTHER BOX TO ESCAPE ME.
DON'T WORRY--

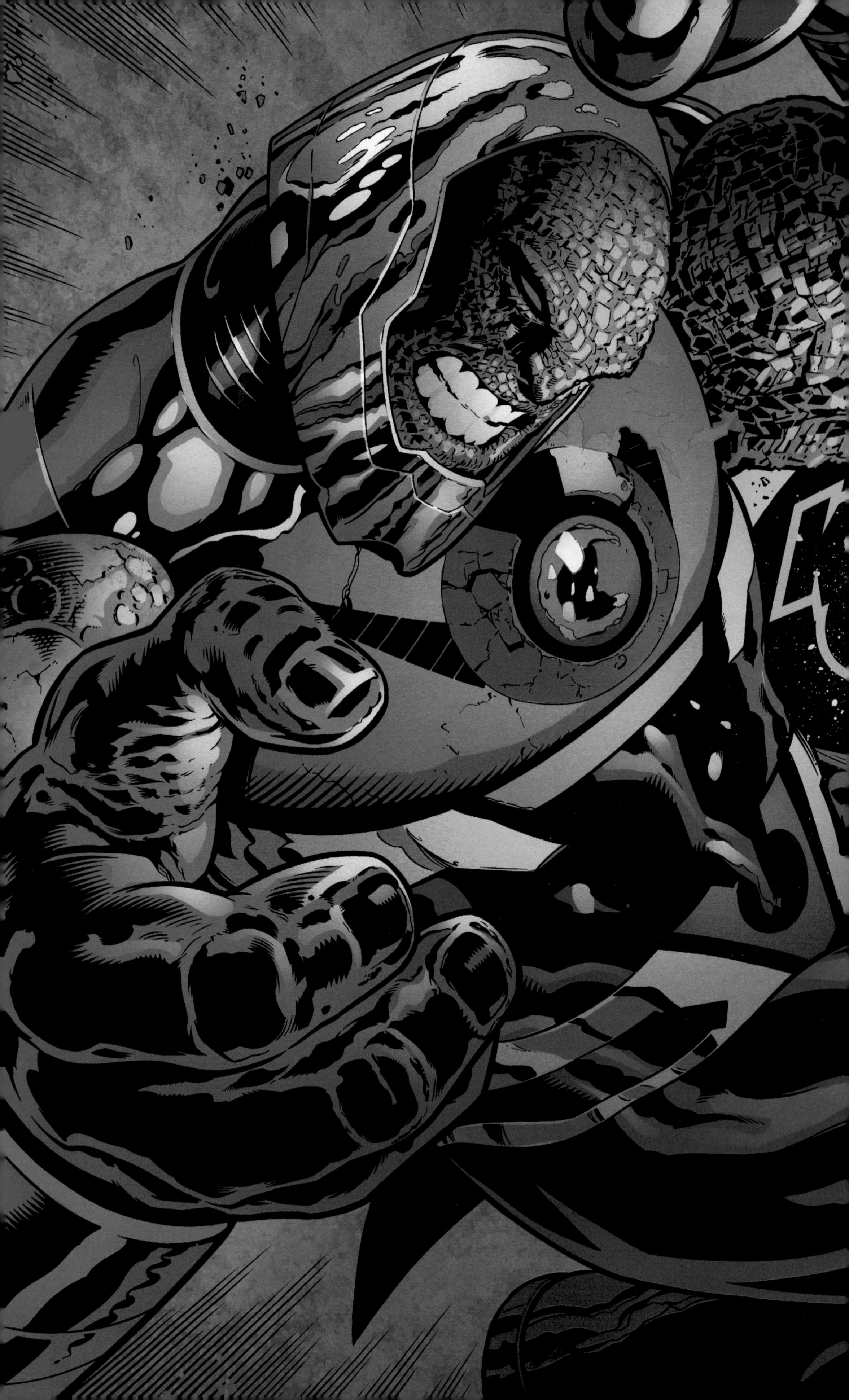

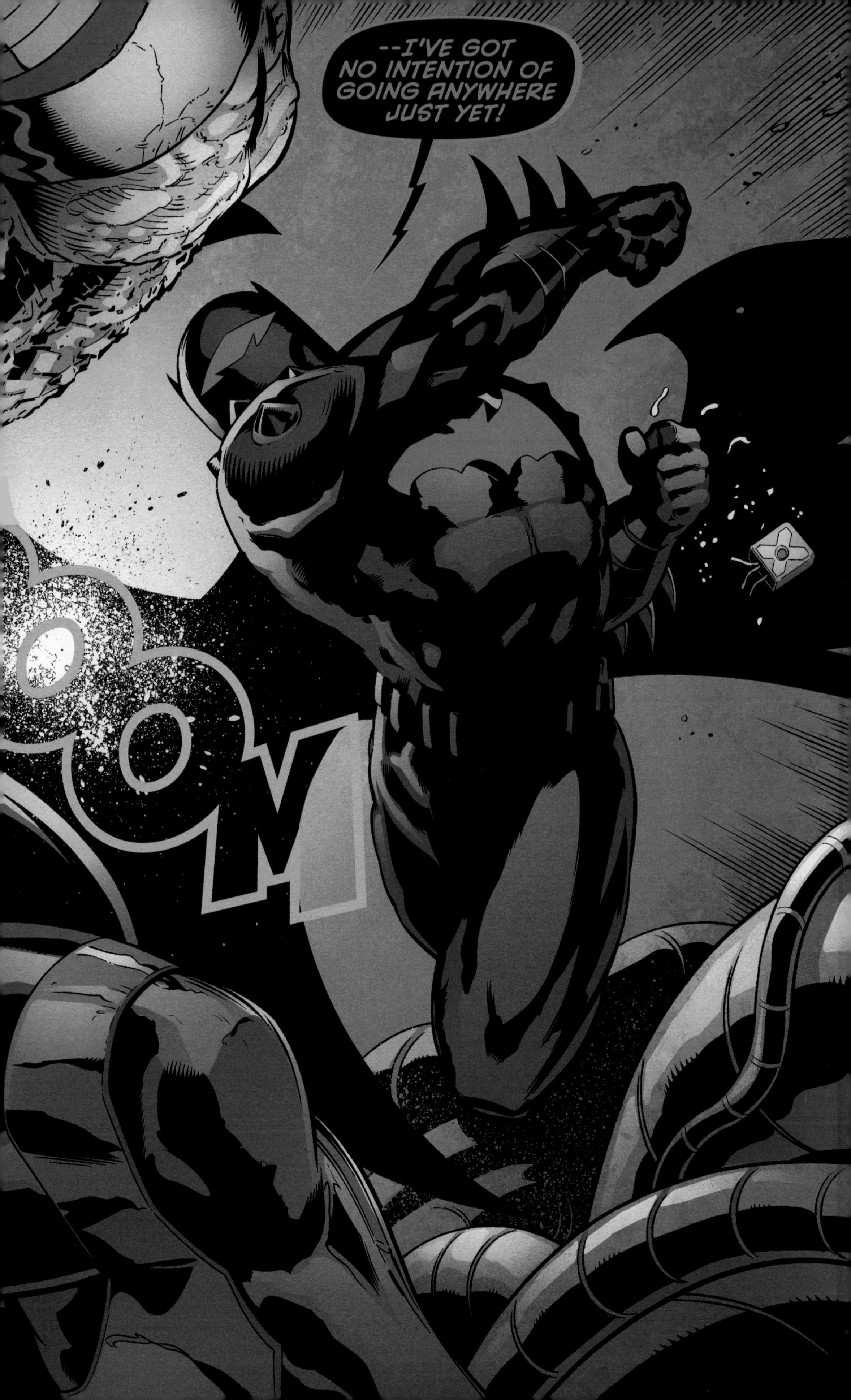
--I'VE GOT NO INTENTION OF GOING ANYWHERE JUST YET!

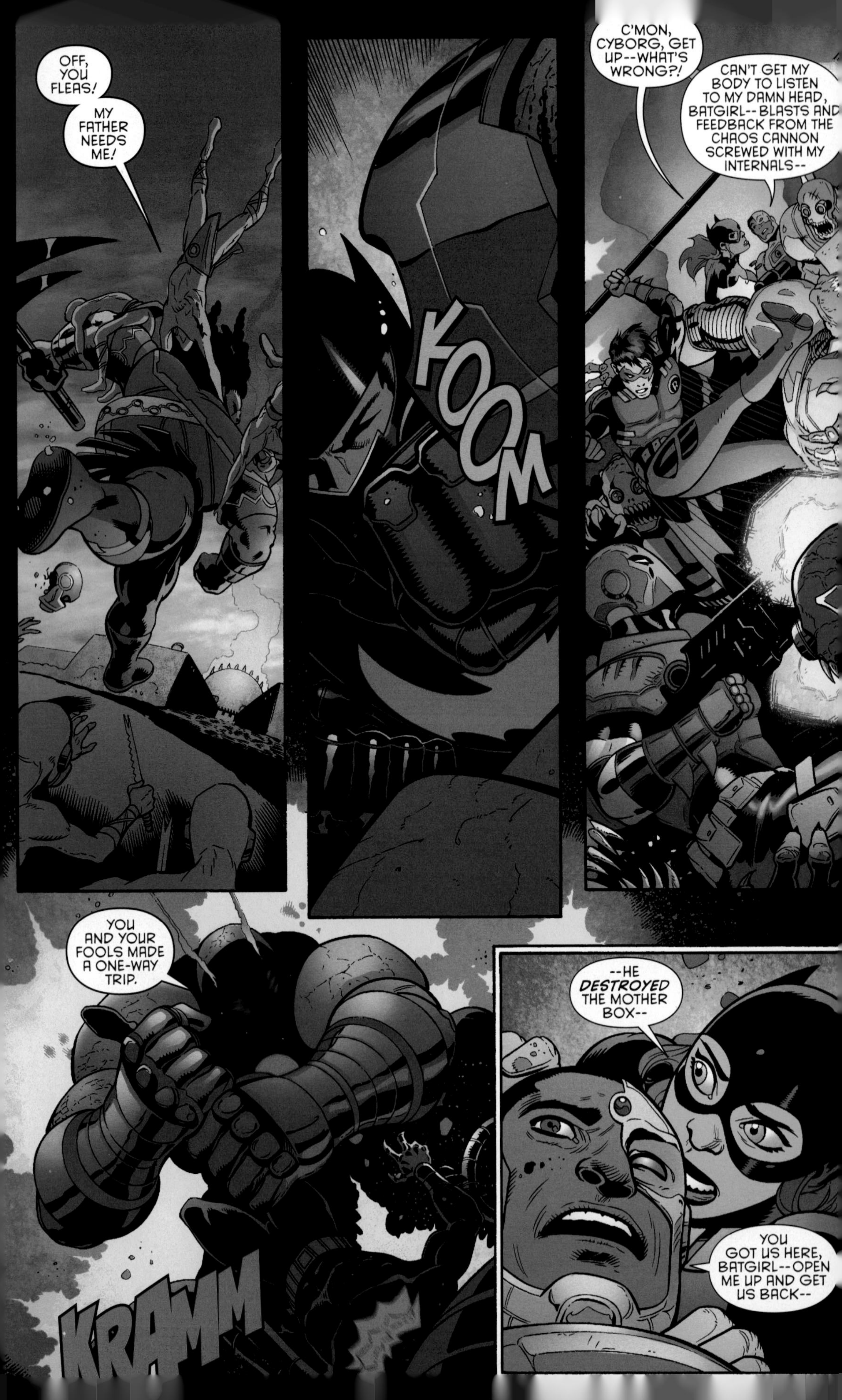
OFF, YOU FLEAS!
MY FATHER NEEDS ME!
KOOM
C'MON, CYBORG, GET UP--WHAT'S WRONG?!
CAN'T GET MY BODY TO LISTEN TO MY DAMN HEAD, BATGIRL--BLASTS AND FEEDBACK FROM THE CHAOS CANNON SCREWED WITH MY INTERNALS--
YOU AND YOUR FOOLS MADE A ONE-WAY TRIP.
KRAMM
--HE DESTROYED THE MOTHER BOX--
YOU GOT US HERE, BATGIRL--OPEN ME UP AND GET US BACK--

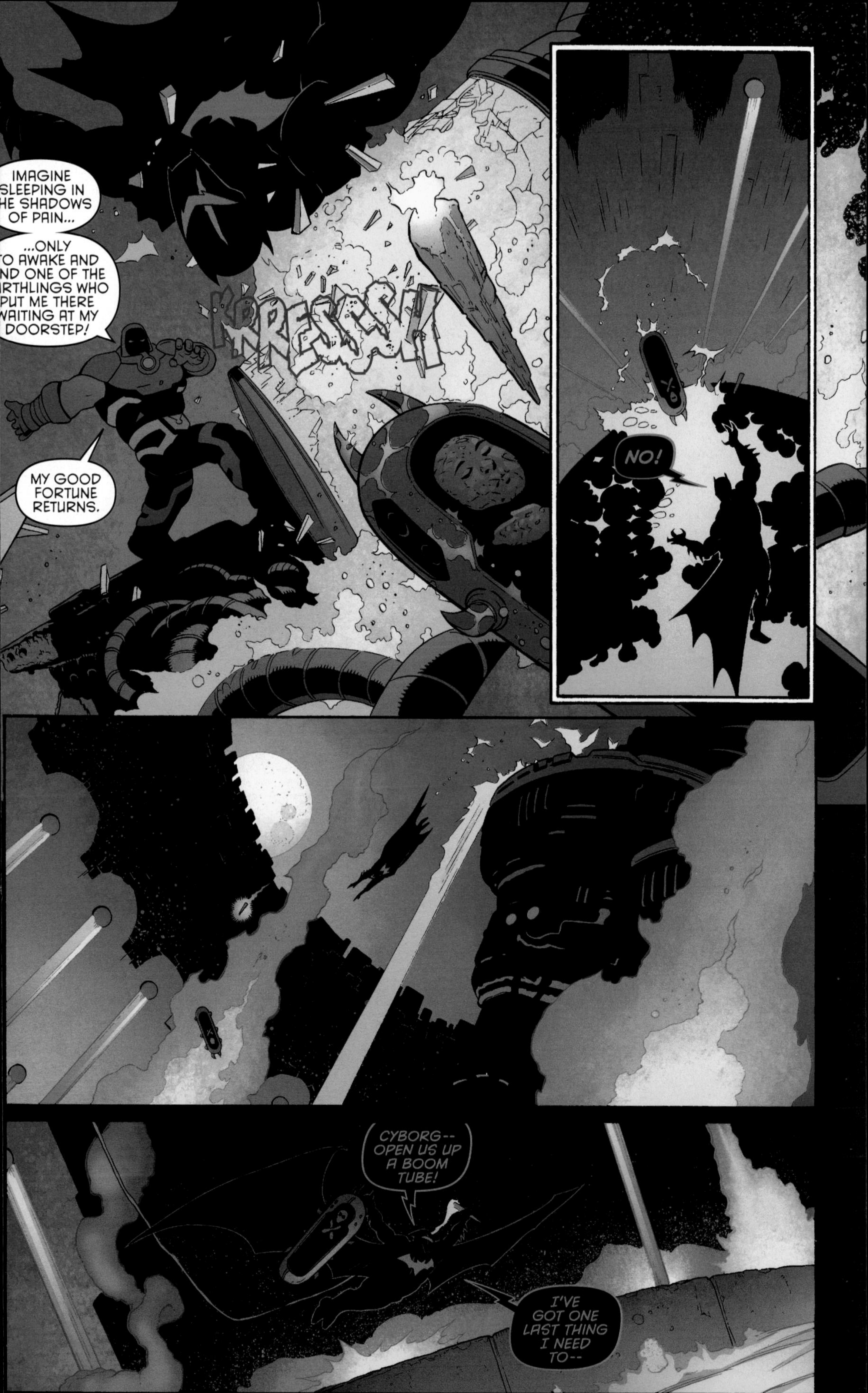
IMAGINE SLEEPING IN HE SHADOWS OF PAIN...
...ONLY TO AWAKE AND ND ONE OF THE ARTHLINGS WHO PUT ME THERE WAITING AT MY DOORSTEP!
MY GOOD FORTUNE RETURNS.
KRESSSH!
NO!
CYBORG-- OPEN US UP A BOOM TUBE!
I'VE GOT ONE LAST THING I NEED TO--

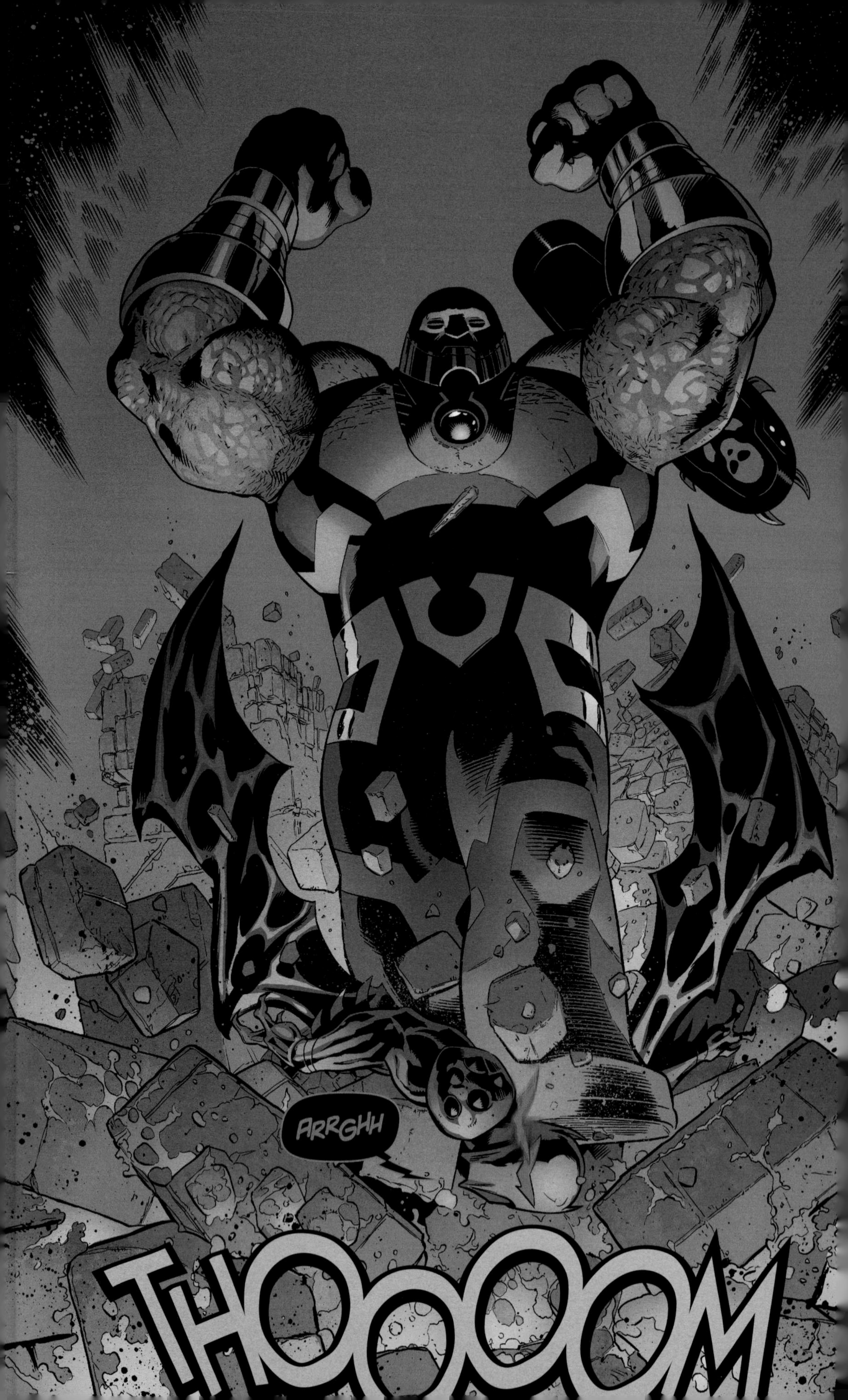
ARRGHH
THOOOOM

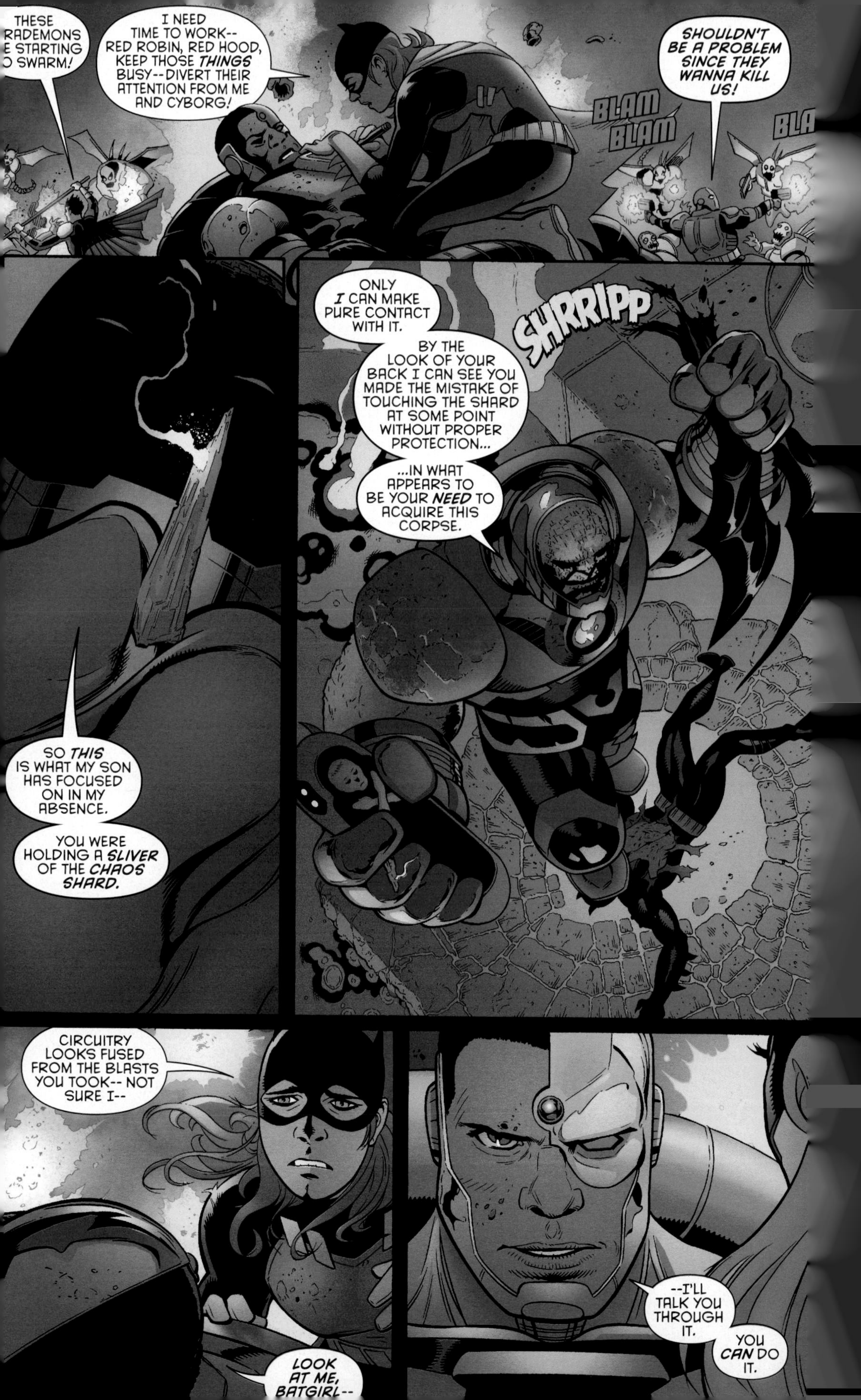

THESE
RADEMONS
E STARTING
O SWARM!
I NEED TIME TO WORK-- RED ROBIN, RED HOOD, KEEP THOSE *THINGS* BUSY--DIVERT THEIR ATTENTION FROM ME AND CYBORG!
BLAM
BLAM
SHOULDN'T BE A PROBLEM SINCE THEY WANNA KILL US!
BLA
SO *THIS* IS WHAT MY SON HAS FOCUSED ON IN MY ABSENCE.
YOU WERE HOLDING A *SLIVER* OF THE *CHAOS SHARD.*
ONLY *I* CAN MAKE PURE CONTACT WITH IT.
SHRRIPP
BY THE LOOK OF YOUR BACK I CAN SEE YOU MADE THE MISTAKE OF TOUCHING THE SHARD AT SOME POINT WITHOUT PROPER PROTECTION...
...IN WHAT APPEARS TO BE YOUR *NEED* TO ACQUIRE THIS CORPSE.
CIRCUITRY LOOKS FUSED FROM THE BLASTS YOU TOOK-- NOT SURE I--
LOOK AT ME, BATGIRL--
--I'LL TALK YOU THROUGH IT.
YOU *CAN* DO IT.

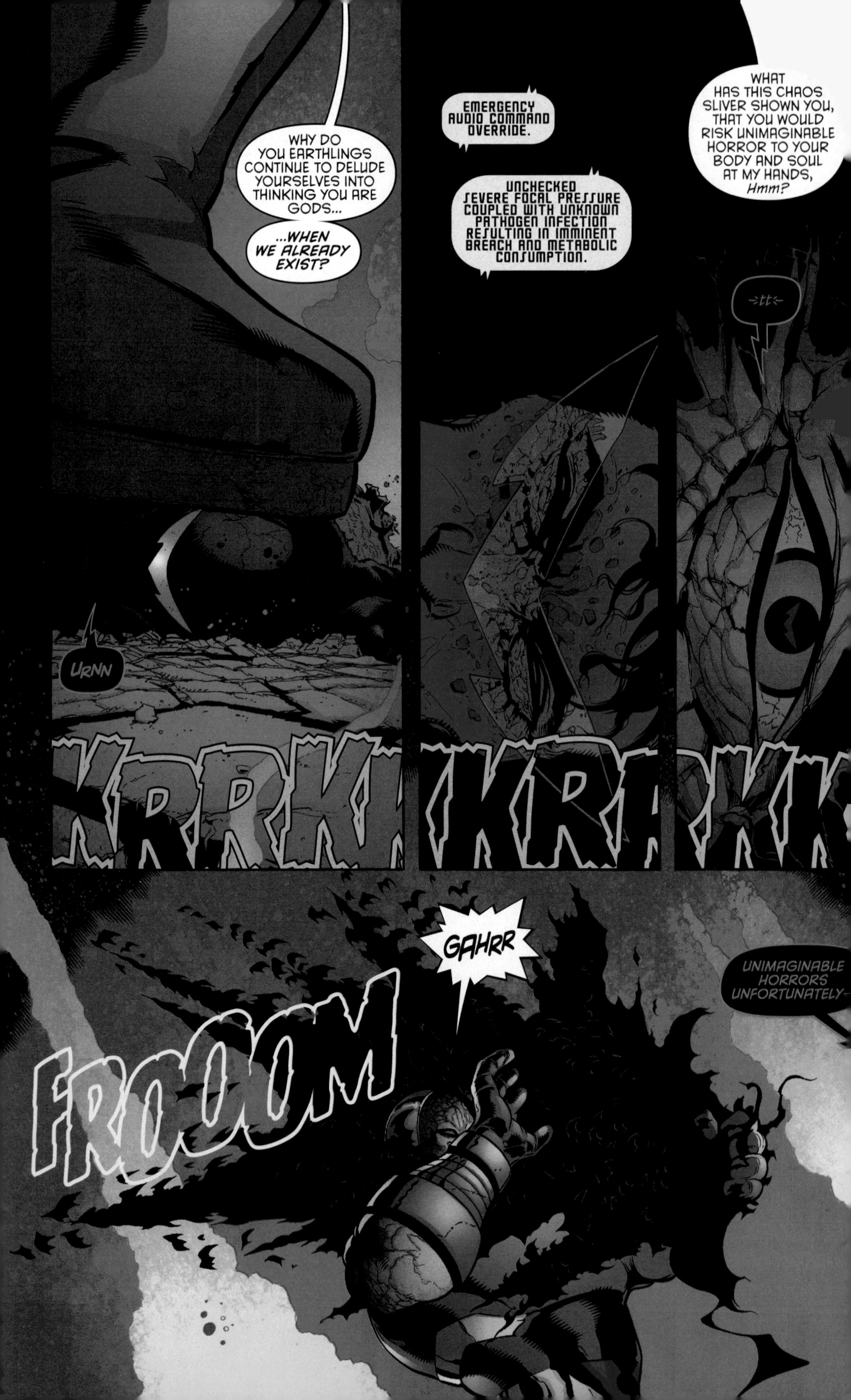
WHY DO YOU EARTHLINGS CONTINUE TO DELUDE YOURSELVES INTO THINKING YOU ARE GODS...
...WHEN WE ALREADY EXIST?
URNN
KRRKK
EMERGENCY AUDIO COMMAND OVERRIDE.
UNCHECKED SEVERE FOCAL PRESSURE COUPLED WITH UNKNOWN PATHOGEN INFECTION RESULTING IN IMMINENT BREACH AND METABOLIC CONSUMPTION.
KRAKK
WHAT HAS THIS CHAOS SLIVER SHOWN YOU, THAT YOU WOULD RISK UNIMAGINABLE HORROR TO YOUR BODY AND SOUL AT MY HANDS, Hmm?
-tt-
RKKK
GAHRR
FROOOM
UNIMAGINABLE HORRORS UNFORTUNATELY--

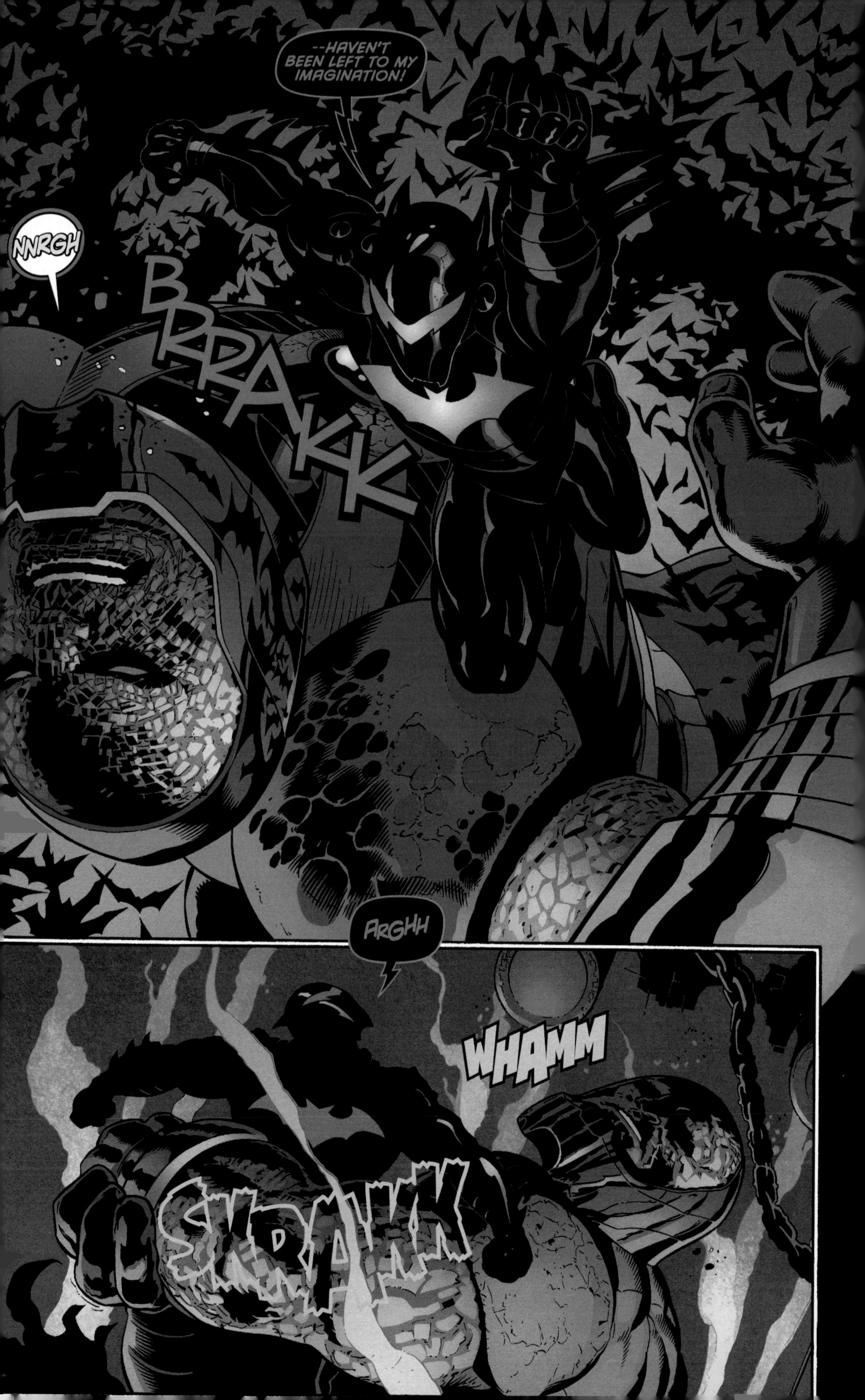
--HAVEN'T BEEN LEFT TO MY IMAGINATION!
NNRGH
BRRRAKKK
ARGHH
WHAMM
SHRAKK

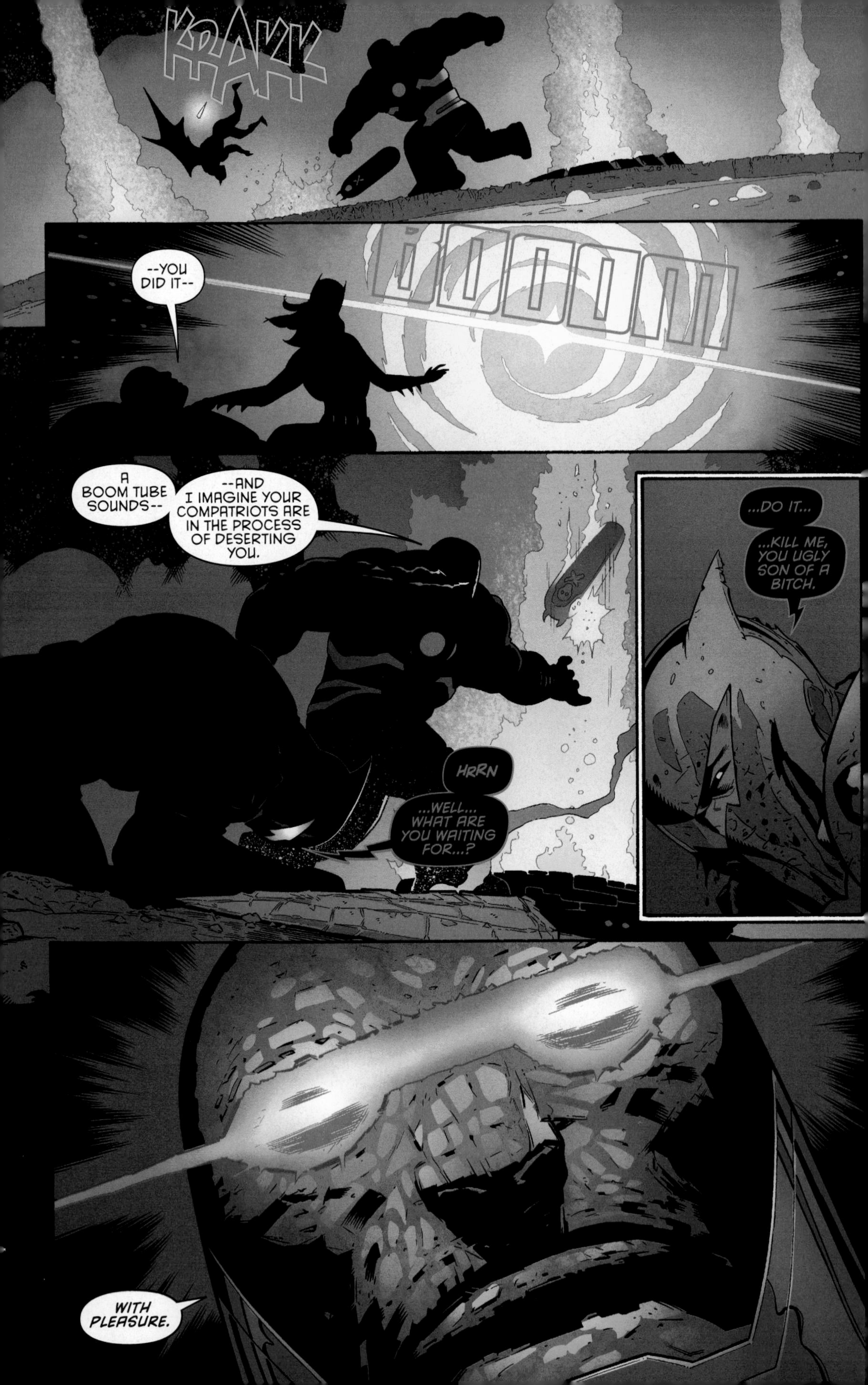
KRAKK
--YOU DID IT--
BOOOOM
A BOOM TUBE SOUNDS--
--AND I IMAGINE YOUR COMPATRIOTS ARE IN THE PROCESS OF DESERTING YOU.
HRRN
...WELL... WHAT ARE YOU WAITING FOR...?
...DO IT...
...KILL ME, YOU UGLY SON OF A BITCH.
WITH PLEASURE.

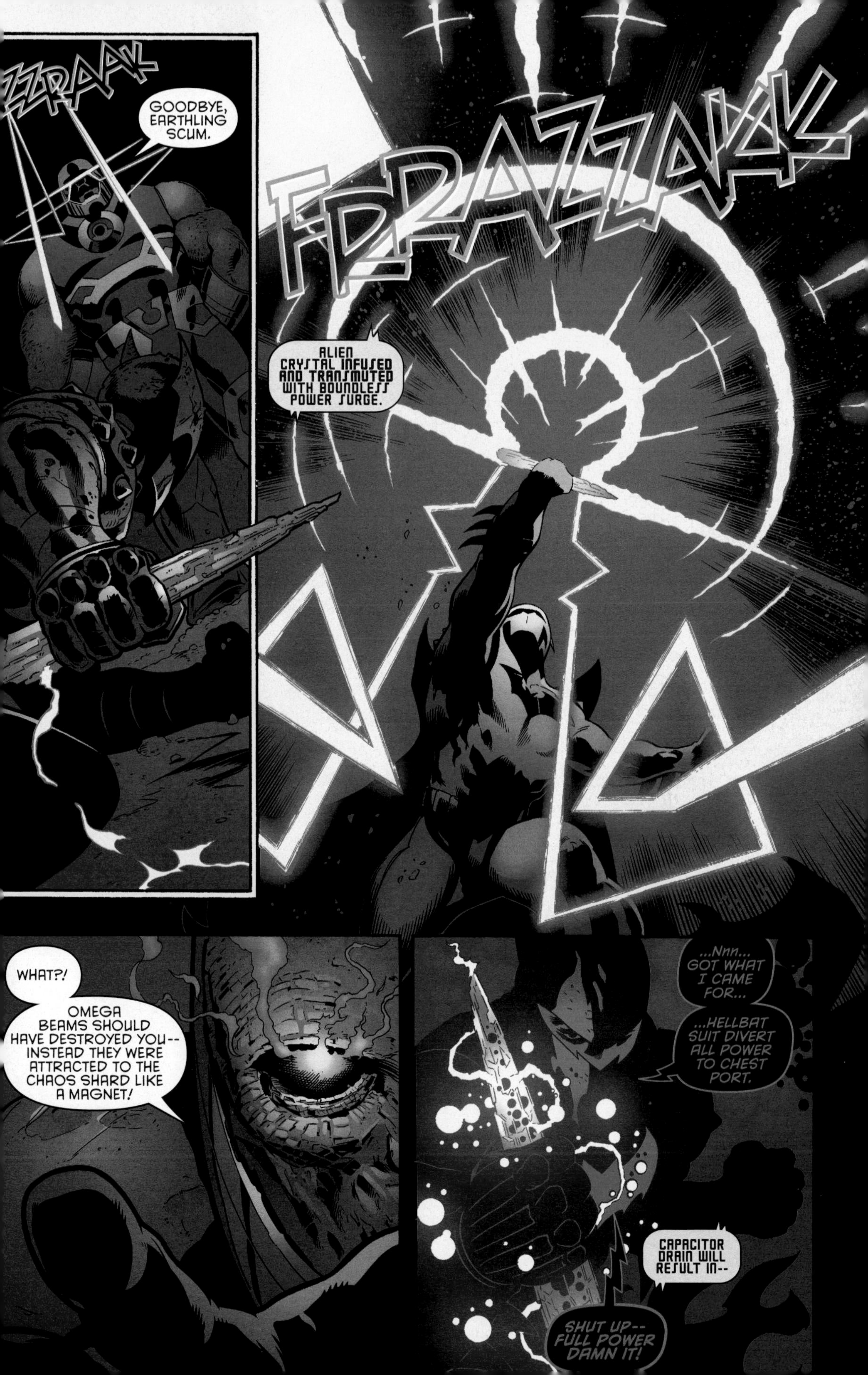
ZZRAAK
GOODBYE, EARTHLING SCUM.
FZRAZZAKK
ALIEN CRYSTAL INFUSED AND TRANSMUTED WITH BOUNDLESS POWER SURGE.
WHAT?!
OMEGA BEAMS SHOULD HAVE DESTROYED YOU-- INSTEAD THEY WERE ATTRACTED TO THE CHAOS SHARD LIKE A MAGNET!
...Nnn... GOT WHAT I CAME FOR...
...HELLBAT SUIT DIVERT ALL POWER TO CHEST PORT.
CAPACITOR DRAIN WILL RESULT IN--
SHUT UP-- FULL POWER DAMN IT!

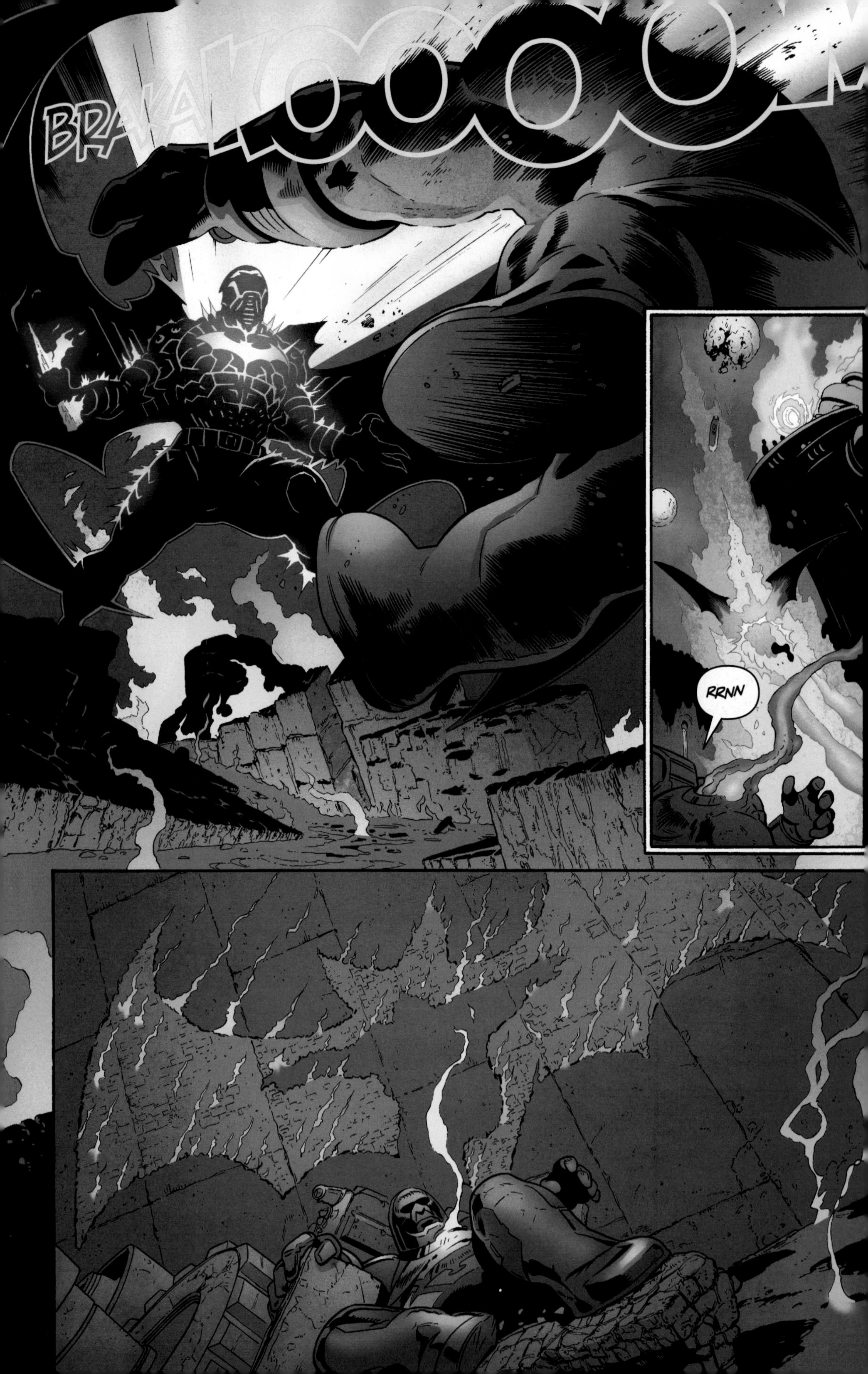
BRAKAKOOOOOM
RRNN

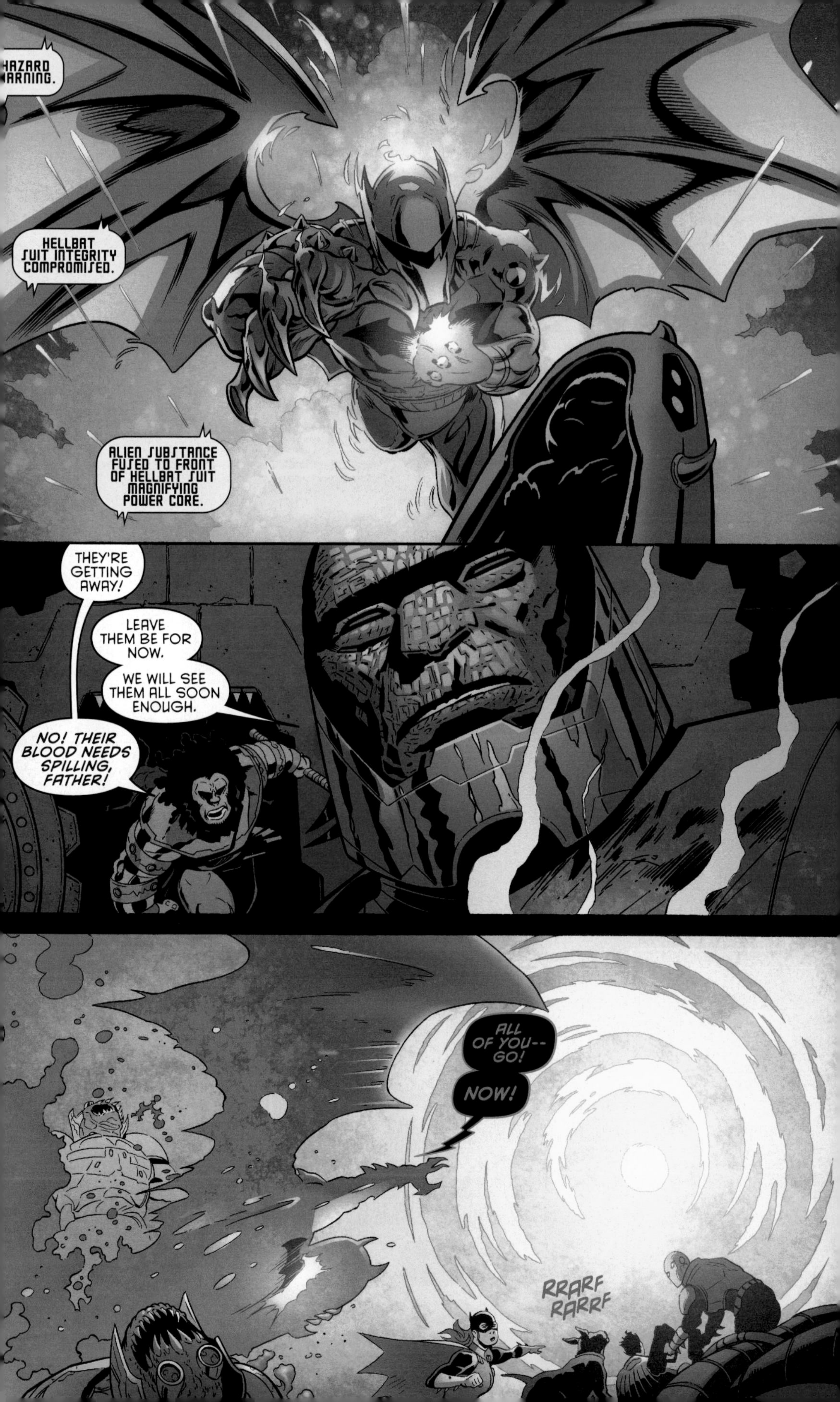
HAZARD WARNING.
HELLBAT SUIT INTEGRITY COMPROMISED.
ALIEN SUBSTANCE FUSED TO FRONT OF HELLBAT SUIT MAGNIFYING POWER CORE.
THEY'RE GETTING AWAY!
LEAVE THEM BE FOR NOW.
WE WILL SEE THEM ALL SOON ENOUGH.
NO! THEIR BLOOD NEEDS SPILLING, FATHER!
ALL OF YOU-- GO!
NOW!
RRARF RARRF

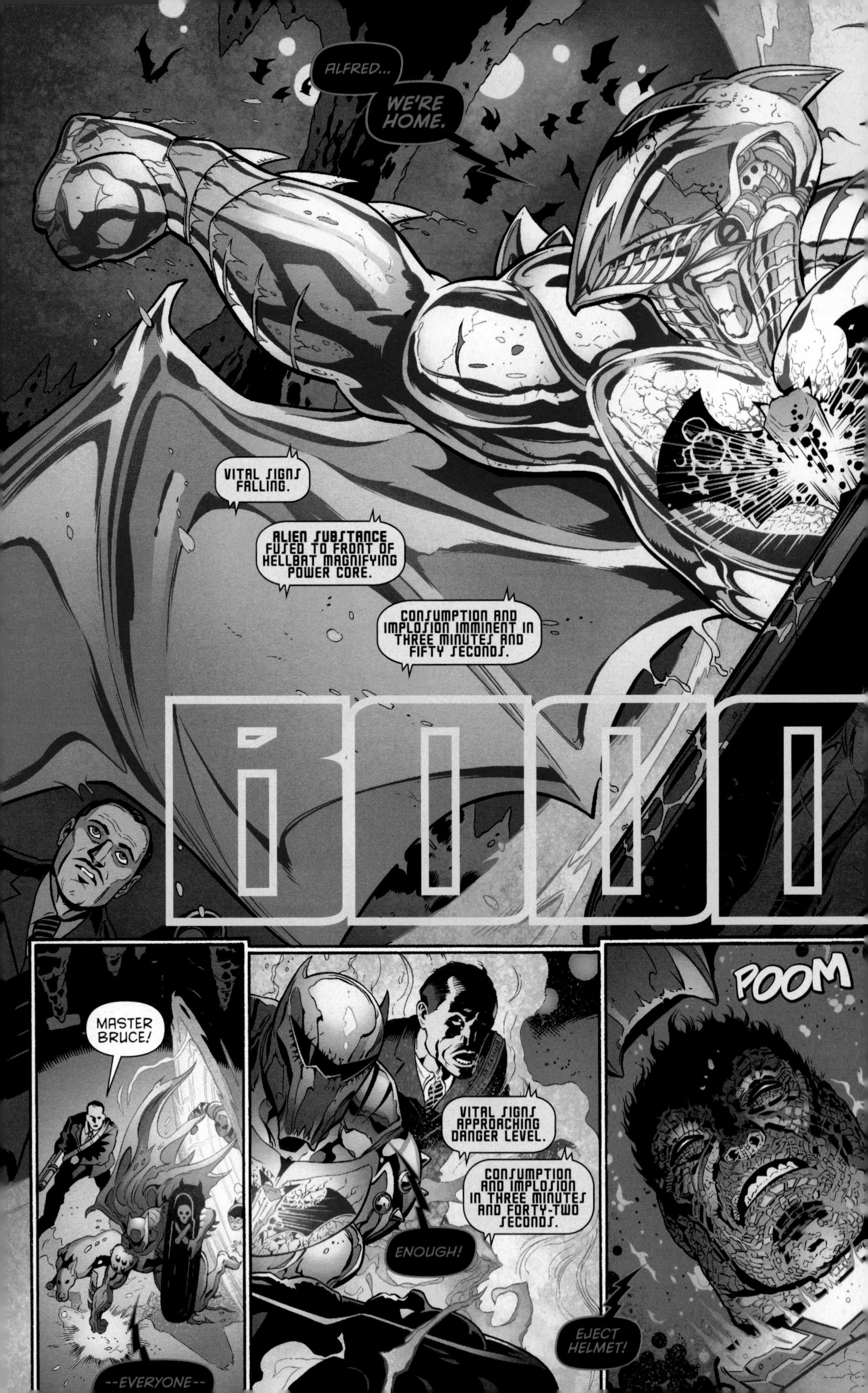
ALFRED...
WE'RE HOME.
VITAL SIGNS FALLING.
ALIEN SUBSTANCE FUSED TO FRONT OF HELLBAT MAGNIFYING POWER CORE.
CONSUMPTION AND IMPLOSION IMMINENT IN THREE MINUTES AND FIFTY SECONDS.
MASTER BRUCE!
--EVERYONE--
VITAL SIGNS APPROACHING DANGER LEVEL.
CONSUMPTION AND IMPLOSION IN THREE MINUTES AND FORTY-TWO SECONDS.
ENOUGH!
POOM
EJECT HELMET!

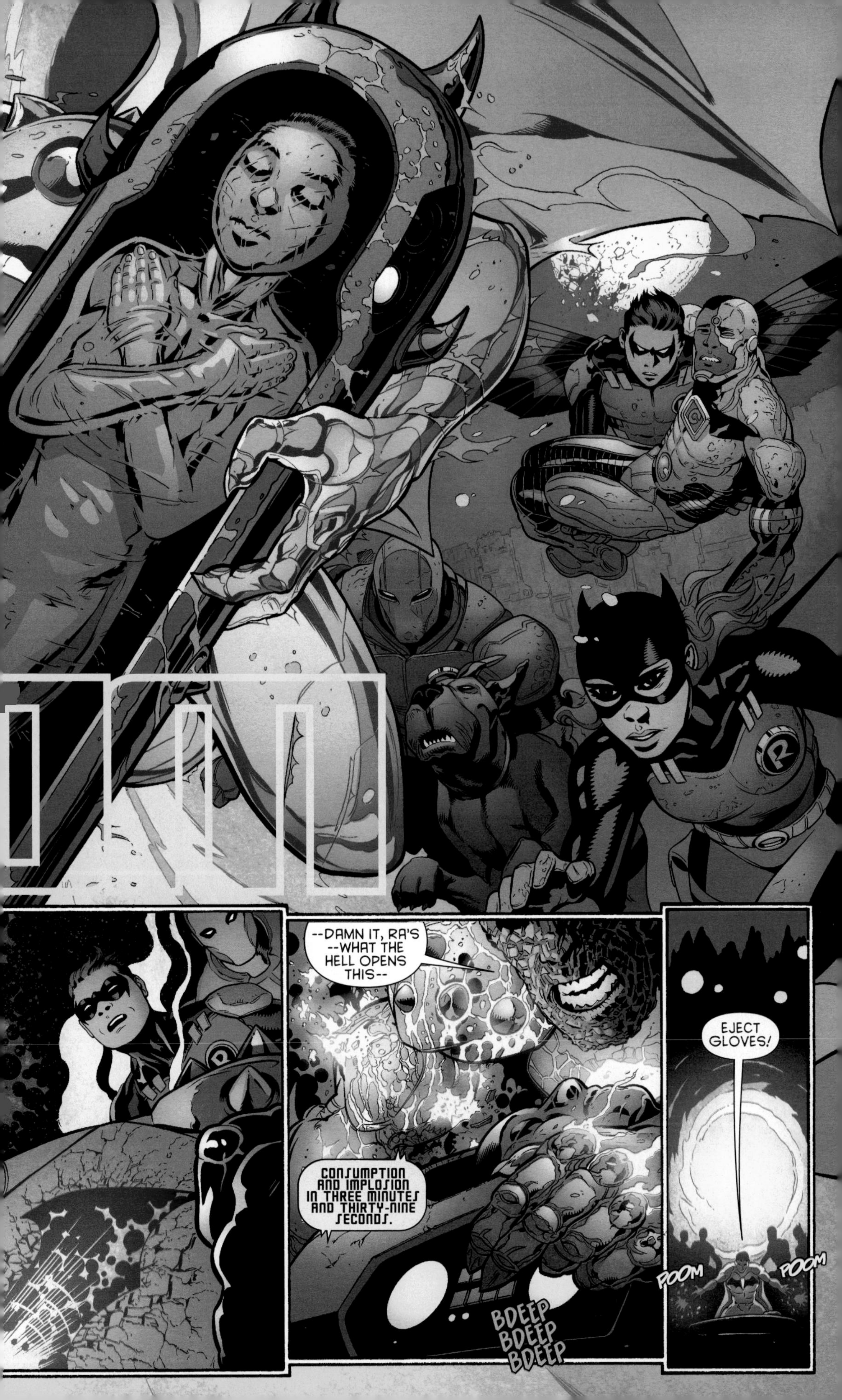

--DAMN IT, RA'S --WHAT THE HELL OPENS THIS--
CONSUMPTION AND IMPLOSION IN THREE MINUTES AND THIRTY-NINE SECONDS.
BDEEP BDEEP BDEEP
EJECT GLOVES!
POOM
POOM

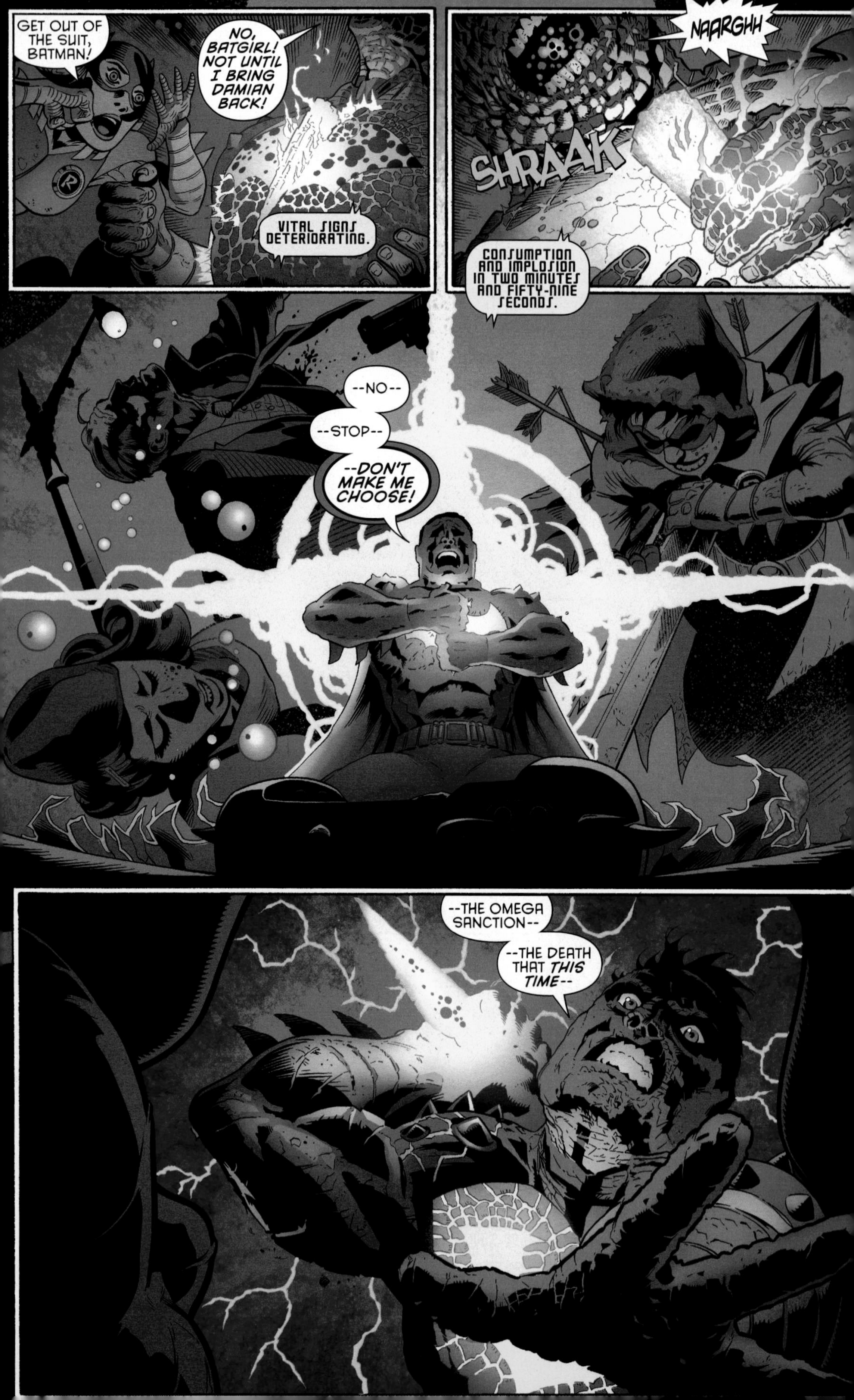
GET OUT OF THE SUIT, BATMAN!
NO, BATGIRL! NOT UNTIL I BRING DAMIAN BACK!
VITAL SIGNS DETERIORATING.
NAARGHH
SHRAAK
CONSUMPTION AND IMPLOSION IN TWO MINUTES AND FIFTY-NINE SECONDS.
--NO--
--STOP--
--DON'T MAKE ME CHOOSE!
--THE OMEGA SANCTION--
--THE DEATH THAT THIS TIME--

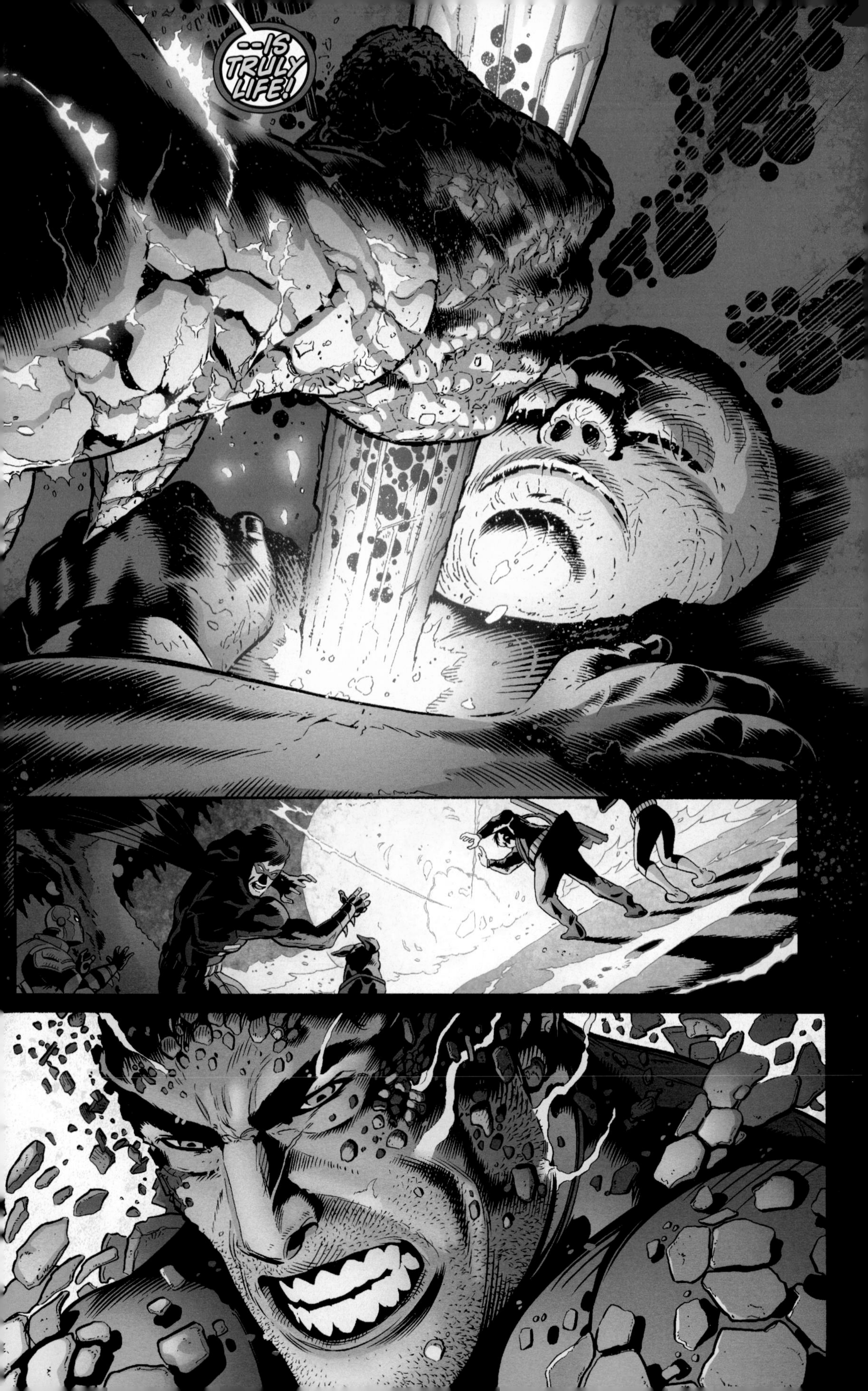
--IS TRULY LIFE!

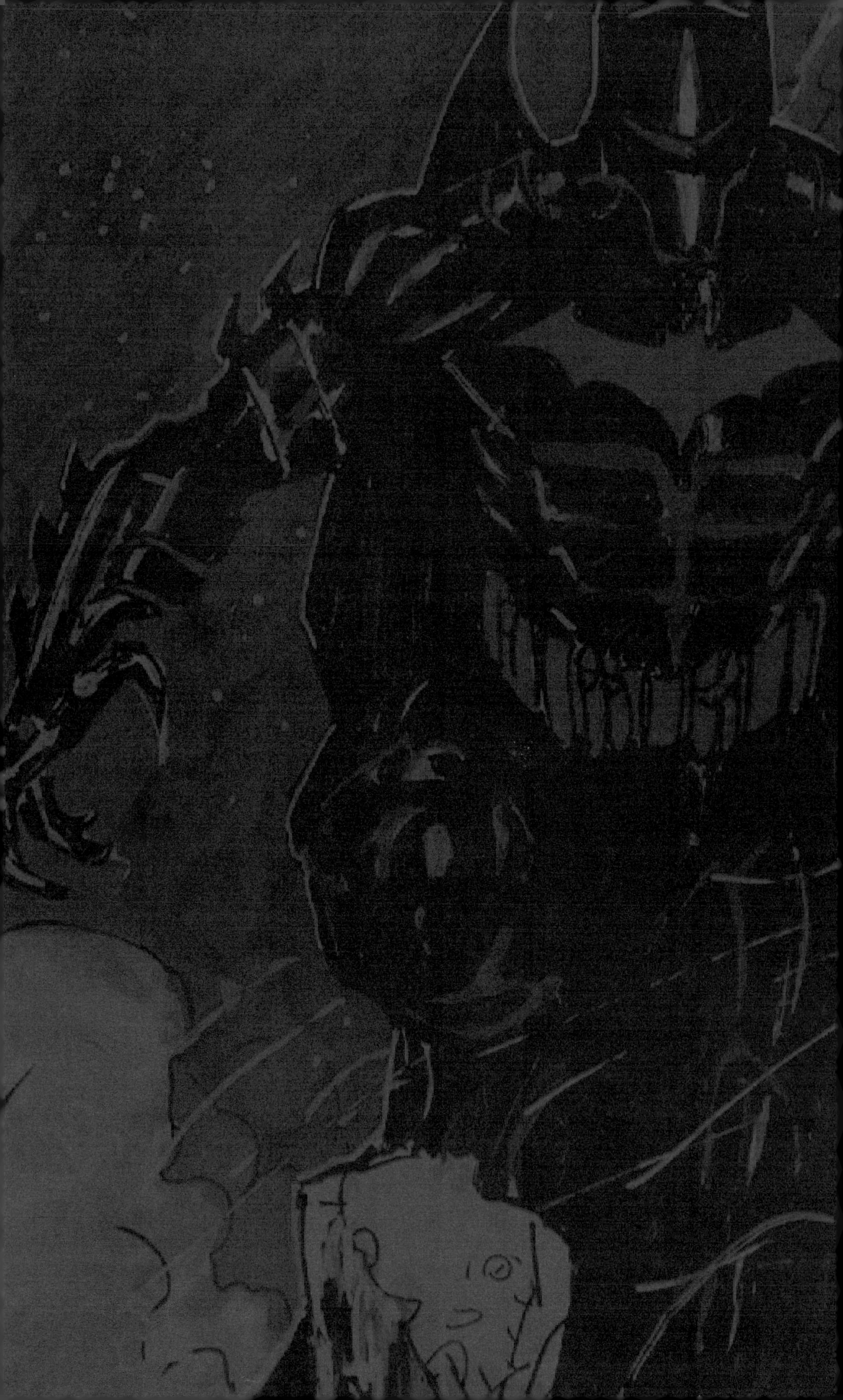

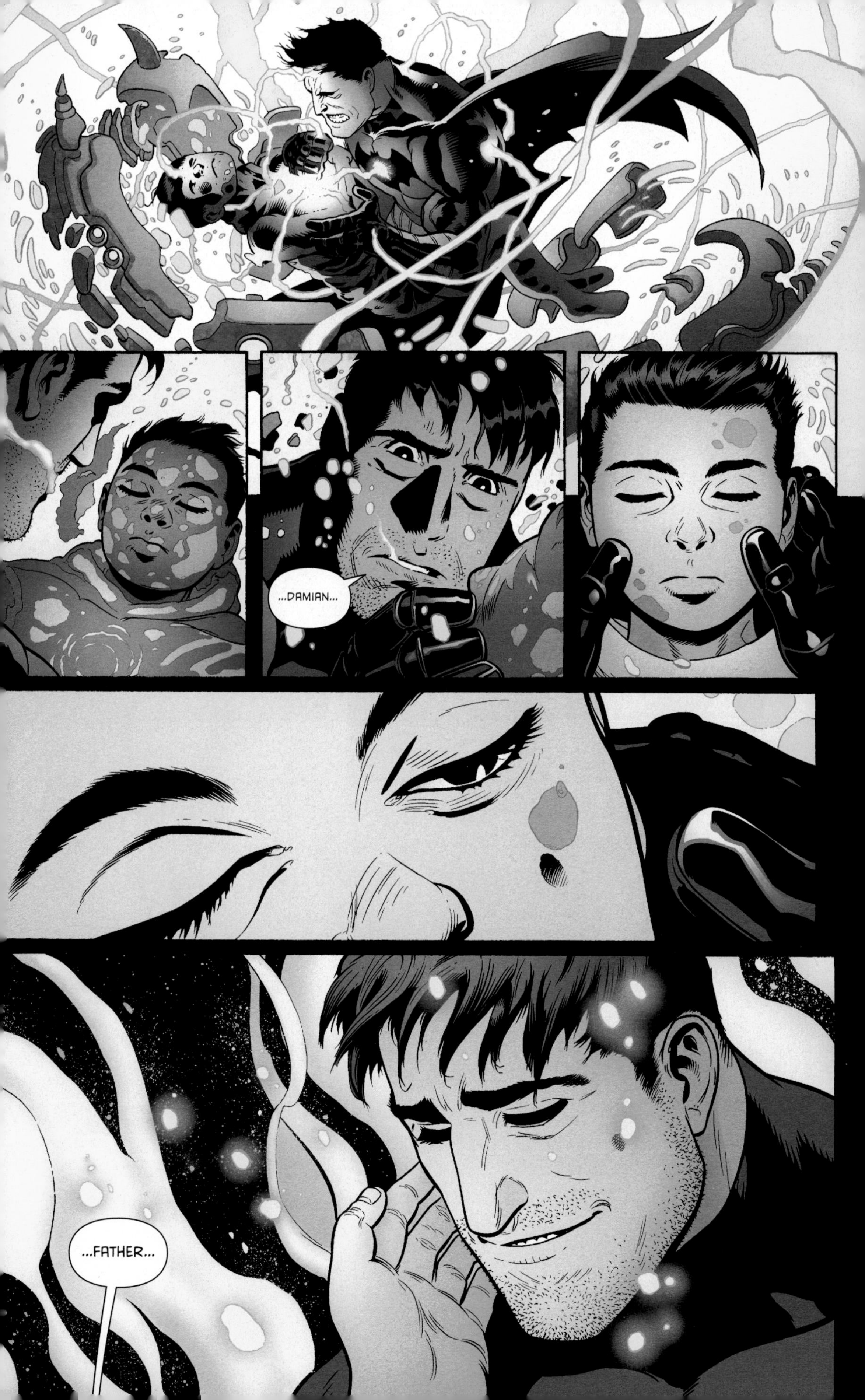
...DAMIAN...
...FATHER...

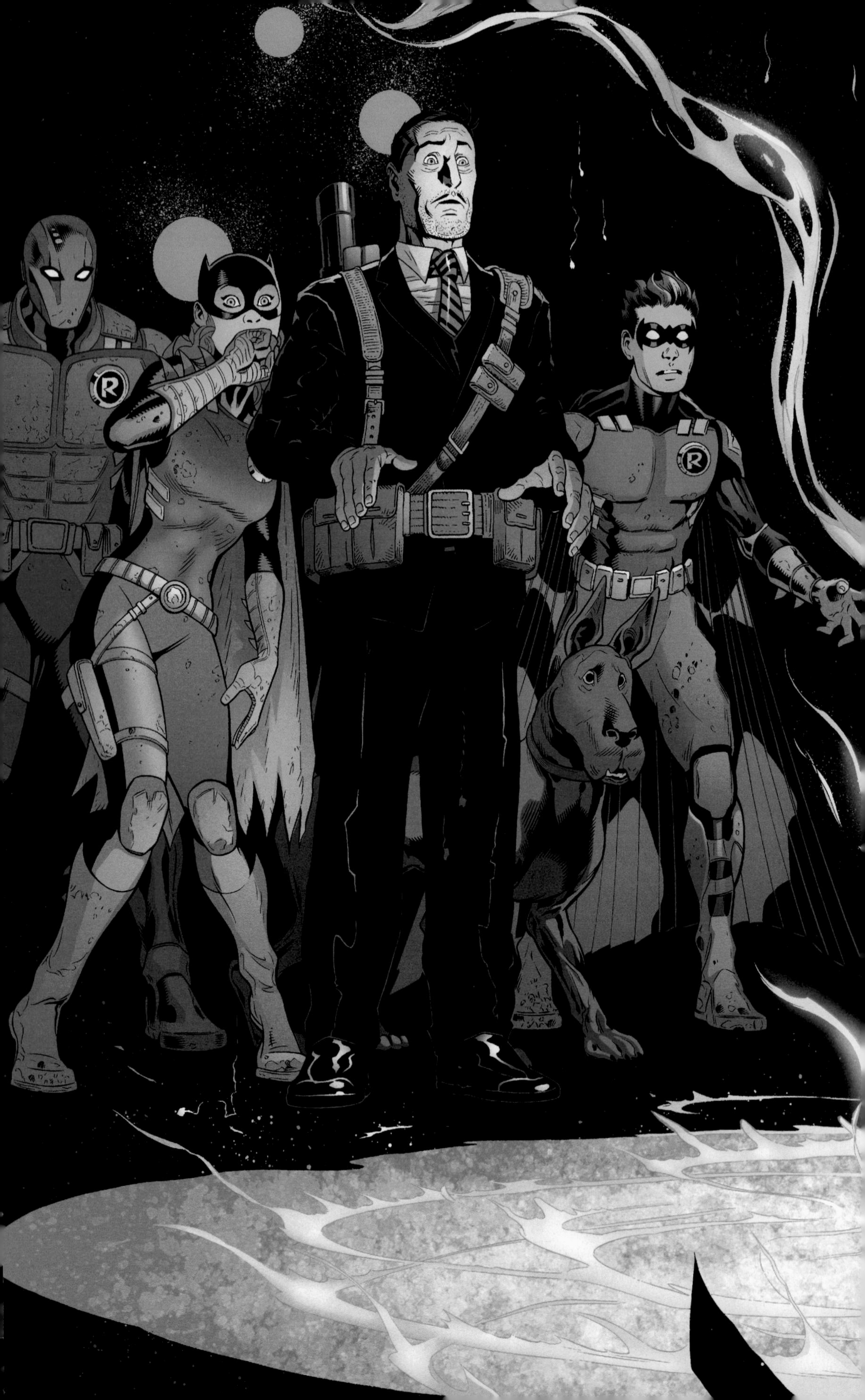

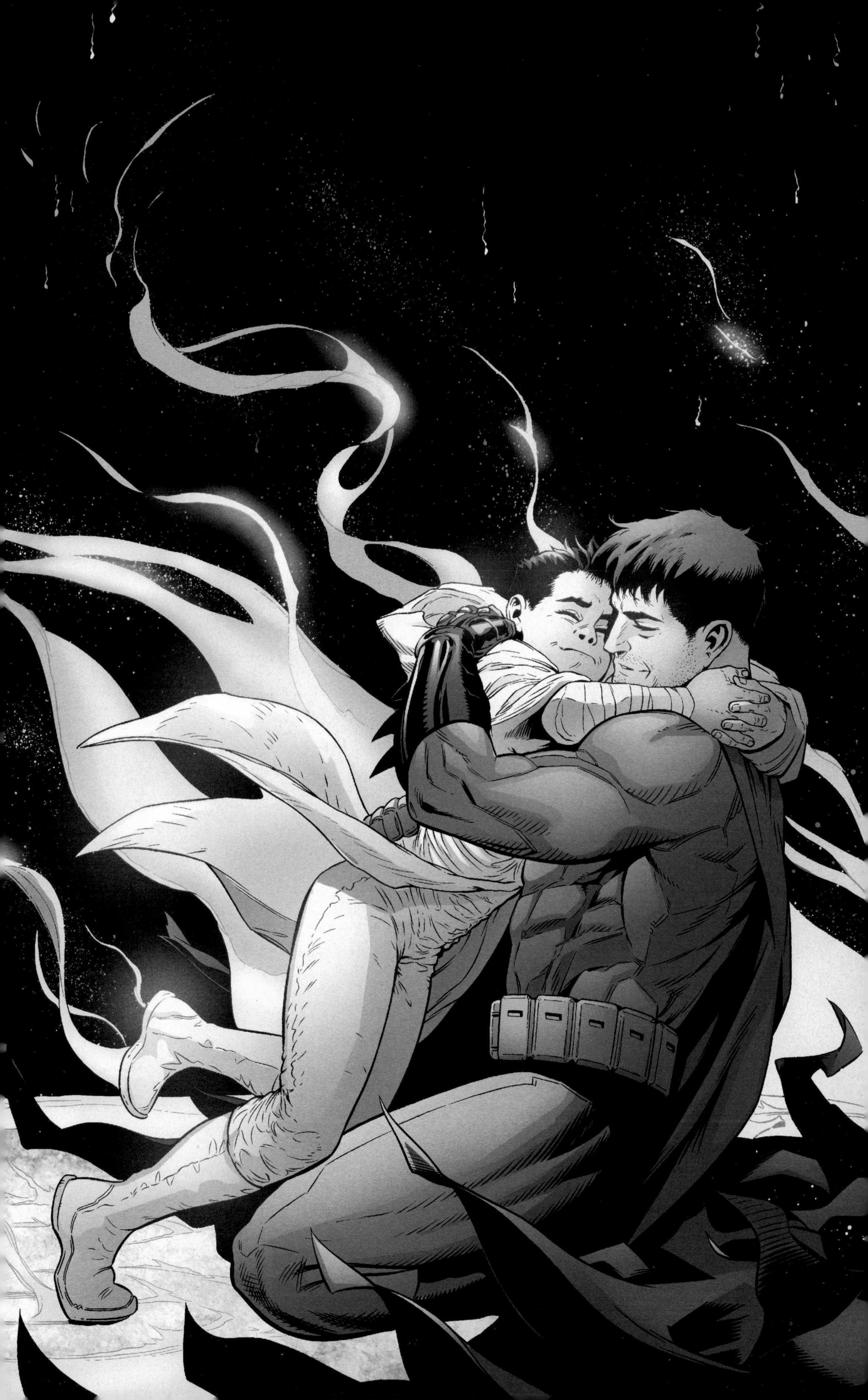

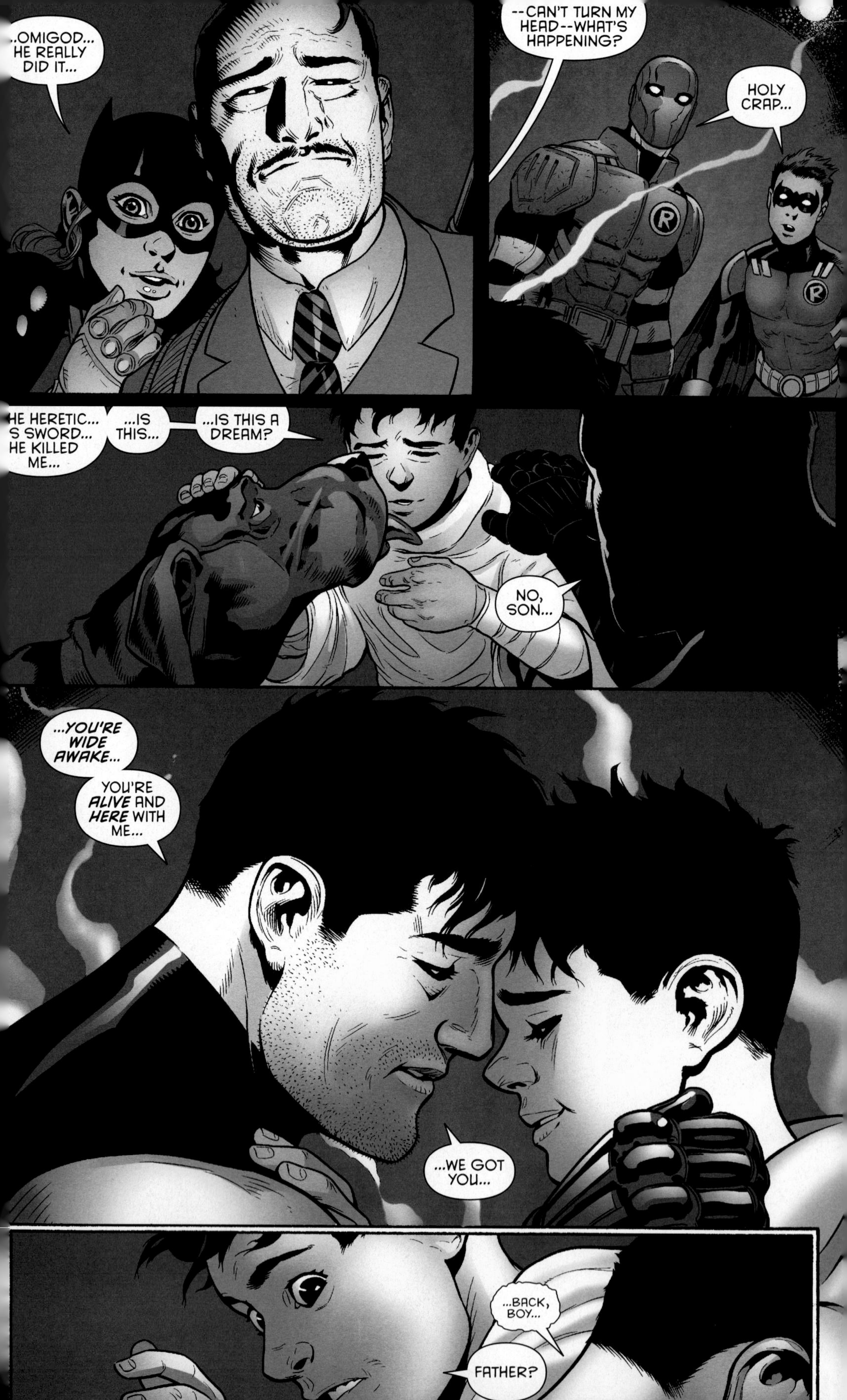
..OMIGOD... HE REALLY DID IT...
--CAN'T TURN MY HEAD--WHAT'S HAPPENING?
HOLY CRAP...
HE HERETIC... S SWORD... HE KILLED ME...
...IS THIS...
...IS THIS A DREAM?
NO, SON...
...YOU'RE WIDE AWAKE...
YOU'RE ALIVE AND HERE WITH ME...
...WE GOT YOU...
...BACK, BOY...
FATHER?

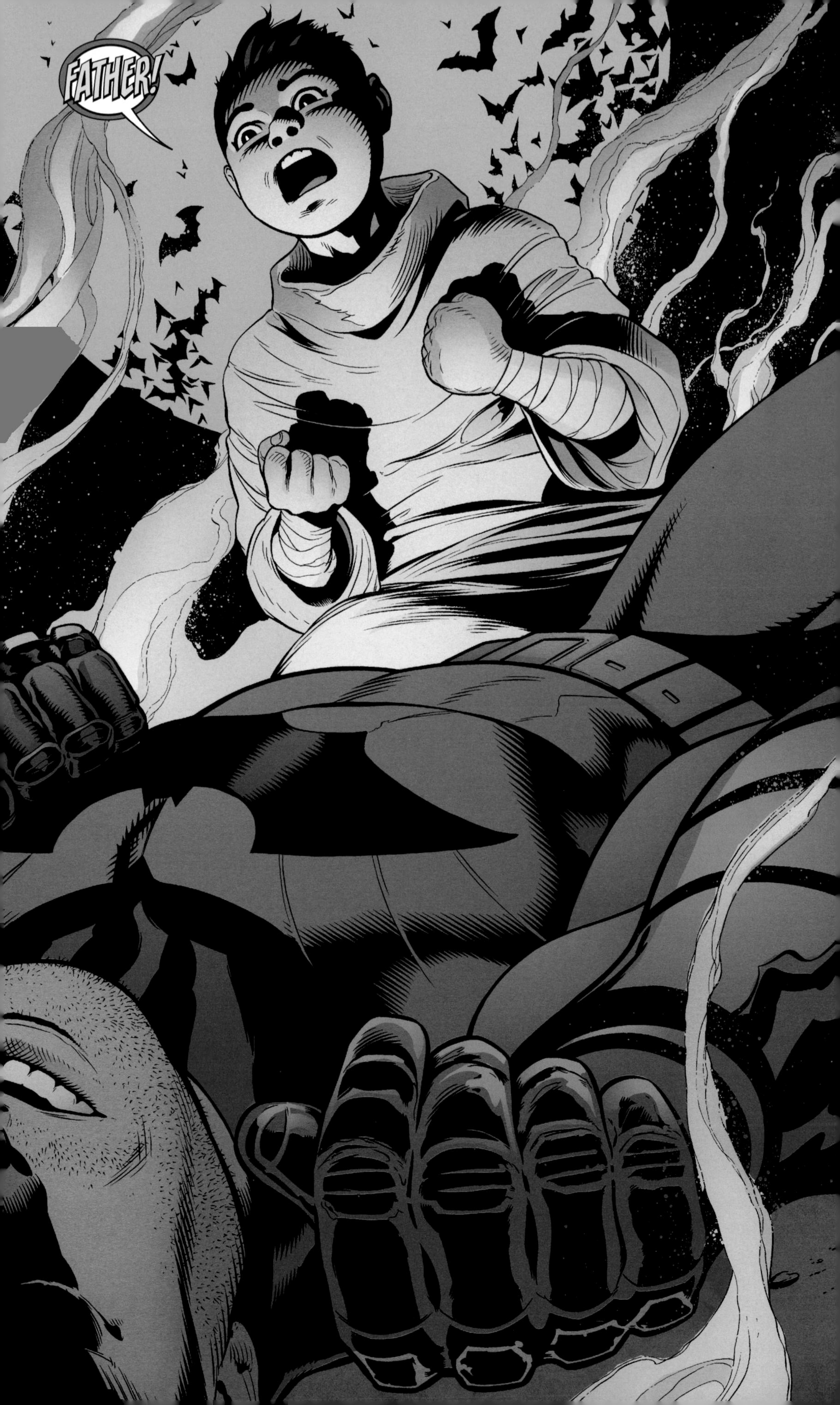
FATHER!

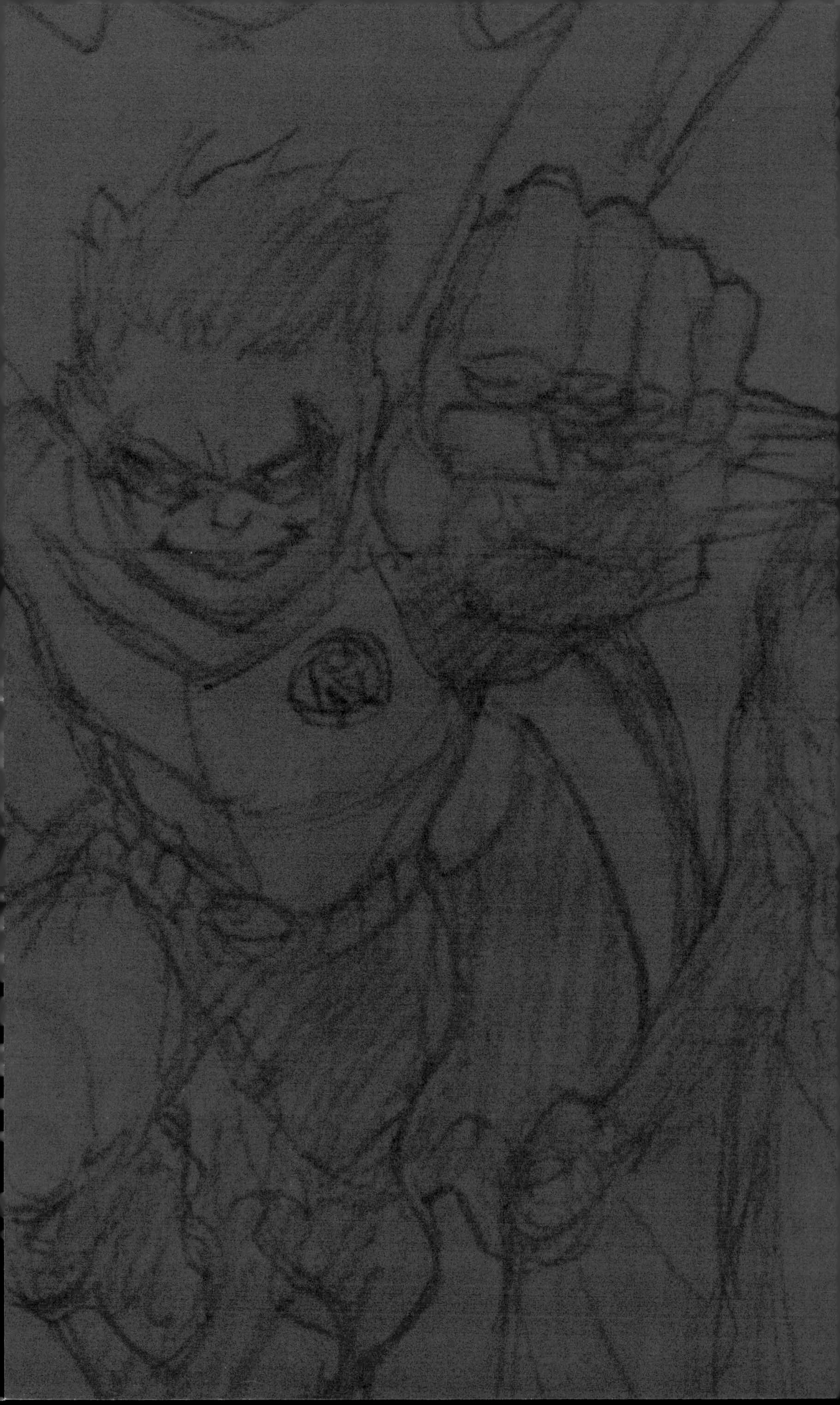

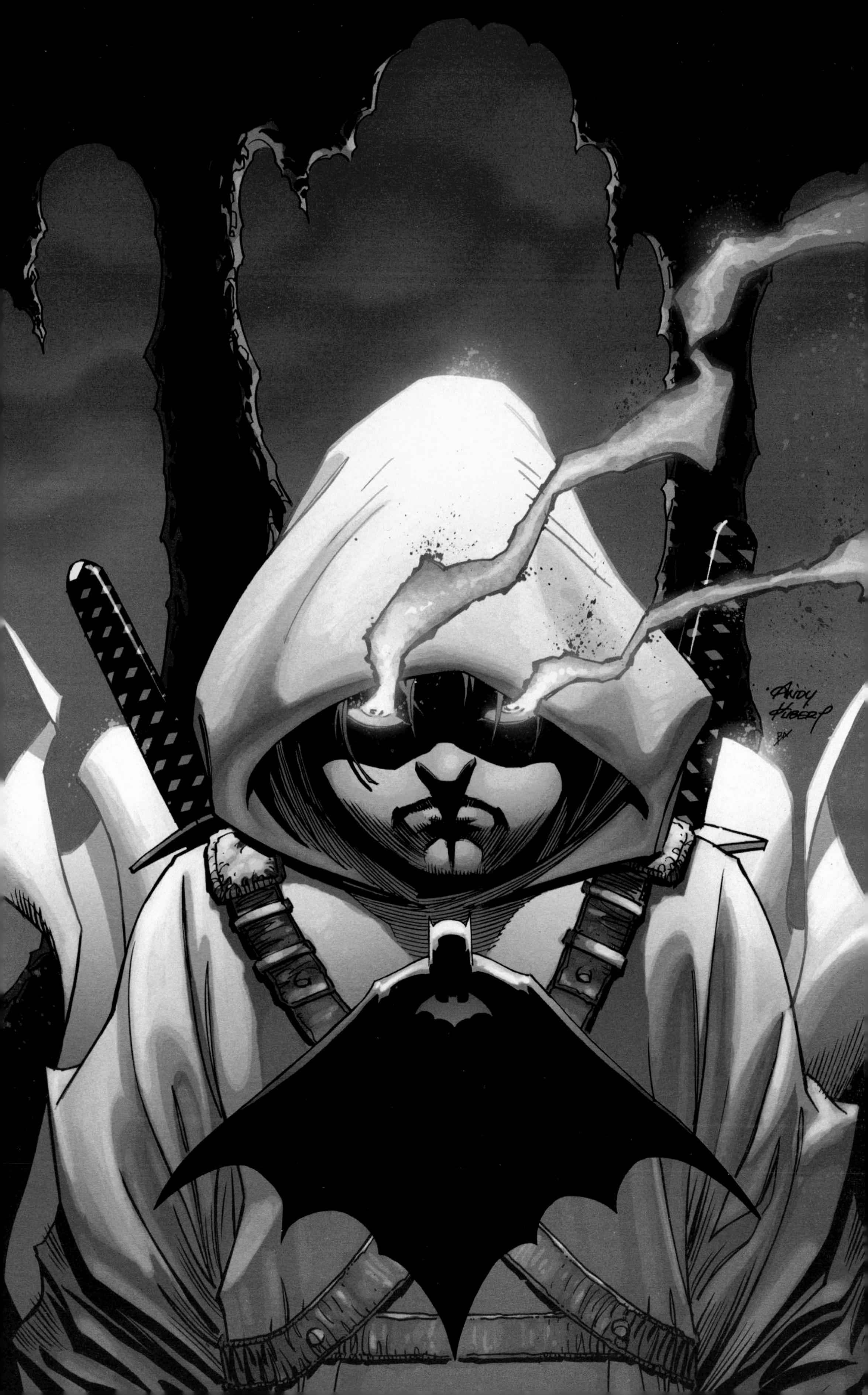
ANDY KUBERT

ANDY KUBERT penciller JONATHAN GLAPION ANDY KUBERT inkers BRAD ANDERSON colorist DEZI SIENTY letterer cover art by KUBERT & ANDERSON

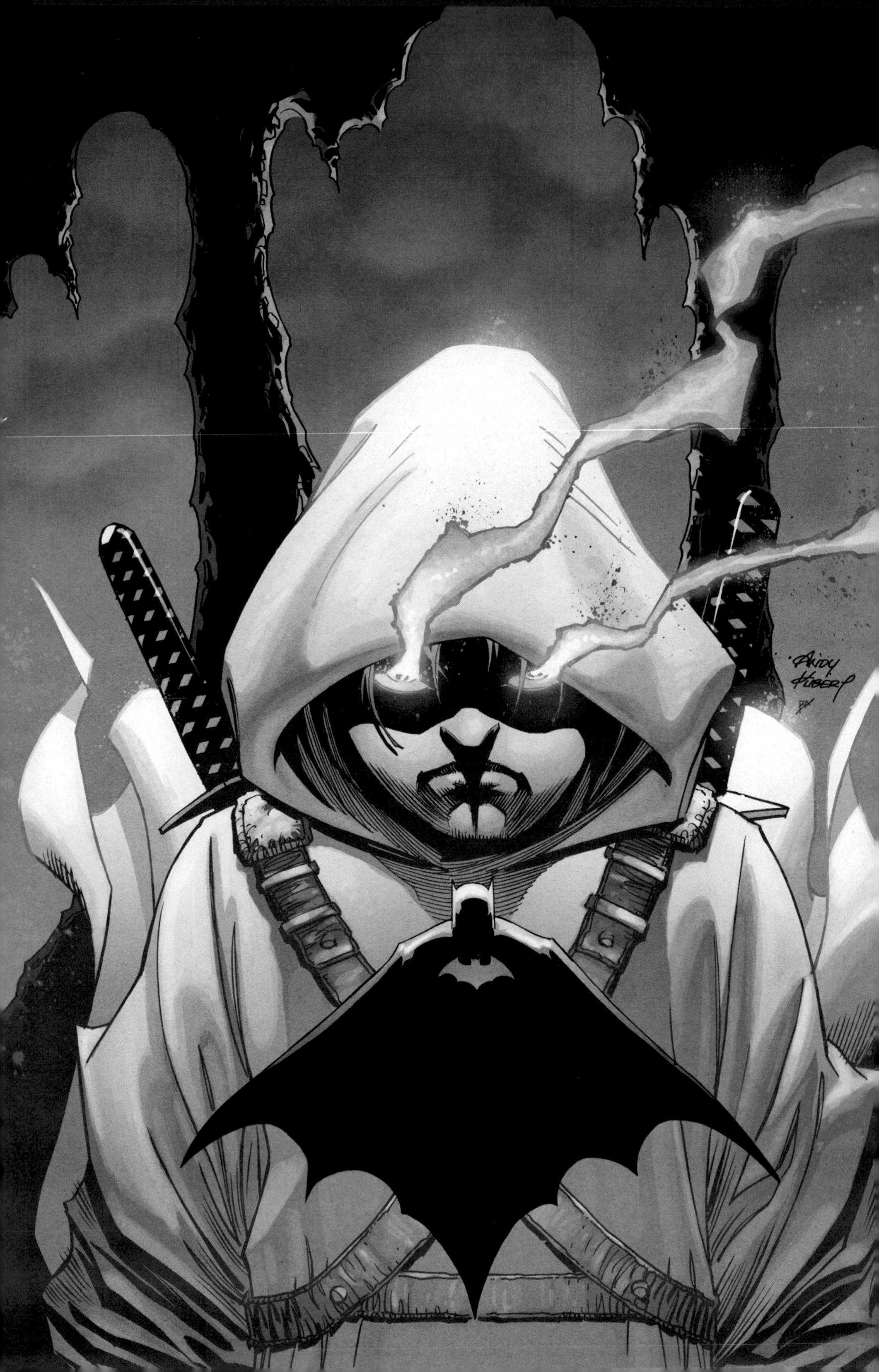
ANDY KUBERT

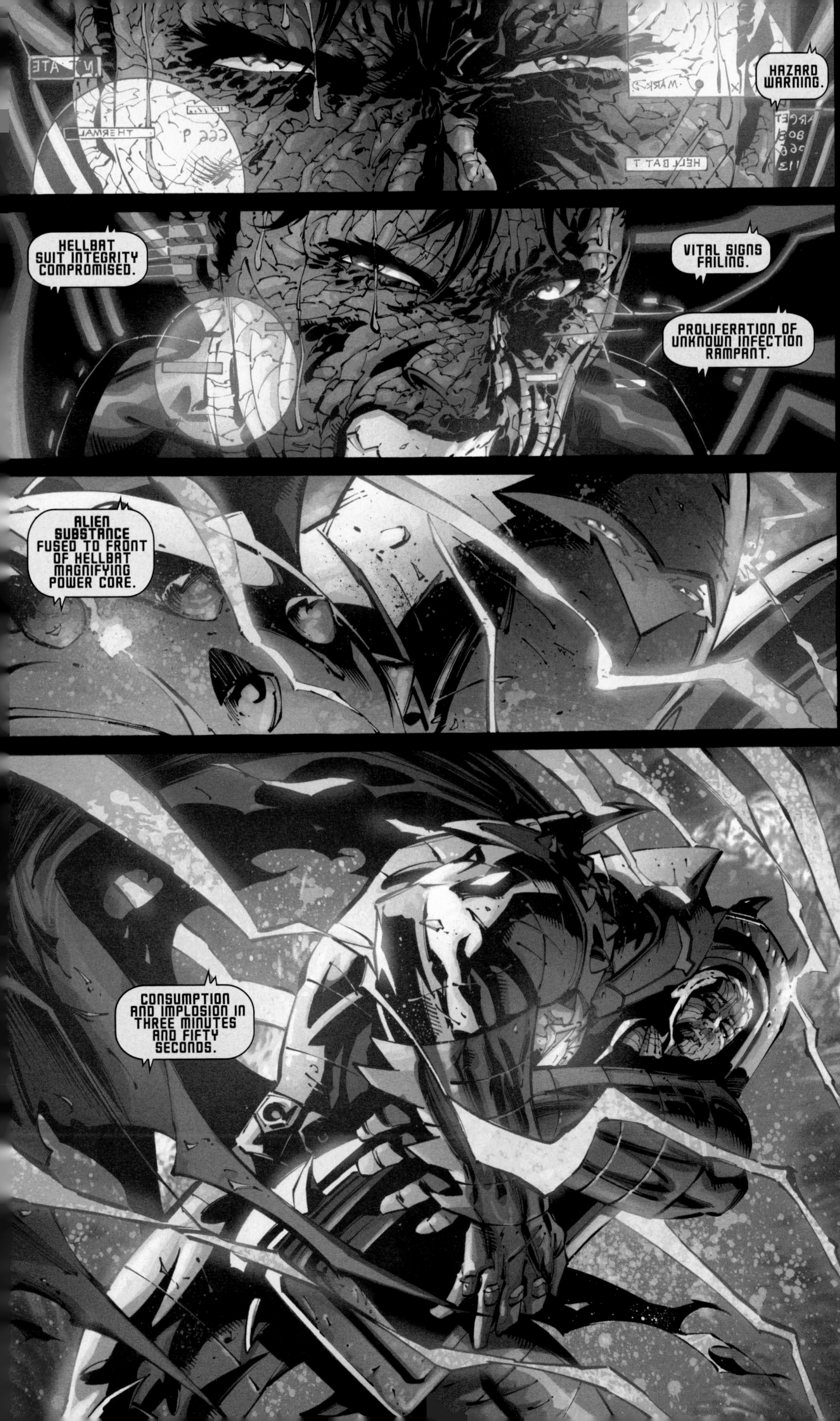
HAZARD WARNING.
HELLBAT SUIT INTEGRITY COMPROMISED.
VITAL SIGNS FAILING.
PROLIFERATION OF UNKNOWN INFECTION RAMPANT.
ALIEN SUBSTANCE FUSED TO FRONT OF HELLBAT MAGNIFYING POWER CORE.
CONSUMPTION AND IMPLOSION IN THREE MINUTES AND FIFTY SECONDS.

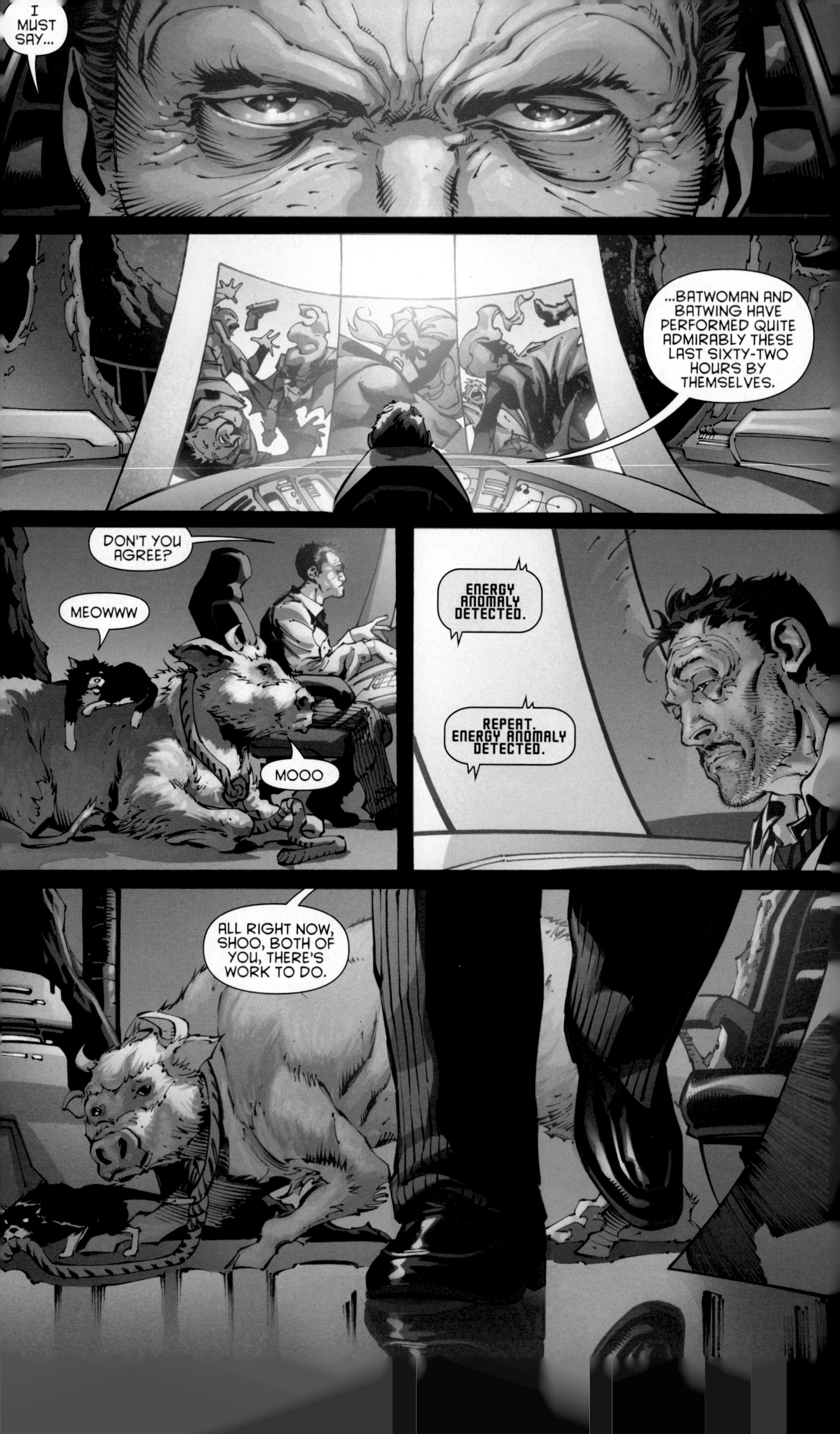
I MUST SAY...
...BATWOMAN AND BATWING HAVE PERFORMED QUITE ADMIRABLY THESE LAST SIXTY-TWO HOURS BY THEMSELVES.
DON'T YOU AGREE?
MEOWWW
MOOO
ENERGY ANOMALY DETECTED.
REPEAT. ENERGY ANOMALY DETECTED.
ALL RIGHT NOW, SHOO, BOTH OF YOU, THERE'S WORK TO DO.

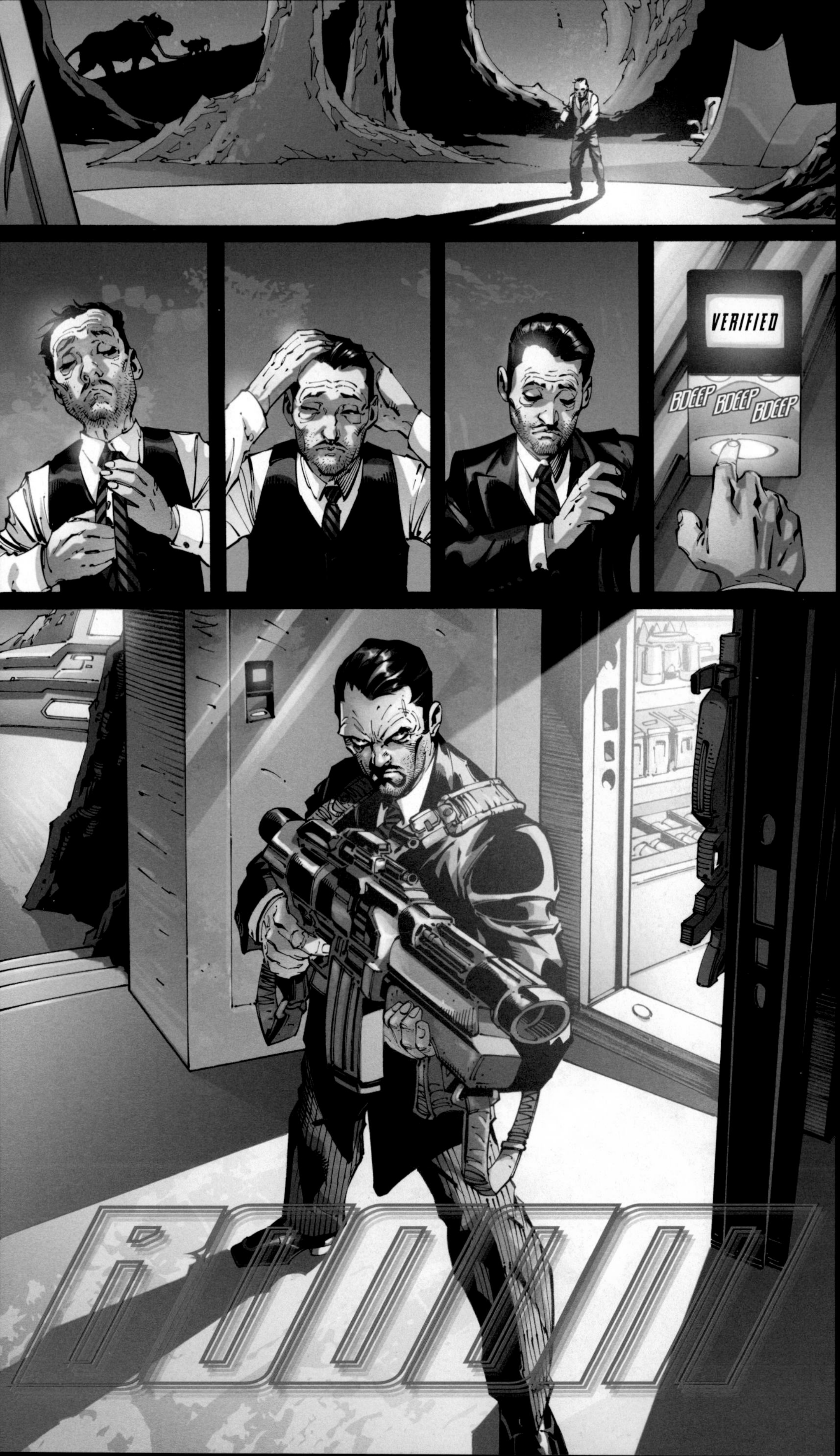
VERIFIED
BDEEP BDEEP BDEEP

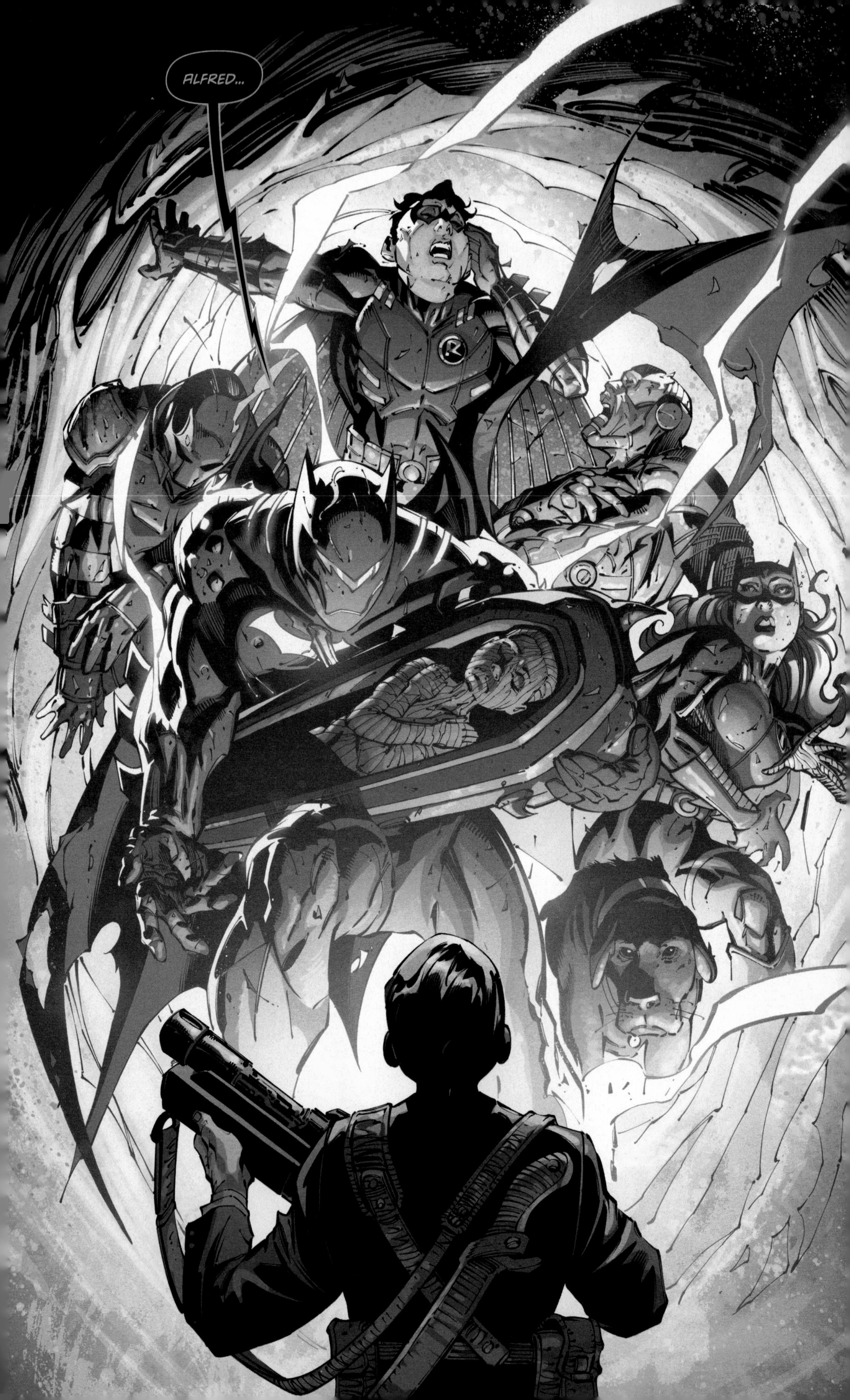
ALFRED...

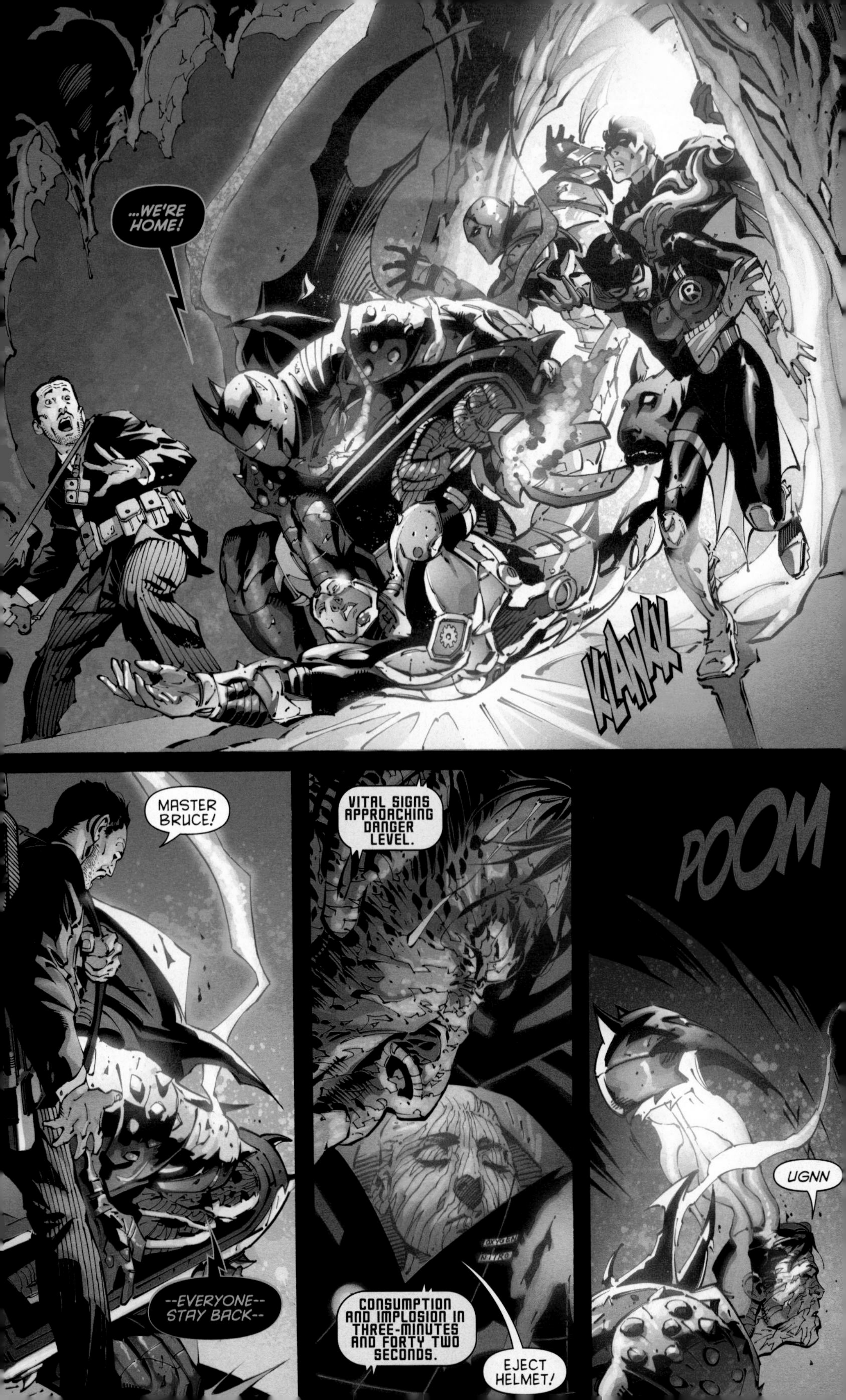
...WE'RE HOME!
KLANKK
MASTER BRUCE!
--EVERYONE-- STAY BACK--
VITAL SIGNS APPROACHING DANGER LEVEL.
CONSUMPTION AND IMPLOSION IN THREE-MINUTES AND FORTY TWO SECONDS.
EJECT HELMET!
POOM
UGNN

--DAMN IT, RA'S--WHAT THE HELL OPENS THIS--

CONSUMPTION AND IMPLOSION IN THREE MINUTES AND THIRTY NINE SECONDS.

BDEEP
BDEEP
BDEEP

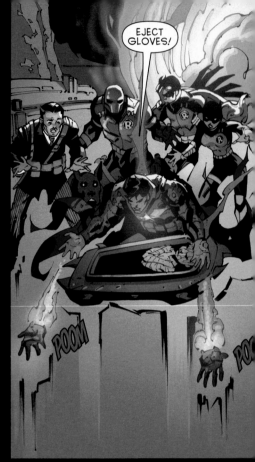

EJECT GLOVES!

POOM

POO

RRAGH!

CONSUMPTION AND IMPLOSION IN THREE MINUTES AND THIRTY FIVE SECONDS.

GET OUT OF THE SUIT, BATMAN!

NO, BATGIRL! NOT UNTIL I BRING DAMIAN BACK!

VITAL SIGNS DETERIORATING.

THREE MINUTES AND THIRTY SECONDS.

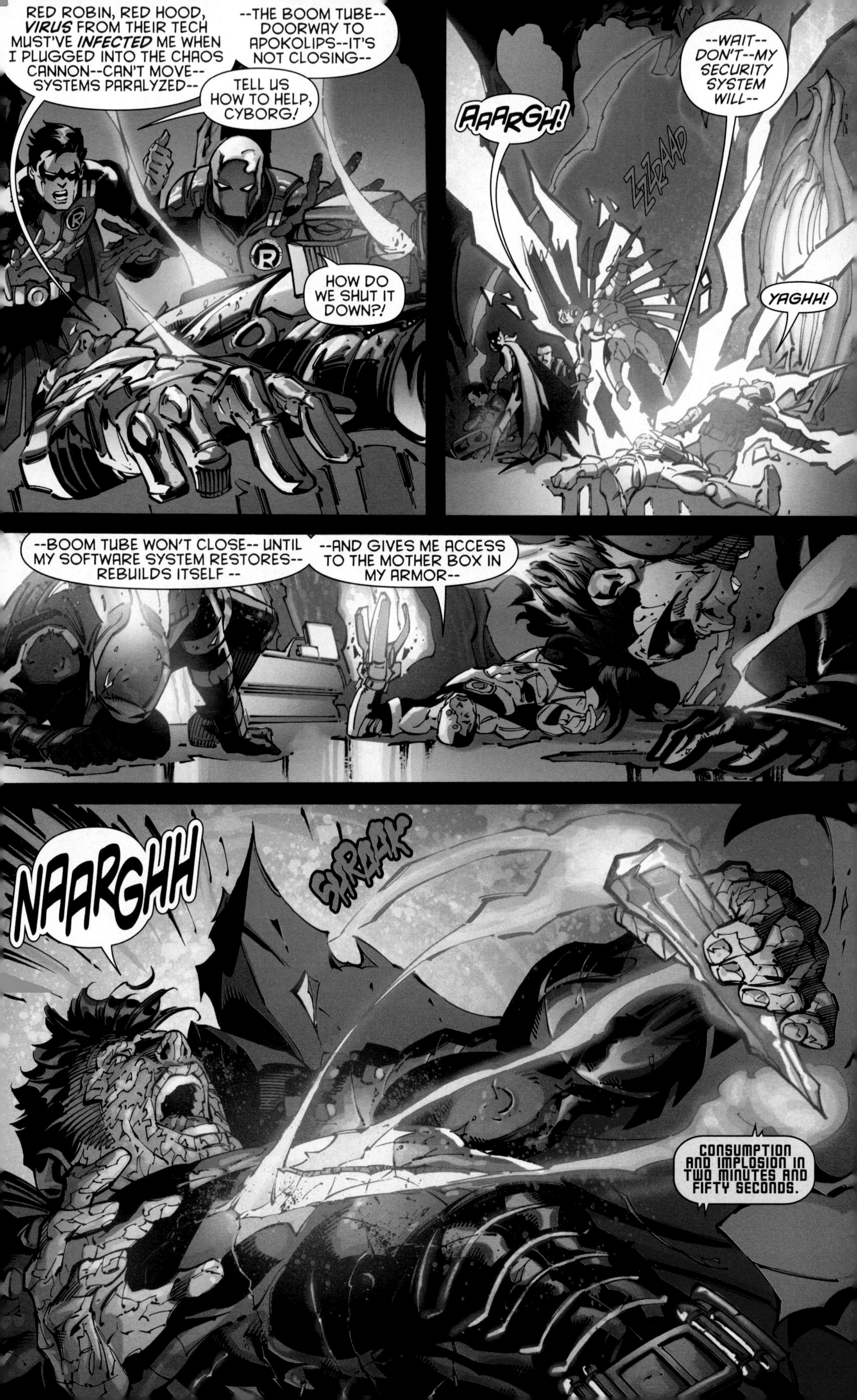

RED ROBIN, RED HOOD, VIRUS FROM THEIR TECH MUST'VE INFECTED ME WHEN I PLUGGED INTO THE CHAOS CANNON--CAN'T MOVE--SYSTEMS PARALYZED--
--THE BOOM TUBE--DOORWAY TO APOKOLIPS--IT'S NOT CLOSING--
TELL US HOW TO HELP, CYBORG!
HOW DO WE SHUT IT DOWN?!
AAARGH!
--WAIT--DON'T--MY SECURITY SYSTEM WILL--
ZZZAAP
YAGHH!
--BOOM TUBE WON'T CLOSE-- UNTIL MY SOFTWARE SYSTEM RESTORES--REBUILDS ITSELF --
--AND GIVES ME ACCESS TO THE MOTHER BOX IN MY ARMOR--
NAARGHH
SKROAK
CONSUMPTION AND IMPLOSION IN TWO MINUTES AND FIFTY SECONDS.

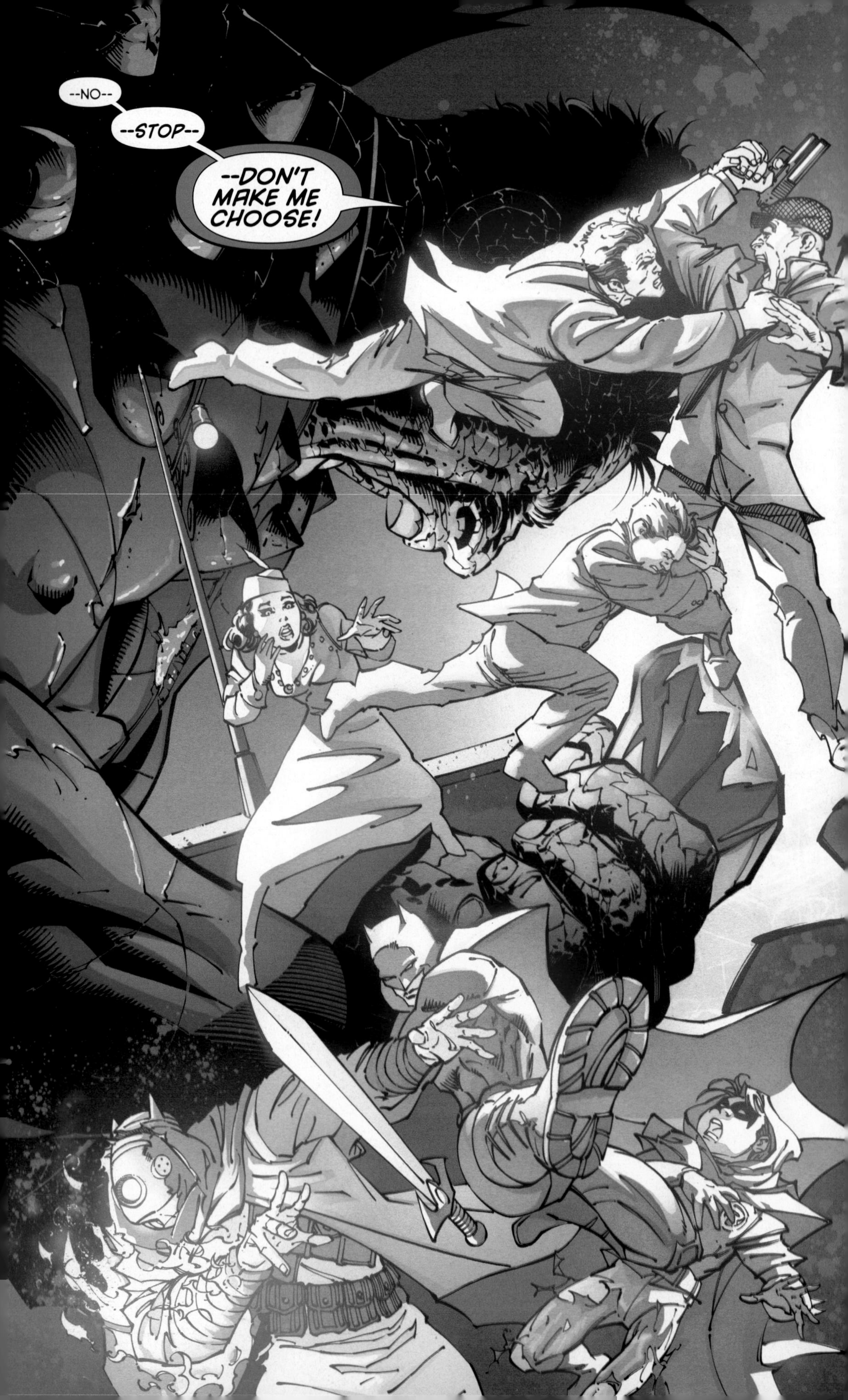
--NO--
--STOP--
--DON'T MAKE ME CHOOSE!

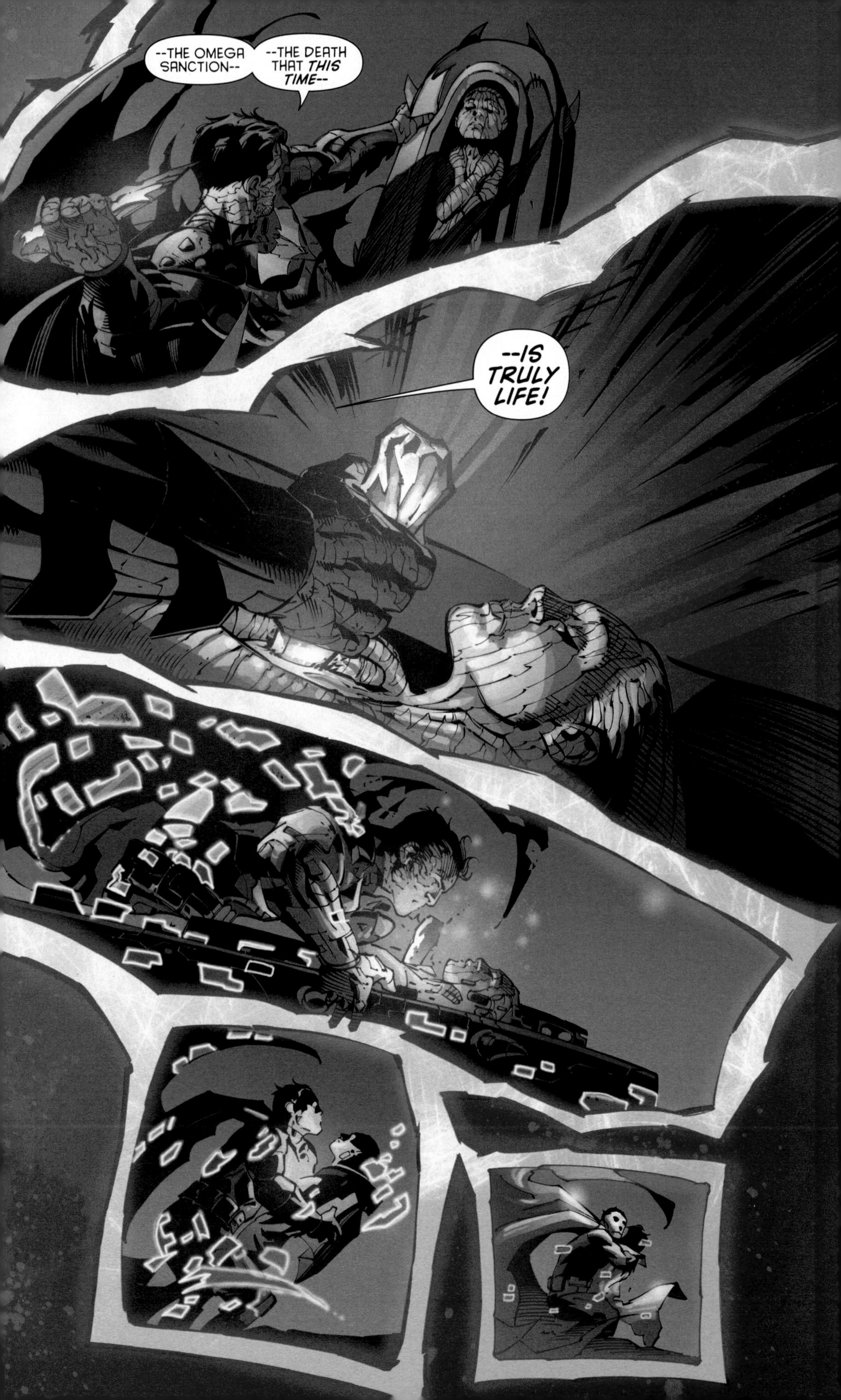
--THE OMEGA SANCTION--
--THE DEATH THAT *THIS TIME*--
--IS TRULY LIFE!

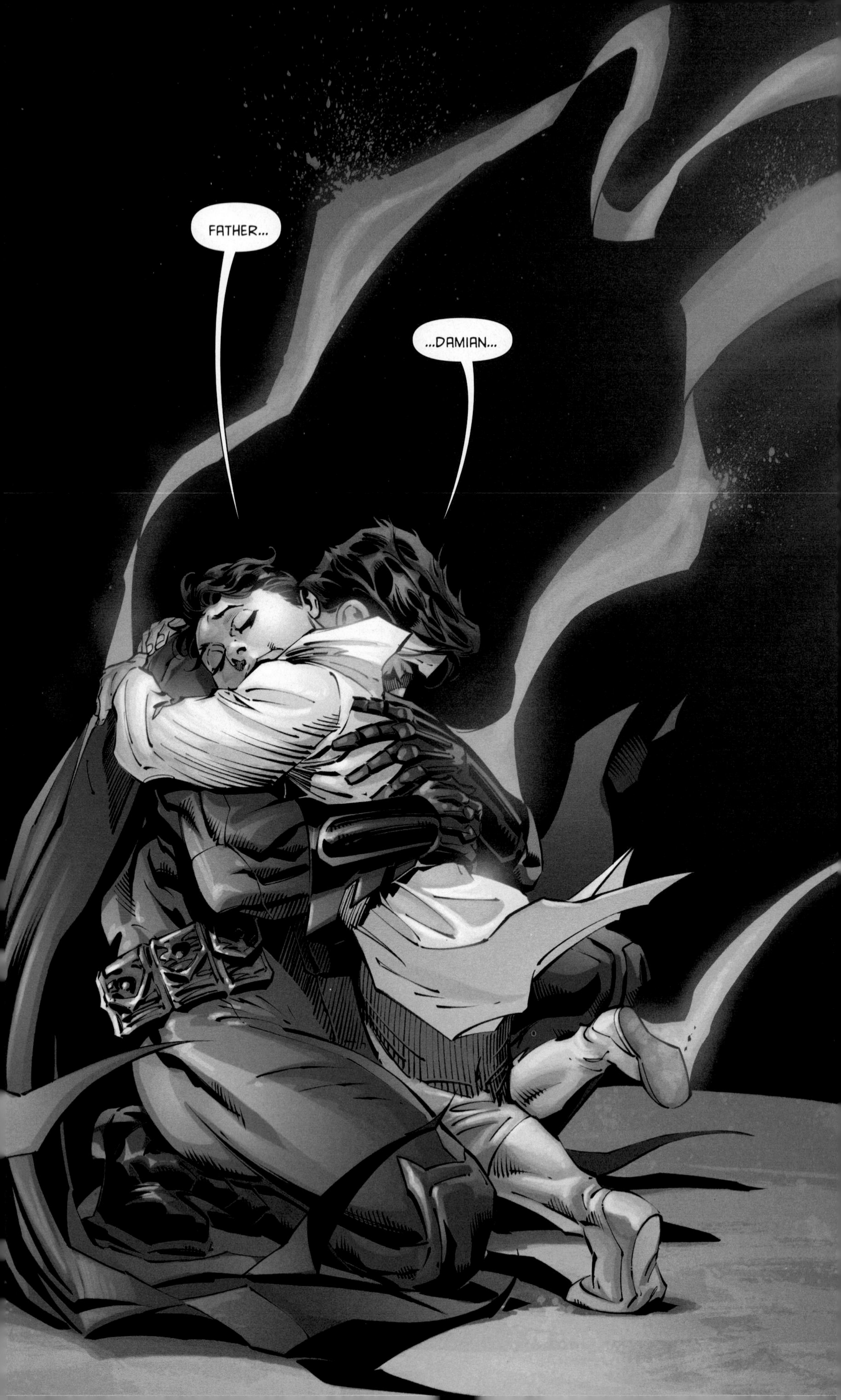
FATHER...
...DAMIAN...

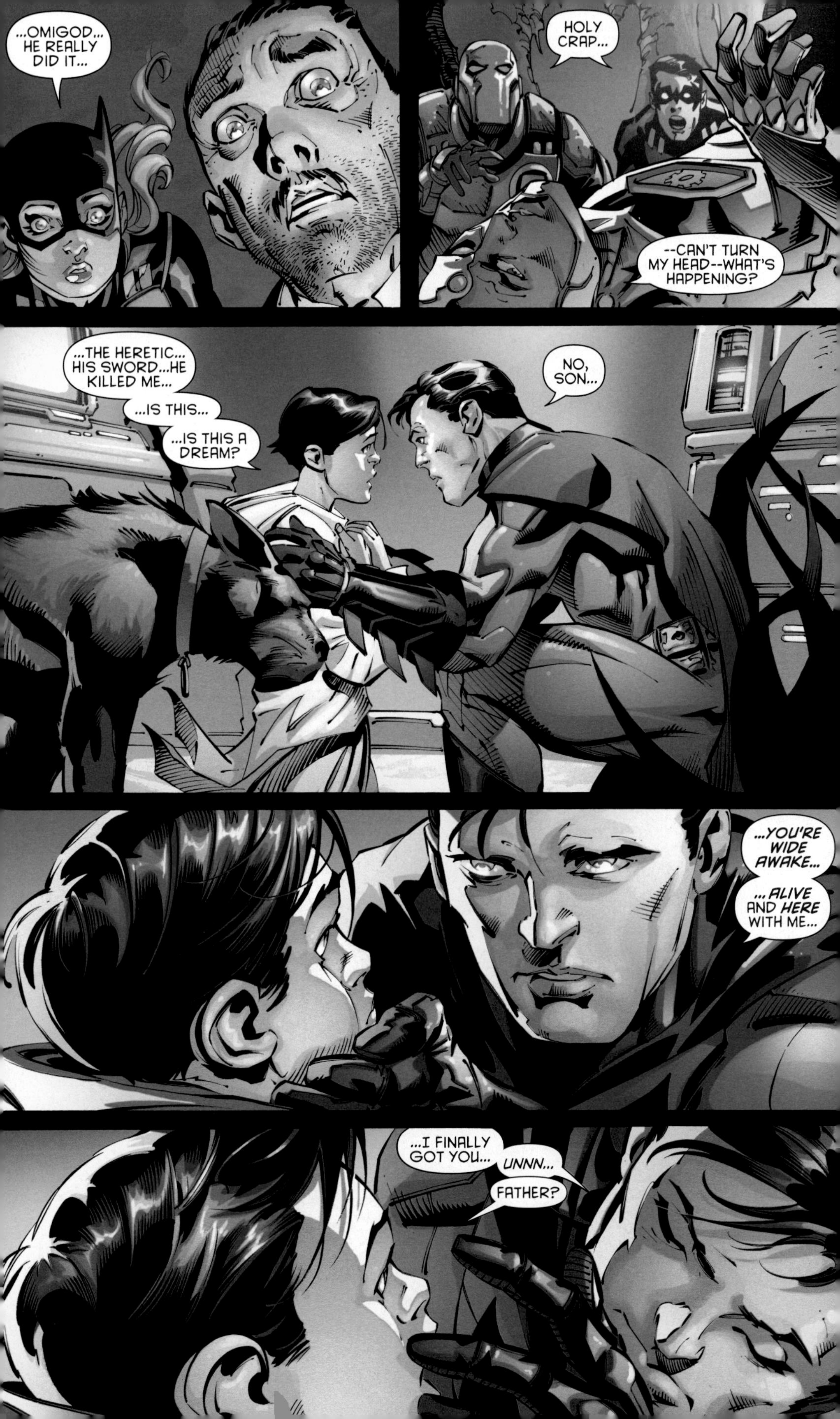
...OMIGOD... HE REALLY DID IT...
HOLY CRAP...
--CAN'T TURN MY HEAD--WHAT'S HAPPENING?
...THE HERETIC... HIS SWORD...HE KILLED ME...
...IS THIS...
...IS THIS A DREAM?
NO, SON...
...YOU'RE WIDE AWAKE...
...ALIVE AND HERE WITH ME...
...I FINALLY GOT YOU...
UNNN...
FATHER?

FATHER!

...BACK, BOY...

PENNYWORTH, WHAT'S WRONG WITH HIM?

HIS PULSE IS STEADY, THANK GOD, AND THERE'S NO TIME TO EXPLAIN.

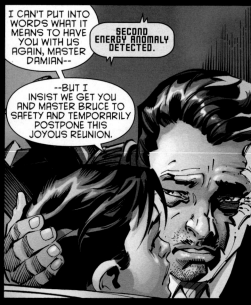

I CAN'T PUT INTO WORDS WHAT IT MEANS TO HAVE YOU WITH US AGAIN, MASTER DAMIAN--

SECOND ENERGY ANOMALY DETECTED.

--BUT I INSIST WE GET YOU AND MASTER BRUCE TO SAFETY AND TEMPORARILY POSTPONE THIS JOYOUS REUNION.

WHATEVER'S HAPPENING IS HAPPENING BECAUSE OF ME.

I'M NOT GOING ANYWHERE.

I'M STAYING RIGHT HERE AT HIS SIDE.

OF COURSE YOU ARE.

REPEAT, SECOND ENERGY ANOMALY DETECTED.

GENTLEMEN, I WOULD APPRECIATE IT IF YOU WOULD SHUT THAT DAMN PORTAL!

WE CAN'T.

AND YOUR WEAPONS SYSTEM, CYBORG?

--WORKING ON IT--

WONDERFUL.

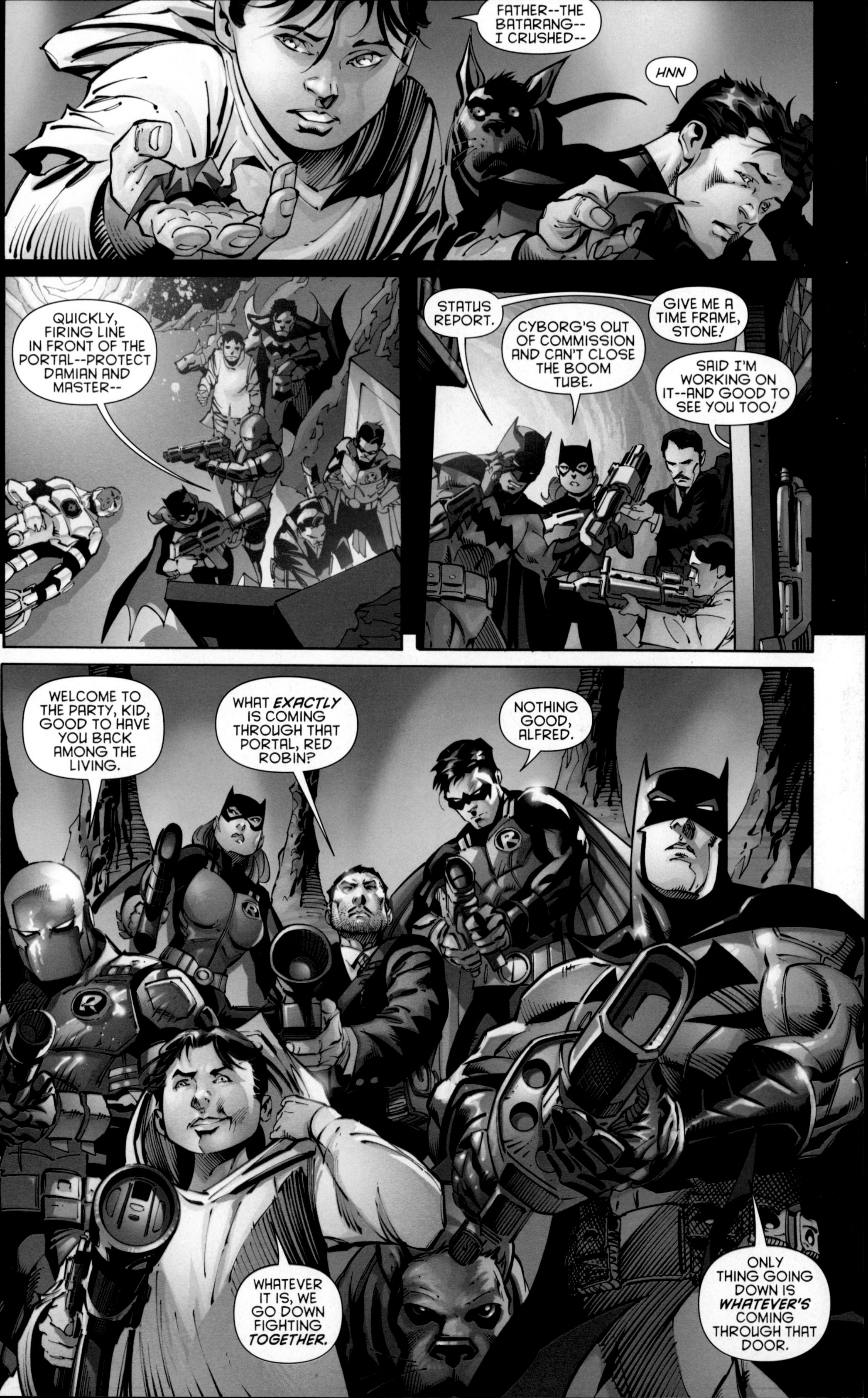
FATHER--THE BATARANG-- I CRUSHED--
HNN
QUICKLY, FIRING LINE IN FRONT OF THE PORTAL--PROTECT DAMIAN AND MASTER--
STATUS REPORT.
CYBORG'S OUT OF COMMISSION AND CAN'T CLOSE THE BOOM TUBE.
GIVE ME A TIME FRAME, STONE!
SAID I'M WORKING ON IT--AND GOOD TO SEE YOU TOO!
WELCOME TO THE PARTY, KID, GOOD TO HAVE YOU BACK AMONG THE LIVING.
WHAT *EXACTLY* IS COMING THROUGH THAT PORTAL, RED ROBIN?
NOTHING GOOD, ALFRED.
WHATEVER IT IS, WE GO DOWN FIGHTING *TOGETHER.*
ONLY THING GOING DOWN IS *WHATEVER'S* COMING THROUGH THAT DOOR.

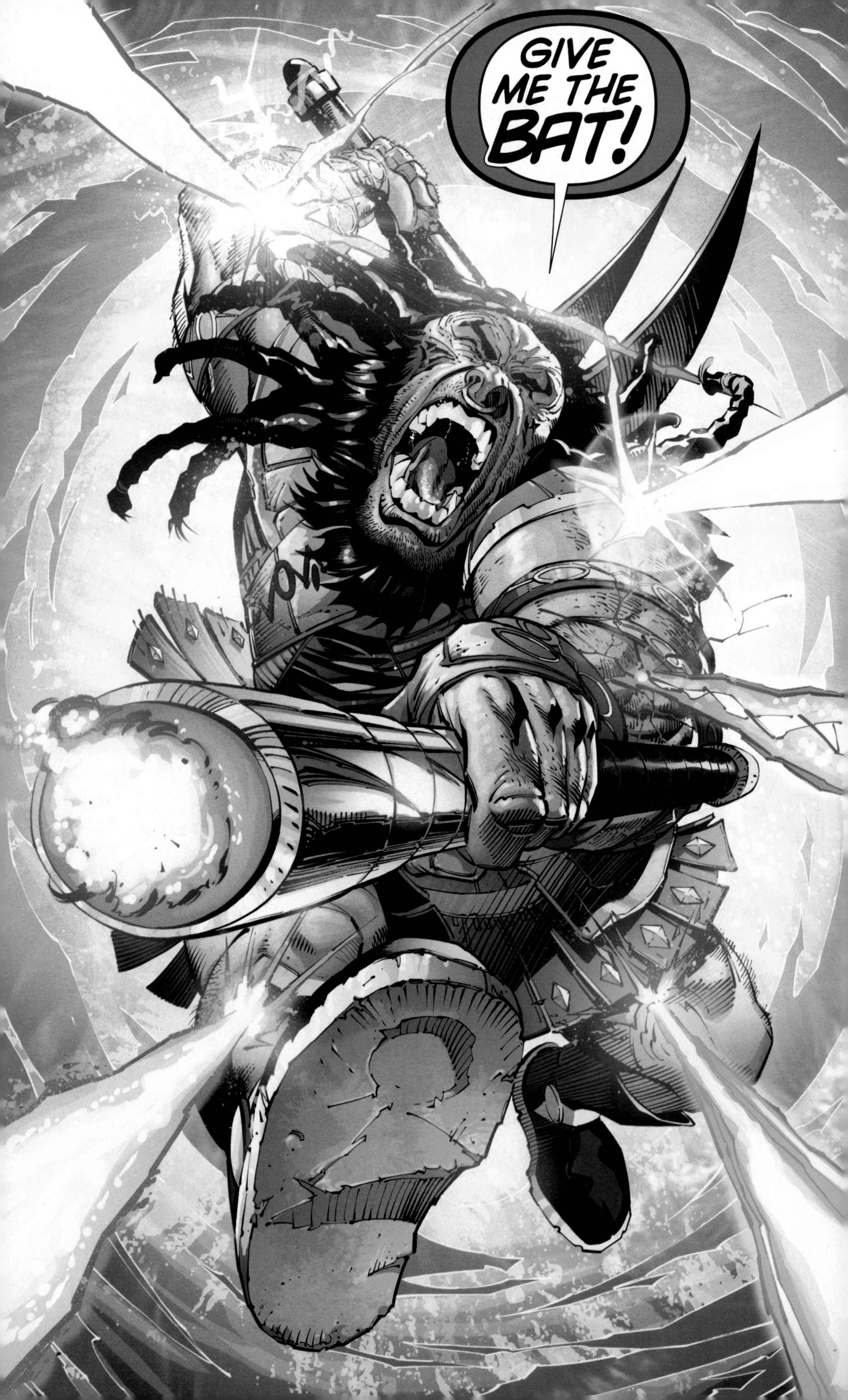
GIVE ME THE BAT!

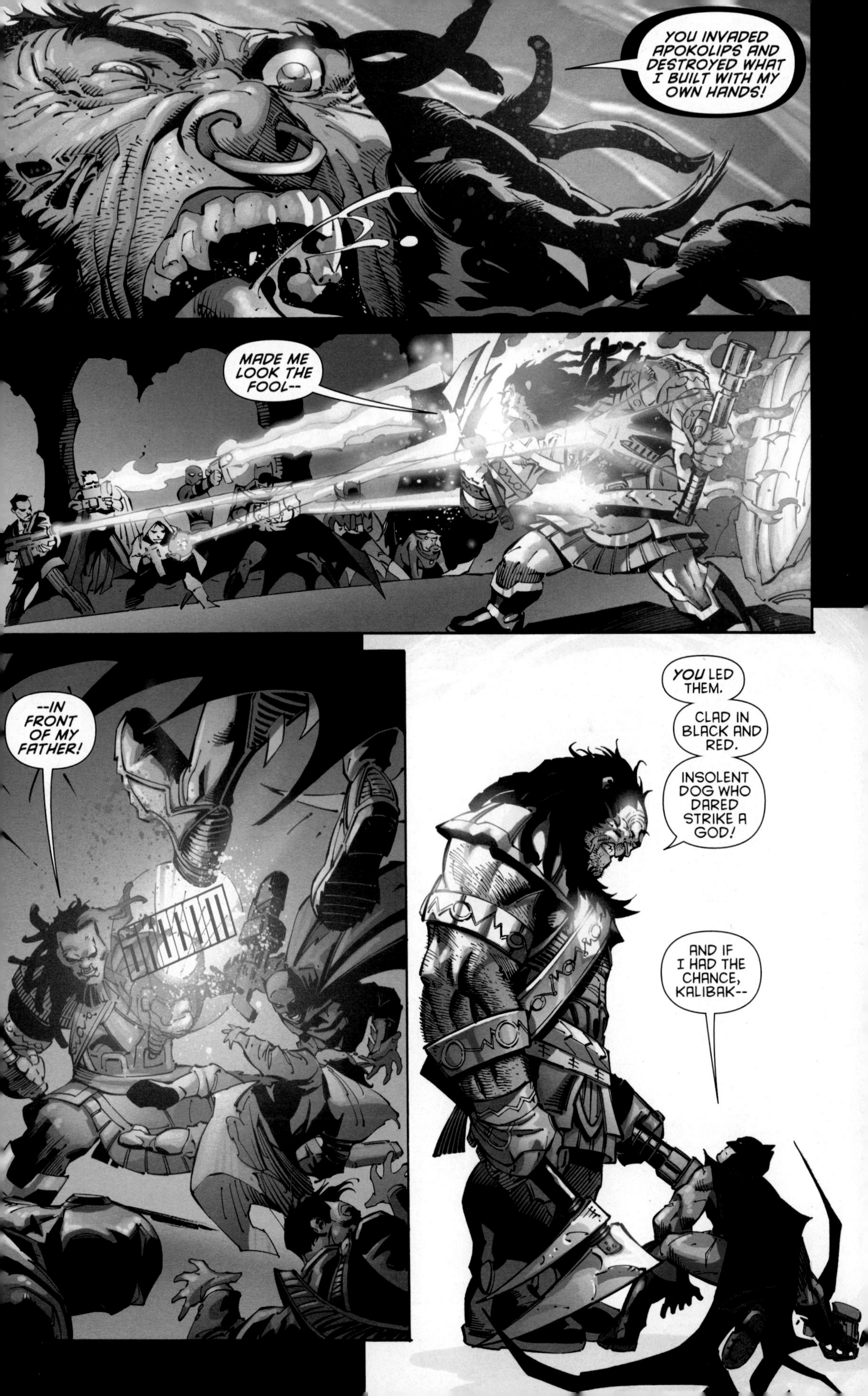
YOU INVADED APOKOLIPS AND DESTROYED WHAT I BUILT WITH MY OWN HANDS!
MADE ME LOOK THE FOOL--
--IN FRONT OF MY FATHER!
YOU LED THEM.
CLAD IN BLACK AND RED.
INSOLENT DOG WHO DARED STRIKE A GOD!
AND IF I HAD THE CHANCE, KALIBAK--

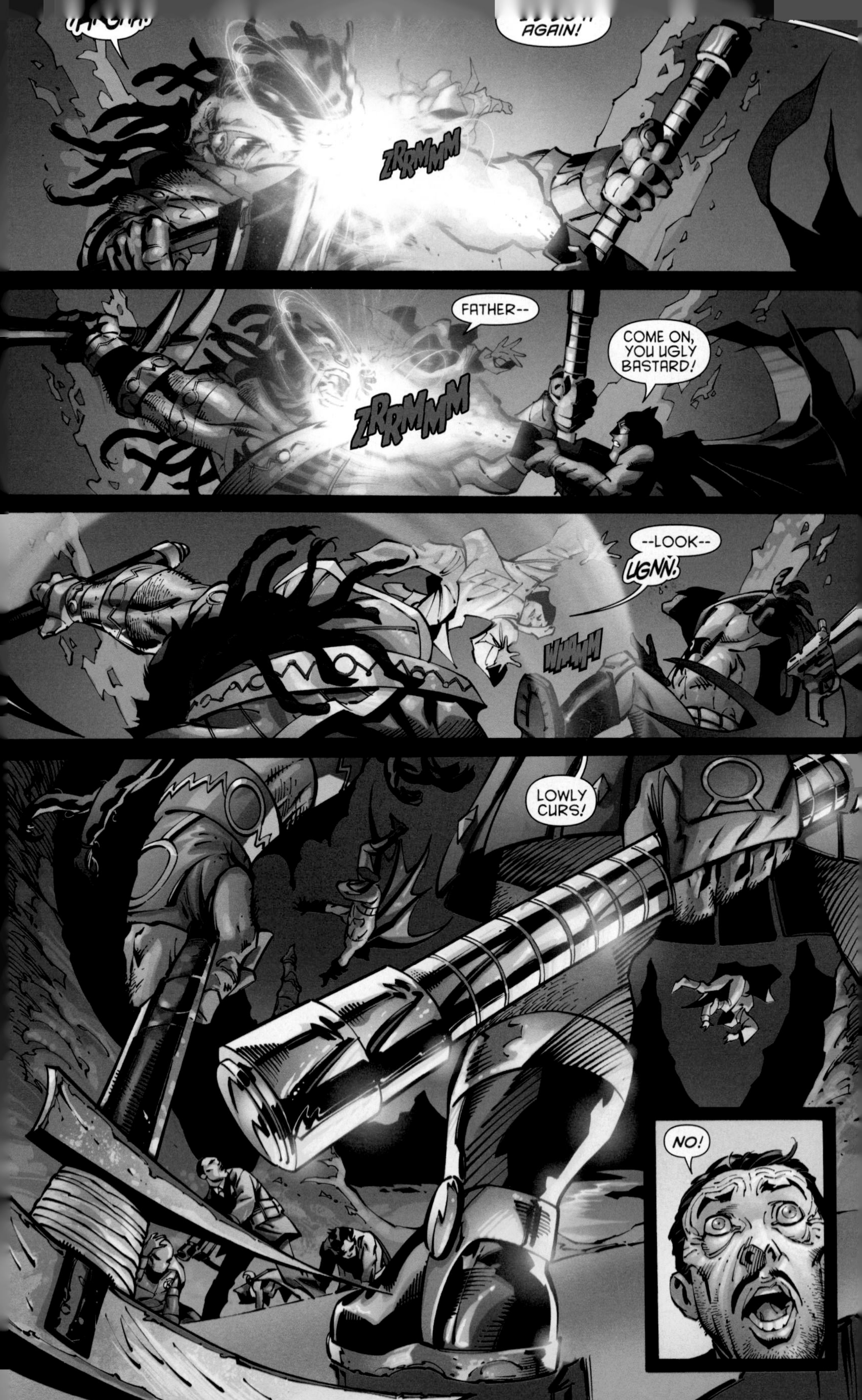
AGAIN!
ZRRMMM
FATHER--
COME ON, YOU UGLY BASTARD!
ZRRMMM
--LOOK--
UGNN!
LOWLY CURS!
NO!

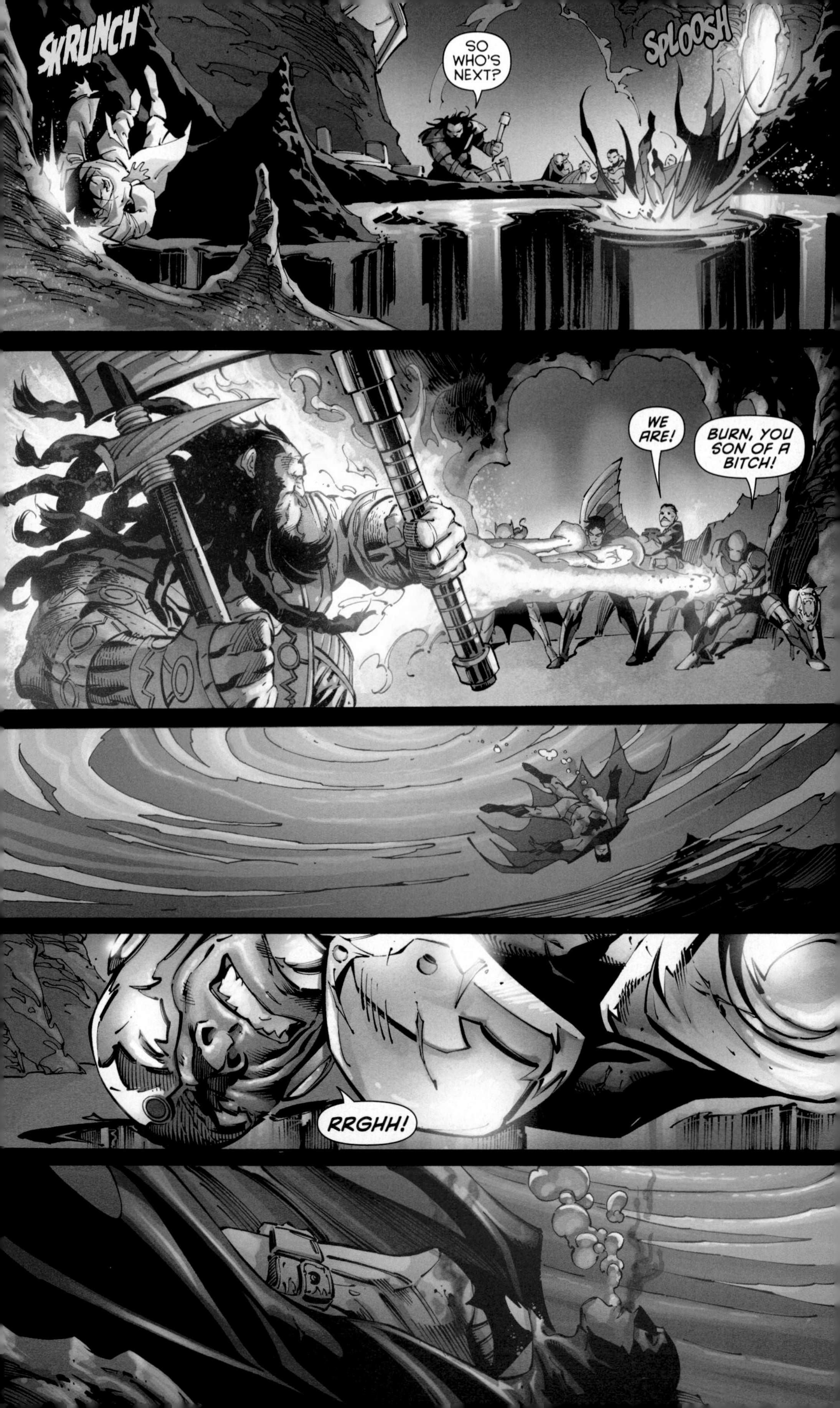
SKRUNCH
SO WHO'S NEXT?
SPLOOSH
WE ARE!
BURN, YOU SON OF A BITCH!
RRGHH!

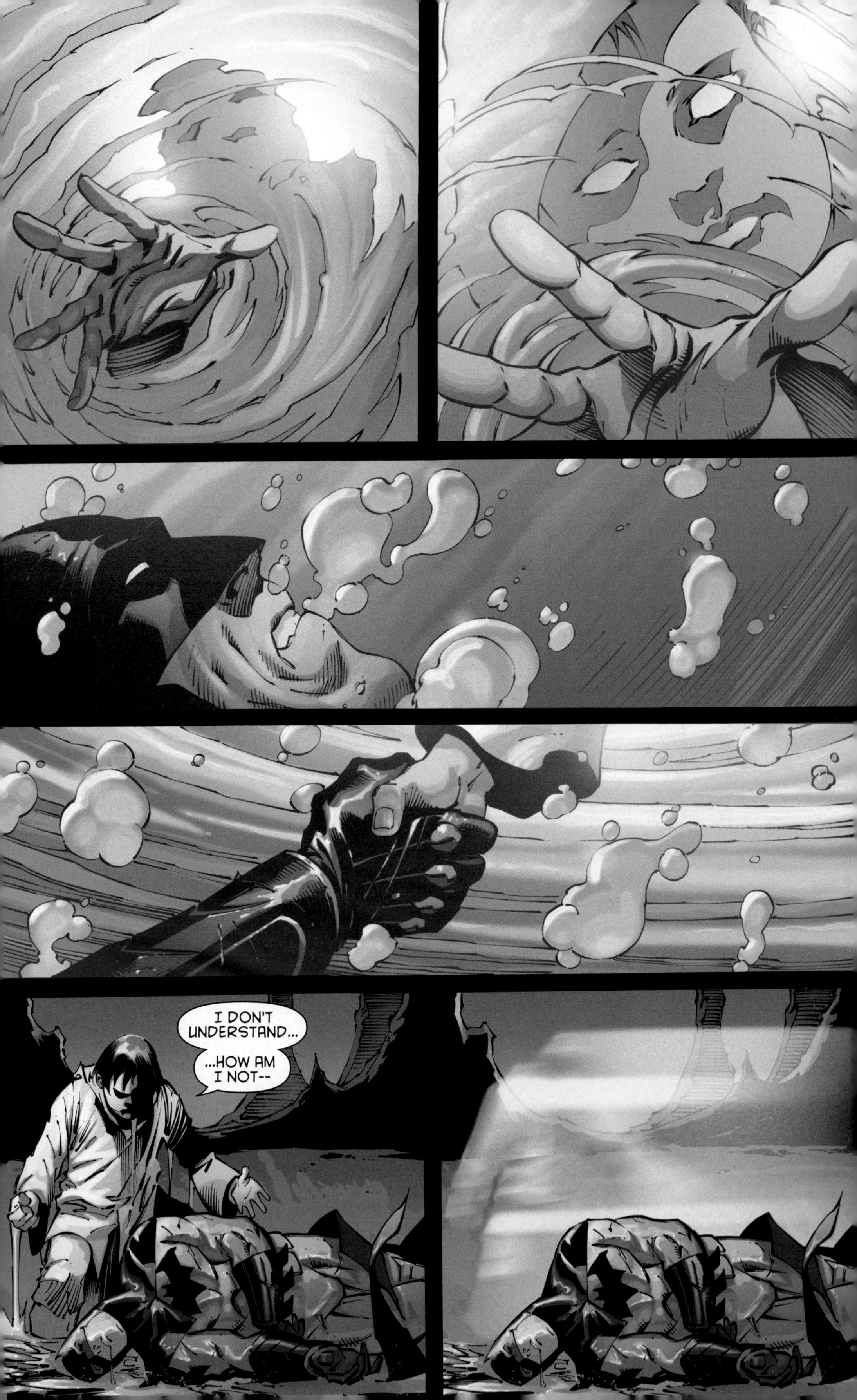
I DON'T UNDERSTAND...
...HOW AM I NOT--

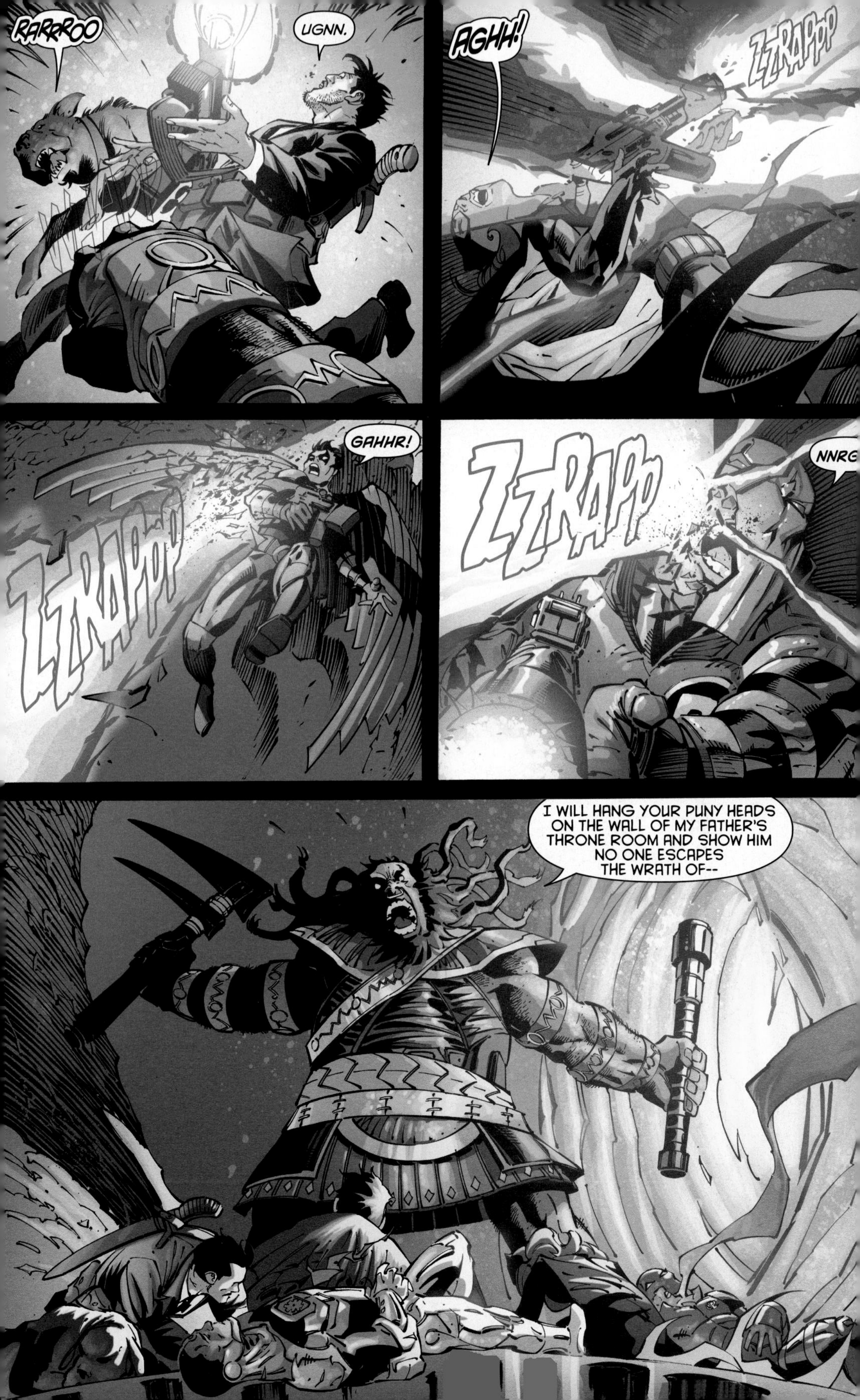
RARRROO
UGNN.
AGHH!
ZZRAPPP
GAHHR!
ZZRAPPP
ZZRAPP
NNRG
I WILL HANG YOUR PUNY HEADS ON THE WALL OF MY FATHER'S THRONE ROOM AND SHOW HIM NO ONE ESCAPES THE WRATH OF--

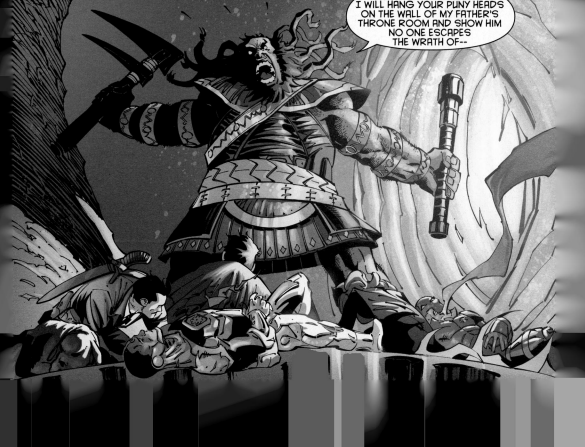

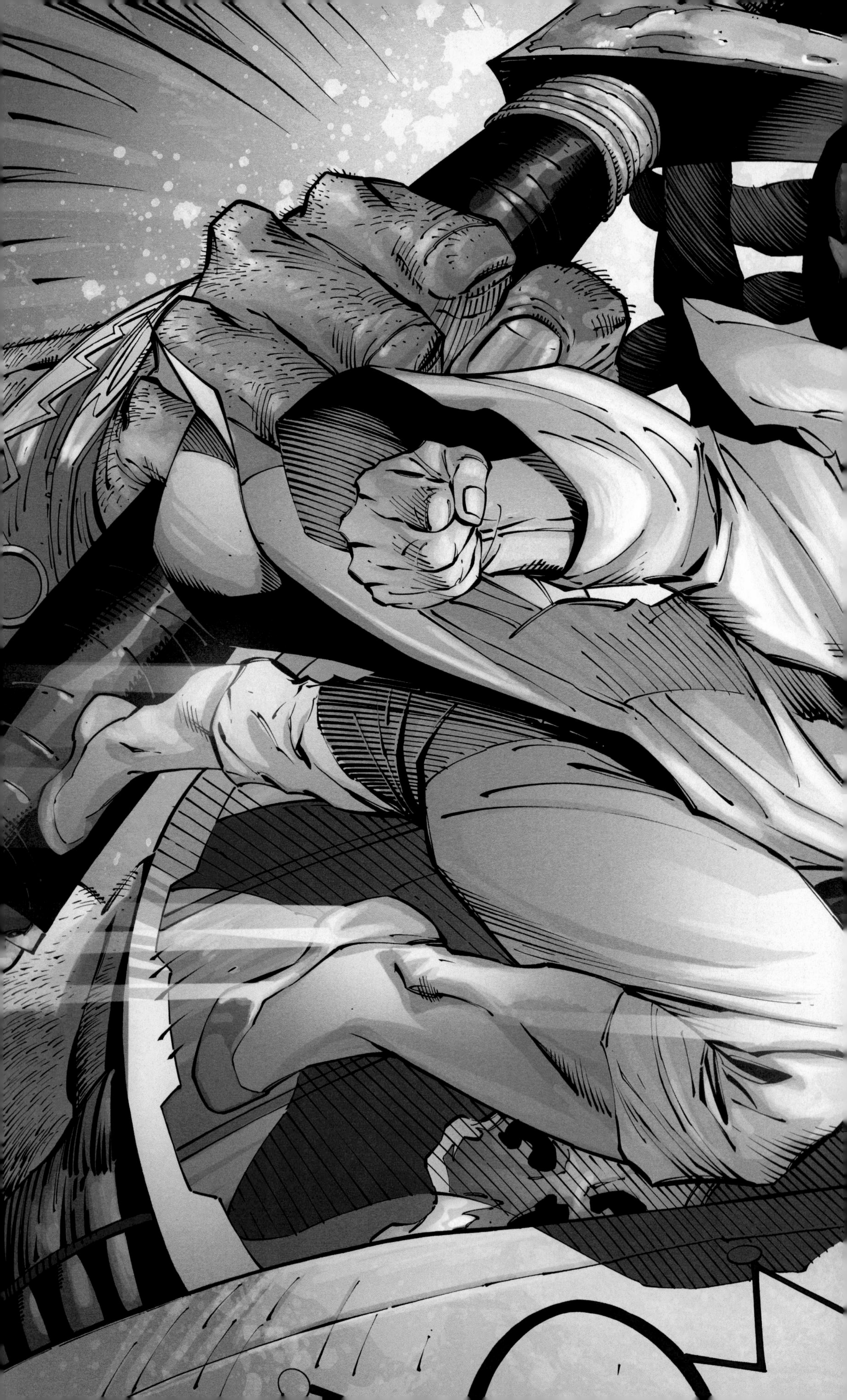

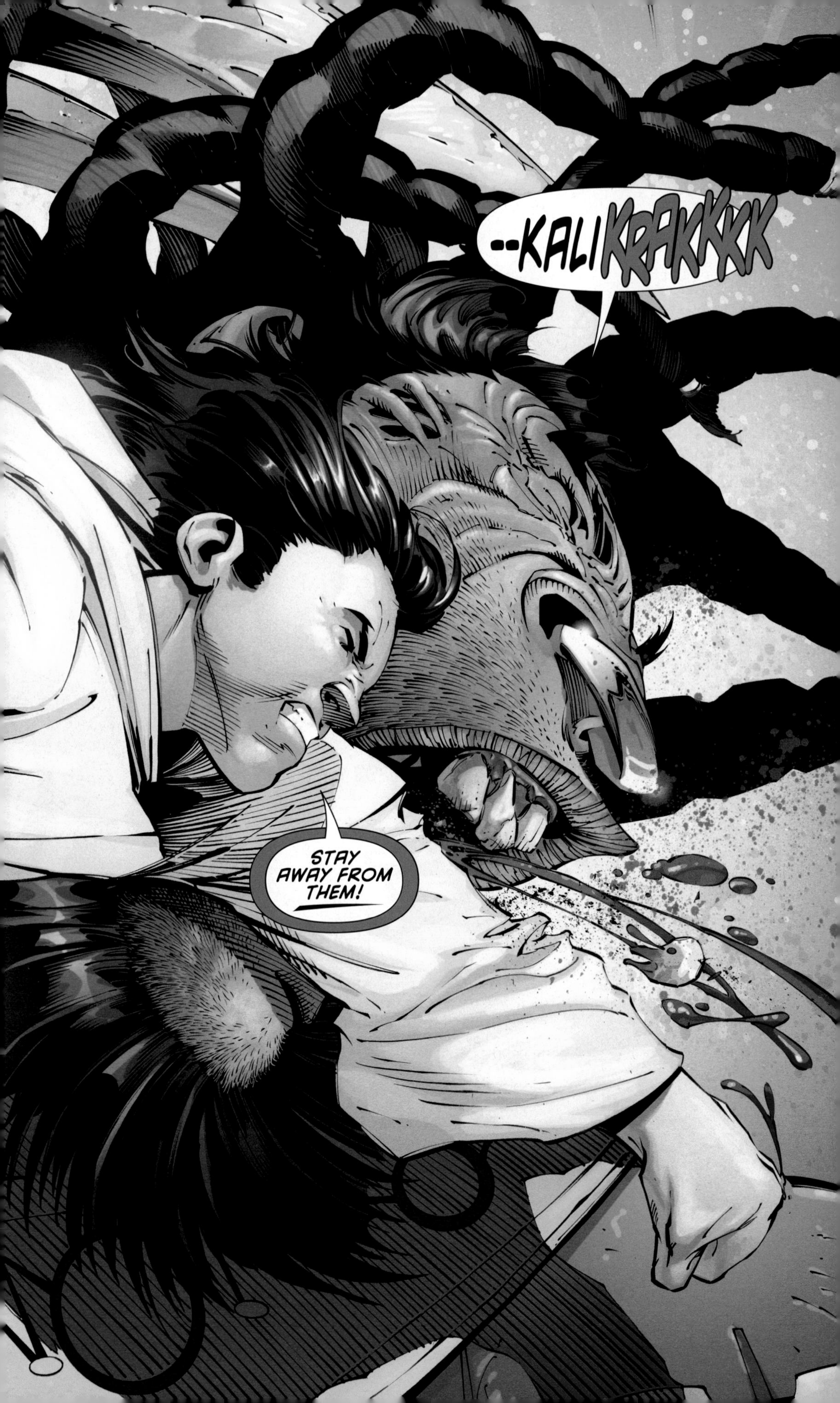
--KALIKRAKKKK
STAY AWAY FROM THEM!

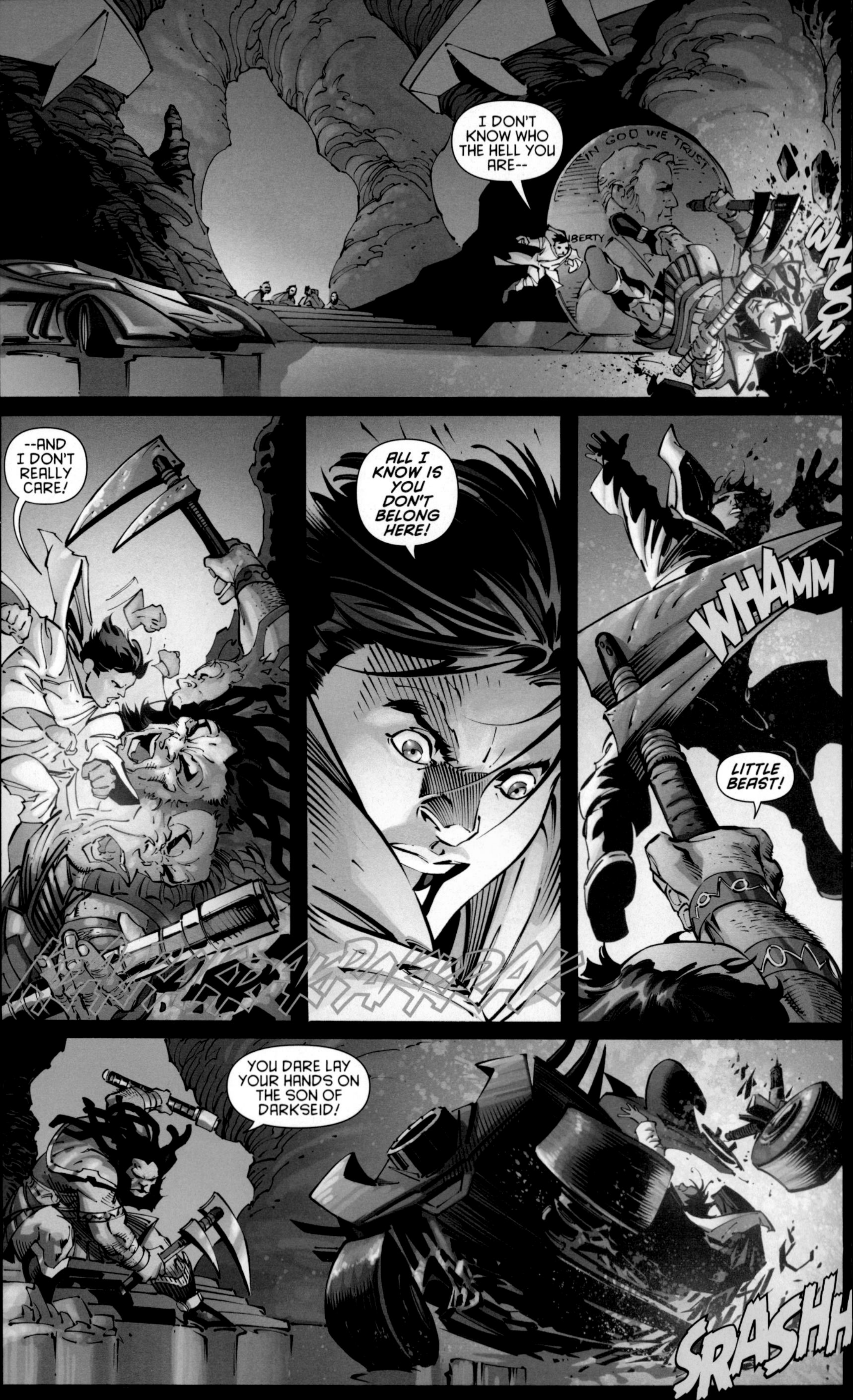

IN GOD WE TRUST
LIBERTY
I DON'T KNOW WHO THE HELL YOU ARE--
--AND I DON'T REALLY CARE!
ALL I KNOW IS YOU DON'T BELONG HERE!
WHAMM
LITTLE BEAST!
YOU DARE LAY YOUR HANDS ON THE SON OF DARKSEID!
SRASHH

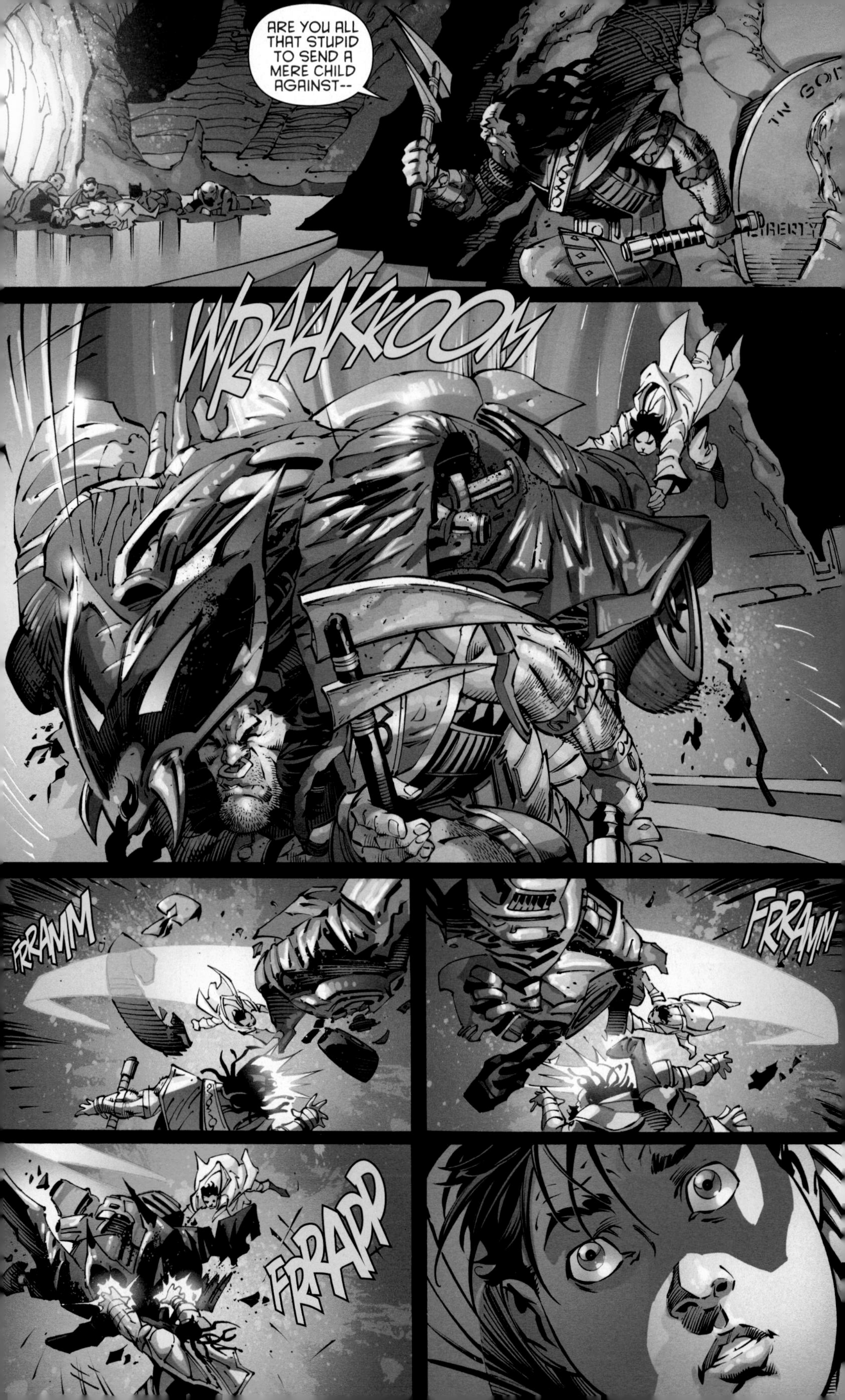
ARE YOU ALL THAT STUPID TO SEND A MERE CHILD AGAINST--
WRAAKKOOM
FRRAMM
FRRAMM
FRRAPP

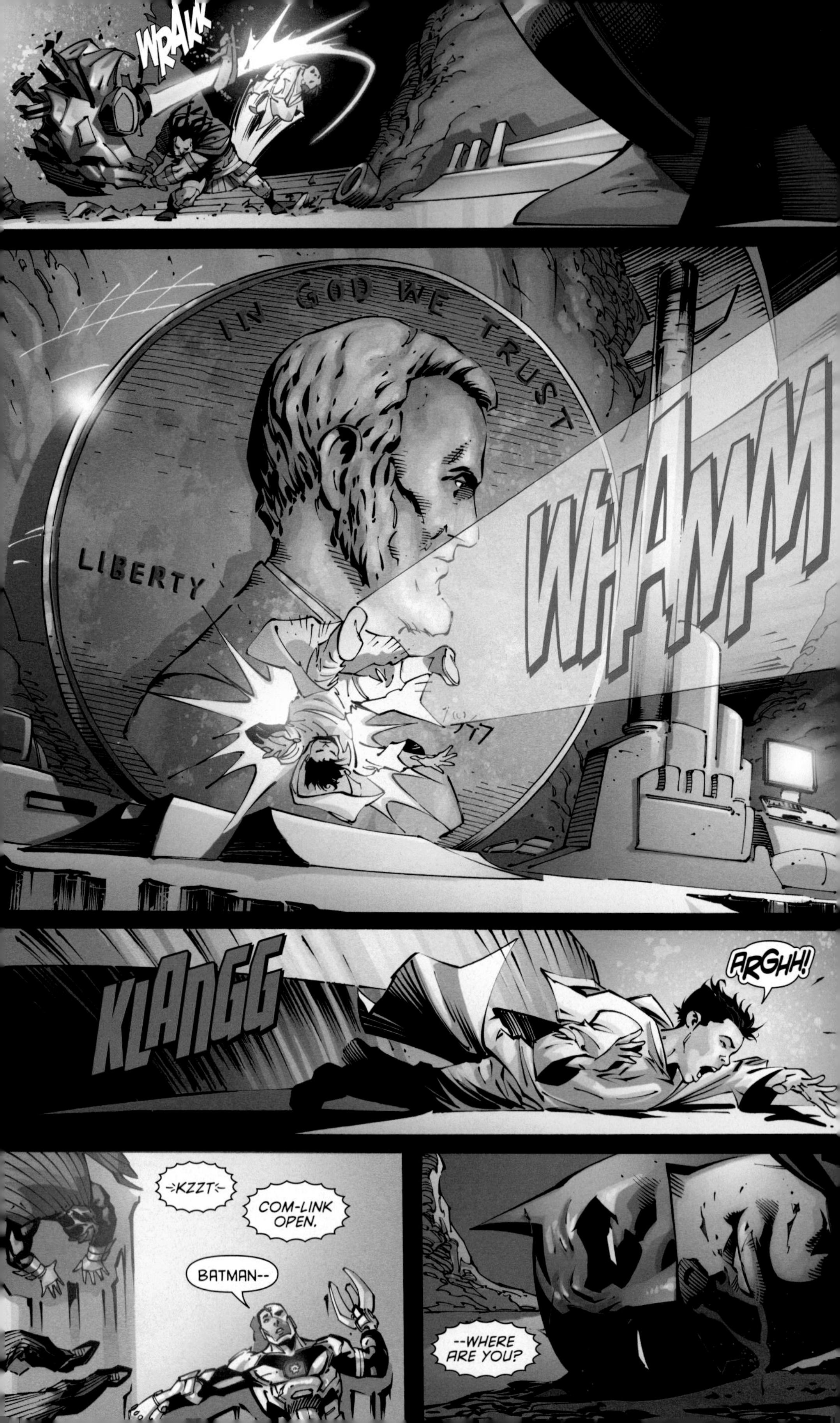
WRAKK
IN GOD WE TRUST
LIBERTY
WHAMM
KLANGG
ARGHH!
-KZZT-
COM-LINK OPEN.
BATMAN--
--WHERE ARE YOU?

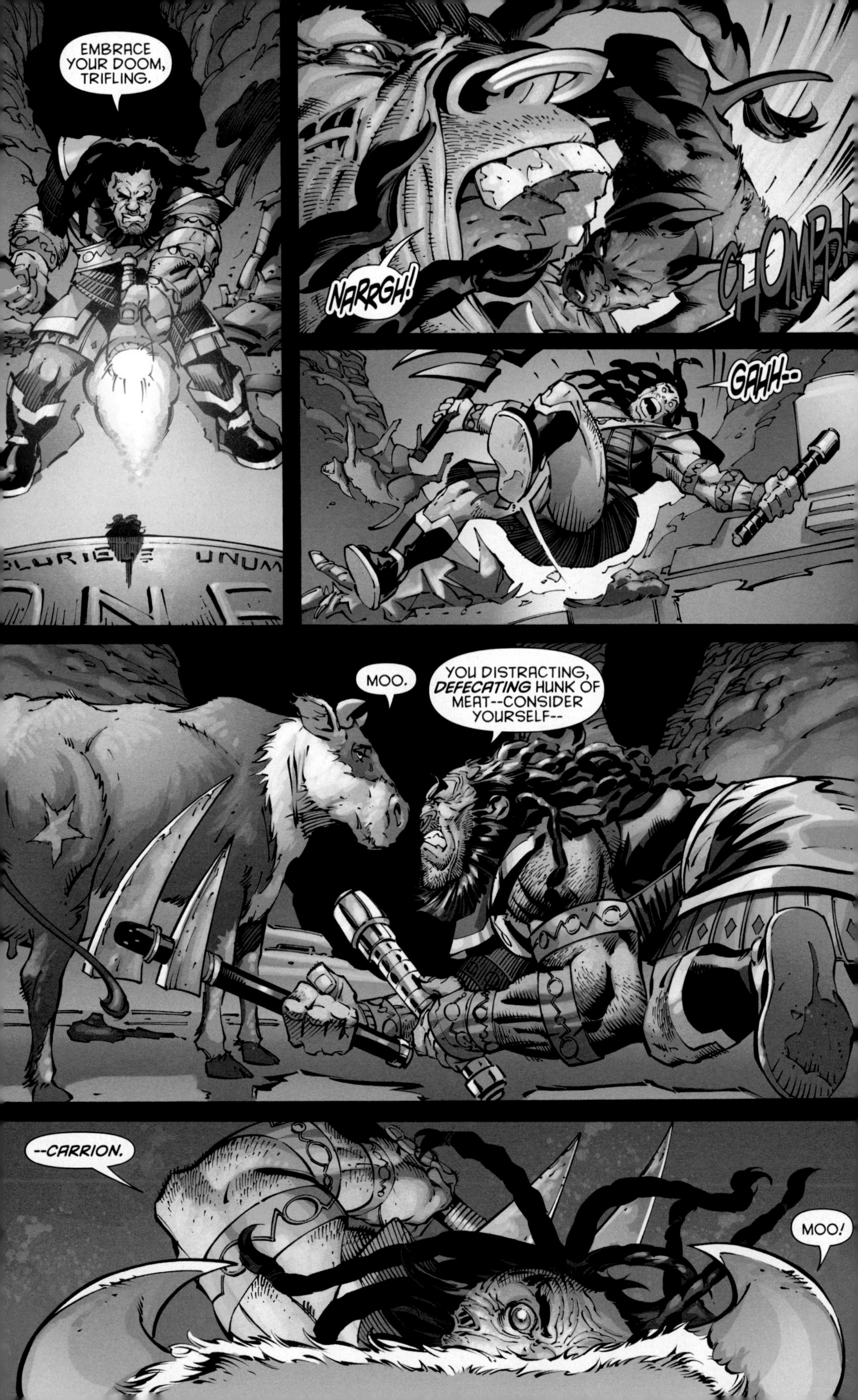
EMBRACE YOUR DOOM, TRIFLING.
NARRGH!
CHOMP!
GAHH--
E PLURIBUS UNUM
MOO.
YOU DISTRACTING, *DEFECATING* HUNK OF MEAT--CONSIDER YOURSELF--
--CARRION.
MOO!

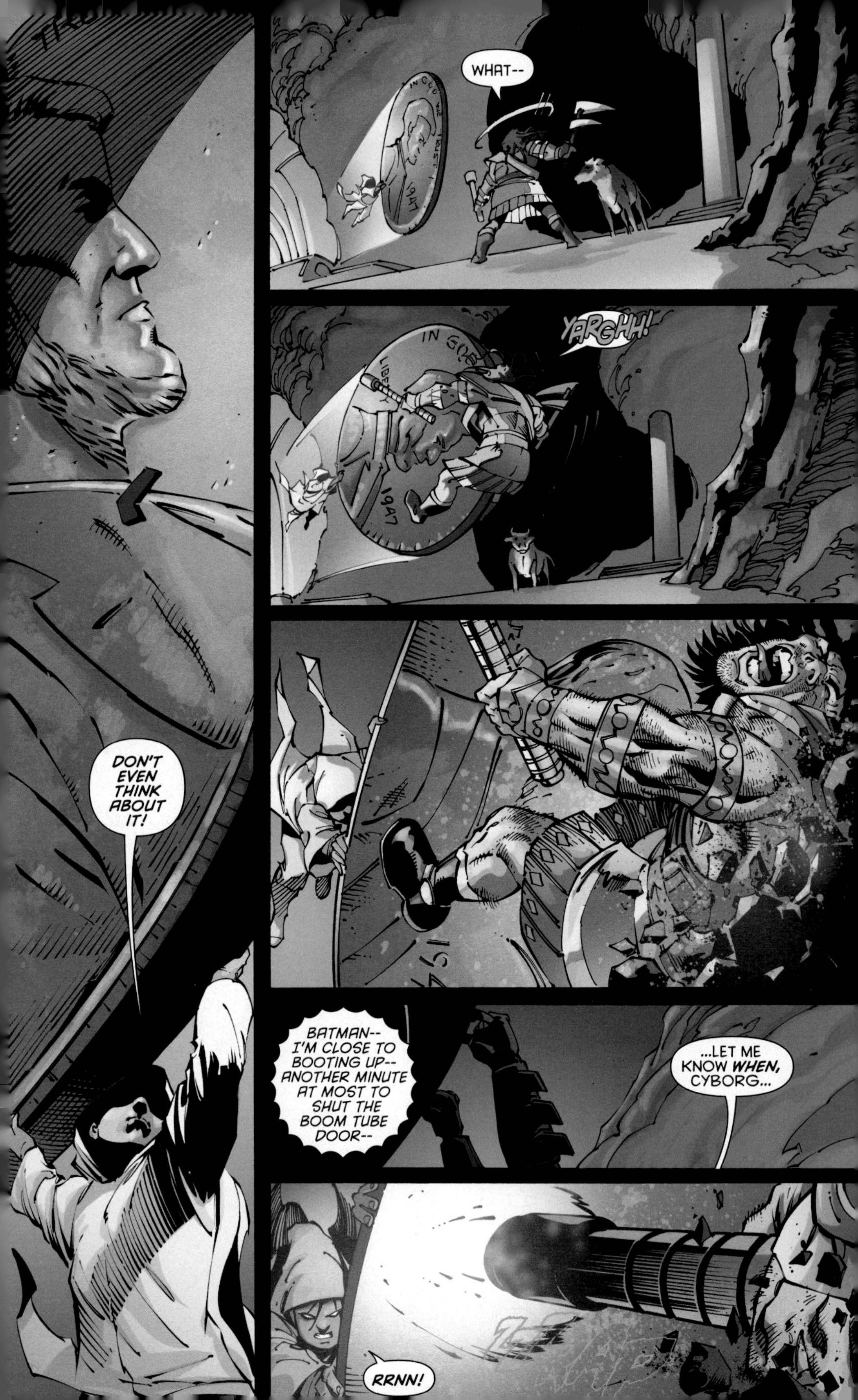
DON'T EVEN THINK ABOUT IT!
WHAT--
YARGHH!
BATMAN-- I'M CLOSE TO BOOTING UP-- ANOTHER MINUTE AT MOST TO SHUT THE BOOM TUBE DOOR--
...LET ME KNOW WHEN, CYBORG...
RRNN!

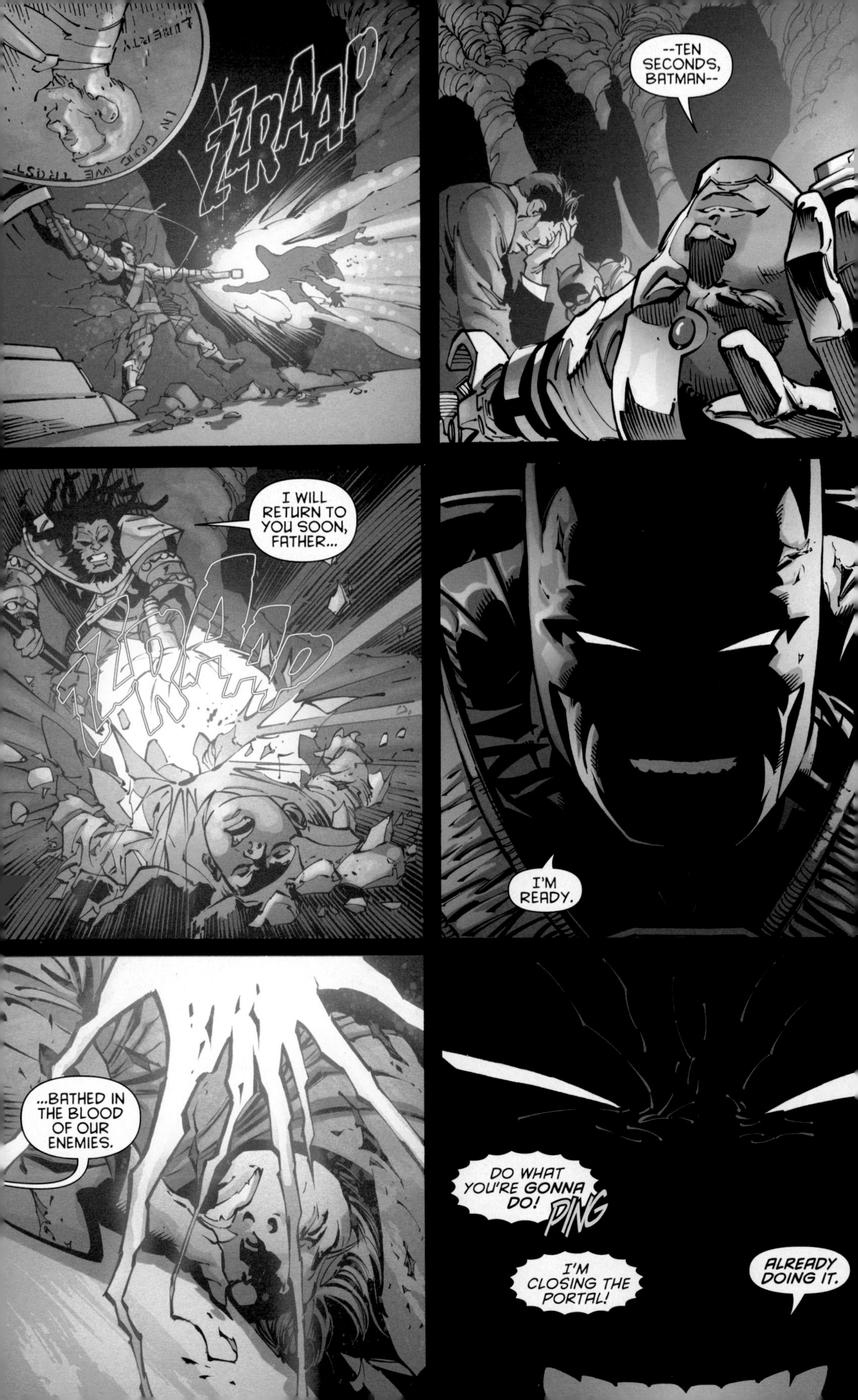
LIBERTY
IN GOD WE TRUST
ZZRAAP
--TEN SECONDS, BATMAN--
I WILL RETURN TO YOU SOON, FATHER...
I'M READY.
...BATHED IN THE BLOOD OF OUR ENEMIES.
DO WHAT YOU'RE GONNA DO!
PING
I'M CLOSING THE PORTAL!
ALREADY DOING IT.

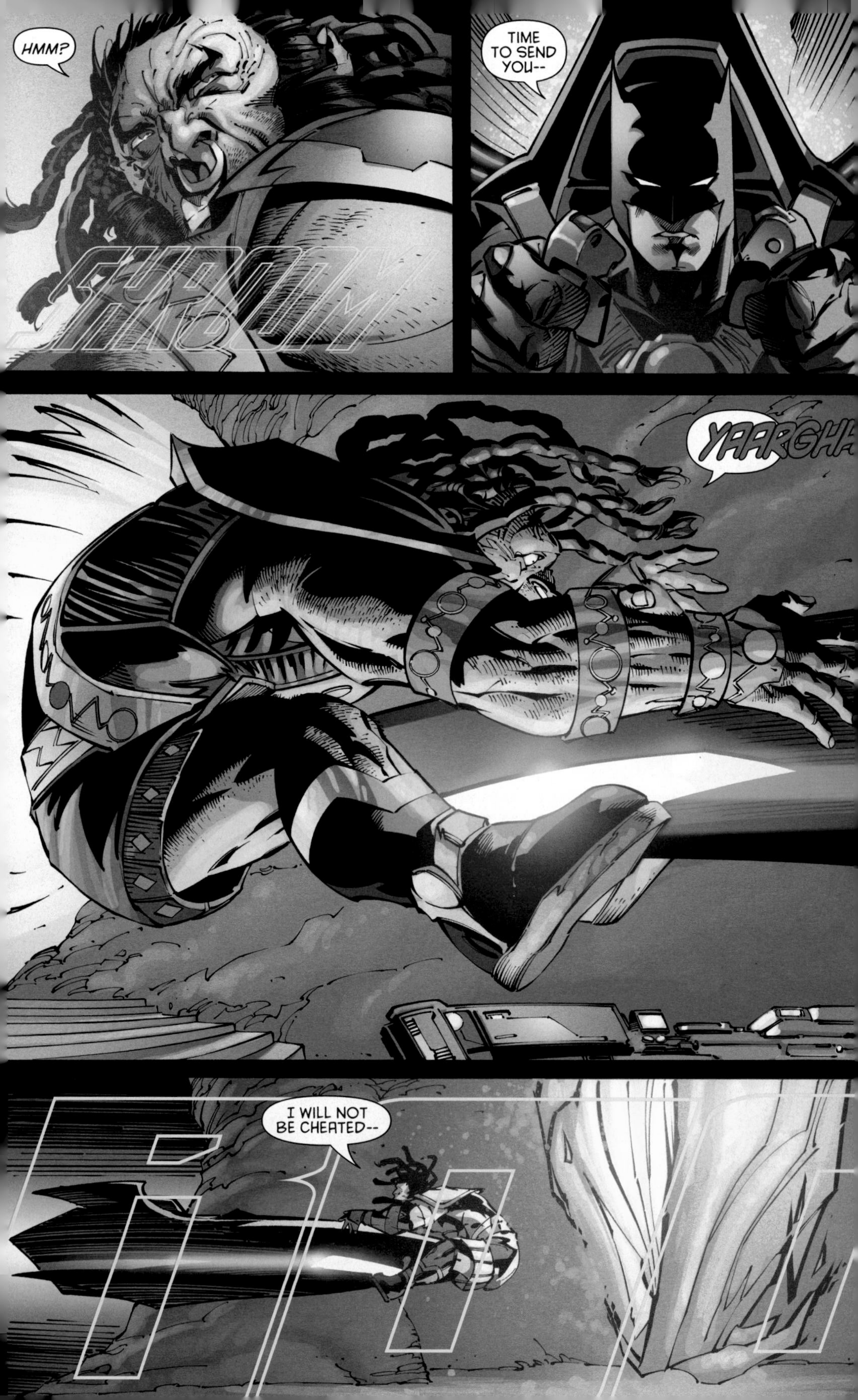
HMM?
SHOOM
TIME TO SEND YOU--
YAARGHH
I WILL NOT BE CHEATED--

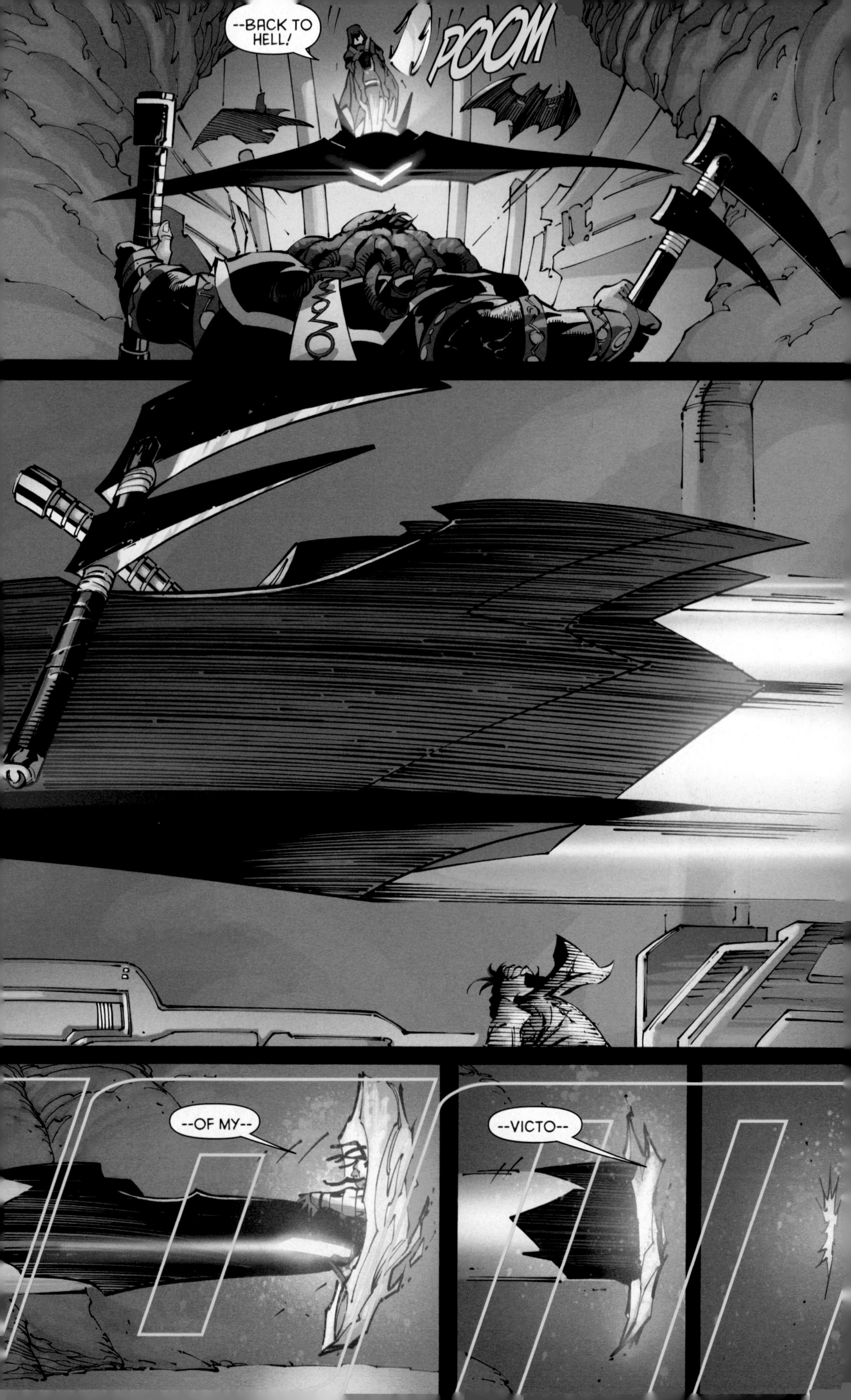
--BACK TO HELL!
POOM
--OF MY--
--VICTO--

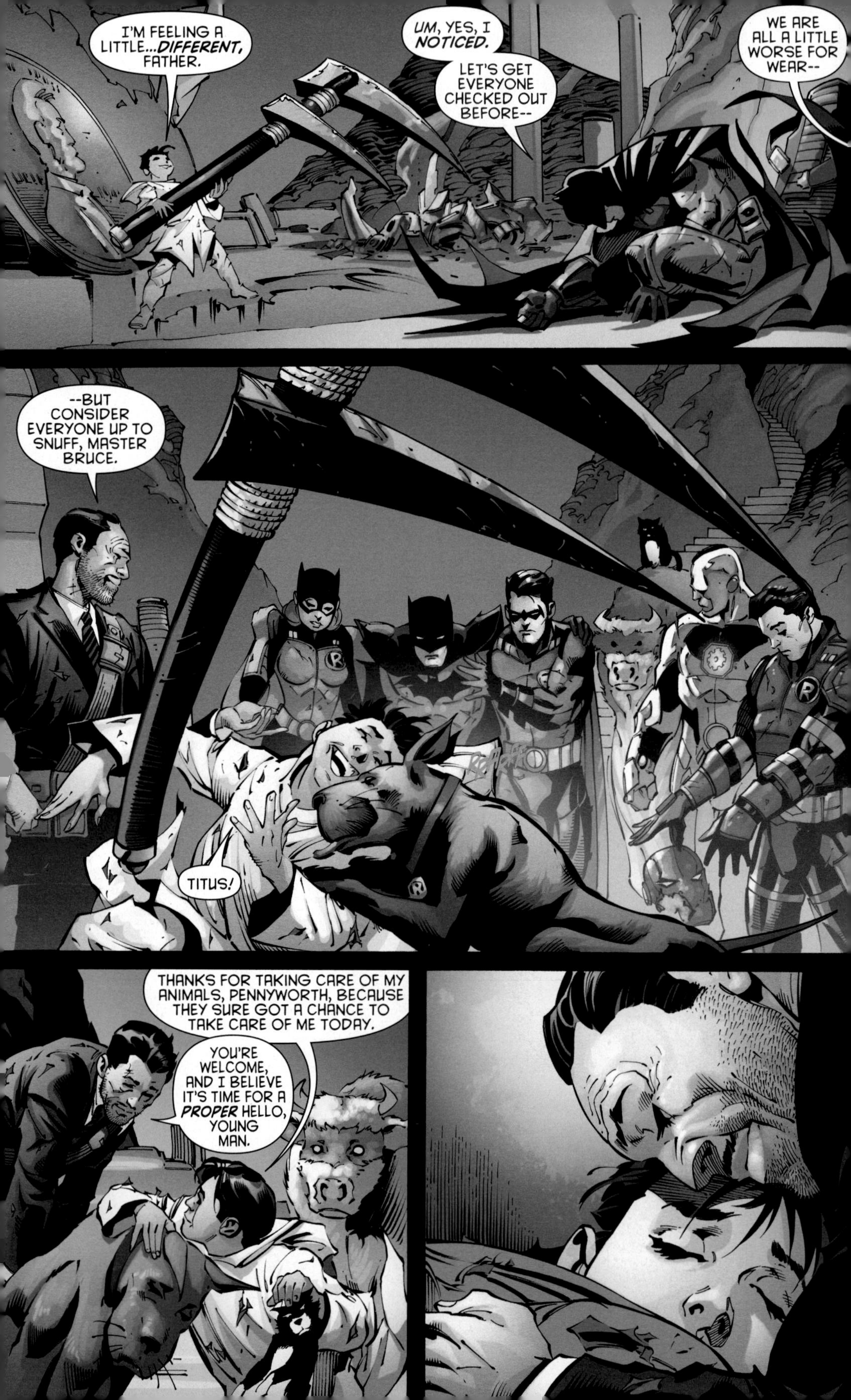
I'M FEELING A LITTLE...*DIFFERENT,* FATHER.
UM, YES, I *NOTICED.*
LET'S GET EVERYONE CHECKED OUT BEFORE--
WE ARE ALL A LITTLE WORSE FOR WEAR--
--BUT CONSIDER EVERYONE UP TO SNUFF, MASTER BRUCE.
TITUS!
THANKS FOR TAKING CARE OF MY ANIMALS, PENNYWORTH, BECAUSE THEY SURE GOT A CHANCE TO TAKE CARE OF ME TODAY.
YOU'RE WELCOME, AND I BELIEVE IT'S TIME FOR A *PROPER* HELLO, YOUNG MAN.

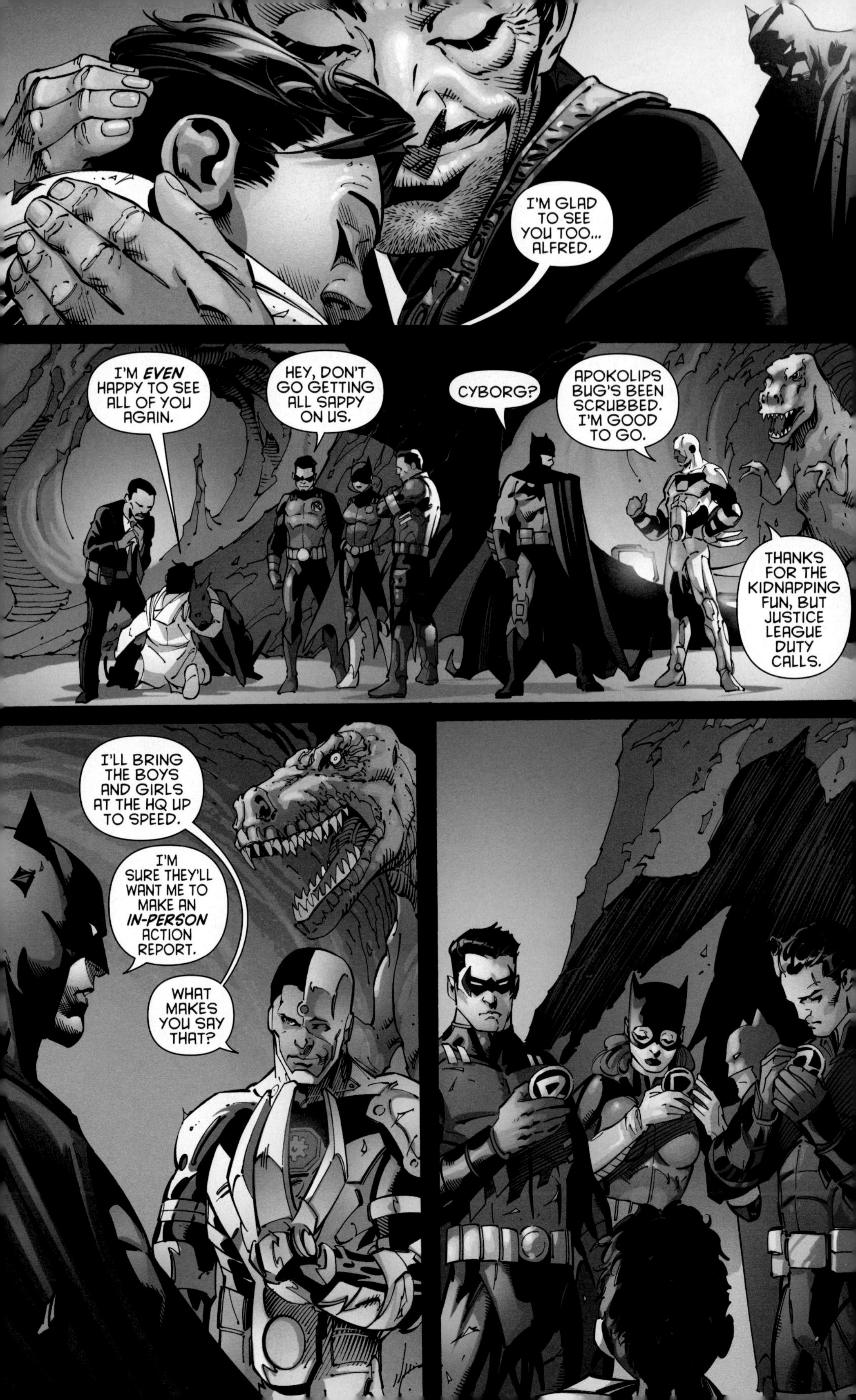
I'M GLAD TO SEE YOU TOO... ALFRED.
I'M *EVEN* HAPPY TO SEE ALL OF YOU AGAIN.
HEY, DON'T GO GETTING ALL SAPPY ON US.
CYBORG?
APOKOLIPS BUG'S BEEN SCRUBBED. I'M GOOD TO GO.
THANKS FOR THE KIDNAPPING FUN, BUT JUSTICE LEAGUE DUTY CALLS.
I'LL BRING THE BOYS AND GIRLS AT THE HQ UP TO SPEED.
I'M SURE THEY'LL WANT ME TO MAKE AN *IN-PERSON* ACTION REPORT.
WHAT MAKES YOU SAY THAT?

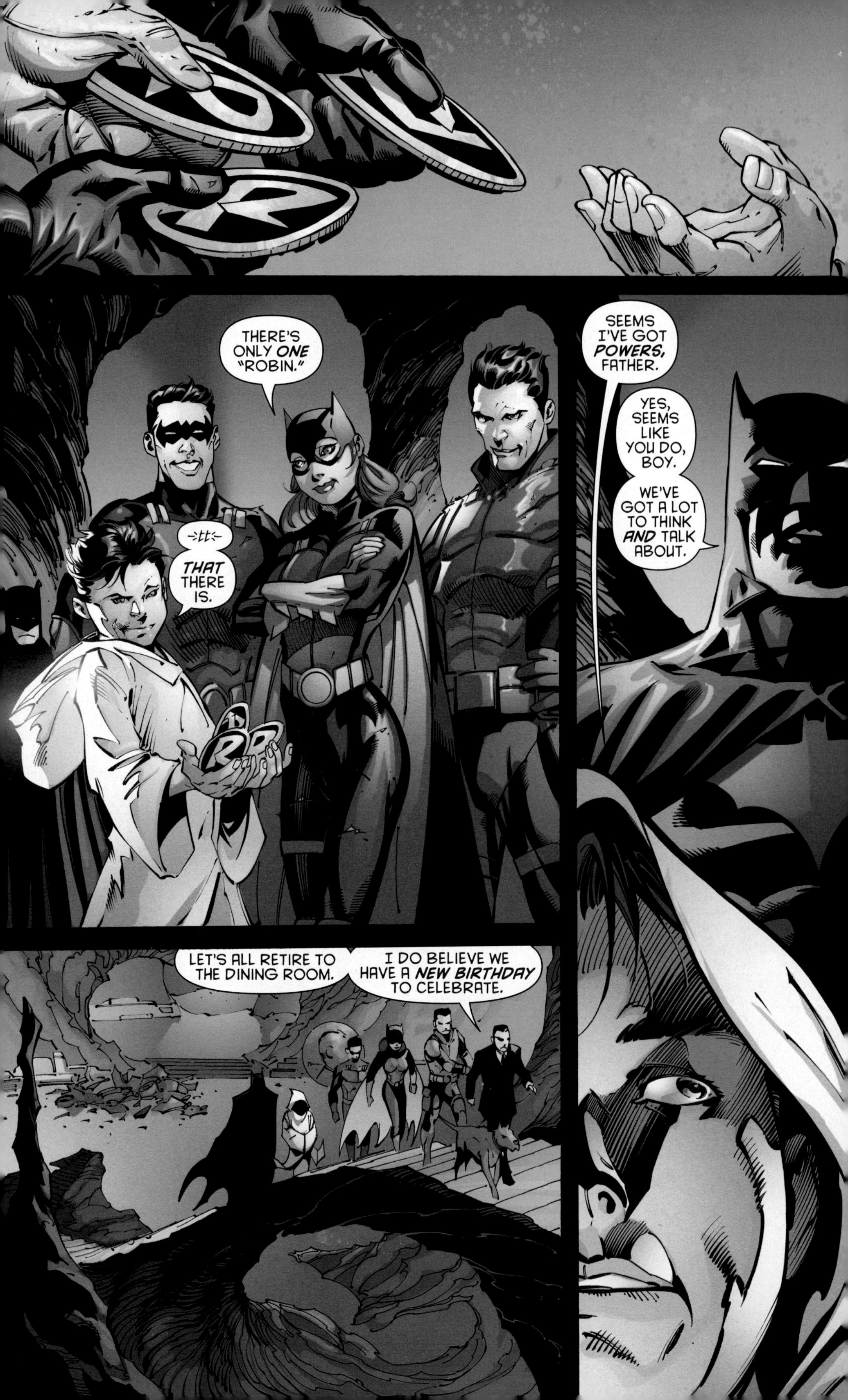

THERE'S ONLY *ONE* "ROBIN."
-tt-
THAT THERE IS.
SEEMS I'VE GOT ***POWERS,*** FATHER.
YES, SEEMS LIKE YOU DO, BOY.
WE'VE GOT A LOT TO THINK ***AND*** TALK ABOUT.
LET'S ALL RETIRE TO THE DINING ROOM.
I DO BELIEVE WE HAVE A ***NEW BIRTHDAY*** TO CELEBRATE.

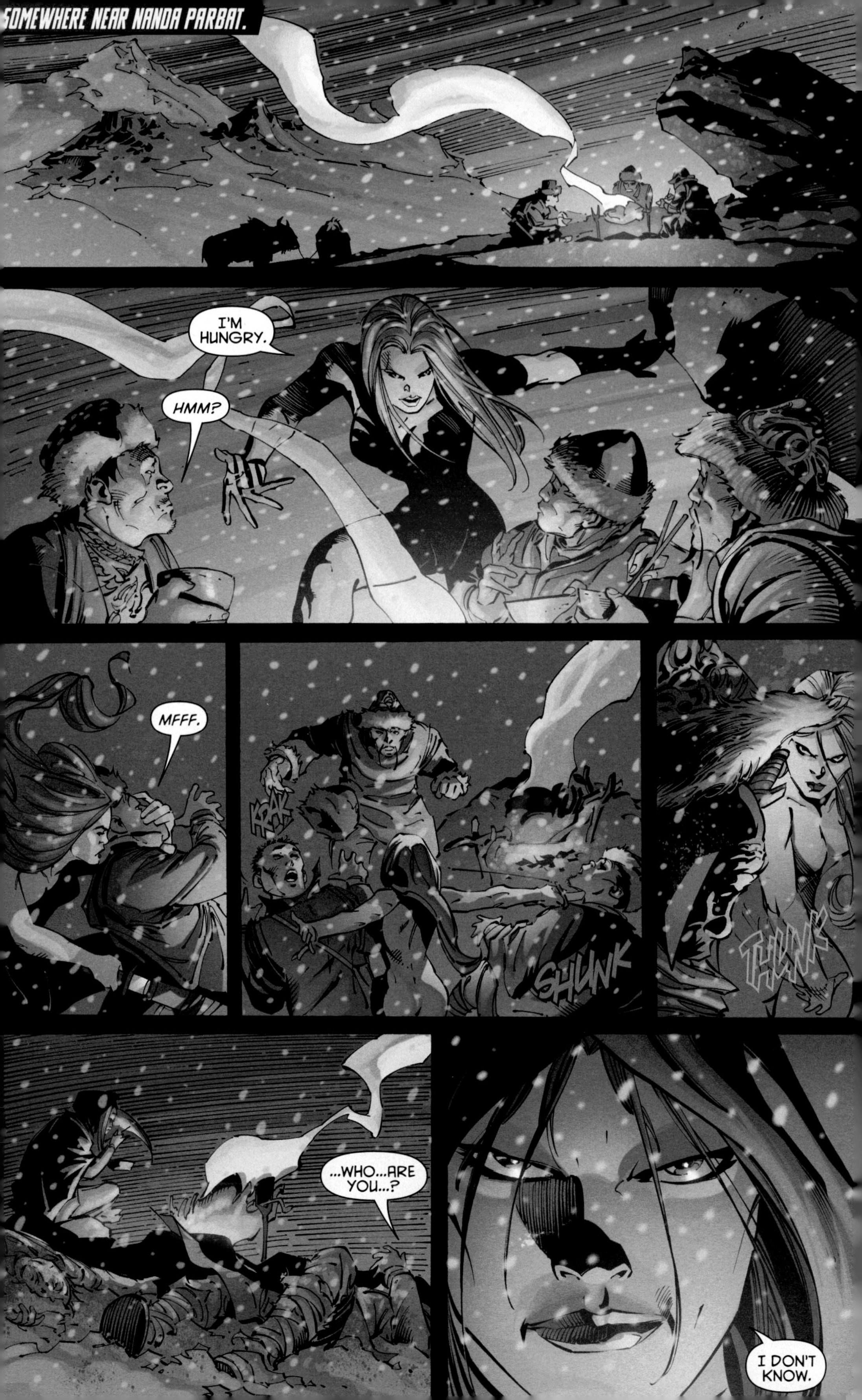

SOMEWHERE NEAR NANDA PARBAT.
I'M HUNGRY.
HMM?
MFFF.
KRAK
SHUNK
THUNK
...WHO...ARE YOU...?
I DON'T KNOW.

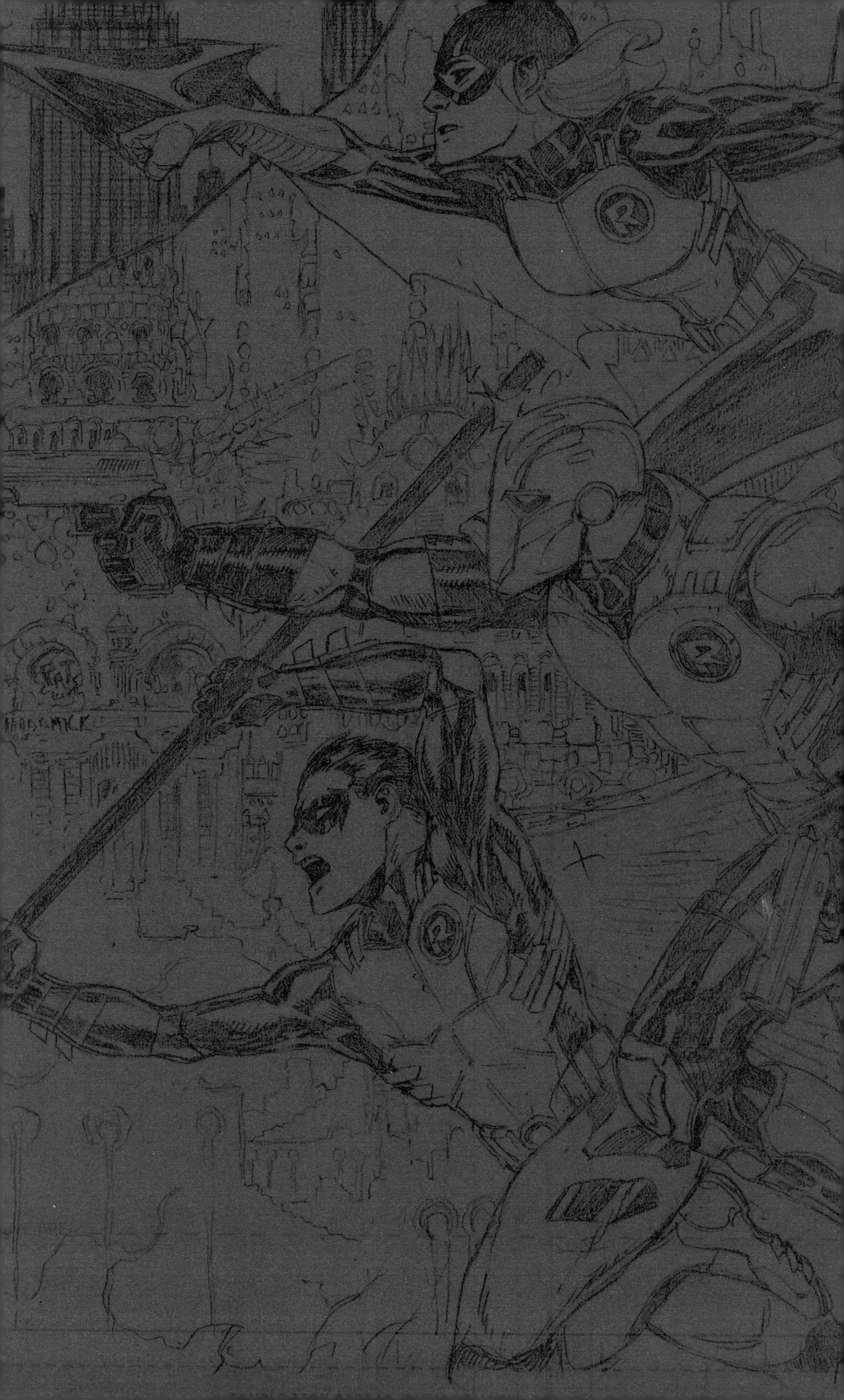

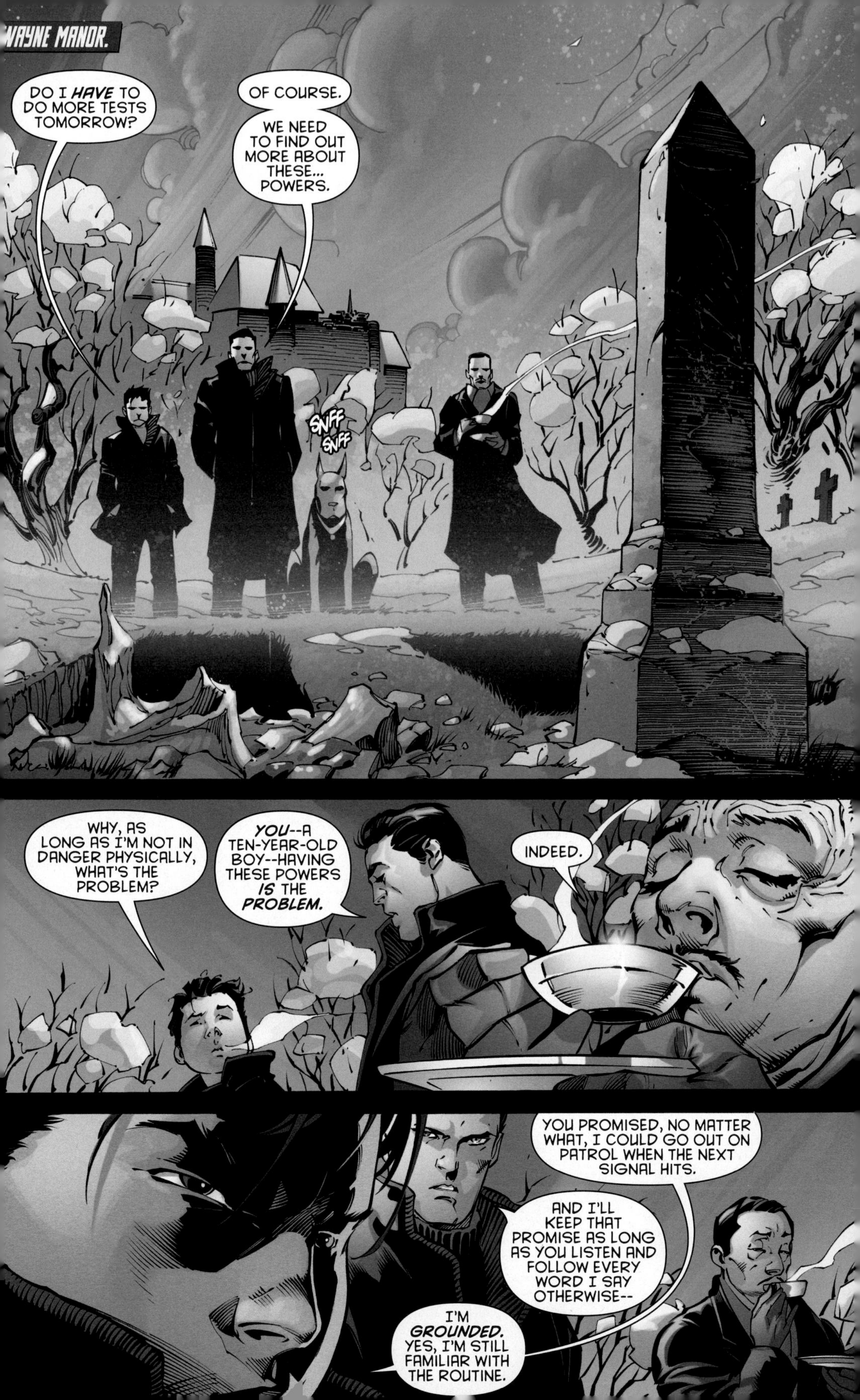
WAYNE MANOR.
DO I HAVE TO DO MORE TESTS TOMORROW?
OF COURSE.
WE NEED TO FIND OUT MORE ABOUT THESE... POWERS.
SNIFF SNIFF
WHY, AS LONG AS I'M NOT IN DANGER PHYSICALLY, WHAT'S THE PROBLEM?
YOU--A TEN-YEAR-OLD BOY--HAVING THESE POWERS IS THE PROBLEM.
INDEED.
YOU PROMISED, NO MATTER WHAT, I COULD GO OUT ON PATROL WHEN THE NEXT SIGNAL HITS.
AND I'LL KEEP THAT PROMISE AS LONG AS YOU LISTEN AND FOLLOW EVERY WORD I SAY OTHERWISE--
I'M GROUNDED. YES, I'M STILL FAMILIAR WITH THE ROUTINE.

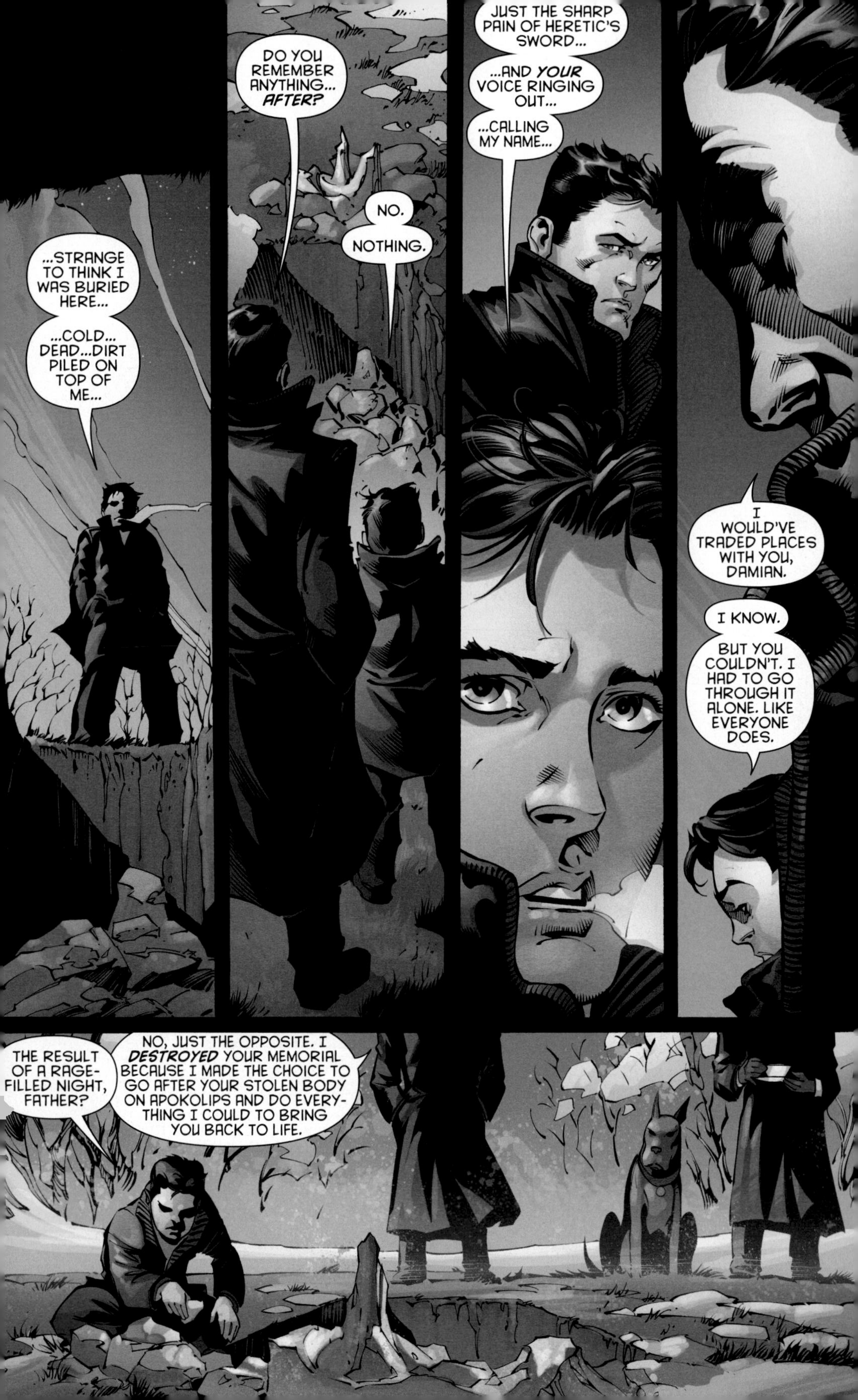
...STRANGE TO THINK I WAS BURIED HERE...
...COLD... DEAD...DIRT PILED ON TOP OF ME...
DO YOU REMEMBER ANYTHING... *AFTER?*
NO.
NOTHING.
JUST THE SHARP PAIN OF HERETIC'S SWORD...
...AND *YOUR* VOICE RINGING OUT...
...CALLING MY NAME...
I WOULD'VE TRADED PLACES WITH YOU, DAMIAN.
I KNOW.
BUT YOU COULDN'T. I HAD TO GO THROUGH IT ALONE. LIKE EVERYONE DOES.
THE RESULT OF A RAGE-FILLED NIGHT, FATHER?
NO, JUST THE OPPOSITE. I *DESTROYED* YOUR MEMORIAL BECAUSE I MADE THE CHOICE TO GO AFTER YOUR STOLEN BODY ON APOKOLIPS AND DO EVERYTHING I COULD TO BRING YOU BACK TO LIFE.

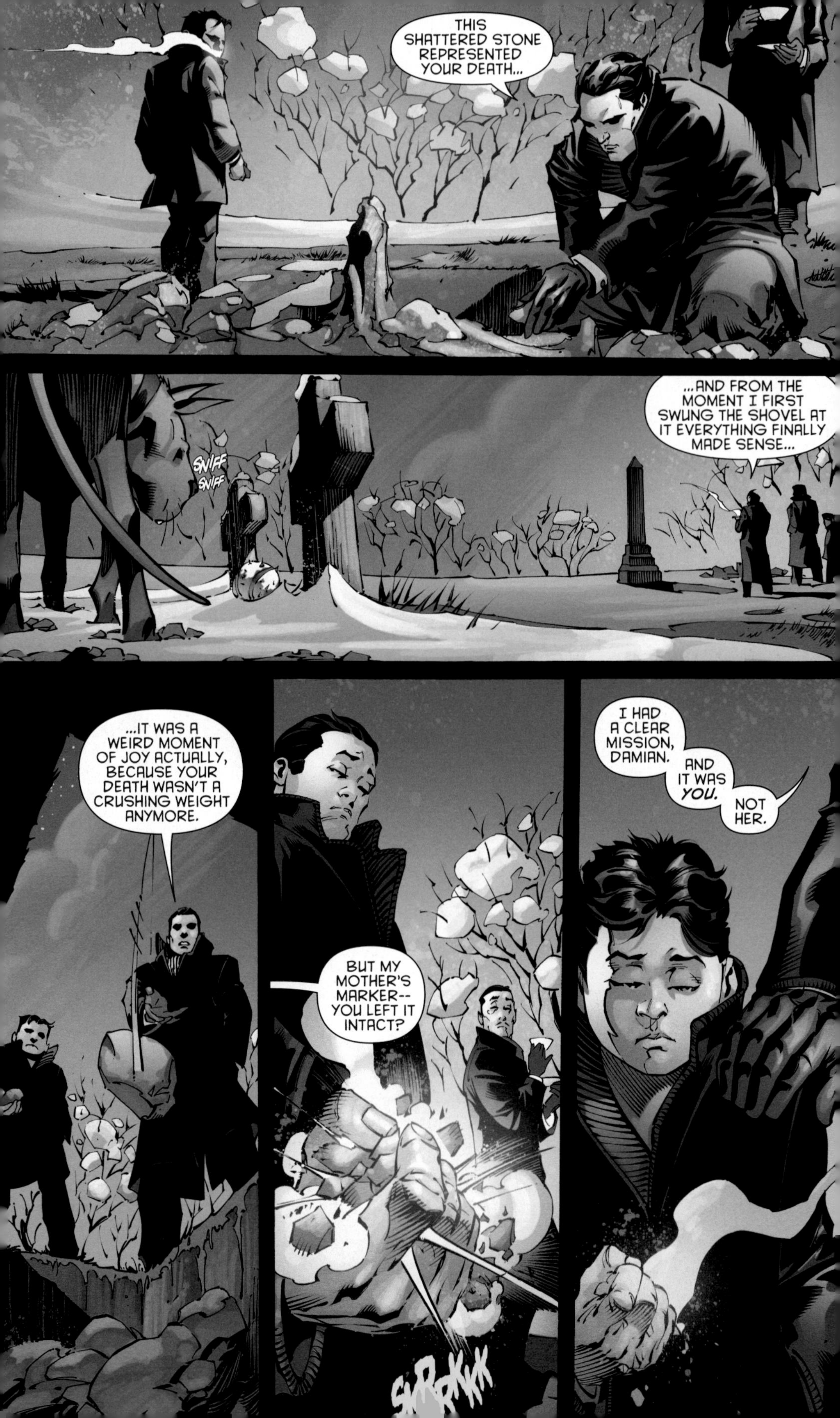
THIS SHATTERED STONE REPRESENTED YOUR DEATH...
SNIFF SNIFF
...AND FROM THE MOMENT I FIRST SWUNG THE SHOVEL AT IT EVERYTHING FINALLY MADE SENSE...
...IT WAS A WEIRD MOMENT OF JOY ACTUALLY, BECAUSE YOUR DEATH WASN'T A CRUSHING WEIGHT ANYMORE.
BUT MY MOTHER'S MARKER-- YOU LEFT IT INTACT?
SKRRKKK
I HAD A CLEAR MISSION, DAMIAN.
AND IT WAS *YOU.*
NOT HER.

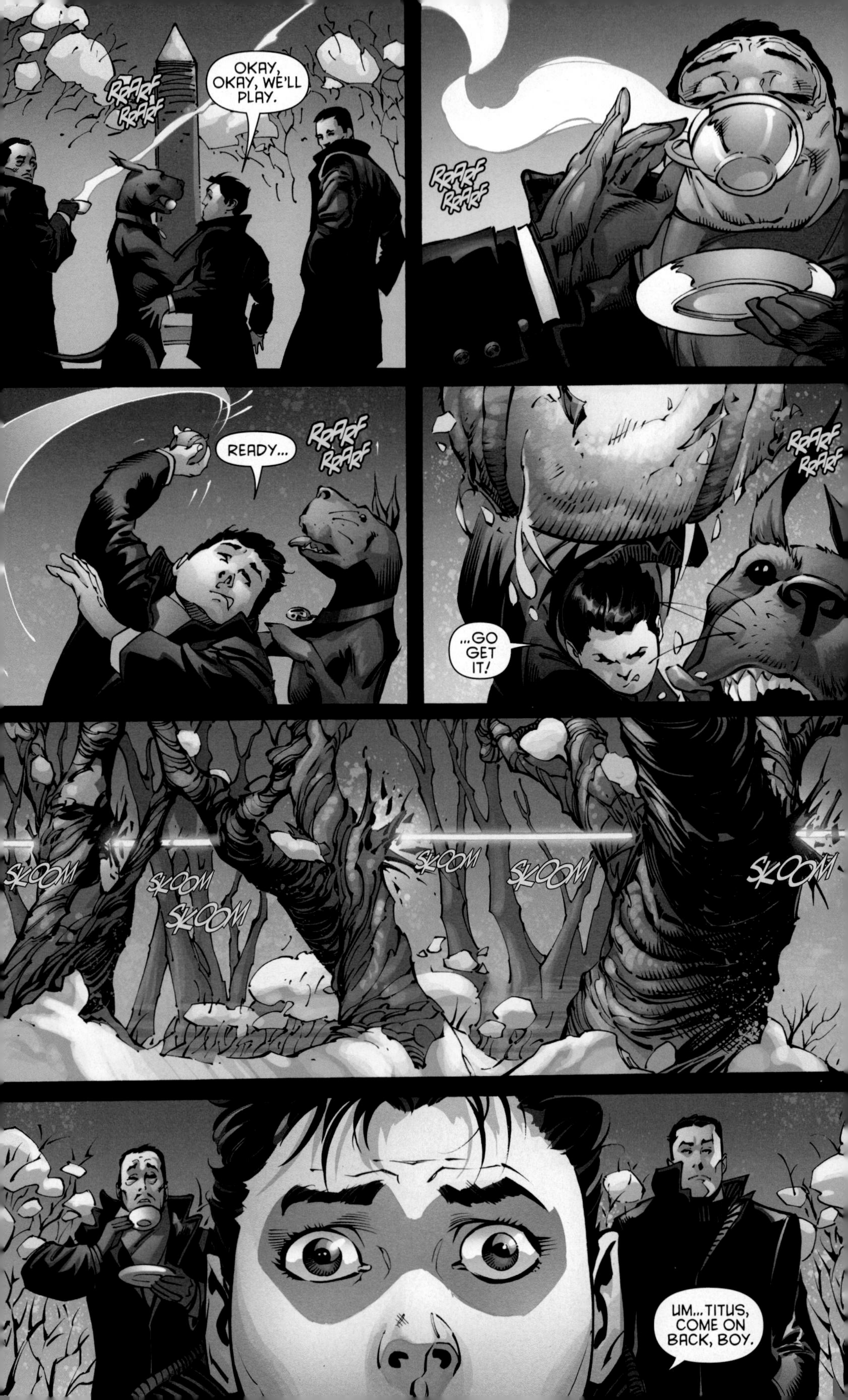
RRARF RRARF
OKAY, OKAY, WE'LL PLAY.
RRARF RRARF
READY...
RRARF RRARF
RRARF RRARF
...GO GET IT!
SKOOM
SKOOM
SKOOM
SKOOM
SKOOM
SKOOM
UM... TITUS, COME ON BACK, BOY.

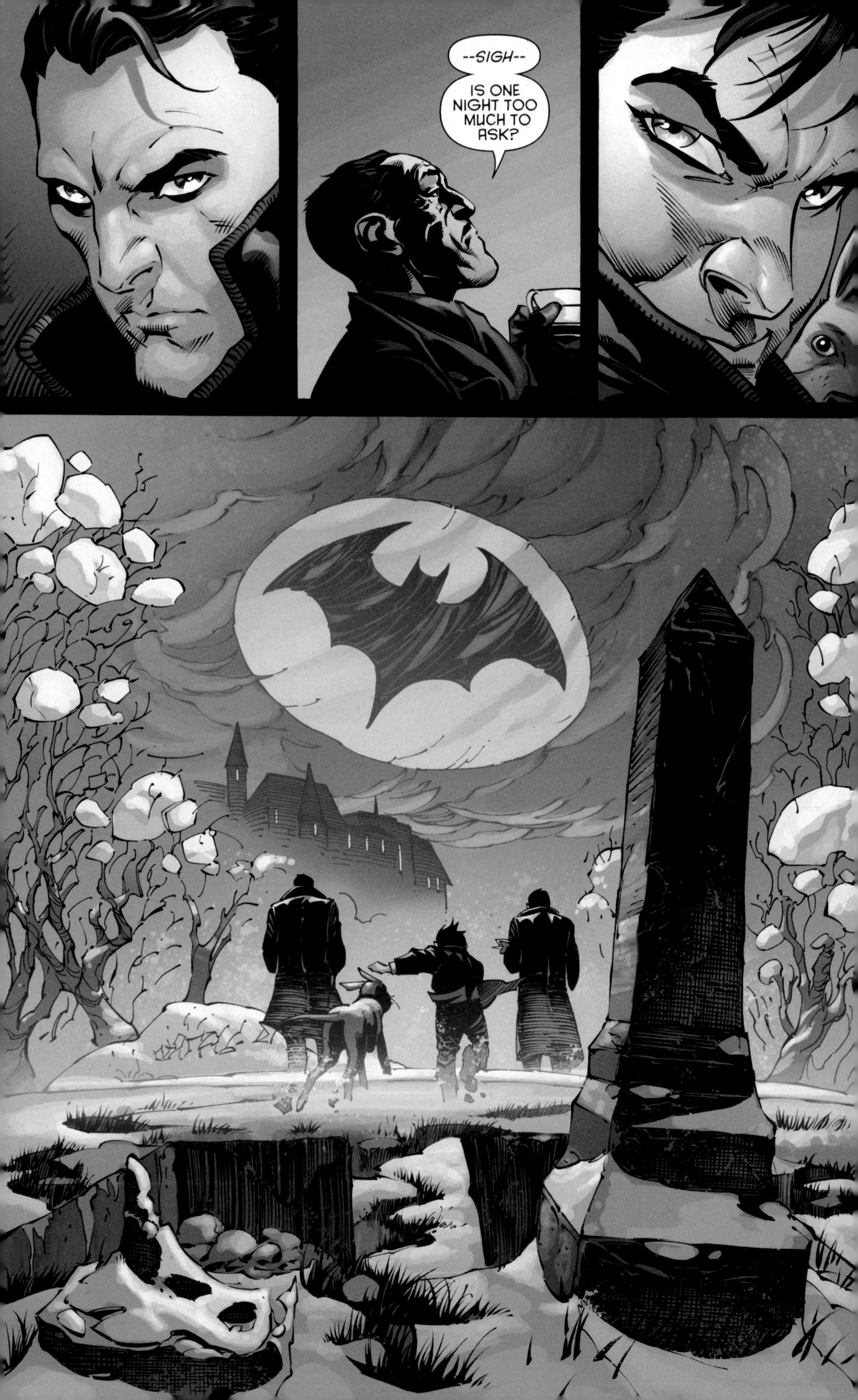
--SIGH--
IS ONE NIGHT TOO MUCH TO ASK?

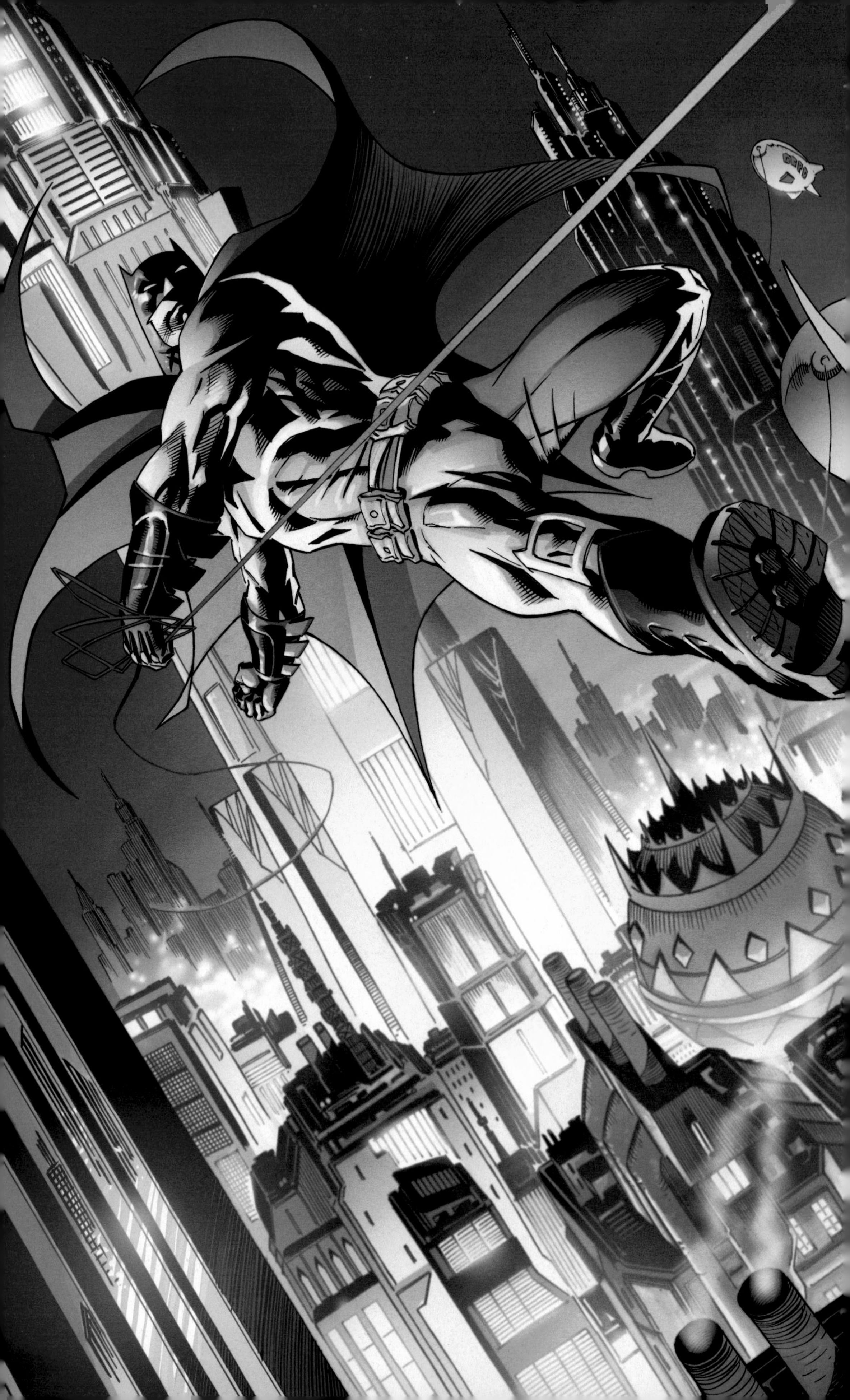
GCPD

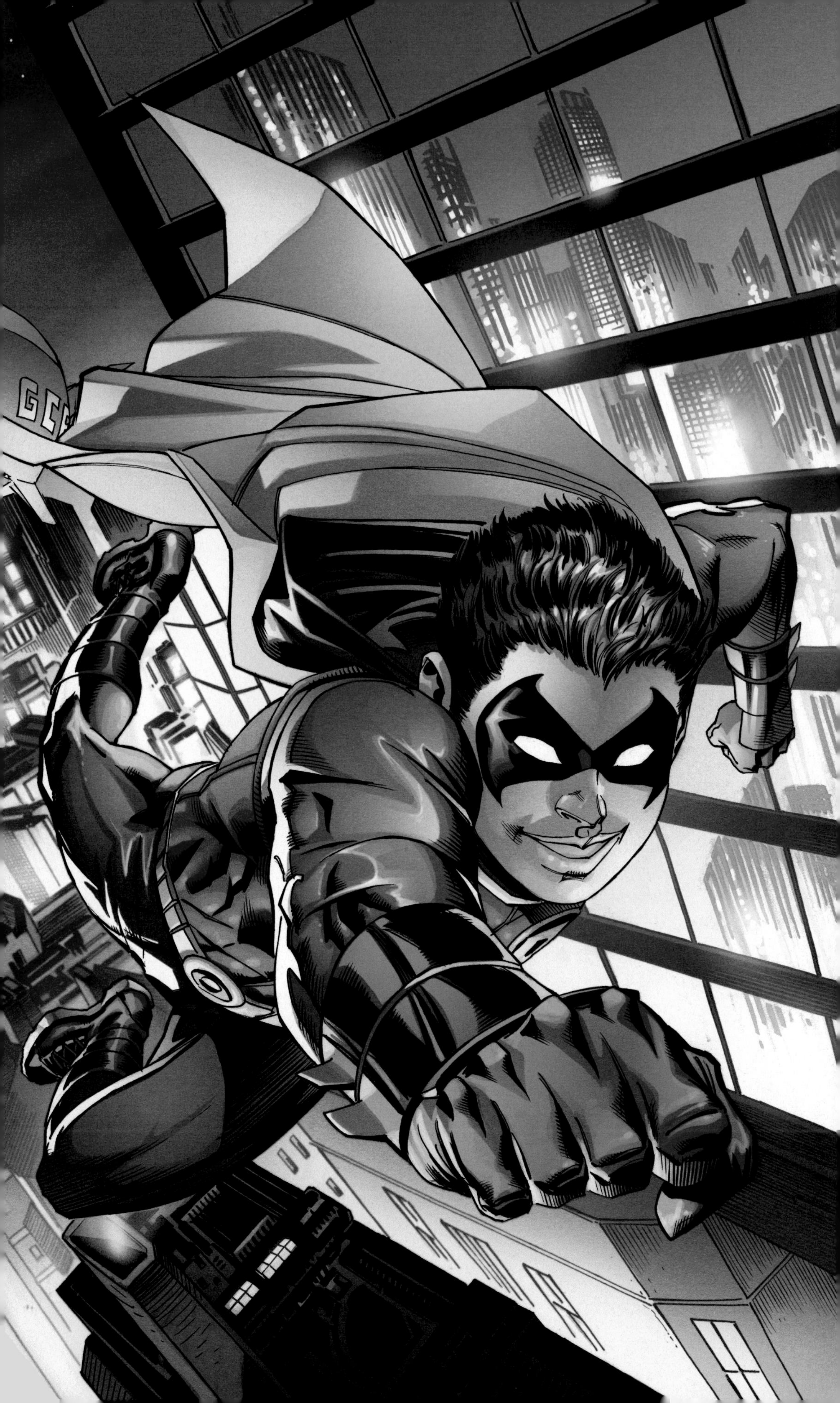

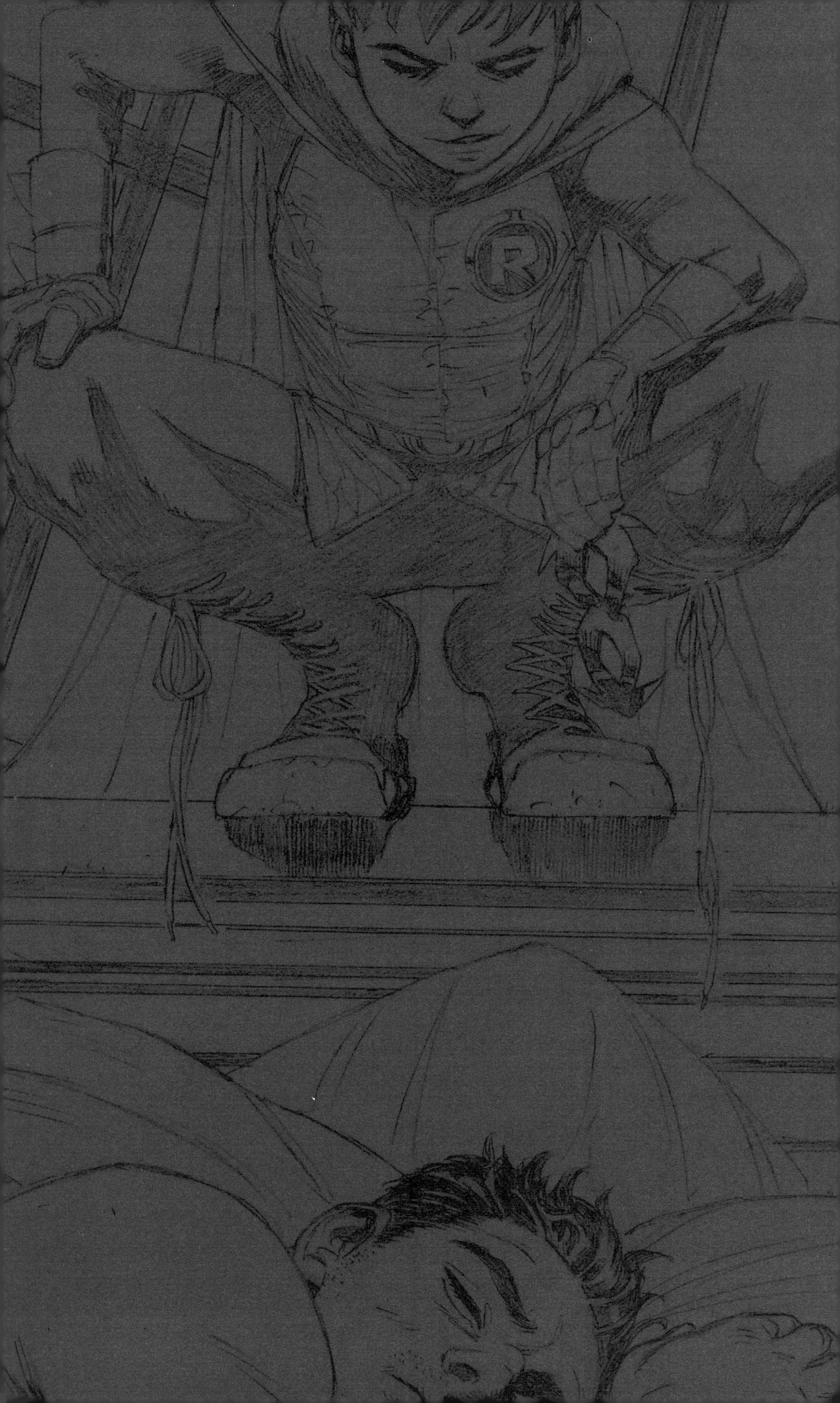

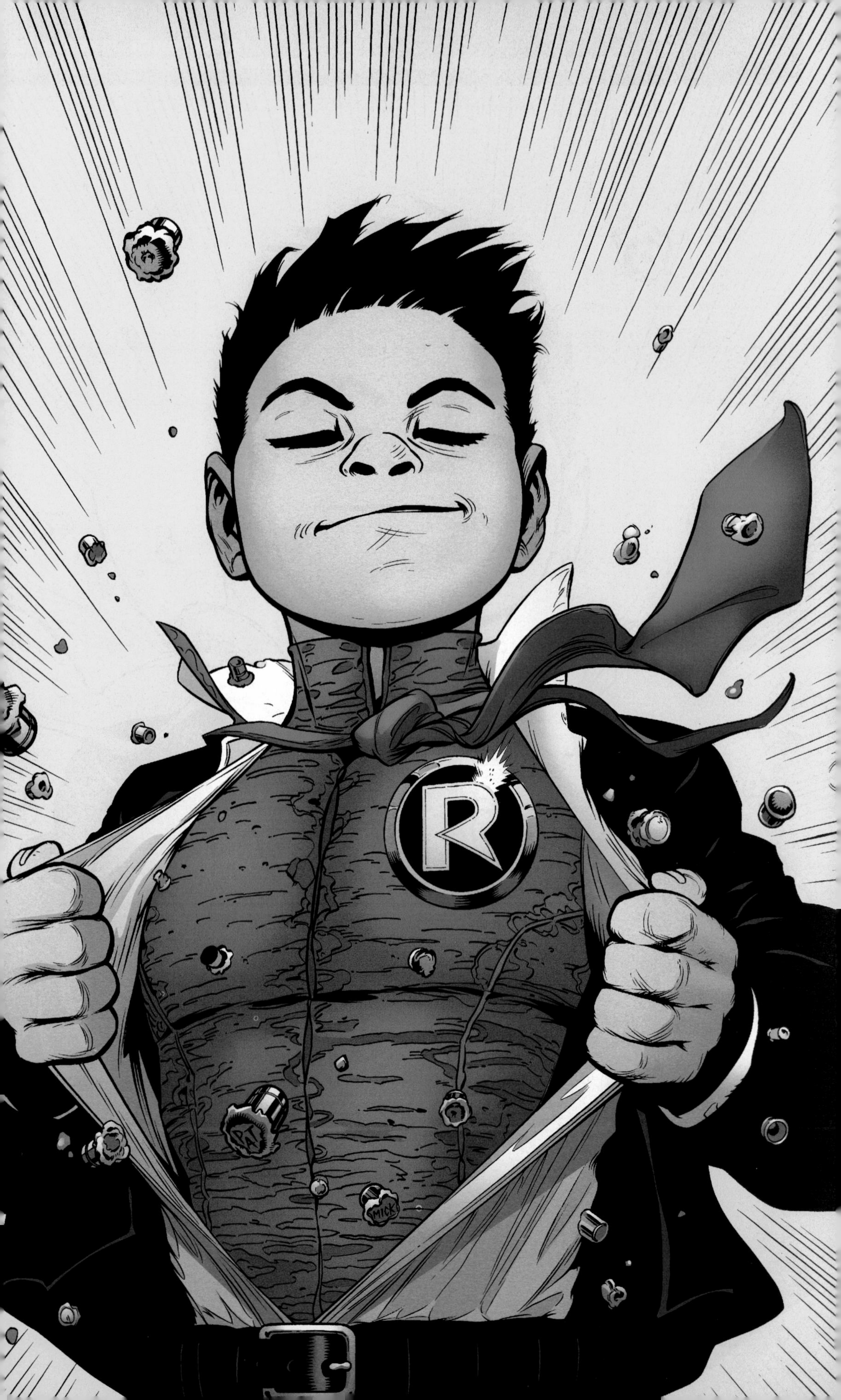

PATRICK GLEASON penciller MICK GRAY inker JOHN KALISZ colorist CARLOS M. MANGUAL letterer cover art by GLEASON, GRAY & KALISZ

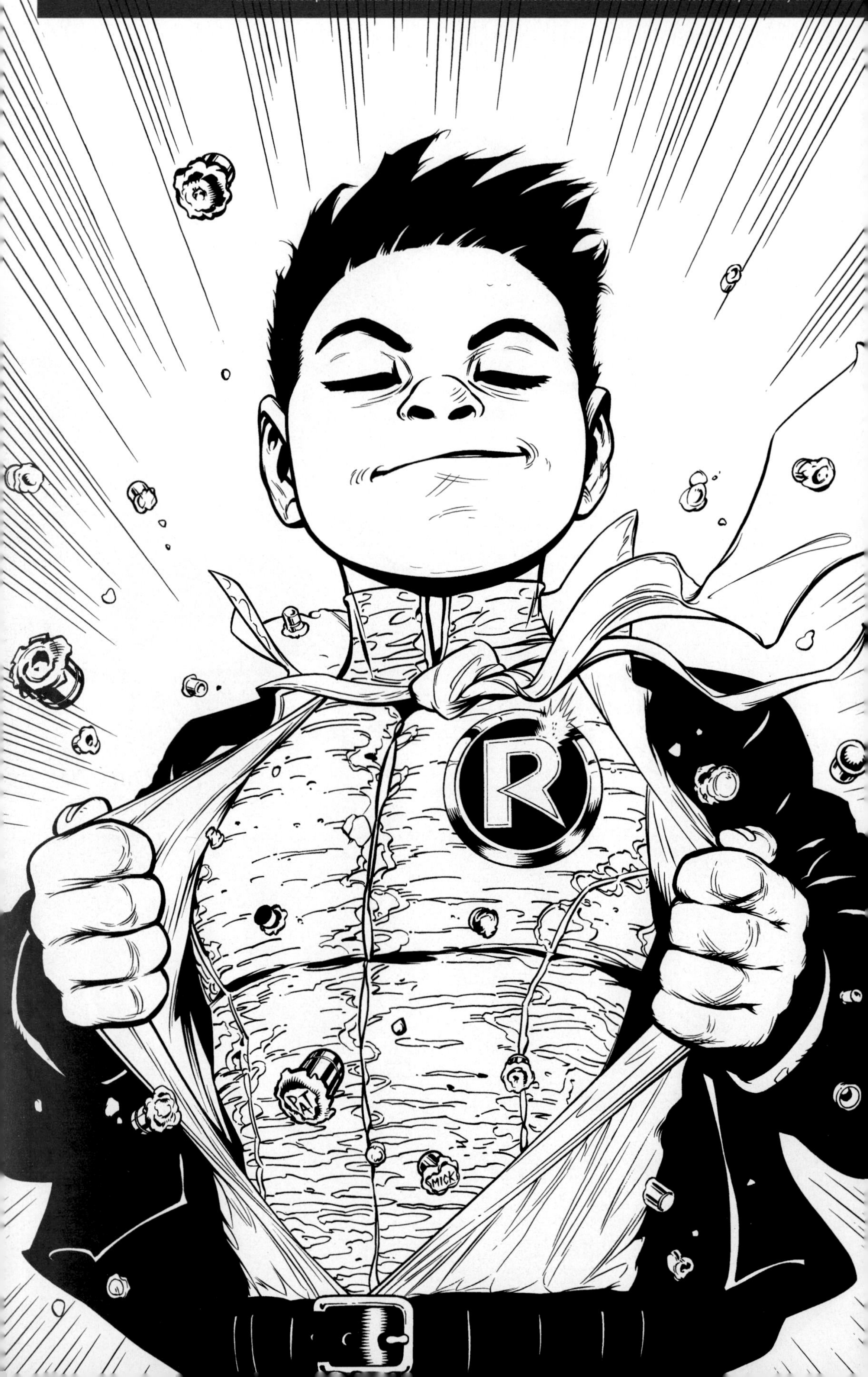

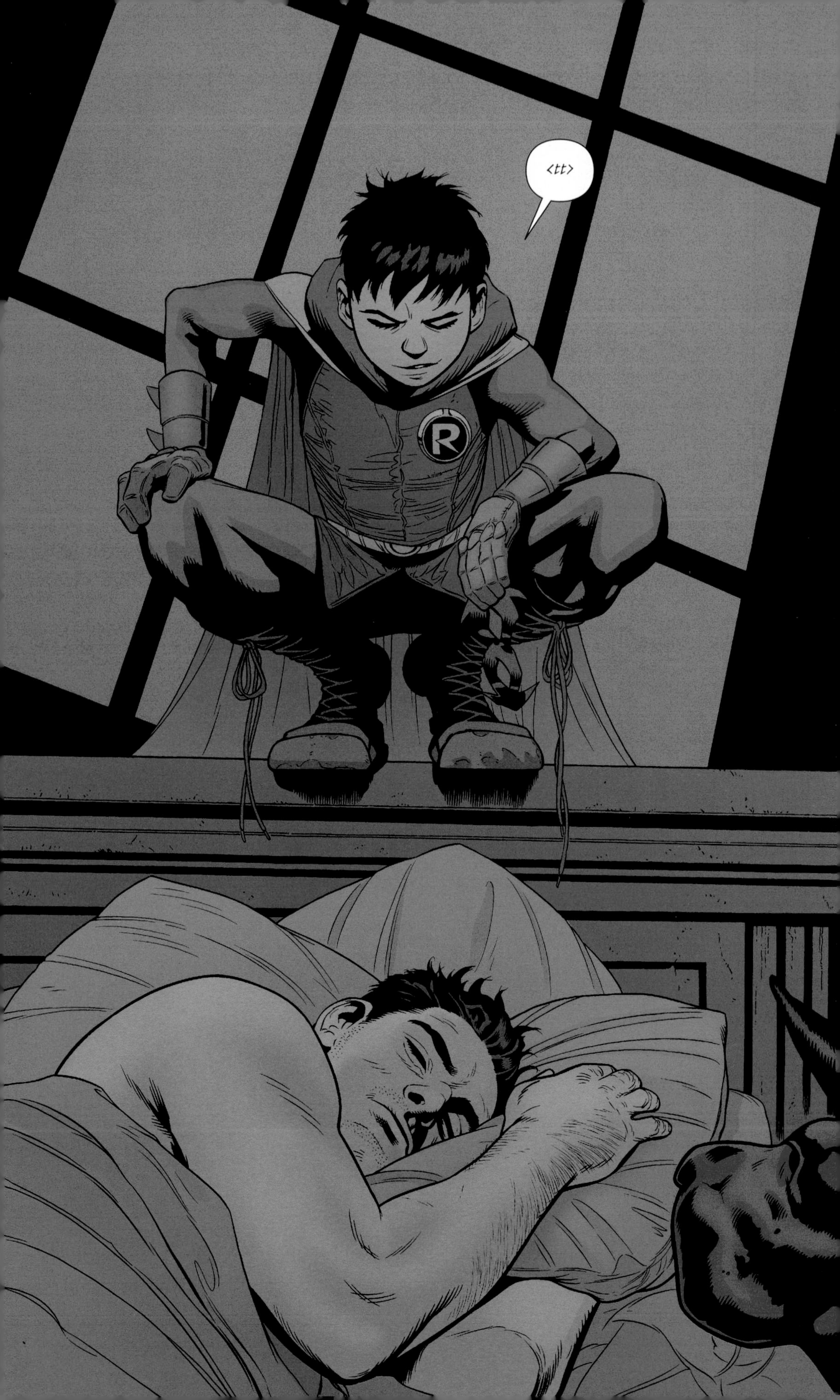
<tt>

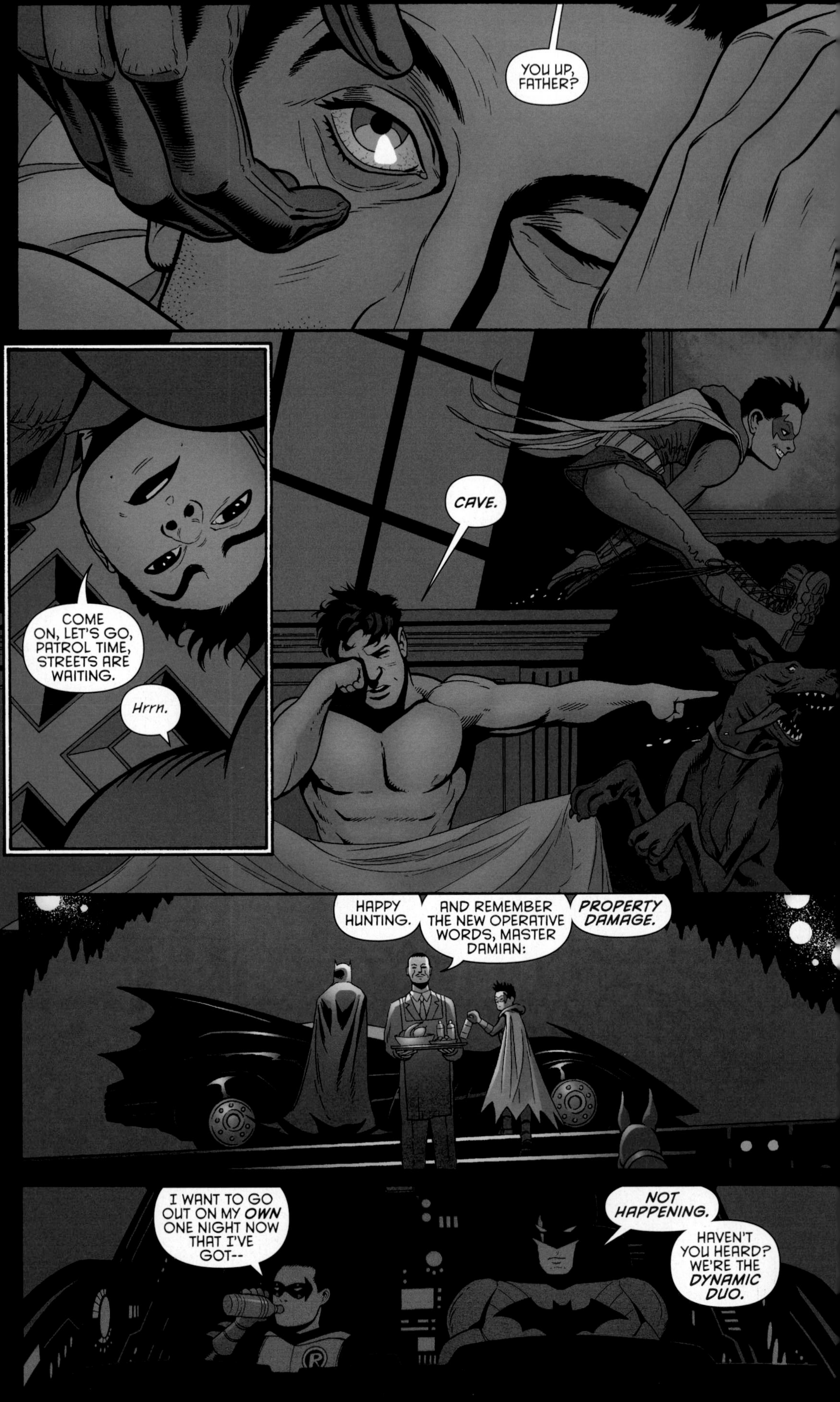

YOU UP, FATHER?
COME ON, LET'S GO, PATROL TIME, STREETS ARE WAITING.
Hrrn.
CAVE.
HAPPY HUNTING.
AND REMEMBER THE NEW OPERATIVE WORDS, MASTER DAMIAN:
PROPERTY DAMAGE.
I WANT TO GO OUT ON MY OWN ONE NIGHT NOW THAT I'VE GOT--
NOT HAPPENING.
HAVEN'T YOU HEARD? WE'RE THE DYNAMIC DUO.

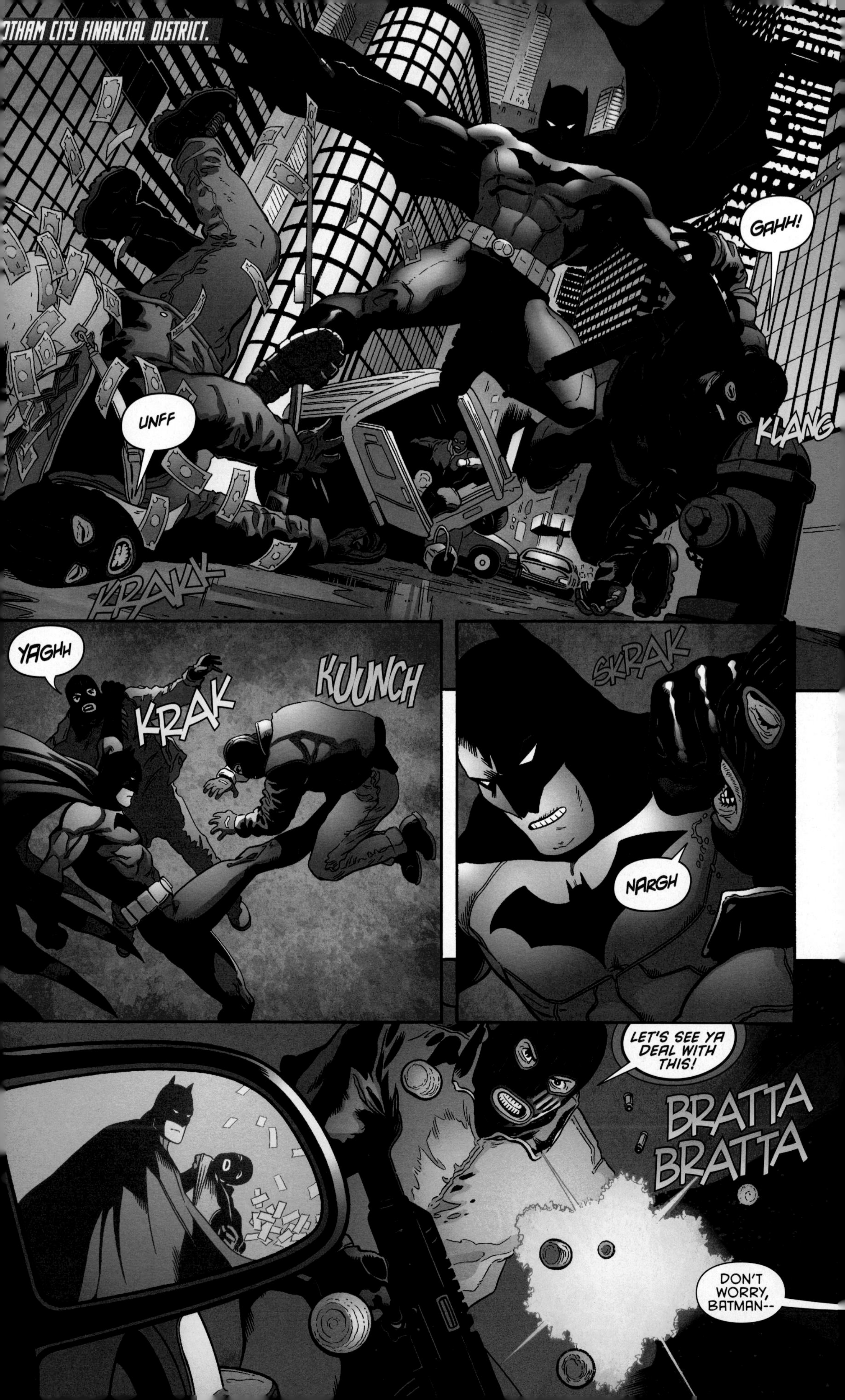
OTHAM CITY FINANCIAL DISTRICT.
GAHH!
UNFF
KLANG
KRAKK
YAGHH
KRAK
KUUNCH
SKRAK
NARGH
LET'S SEE YA DEAL WITH THIS!
BRATTA BRATTA
DON'T WORRY, BATMAN--

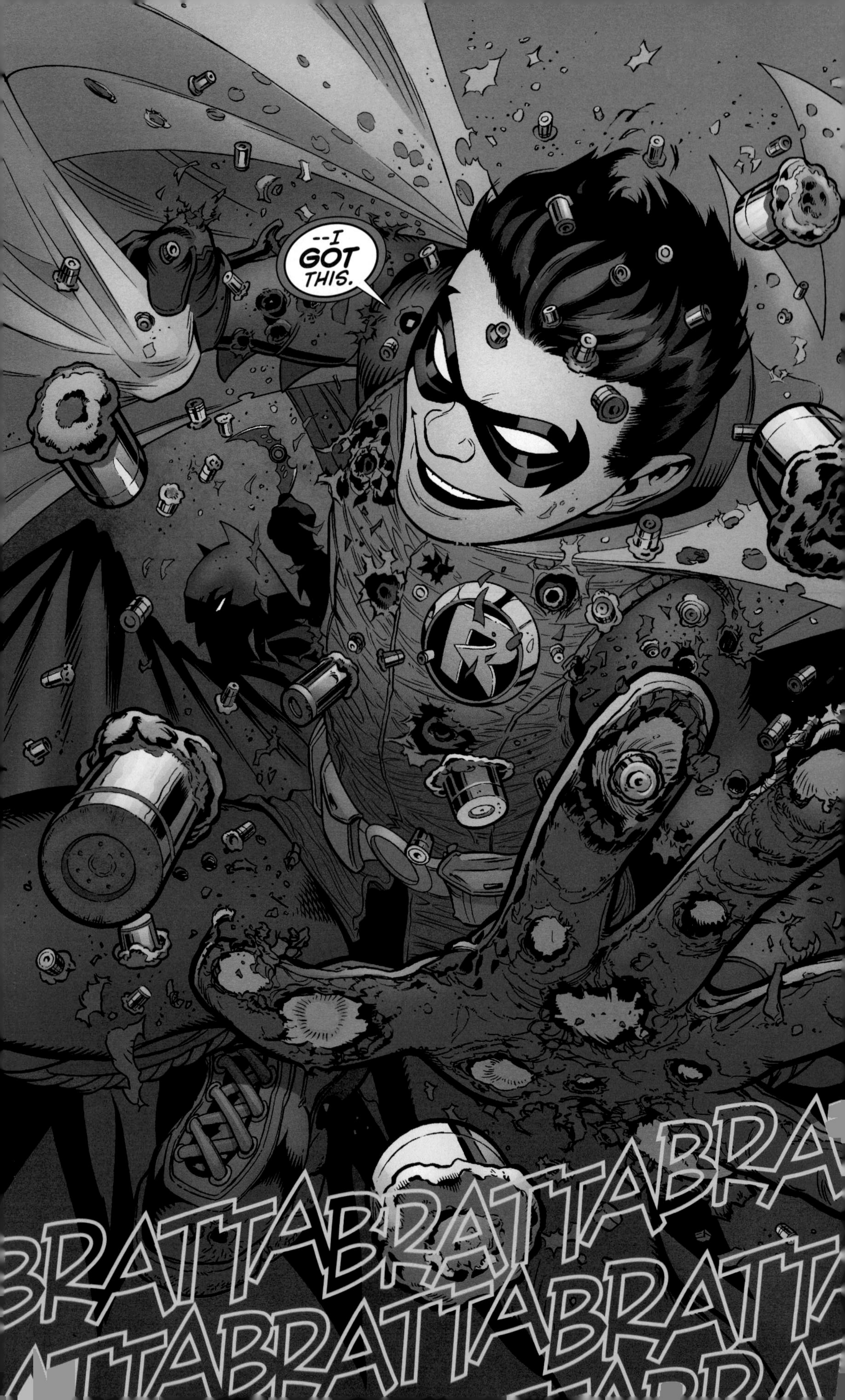
--I GOT THIS.
BRATTATBRATTATBRA
TTATBRATTATBRATTA

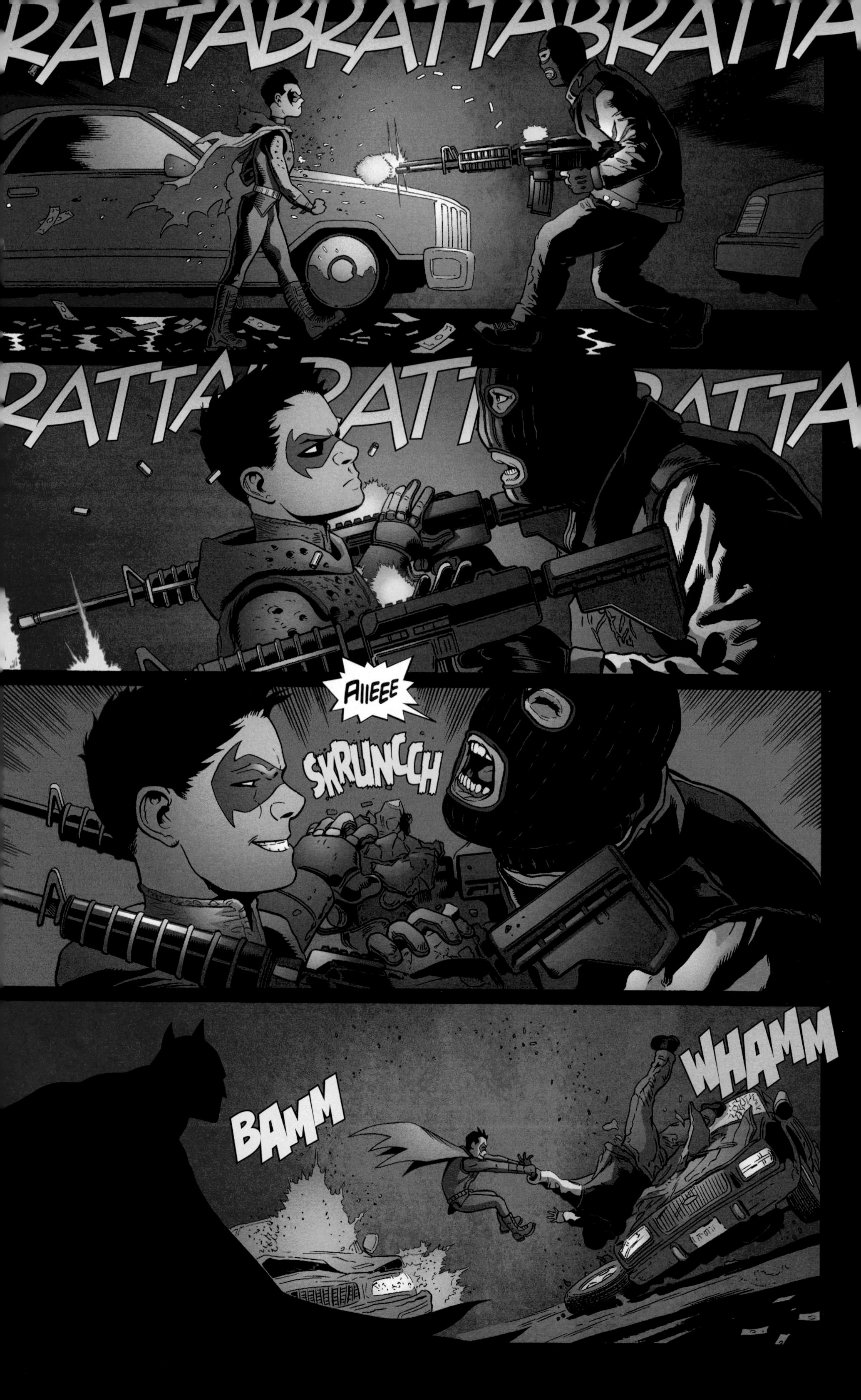
RATTABRATTABRATTA
RATTARATTARATTA
AIIEEE
SKRUNCCH
BAMM
WHAMM

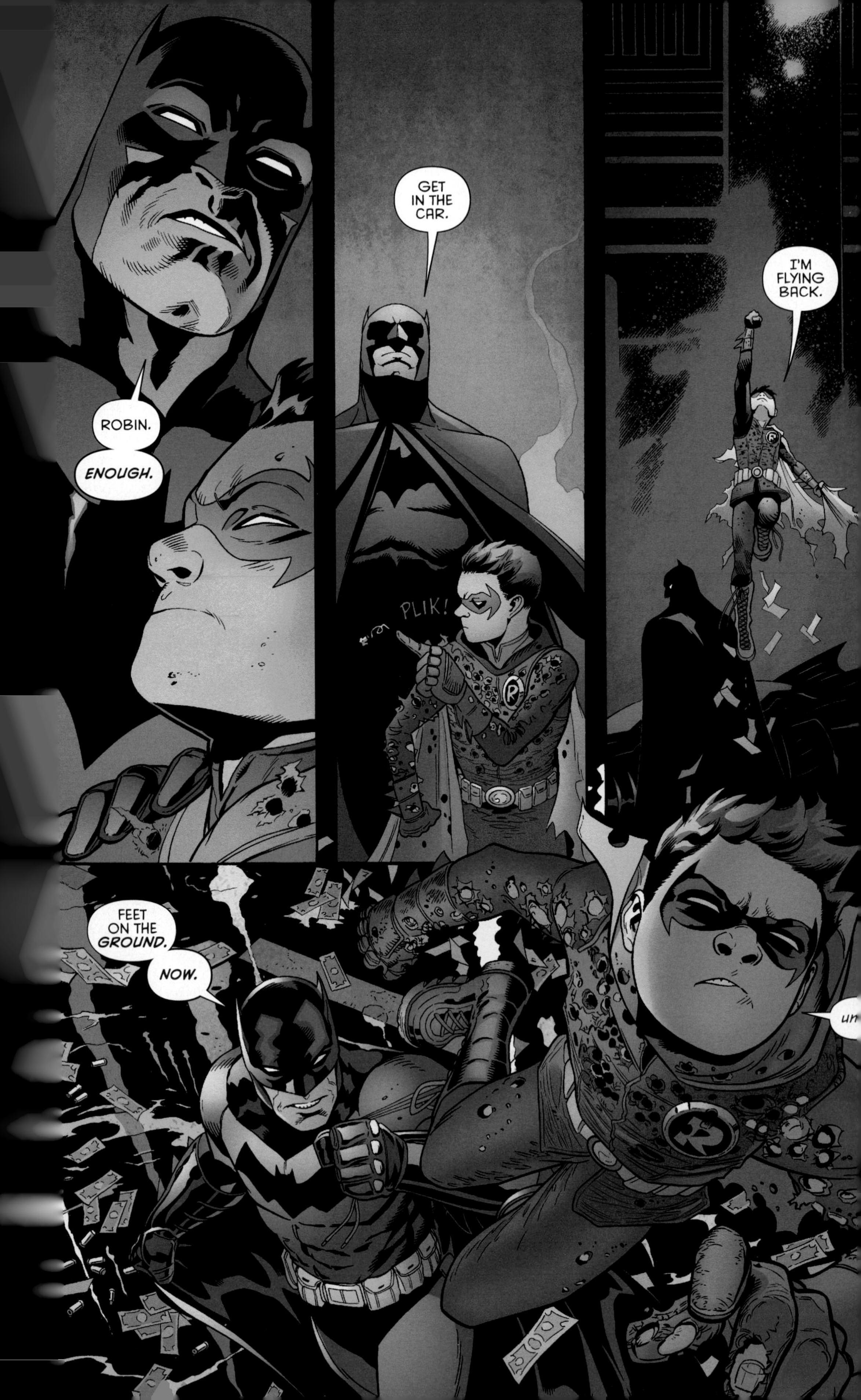

ROBIN.
ENOUGH.
GET IN THE CAR.
PLIK!
I'M FLYING BACK.
FEET ON THE *GROUND.*
NOW.

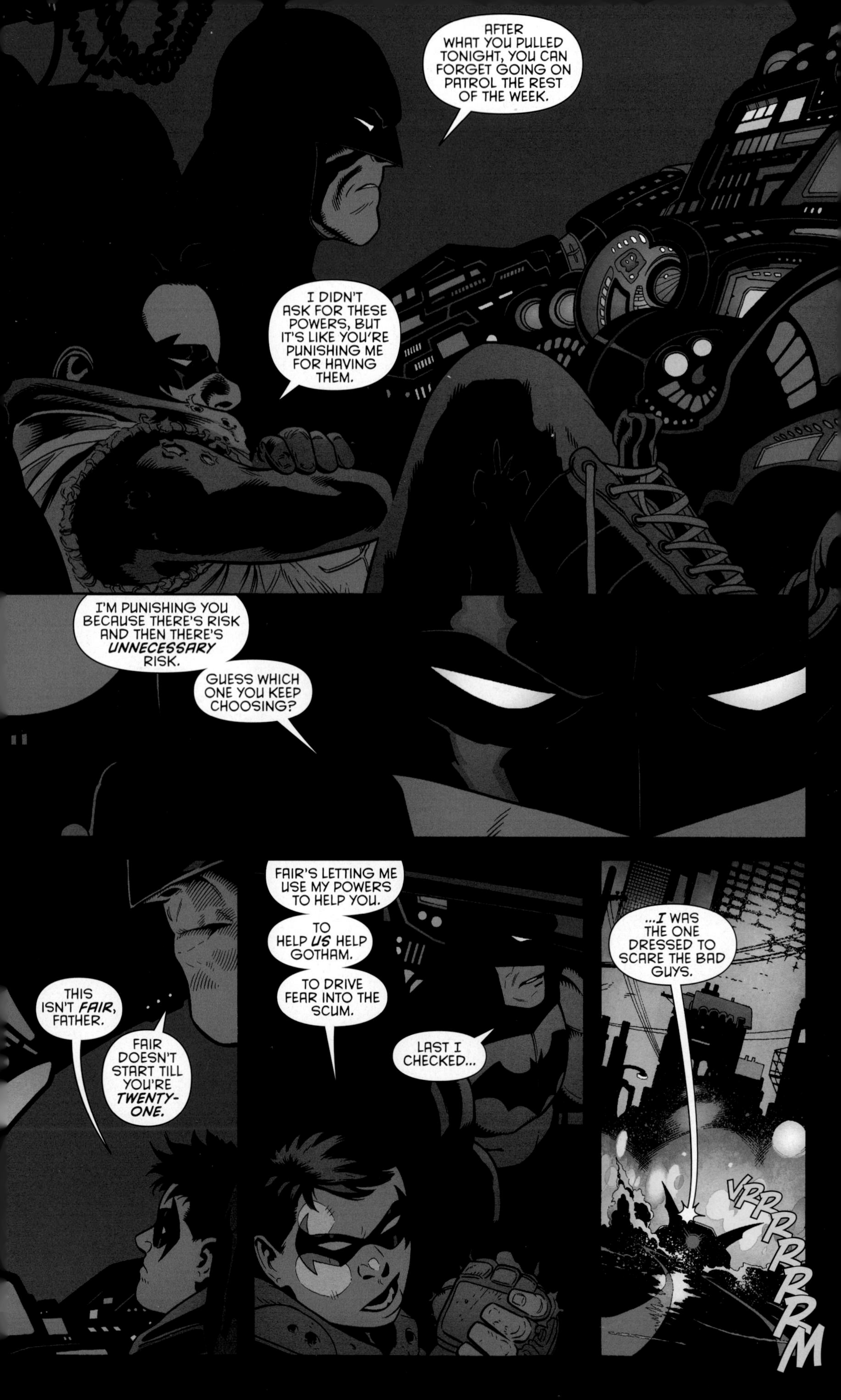
AFTER WHAT YOU PULLED TONIGHT, YOU CAN FORGET GOING ON PATROL THE REST OF THE WEEK.
I DIDN'T ASK FOR THESE POWERS, BUT IT'S LIKE YOU'RE PUNISHING ME FOR HAVING THEM.
I'M PUNISHING YOU BECAUSE THERE'S RISK AND THEN THERE'S *UNNECESSARY* RISK.
GUESS WHICH ONE YOU KEEP CHOOSING?
THIS ISN'T *FAIR*, FATHER.
FAIR DOESN'T START TILL YOU'RE *TWENTY-ONE.*
FAIR'S LETTING ME USE MY POWERS TO HELP YOU.
TO HELP *US* HELP GOTHAM.
TO DRIVE FEAR INTO THE SCUM.
LAST I CHECKED...
...*I* WAS THE ONE DRESSED TO SCARE THE BAD GUYS.
VRRRRRRM

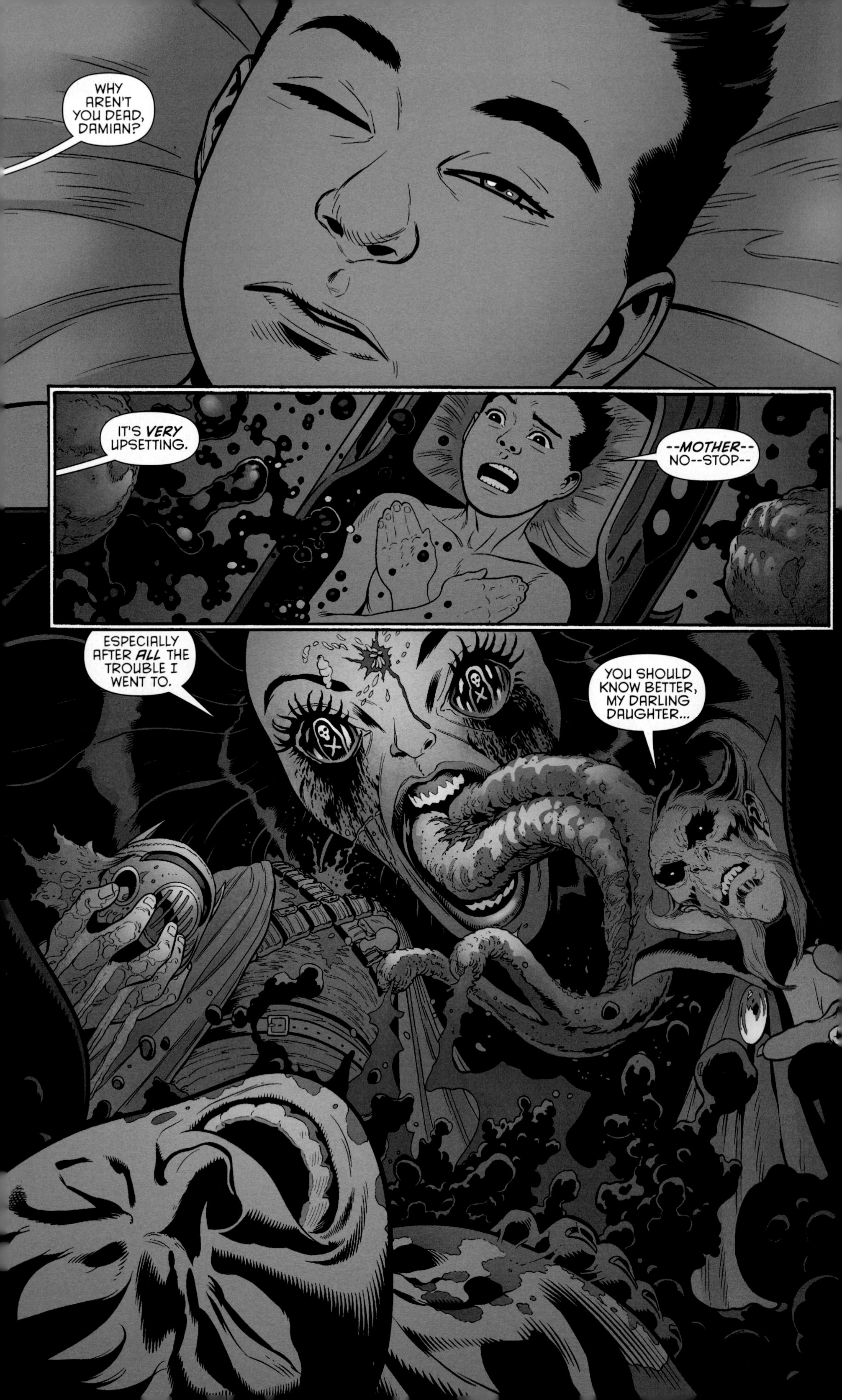
WHY AREN'T YOU DEAD, DAMIAN?
IT'S VERY UPSETTING.
--MOTHER-- NO--STOP--
ESPECIALLY AFTER ALL THE TROUBLE I WENT TO.
YOU SHOULD KNOW BETTER, MY DARLING DAUGHTER...

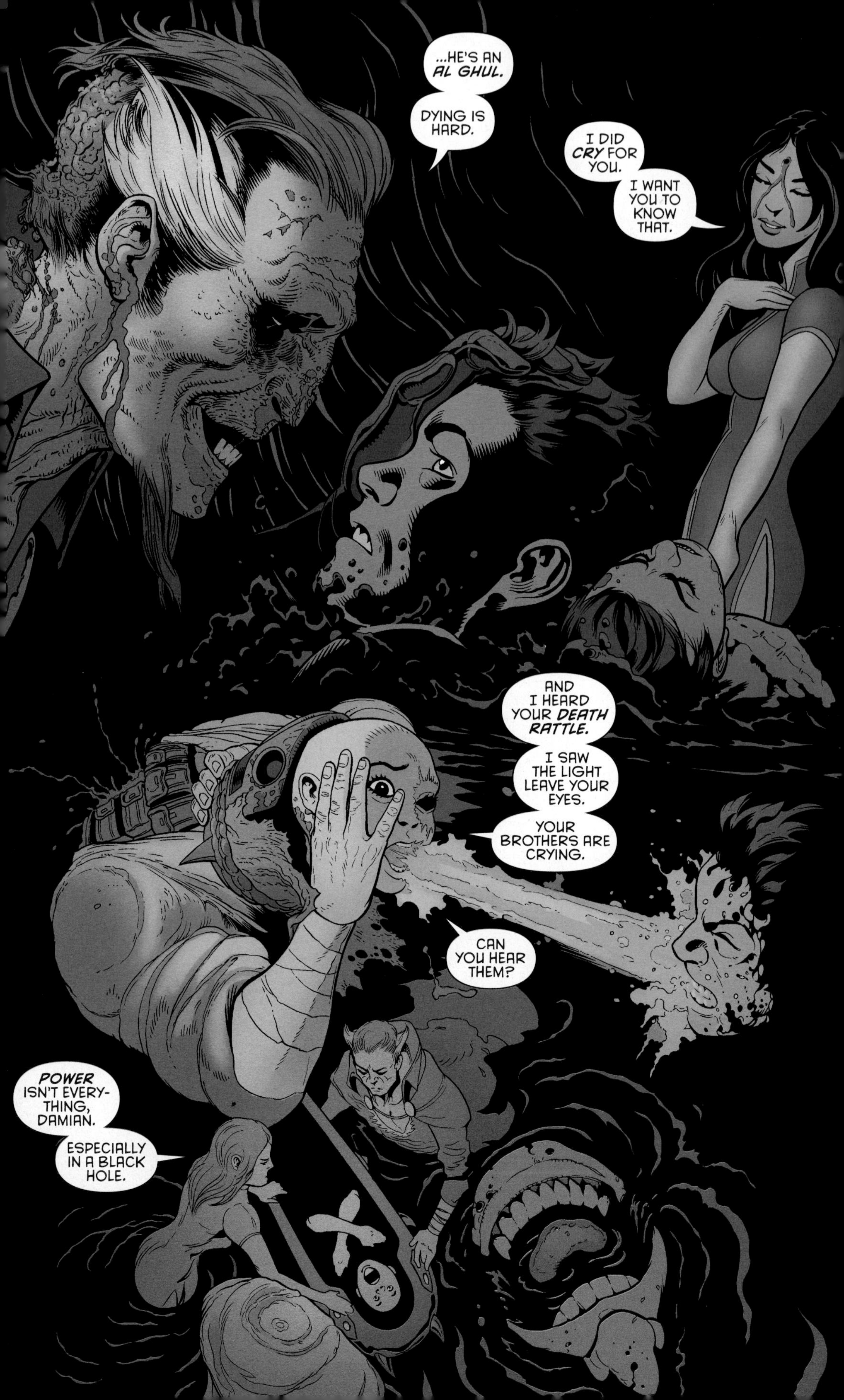
...HE'S AN AL GHUL.
DYING IS HARD.
I DID CRY FOR YOU.
I WANT YOU TO KNOW THAT.
AND I HEARD YOUR DEATH RATTLE.
I SAW THE LIGHT LEAVE YOUR EYES.
YOUR BROTHERS ARE CRYING.
CAN YOU HEAR THEM?
POWER ISN'T EVERY-THING, DAMIAN.
ESPECIALLY IN A BLACK HOLE.

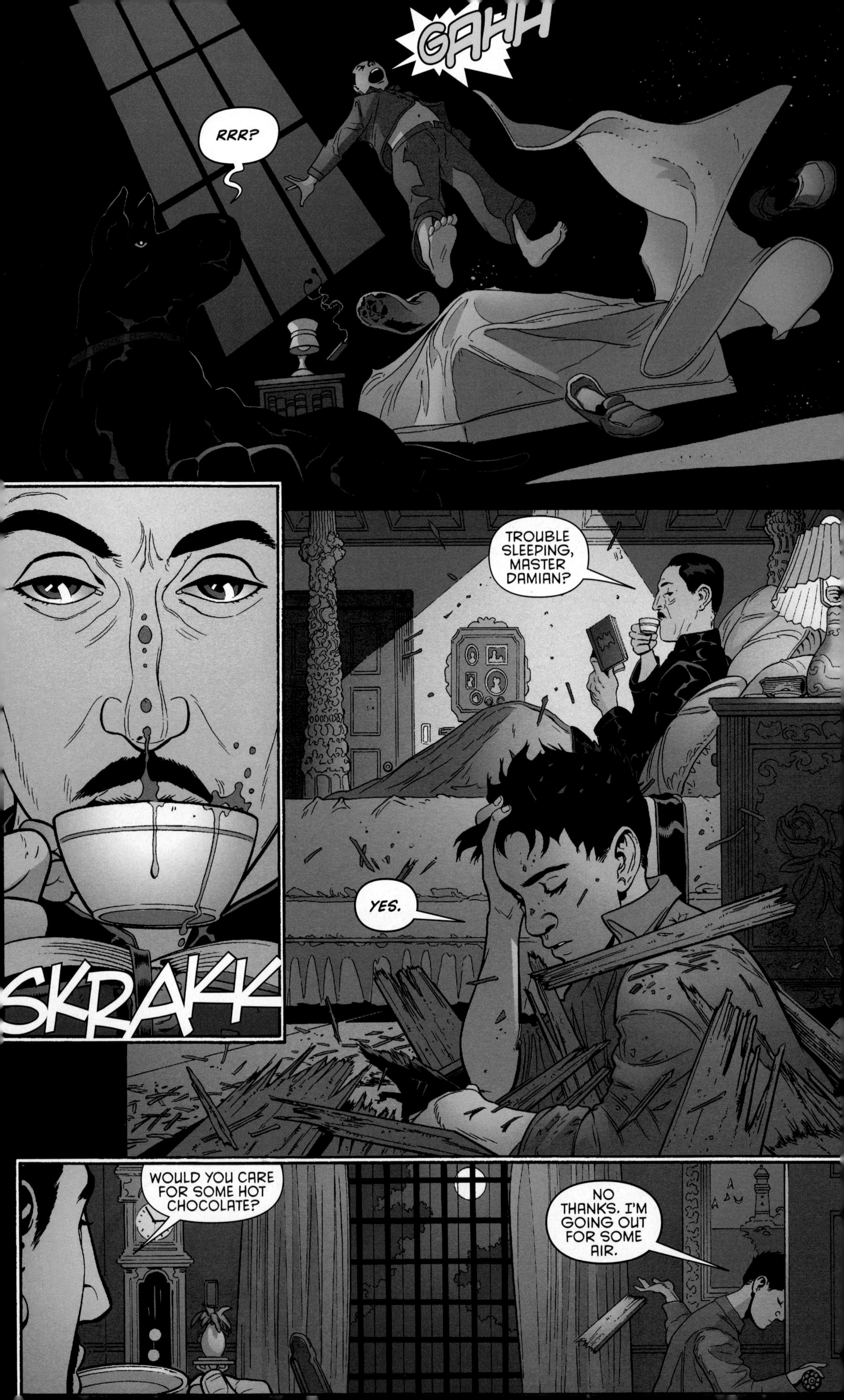
GAHH
RRR?
SKRAKK
TROUBLE SLEEPING, MASTER DAMIAN?
YES.
WOULD YOU CARE FOR SOME HOT CHOCOLATE?
NO THANKS. I'M GOING OUT FOR SOME AIR.

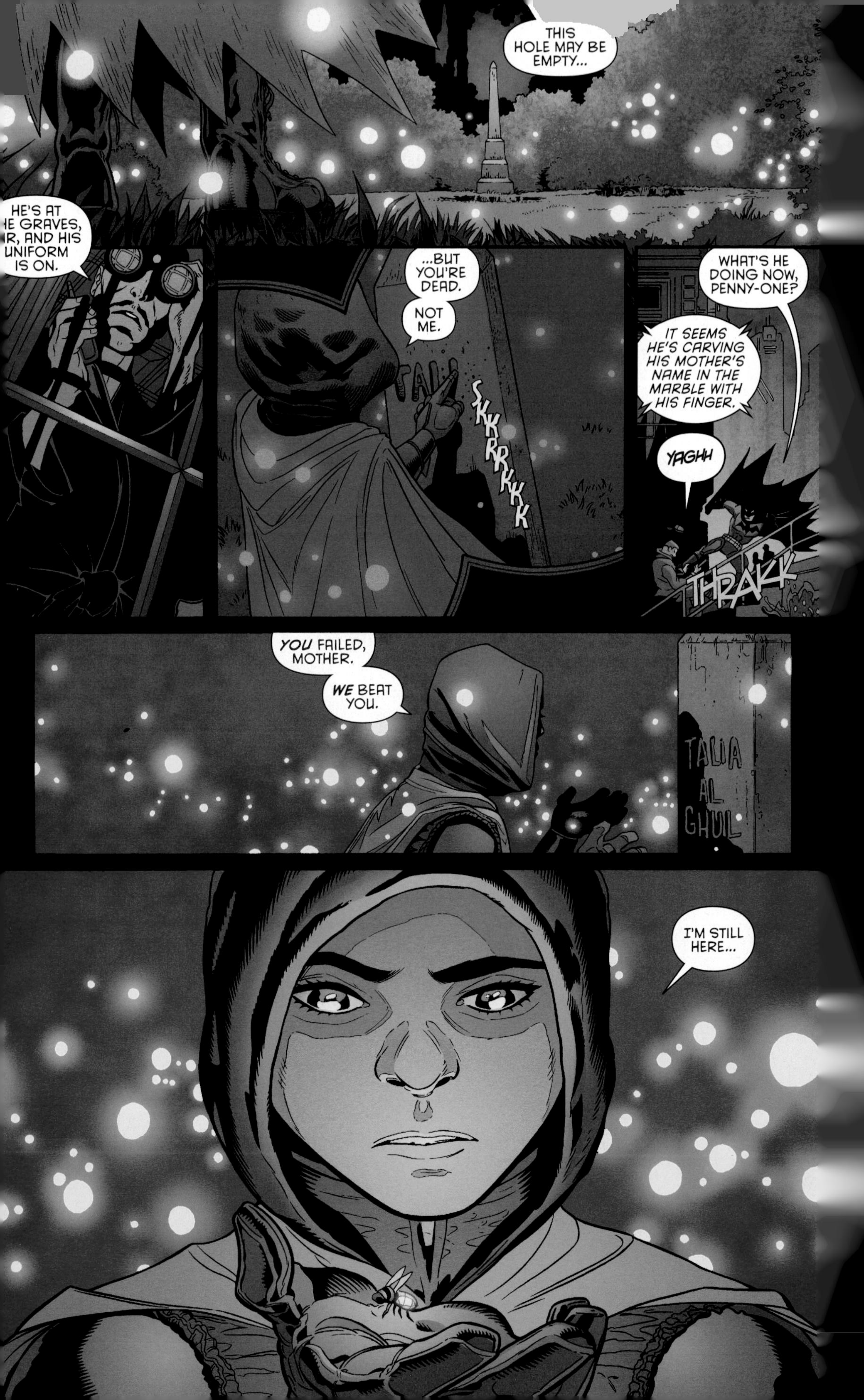
THIS HOLE MAY BE EMPTY...
HE'S AT
IE GRAVES,
R, AND HIS
UNIFORM
IS ON.
...BUT YOU'RE DEAD.
NOT ME.
SKKRRKKKK
WHAT'S HE DOING NOW, PENNY-ONE?
IT SEEMS HE'S CARVING HIS MOTHER'S NAME IN THE MARBLE WITH HIS FINGER.
YAGHH
THRAKK
YOU FAILED, MOTHER.
WE BEAT YOU.
TALIA AL GHUL
I'M STILL HERE...

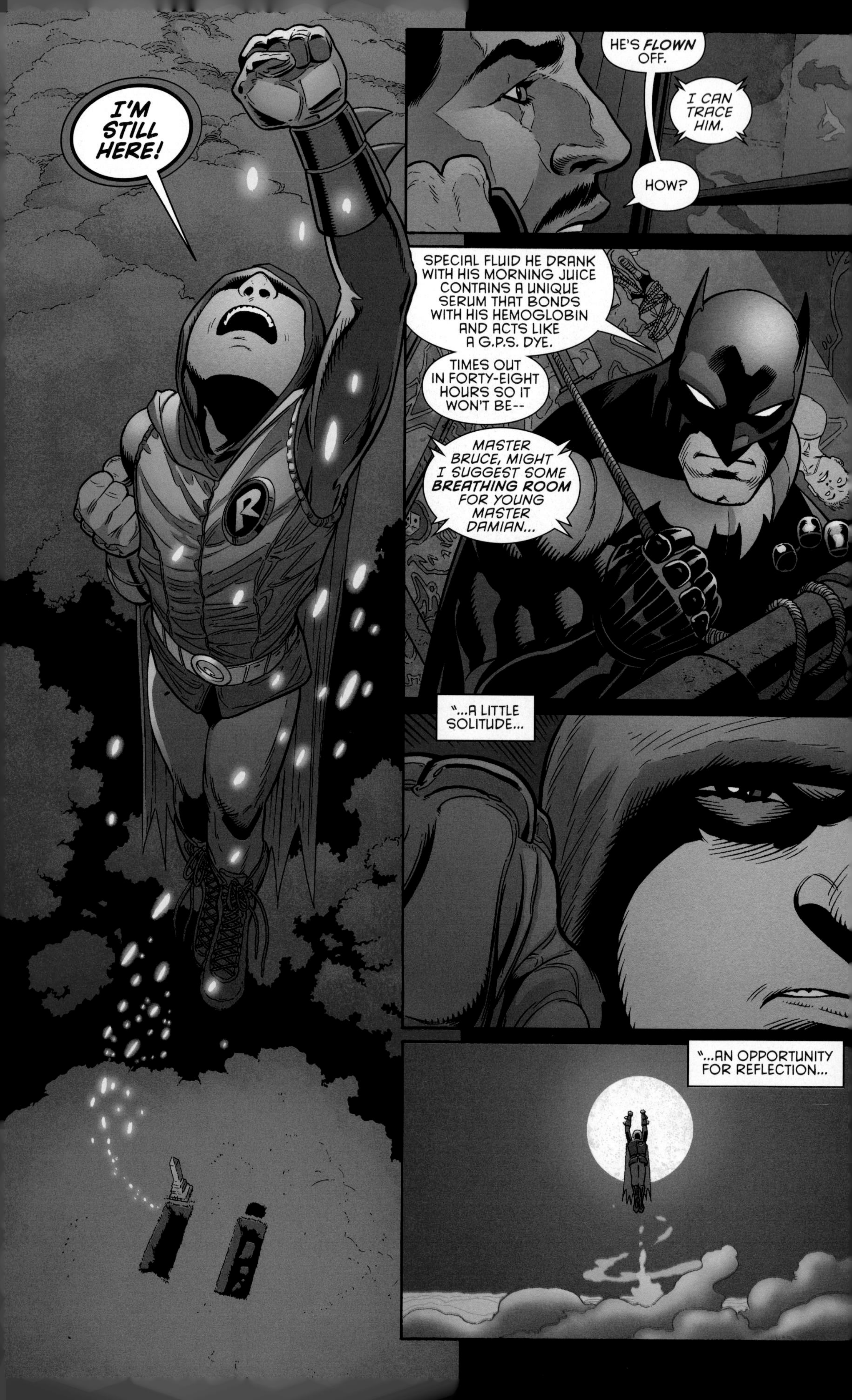
I'M STILL HERE!
HE'S FLOWN OFF.
I CAN TRACE HIM.
HOW?
SPECIAL FLUID HE DRANK WITH HIS MORNING JUICE CONTAINS A UNIQUE SERUM THAT BONDS WITH HIS HEMOGLOBIN AND ACTS LIKE A G.P.S. DYE.
TIMES OUT IN FORTY-EIGHT HOURS SO IT WON'T BE--
MASTER BRUCE, MIGHT I SUGGEST SOME BREATHING ROOM FOR YOUNG MASTER DAMIAN...
"...A LITTLE SOLITUDE...
"...AN OPPORTUNITY FOR REFLECTION...

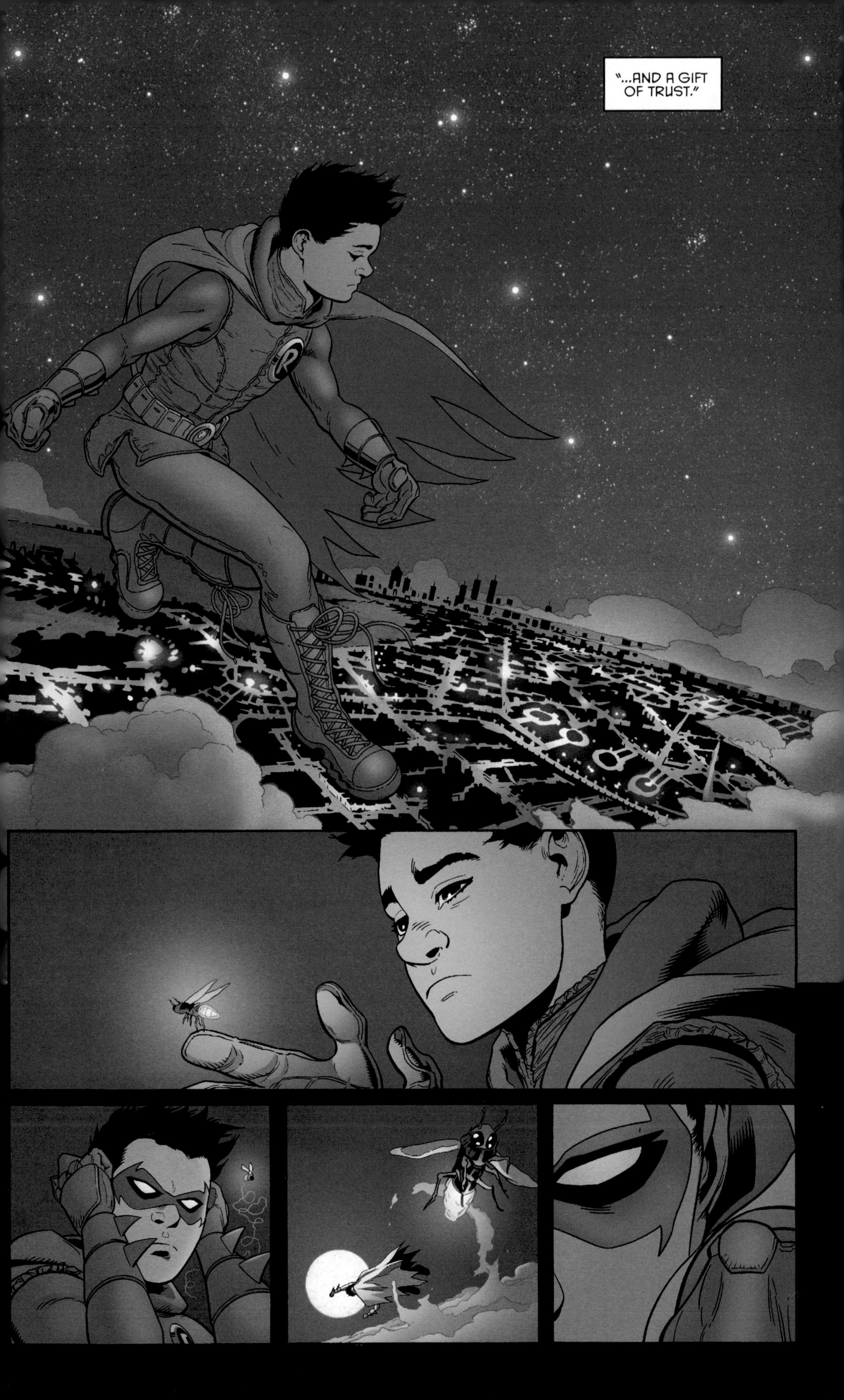
"...AND A GIFT
OF TRUST."

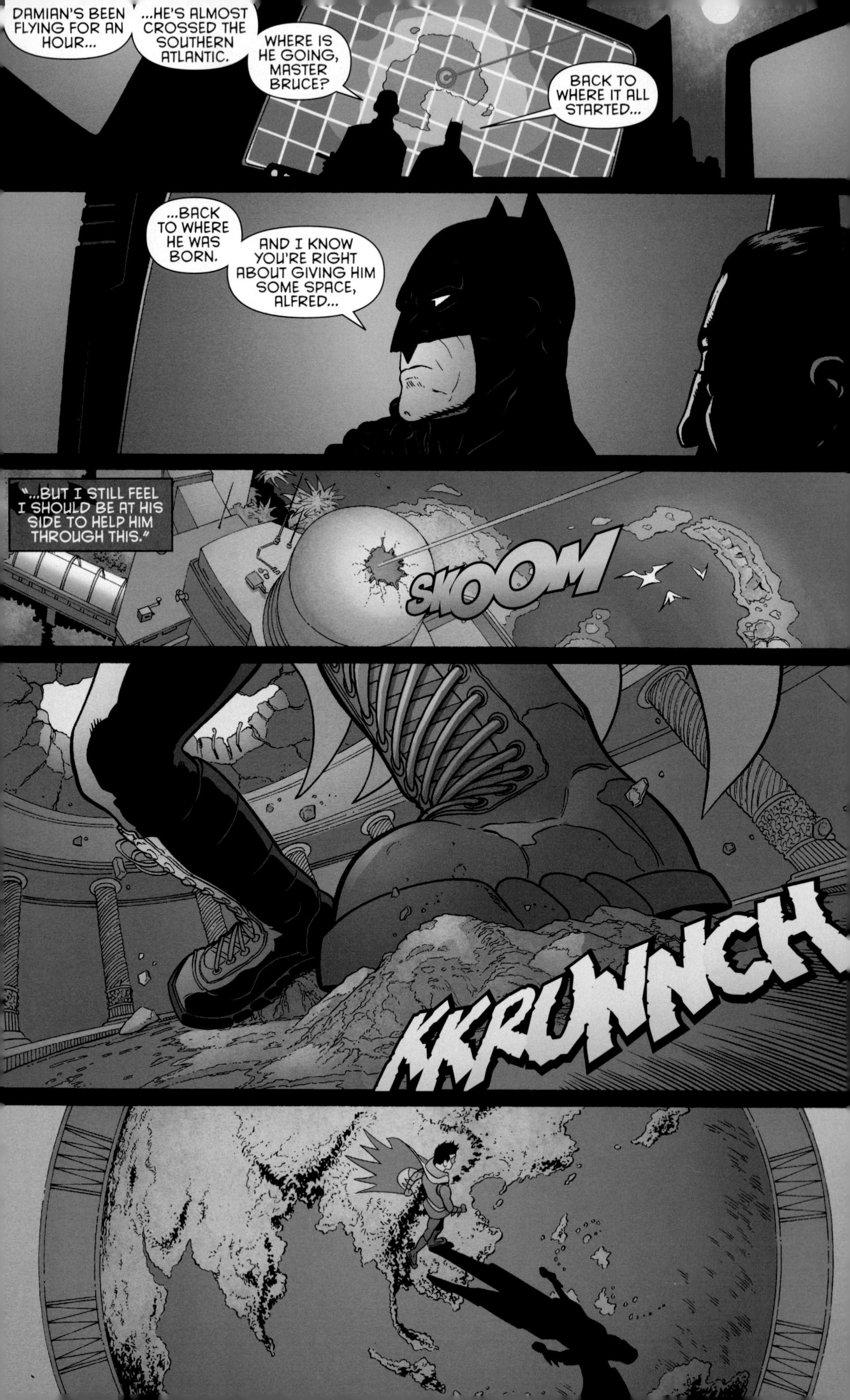
DAMIAN'S BEEN FLYING FOR AN HOUR...
...HE'S ALMOST CROSSED THE SOUTHERN ATLANTIC.
WHERE IS HE GOING, MASTER BRUCE?
BACK TO WHERE IT ALL STARTED...
...BACK TO WHERE HE WAS BORN.
AND I KNOW YOU'RE RIGHT ABOUT GIVING HIM SOME SPACE, ALFRED...
"...BUT I STILL FEEL I SHOULD BE AT HIS SIDE TO HELP HIM THROUGH THIS."
SKOOM
KKRUNNCH

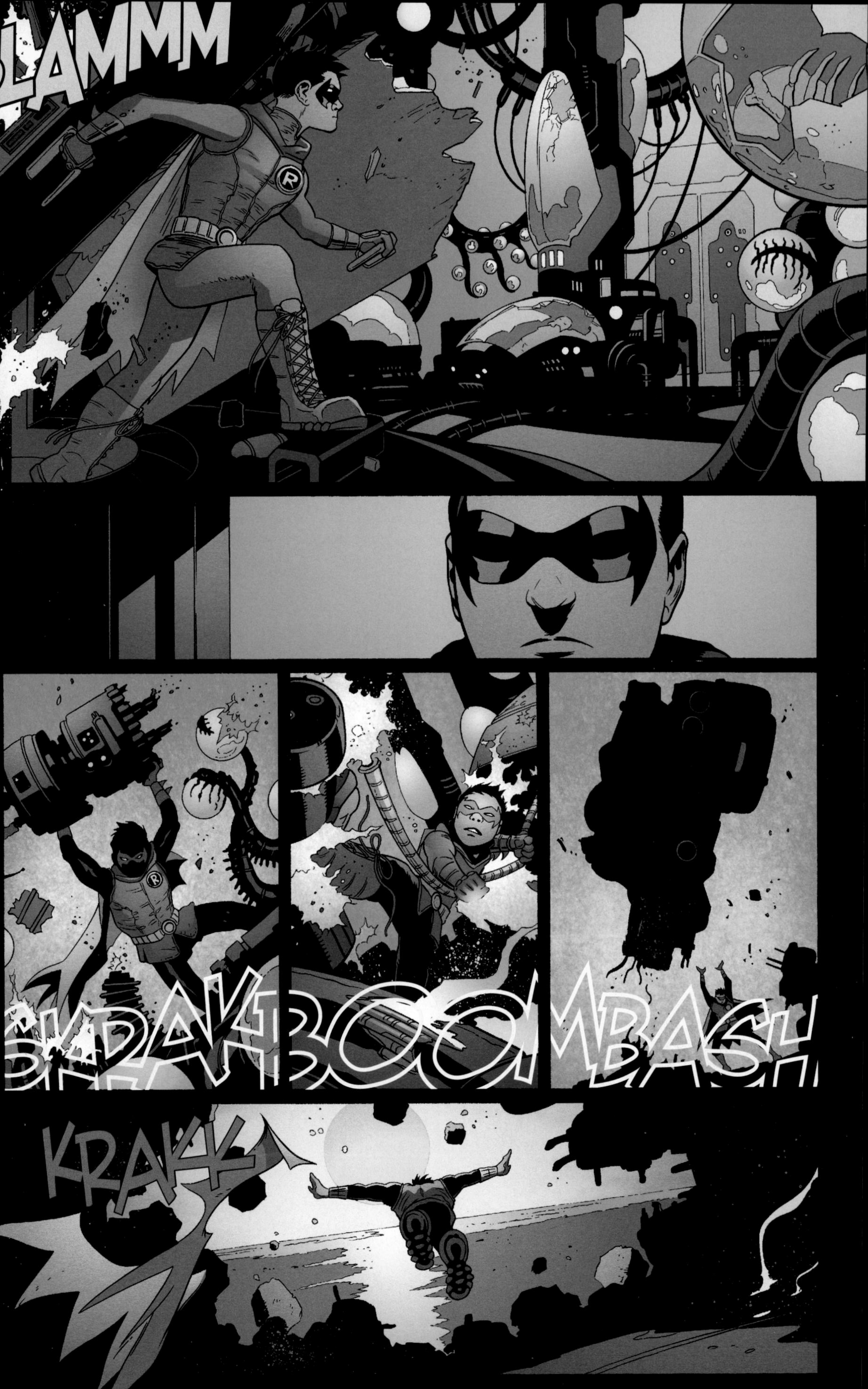
SLAMMM
SKRAK
BOOM
BASH
KRAKK

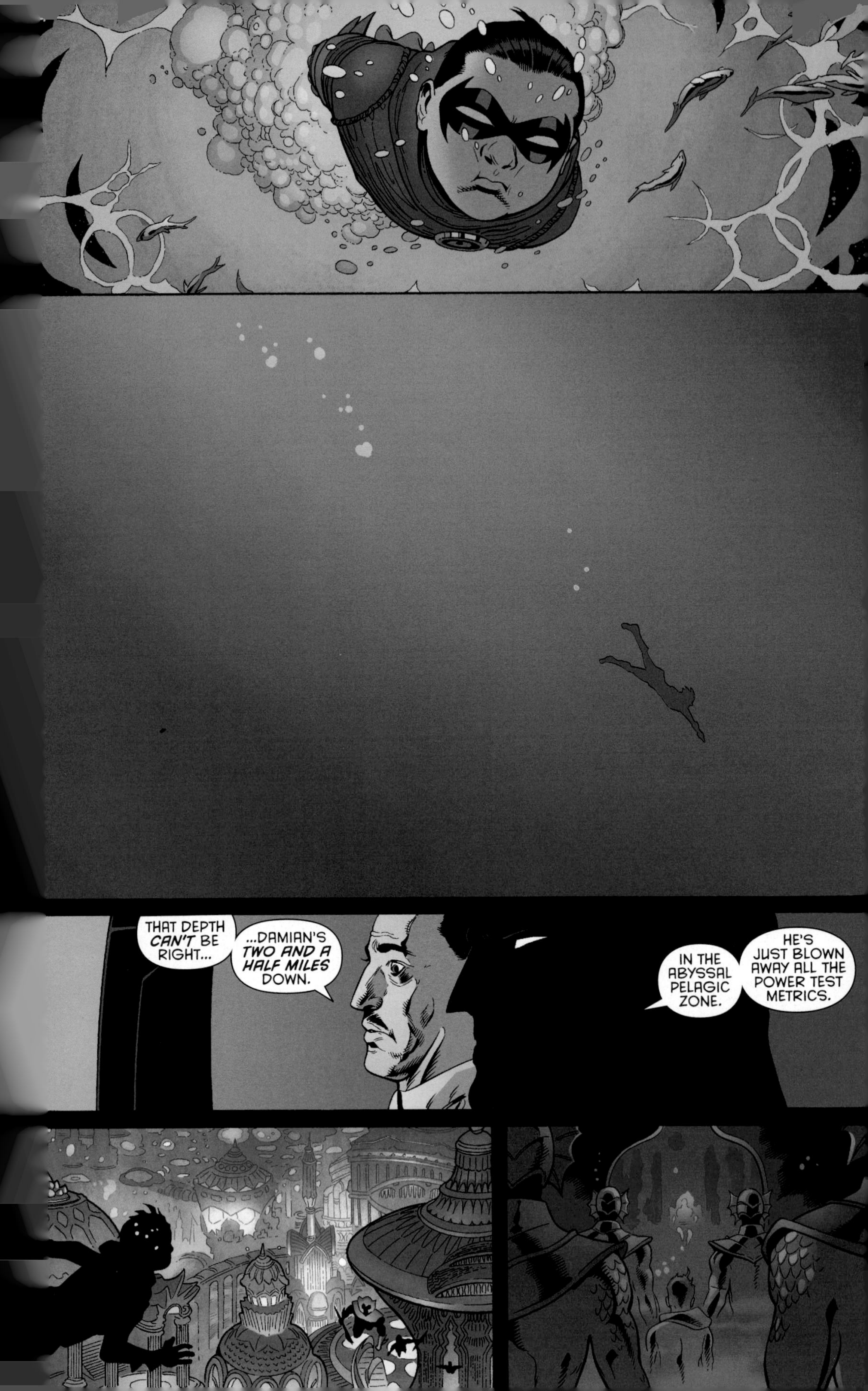
THAT DEPTH CAN'T BE RIGHT...
...DAMIAN'S TWO AND A HALF MILES DOWN.
IN THE ABYSSAL PELAGIC ZONE.
HE'S JUST BLOWN AWAY ALL THE POWER TEST METRICS.

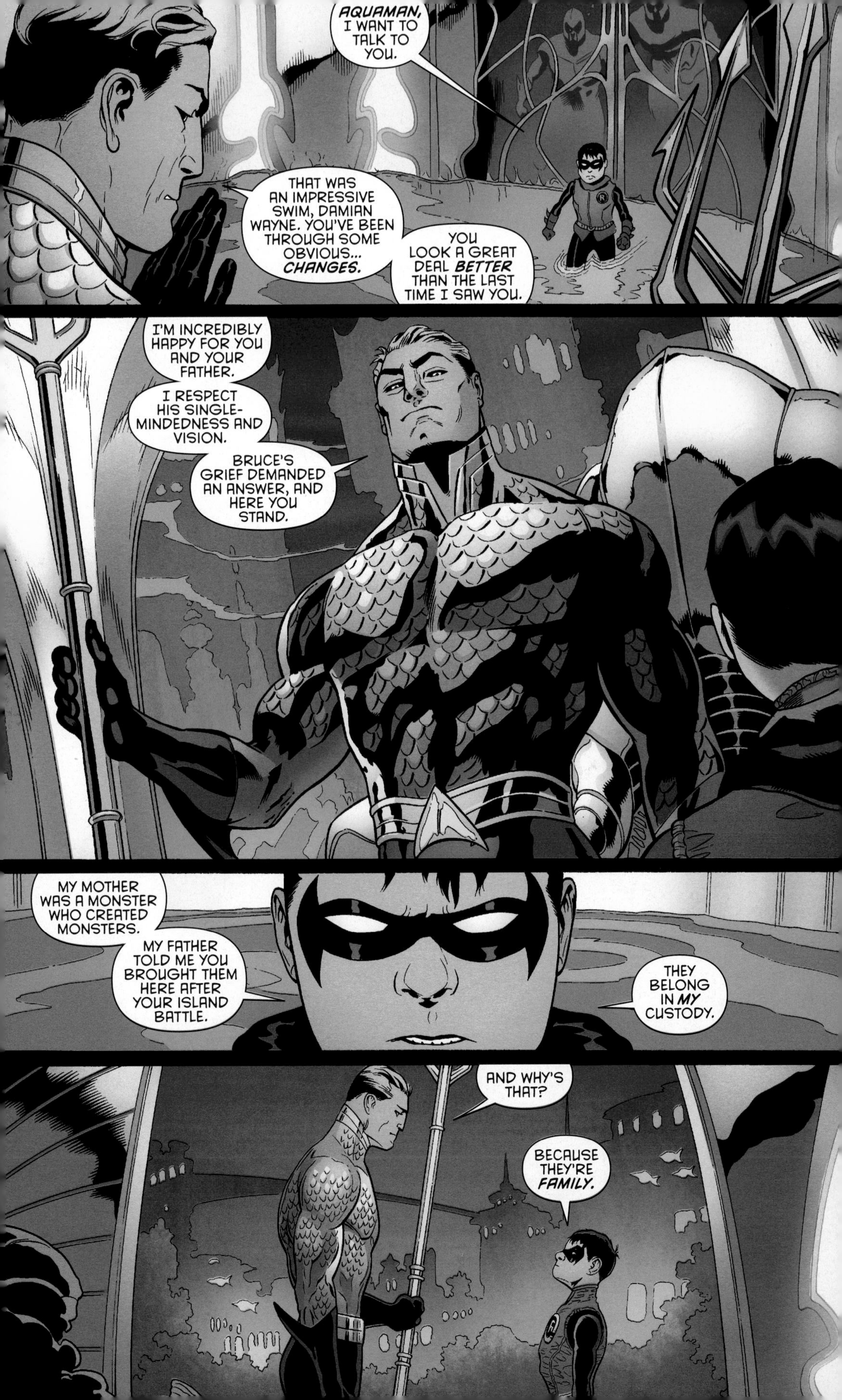
AQUAMAN, I WANT TO TALK TO YOU.
THAT WAS AN IMPRESSIVE SWIM, DAMIAN WAYNE. YOU'VE BEEN THROUGH SOME OBVIOUS... CHANGES.
YOU LOOK A GREAT DEAL BETTER THAN THE LAST TIME I SAW YOU.
I'M INCREDIBLY HAPPY FOR YOU AND YOUR FATHER.
I RESPECT HIS SINGLE-MINDEDNESS AND VISION.
BRUCE'S GRIEF DEMANDED AN ANSWER, AND HERE YOU STAND.
MY MOTHER WAS A MONSTER WHO CREATED MONSTERS.
MY FATHER TOLD ME YOU BROUGHT THEM HERE AFTER YOUR ISLAND BATTLE.
THEY BELONG IN MY CUSTODY.
AND WHY'S THAT?
BECAUSE THEY'RE FAMILY.

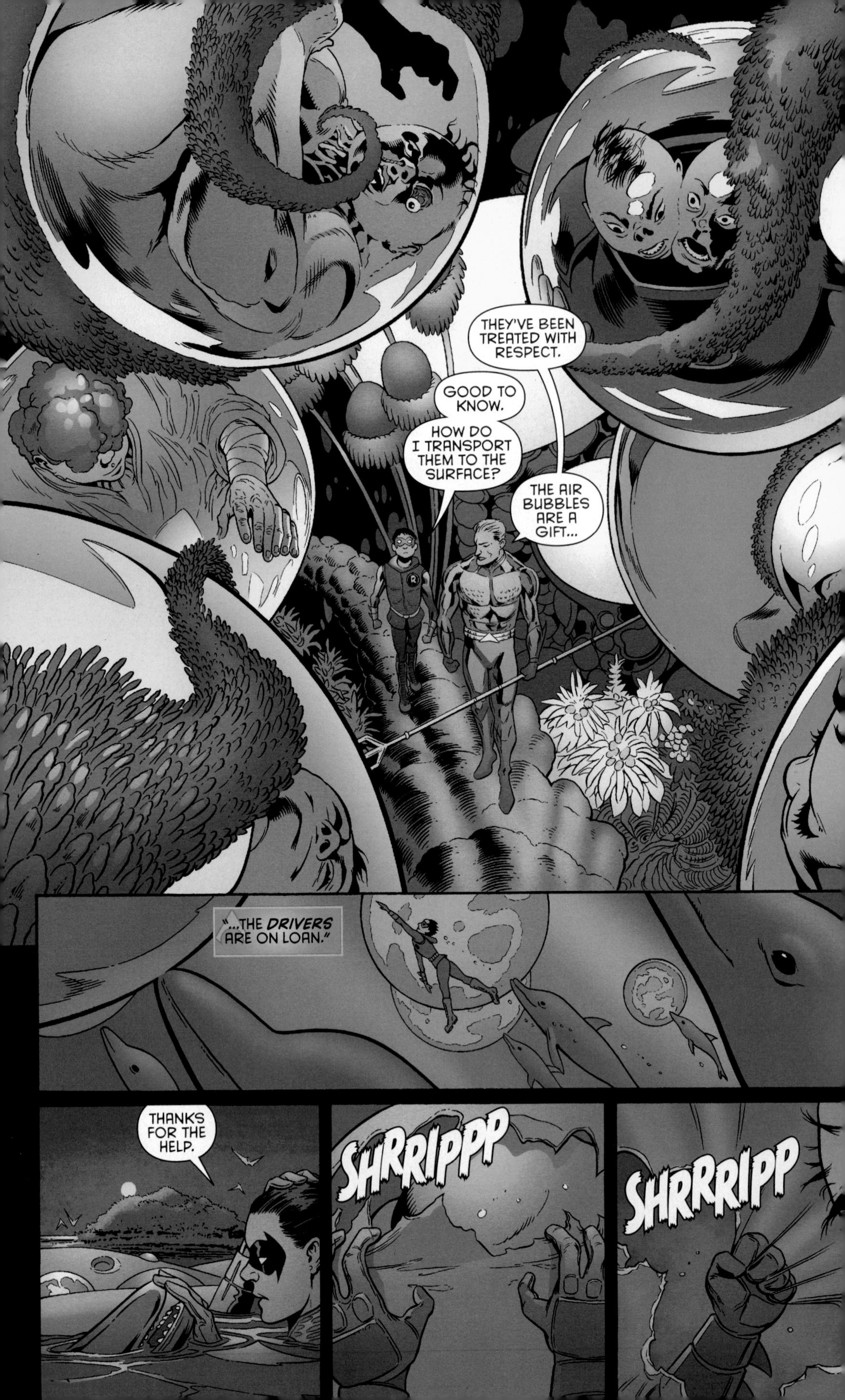
THEY'VE BEEN TREATED WITH RESPECT.
GOOD TO KNOW.
HOW DO I TRANSPORT THEM TO THE SURFACE?
THE AIR BUBBLES ARE A GIFT...
"...THE DRIVERS ARE ON LOAN."
THANKS FOR THE HELP.
SHRRIPPP
SHRRRIPP

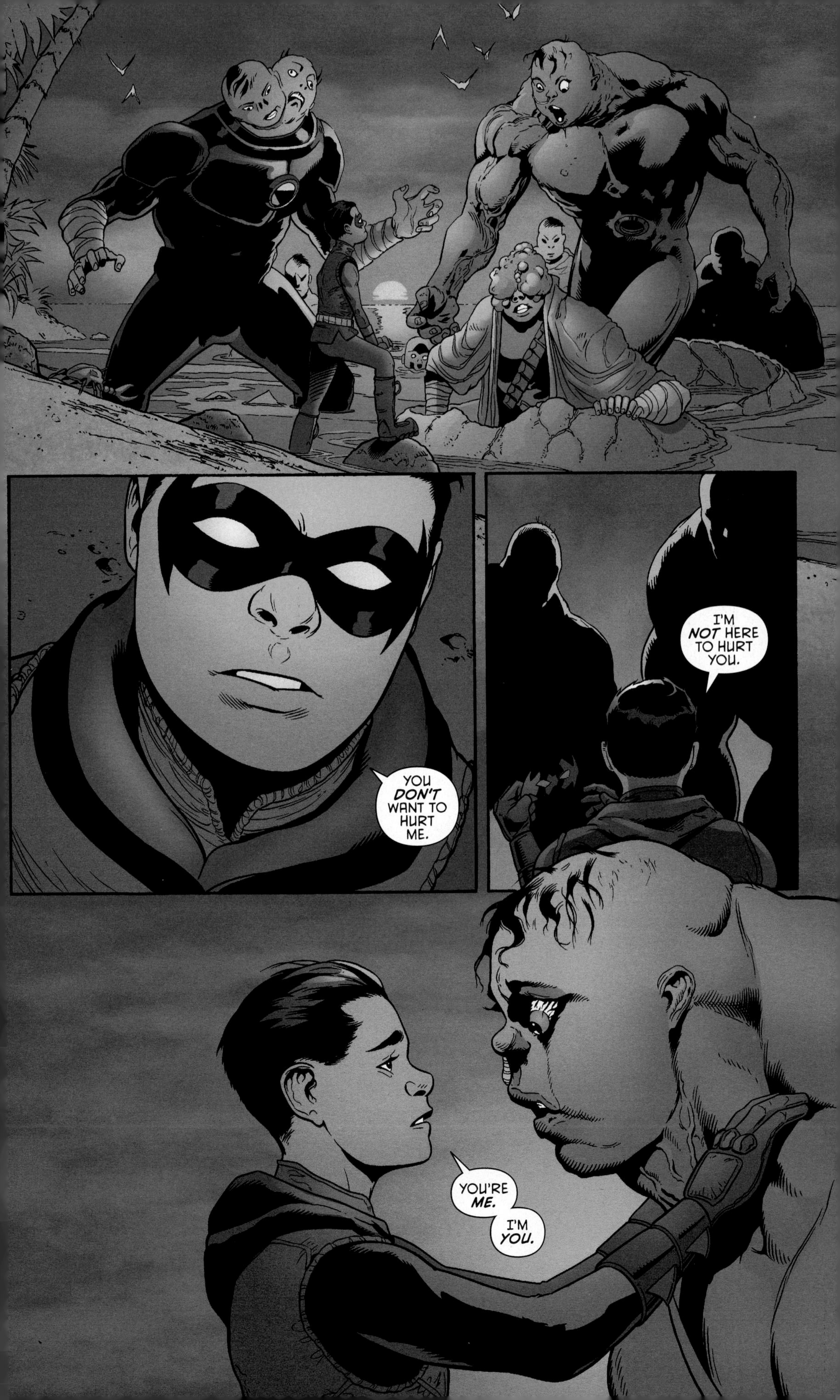
YOU DON'T WANT TO HURT ME.
I'M NOT HERE TO HURT YOU.
YOU'RE ME.
I'M YOU.

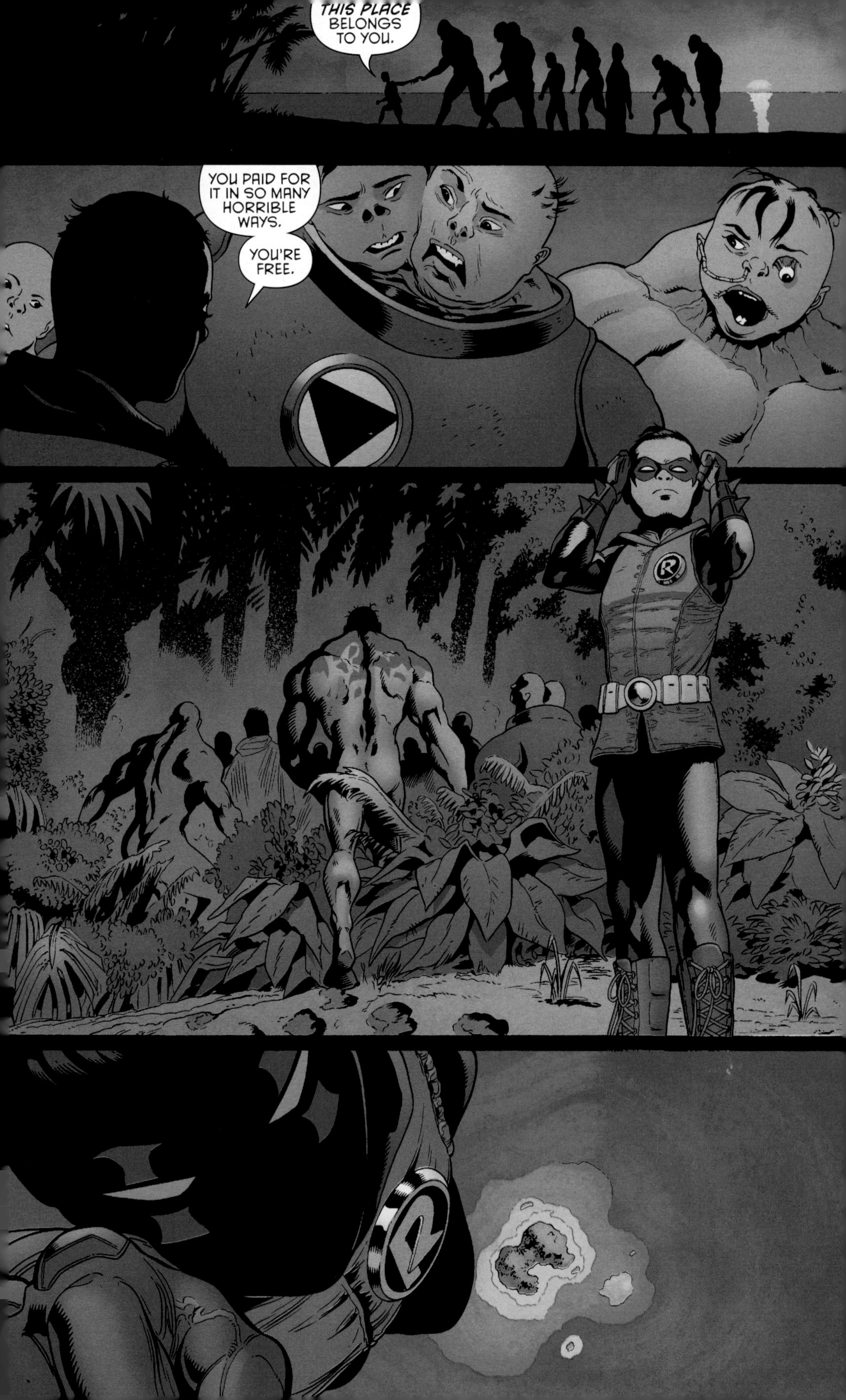
THIS PLACE BELONGS TO YOU.
YOU PAID FOR IT IN SO MANY HORRIBLE WAYS.
YOU'RE FREE.

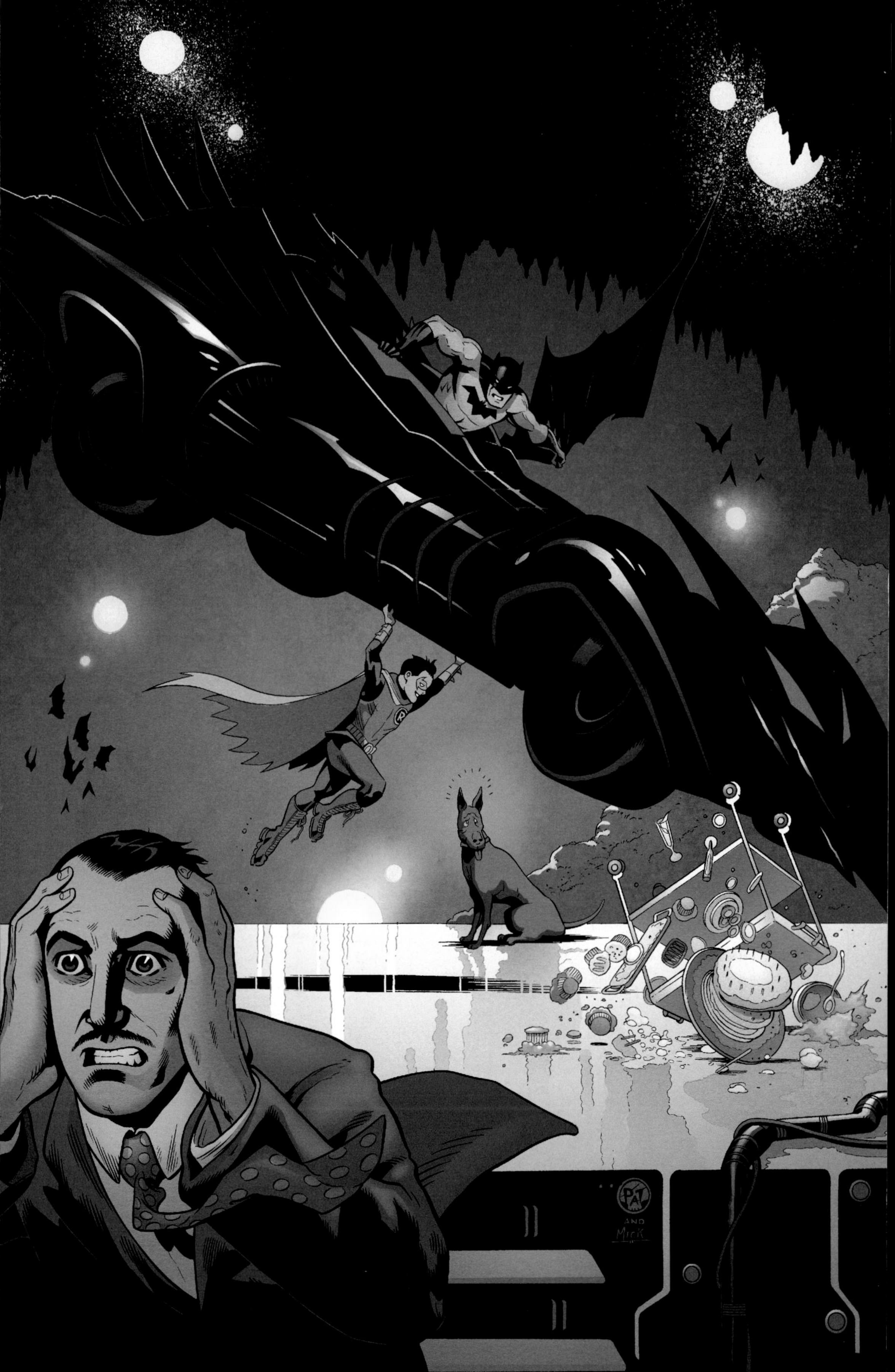

PATRICK GLEASON penciller MICK GRAY inker JOHN KALISZ colorist CARLOS M. MANGUAL letterer cover art by GLEASON, GRAY & KALISZ

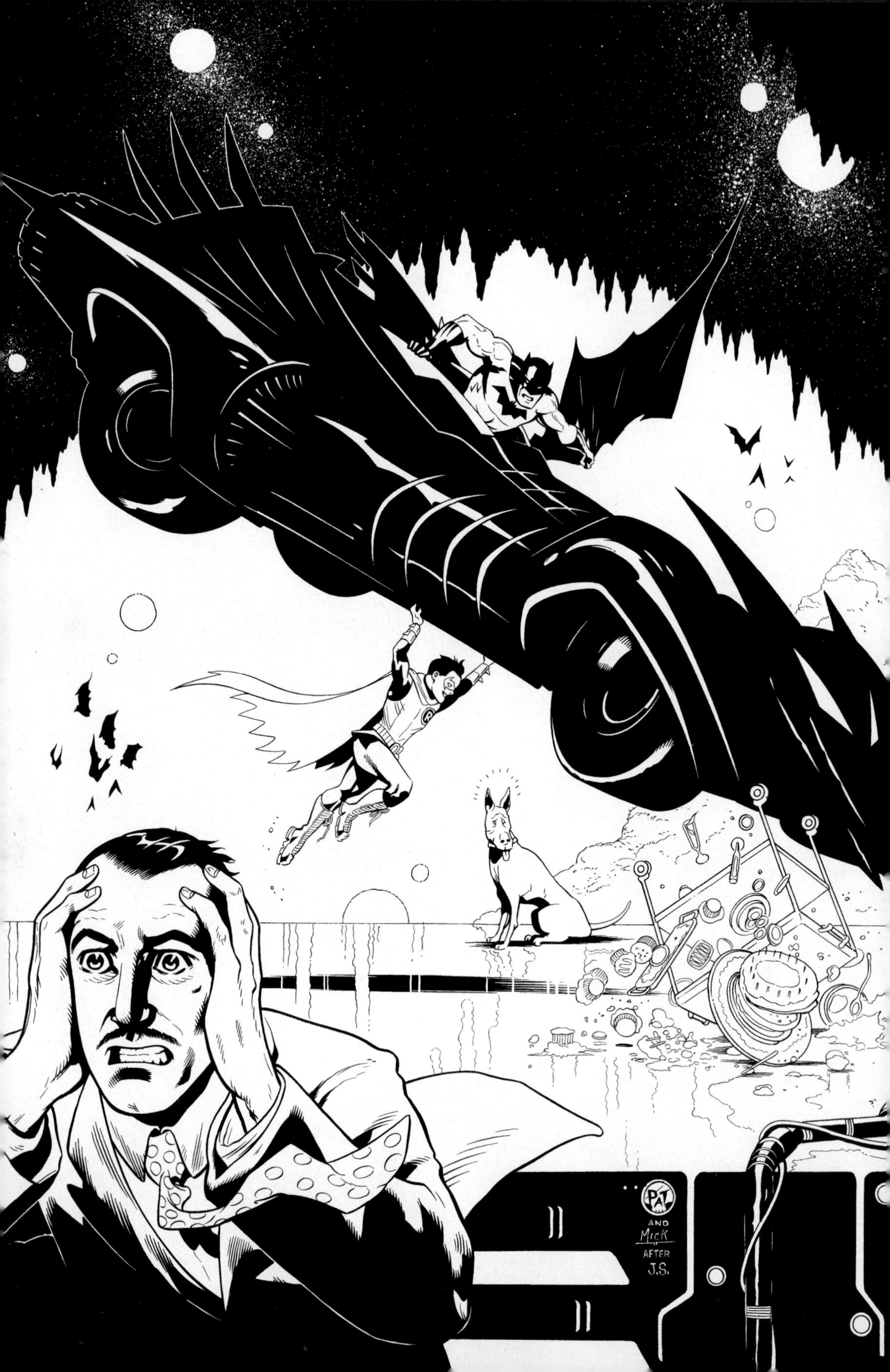
PAT AND MICK AFTER J.S.

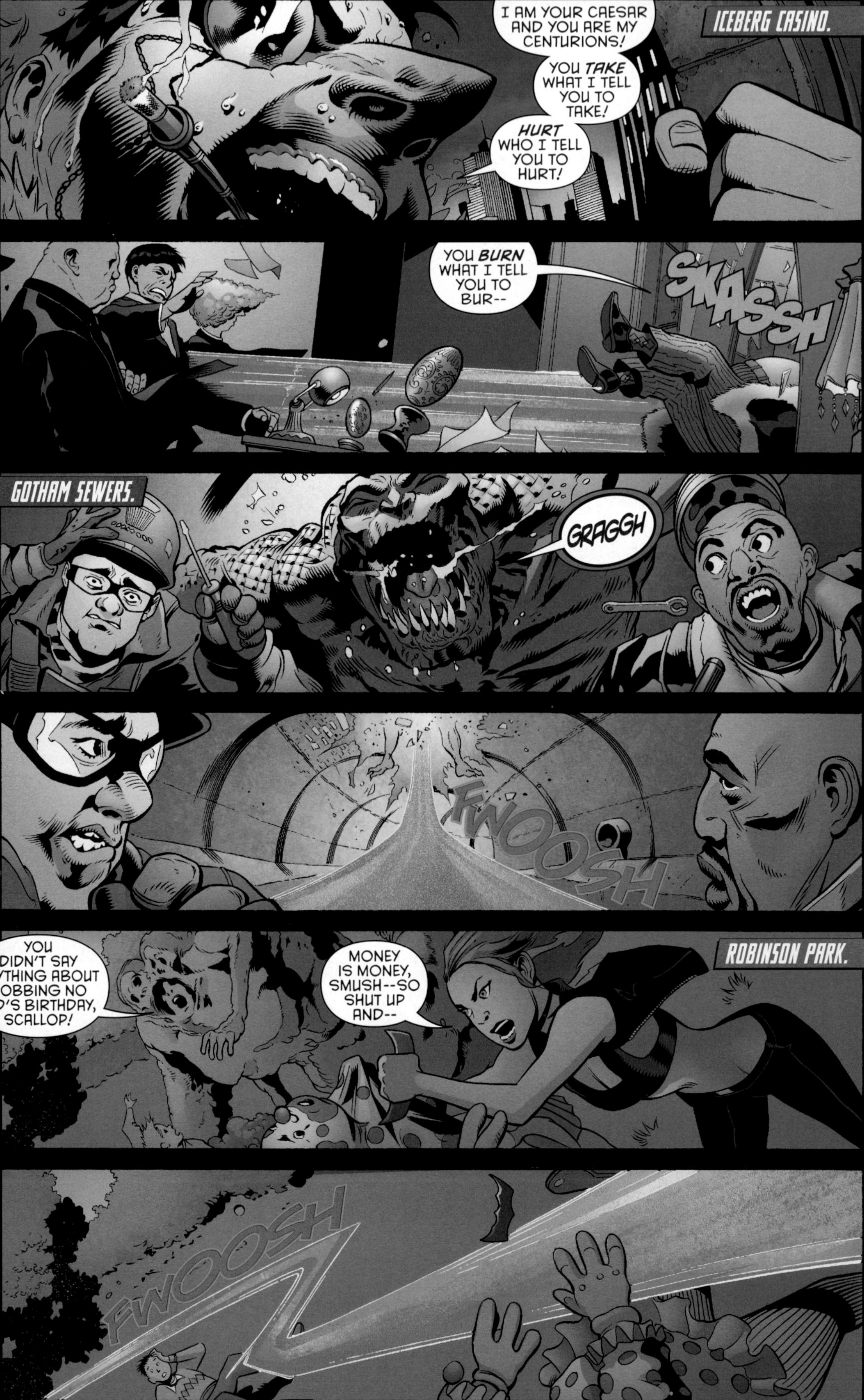
ICEBERG CASINO.
I AM YOUR CAESAR AND YOU ARE MY CENTURIONS!
YOU TAKE WHAT I TELL YOU TO TAKE!
HURT WHO I TELL YOU TO HURT!
YOU BURN WHAT I TELL YOU TO BUR--
SKASSSH
GOTHAM SEWERS.
GRAGGH
FWOOSH
YOU
DIDN'T SAY
YTHING ABOUT
OBBING NO
D'S BIRTHDAY,
SCALLOP!
MONEY IS MONEY, SMUSH--SO SHUT UP AND--
ROBINSON PARK.
FWOOSH

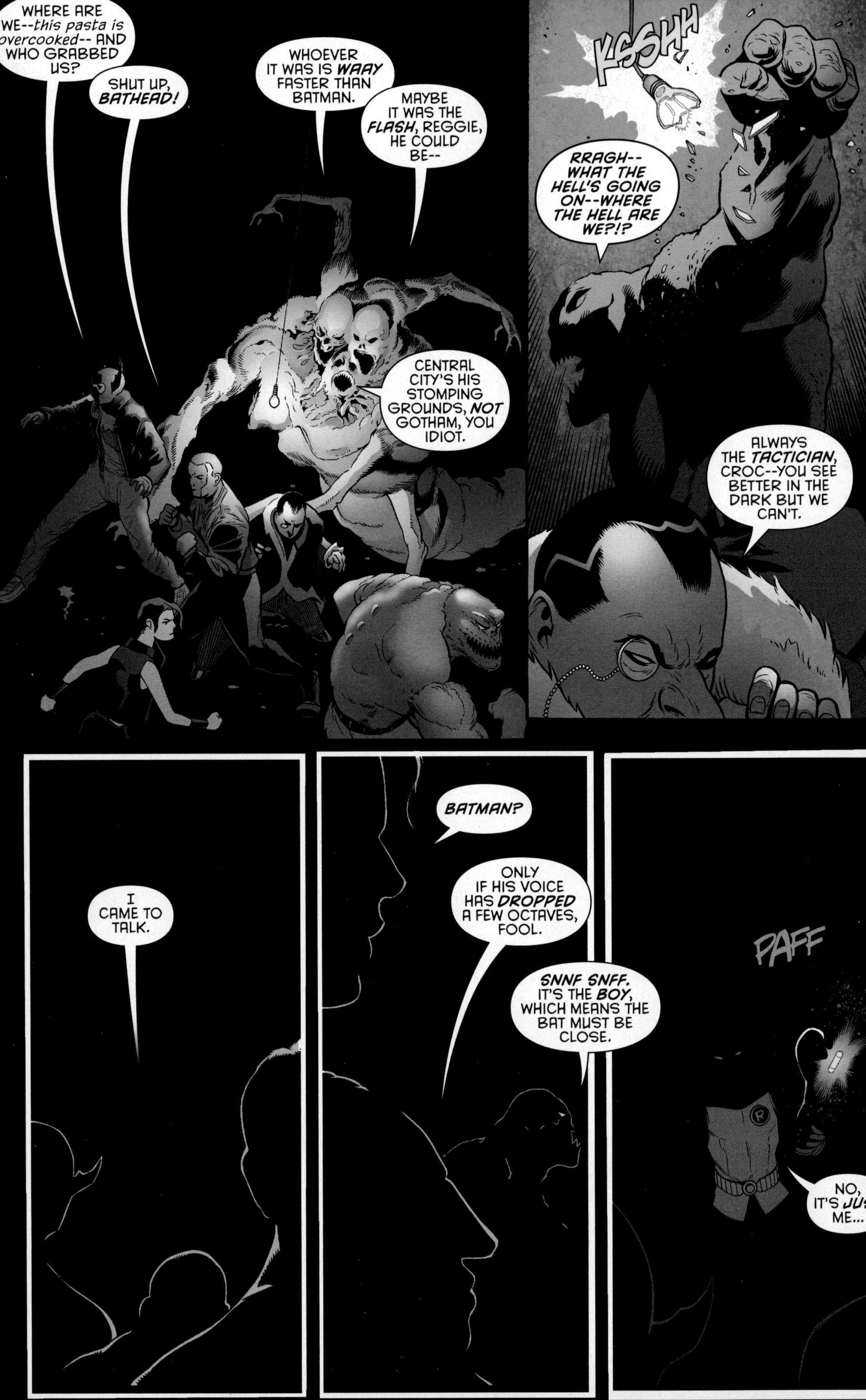
WHERE ARE WE--*this pasta is overcooked*-- AND WHO GRABBED US?
SHUT UP, ***BATHEAD!***
WHOEVER IT WAS IS ***WAAY*** FASTER THAN BATMAN.
MAYBE IT WAS THE ***FLASH***, REGGIE, HE COULD BE--
CENTRAL CITY'S HIS STOMPING GROUNDS, ***NOT*** GOTHAM, YOU IDIOT.
KSSHH
RRAGH-- WHAT THE HELL'S GOING ON--WHERE THE HELL ARE WE?!?
ALWAYS THE ***TACTICIAN***, CROC--YOU SEE BETTER IN THE DARK BUT WE CAN'T.
I CAME TO TALK.
BATMAN?
ONLY IF HIS VOICE HAS ***DROPPED*** A FEW OCTAVES, FOOL.
SNNF SNFF. IT'S THE ***BOY***, WHICH MEANS THE BAT MUST BE CLOSE.
PAFF
NO, IT'S JU ME...

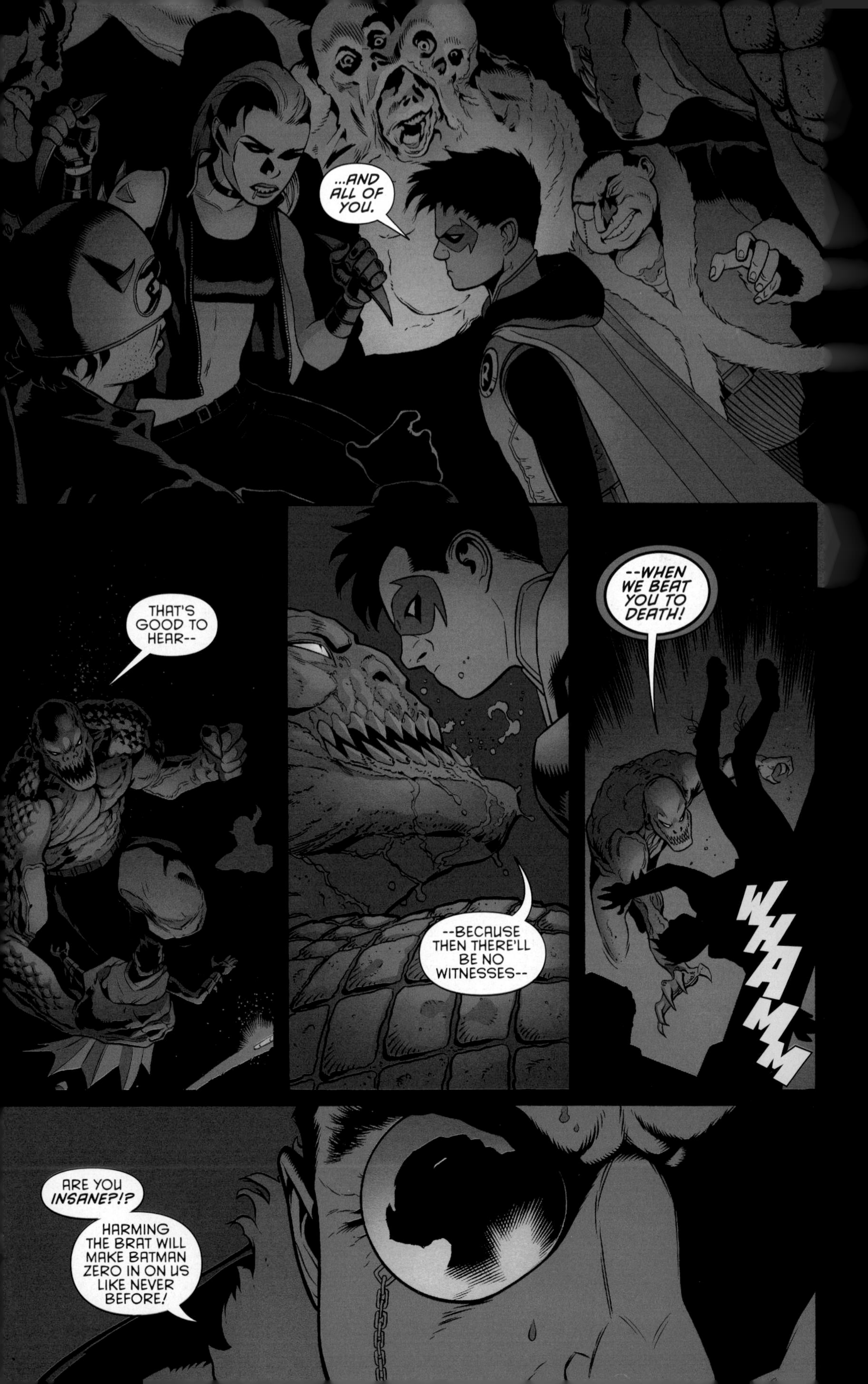
...AND ALL OF YOU.
THAT'S GOOD TO HEAR--
--BECAUSE THEN THERE'LL BE NO WITNESSES--
--WHEN WE BEAT YOU TO DEATH!
WHAMM
ARE YOU *INSANE?!?*
HARMING THE BRAT WILL MAKE BATMAN ZERO IN ON US LIKE NEVER BEFORE!

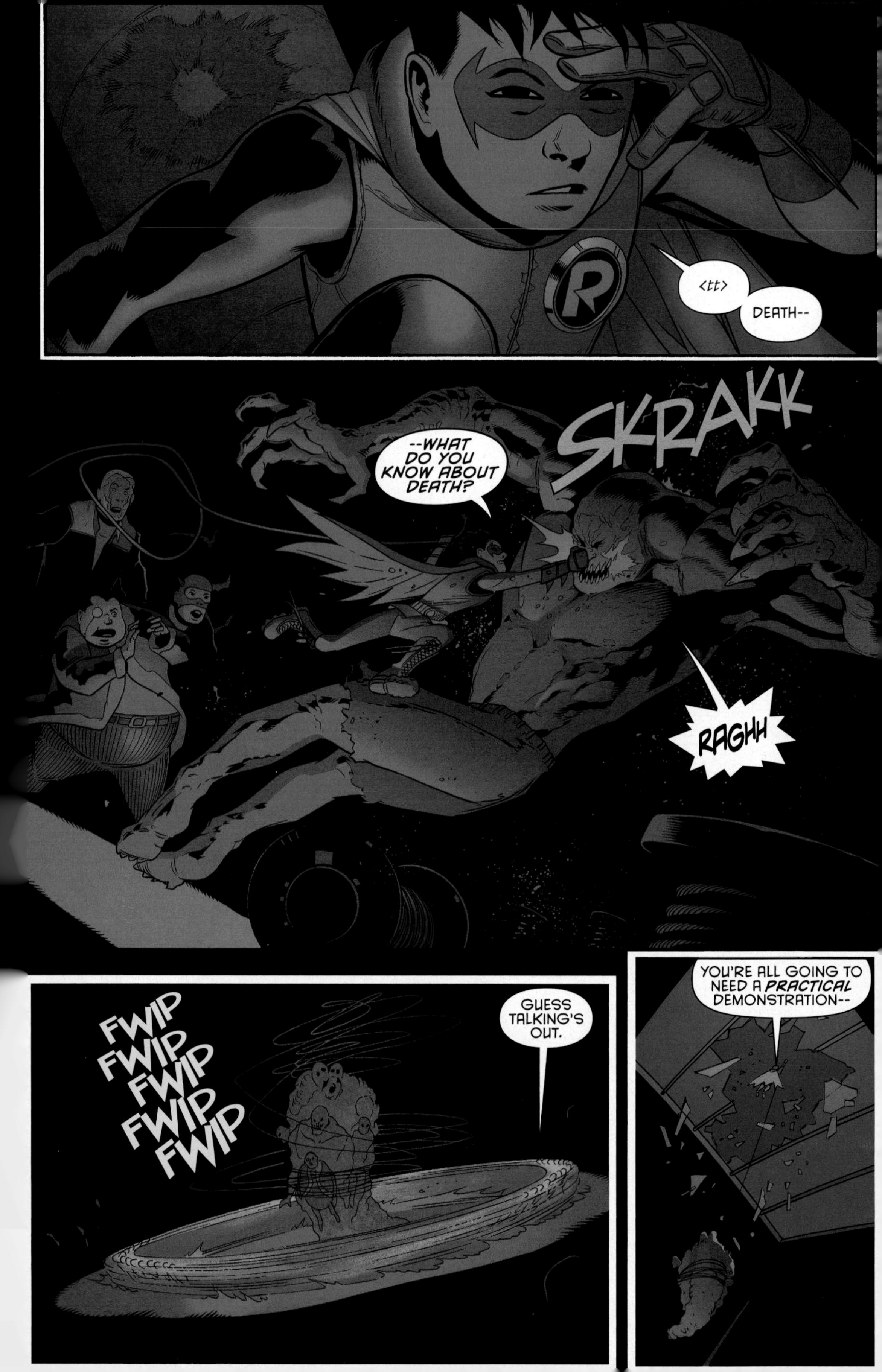

<tt>
DEATH--
SKRAKK
--WHAT DO YOU KNOW ABOUT DEATH?
RAGHH
FWIP FWIP FWIP FWIP FWIP
GUESS TALKING'S OUT.
YOU'RE ALL GOING TO NEED A *PRACTICAL* DEMONSTRATION--

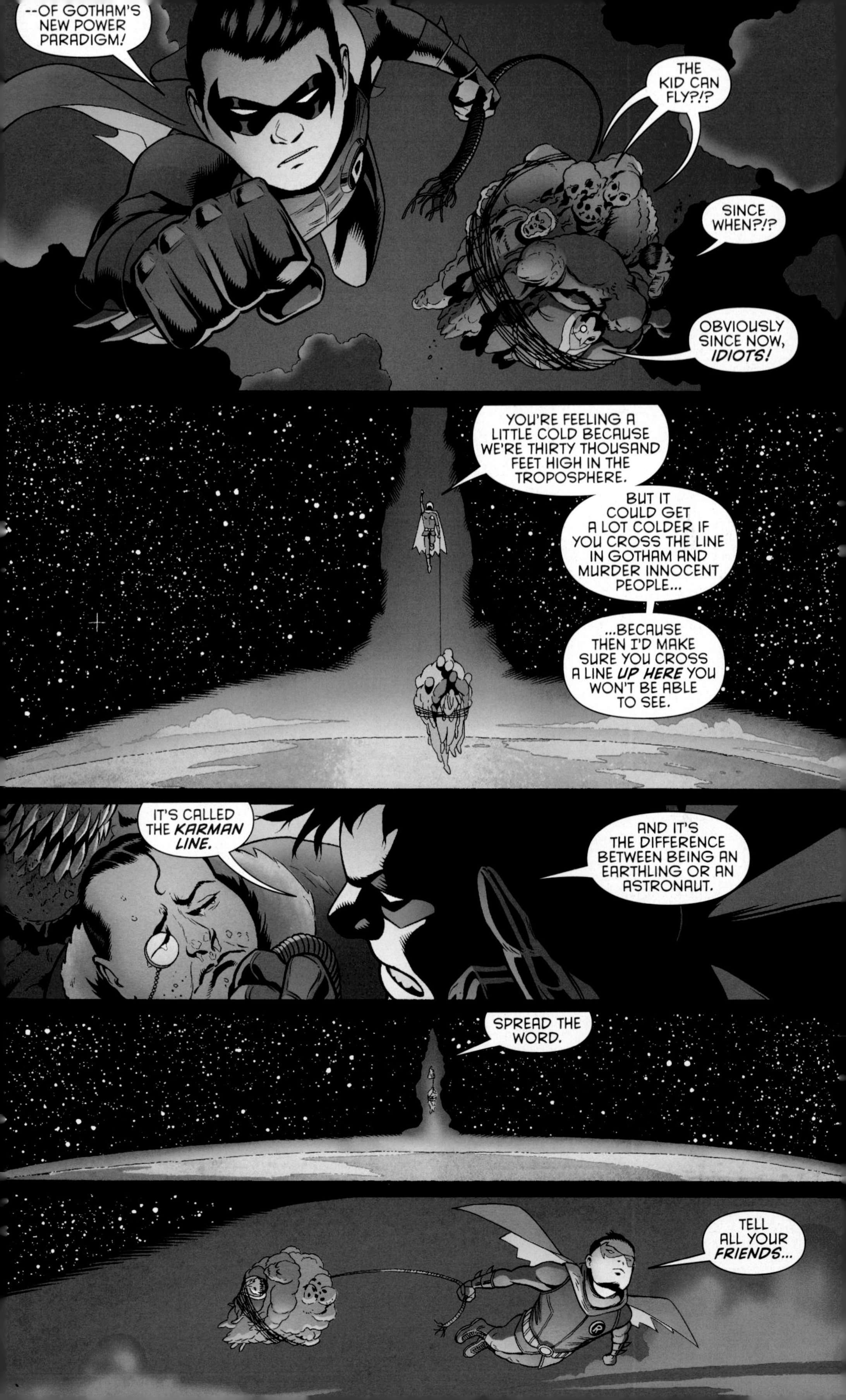
--OF GOTHAM'S NEW POWER PARADIGM!
THE KID CAN FLY?!?
SINCE WHEN?!?
OBVIOUSLY SINCE NOW, *IDIOTS!*
YOU'RE FEELING A LITTLE COLD BECAUSE WE'RE THIRTY THOUSAND FEET HIGH IN THE TROPOSPHERE.
BUT IT COULD GET A LOT COLDER IF YOU CROSS THE LINE IN GOTHAM AND MURDER INNOCENT PEOPLE...
...BECAUSE THEN I'D MAKE SURE YOU CROSS A LINE *UP HERE* YOU WON'T BE ABLE TO SEE.
IT'S CALLED THE *KARMAN LINE.*
AND IT'S THE DIFFERENCE BETWEEN BEING AN EARTHLING OR AN ASTRONAUT.
SPREAD THE WORD.
TELL ALL YOUR *FRIENDS...*

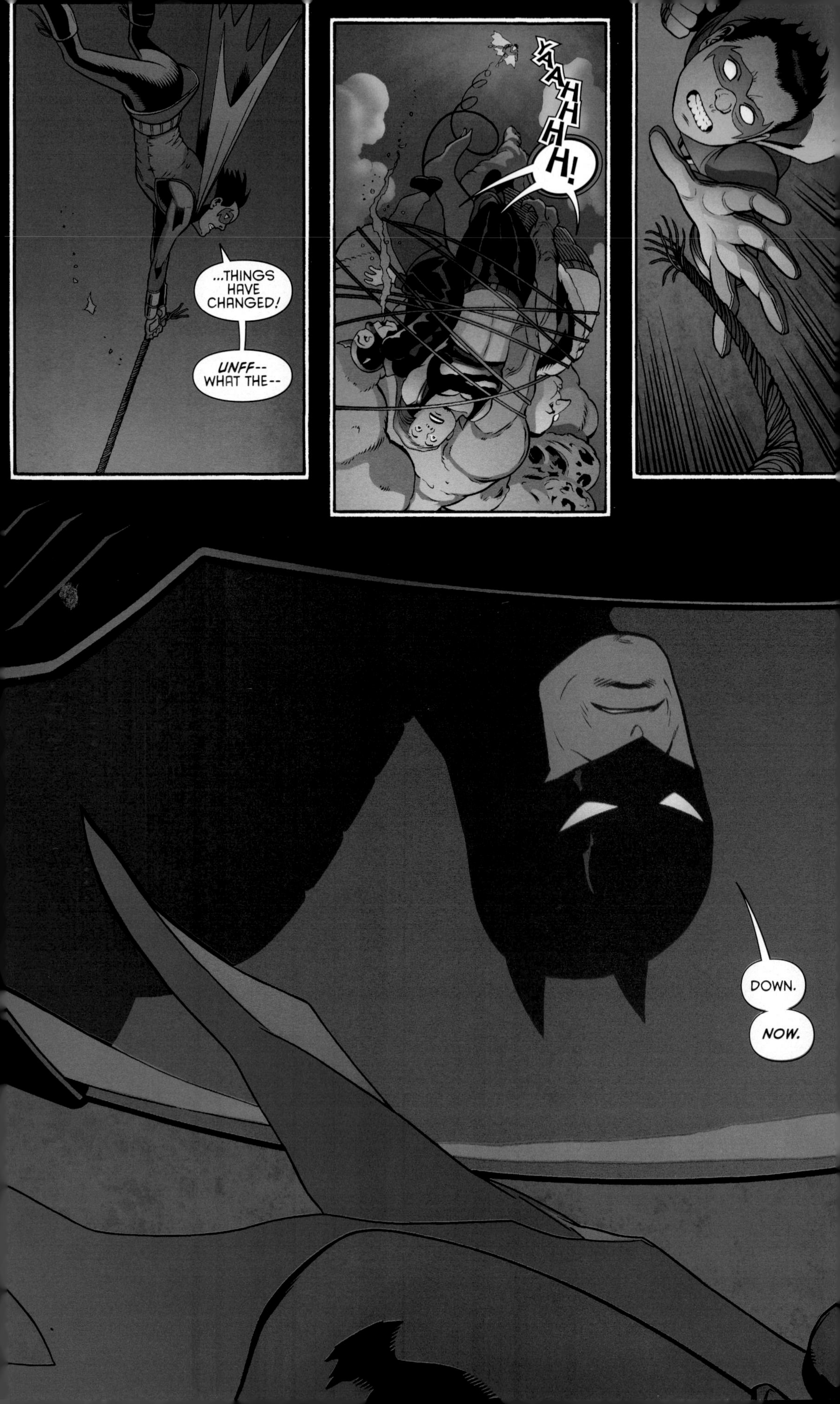

...THINGS HAVE CHANGED!
UNFF-- WHAT THE--
YAAHHHH!
DOWN.
NOW.

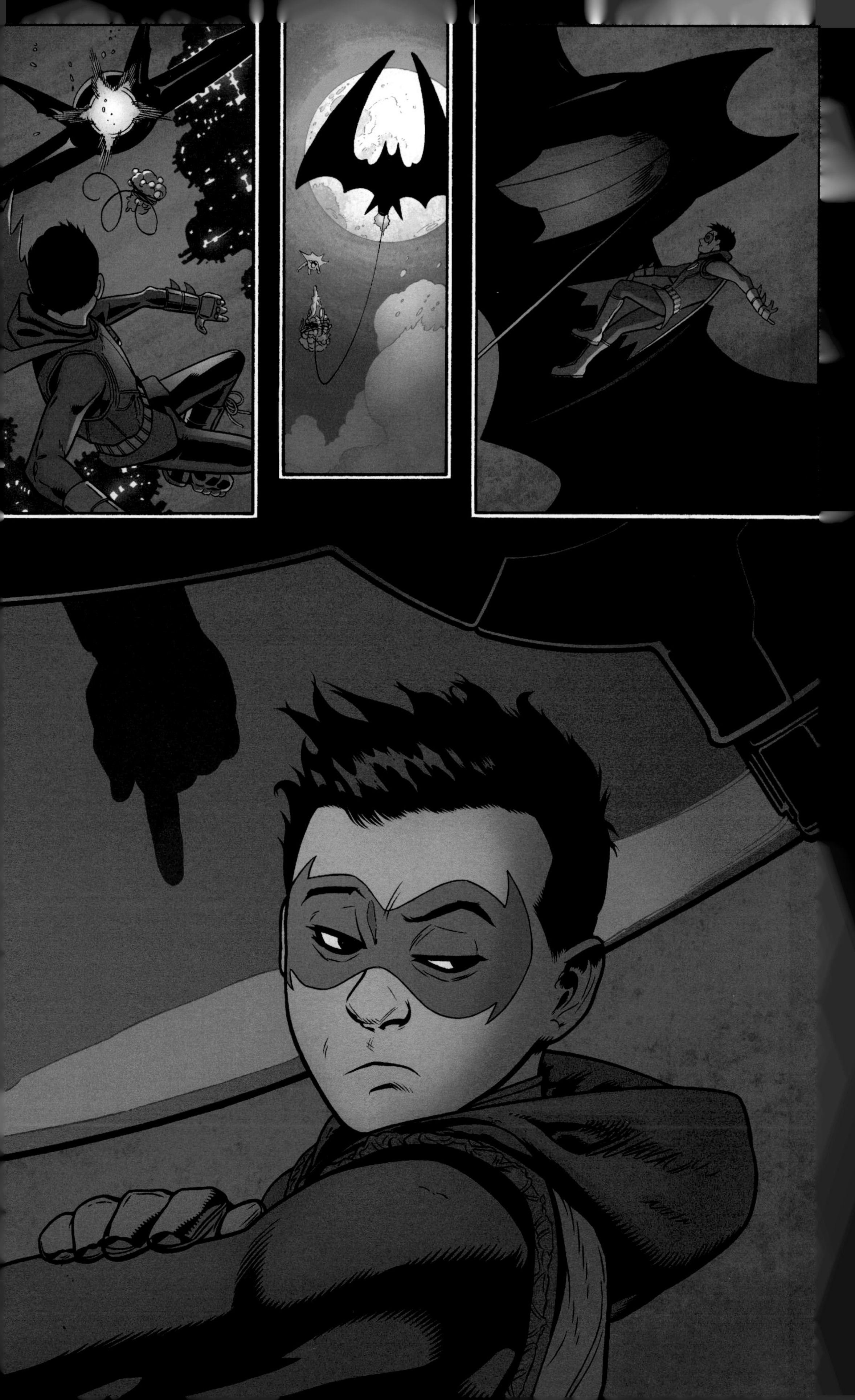

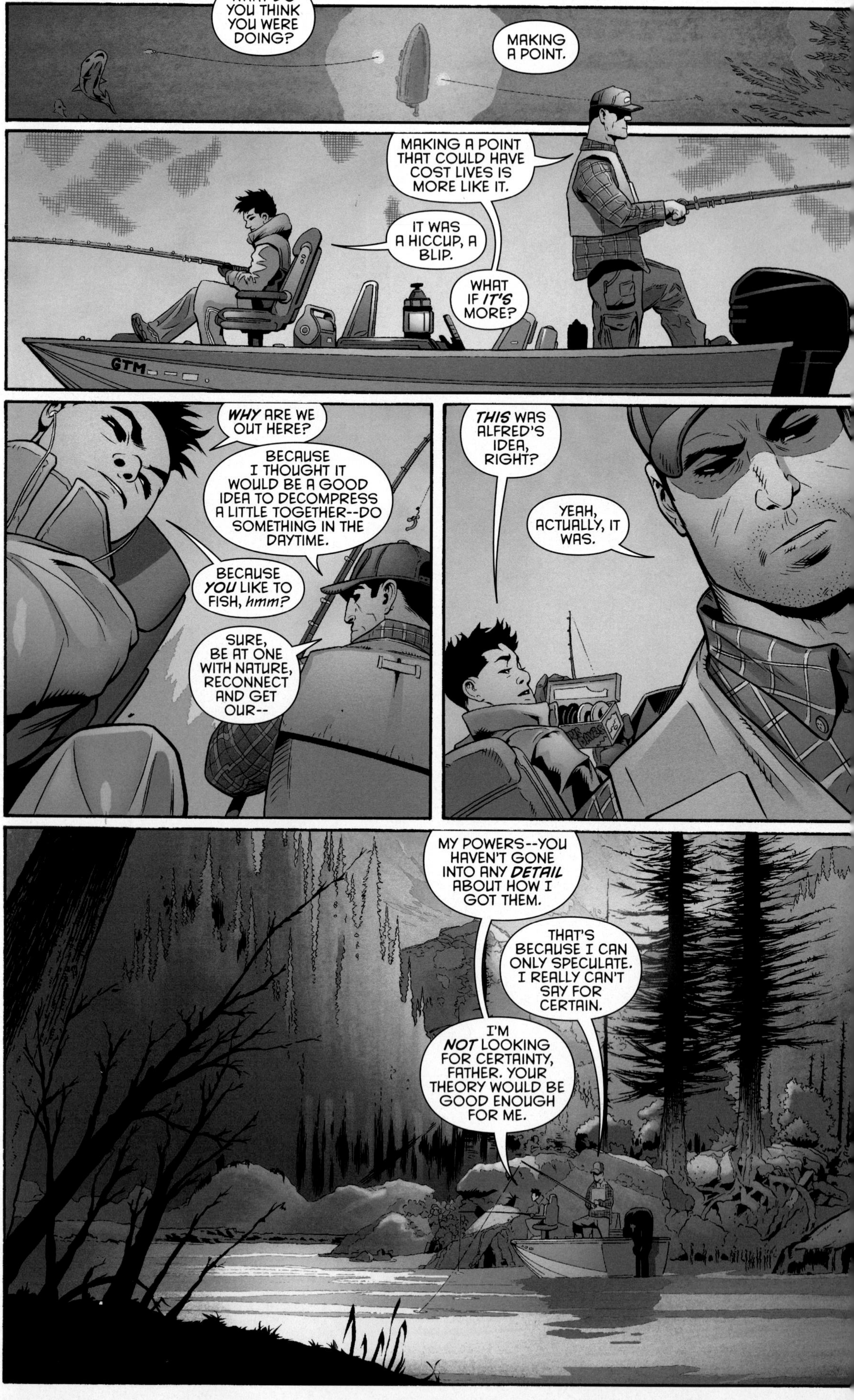
WHAT DO YOU THINK YOU WERE DOING?
MAKING A POINT.
MAKING A POINT THAT COULD HAVE COST LIVES IS MORE LIKE IT.
IT WAS A HICCUP, A BLIP.
WHAT IF IT'S MORE?
GTM
WHY ARE WE OUT HERE?
BECAUSE I THOUGHT IT WOULD BE A GOOD IDEA TO DECOMPRESS A LITTLE TOGETHER--DO SOMETHING IN THE DAYTIME.
BECAUSE YOU LIKE TO FISH, hmm?
SURE, BE AT ONE WITH NATURE, RECONNECT AND GET OUR--
THIS WAS ALFRED'S IDEA, RIGHT?
YEAH, ACTUALLY, IT WAS.
MY POWERS--YOU HAVEN'T GONE INTO ANY DETAIL ABOUT HOW I GOT THEM.
THAT'S BECAUSE I CAN ONLY SPECULATE. I REALLY CAN'T SAY FOR CERTAIN.
I'M NOT LOOKING FOR CERTAINTY, FATHER. YOUR THEORY WOULD BE GOOD ENOUGH FOR ME.

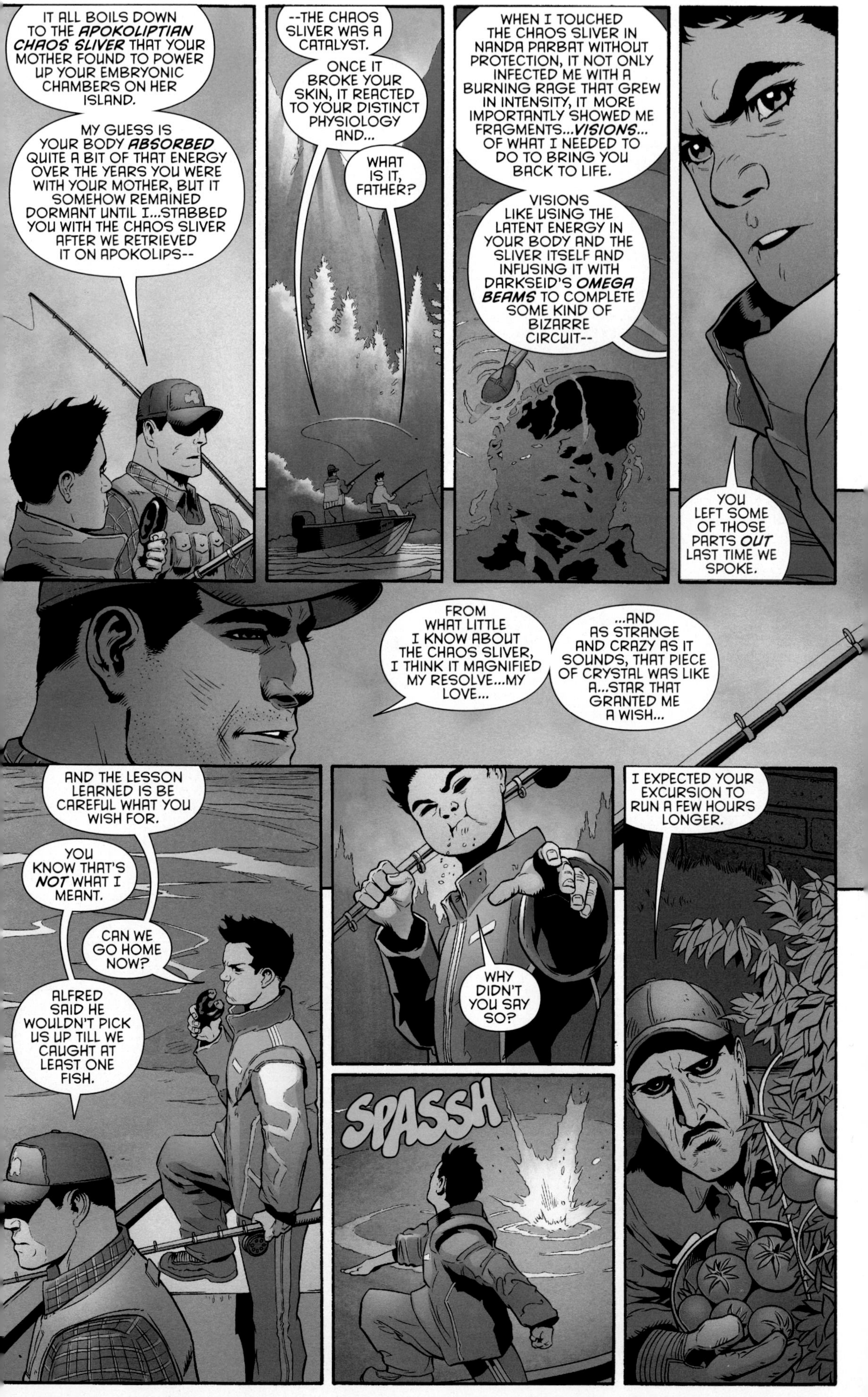
IT ALL BOILS DOWN TO THE APOKOLIPTIAN CHAOS SLIVER THAT YOUR MOTHER FOUND TO POWER UP YOUR EMBRYONIC CHAMBERS ON HER ISLAND.
MY GUESS IS YOUR BODY ABSORBED QUITE A BIT OF THAT ENERGY OVER THE YEARS YOU WERE WITH YOUR MOTHER, BUT IT SOMEHOW REMAINED DORMANT UNTIL I...STABBED YOU WITH THE CHAOS SLIVER AFTER WE RETRIEVED IT ON APOKOLIPS--
--THE CHAOS SLIVER WAS A CATALYST.
ONCE IT BROKE YOUR SKIN, IT REACTED TO YOUR DISTINCT PHYSIOLOGY AND...
WHAT IS IT, FATHER?
WHEN I TOUCHED THE CHAOS SLIVER IN NANDA PARBAT WITHOUT PROTECTION, IT NOT ONLY INFECTED ME WITH A BURNING RAGE THAT GREW IN INTENSITY, IT MORE IMPORTANTLY SHOWED ME FRAGMENTS...VISIONS...OF WHAT I NEEDED TO DO TO BRING YOU BACK TO LIFE.
VISIONS LIKE USING THE LATENT ENERGY IN YOUR BODY AND THE SLIVER ITSELF AND INFUSING IT WITH DARKSEID'S OMEGA BEAMS TO COMPLETE SOME KIND OF BIZARRE CIRCUIT--
YOU LEFT SOME OF THOSE PARTS OUT LAST TIME WE SPOKE.
FROM WHAT LITTLE I KNOW ABOUT THE CHAOS SLIVER, I THINK IT MAGNIFIED MY RESOLVE...MY LOVE...
...AND AS STRANGE AND CRAZY AS IT SOUNDS, THAT PIECE OF CRYSTAL WAS LIKE A...STAR THAT GRANTED ME A WISH...
AND THE LESSON LEARNED IS BE CAREFUL WHAT YOU WISH FOR.
YOU KNOW THAT'S NOT WHAT I MEANT.
CAN WE GO HOME NOW?
ALFRED SAID HE WOULDN'T PICK US UP TILL WE CAUGHT AT LEAST ONE FISH.
WHY DIDN'T YOU SAY SO?
SPASSH
I EXPECTED YOUR EXCURSION TO RUN A FEW HOURS LONGER.

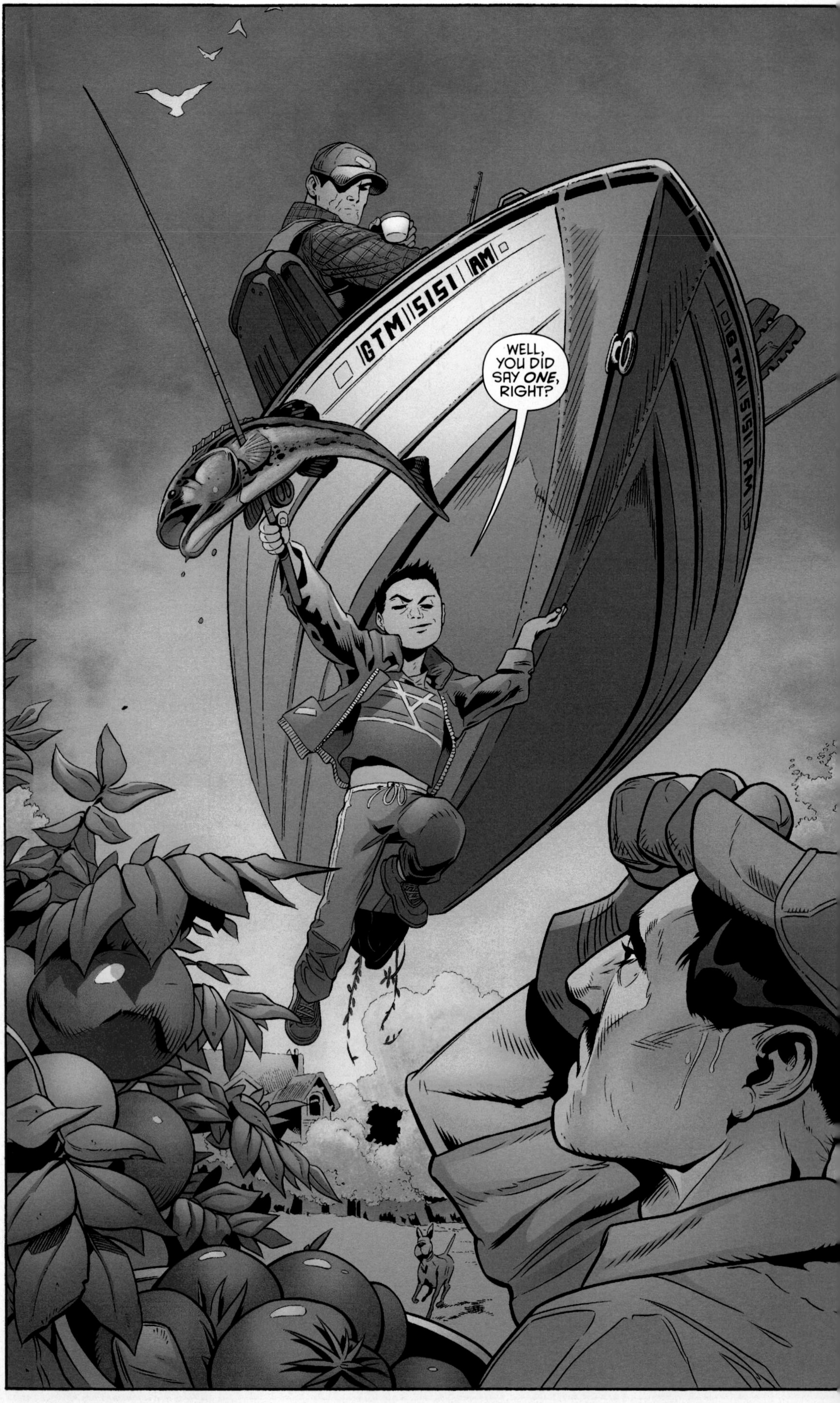
WELL, YOU DID SAY ONE, RIGHT?
GTM 5151 AM

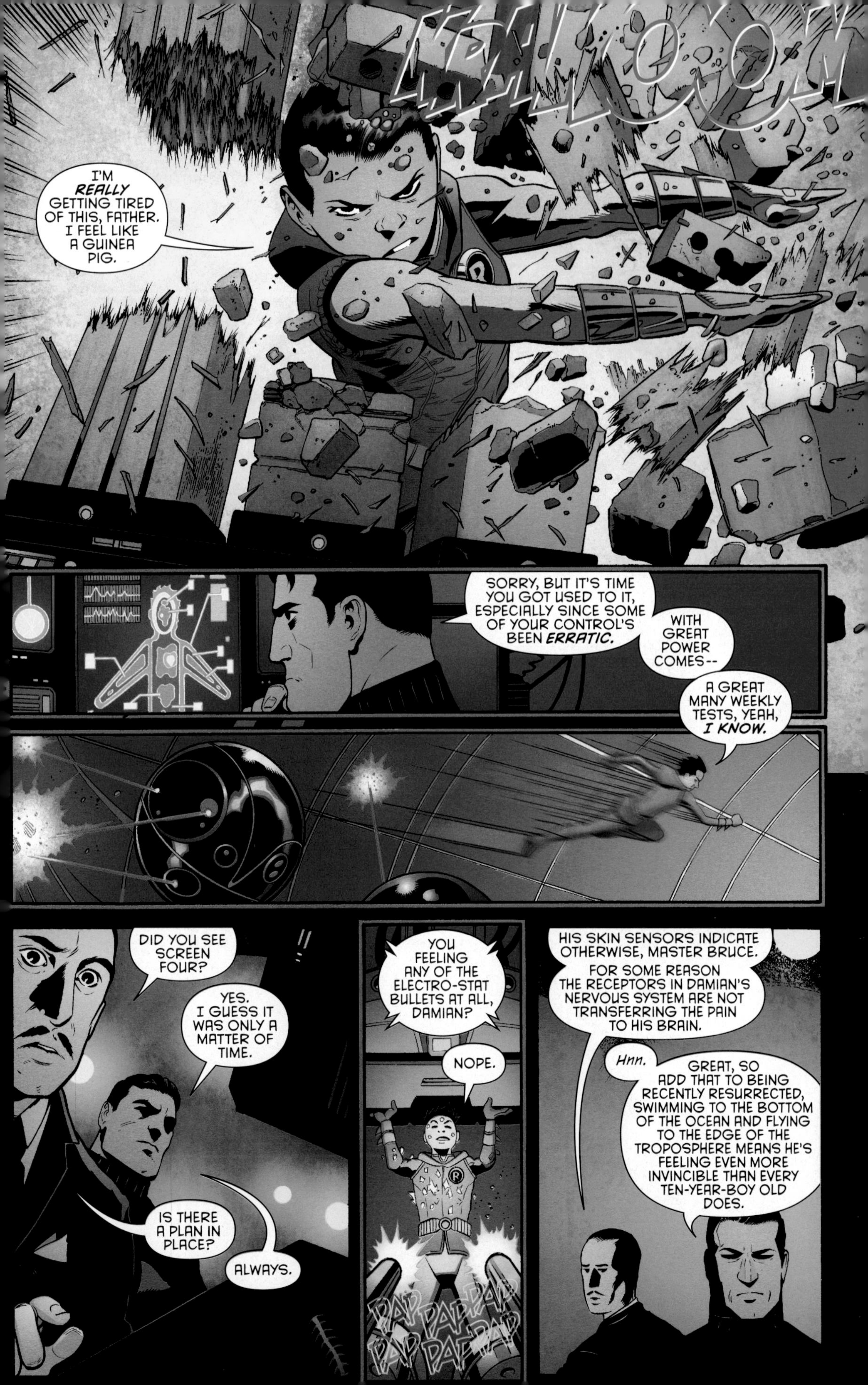
I'M *REALLY* GETTING TIRED OF THIS, FATHER. I FEEL LIKE A GUINEA PIG.
SORRY, BUT IT'S TIME YOU GOT USED TO IT, ESPECIALLY SINCE SOME OF YOUR CONTROL'S BEEN *ERRATIC.*
WITH GREAT POWER COMES--
A GREAT MANY WEEKLY TESTS, YEAH, *I KNOW.*
DID YOU SEE SCREEN FOUR?
YES. I GUESS IT WAS ONLY A MATTER OF TIME.
IS THERE A PLAN IN PLACE?
ALWAYS.
YOU FEELING ANY OF THE ELECTRO-STAT BULLETS AT ALL, DAMIAN?
NOPE.
PAP PAP PAP
PAP PAP PAP
HIS SKIN SENSORS INDICATE OTHERWISE, MASTER BRUCE.
FOR SOME REASON THE RECEPTORS IN DAMIAN'S NERVOUS SYSTEM ARE NOT TRANSFERRING THE PAIN TO HIS BRAIN.
Hnn.
GREAT, SO ADD THAT TO BEING RECENTLY RESURRECTED, SWIMMING TO THE BOTTOM OF THE OCEAN AND FLYING TO THE EDGE OF THE TROPOSPHERE MEANS HE'S FEELING EVEN MORE INVINCIBLE THAN EVERY TEN-YEAR-BOY OLD DOES.

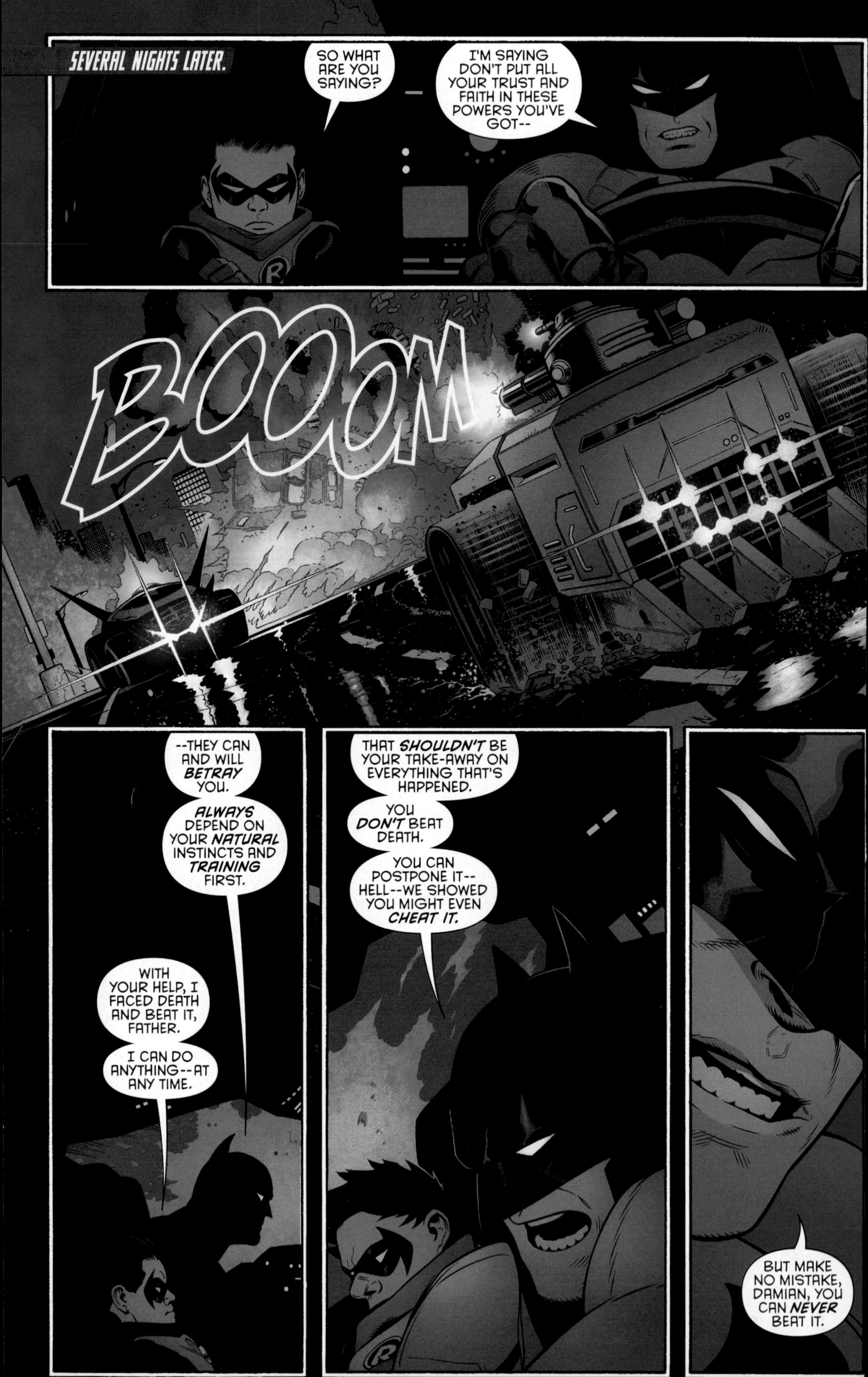
SEVERAL NIGHTS LATER.
SO WHAT ARE YOU SAYING?
I'M SAYING DON'T PUT ALL YOUR TRUST AND FAITH IN THESE POWERS YOU'VE GOT--
BOOOM
--THEY CAN AND WILL BETRAY YOU.
ALWAYS DEPEND ON YOUR NATURAL INSTINCTS AND TRAINING FIRST.
WITH YOUR HELP, I FACED DEATH AND BEAT IT, FATHER.
I CAN DO ANYTHING--AT ANY TIME.
THAT SHOULDN'T BE YOUR TAKE-AWAY ON EVERYTHING THAT'S HAPPENED.
YOU DON'T BEAT DEATH.
YOU CAN POSTPONE IT--HELL--WE SHOWED YOU MIGHT EVEN CHEAT IT.
BUT MAKE NO MISTAKE, DAMIAN, YOU CAN NEVER BEAT IT.

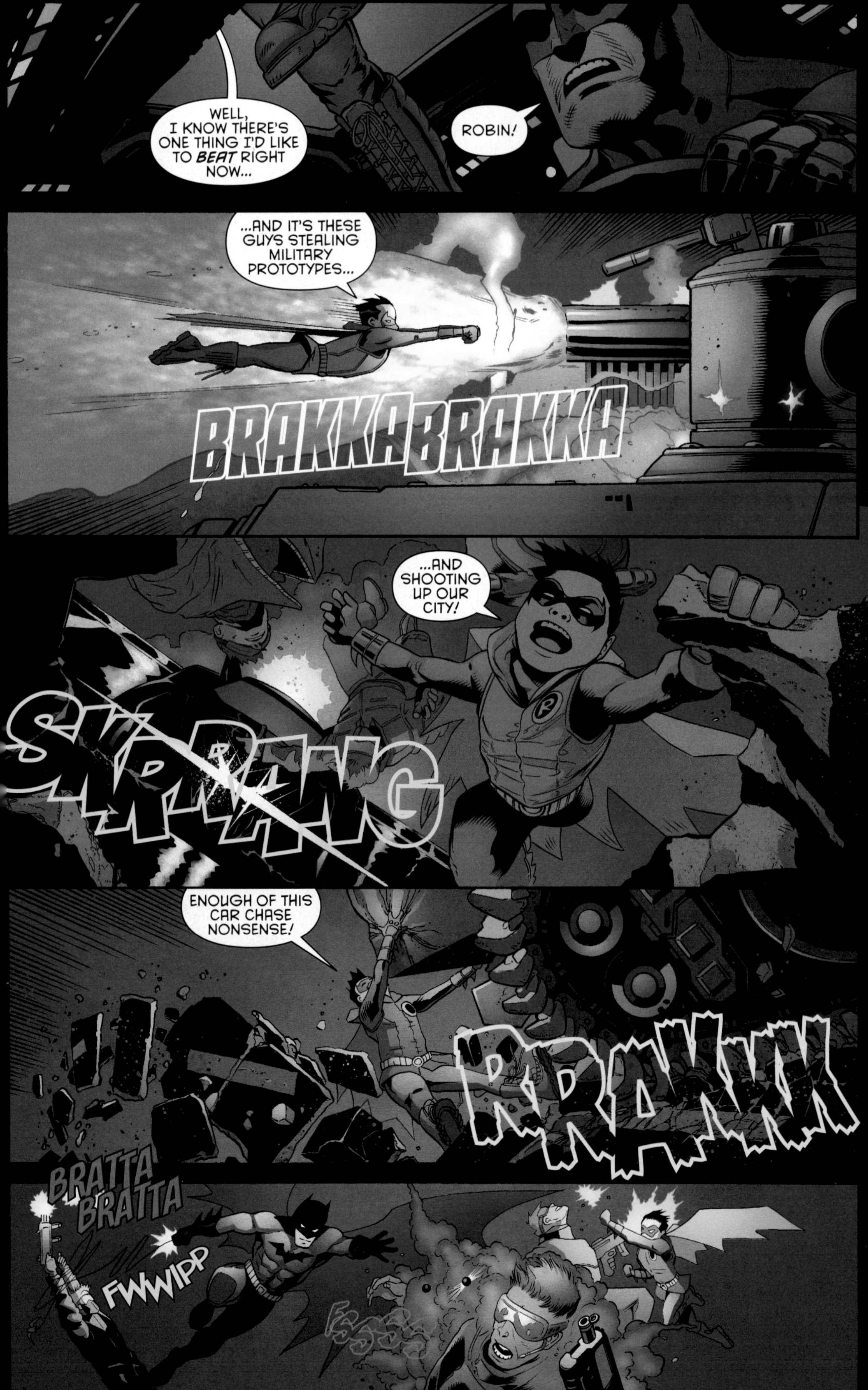
WELL, I KNOW THERE'S ONE THING I'D LIKE TO BEAT RIGHT NOW...
ROBIN!
...AND IT'S THESE GUYS STEALING MILITARY PROTOTYPES...
BRAKKA BRAKKA
...AND SHOOTING UP OUR CITY!
SKRANG
ENOUGH OF THIS CAR CHASE NONSENSE!
RRAKKK
BRATTA BRATTA
FWWIPP

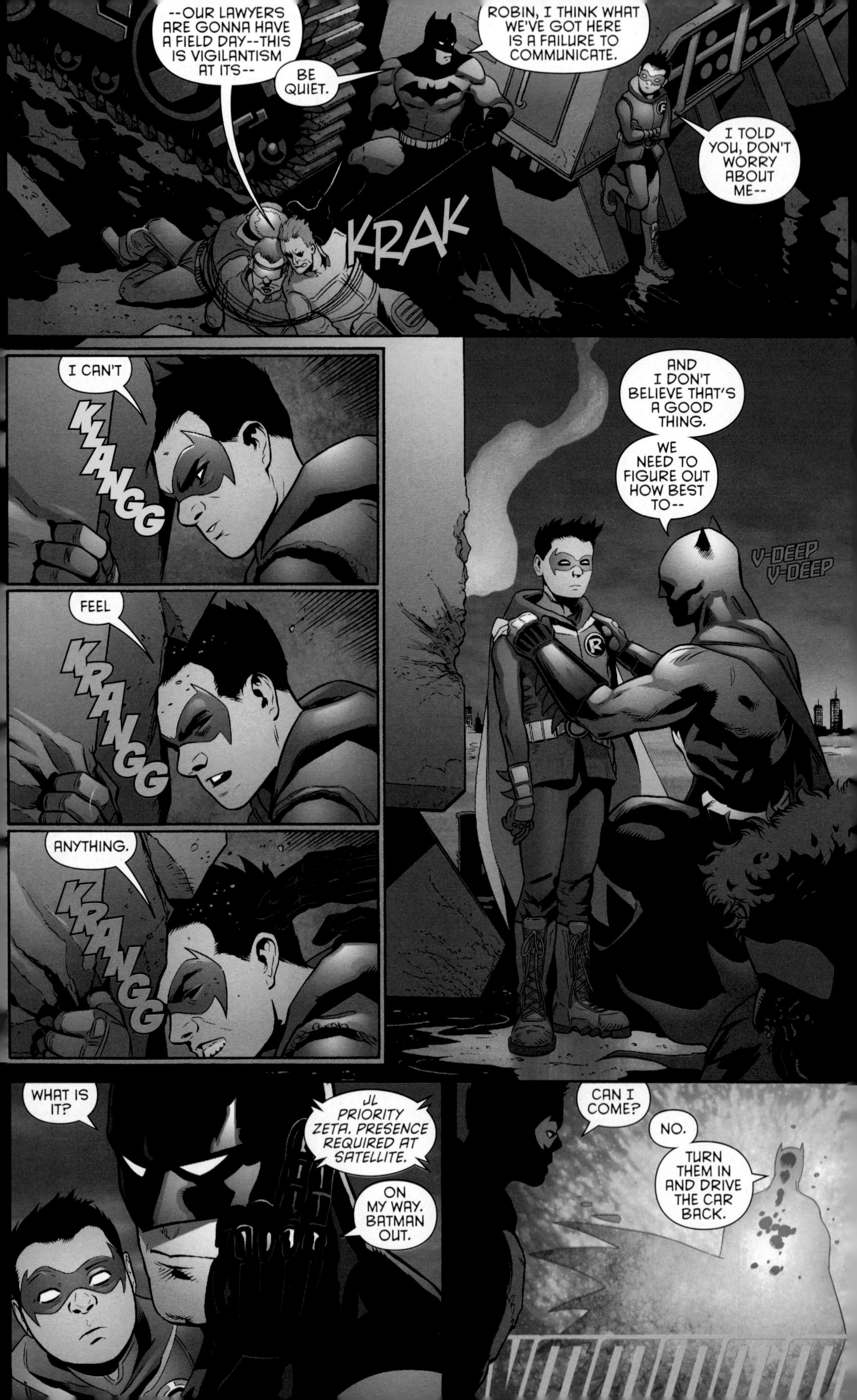
--OUR LAWYERS ARE GONNA HAVE A FIELD DAY--THIS IS VIGILANTISM AT ITS--
BE QUIET.
ROBIN, I THINK WHAT WE'VE GOT HERE IS A FAILURE TO COMMUNICATE.
I TOLD YOU, DON'T WORRY ABOUT ME--
KRAK
I CAN'T
KLANGG
FEEL
KRANGG
ANYTHING.
KRANGG
AND I DON'T BELIEVE THAT'S A GOOD THING.
WE NEED TO FIGURE OUT HOW BEST TO--
V-DEEP V-DEEP
WHAT IS IT?
JL PRIORITY ZETA. PRESENCE REQUIRED AT SATELLITE.
ON MY WAY. BATMAN OUT.
CAN I COME?
NO.
TURN THEM IN AND DRIVE THE CAR BACK.

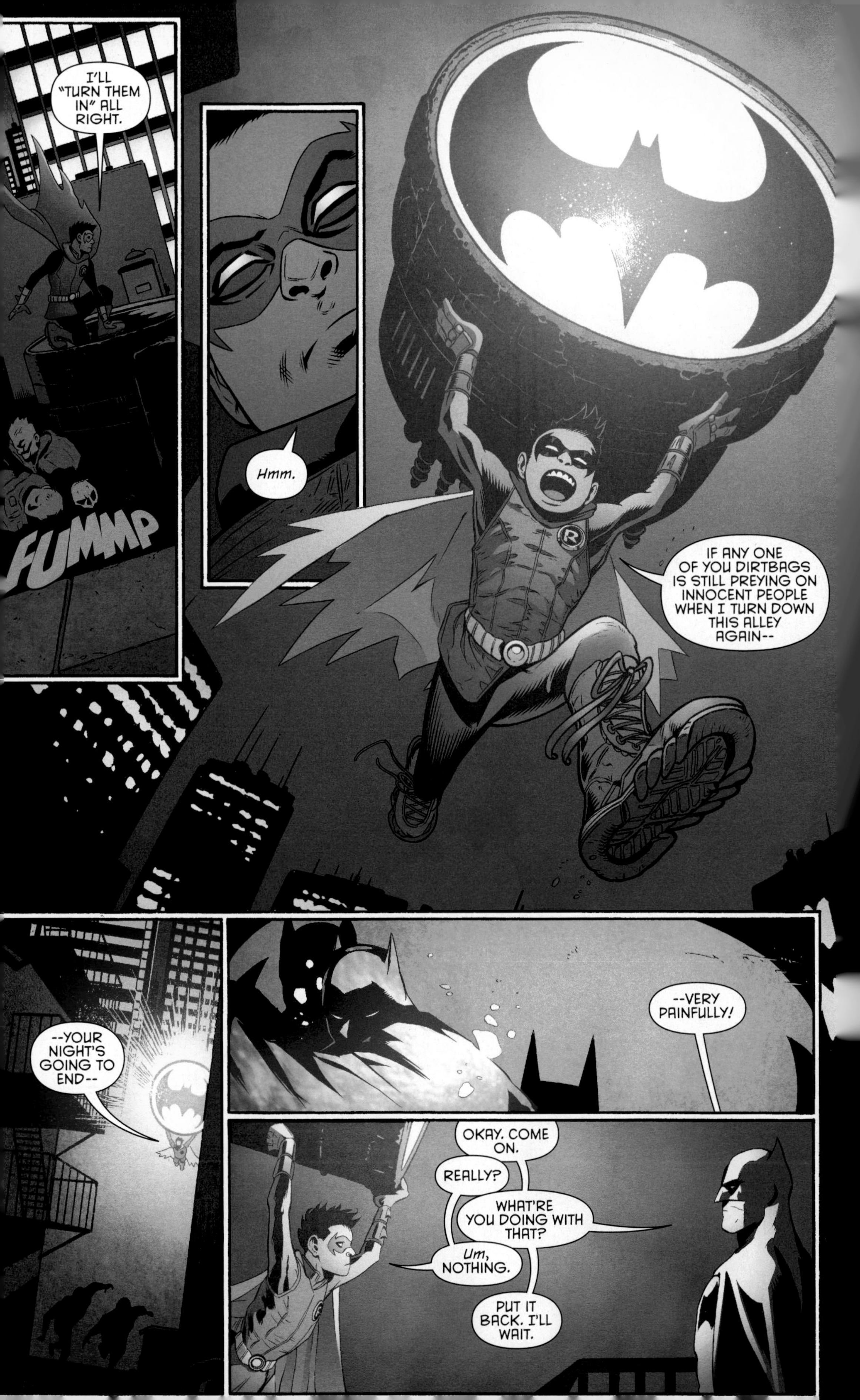
I'LL "TURN THEM IN" ALL RIGHT.
FUMMP
Hmm.
IF ANY ONE OF YOU DIRTBAGS IS STILL PREYING ON INNOCENT PEOPLE WHEN I TURN DOWN THIS ALLEY AGAIN--
--YOUR NIGHT'S GOING TO END--
--VERY PAINFULLY!
OKAY. COME ON.
REALLY?
WHAT'RE YOU DOING WITH THAT?
Um, NOTHING.
PUT IT BACK. I'LL WAIT.

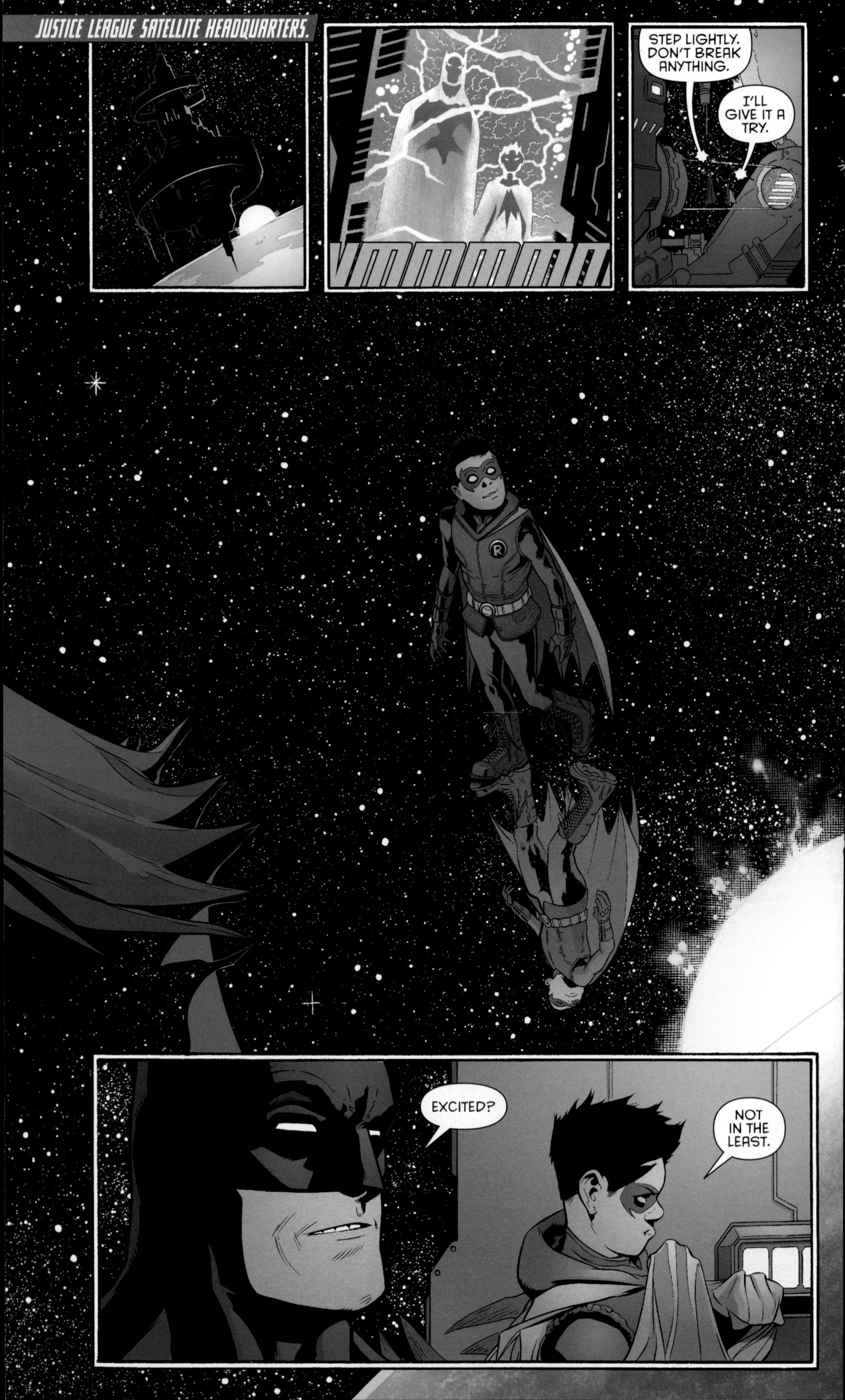

JUSTICE LEAGUE SATELLITE HEADQUARTERS.
VMMMMMN
STEP LIGHTLY. DON'T BREAK ANYTHING.
I'LL GIVE IT A TRY.
EXCITED?
NOT IN THE LEAST.

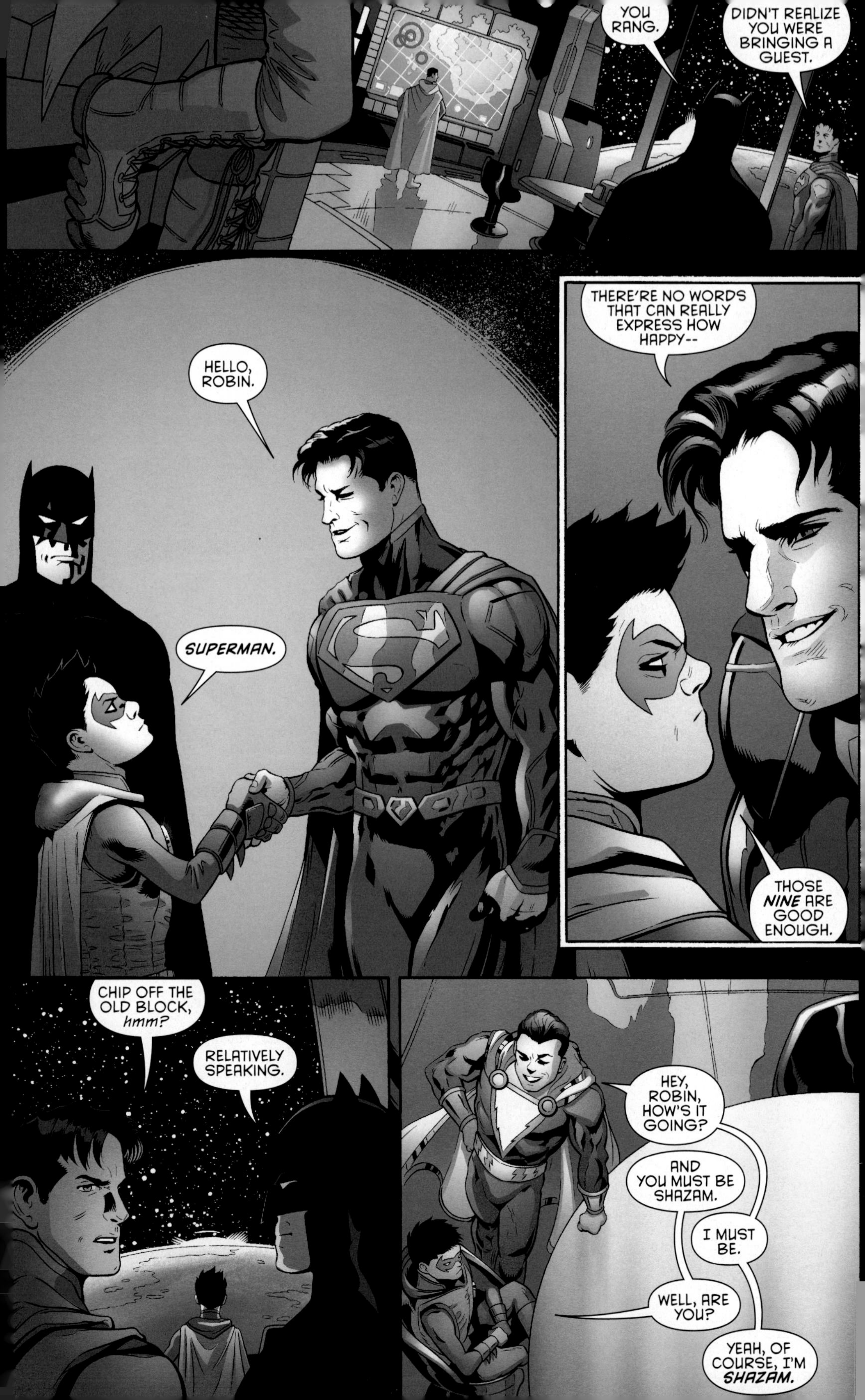
YOU RANG.
DIDN'T REALIZE YOU WERE BRINGING A GUEST.
HELLO, ROBIN.
SUPERMAN.
THERE'RE NO WORDS THAT CAN REALLY EXPRESS HOW HAPPY--
THOSE NINE ARE GOOD ENOUGH.
CHIP OFF THE OLD BLOCK, hmm?
RELATIVELY SPEAKING.
HEY, ROBIN, HOW'S IT GOING?
AND YOU MUST BE SHAZAM.
I MUST BE.
WELL, ARE YOU?
YEAH, OF COURSE, I'M SHAZAM.

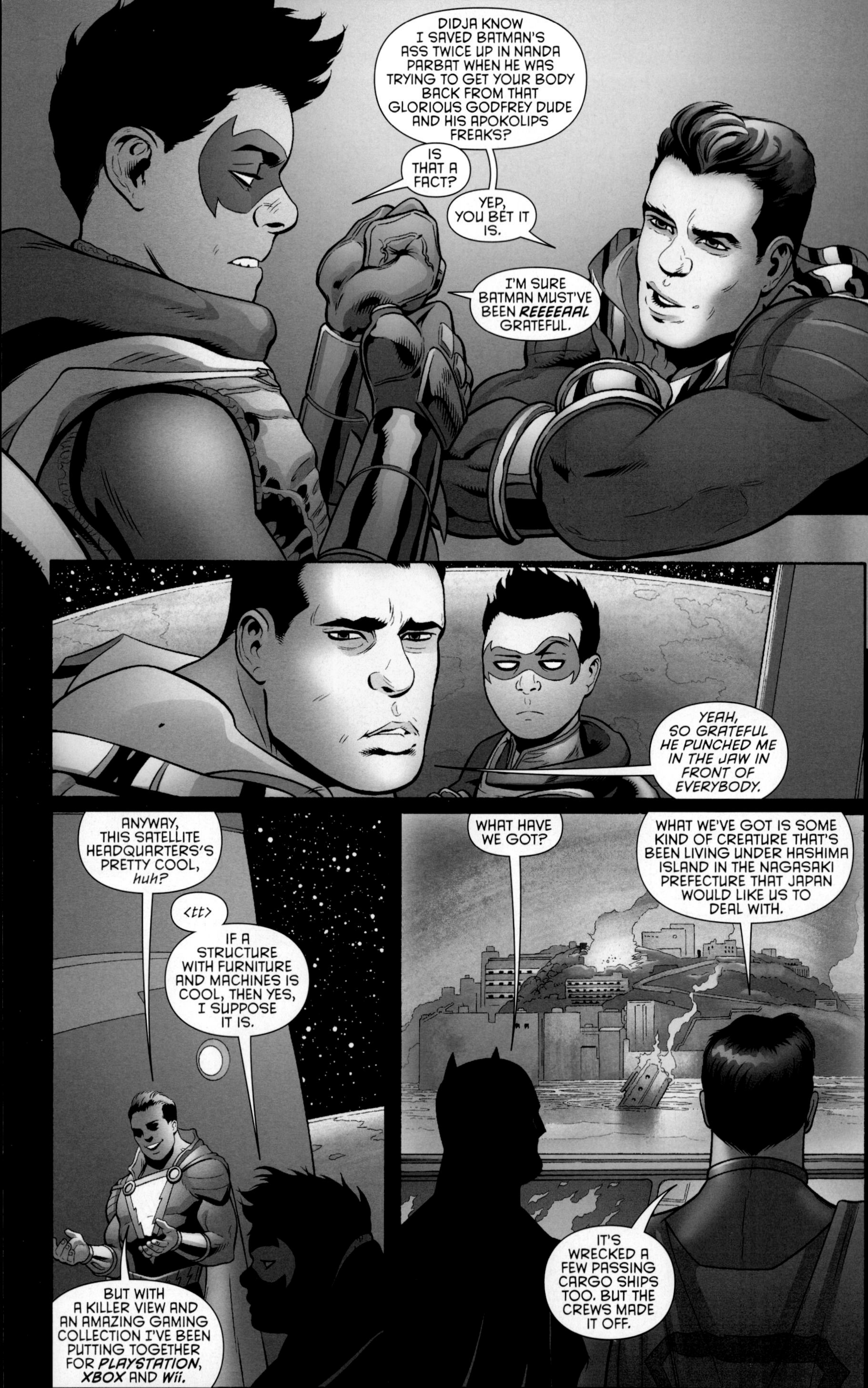
DIDJA KNOW I SAVED BATMAN'S ASS TWICE UP IN NANDA PARBAT WHEN HE WAS TRYING TO GET YOUR BODY BACK FROM THAT GLORIOUS GODFREY DUDE AND HIS APOKOLIPS FREAKS?
IS THAT A FACT?
YEP, YOU BET IT IS.
I'M SURE BATMAN MUST'VE BEEN ***REEEEAAL*** GRATEFUL.
YEAH, SO GRATEFUL HE PUNCHED ME IN THE JAW IN FRONT OF EVERYBODY.
ANYWAY, THIS SATELLITE HEADQUARTERS'S PRETTY COOL, *huh?*
<tt>
IF A STRUCTURE WITH FURNITURE AND MACHINES IS COOL, THEN YES, I SUPPOSE IT IS.
BUT WITH A KILLER VIEW AND AN AMAZING GAMING COLLECTION I'VE BEEN PUTTING TOGETHER FOR ***PLAYSTATION, XBOX*** AND ***Wii.***
WHAT HAVE WE GOT?
WHAT WE'VE GOT IS SOME KIND OF CREATURE THAT'S BEEN LIVING UNDER HASHIMA ISLAND IN THE NAGASAKI PREFECTURE THAT JAPAN WOULD LIKE US TO DEAL WITH.
IT'S WRECKED A FEW PASSING CARGO SHIPS TOO. BUT THE CREWS MADE IT OFF.

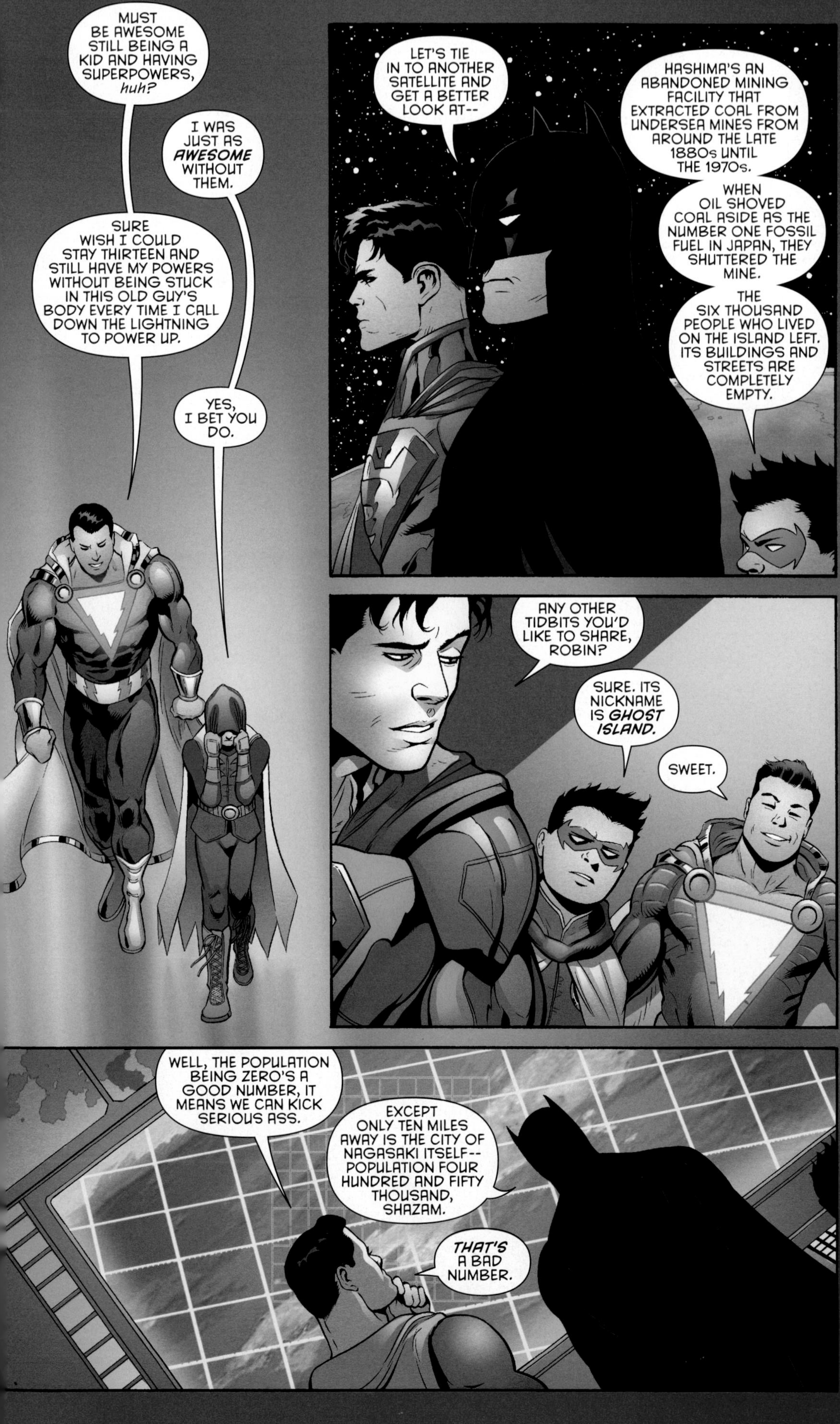
MUST BE AWESOME STILL BEING A KID AND HAVING SUPERPOWERS, *huh?*
I WAS JUST AS ***AWESOME*** WITHOUT THEM.
SURE WISH I COULD STAY THIRTEEN AND STILL HAVE MY POWERS WITHOUT BEING STUCK IN THIS OLD GUY'S BODY EVERY TIME I CALL DOWN THE LIGHTNING TO POWER UP.
YES, I BET YOU DO.
LET'S TIE IN TO ANOTHER SATELLITE AND GET A BETTER LOOK AT--
HASHIMA'S AN ABANDONED MINING FACILITY THAT EXTRACTED COAL FROM UNDERSEA MINES FROM AROUND THE LATE 1880s UNTIL THE 1970s.
WHEN OIL SHOVED COAL ASIDE AS THE NUMBER ONE FOSSIL FUEL IN JAPAN, THEY SHUTTERED THE MINE.
THE SIX THOUSAND PEOPLE WHO LIVED ON THE ISLAND LEFT. ITS BUILDINGS AND STREETS ARE COMPLETELY EMPTY.
ANY OTHER TIDBITS YOU'D LIKE TO SHARE, ROBIN?
SURE. ITS NICKNAME IS ***GHOST ISLAND.***
SWEET.
WELL, THE POPULATION BEING ZERO'S A GOOD NUMBER, IT MEANS WE CAN KICK SERIOUS ASS.
EXCEPT ONLY TEN MILES AWAY IS THE CITY OF NAGASAKI ITSELF--POPULATION FOUR HUNDRED AND FIFTY THOUSAND, SHAZAM.
THAT'S A BAD NUMBER.

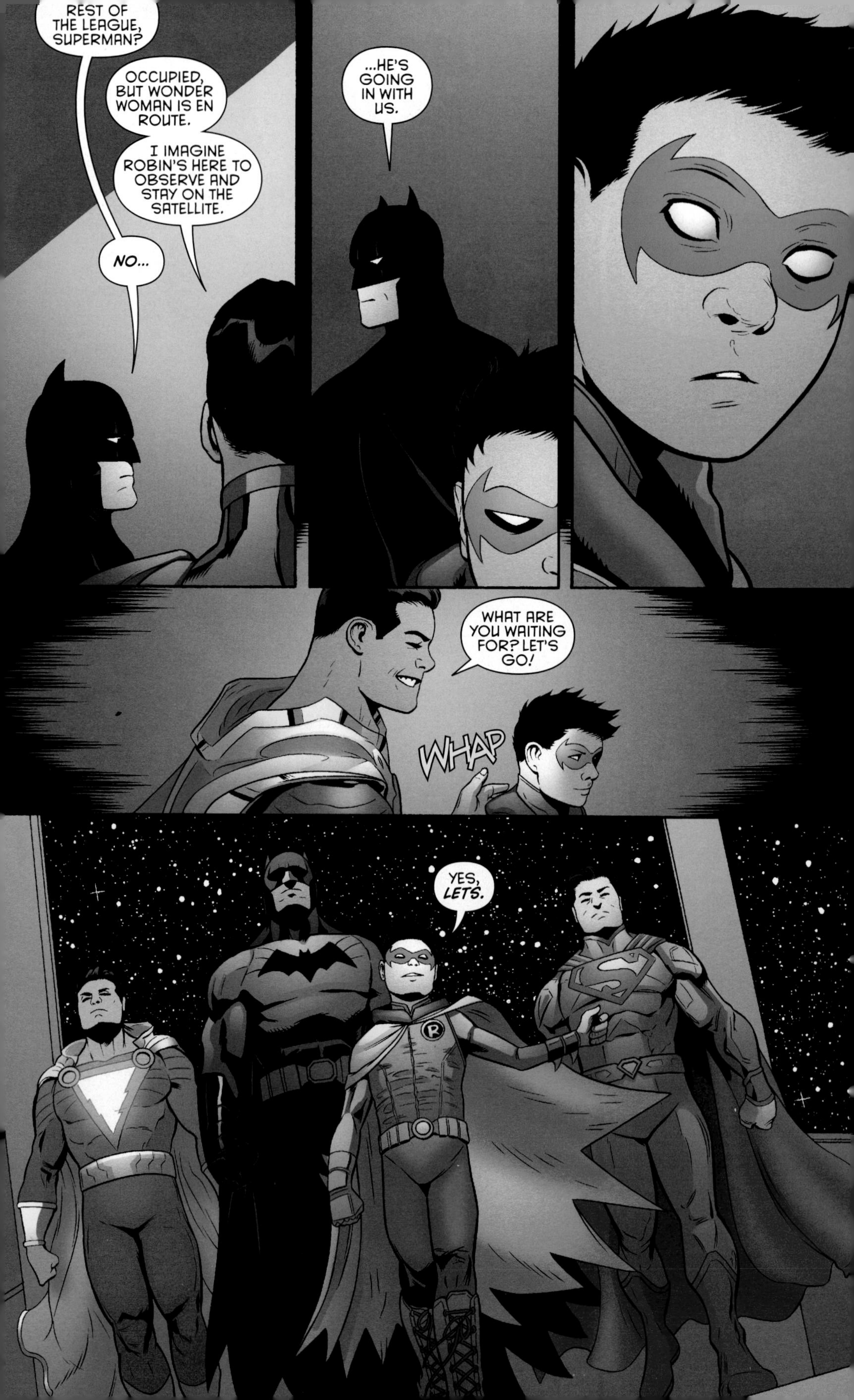

REST OF THE LEAGUE, SUPERMAN?
OCCUPIED, BUT WONDER WOMAN IS EN ROUTE.
I IMAGINE ROBIN'S HERE TO OBSERVE AND STAY ON THE SATELLITE.
NO...
...HE'S GOING IN WITH US.
WHAT ARE YOU WAITING FOR? LET'S GO!
WHAP
YES, LETS.

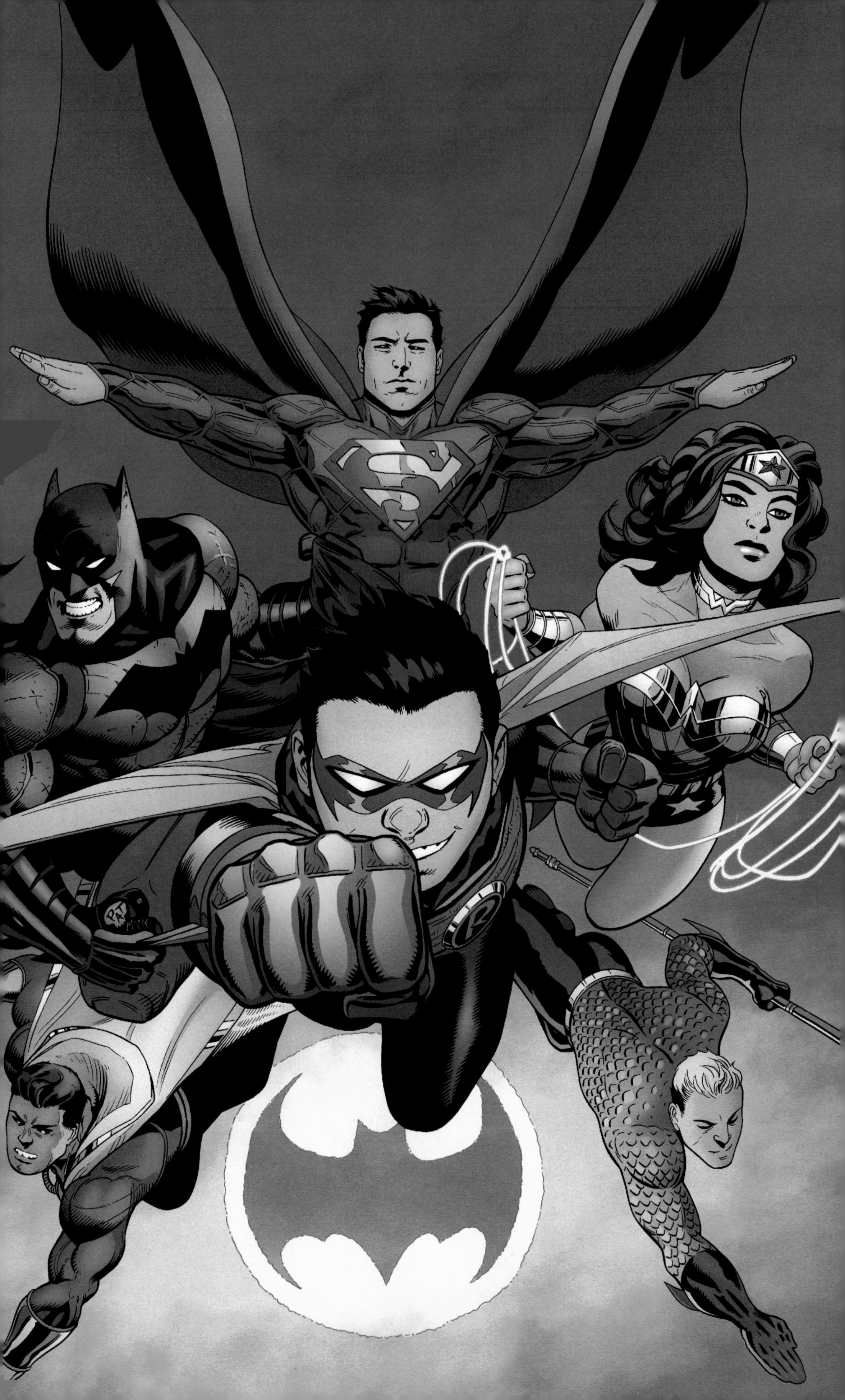

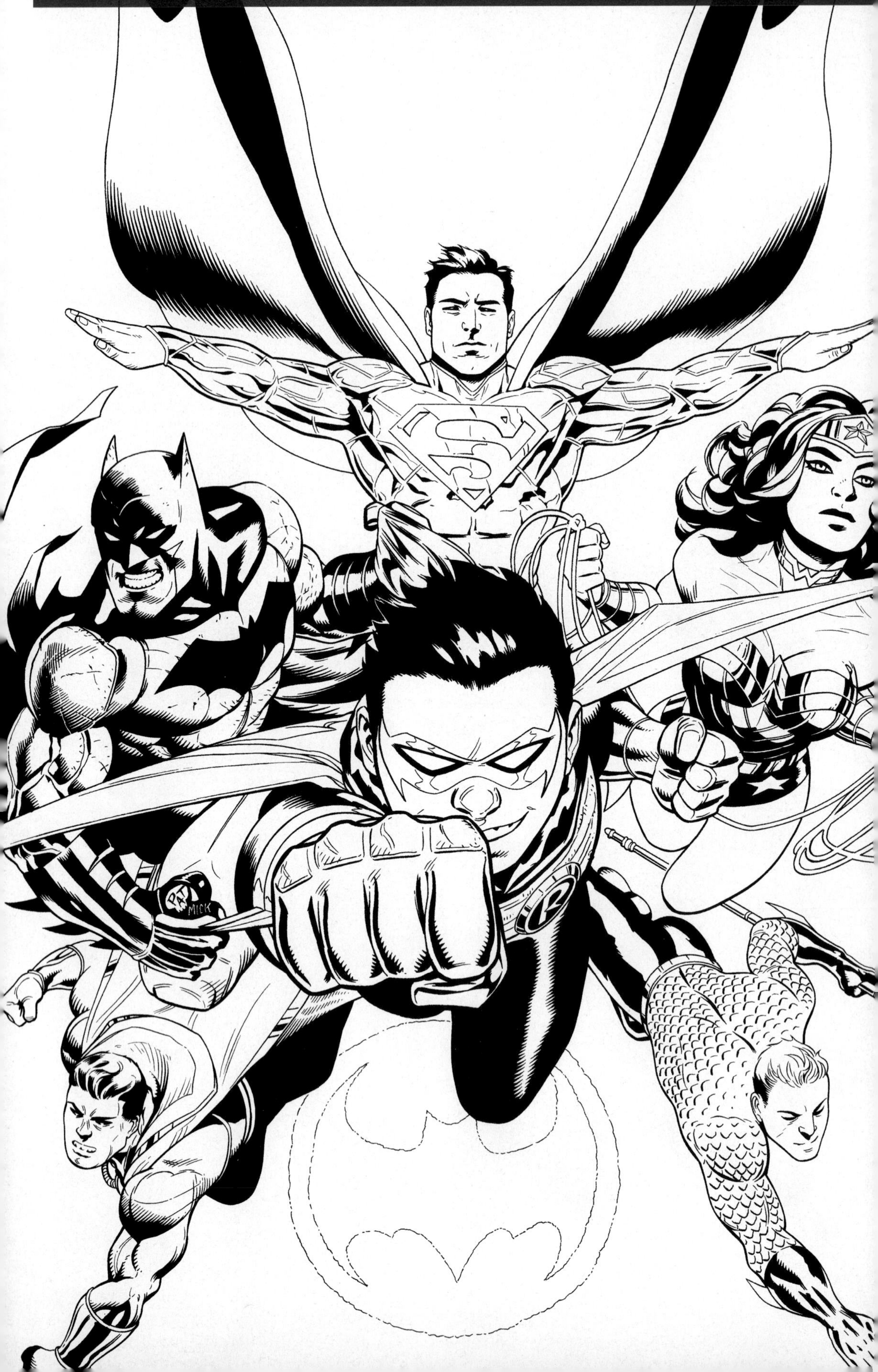
MICK

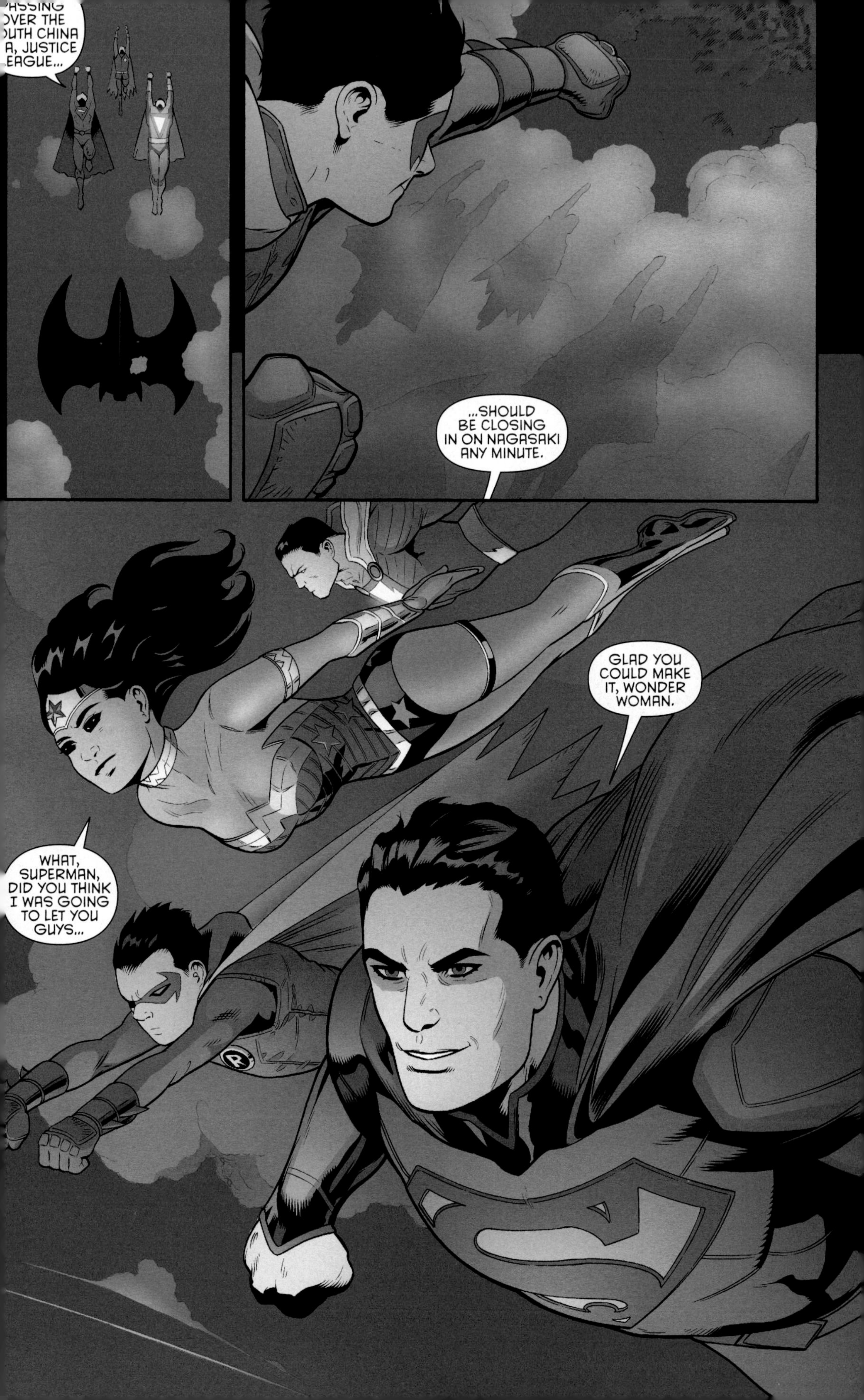
ASSING OVER THE UTH CHINA A, JUSTICE EAGUE...
...SHOULD BE CLOSING IN ON NAGASAKI ANY MINUTE.
GLAD YOU COULD MAKE IT, WONDER WOMAN.
WHAT, SUPERMAN, DID YOU THINK I WAS GOING TO LET YOU GUYS...

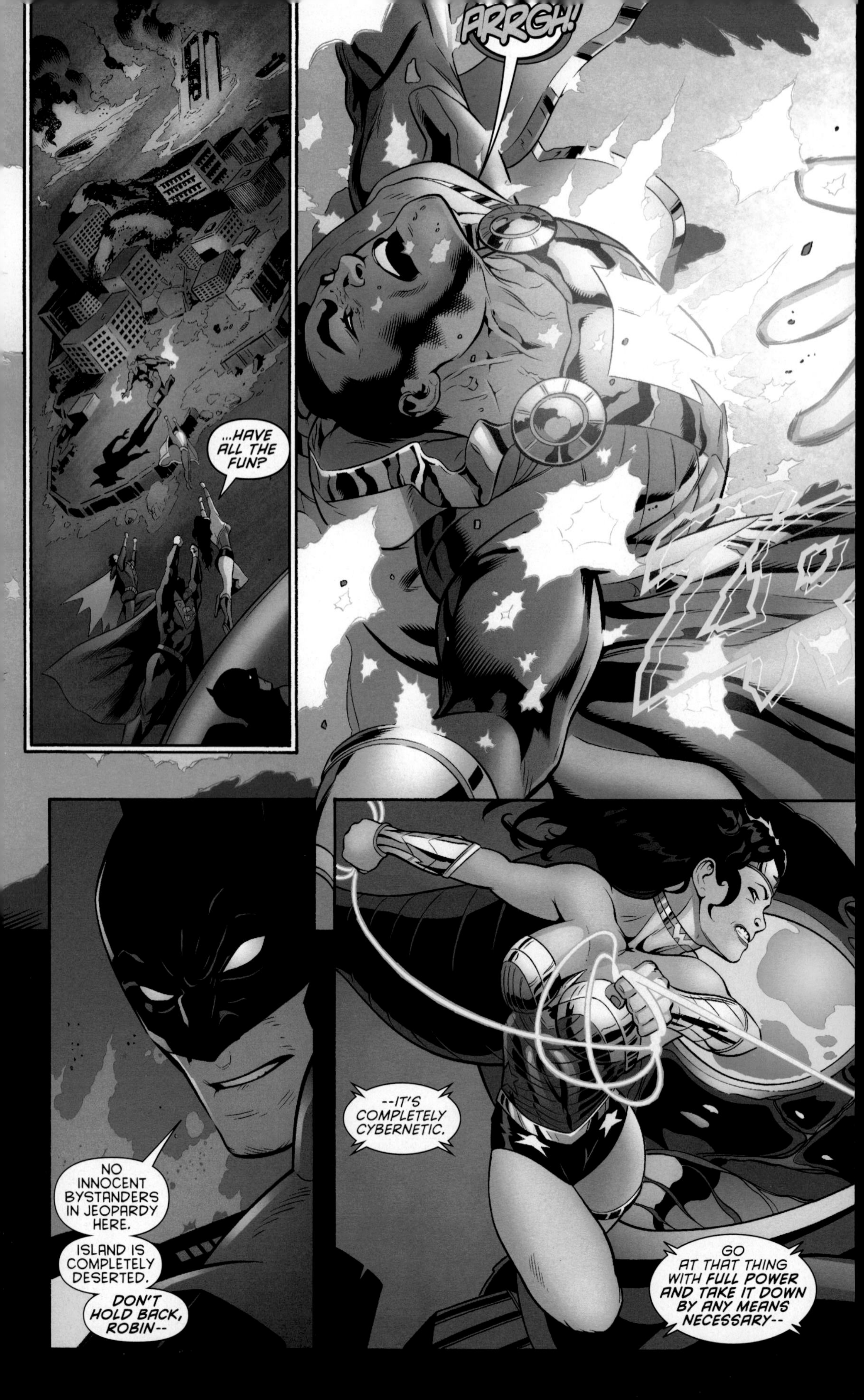
...HAVE ALL THE FUN?
ARRGH!
NO INNOCENT BYSTANDERS IN JEOPARDY HERE.
ISLAND IS COMPLETELY DESERTED.
DON'T HOLD BACK, ROBIN--
--IT'S COMPLETELY CYBERNETIC.
GO AT THAT THING WITH FULL POWER AND TAKE IT DOWN BY ANY MEANS NECESSARY--

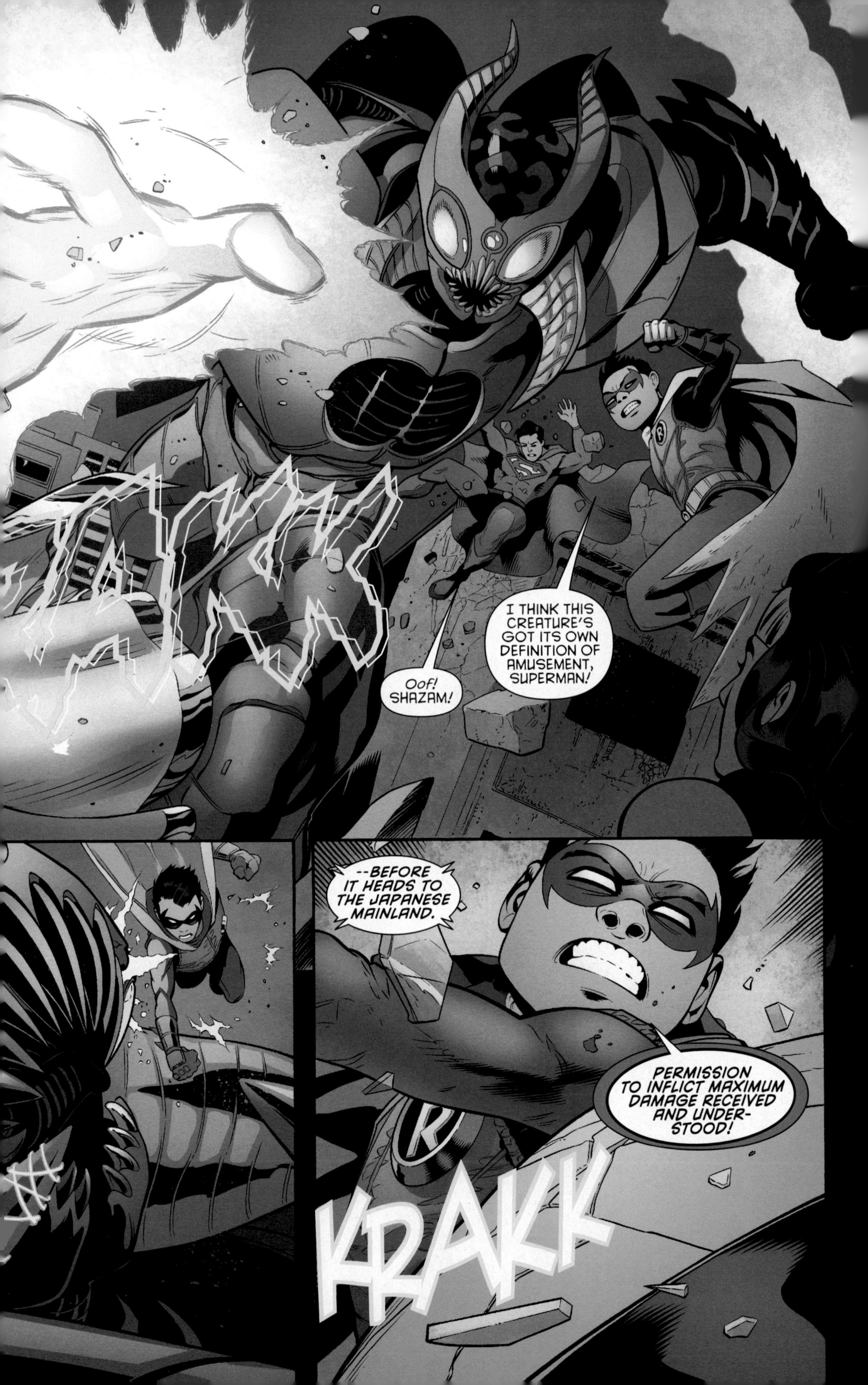
I THINK THIS CREATURE'S GOT ITS OWN DEFINITION OF AMUSEMENT, SUPERMAN!
Oof! SHAZAM!
--BEFORE IT HEADS TO THE JAPANESE MAINLAND.
PERMISSION TO INFLICT MAXIMUM DAMAGE RECEIVED AND UNDER-STOOD!
KRAKK

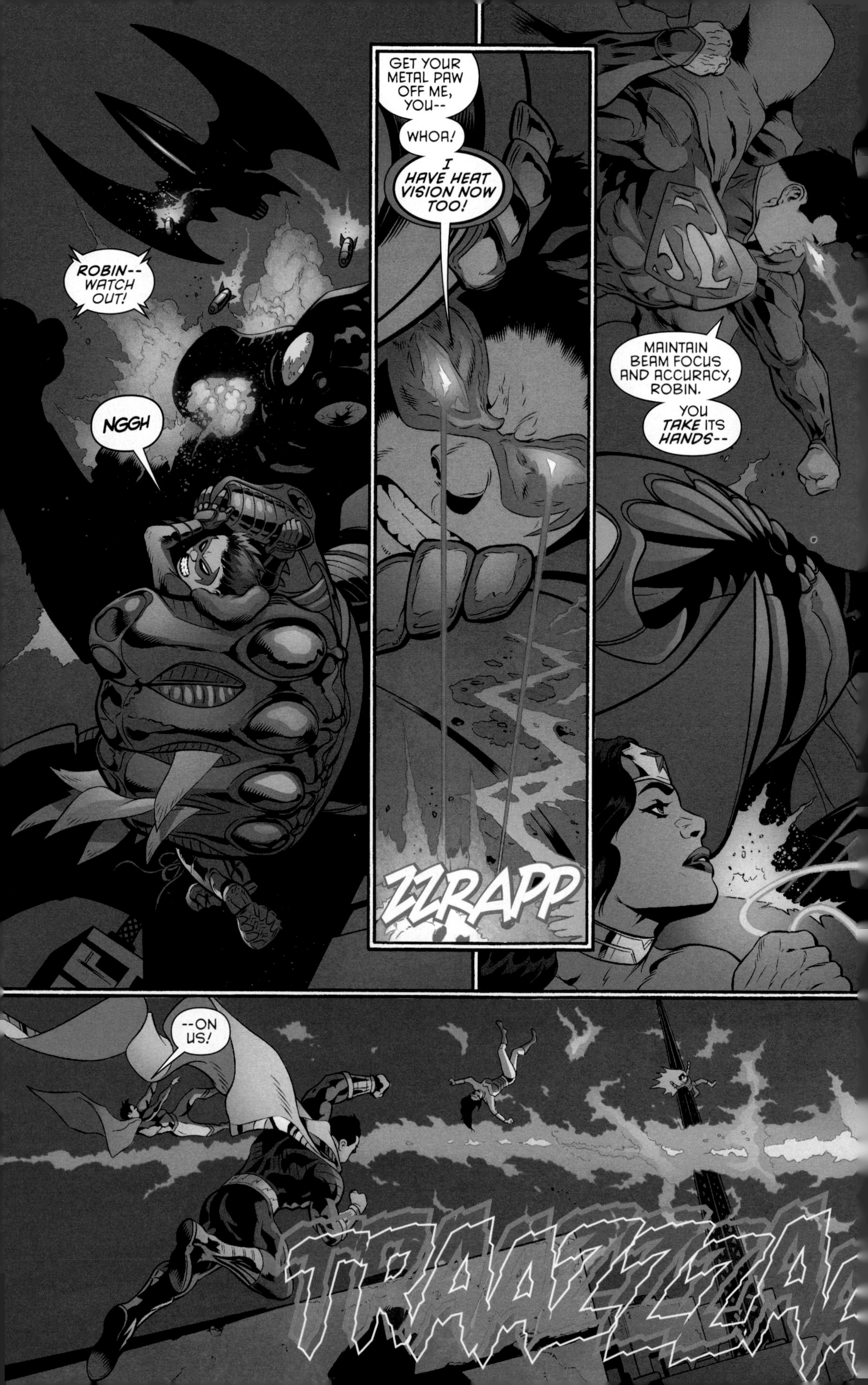
ROBIN-- WATCH OUT!
NGGH
GET YOUR METAL PAW OFF ME, YOU--
WHOA!
I HAVE HEAT VISION NOW TOO!
ZZRAPP
MAINTAIN BEAM FOCUS AND ACCURACY, ROBIN.
YOU TAKE ITS HANDS--
--ON US!
TRAAZZZA

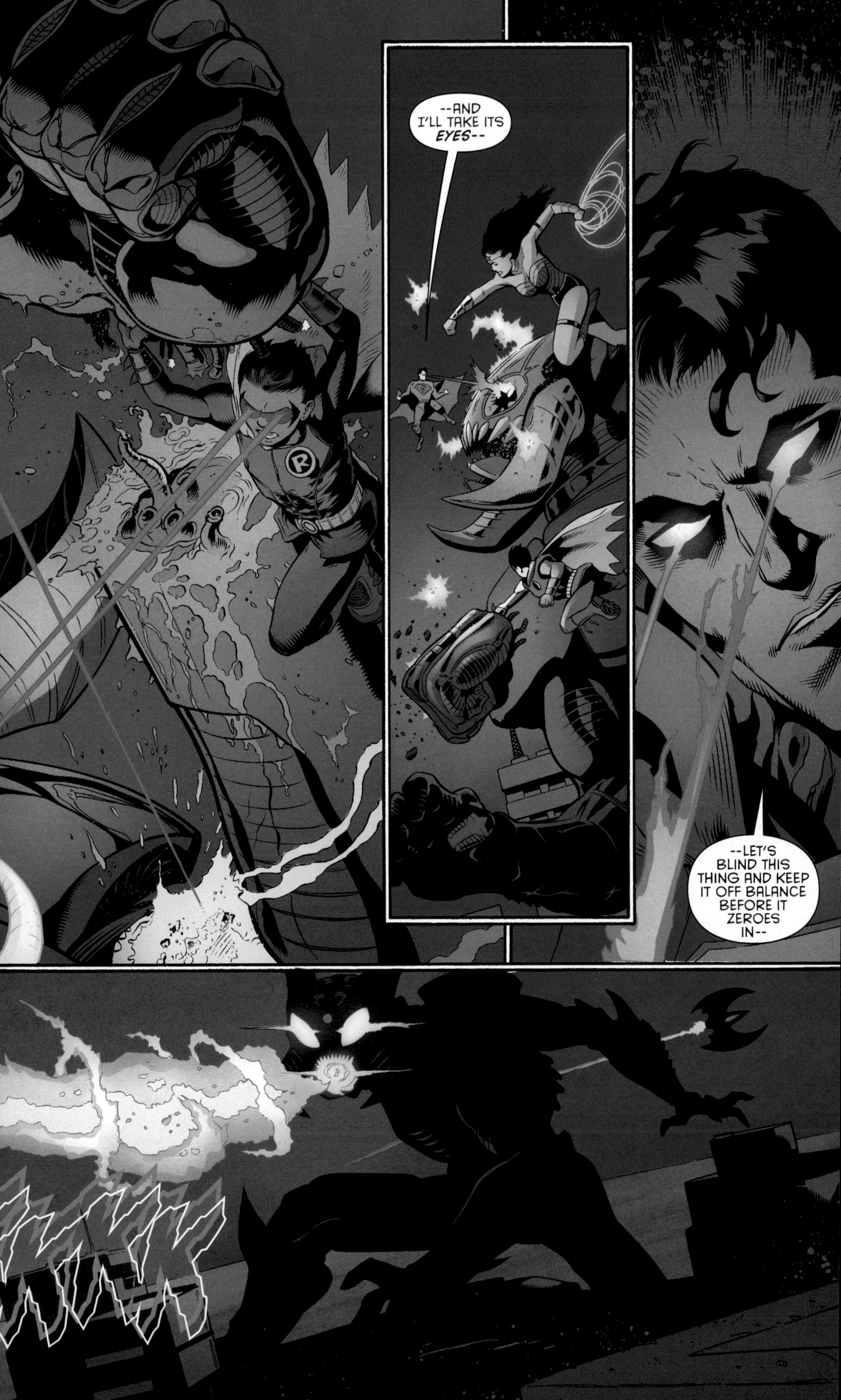
--AND I'LL TAKE ITS *EYES*--
--LET'S BLIND THIS THING AND KEEP IT OFF BALANCE BEFORE IT ZEROES IN--

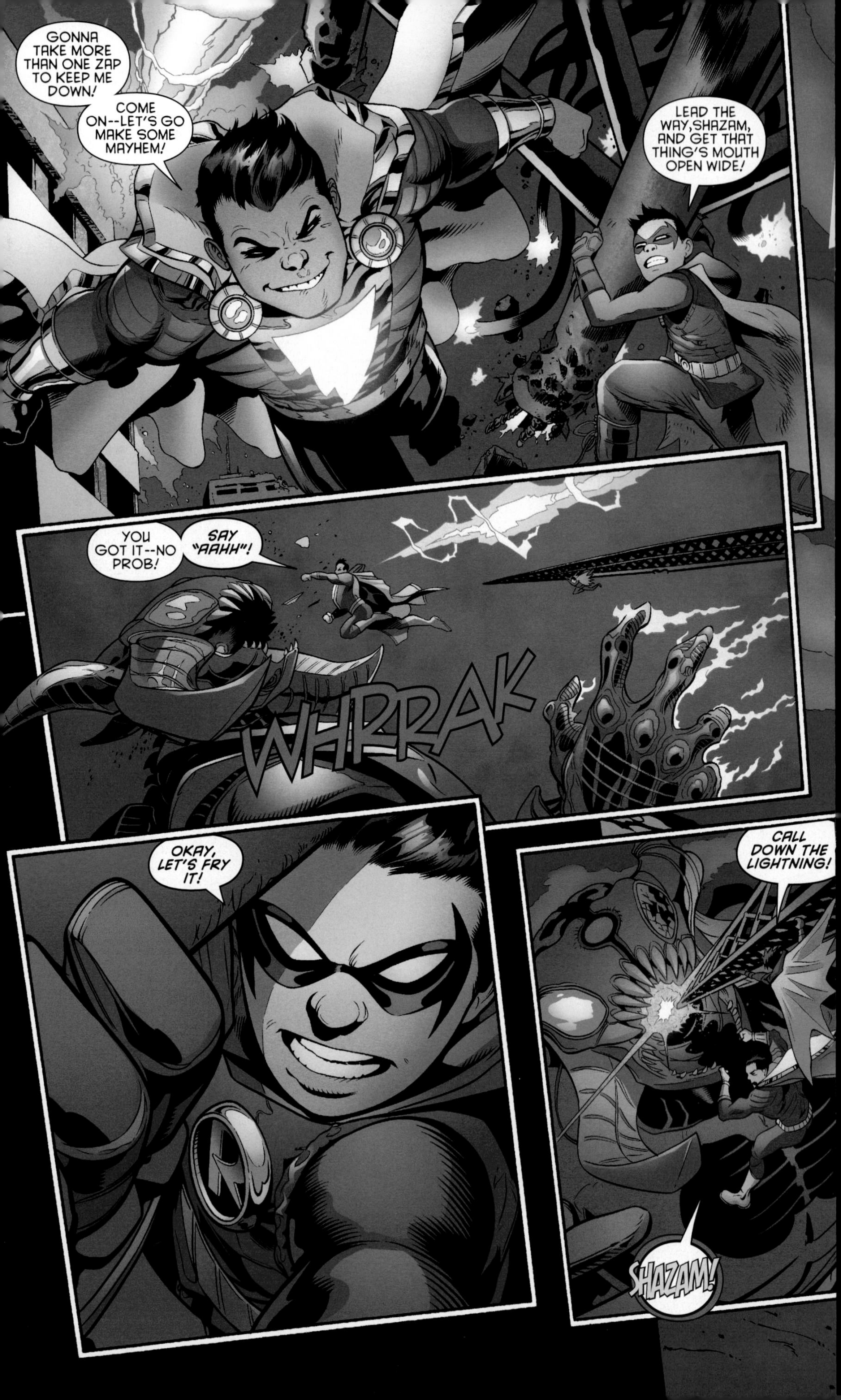
GONNA TAKE MORE THAN ONE ZAP TO KEEP ME DOWN!
COME ON--LET'S GO MAKE SOME MAYHEM!
LEAD THE WAY, SHAZAM, AND GET THAT THING'S MOUTH OPEN WIDE!
YOU GOT IT--NO PROB!
SAY "AAHH"!
WHRRAK
OKAY, LET'S FRY IT!
CALL DOWN THE LIGHTNING!
SHAZAM!

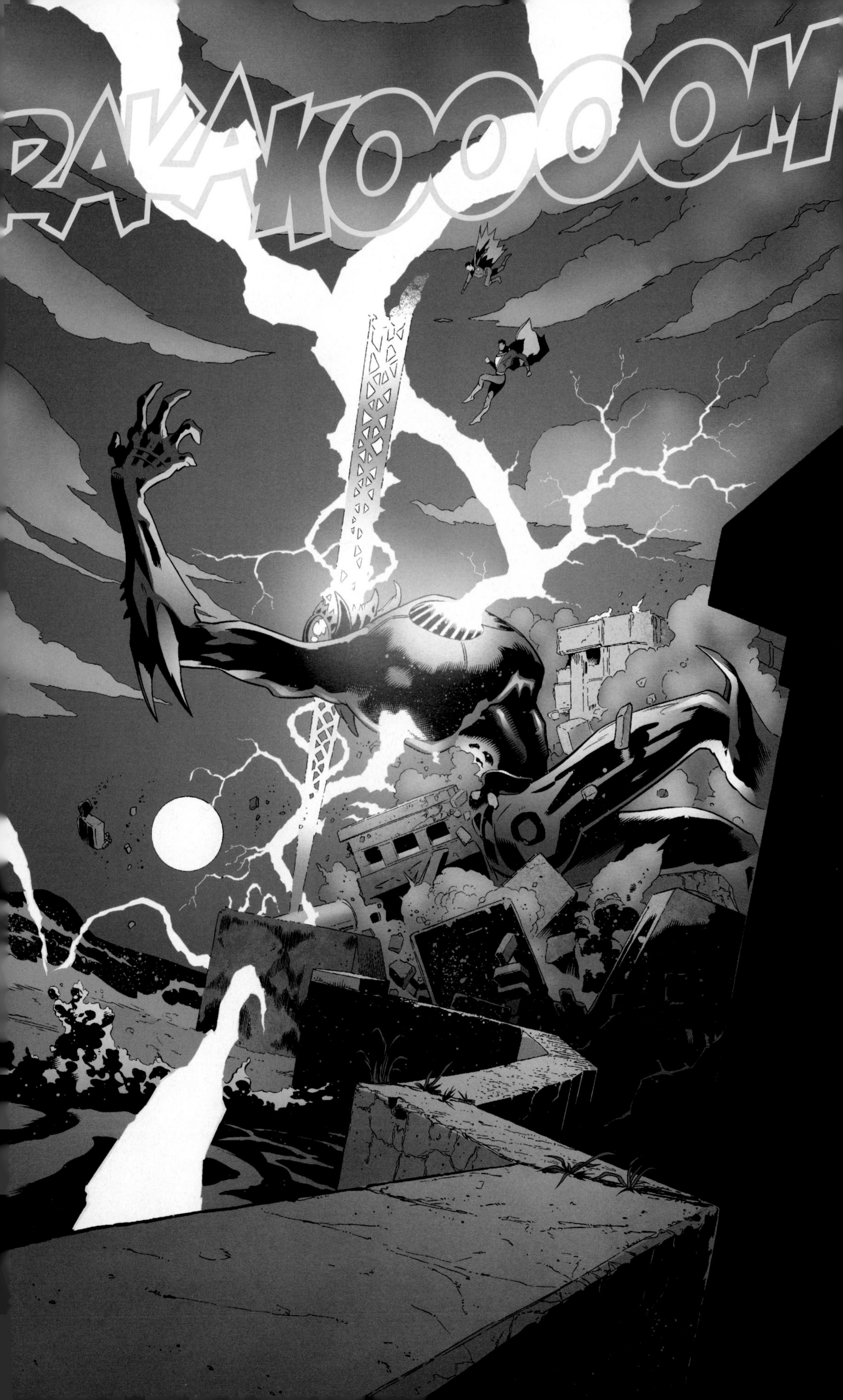
RAKAKOOOOM

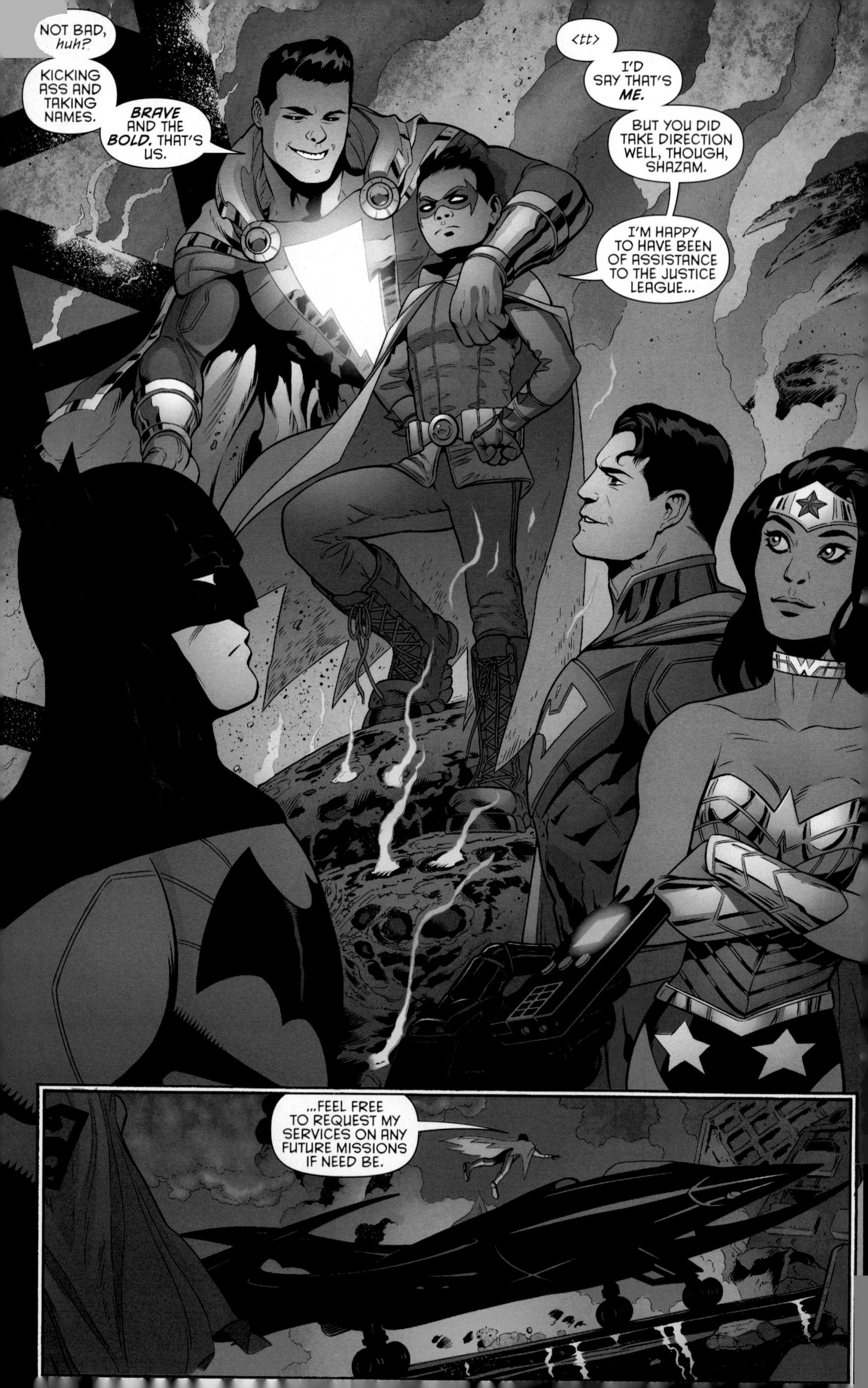
NOT BAD, *huh?*
KICKING ASS AND TAKING NAMES.
BRAVE AND THE ***BOLD.*** THAT'S US.
<tt>
I'D SAY THAT'S ***ME.***
BUT YOU DID TAKE DIRECTION WELL, THOUGH, SHAZAM.
I'M HAPPY TO HAVE BEEN OF ASSISTANCE TO THE JUSTICE LEAGUE...
...FEEL FREE TO REQUEST MY SERVICES ON ANY FUTURE MISSIONS IF NEED BE.

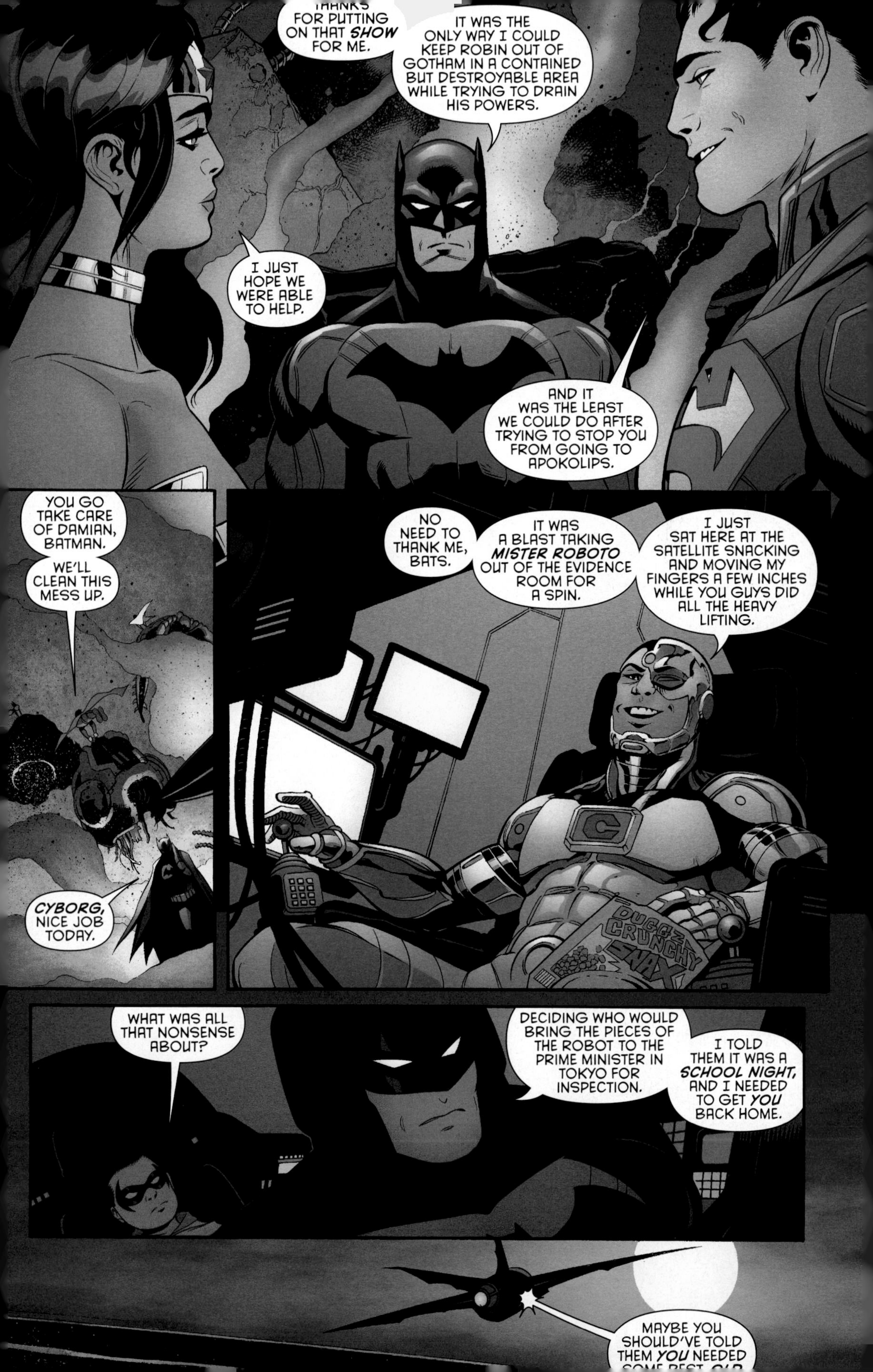
THANKS FOR PUTTING ON THAT SHOW FOR ME.
IT WAS THE ONLY WAY I COULD KEEP ROBIN OUT OF GOTHAM IN A CONTAINED BUT DESTROYABLE AREA WHILE TRYING TO DRAIN HIS POWERS.
I JUST HOPE WE WERE ABLE TO HELP.
AND IT WAS THE LEAST WE COULD DO AFTER TRYING TO STOP YOU FROM GOING TO APOKOLIPS.
YOU GO TAKE CARE OF DAMIAN, BATMAN.
WE'LL CLEAN THIS MESS UP.
CYBORG, NICE JOB TODAY.
NO NEED TO THANK ME, BATS.
IT WAS A BLAST TAKING MISTER ROBOTO OUT OF THE EVIDENCE ROOM FOR A SPIN.
I JUST SAT HERE AT THE SATELLITE SNACKING AND MOVING MY FINGERS A FEW INCHES WHILE YOU GUYS DID ALL THE HEAVY LIFTING.
DUGGZY CRUNCHY SNAX
WHAT WAS ALL THAT NONSENSE ABOUT?
DECIDING WHO WOULD BRING THE PIECES OF THE ROBOT TO THE PRIME MINISTER IN TOKYO FOR INSPECTION.
I TOLD THEM IT WAS A SCHOOL NIGHT, AND I NEEDED TO GET YOU BACK HOME.
MAYBE YOU SHOULD'VE TOLD THEM YOU NEEDED

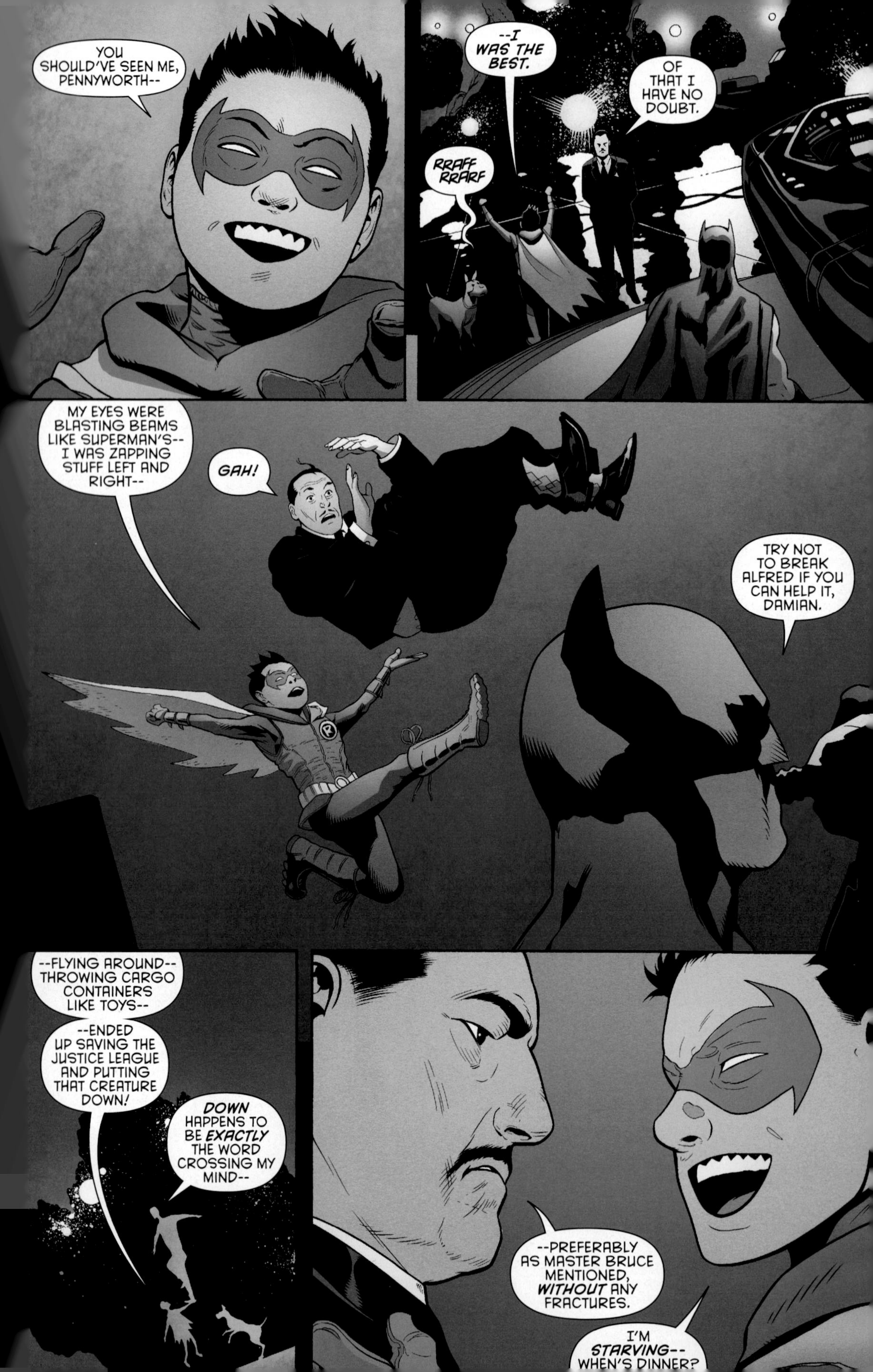
YOU SHOULD'VE SEEN ME, PENNYWORTH--
--I WAS THE BEST.
OF THAT I HAVE NO DOUBT.
RRAFF RRARF
MY EYES WERE BLASTING BEAMS LIKE SUPERMAN'S-- I WAS ZAPPING STUFF LEFT AND RIGHT--
GAH!
TRY NOT TO BREAK ALFRED IF YOU CAN HELP IT, DAMIAN.
--FLYING AROUND-- THROWING CARGO CONTAINERS LIKE TOYS--
--ENDED UP SAVING THE JUSTICE LEAGUE AND PUTTING THAT CREATURE DOWN!
DOWN HAPPENS TO BE EXACTLY THE WORD CROSSING MY MIND--
--PREFERABLY AS MASTER BRUCE MENTIONED, WITHOUT ANY FRACTURES.
I'M STARVING-- WHEN'S DINNER?

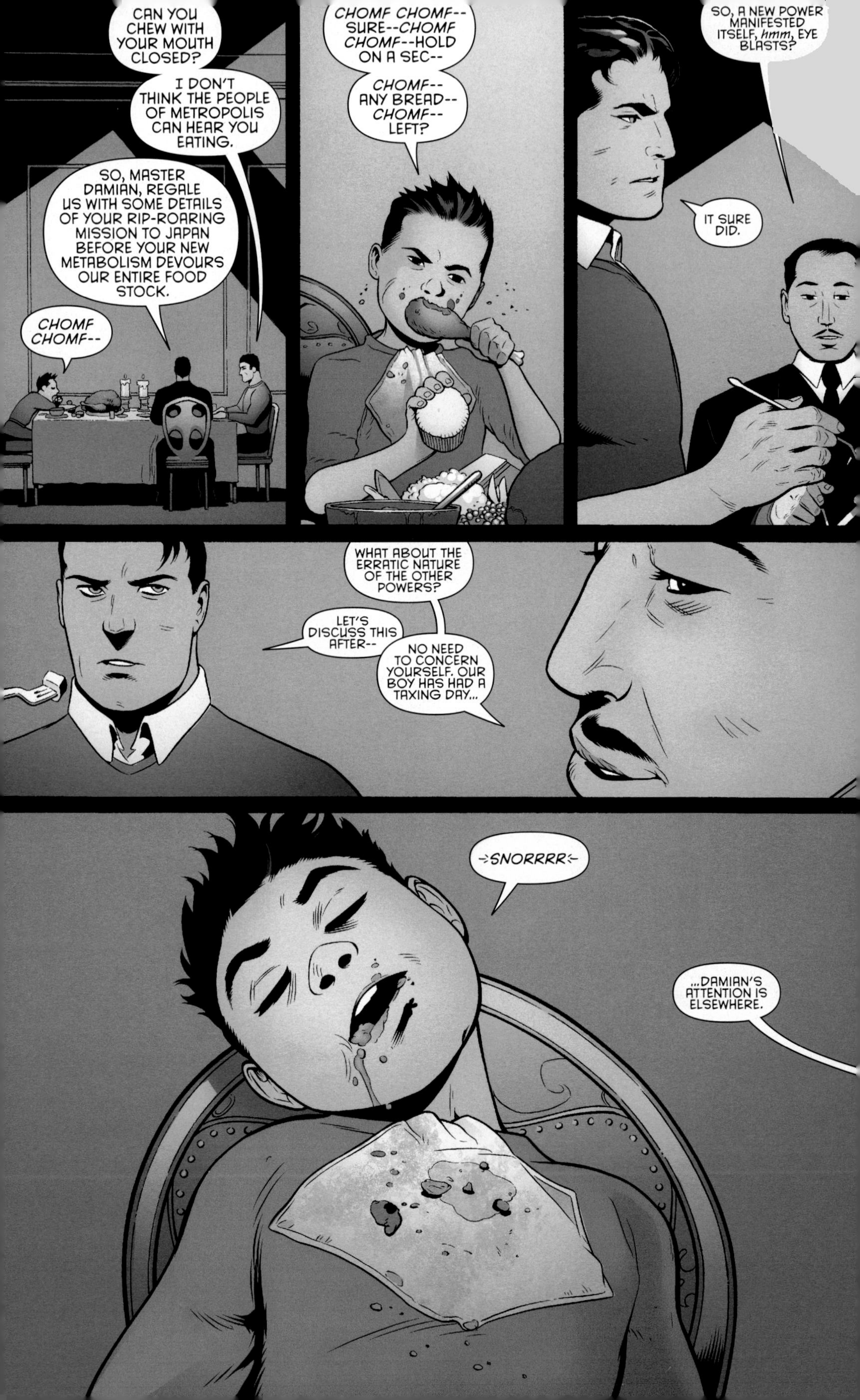
CAN YOU CHEW WITH YOUR MOUTH CLOSED?
I DON'T THINK THE PEOPLE OF METROPOLIS CAN HEAR YOU EATING.
SO, MASTER DAMIAN, REGALE US WITH SOME DETAILS OF YOUR RIP-ROARING MISSION TO JAPAN BEFORE YOUR NEW METABOLISM DEVOURS OUR ENTIRE FOOD STOCK.
CHOMF CHOMF--
CHOMF CHOMF-- SURE--CHOMF CHOMF--HOLD ON A SEC--
CHOMF-- ANY BREAD-- CHOMF-- LEFT?
SO, A NEW POWER MANIFESTED ITSELF, hmm, EYE BLASTS?
IT SURE DID.
WHAT ABOUT THE ERRATIC NATURE OF THE OTHER POWERS?
LET'S DISCUSS THIS AFTER--
NO NEED TO CONCERN YOURSELF. OUR BOY HAS HAD A TAXING DAY...
SNORRRR
...DAMIAN'S ATTENTION IS ELSEWHERE.

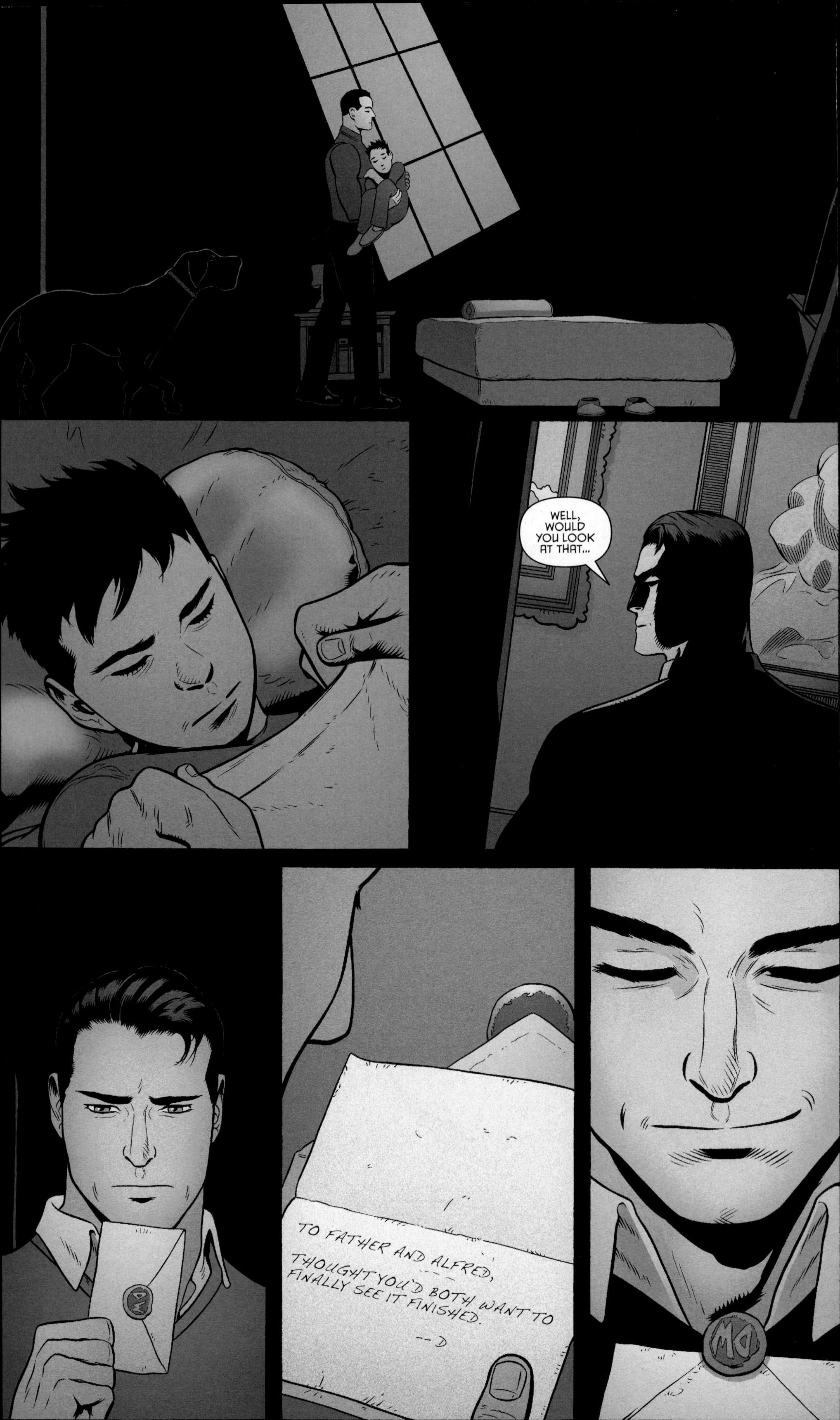
WELL, WOULD YOU LOOK AT THAT...
TO FATHER AND ALFRED,
THOUGHT YOU'D BOTH WANT TO FINALLY SEE IT FINISHED.
--D

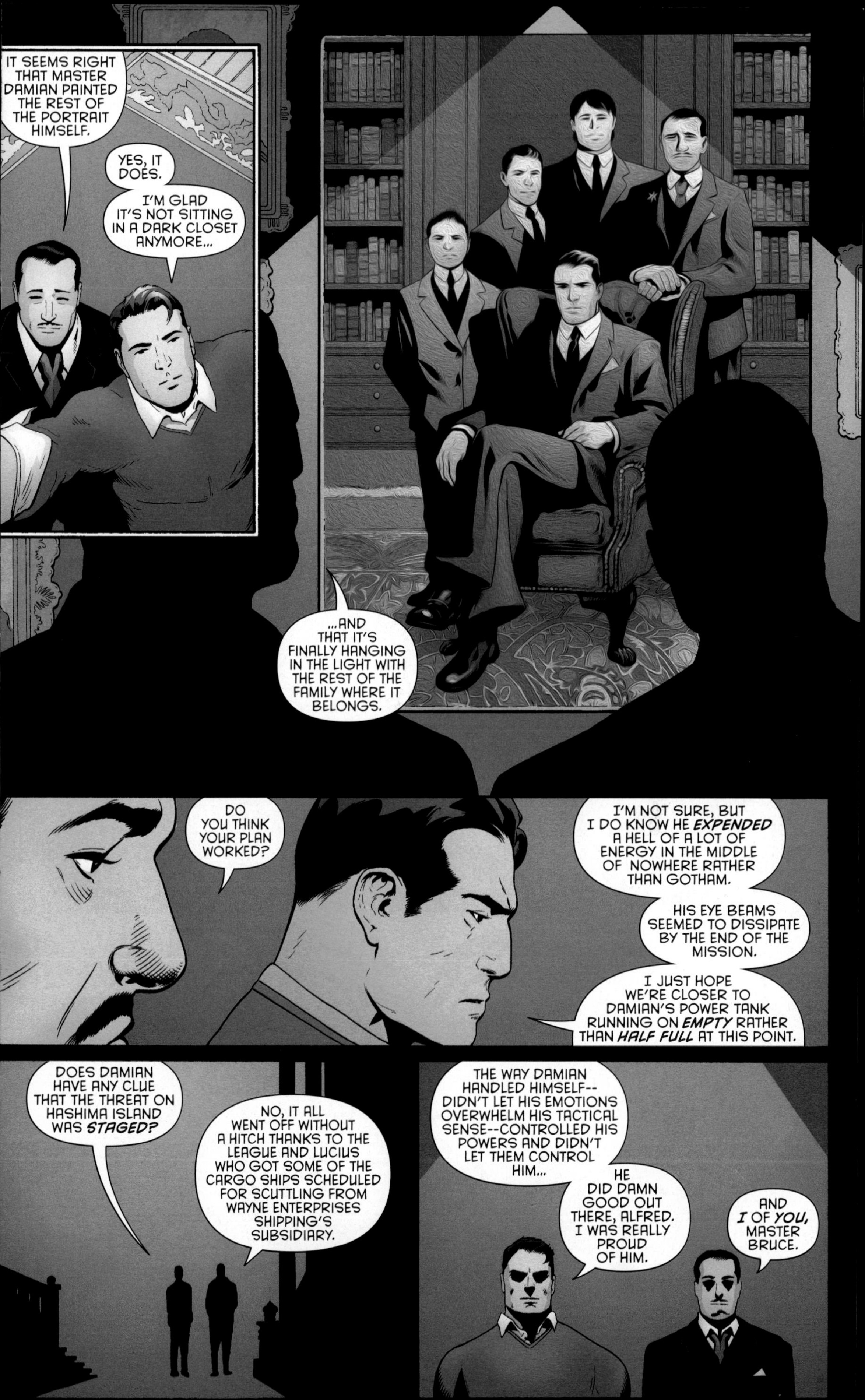
IT SEEMS RIGHT THAT MASTER DAMIAN PAINTED THE REST OF THE PORTRAIT HIMSELF.
YES, IT DOES.
I'M GLAD IT'S NOT SITTING IN A DARK CLOSET ANYMORE...
...AND THAT IT'S FINALLY HANGING IN THE LIGHT WITH THE REST OF THE FAMILY WHERE IT BELONGS.
DO YOU THINK YOUR PLAN WORKED?
I'M NOT SURE, BUT I DO KNOW HE *EXPENDED* A HELL OF A LOT OF ENERGY IN THE MIDDLE OF NOWHERE RATHER THAN GOTHAM.
HIS EYE BEAMS SEEMED TO DISSIPATE BY THE END OF THE MISSION.
I JUST HOPE WE'RE CLOSER TO DAMIAN'S POWER TANK RUNNING ON *EMPTY* RATHER THAN *HALF FULL* AT THIS POINT.
DOES DAMIAN HAVE ANY CLUE THAT THE THREAT ON HASHIMA ISLAND WAS *STAGED?*
NO, IT ALL WENT OFF WITHOUT A HITCH THANKS TO THE LEAGUE AND LUCIUS WHO GOT SOME OF THE CARGO SHIPS SCHEDULED FOR SCUTTLING FROM WAYNE ENTERPRISES SHIPPING'S SUBSIDIARY.
THE WAY DAMIAN HANDLED HIMSELF--DIDN'T LET HIS EMOTIONS OVERWHELM HIS TACTICAL SENSE--CONTROLLED HIS POWERS AND DIDN'T LET THEM CONTROL HIM...
HE DID DAMN GOOD OUT THERE, ALFRED. I WAS REALLY PROUD OF HIM.
AND *I* OF *YOU,* MASTER BRUCE.

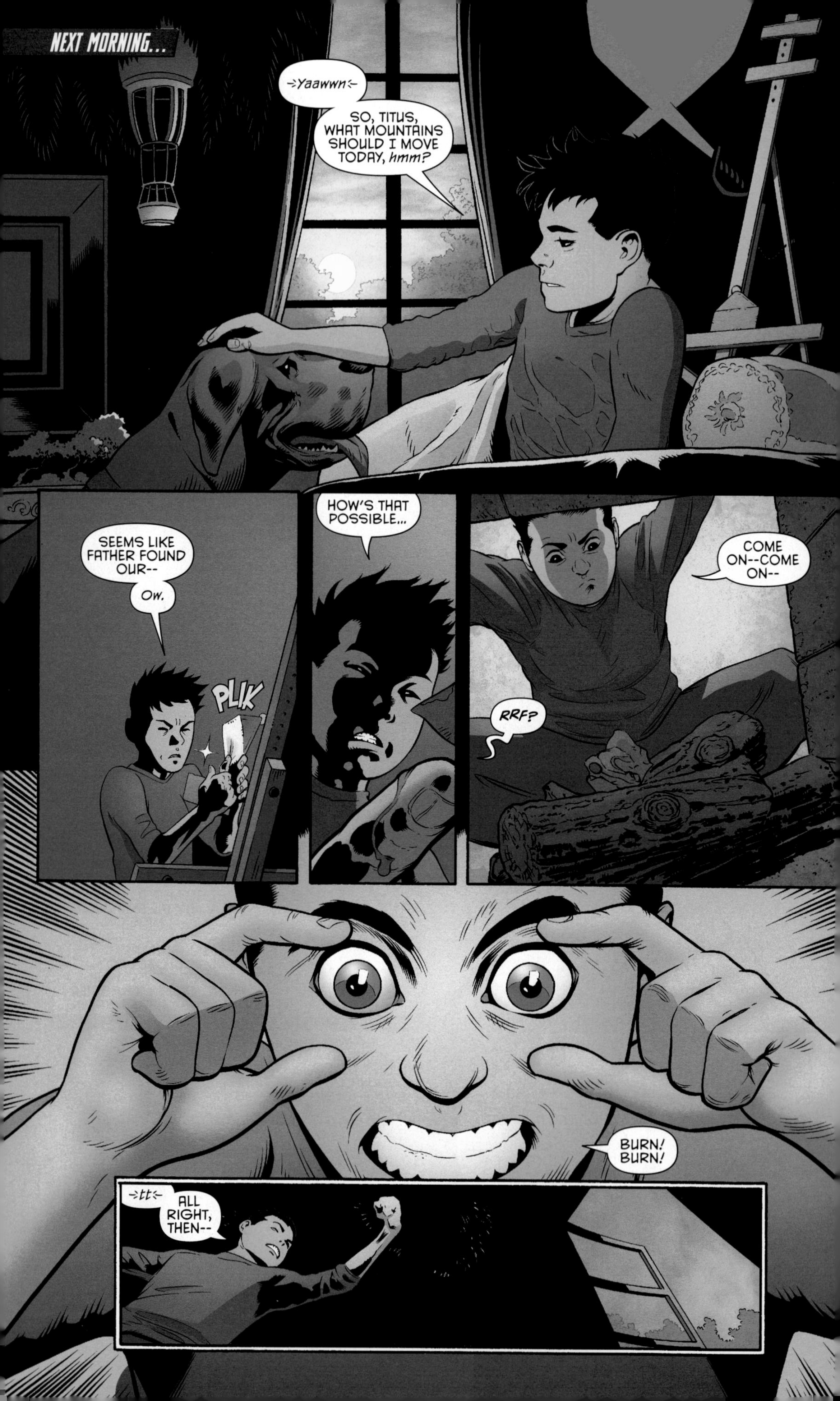
NEXT MORNING...
-Yaawwn-
SO, TITUS, WHAT MOUNTAINS SHOULD I MOVE TODAY, hmm?
SEEMS LIKE FATHER FOUND OUR--
Ow.
PLIK
HOW'S THAT POSSIBLE...
COME ON--COME ON--
RRF?
BURN! BURN!
-tt-
ALL RIGHT, THEN--

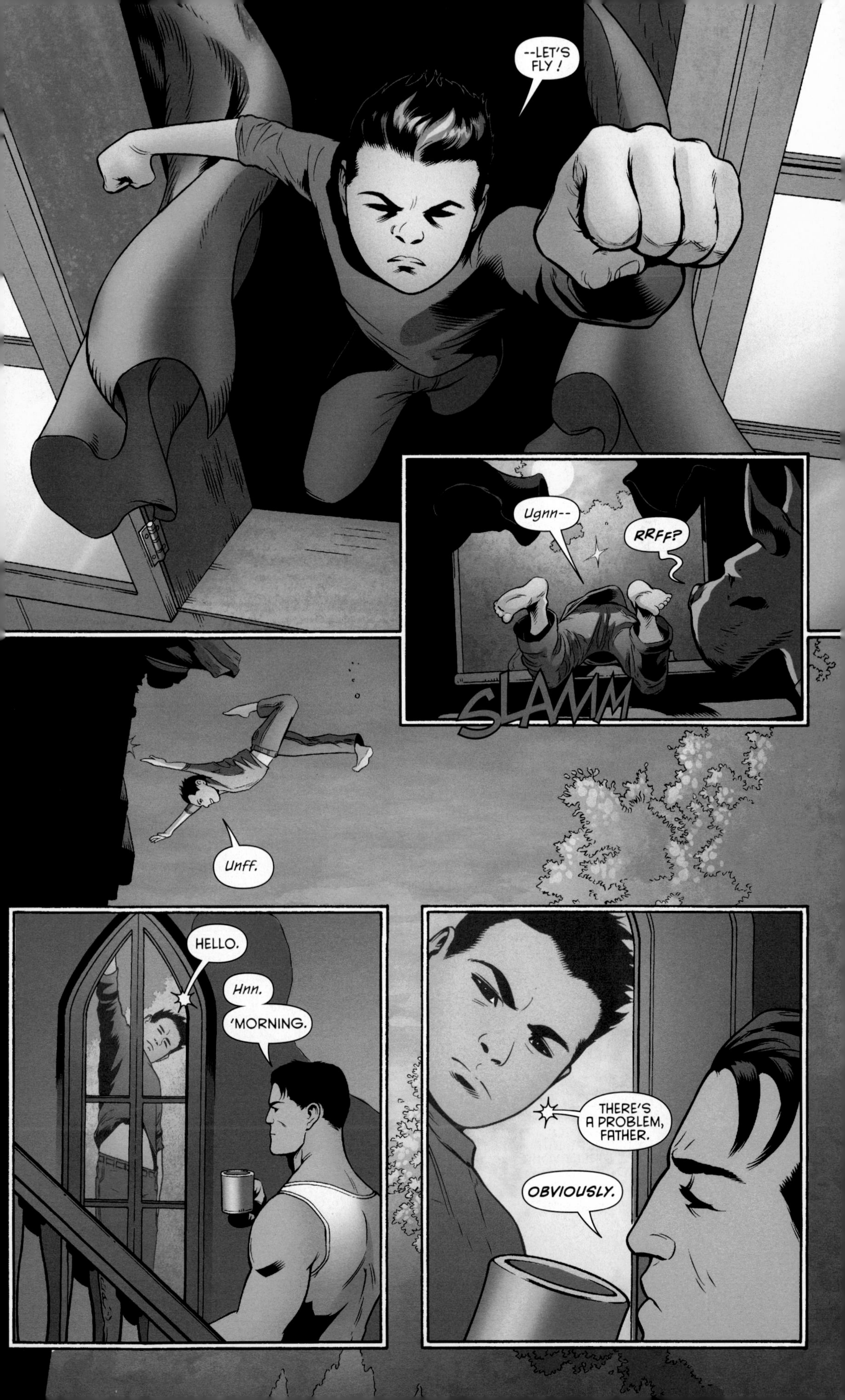

--LET'S FLY!
Ugnn--
RRFF?
SLAMM
Unff.
HELLO.
Hnn.
'MORNING.
THERE'S A PROBLEM, FATHER.
OBVIOUSLY.

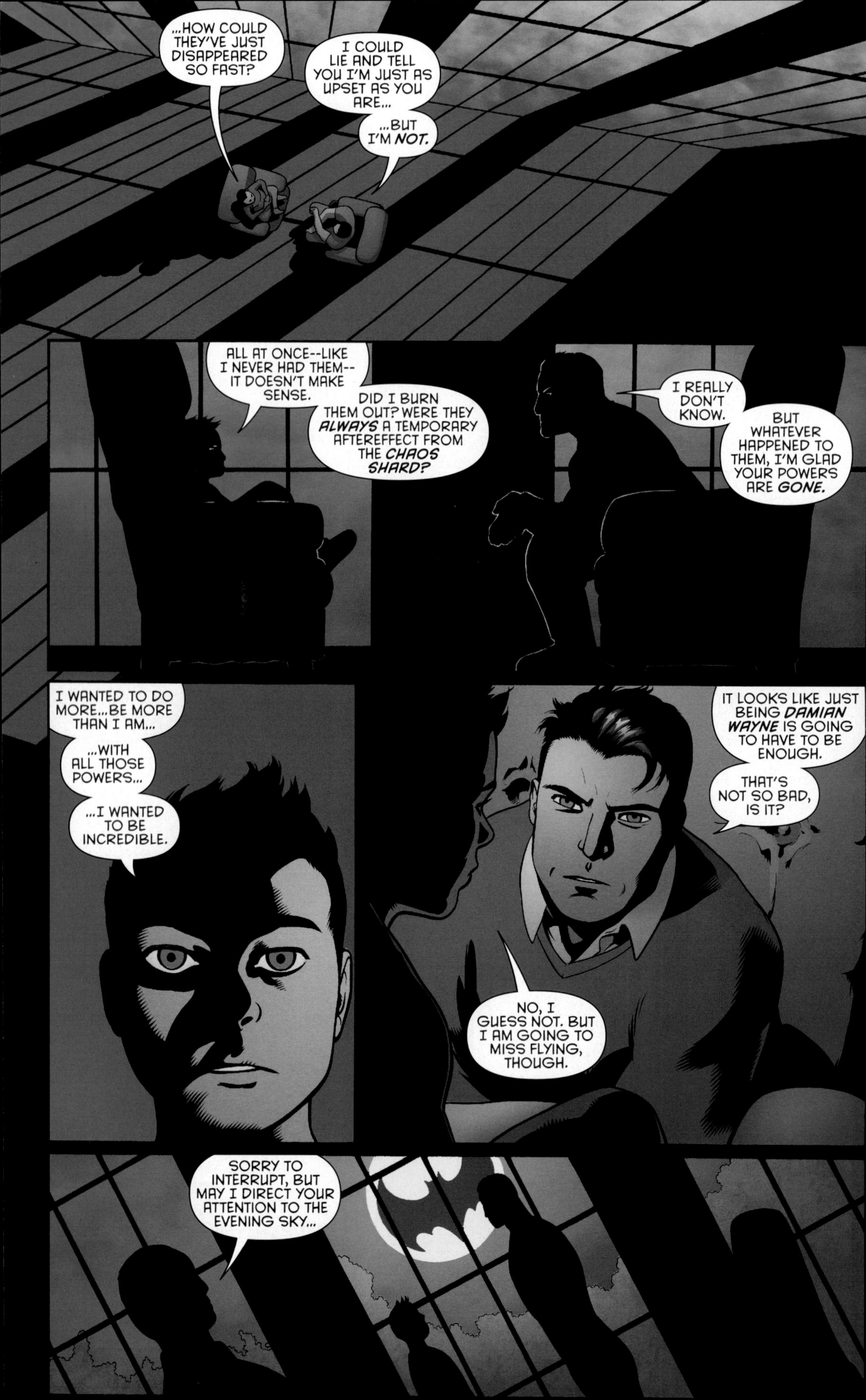
...HOW COULD THEY'VE JUST DISAPPEARED SO FAST?
I COULD LIE AND TELL YOU I'M JUST AS UPSET AS YOU ARE...
...BUT I'M NOT.
ALL AT ONCE--LIKE I NEVER HAD THEM--IT DOESN'T MAKE SENSE.
DID I BURN THEM OUT? WERE THEY ALWAYS A TEMPORARY AFTEREFFECT FROM THE CHAOS SHARD?
I REALLY DON'T KNOW.
BUT WHATEVER HAPPENED TO THEM, I'M GLAD YOUR POWERS ARE GONE.
I WANTED TO DO MORE...BE MORE THAN I AM...
...WITH ALL THOSE POWERS...
...I WANTED TO BE INCREDIBLE.
IT LOOKS LIKE JUST BEING DAMIAN WAYNE IS GOING TO HAVE TO BE ENOUGH.
THAT'S NOT SO BAD, IS IT?
NO, I GUESS NOT. BUT I AM GOING TO MISS FLYING, THOUGH.
SORRY TO INTERRUPT, BUT MAY I DIRECT YOUR ATTENTION TO THE EVENING SKY...

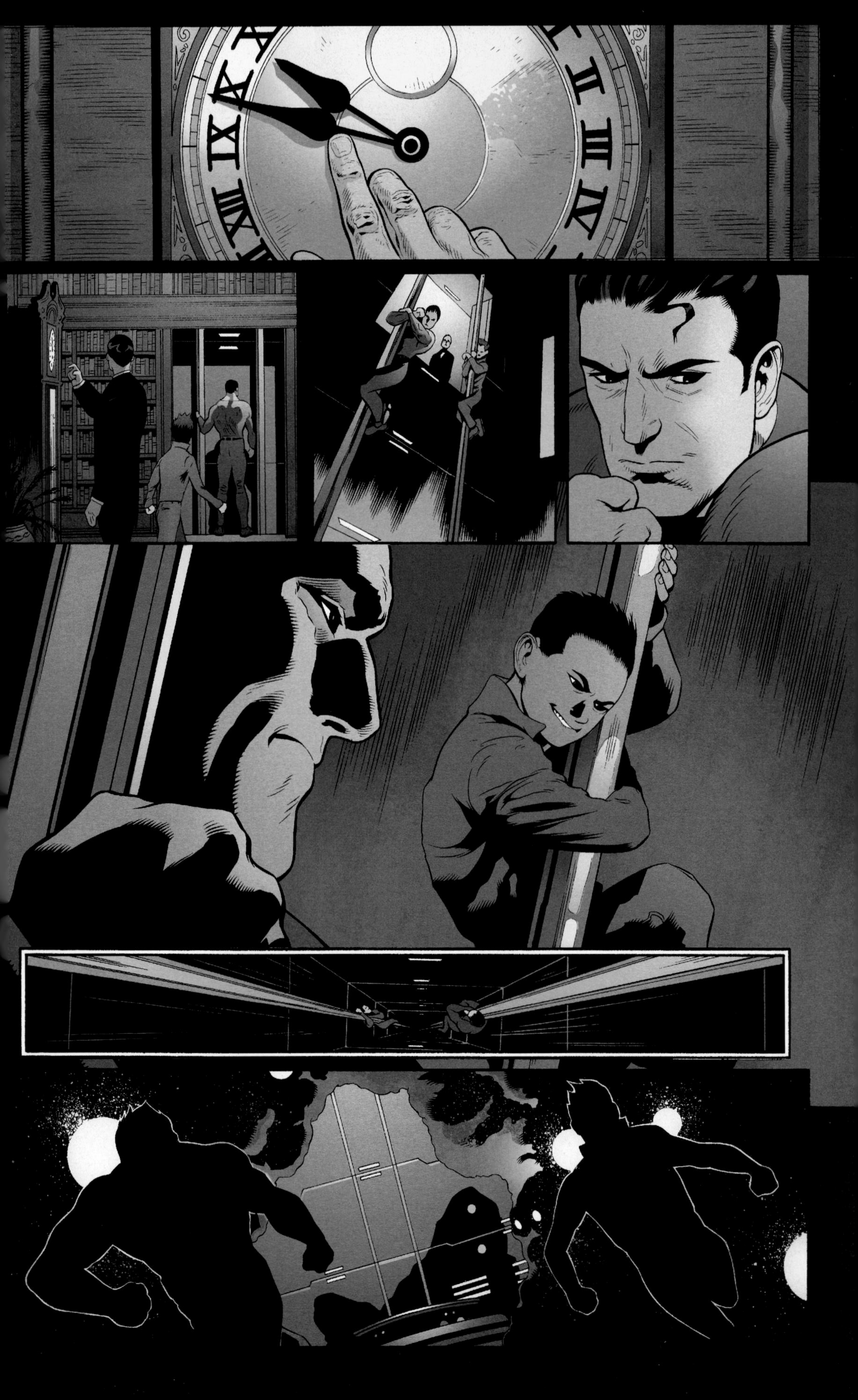

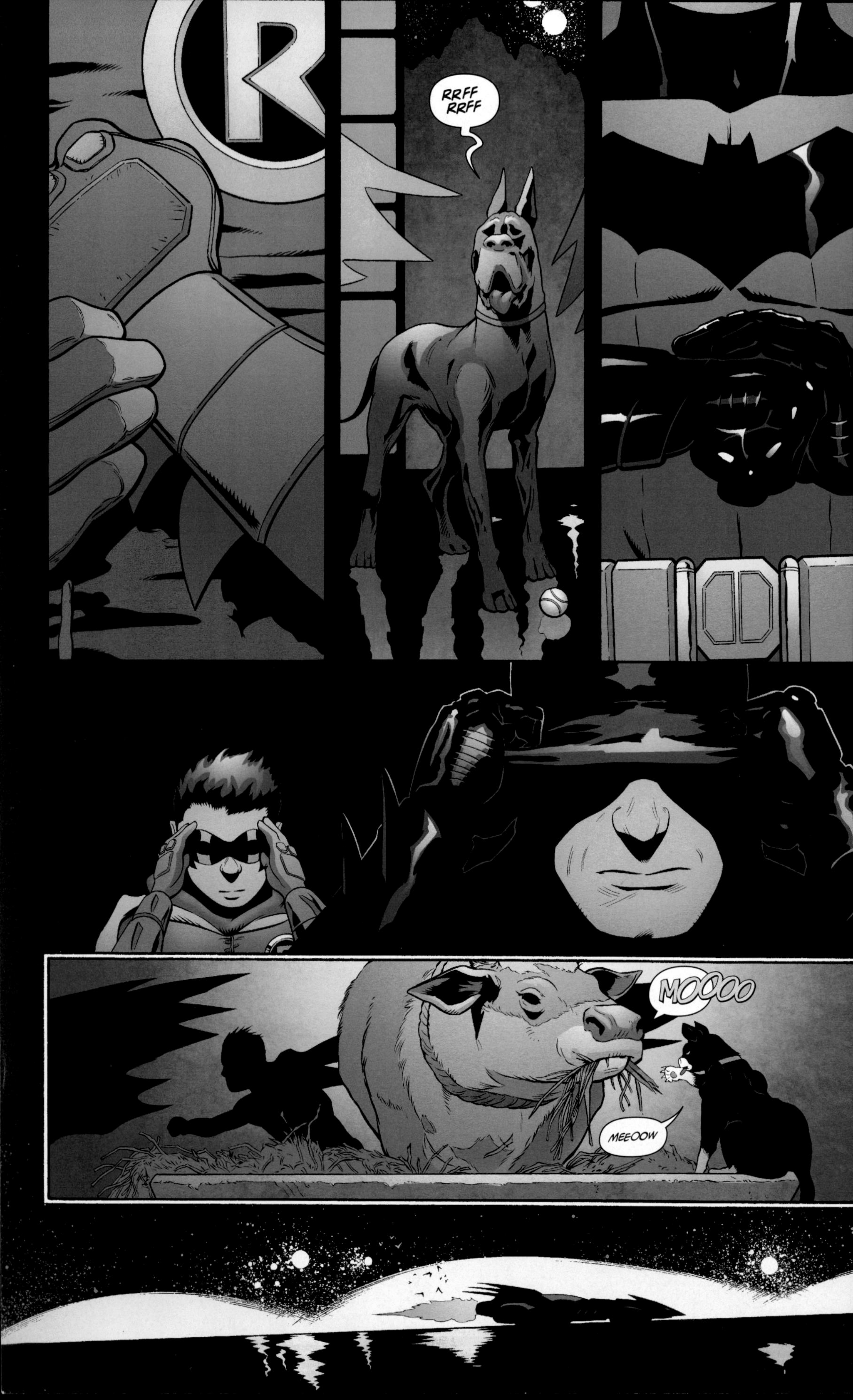
RRFF RRFF
MOOOO
MEEOOW

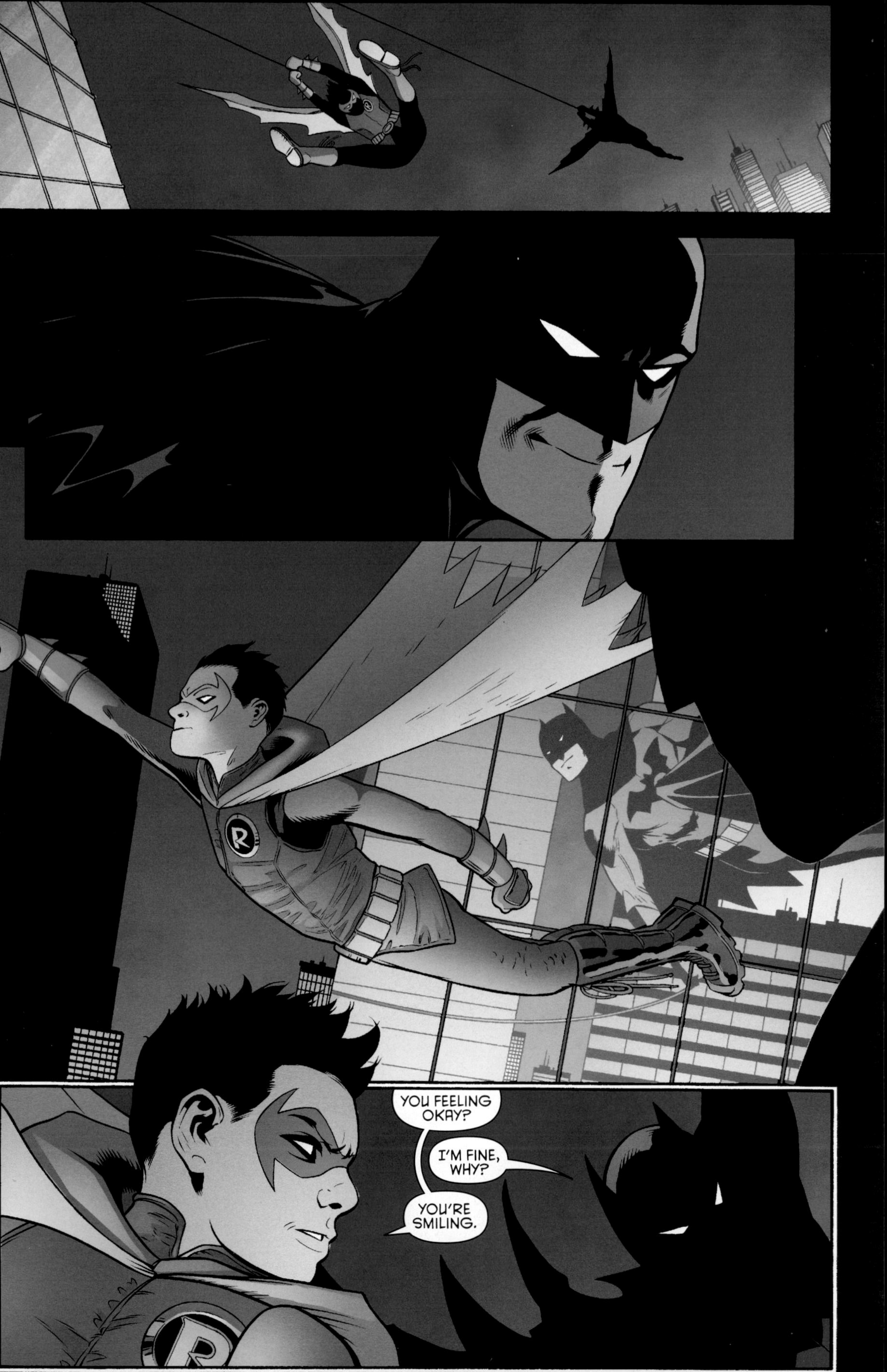
YOU FEELING OKAY?
I'M FINE, WHY?
YOU'RE SMILING.

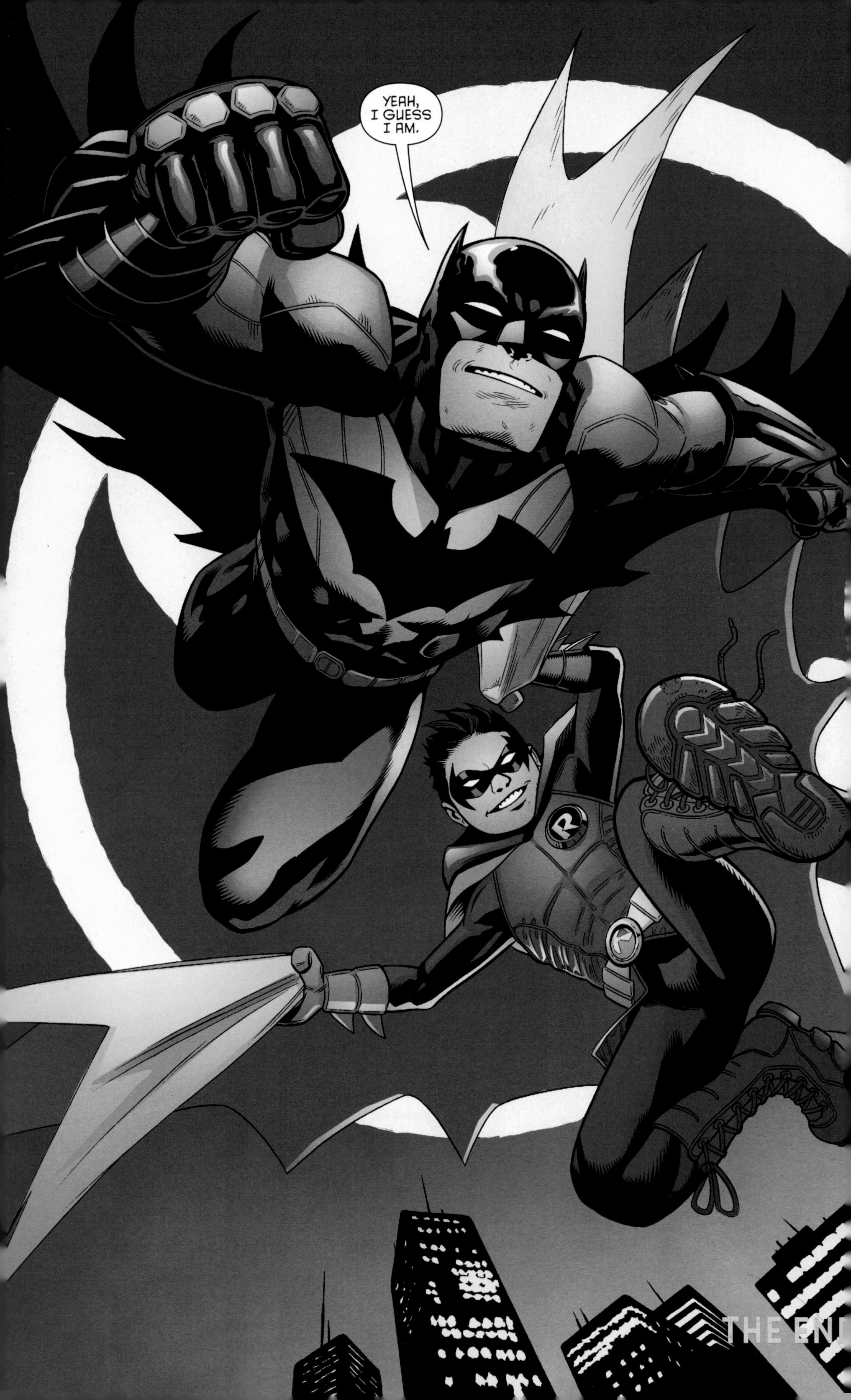
YEAH, I GUESS I AM.
THE EN

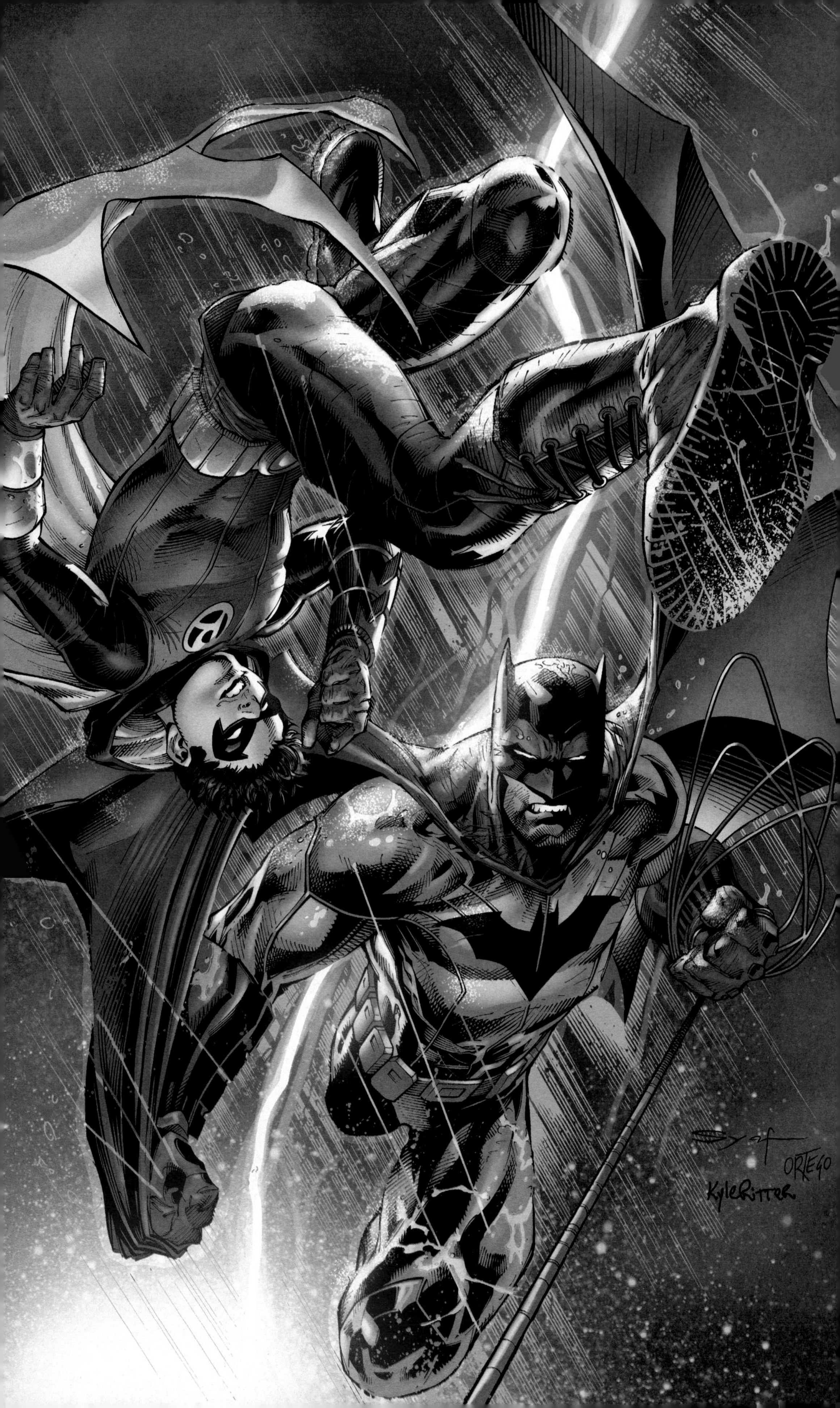
ORTEGO
KyleRitter

[redacted]

TOM NAPOLITANO letterer cover art by ARDIAN SYAF, GUILLERMO ORTEGO & KYLE RITTER

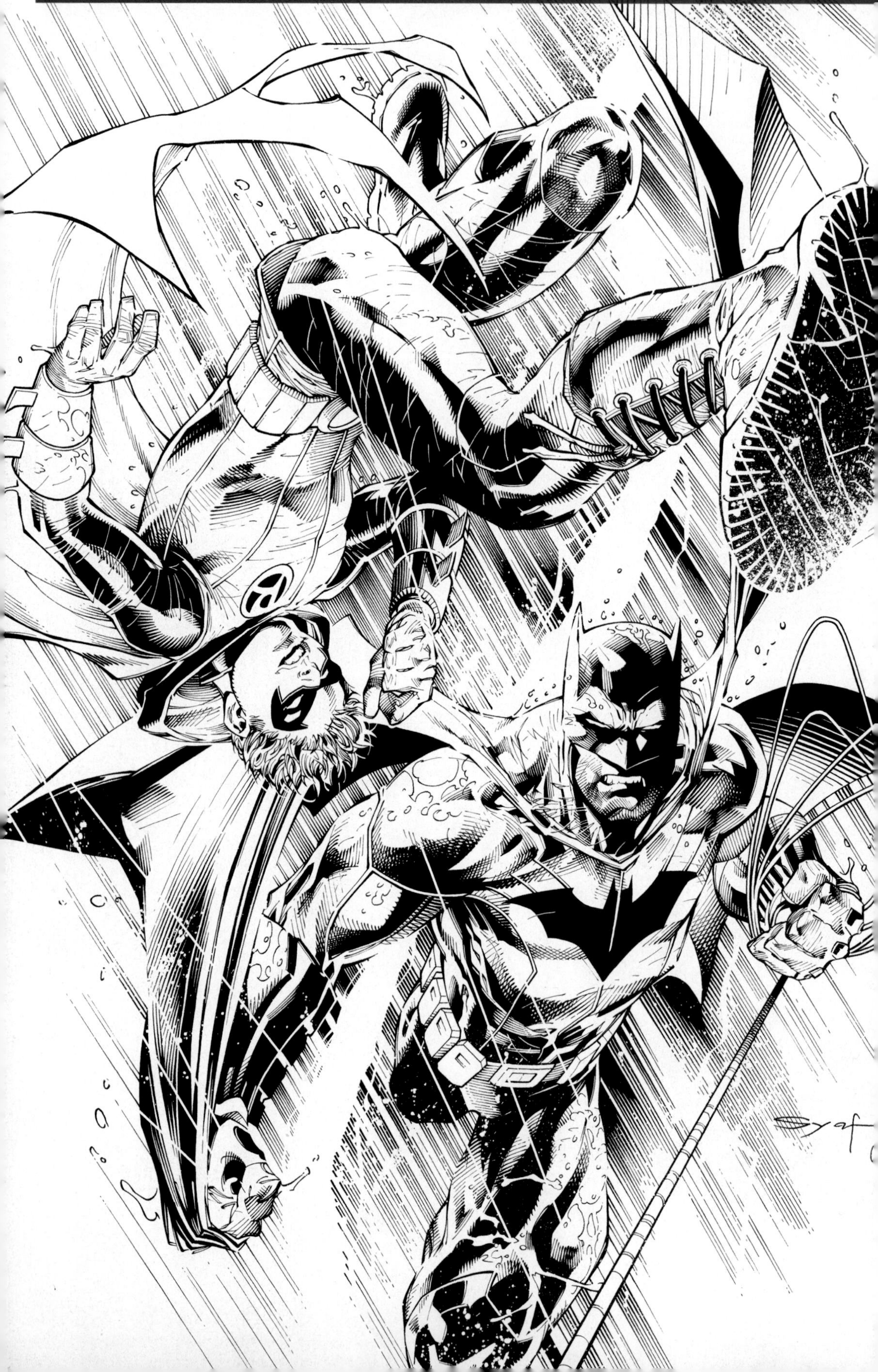
Syaf

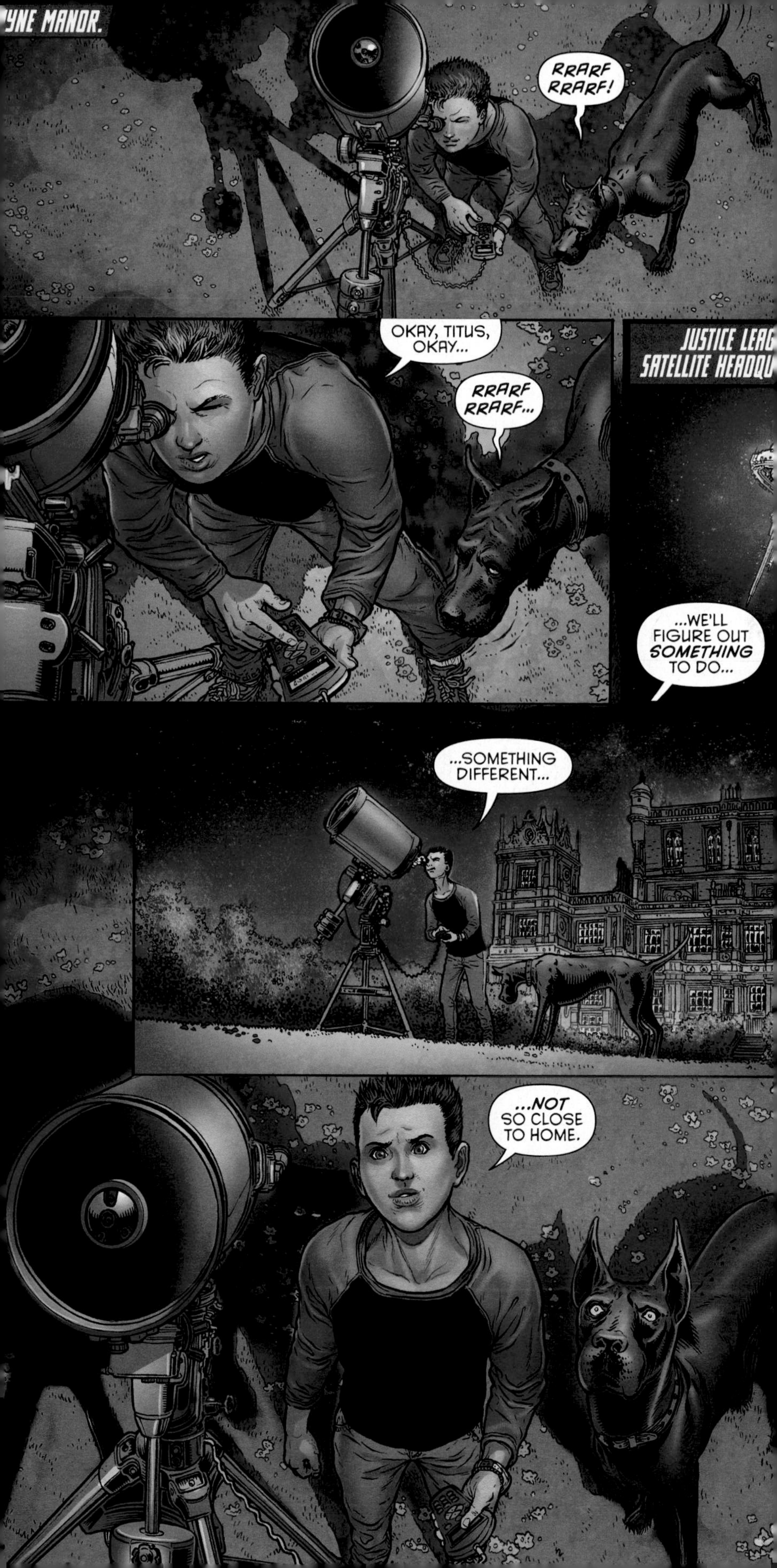
YNE MANOR.
RRARF RRARF!
OKAY, TITUS, OKAY...
RRARF RRARF...
JUSTICE LEAG
SATELLITE HEADQU
...WE'LL FIGURE OUT SOMETHING TO DO...
...SOMETHING DIFFERENT...
...NOT SO CLOSE TO HOME.

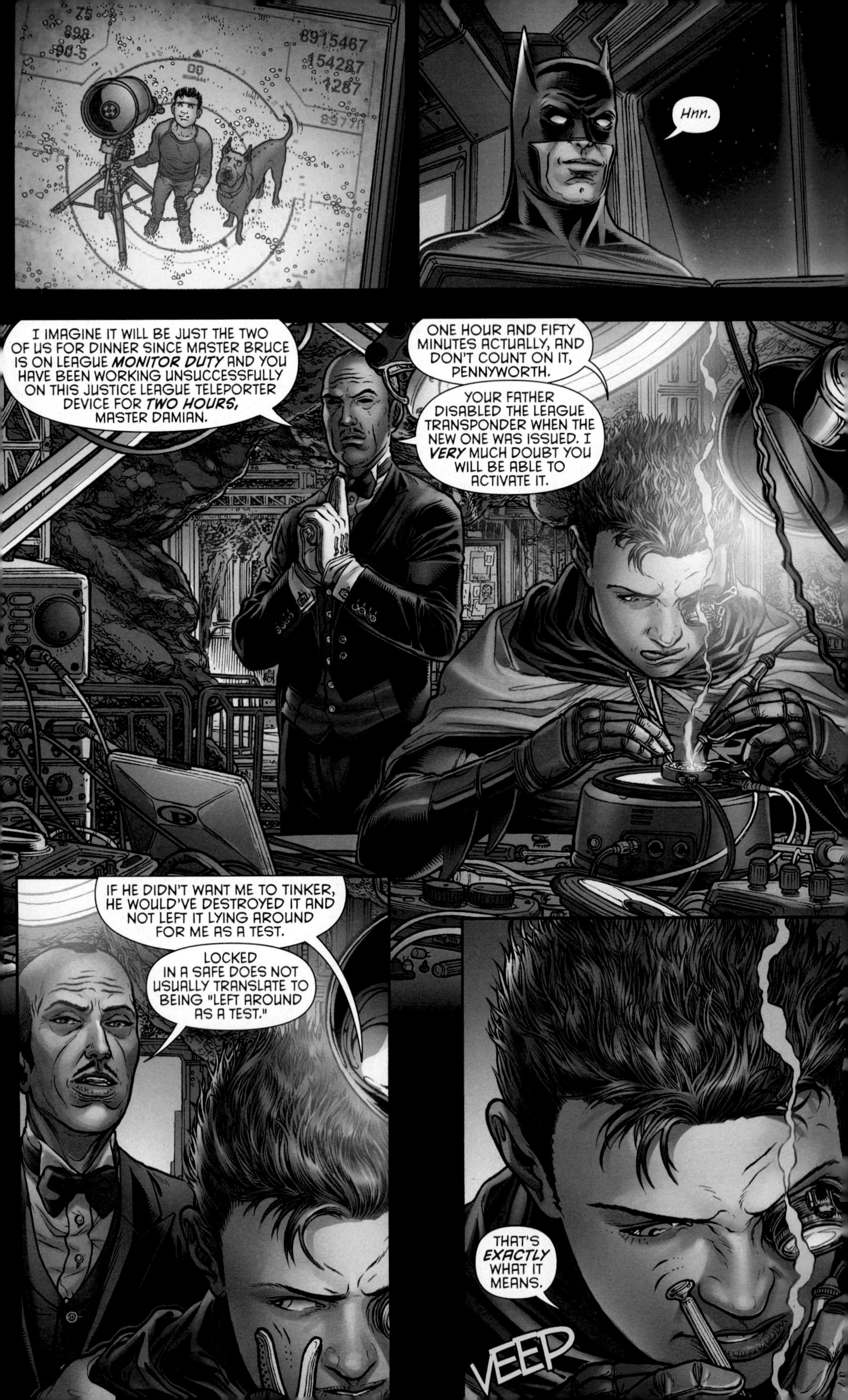
8915467
154287
1287
Hnn.
I IMAGINE IT WILL BE JUST THE TWO OF US FOR DINNER SINCE MASTER BRUCE IS ON LEAGUE *MONITOR DUTY* AND YOU HAVE BEEN WORKING UNSUCCESSFULLY ON THIS JUSTICE LEAGUE TELEPORTER DEVICE FOR *TWO HOURS,* MASTER DAMIAN.
ONE HOUR AND FIFTY MINUTES ACTUALLY, AND DON'T COUNT ON IT, PENNYWORTH.
YOUR FATHER DISABLED THE LEAGUE TRANSPONDER WHEN THE NEW ONE WAS ISSUED. I *VERY* MUCH DOUBT YOU WILL BE ABLE TO ACTIVATE IT.
IF HE DIDN'T WANT ME TO TINKER, HE WOULD'VE DESTROYED IT AND NOT LEFT IT LYING AROUND FOR ME AS A TEST.
LOCKED IN A SAFE DOES NOT USUALLY TRANSLATE TO BEING "LEFT AROUND AS A TEST."
THAT'S *EXACTLY* WHAT IT MEANS.
VEEP

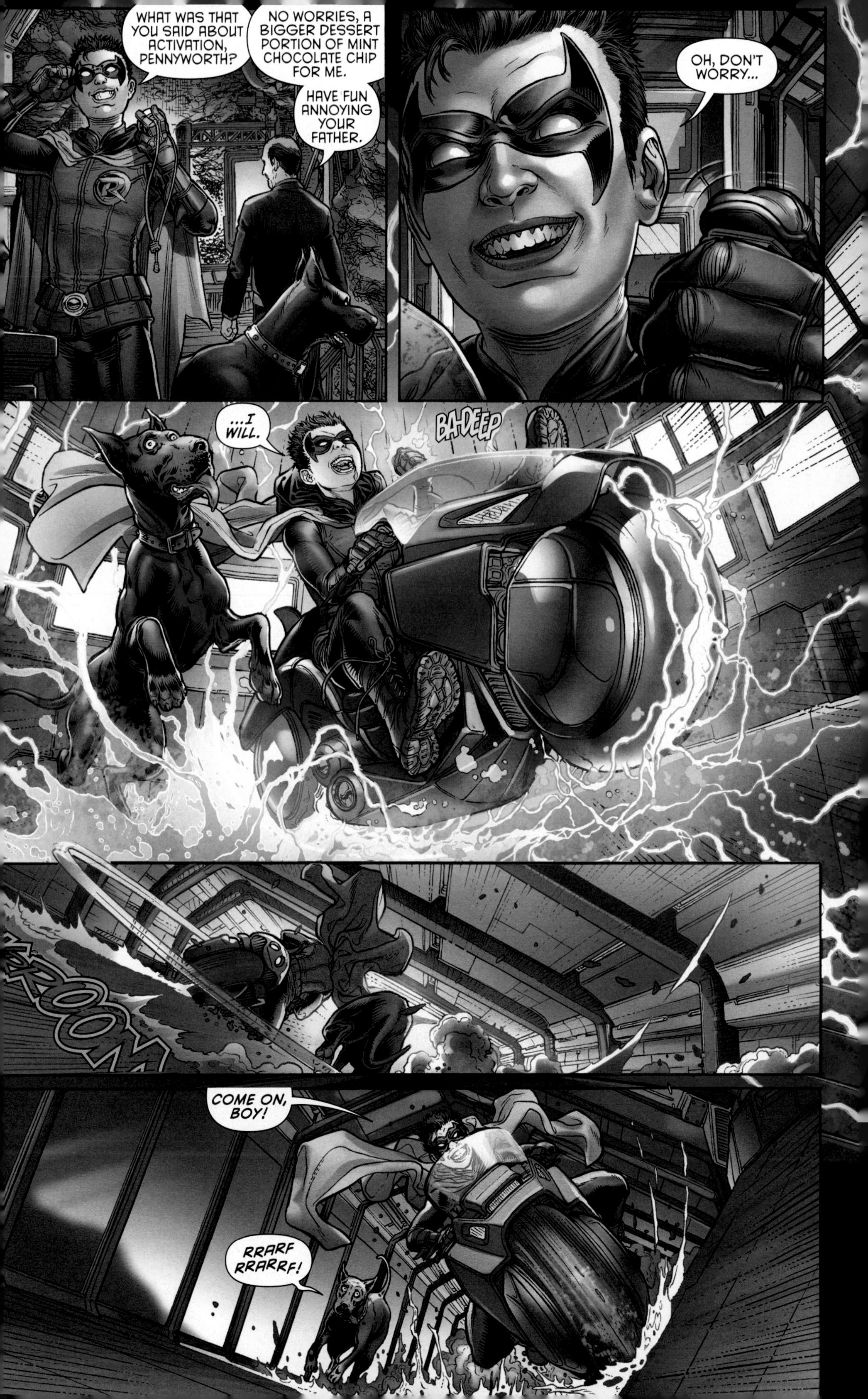
WHAT WAS THAT YOU SAID ABOUT ACTIVATION, PENNYWORTH?
NO WORRIES, A BIGGER DESSERT PORTION OF MINT CHOCOLATE CHIP FOR ME.
HAVE FUN ANNOYING YOUR FATHER.
OH, DON'T WORRY...
...I WILL.
BA-DEEP
COME ON, BOY!
RRARF RRARRF!

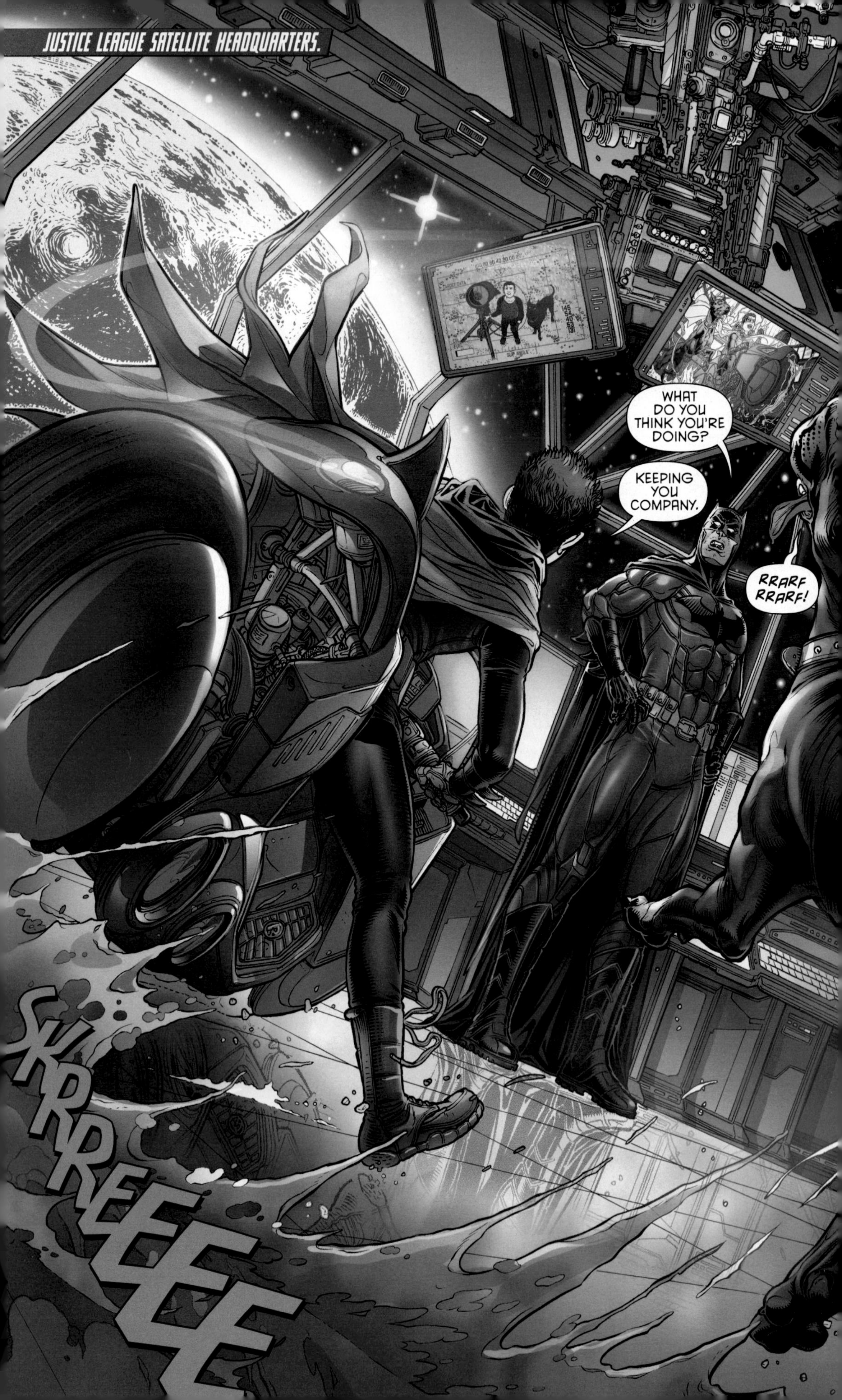
JUSTICE LEAGUE SATELLITE HEADQUARTERS.
WHAT DO YOU THINK YOU'RE DOING?
KEEPING YOU COMPANY.
RRARF RRARF!
SKRREEEE

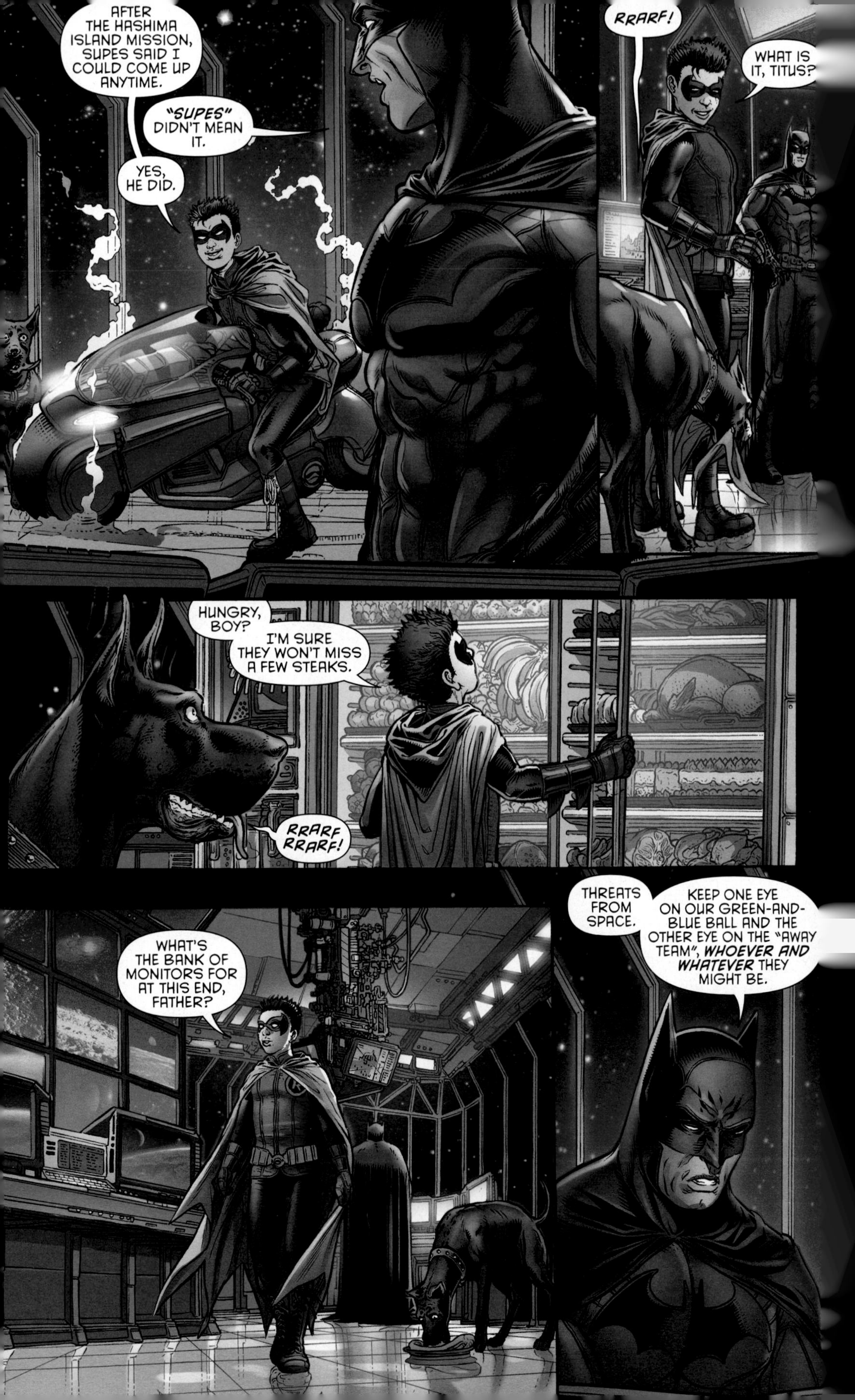

AFTER THE HASHIMA ISLAND MISSION, SUPES SAID I COULD COME UP ANYTIME.
"SUPES" DIDN'T MEAN IT.
YES, HE DID.
RRARF!
WHAT IS IT, TITUS?
HUNGRY, BOY?
I'M SURE THEY WON'T MISS A FEW STEAKS.
RRARF RRARF!
WHAT'S THE BANK OF MONITORS FOR AT THIS END, FATHER?
THREATS FROM SPACE.
KEEP ONE EYE ON OUR GREEN-AND-BLUE BALL AND THE OTHER EYE ON THE "AWAY TEAM", WHOEVER AND WHATEVER THEY MIGHT BE.

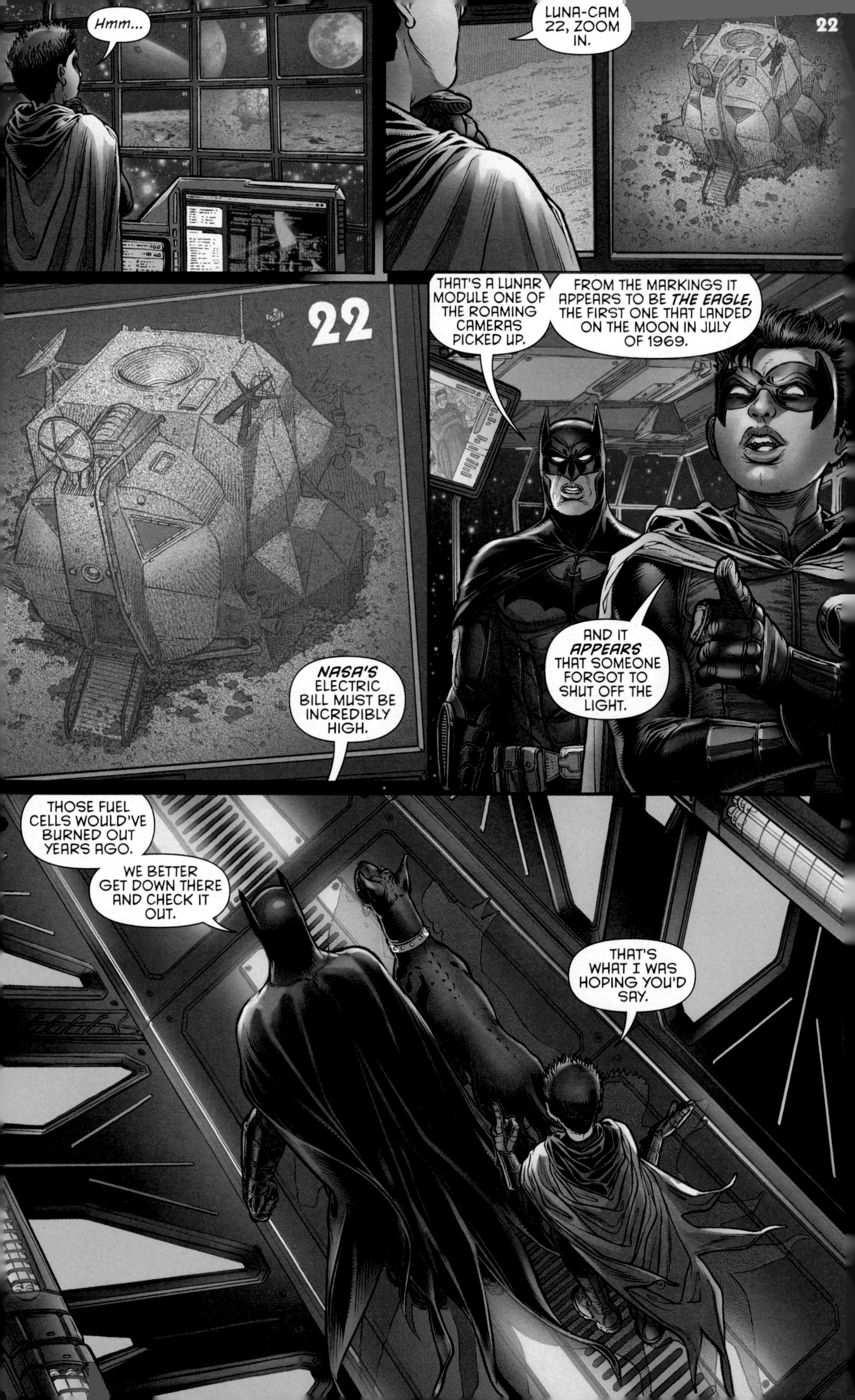
Hmm...
LUNA-CAM 22, ZOOM IN.
22
22
THAT'S A LUNAR MODULE ONE OF THE ROAMING CAMERAS PICKED UP.
FROM THE MARKINGS IT APPEARS TO BE *THE EAGLE,* THE FIRST ONE THAT LANDED ON THE MOON IN JULY OF 1969.
NASA'S ELECTRIC BILL MUST BE INCREDIBLY HIGH.
AND IT *APPEARS* THAT SOMEONE FORGOT TO SHUT OFF THE LIGHT.
THOSE FUEL CELLS WOULD'VE BURNED OUT YEARS AGO.
WE BETTER GET DOWN THERE AND CHECK IT OUT.
THAT'S WHAT I WAS HOPING YOU'D SAY.

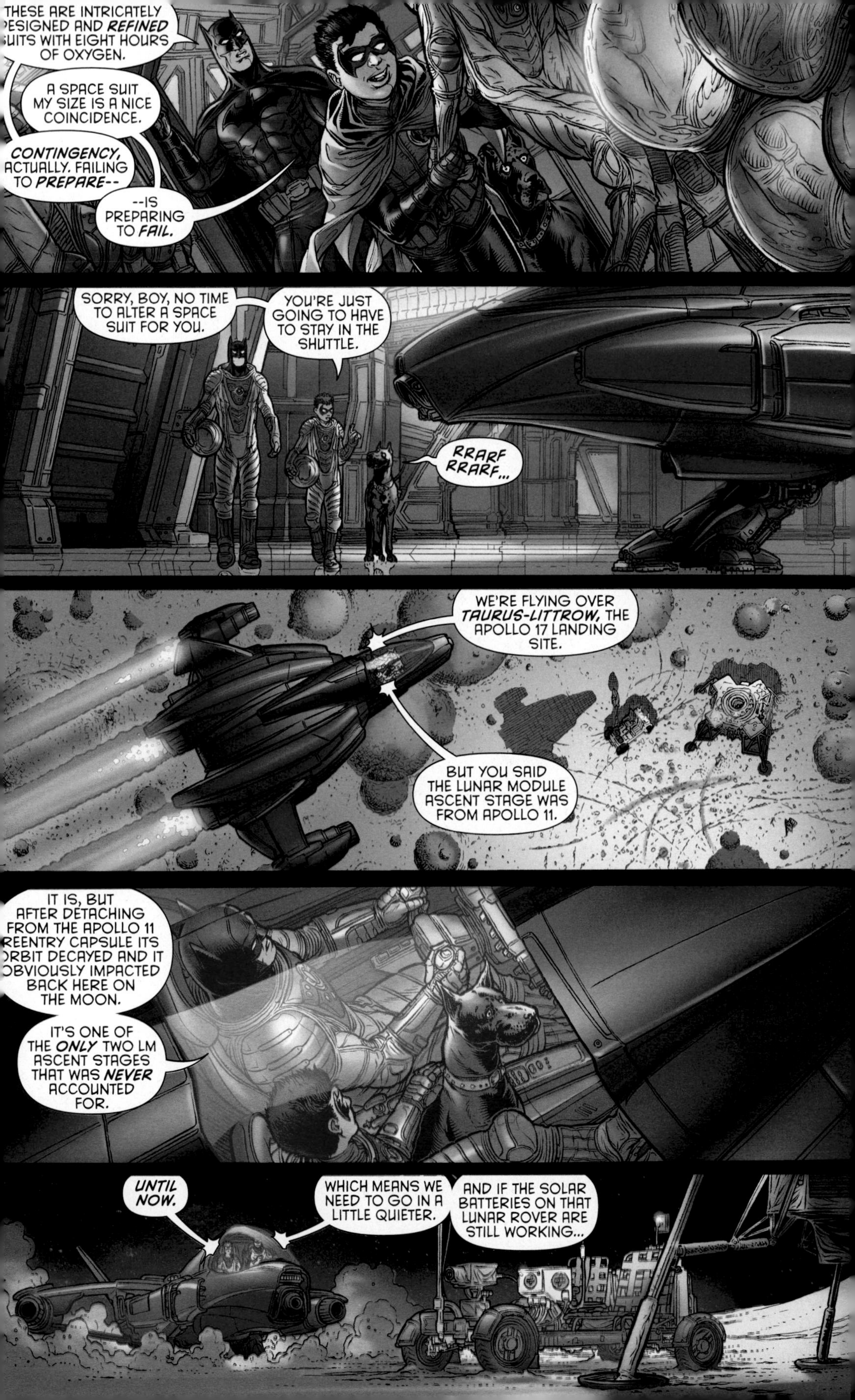
THESE ARE INTRICATELY DESIGNED AND REFINED SUITS WITH EIGHT HOURS OF OXYGEN.
A SPACE SUIT MY SIZE IS A NICE COINCIDENCE.
CONTINGENCY, ACTUALLY. FAILING TO PREPARE--
--IS PREPARING TO FAIL.
SORRY, BOY, NO TIME TO ALTER A SPACE SUIT FOR YOU.
YOU'RE JUST GOING TO HAVE TO STAY IN THE SHUTTLE.
RRARF RRARF...
WE'RE FLYING OVER TAURUS-LITTROW, THE APOLLO 17 LANDING SITE.
BUT YOU SAID THE LUNAR MODULE ASCENT STAGE WAS FROM APOLLO 11.
IT IS, BUT AFTER DETACHING FROM THE APOLLO 11 REENTRY CAPSULE ITS ORBIT DECAYED AND IT OBVIOUSLY IMPACTED BACK HERE ON THE MOON.
IT'S ONE OF THE ONLY TWO LM ASCENT STAGES THAT WAS NEVER ACCOUNTED FOR.
UNTIL NOW.
WHICH MEANS WE NEED TO GO IN A LITTLE QUIETER.
AND IF THE SOLAR BATTERIES ON THAT LUNAR ROVER ARE STILL WORKING...

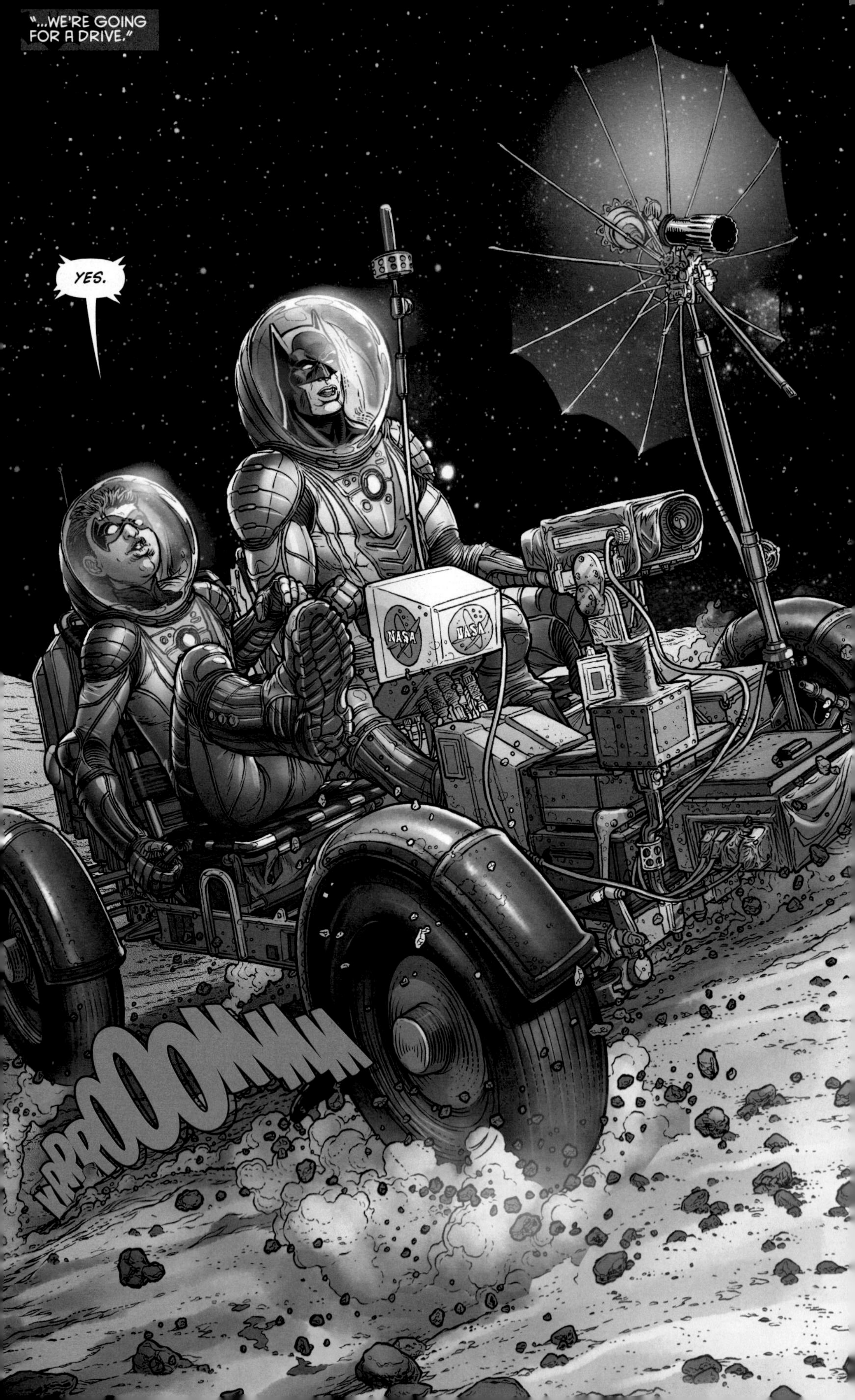
"...WE'RE GOING FOR A DRIVE."
YES.
NASA
NASA
VRRROOOMMM

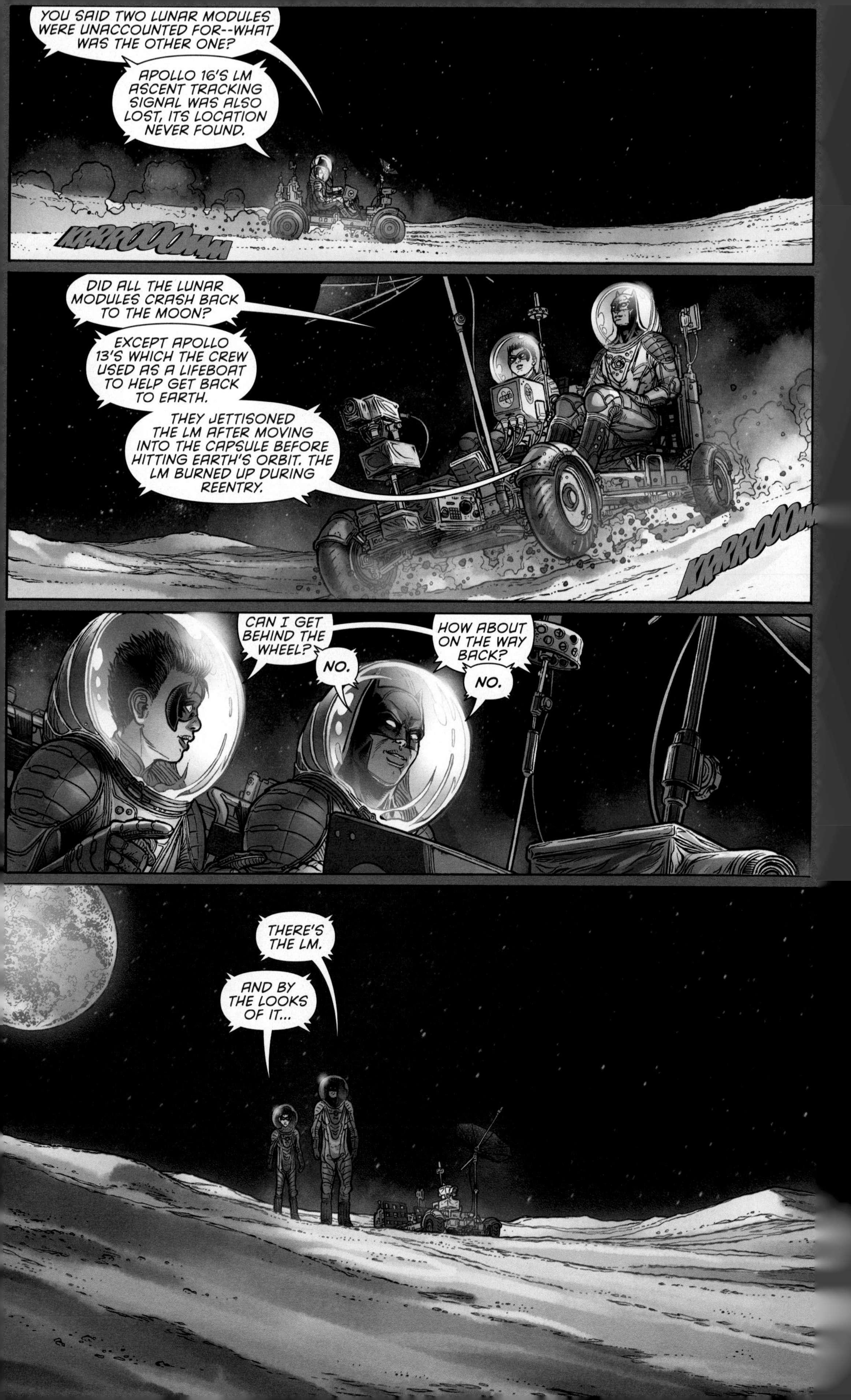
YOU SAID TWO LUNAR MODULES WERE UNACCOUNTED FOR--WHAT WAS THE OTHER ONE?
APOLLO 16'S LM ASCENT TRACKING SIGNAL WAS ALSO LOST, ITS LOCATION NEVER FOUND.
KRRROOOMM
DID ALL THE LUNAR MODULES CRASH BACK TO THE MOON?
EXCEPT APOLLO 13'S WHICH THE CREW USED AS A LIFEBOAT TO HELP GET BACK TO EARTH.
THEY JETTISONED THE LM AFTER MOVING INTO THE CAPSULE BEFORE HITTING EARTH'S ORBIT. THE LM BURNED UP DURING REENTRY.
KRRROOOM
CAN I GET BEHIND THE WHEEL?
NO.
HOW ABOUT ON THE WAY BACK?
NO.
THERE'S THE LM.
AND BY THE LOOKS OF IT...

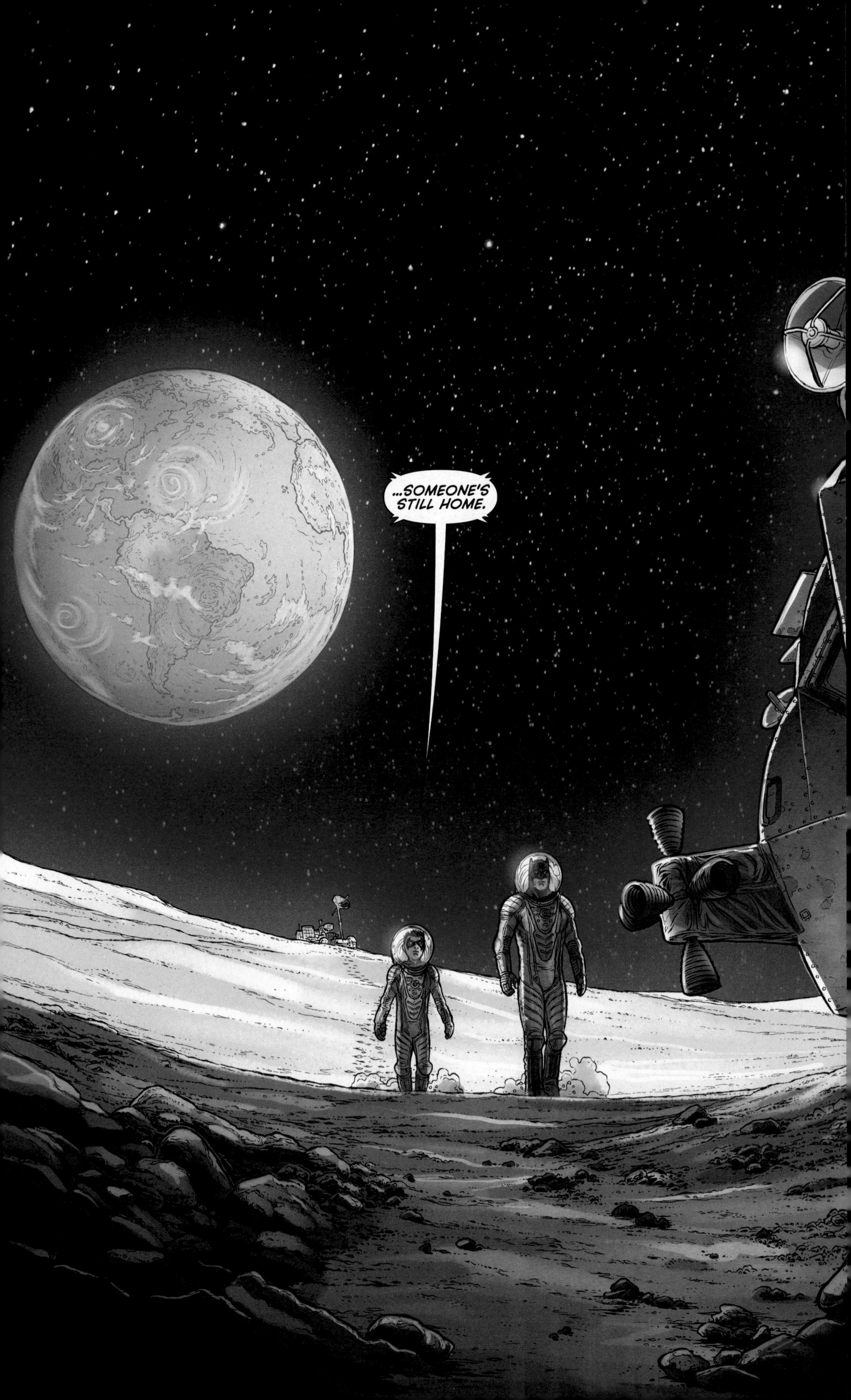
...SOMEONE'S STILL HOME.

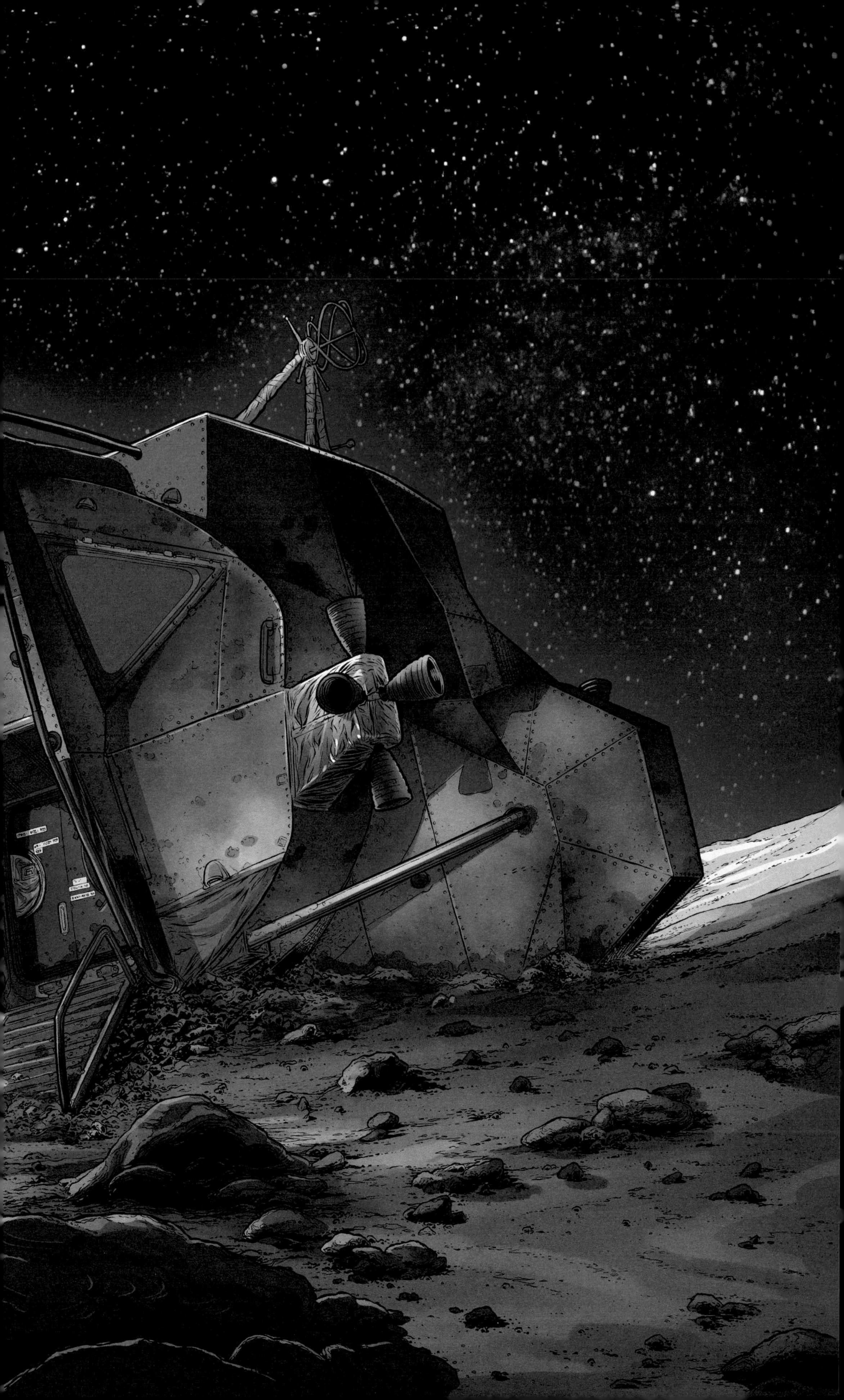

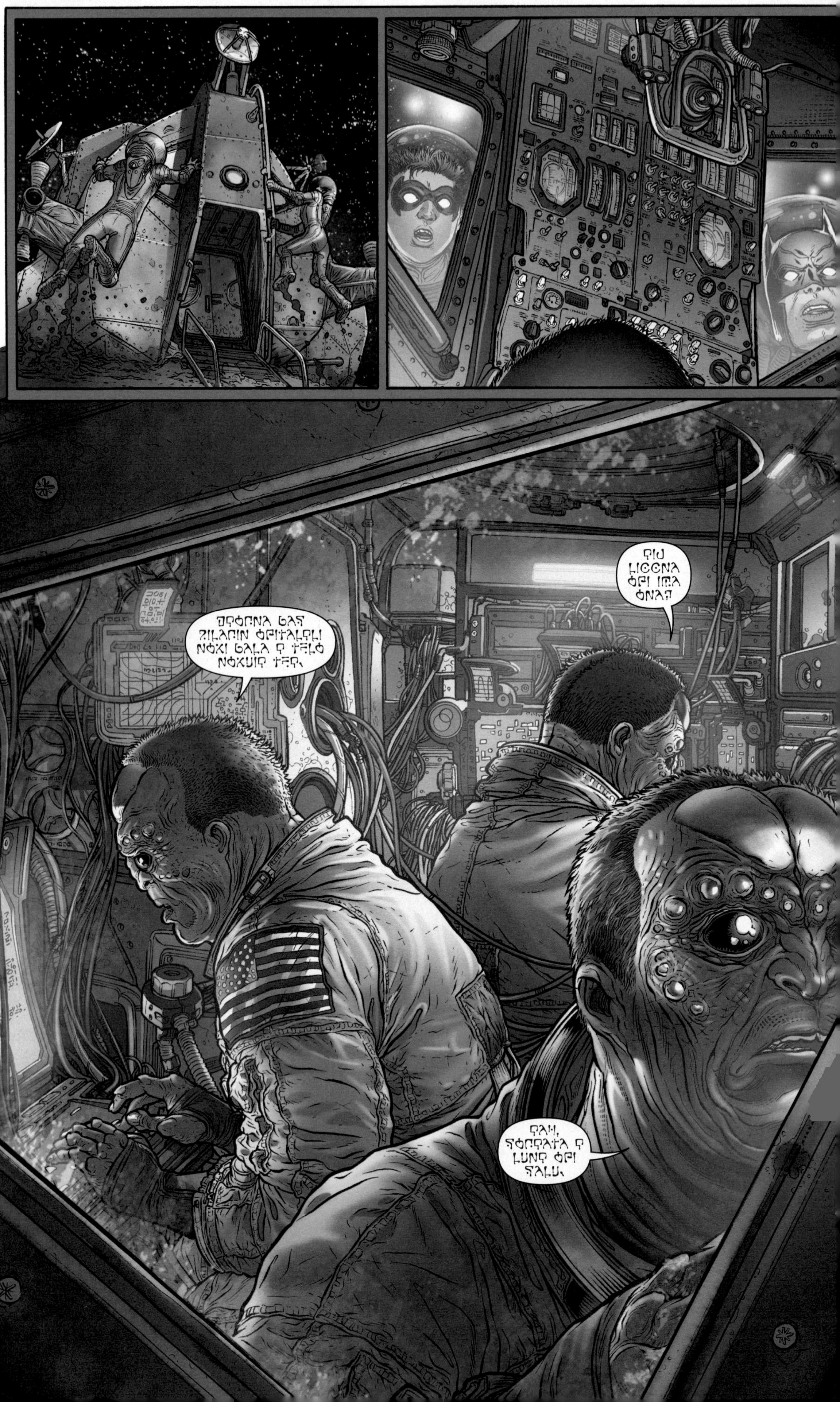

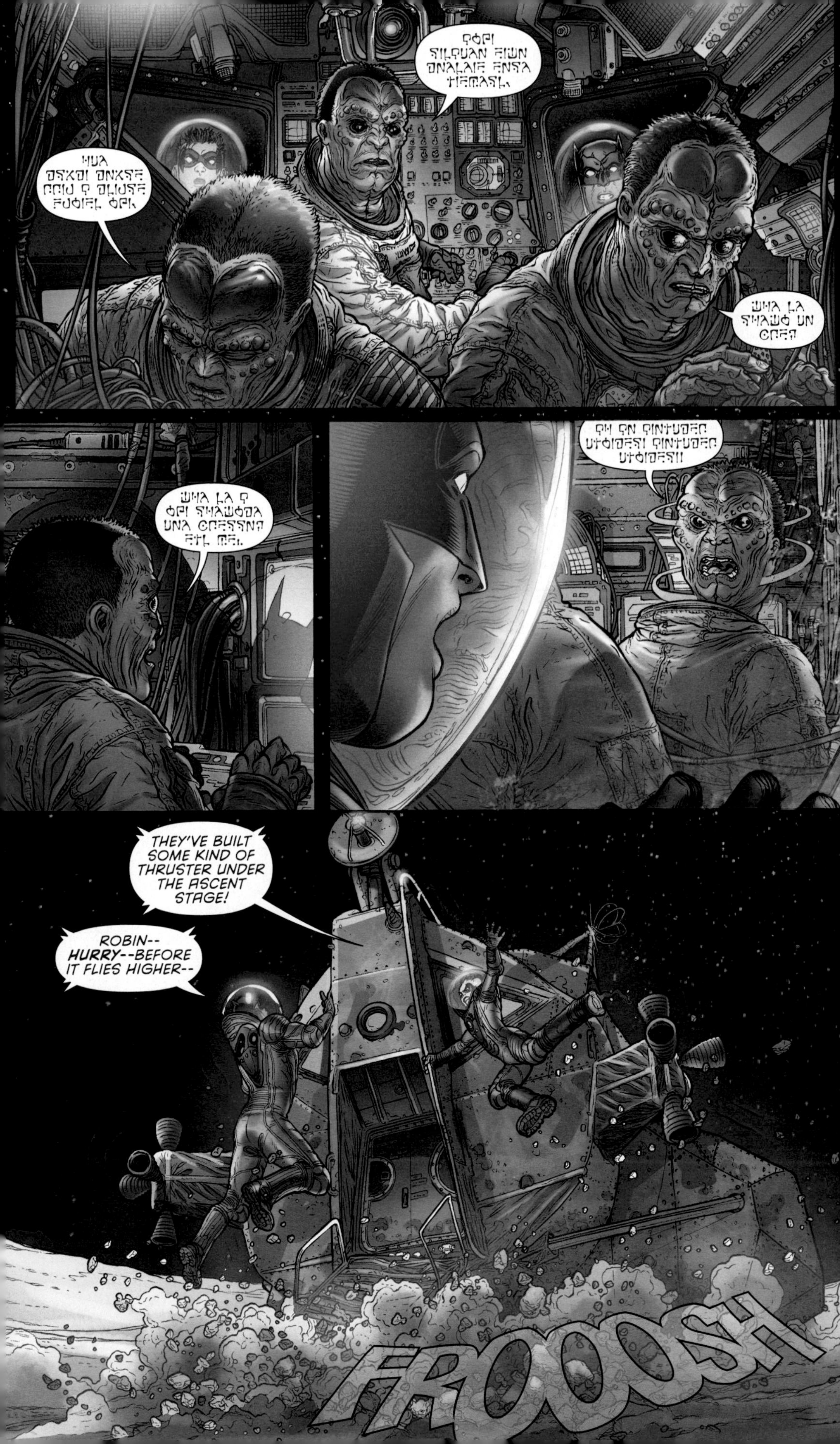
THEY'VE BUILT SOME KIND OF THRUSTER UNDER THE ASCENT STAGE!
ROBIN-- HURRY--BEFORE IT FLIES HIGHER--
FROOOSH

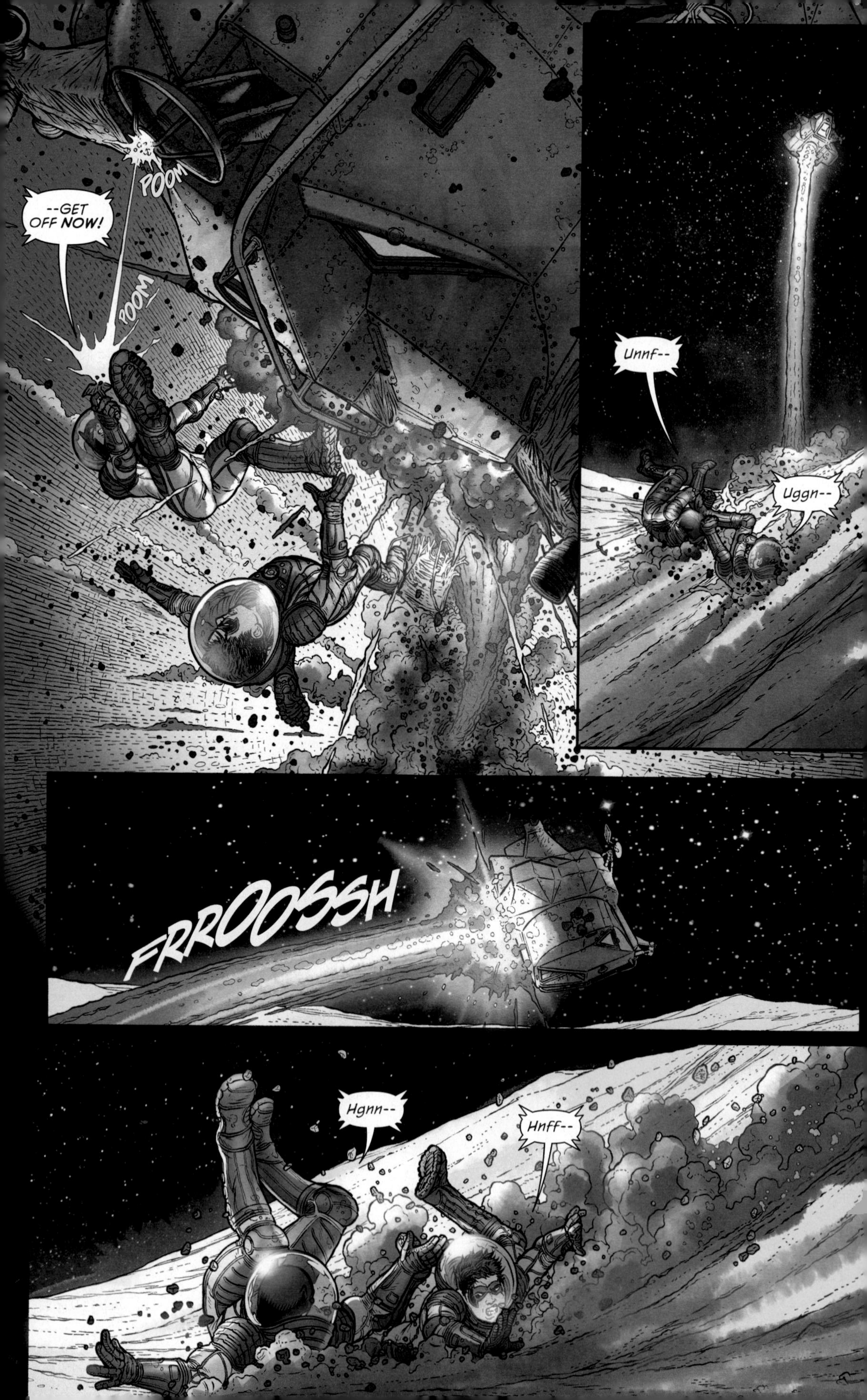
POOM
--GET OFF NOW!
POOM
Unnf--
Uggn--
FRROOSSH
Hgnn--
Hnff--

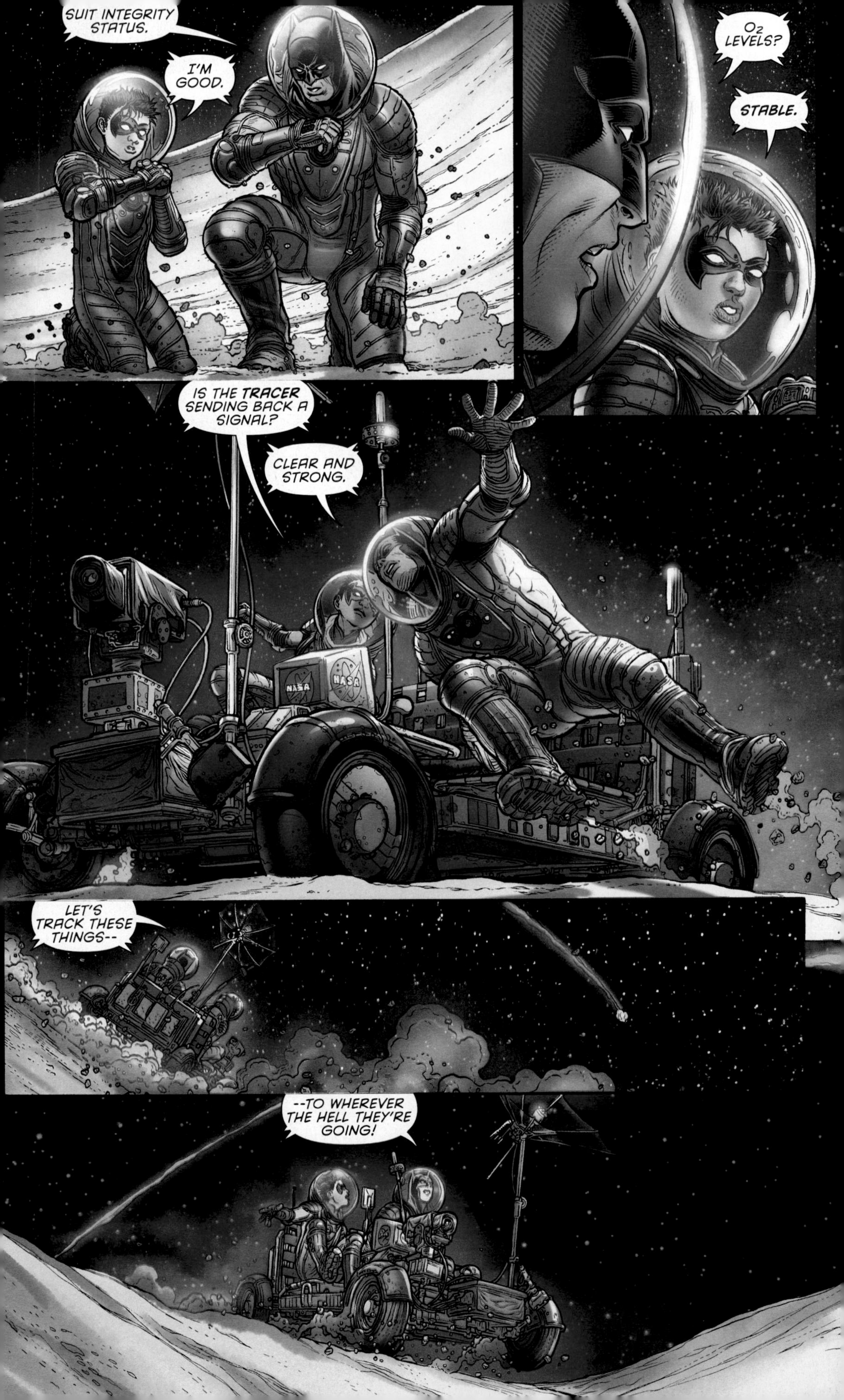
SUIT INTEGRITY STATUS.
I'M GOOD.
O2 LEVELS?
STABLE.
IS THE TRACER SENDING BACK A SIGNAL?
CLEAR AND STRONG.
NASA
NASA
LET'S TRACK THESE THINGS--
--TO WHEREVER THE HELL THEY'RE GOING!

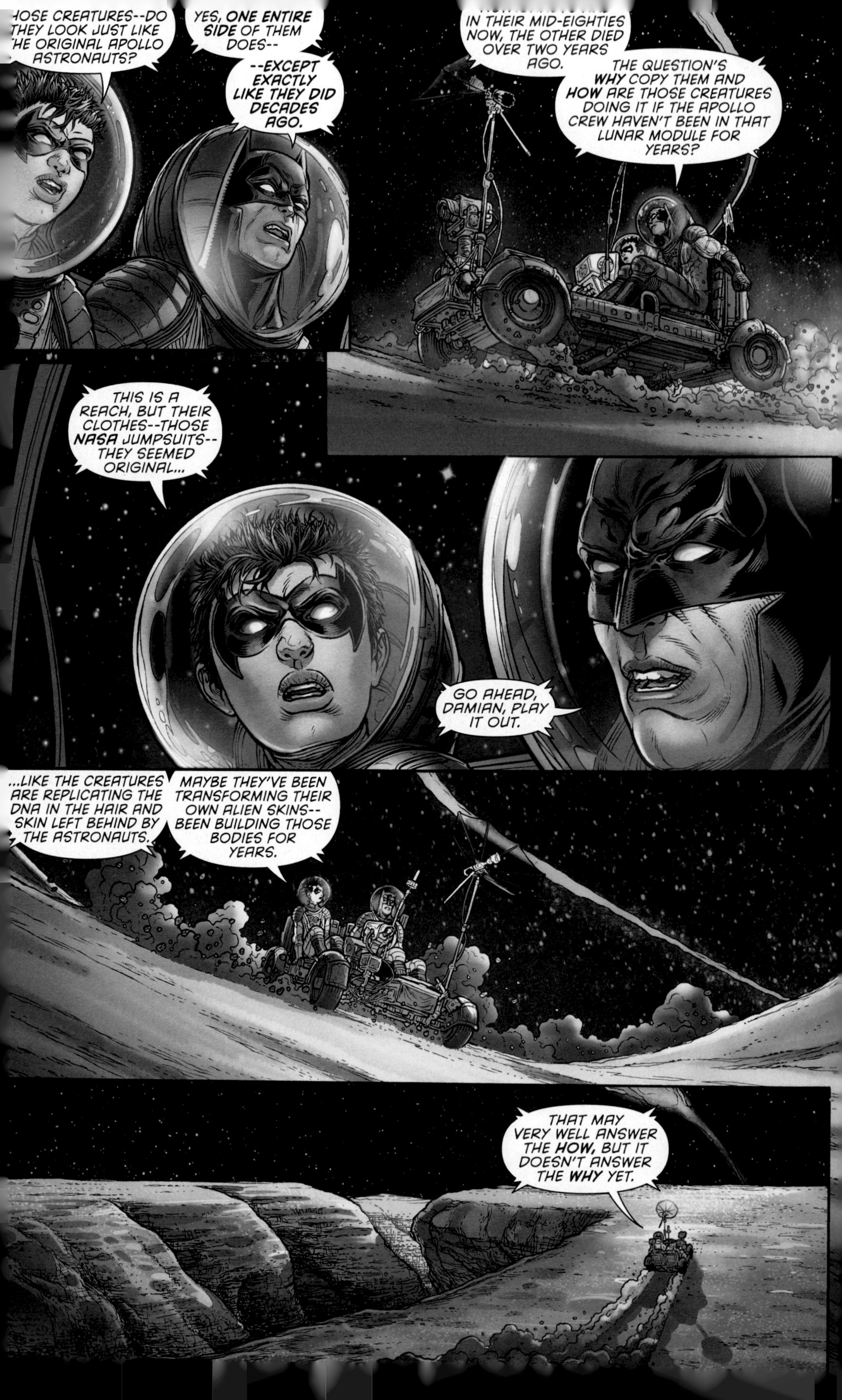
HOSE CREATURES--DO THEY LOOK JUST LIKE THE ORIGINAL APOLLO ASTRONAUTS?
YES, ONE ENTIRE SIDE OF THEM DOES--
--EXCEPT EXACTLY LIKE THEY DID DECADES AGO.
IN THEIR MID-EIGHTIES NOW, THE OTHER DIED OVER TWO YEARS AGO.
THE QUESTION'S WHY COPY THEM AND HOW ARE THOSE CREATURES DOING IT IF THE APOLLO CREW HAVEN'T BEEN IN THAT LUNAR MODULE FOR YEARS?
THIS IS A REACH, BUT THEIR CLOTHES--THOSE NASA JUMPSUITS--THEY SEEMED ORIGINAL...
GO AHEAD, DAMIAN, PLAY IT OUT.
...LIKE THE CREATURES ARE REPLICATING THE DNA IN THE HAIR AND SKIN LEFT BEHIND BY THE ASTRONAUTS.
MAYBE THEY'VE BEEN TRANSFORMING THEIR OWN ALIEN SKINS--BEEN BUILDING THOSE BODIES FOR YEARS.
THAT MAY VERY WELL ANSWER THE HOW, BUT IT DOESN'T ANSWER THE WHY YET.

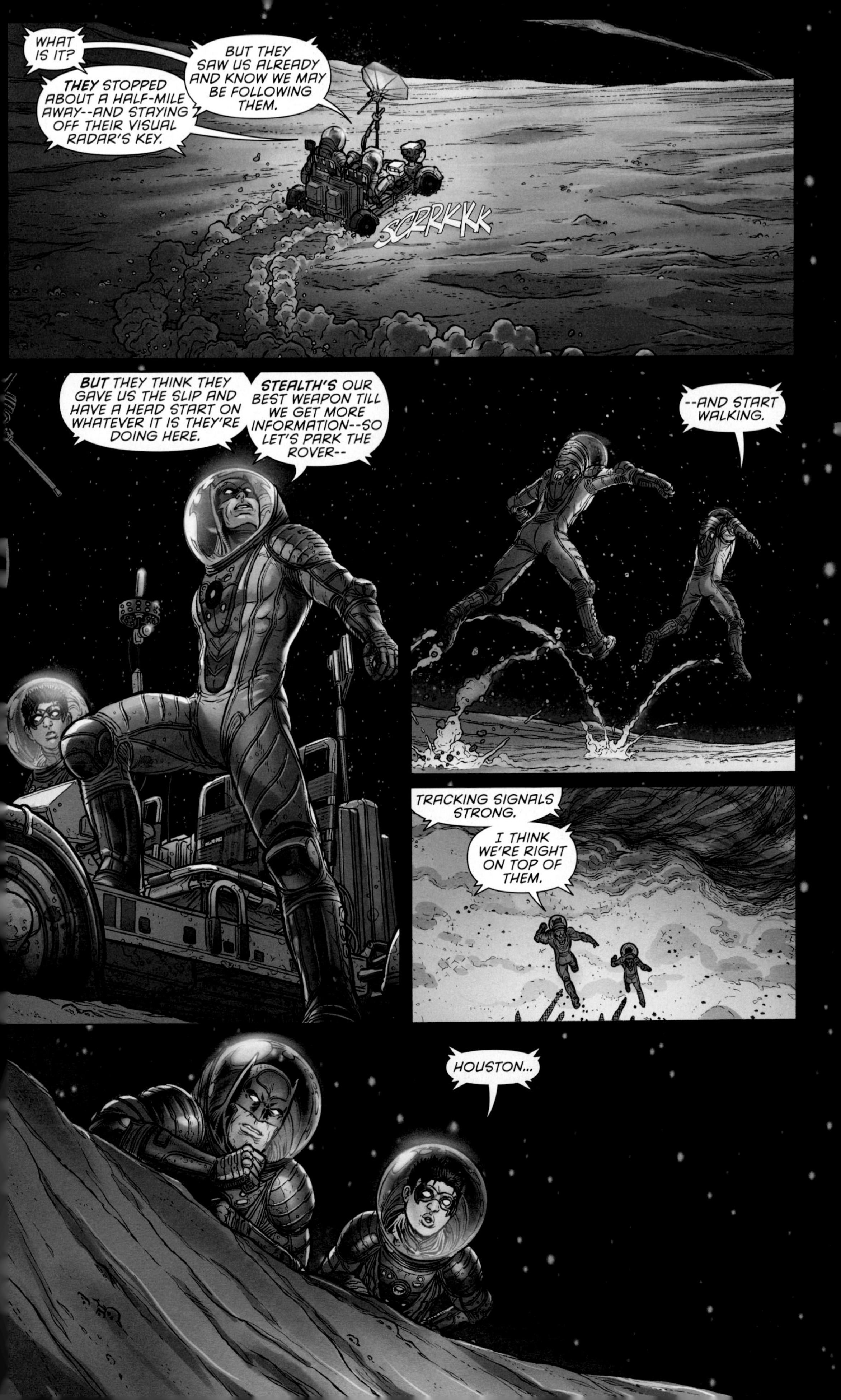
WHAT IS IT?
THEY STOPPED ABOUT A HALF-MILE AWAY--AND STAYING OFF THEIR VISUAL RADAR'S KEY.
BUT THEY SAW US ALREADY AND KNOW WE MAY BE FOLLOWING THEM.
SCRRKKK
BUT THEY THINK THEY GAVE US THE SLIP AND HAVE A HEAD START ON WHATEVER IT IS THEY'RE DOING HERE.
STEALTH'S OUR BEST WEAPON TILL WE GET MORE INFORMATION--SO LET'S PARK THE ROVER--
--AND START WALKING.
TRACKING SIGNALS STRONG.
I THINK WE'RE RIGHT ON TOP OF THEM.
HOUSTON...

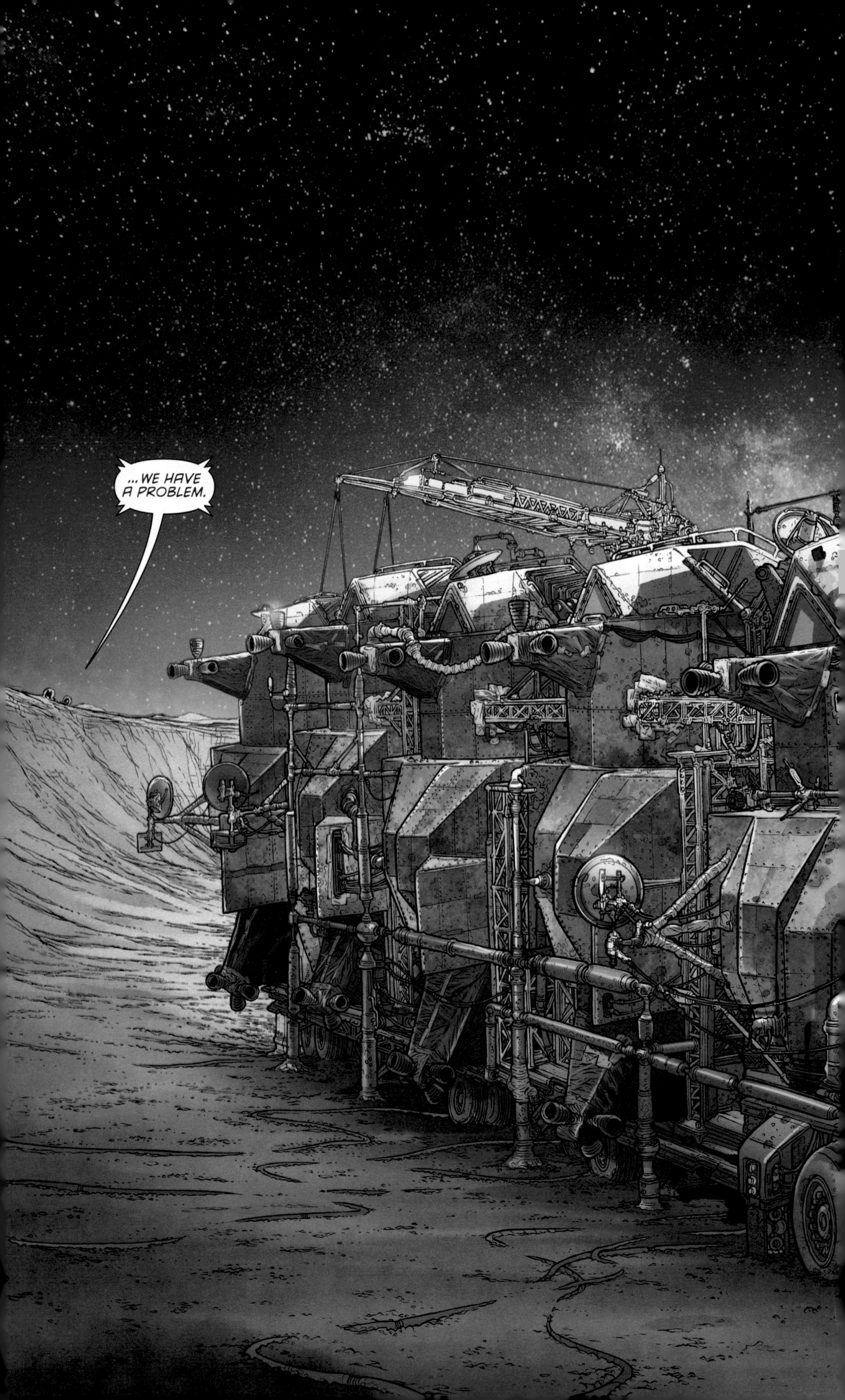
...WE HAVE A PROBLEM.

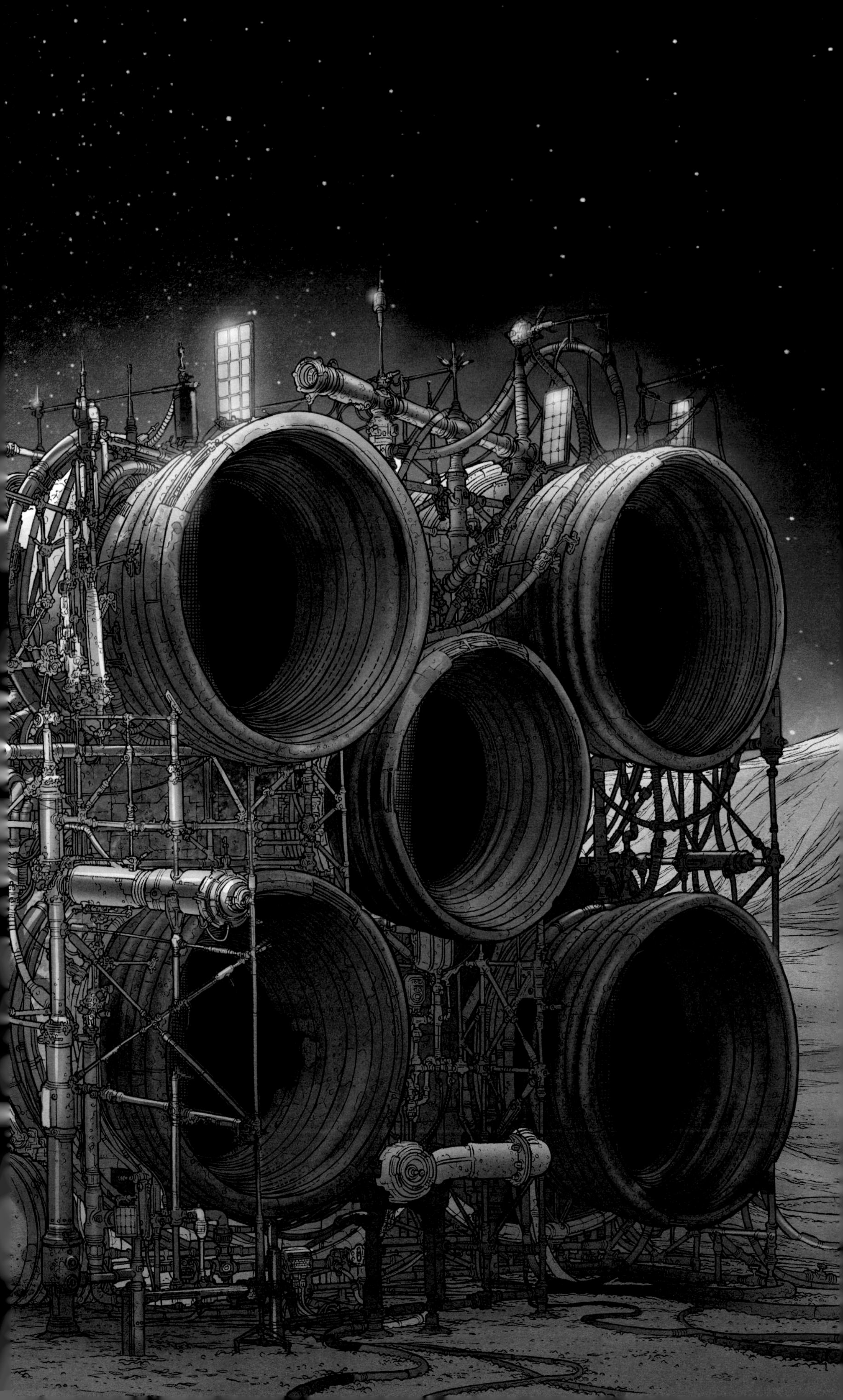

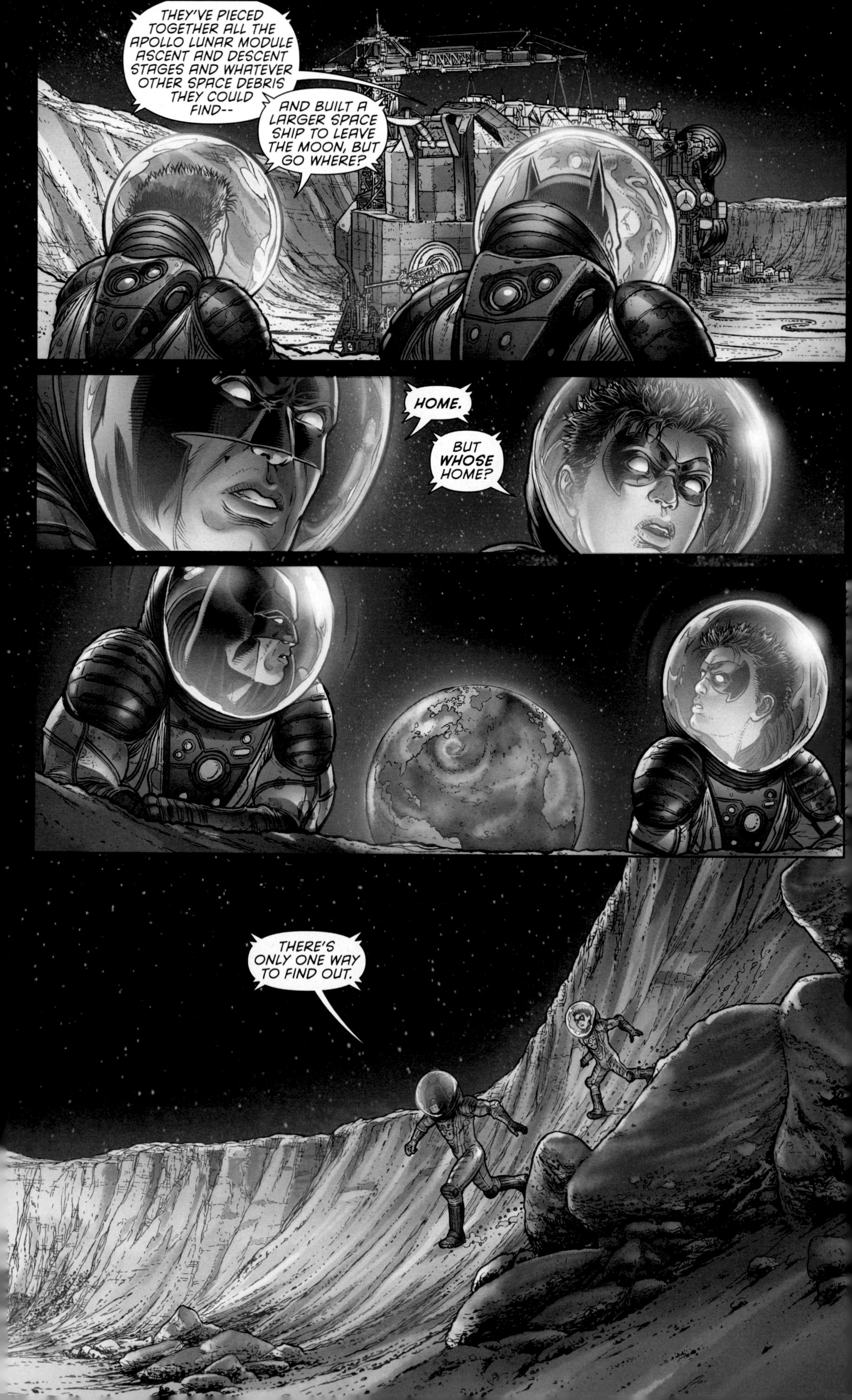
THEY'VE PIECED TOGETHER ALL THE APOLLO LUNAR MODULE ASCENT AND DESCENT STAGES AND WHATEVER OTHER SPACE DEBRIS THEY COULD FIND--
AND BUILT A LARGER SPACE SHIP TO LEAVE THE MOON, BUT GO WHERE?
HOME.
BUT WHOSE HOME?
THERE'S ONLY ONE WAY TO FIND OUT.

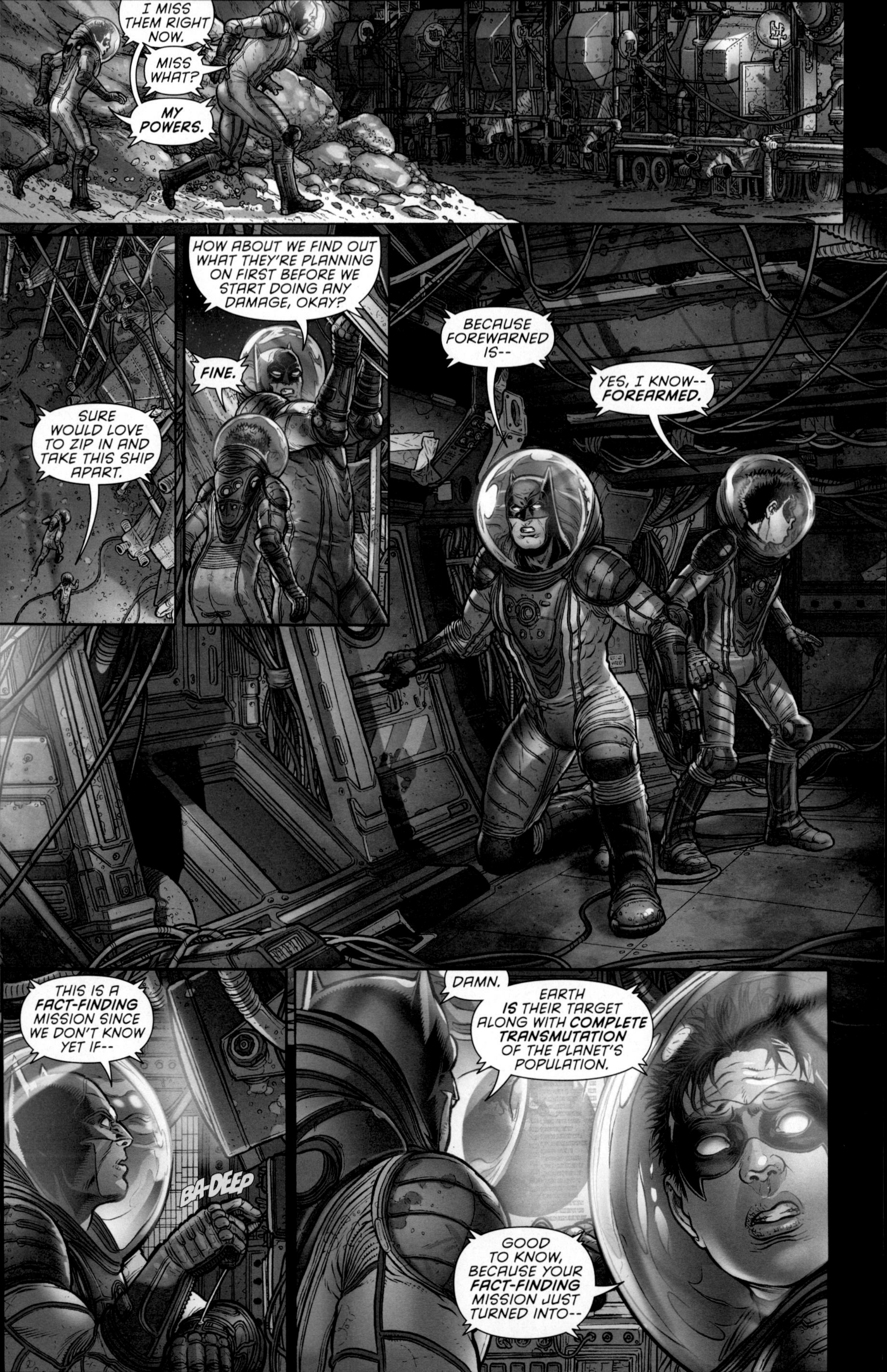
I MISS THEM RIGHT NOW.
MISS WHAT?
MY POWERS.
SURE WOULD LOVE TO ZIP IN AND TAKE THIS SHIP APART.
HOW ABOUT WE FIND OUT WHAT THEY'RE PLANNING ON FIRST BEFORE WE START DOING ANY DAMAGE, OKAY?
FINE.
BECAUSE FOREWARNED IS--
YES, I KNOW-- FOREARMED.
THIS IS A FACT-FINDING MISSION SINCE WE DON'T KNOW YET IF--
BA-DEEP
DAMN.
EARTH IS THEIR TARGET ALONG WITH COMPLETE TRANSMUTATION OF THE PLANET'S POPULATION.
GOOD TO KNOW, BECAUSE YOUR FACT-FINDING MISSION JUST TURNED INTO--

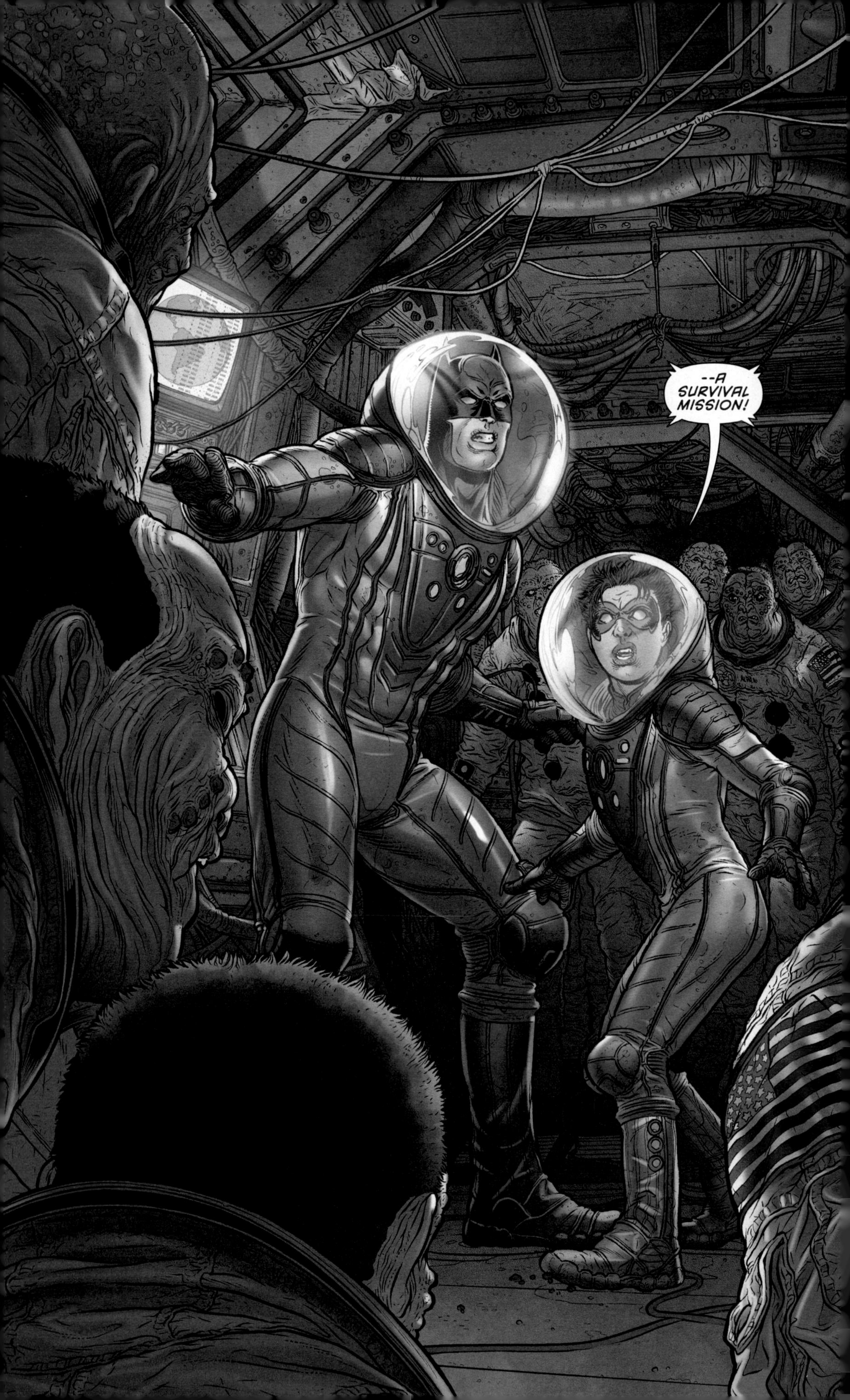
--A SURVIVAL MISSION!

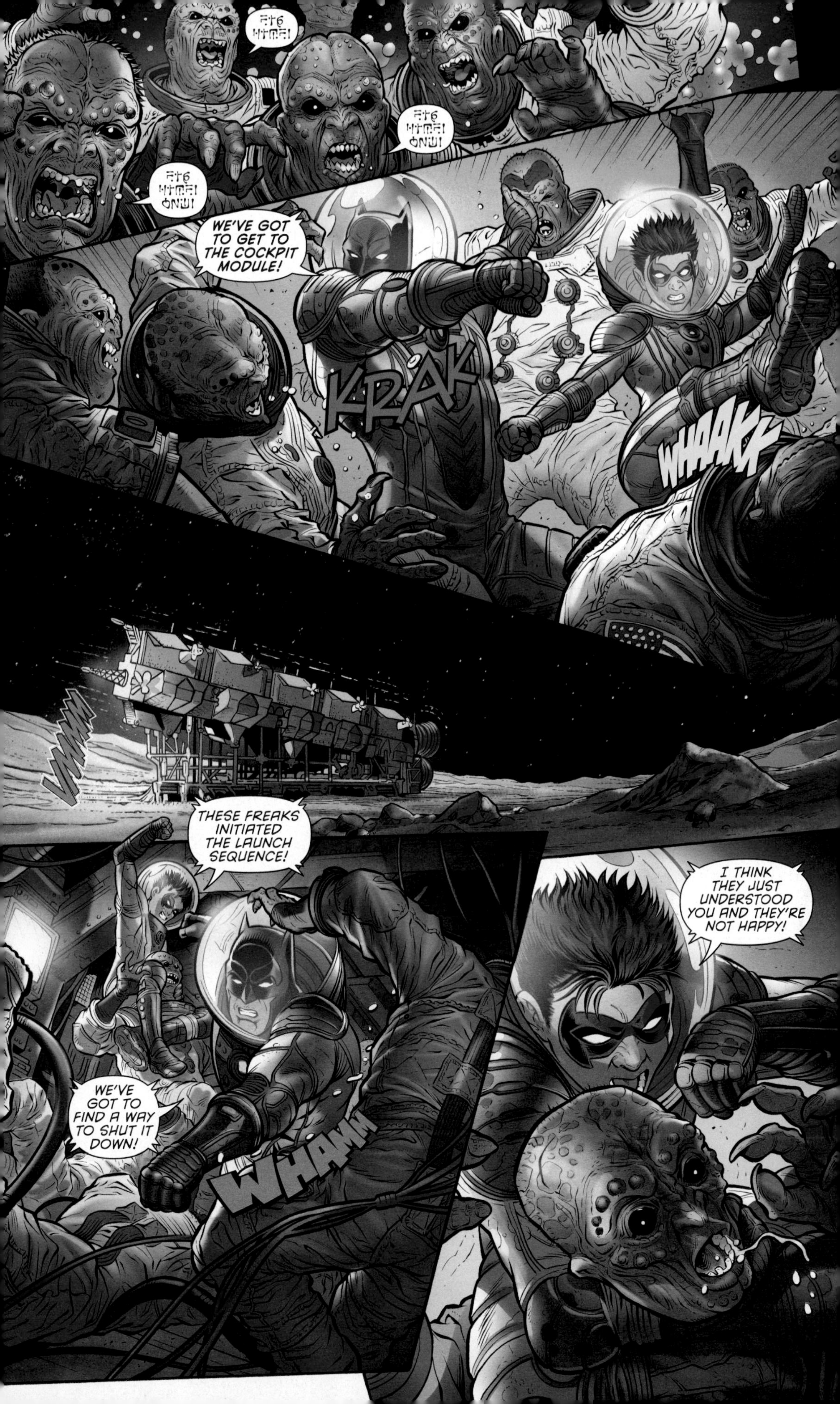

WE'VE GOT TO GET TO THE COCKPIT MODULE!
KRAK
WHAAKK
THESE FREAKS INITIATED THE LAUNCH SEQUENCE!
WE'VE GOT TO FIND A WAY TO SHUT IT DOWN!
WHAMM
I THINK THEY JUST UNDERSTOOD YOU AND THEY'RE NOT HAPPY!

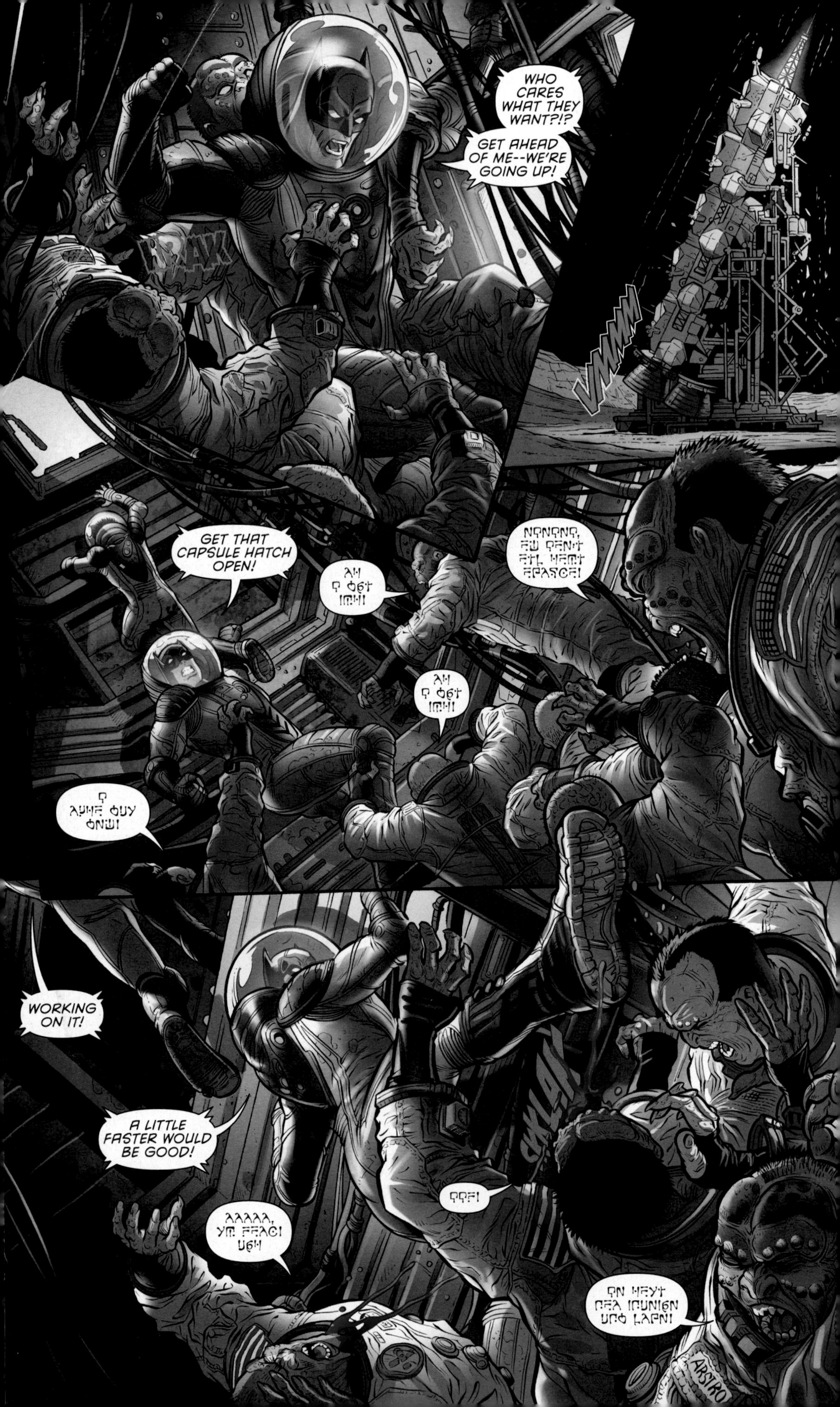
WHO CARES WHAT THEY WANT?!?
GET AHEAD OF ME--WE'RE GOING UP!
GET THAT CAPSULE HATCH OPEN!
WORKING ON IT!
A LITTLE FASTER WOULD BE GOOD!
ASTRO

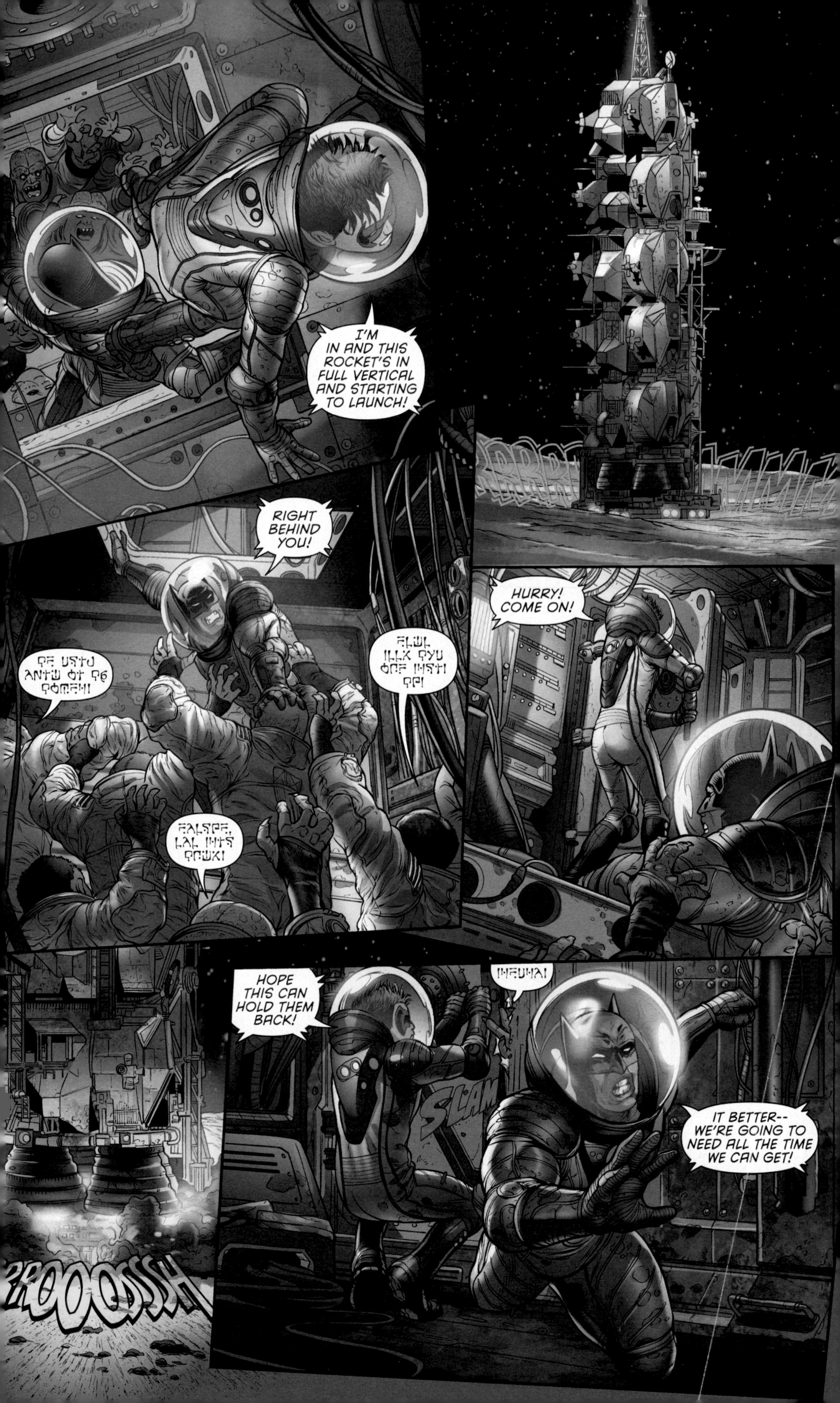
I'M IN AND THIS ROCKET'S IN FULL VERTICAL AND STARTING TO LAUNCH!
RIGHT BEHIND YOU!
HURRY! COME ON!
HOPE THIS CAN HOLD THEM BACK!
SLAM
IT BETTER-- WE'RE GOING TO NEED ALL THE TIME WE CAN GET!

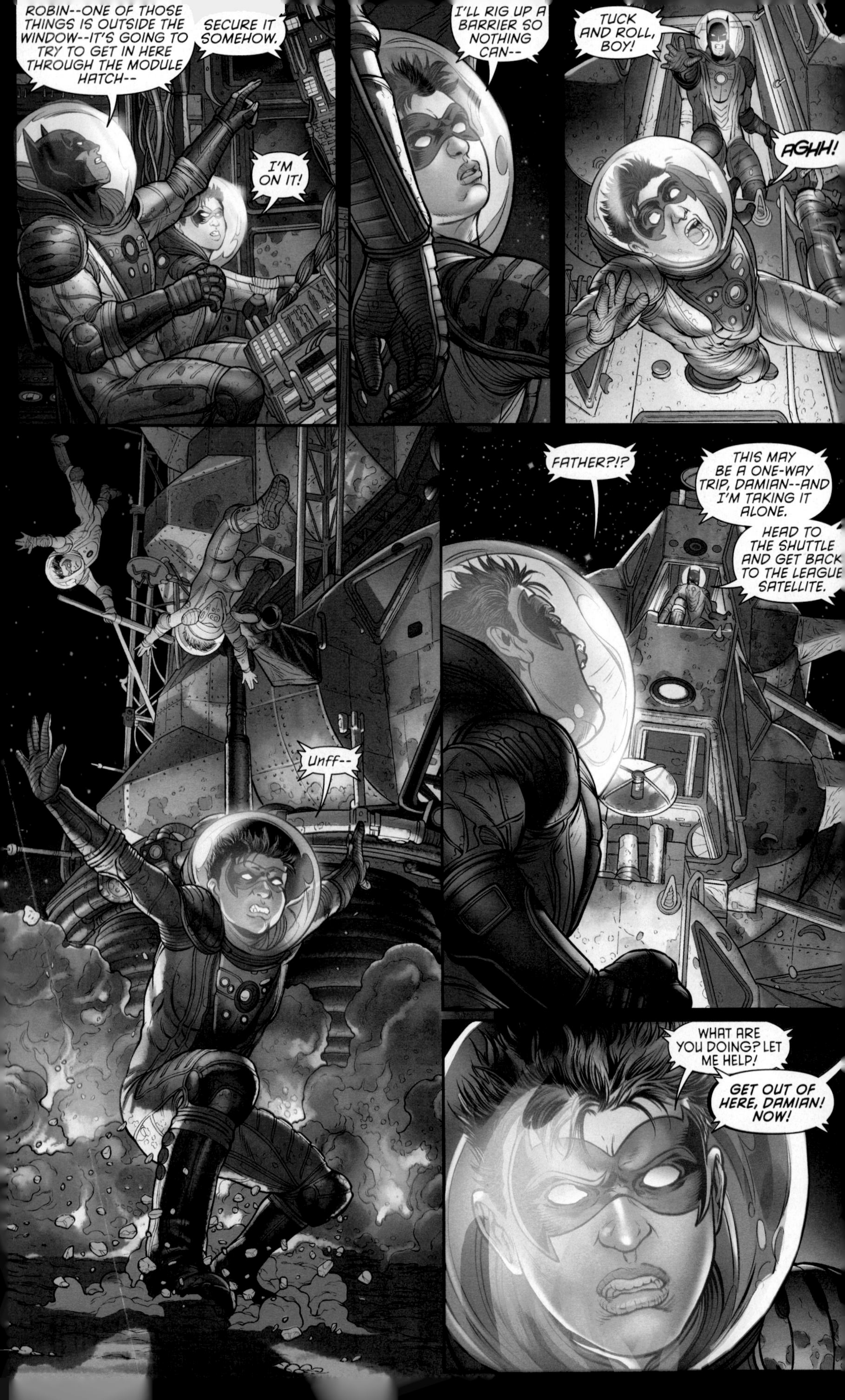

ROBIN--ONE OF THOSE THINGS IS OUTSIDE THE WINDOW--IT'S GOING TO TRY TO GET IN HERE THROUGH THE MODULE HATCH--
SECURE IT SOMEHOW.
I'M ON IT!
I'LL RIG UP A BARRIER SO NOTHING CAN--
TUCK AND ROLL, BOY!
AGHH!
Unff--
FATHER?!?
THIS MAY BE A ONE-WAY TRIP, DAMIAN--AND I'M TAKING IT ALONE.
HEAD TO THE SHUTTLE AND GET BACK TO THE LEAGUE SATELLITE.
WHAT ARE YOU DOING? LET ME HELP!
GET OUT OF HERE, DAMIAN! NOW!

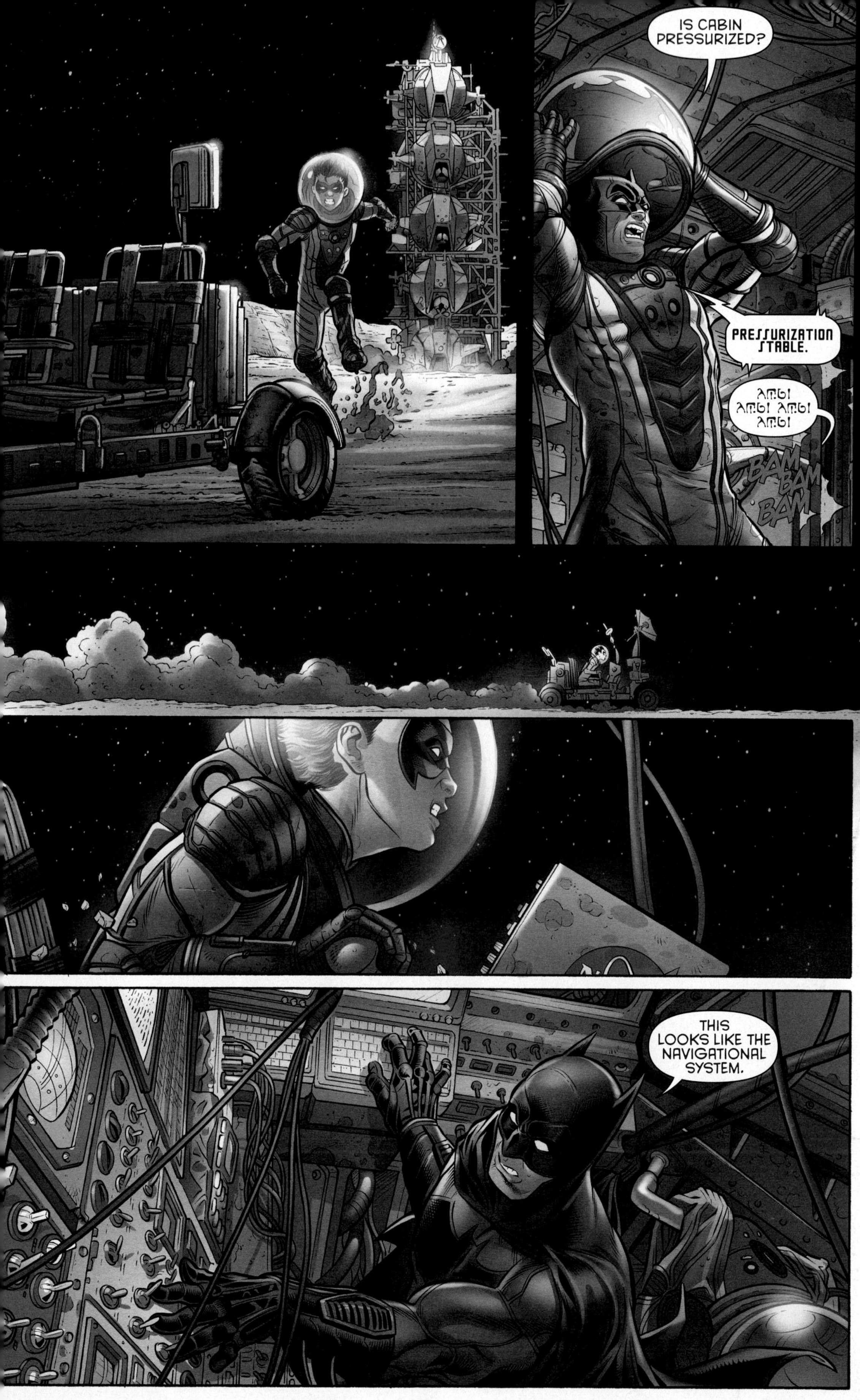
IS CABIN PRESSURIZED?
PRESSURIZATION STABLE.
BAM BAM BAM
THIS LOOKS LIKE THE NAVIGATIONAL SYSTEM.

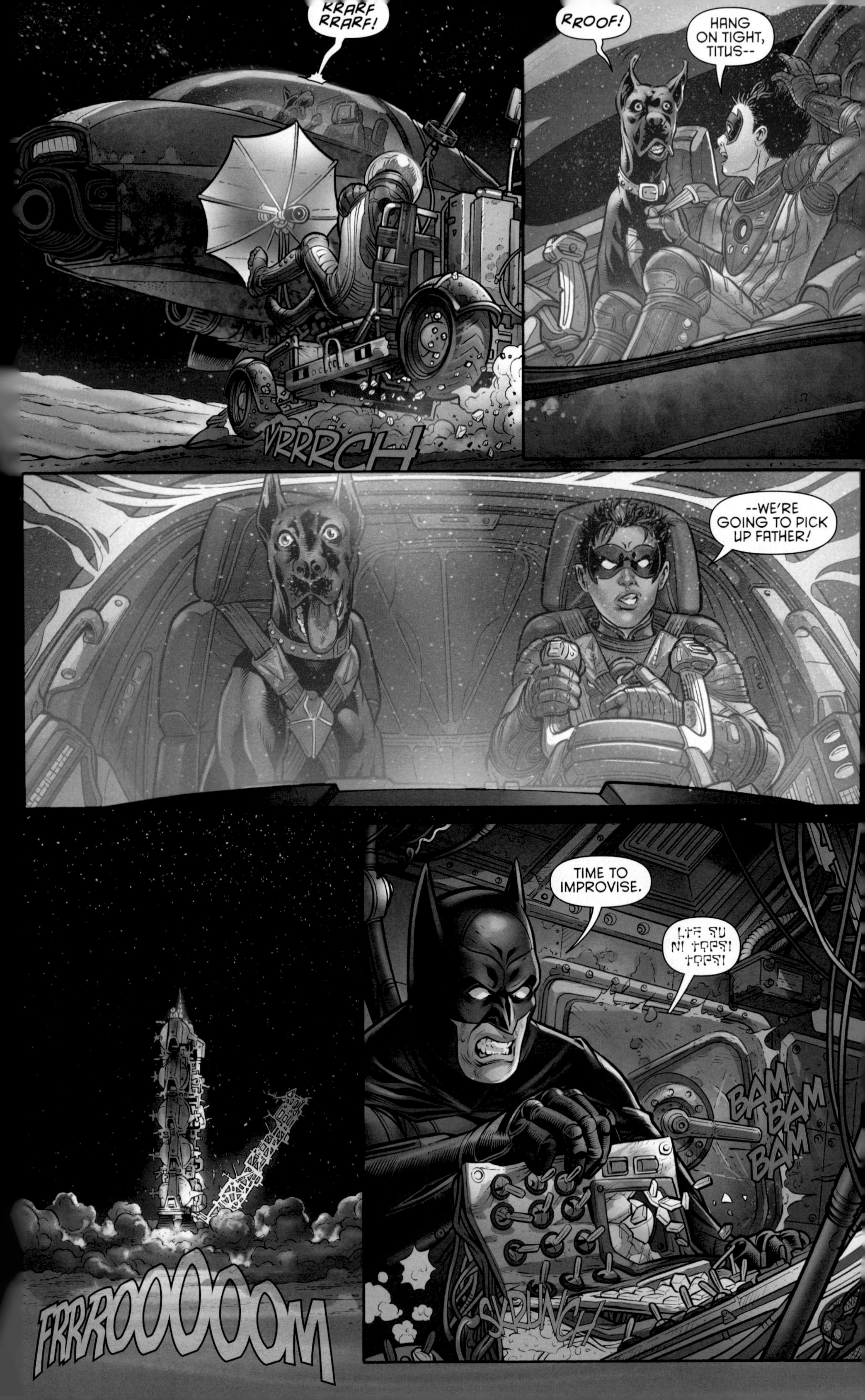
KRARF RRARF!
VRRRCH
RROOF!
HANG ON TIGHT, TITUS--
--WE'RE GOING TO PICK UP FATHER!
FRRROOOOOOM
TIME TO IMPROVISE.
BAM BAM BAM
SKRUNCH

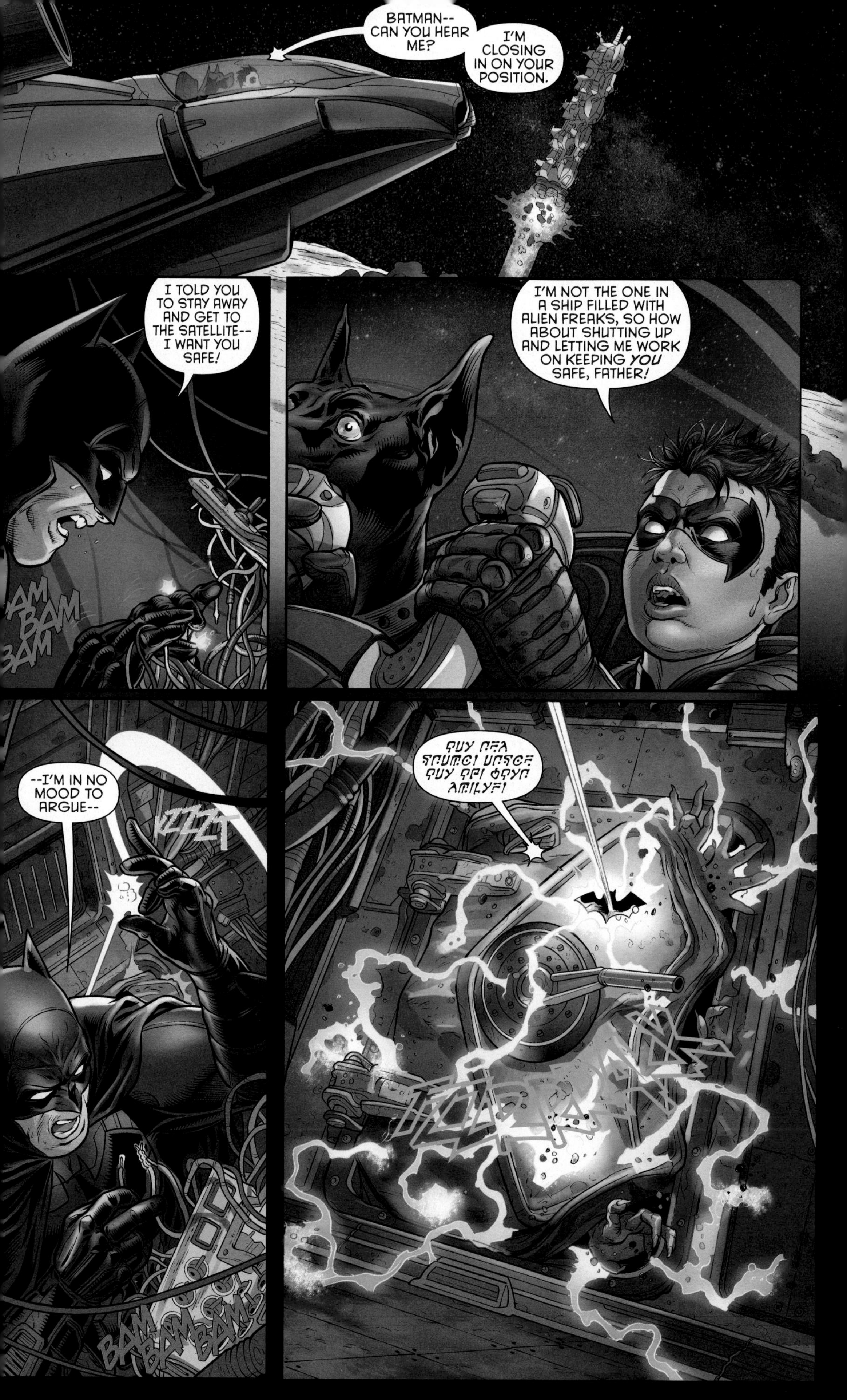
BATMAN-- CAN YOU HEAR ME?
I'M CLOSING IN ON YOUR POSITION.
I TOLD YOU TO STAY AWAY AND GET TO THE SATELLITE-- I WANT YOU SAFE!
BAM BAM BAM
I'M NOT THE ONE IN A SHIP FILLED WITH ALIEN FREAKS, SO HOW ABOUT SHUTTING UP AND LETTING ME WORK ON KEEPING *YOU* SAFE, FATHER!
--I'M IN NO MOOD TO ARGUE--
VZZZT
BAM BAM BAM

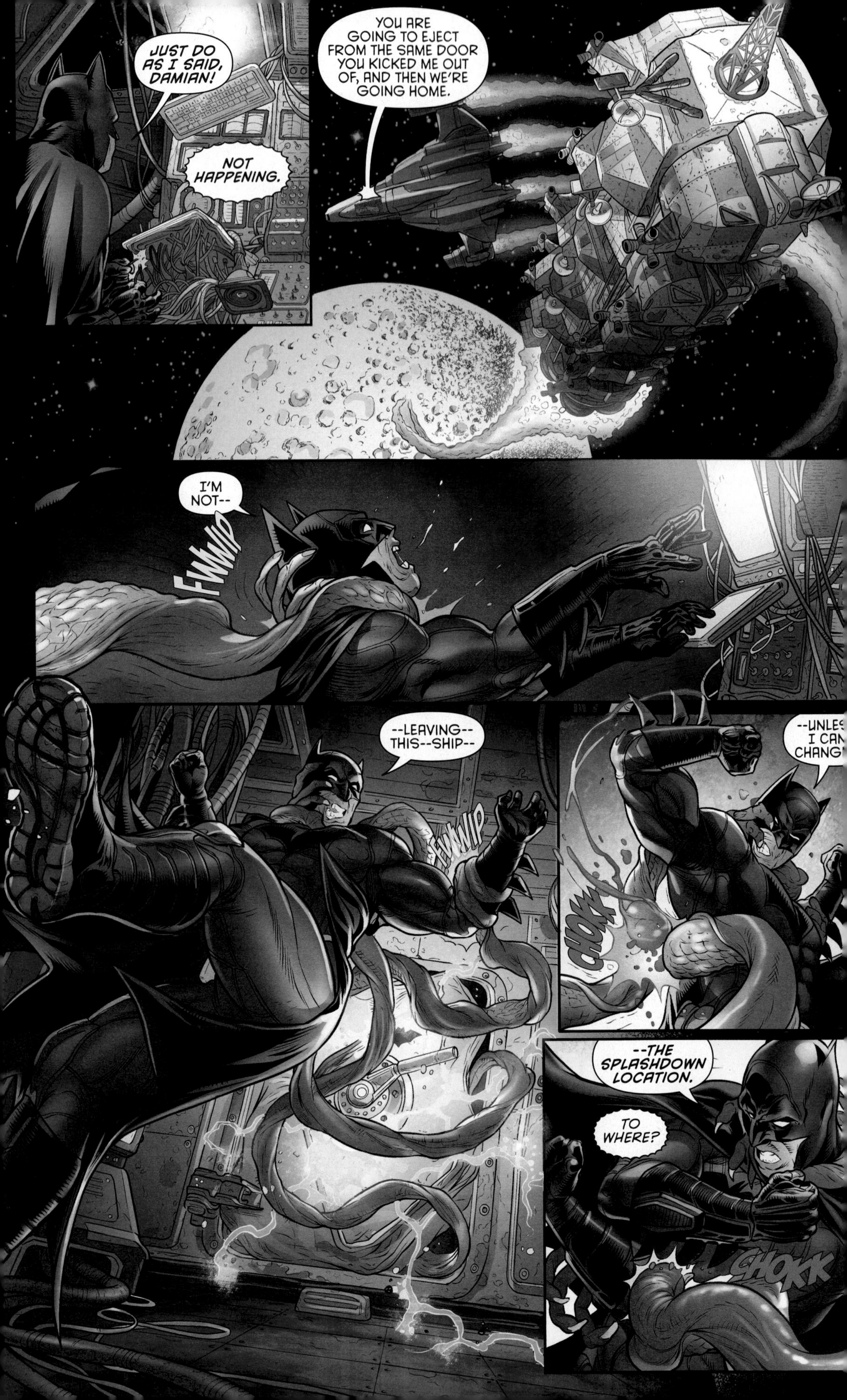
JUST DO AS I SAID, DAMIAN!
NOT HAPPENING.
YOU ARE GOING TO EJECT FROM THE SAME DOOR YOU KICKED ME OUT OF, AND THEN WE'RE GOING HOME.
I'M NOT--
FWWIP
--LEAVING-- THIS--SHIP--
FWWIP
--UNLES I CAN CHANG
CHOKK
--THE SPLASHDOWN LOCATION.
TO WHERE?
CHOKK

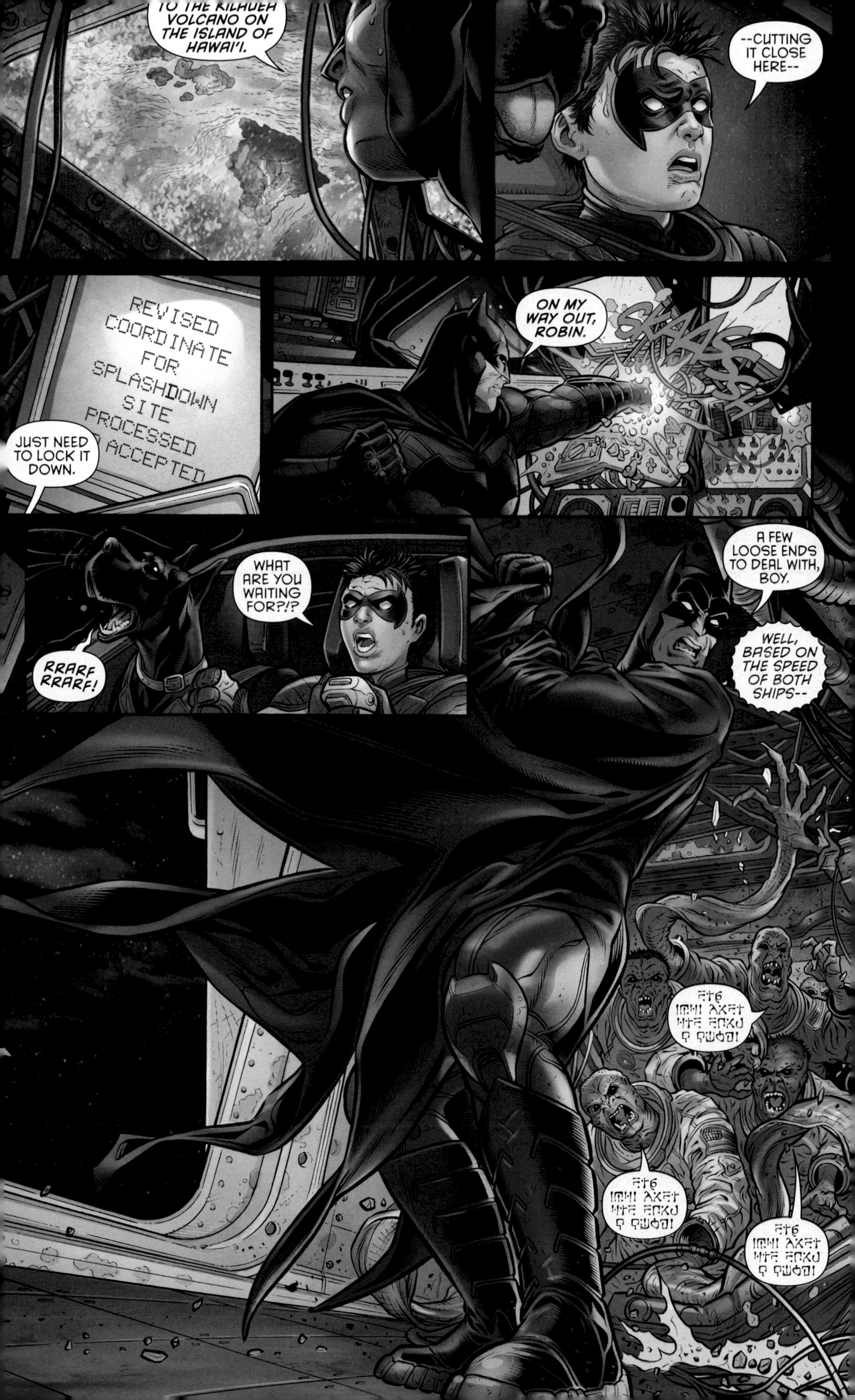
TO THE KILAUEA VOLCANO ON THE ISLAND OF HAWAI'I.
--CUTTING IT CLOSE HERE--
REVISED COORDINATE FOR SPLASHDOWN SITE PROCESSED ACCEPTED
JUST NEED TO LOCK IT DOWN.
ON MY WAY OUT, ROBIN.
SKASSH
WHAT ARE YOU WAITING FOR?!?
RRARF RRARF!
A FEW LOOSE ENDS TO DEAL WITH, BOY.
WELL, BASED ON THE SPEED OF BOTH SHIPS--

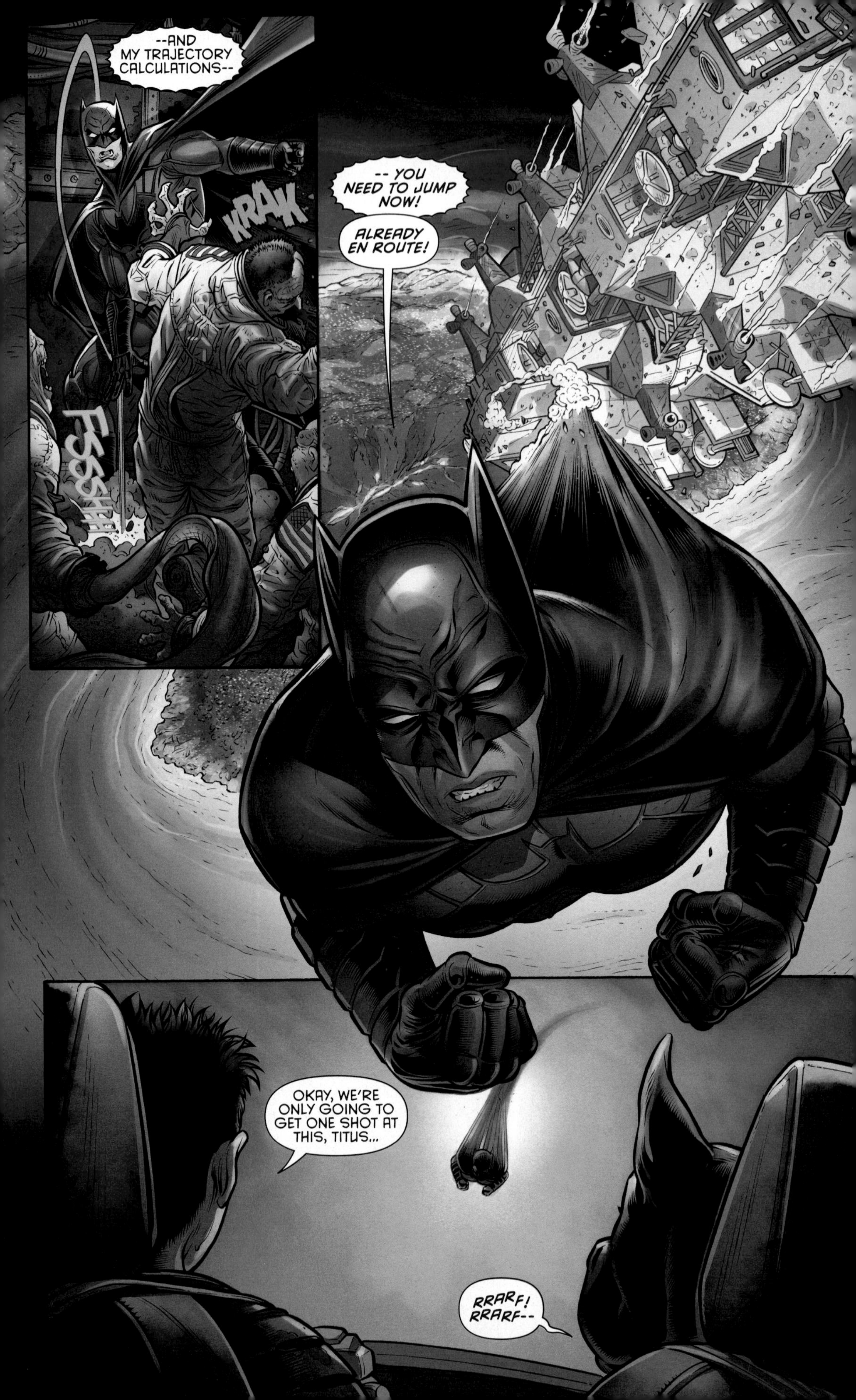
--AND MY TRAJECTORY CALCULATIONS--
KRAK
FSSSHH
-- YOU NEED TO JUMP NOW!
ALREADY EN ROUTE!
OKAY, WE'RE ONLY GOING TO GET ONE SHOT AT THIS, TITUS...
RRARF! RRARF--

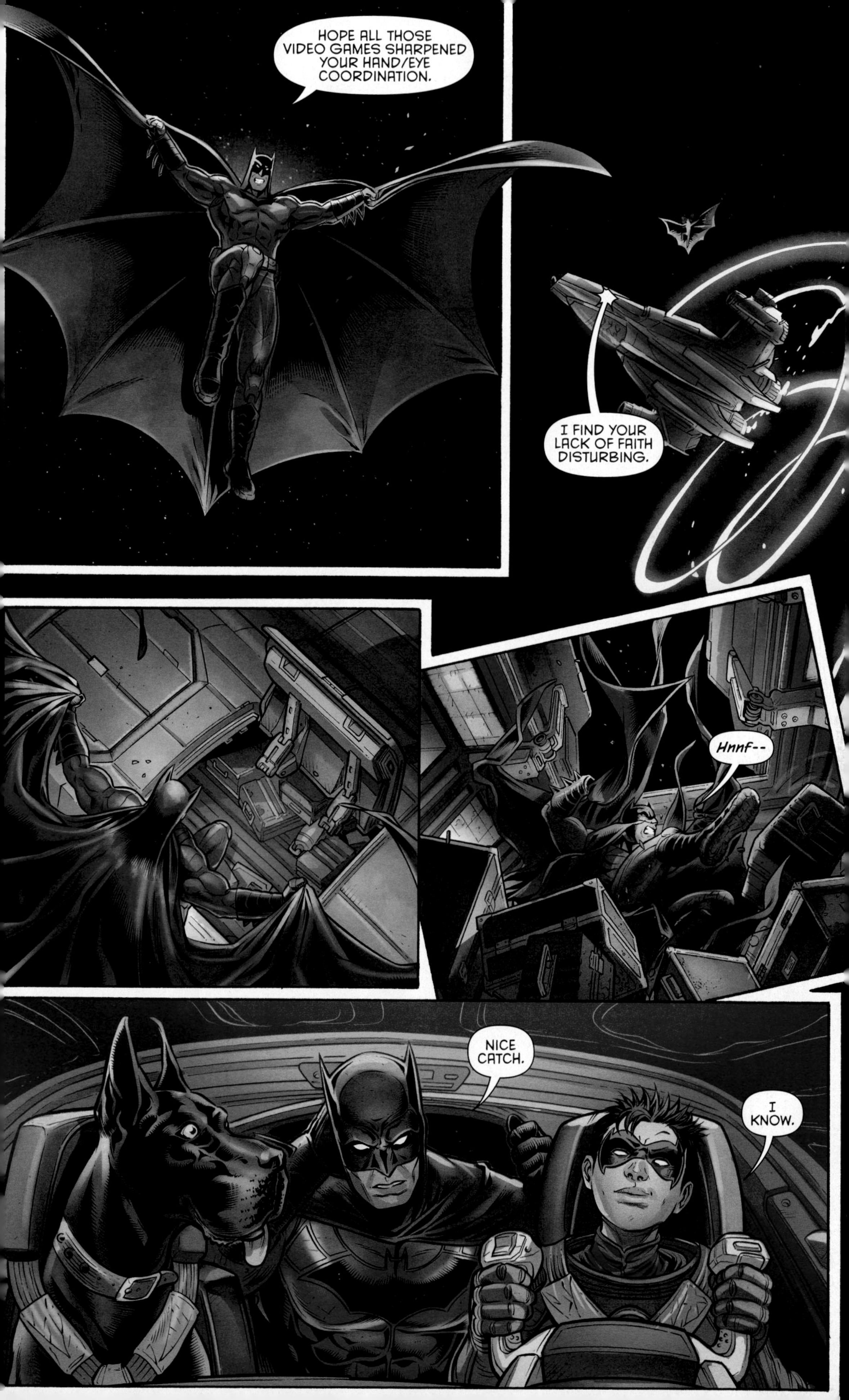
HOPE ALL THOSE VIDEO GAMES SHARPENED YOUR HAND/EYE COORDINATION.
I FIND YOUR LACK OF FAITH DISTURBING.
Hnnf--
NICE CATCH.
I KNOW.

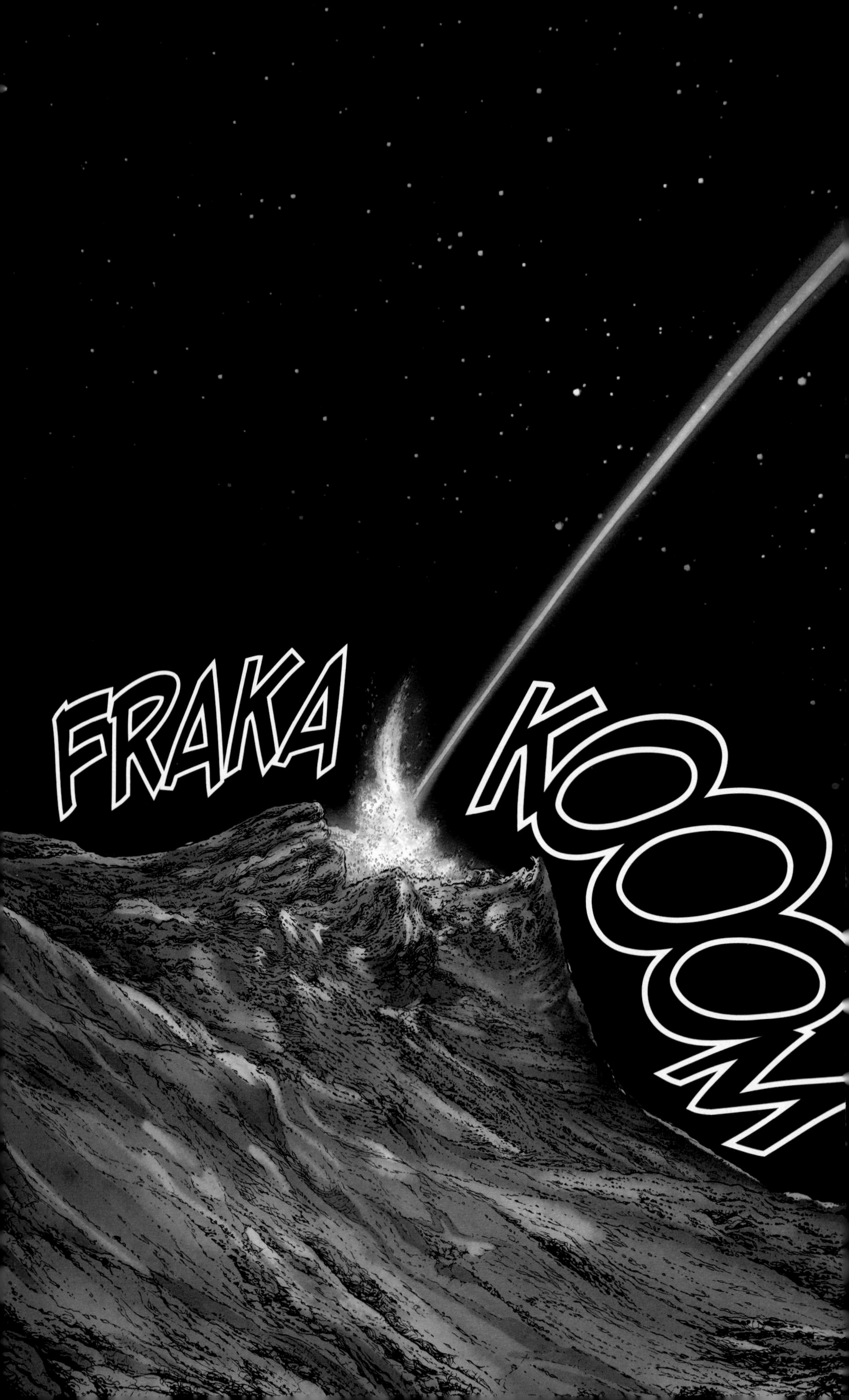
FRAKA
KOOOM

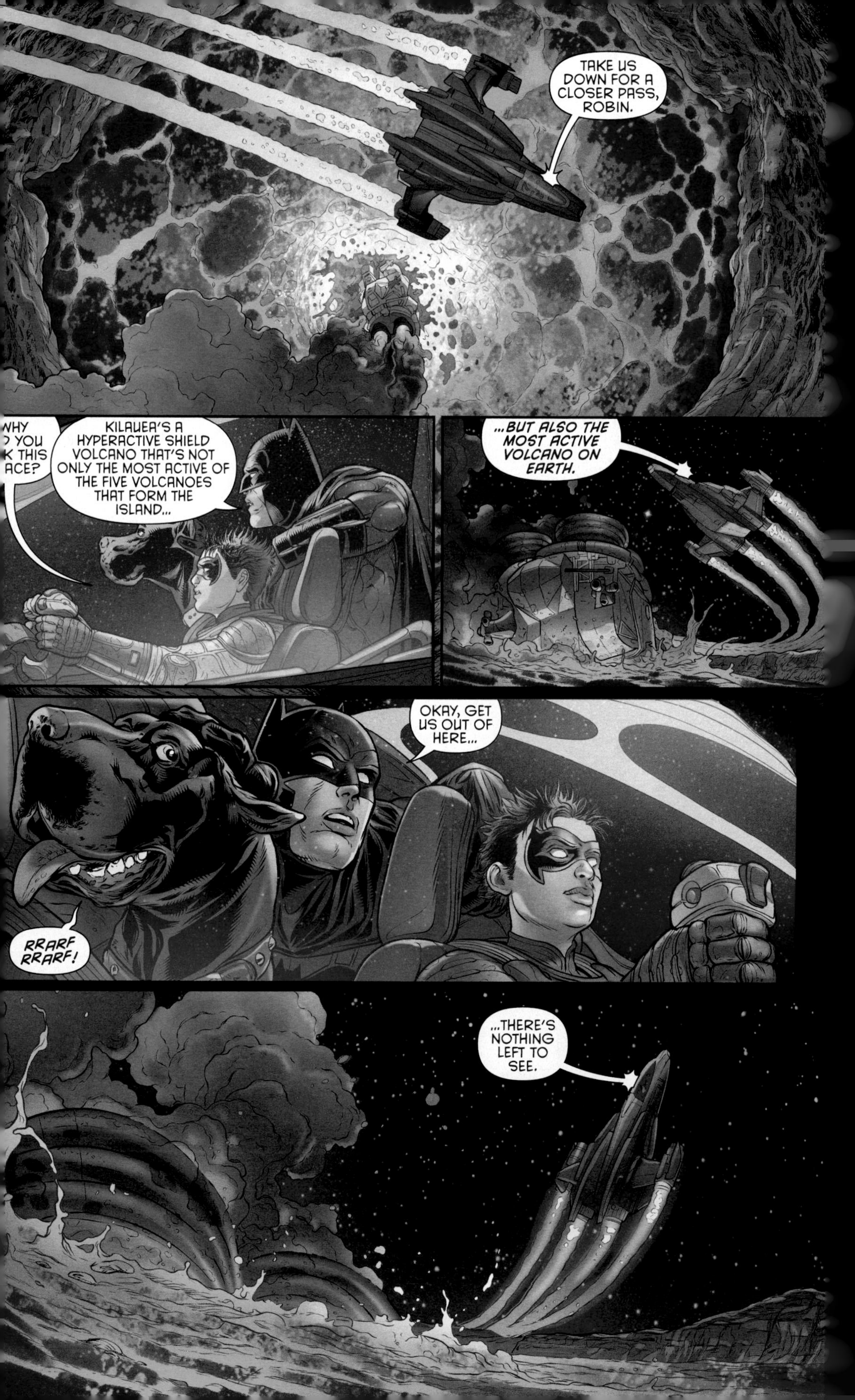
TAKE US DOWN FOR A CLOSER PASS, ROBIN.
WHY D YOU K THIS ACE?
KILAUEA'S A HYPERACTIVE SHIELD VOLCANO THAT'S NOT ONLY THE MOST ACTIVE OF THE FIVE VOLCANOES THAT FORM THE ISLAND...
...BUT ALSO THE MOST ACTIVE VOLCANO ON EARTH.
OKAY, GET US OUT OF HERE...
RRARF RRARF!
...THERE'S NOTHING LEFT TO SEE.

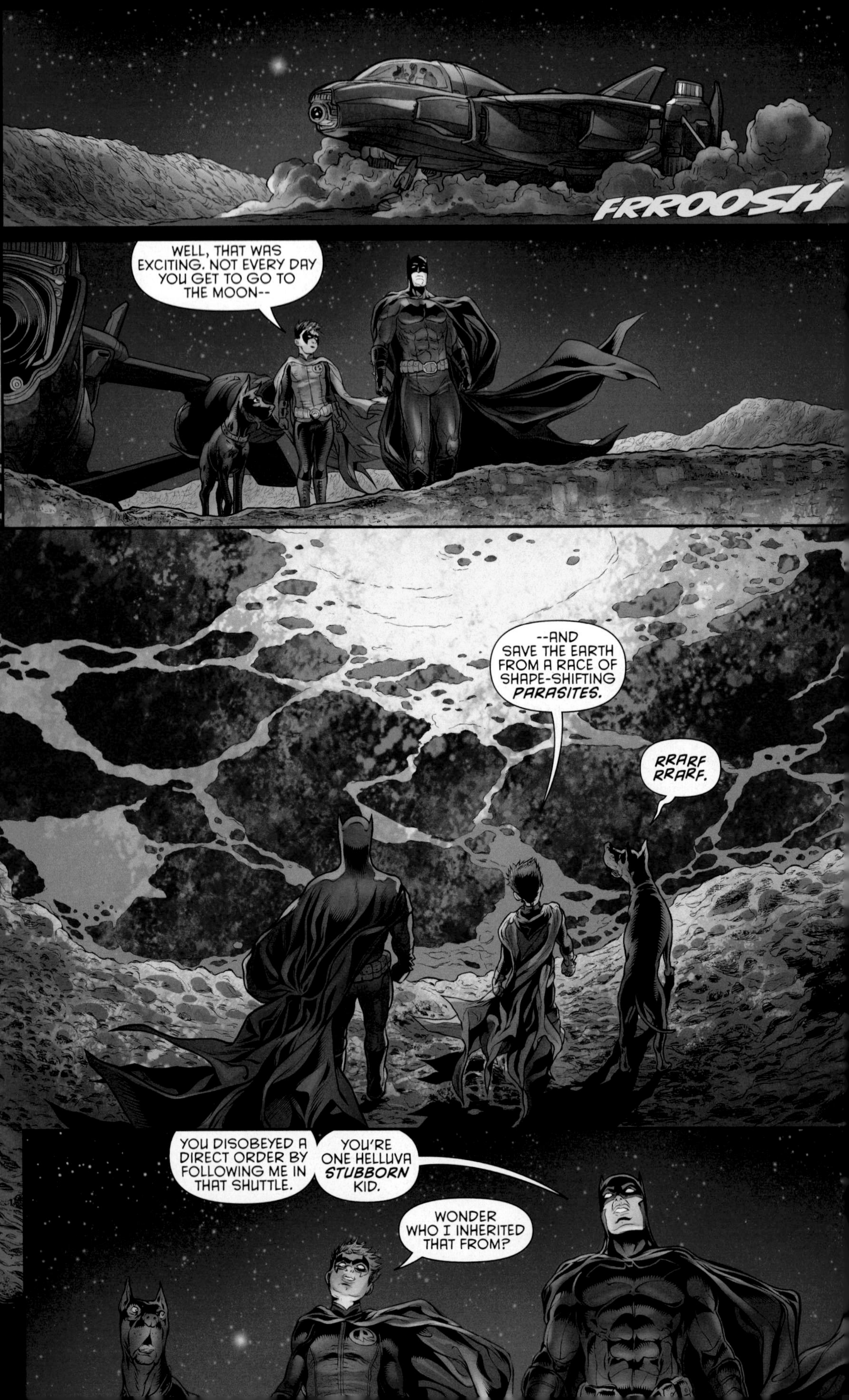
FRROOSH
WELL, THAT WAS EXCITING. NOT EVERY DAY YOU GET TO GO TO THE MOON--
--AND SAVE THE EARTH FROM A RACE OF SHAPE-SHIFTING PARASITES.
RRARF RRARF.
YOU DISOBEYED A DIRECT ORDER BY FOLLOWING ME IN THAT SHUTTLE.
YOU'RE ONE HELLUVA STUBBORN KID.
WONDER WHO I INHERITED THAT FROM?

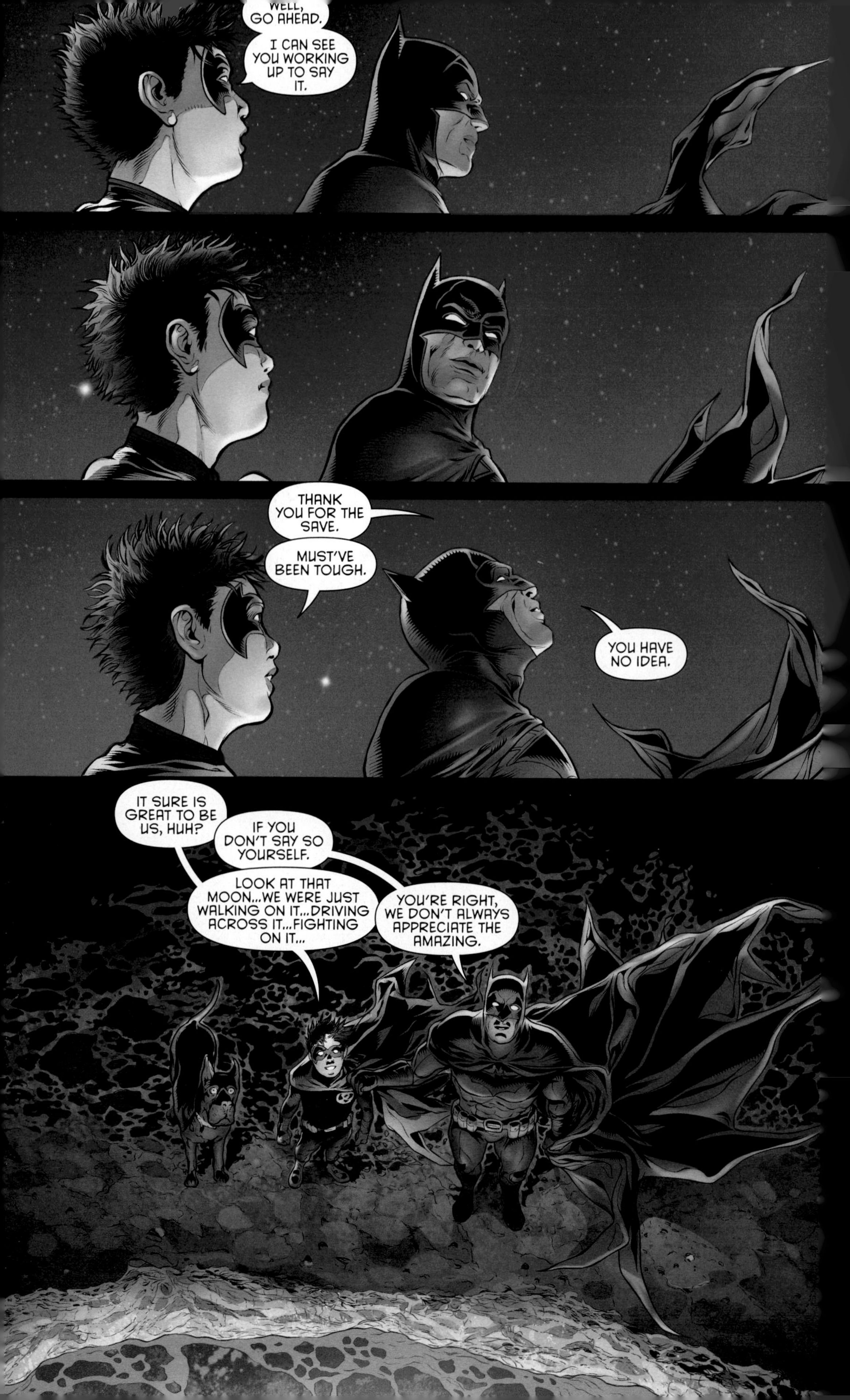
WELL, GO AHEAD.
I CAN SEE YOU WORKING UP TO SAY IT.
THANK YOU FOR THE SAVE.
MUST'VE BEEN TOUGH.
YOU HAVE NO IDEA.
IT SURE IS GREAT TO BE US, HUH?
IF YOU DON'T SAY SO YOURSELF.
LOOK AT THAT MOON...WE WERE JUST WALKING ON IT...DRIVING ACROSS IT...FIGHTING ON IT...
YOU'RE RIGHT, WE DON'T ALWAYS APPRECIATE THE AMAZING.

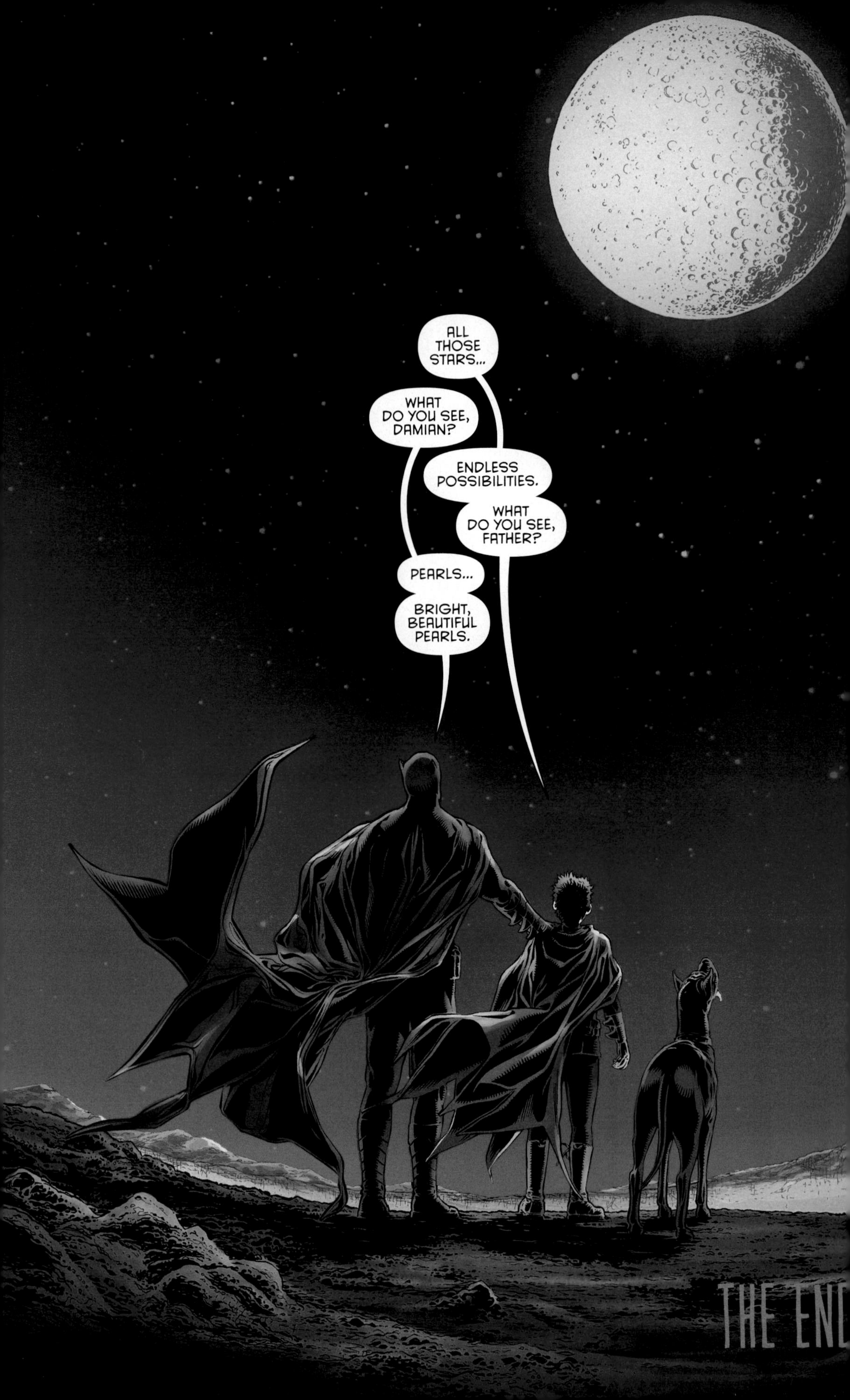
ALL THOSE STARS...
WHAT DO YOU SEE, DAMIAN?
ENDLESS POSSIBILITIES.
WHAT DO YOU SEE, FATHER?
PEARLS...
BRIGHT, BEAUTIFUL PEARLS.
THE END

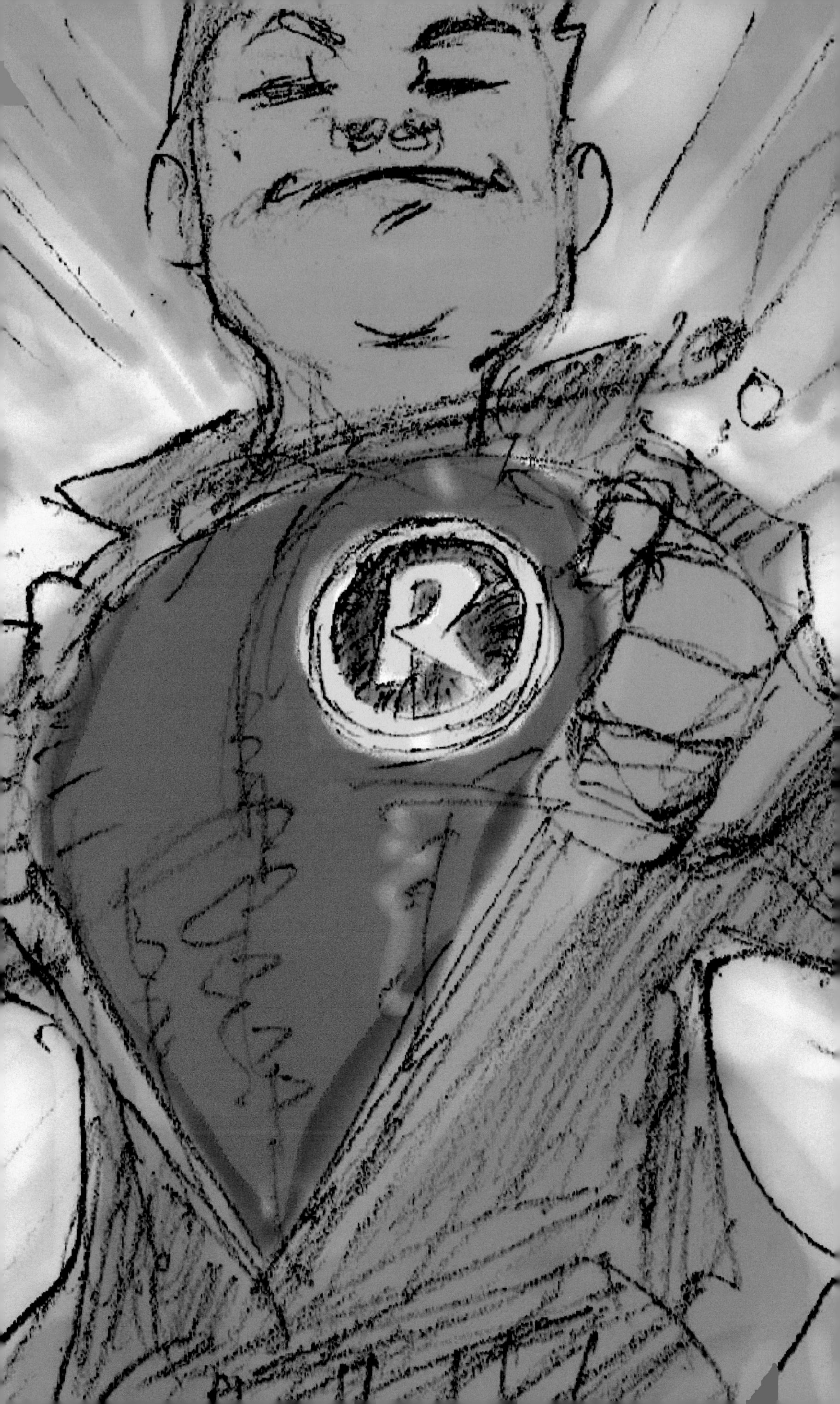

A BOY'S LIFE: DAMIAN WAYNE ROBIN

IAN BERTRAM artist DAVE STEWART colorist STEVE WANDS coloris

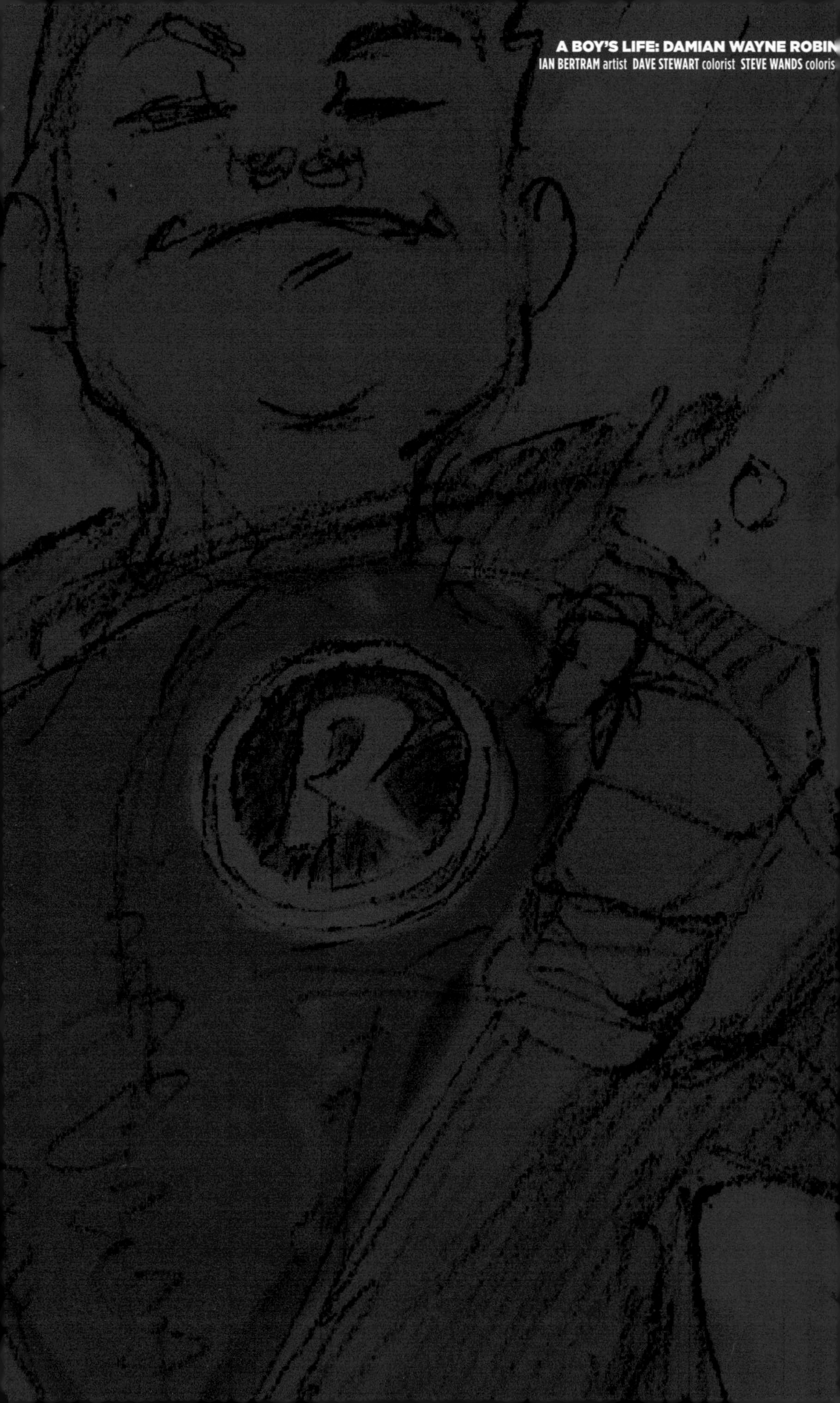

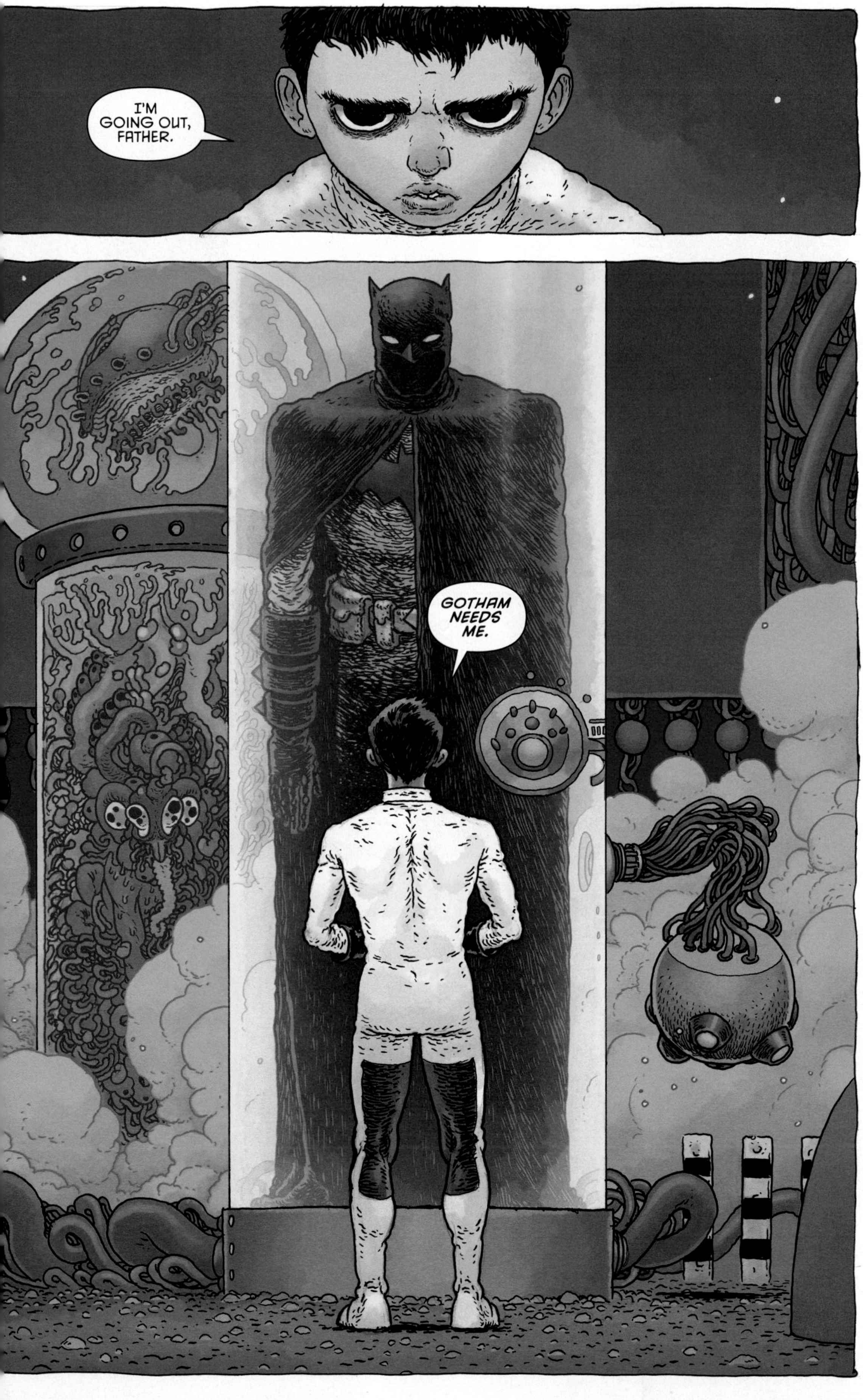
I'M GOING OUT, FATHER.
GOTHAM NEEDS ME.

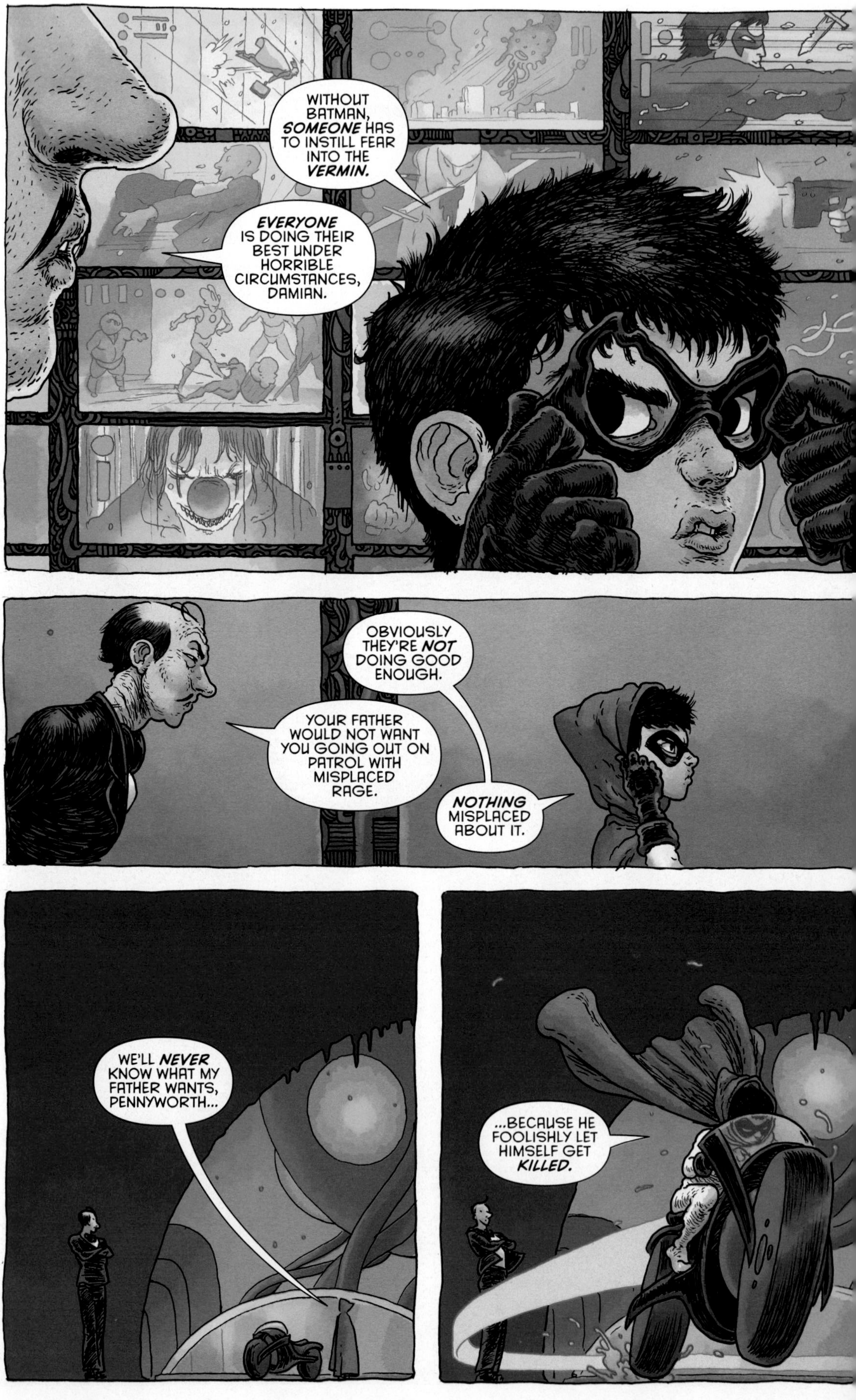

WITHOUT BATMAN, SOMEONE HAS TO INSTILL FEAR INTO THE VERMIN.
EVERYONE IS DOING THEIR BEST UNDER HORRIBLE CIRCUMSTANCES, DAMIAN.
OBVIOUSLY THEY'RE NOT DOING GOOD ENOUGH.
YOUR FATHER WOULD NOT WANT YOU GOING OUT ON PATROL WITH MISPLACED RAGE.
NOTHING MISPLACED ABOUT IT.
WE'LL NEVER KNOW WHAT MY FATHER WANTS, PENNYWORTH...
...BECAUSE HE FOOLISHLY LET HIMSELF GET KILLED.

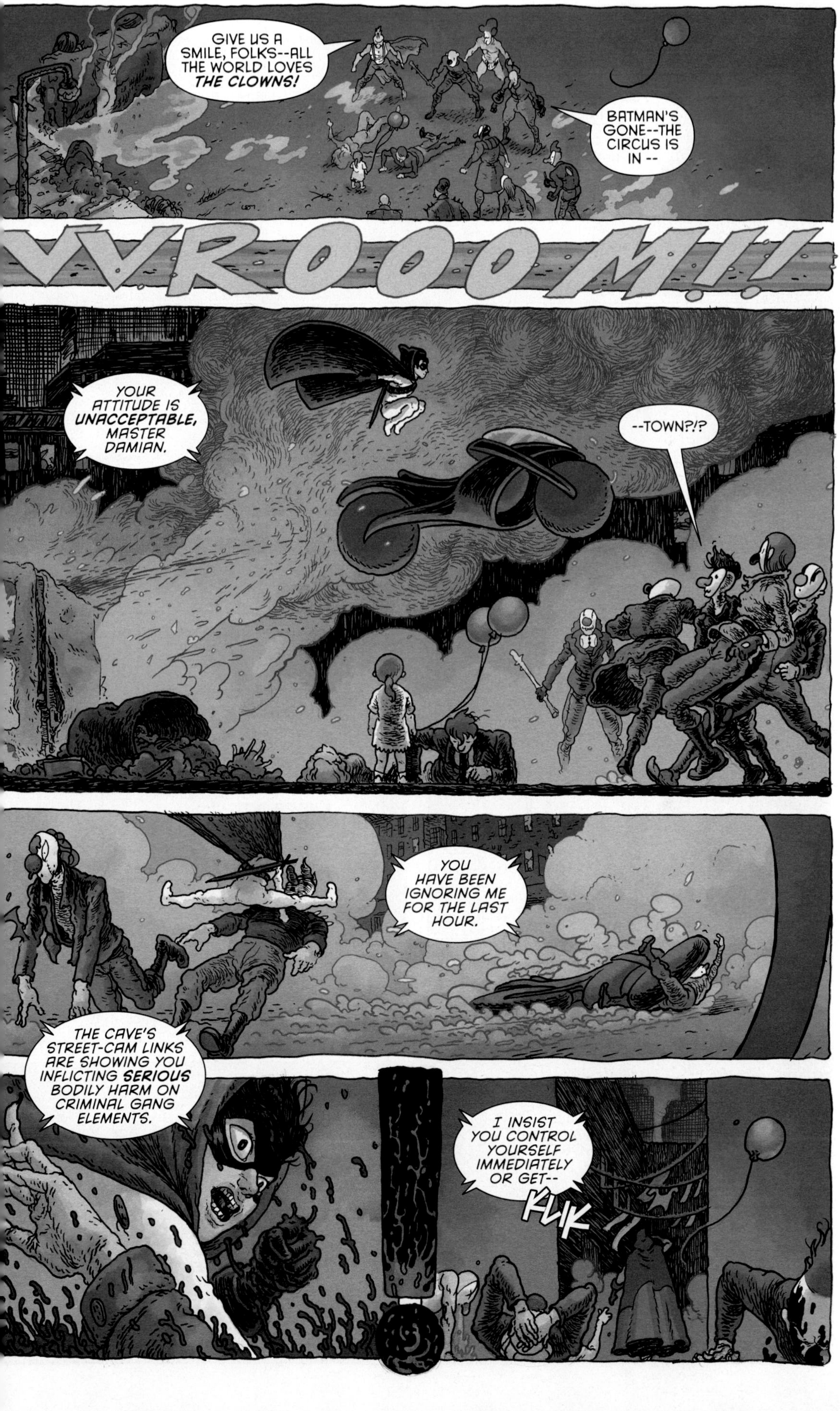
GIVE US A SMILE, FOLKS--ALL THE WORLD LOVES ***THE CLOWNS!***
BATMAN'S GONE--THE CIRCUS IS IN --
VVROOOM!!
YOUR ATTITUDE IS ***UNACCEPTABLE,*** MASTER DAMIAN.
--TOWN?!?
YOU HAVE BEEN IGNORING ME FOR THE LAST HOUR.
THE CAVE'S STREET-CAM LINKS ARE SHOWING YOU INFLICTING **SERIOUS** BODILY HARM ON CRIMINAL GANG ELEMENTS.
I INSIST YOU CONTROL YOURSELF IMMEDIATELY OR GET--
KLIK

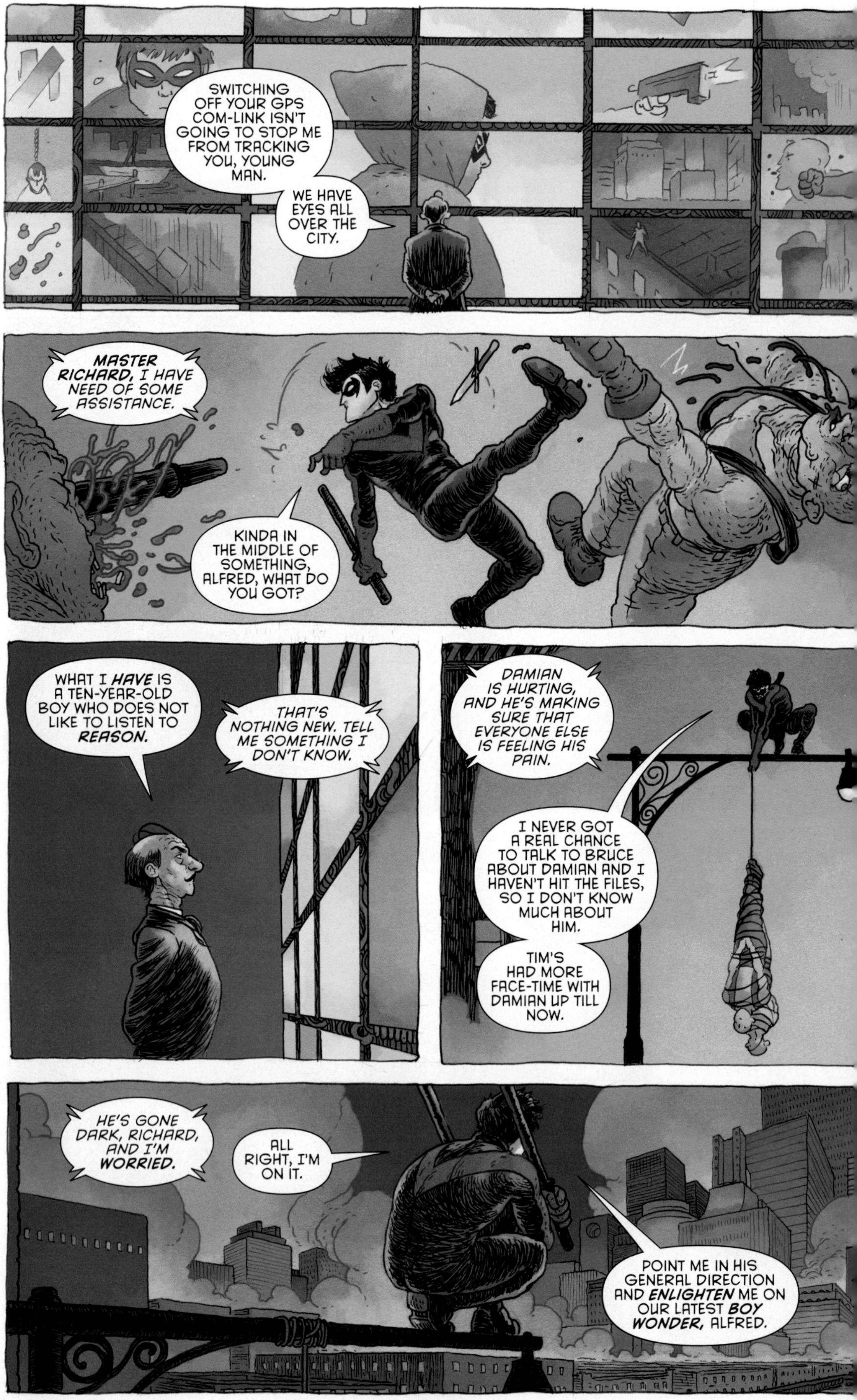
SWITCHING OFF YOUR GPS COM-LINK ISN'T GOING TO STOP ME FROM TRACKING YOU, YOUNG MAN.
WE HAVE EYES ALL OVER THE CITY.
MASTER RICHARD, I HAVE NEED OF SOME ASSISTANCE.
KINDA IN THE MIDDLE OF SOMETHING, ALFRED, WHAT DO YOU GOT?
WHAT I HAVE IS A TEN-YEAR-OLD BOY WHO DOES NOT LIKE TO LISTEN TO REASON.
THAT'S NOTHING NEW. TELL ME SOMETHING I DON'T KNOW.
DAMIAN IS HURTING, AND HE'S MAKING SURE THAT EVERYONE ELSE IS FEELING HIS PAIN.
I NEVER GOT A REAL CHANCE TO TALK TO BRUCE ABOUT DAMIAN AND I HAVEN'T HIT THE FILES, SO I DON'T KNOW MUCH ABOUT HIM.
TIM'S HAD MORE FACE-TIME WITH DAMIAN UP TILL NOW.
HE'S GONE DARK, RICHARD, AND I'M WORRIED.
ALL RIGHT, I'M ON IT.
POINT ME IN HIS GENERAL DIRECTION AND ENLIGHTEN ME ON OUR LATEST BOY WONDER, ALFRED.

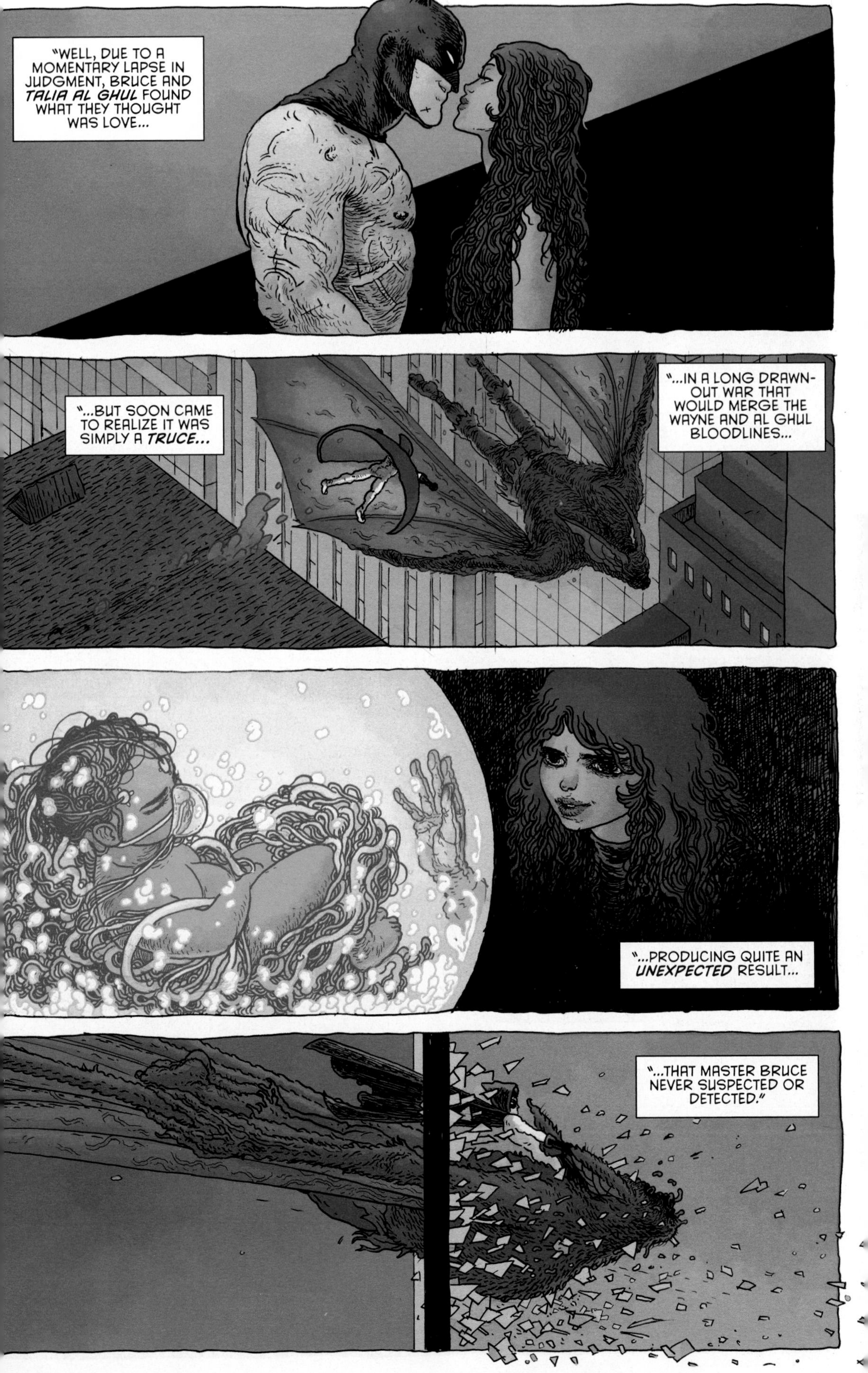

"WELL, DUE TO A MOMENTARY LAPSE IN JUDGMENT, BRUCE AND TALIA AL GHUL FOUND WHAT THEY THOUGHT WAS LOVE...
"...BUT SOON CAME TO REALIZE IT WAS SIMPLY A TRUCE...
"...IN A LONG DRAWN-OUT WAR THAT WOULD MERGE THE WAYNE AND AL GHUL BLOODLINES...
"...PRODUCING QUITE AN UNEXPECTED RESULT...
"...THAT MASTER BRUCE NEVER SUSPECTED OR DETECTED."

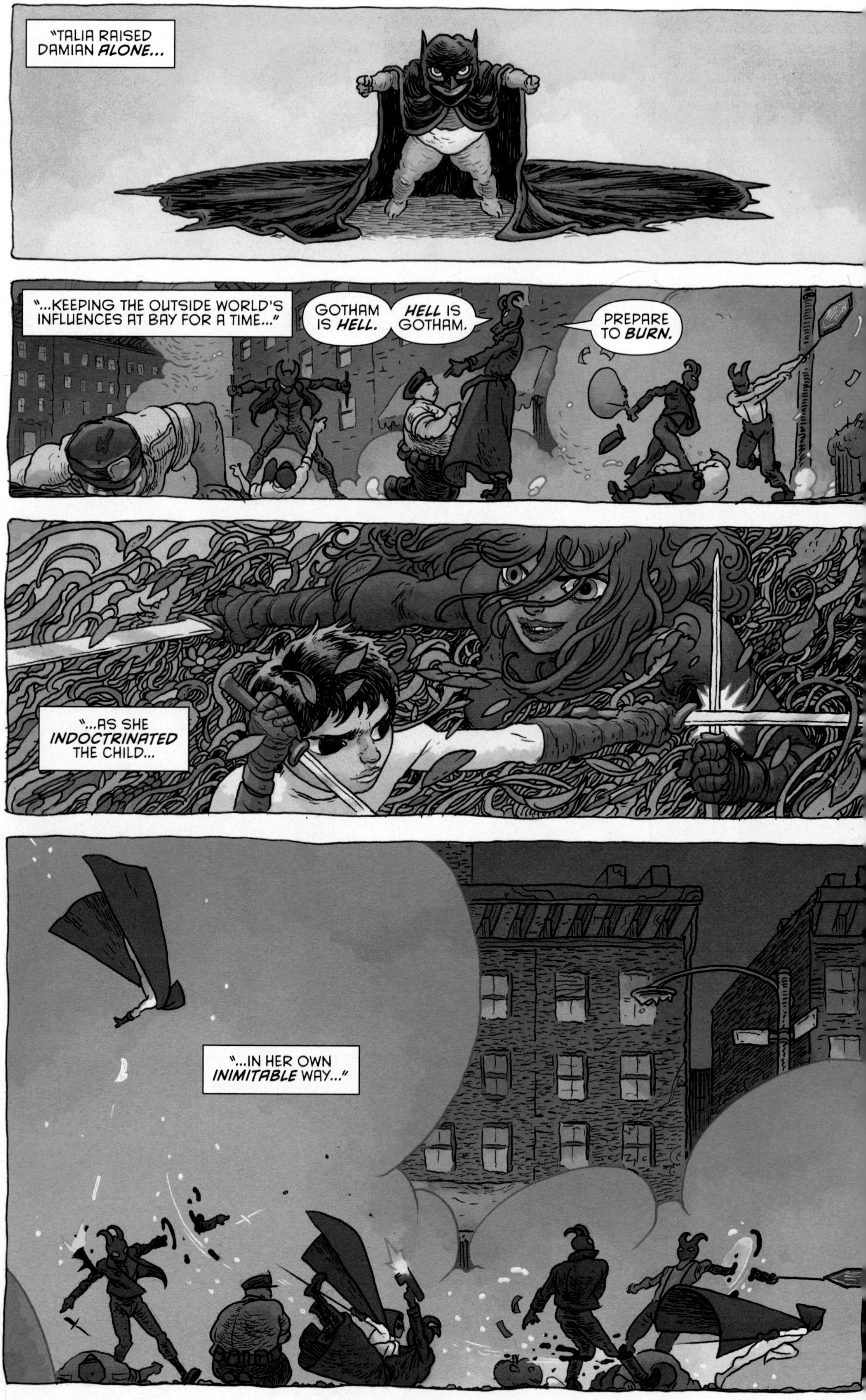
"TALIA RAISED DAMIAN ALONE...
"...KEEPING THE OUTSIDE WORLD'S INFLUENCES AT BAY FOR A TIME..."
GOTHAM IS HELL.
HELL IS GOTHAM.
PREPARE TO BURN.
"...AS SHE INDOCTRINATED THE CHILD...
"...IN HER OWN INIMITABLE WAY..."

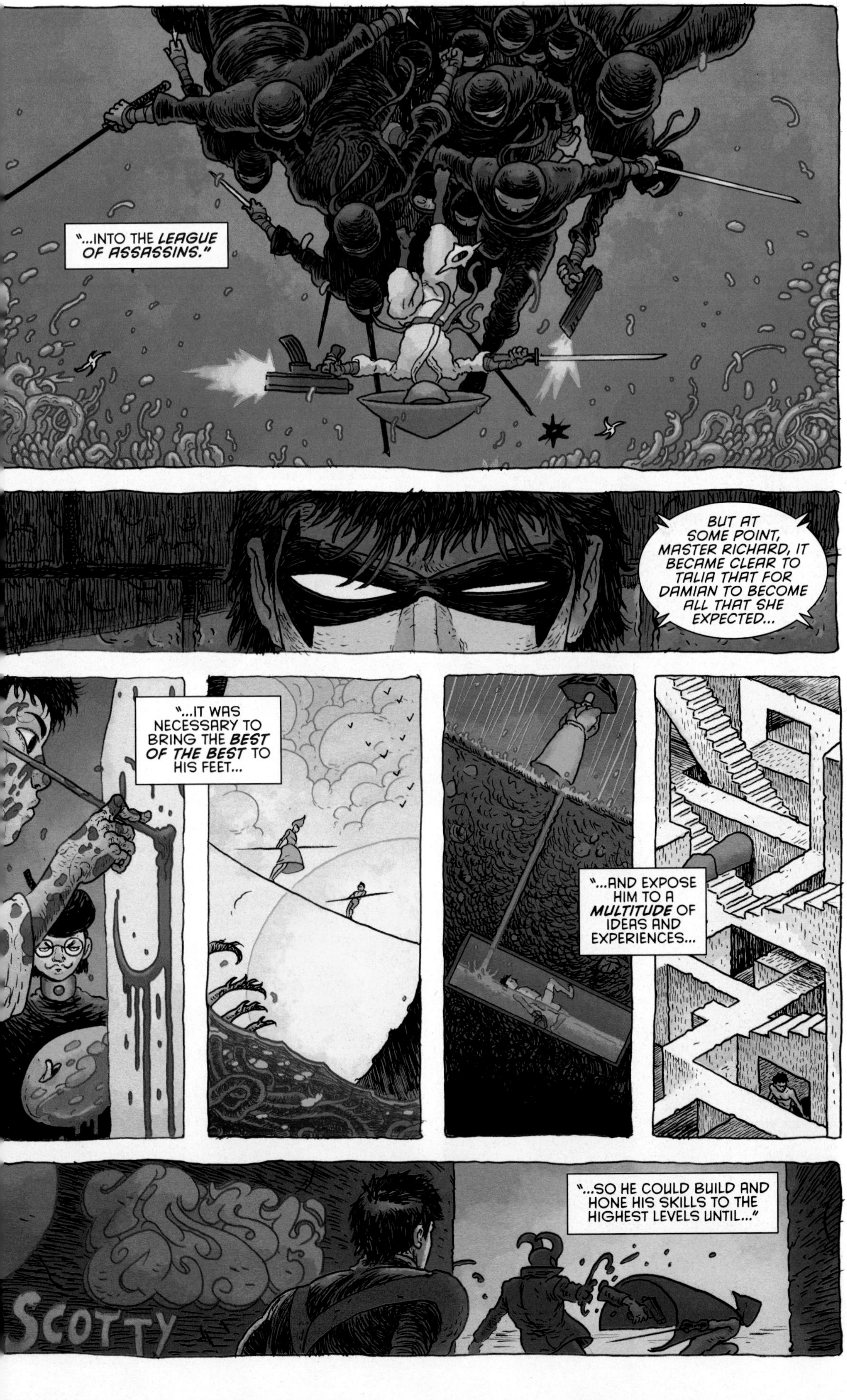
"...INTO THE LEAGUE OF ASSASSINS."
BUT AT SOME POINT, MASTER RICHARD, IT BECAME CLEAR TO TALIA THAT FOR DAMIAN TO BECOME ALL THAT SHE EXPECTED...
"...IT WAS NECESSARY TO BRING THE BEST OF THE BEST TO HIS FEET...
"...AND EXPOSE HIM TO A MULTITUDE OF IDEAS AND EXPERIENCES...
"...SO HE COULD BUILD AND HONE HIS SKILLS TO THE HIGHEST LEVELS UNTIL..."
SCOTTY

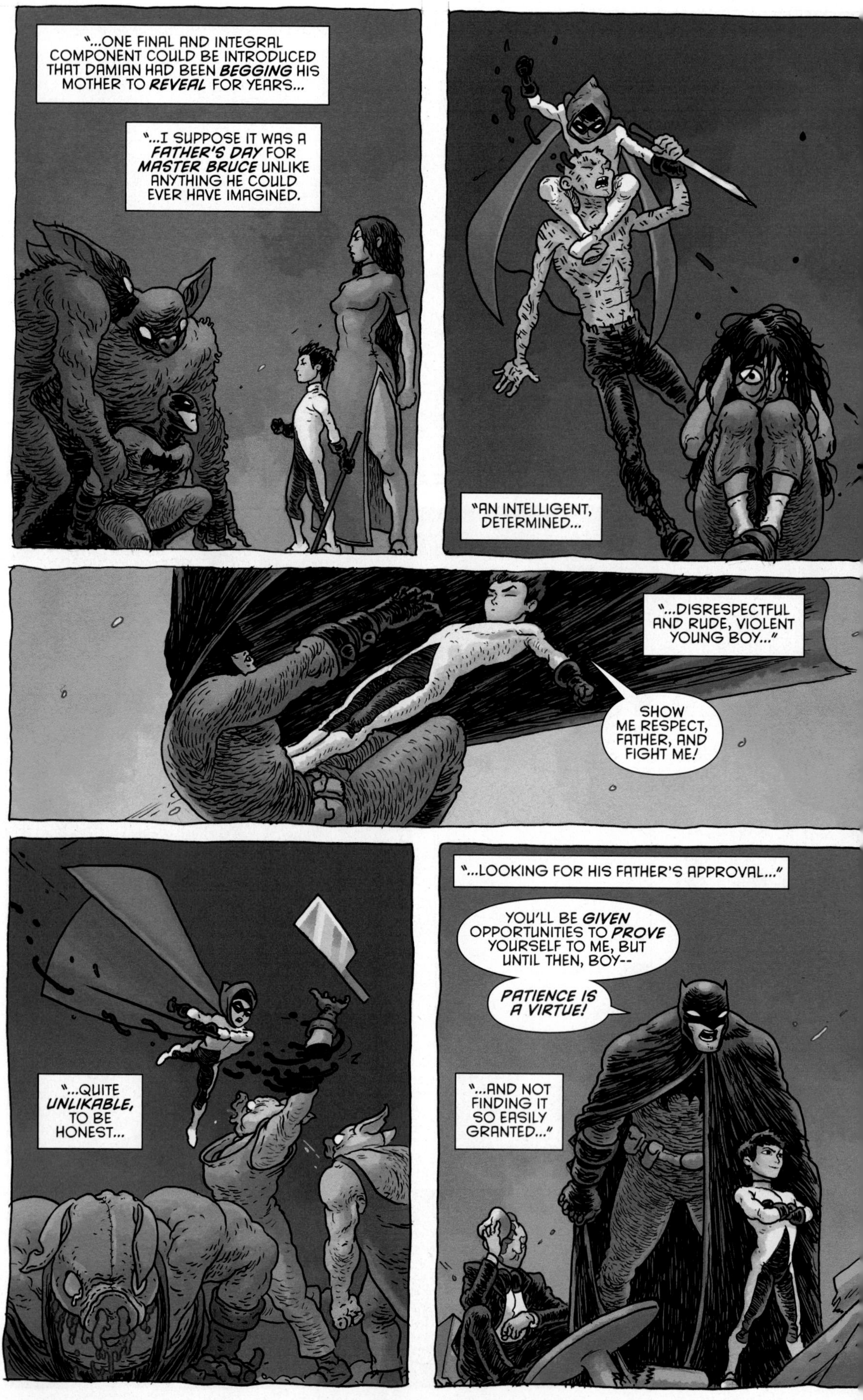
"...ONE FINAL AND INTEGRAL COMPONENT COULD BE INTRODUCED THAT DAMIAN HAD BEEN *BEGGING* HIS MOTHER TO *REVEAL* FOR YEARS...
"...I SUPPOSE IT WAS A *FATHER'S DAY* FOR *MASTER BRUCE* UNLIKE ANYTHING HE COULD EVER HAVE IMAGINED.
"AN INTELLIGENT, DETERMINED...
"...DISRESPECTFUL AND RUDE, VIOLENT YOUNG BOY..."
SHOW ME RESPECT, FATHER, AND FIGHT ME!
"...QUITE *UNLIKABLE,* TO BE HONEST...
"...LOOKING FOR HIS FATHER'S APPROVAL..."
YOU'LL BE *GIVEN* OPPORTUNITIES TO *PROVE* YOURSELF TO ME, BUT UNTIL THEN, BOY--
PATIENCE IS A VIRTUE!
"...AND NOT FINDING IT SO EASILY GRANTED..."

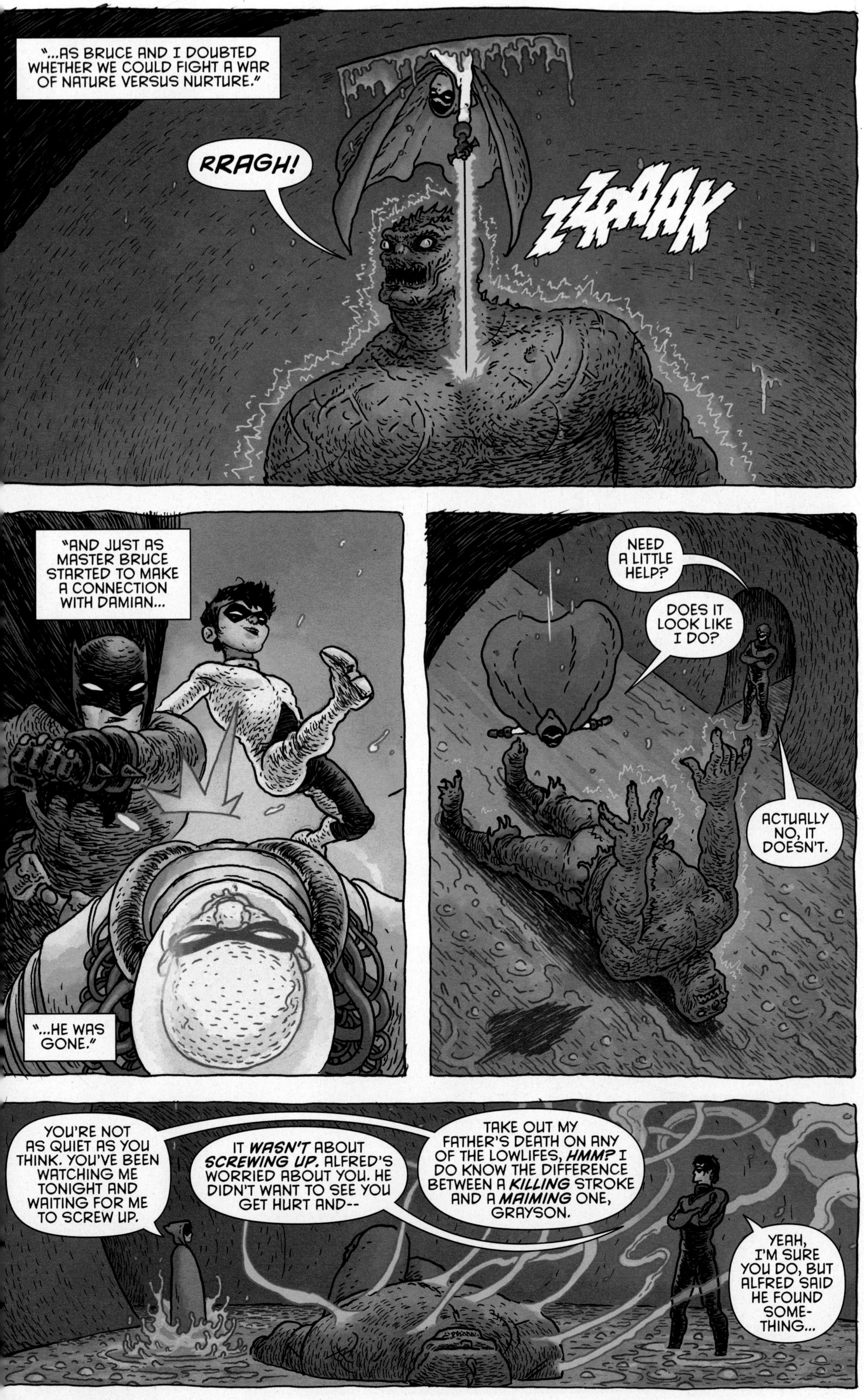
"...AS BRUCE AND I DOUBTED WHETHER WE COULD FIGHT A WAR OF NATURE VERSUS NURTURE."
RRAGH!
ZZRAAK
"AND JUST AS MASTER BRUCE STARTED TO MAKE A CONNECTION WITH DAMIAN...
"...HE WAS GONE."
NEED A LITTLE HELP?
DOES IT LOOK LIKE I DO?
ACTUALLY NO, IT DOESN'T.
YOU'RE NOT AS QUIET AS YOU THINK. YOU'VE BEEN WATCHING ME TONIGHT AND WAITING FOR ME TO SCREW UP.
IT WASN'T ABOUT SCREWING UP. ALFRED'S WORRIED ABOUT YOU. HE DIDN'T WANT TO SEE YOU GET HURT AND--
TAKE OUT MY FATHER'S DEATH ON ANY OF THE LOWLIFES, HMM? I DO KNOW THE DIFFERENCE BETWEEN A KILLING STROKE AND A MAIMING ONE, GRAYSON.
YEAH, I'M SURE YOU DO, BUT ALFRED SAID HE FOUND SOME-THING...

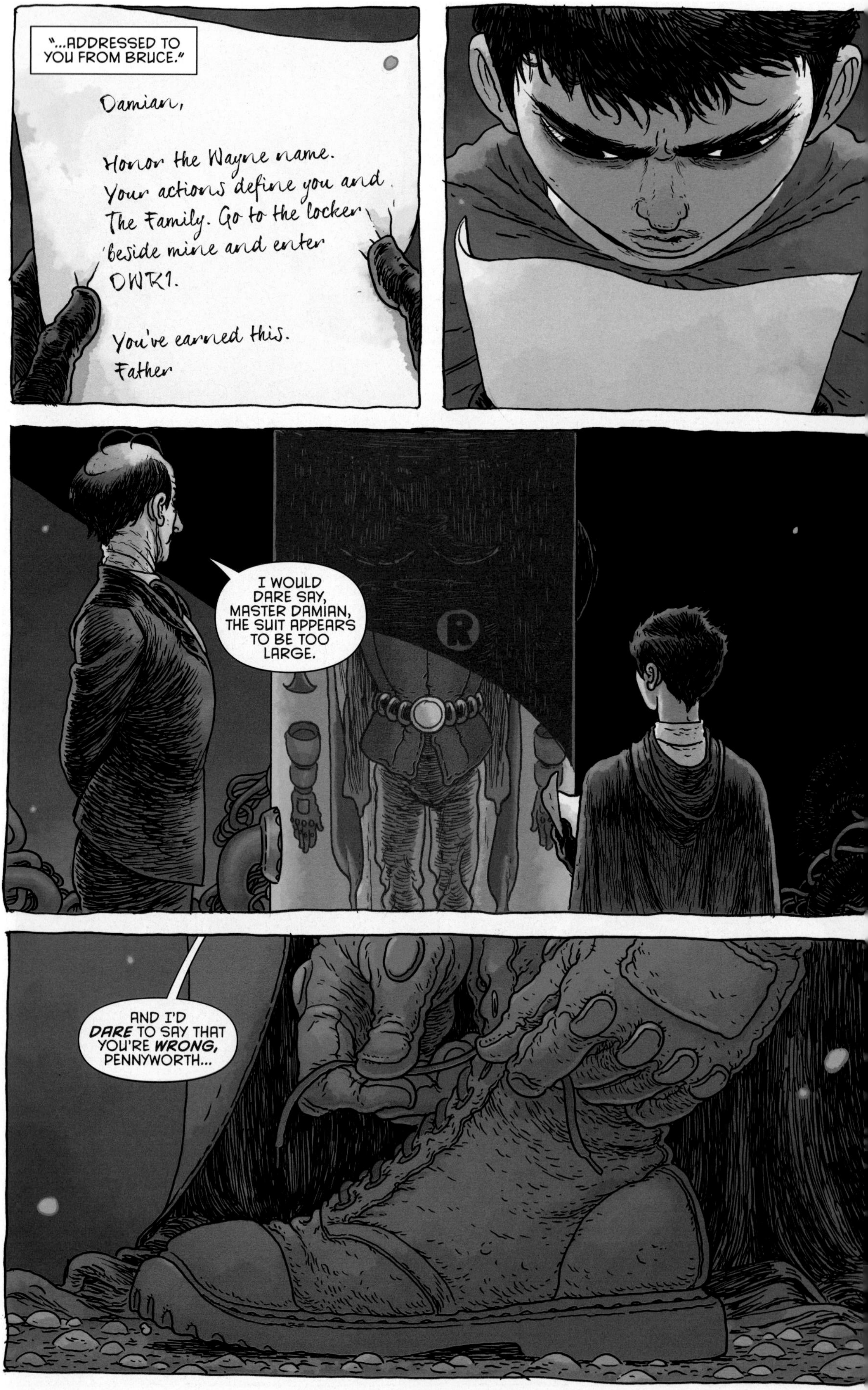
"...ADDRESSED TO YOU FROM BRUCE."
Damian,
Honor the Wayne name. Your actions define you and The Family. Go to the locker beside mine and enter DWR1.
You've earned this.
Father
I WOULD DARE SAY, MASTER DAMIAN, THE SUIT APPEARS TO BE TOO LARGE.
AND I'D ***DARE*** TO SAY THAT YOU'RE ***WRONG,*** PENNYWORTH...

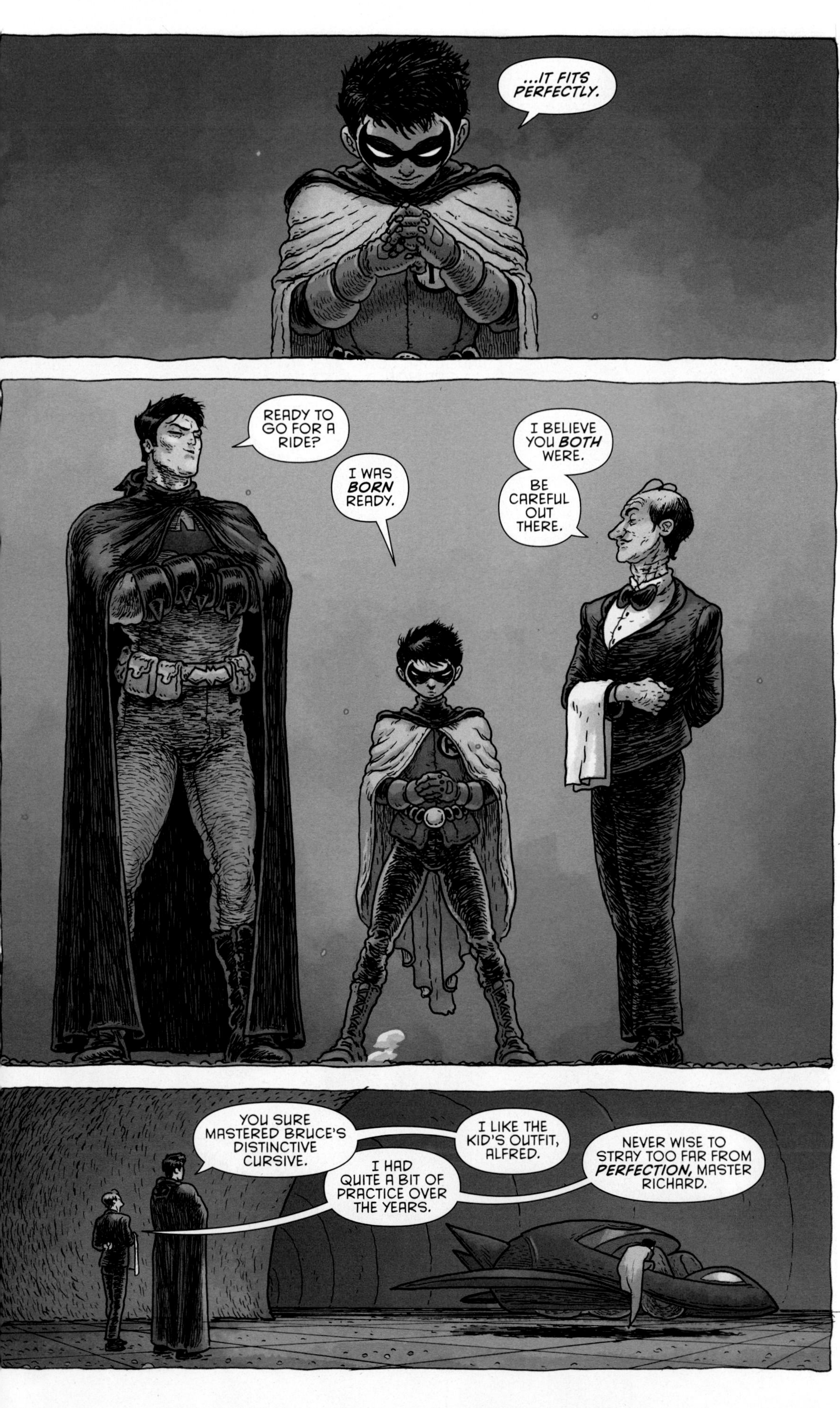
...IT FITS PERFECTLY.
READY TO GO FOR A RIDE?
I WAS BORN READY.
I BELIEVE YOU BOTH WERE.
BE CAREFUL OUT THERE.
YOU SURE MASTERED BRUCE'S DISTINCTIVE CURSIVE.
I HAD QUITE A BIT OF PRACTICE OVER THE YEARS.
I LIKE THE KID'S OUTFIT, ALFRED.
NEVER WISE TO STRAY TOO FAR FROM PERFECTION, MASTER RICHARD.

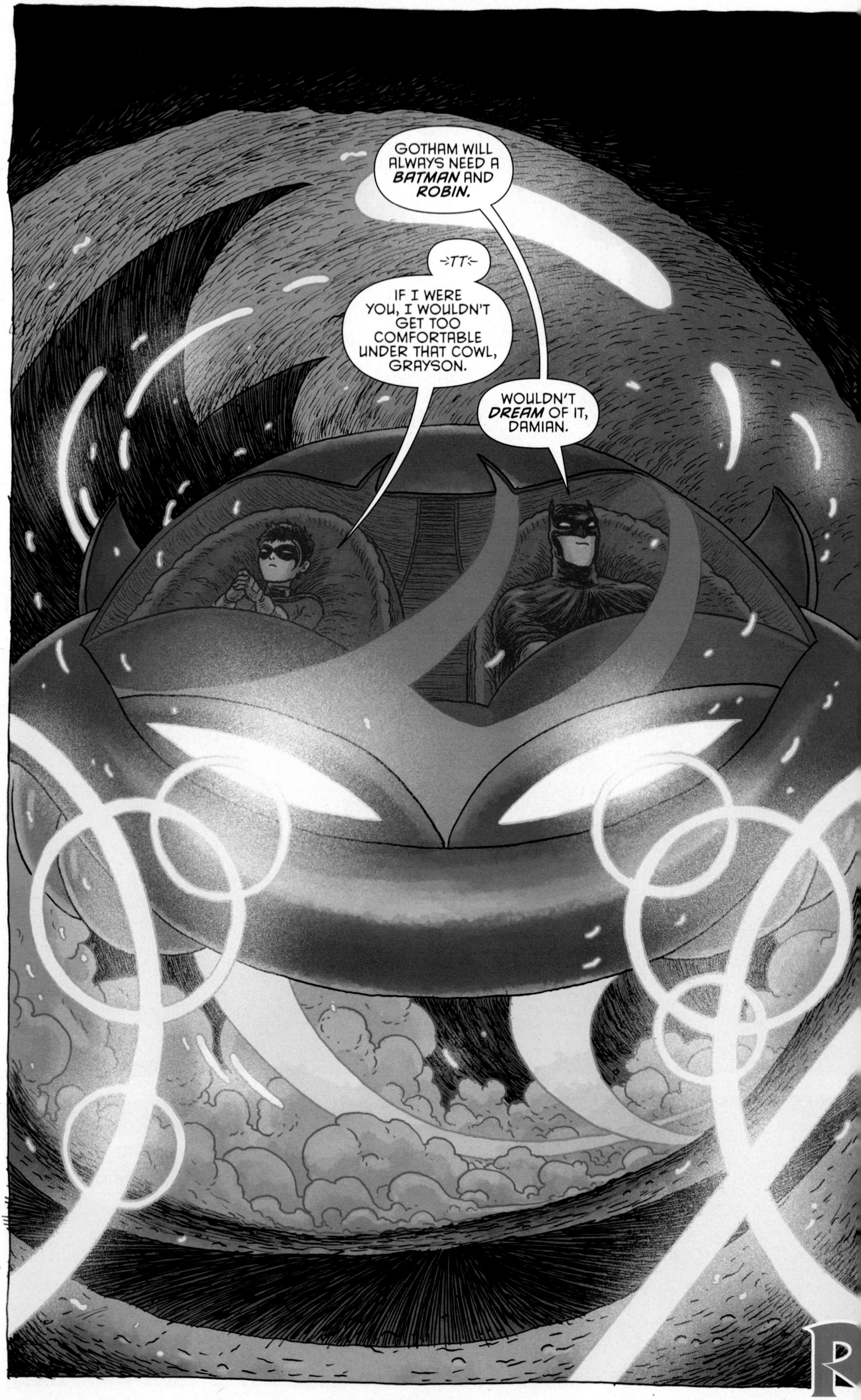
GOTHAM WILL ALWAYS NEED A BATMAN AND ROBIN.
TT
IF I WERE YOU, I WOULDN'T GET TOO COMFORTABLE UNDER THAT COWL, GRAYSON.
WOULDN'T DREAM OF IT, DAMIAN.

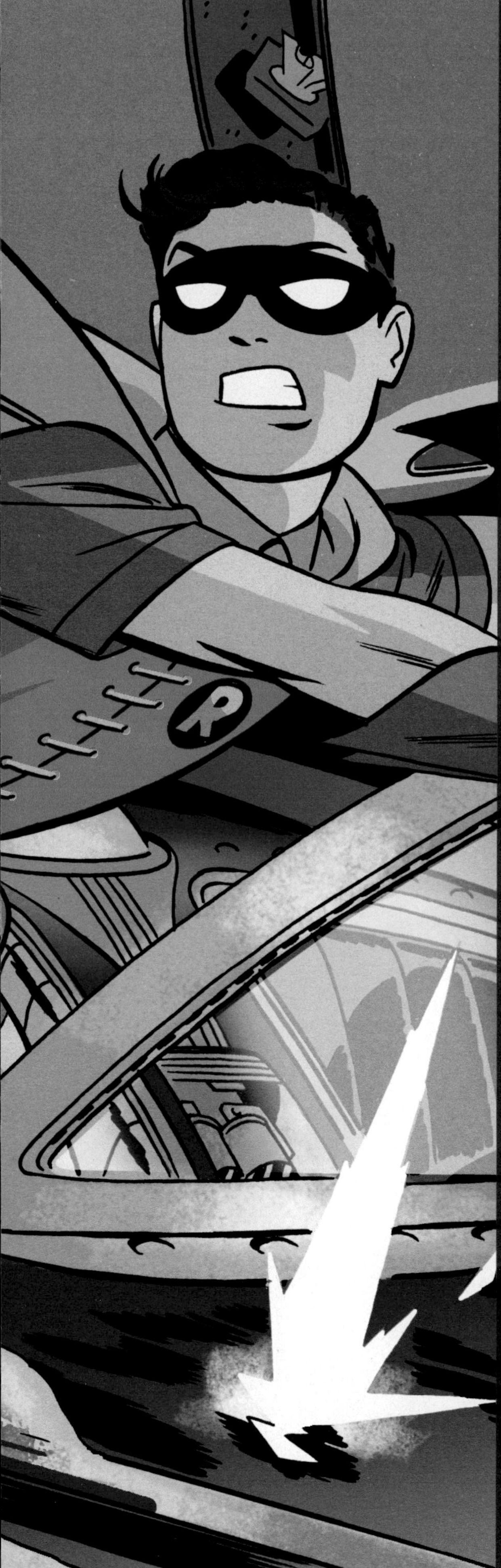

VARIANT COVER GALLERY

BATMAN AND ROBIN #35
MONSTER VARIANT BY
CHRIS BURNHAM &
NATHAN FAIRBAIRN

BATMAN AND ROBIN #36
LEGO VARIANT

BATMAN AND ROBIN #37
VARIANT BY DWARYN COOKE

ROBIN RISES: ALPHA #1
VARIANT BY CLIFF CHIANG

BATMAN AND ROBIN #38
THE FLASH 75TH ANNIVERSARY
VARIANT BY
DAVE BULLOCK, after BOB KANE
& JERRY ROBINSON

BATMAN AND ROBIN #39
HARLEY QUINN VARIANT BY
EMANUELA LUPACCHINO
& TOMEU MOREY

BATMAN AND ROBIN #40
MOVIE POSTER VARIANT BY
TOMMY LEE EDWARDS

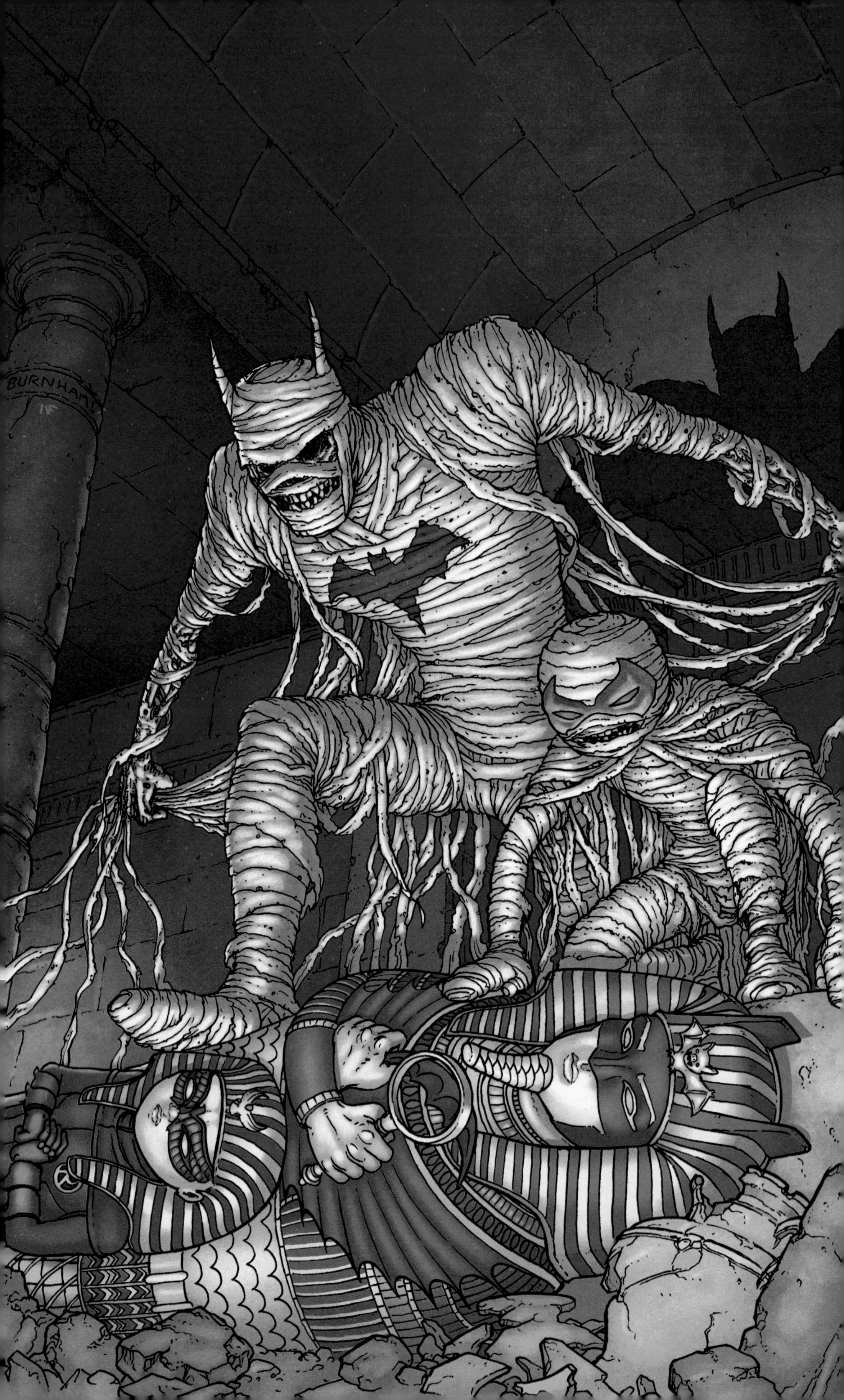
BURNHAM

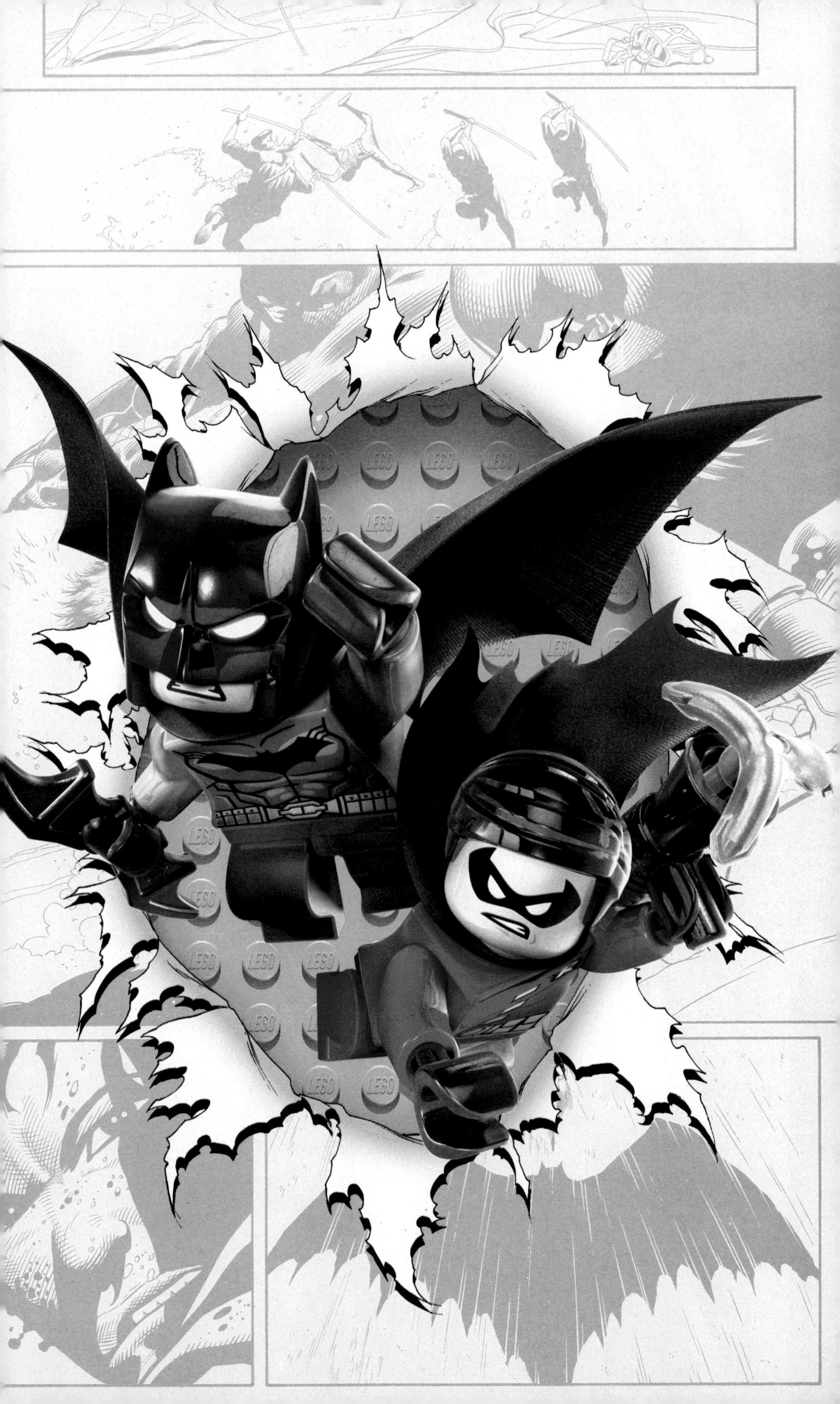

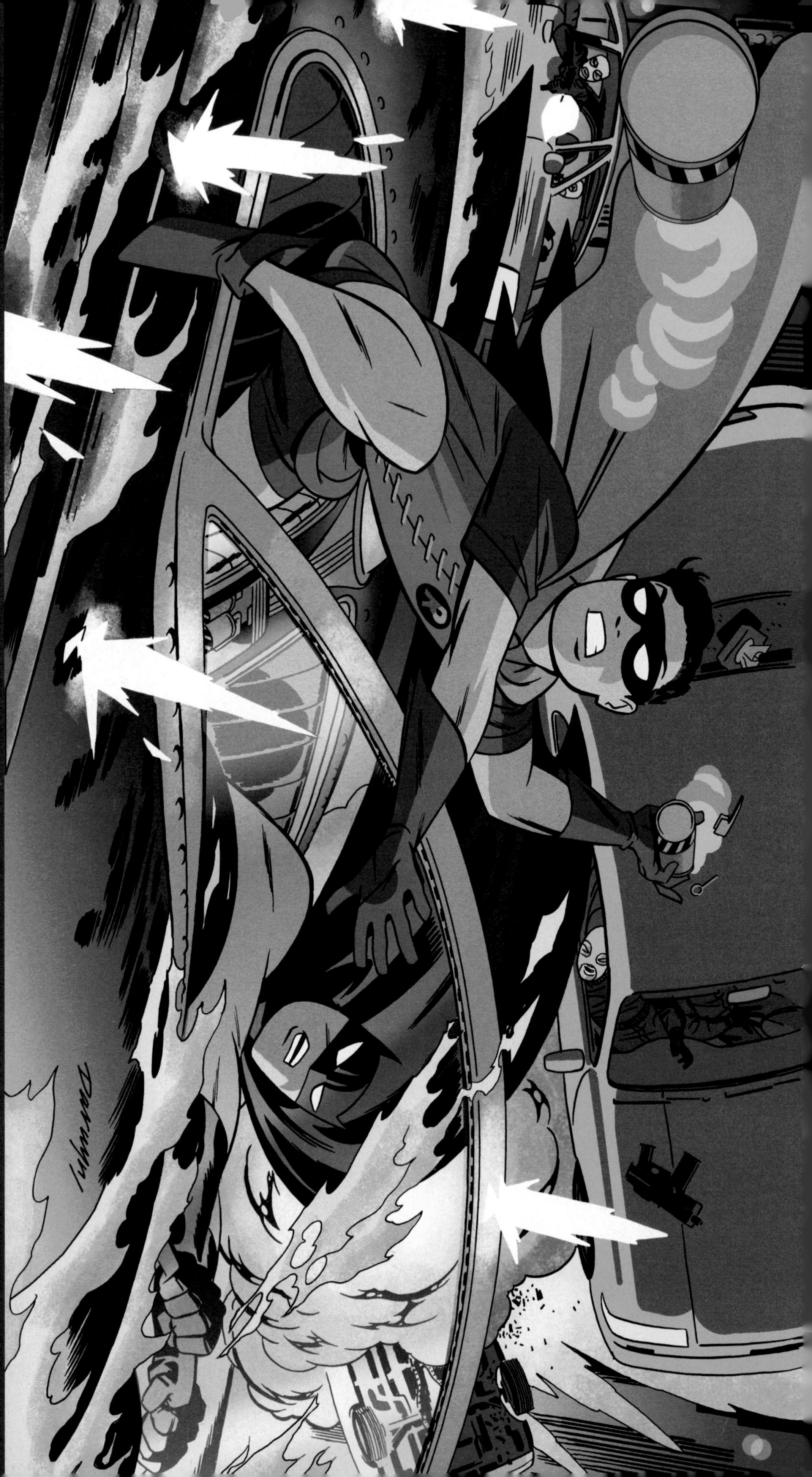

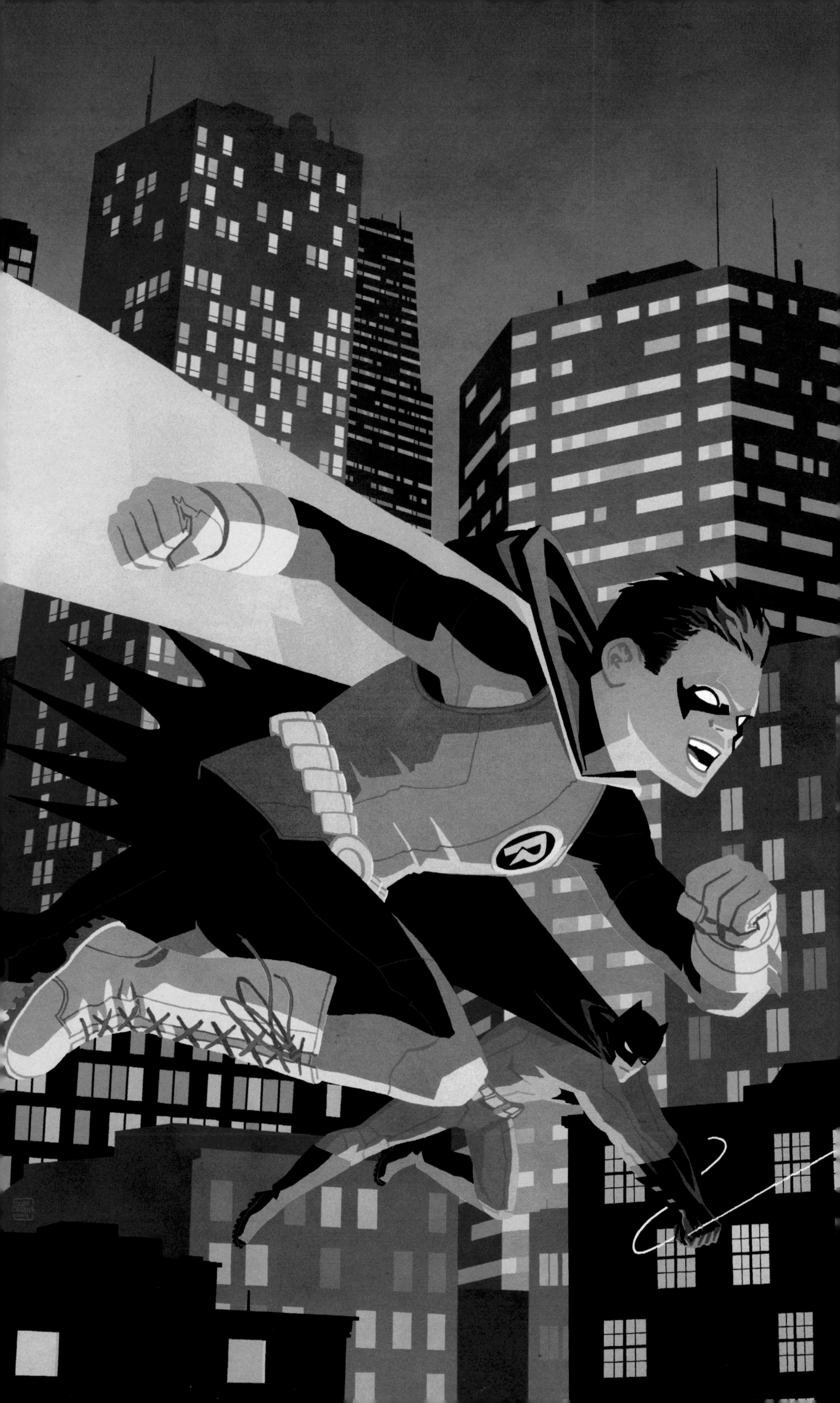

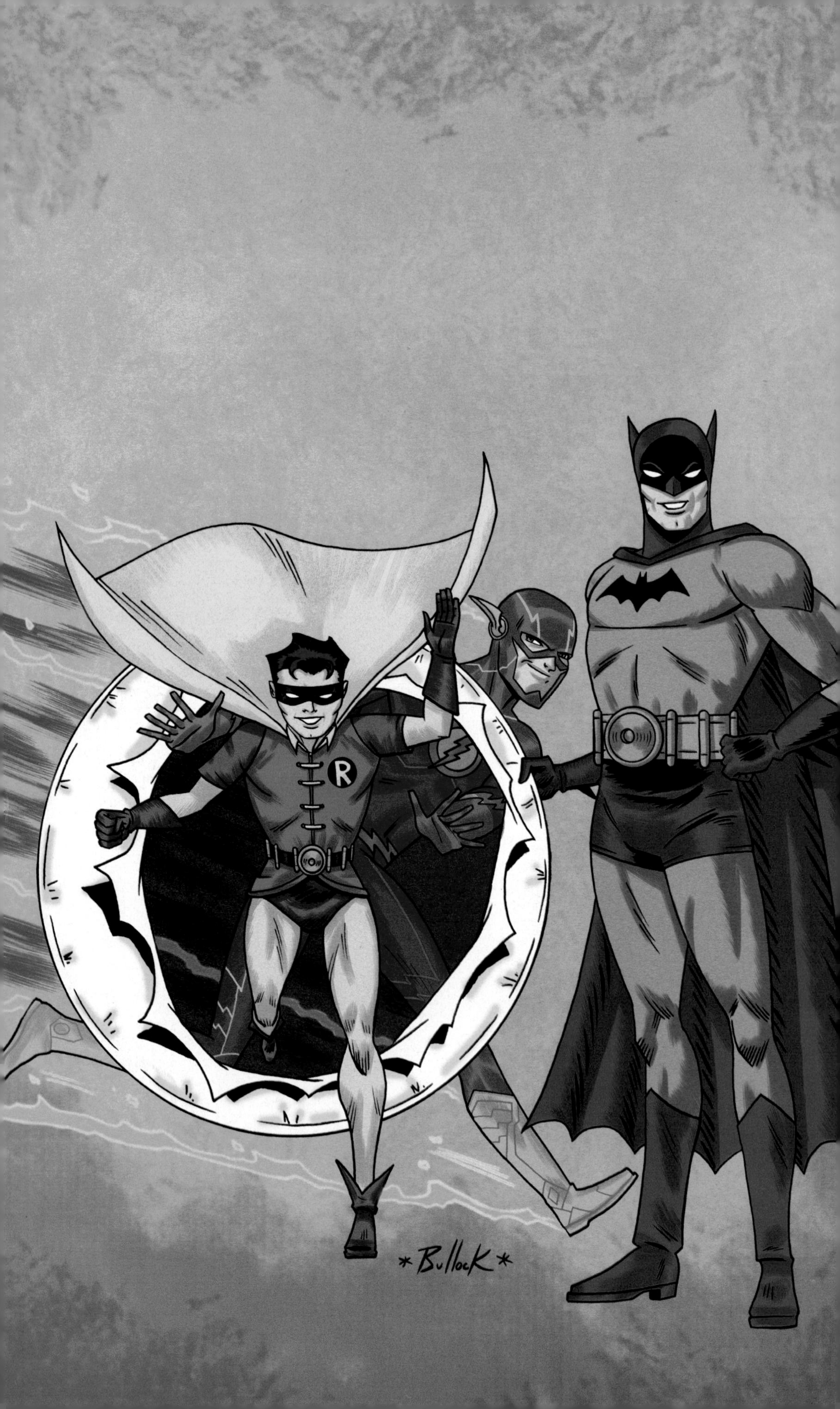
Bullock

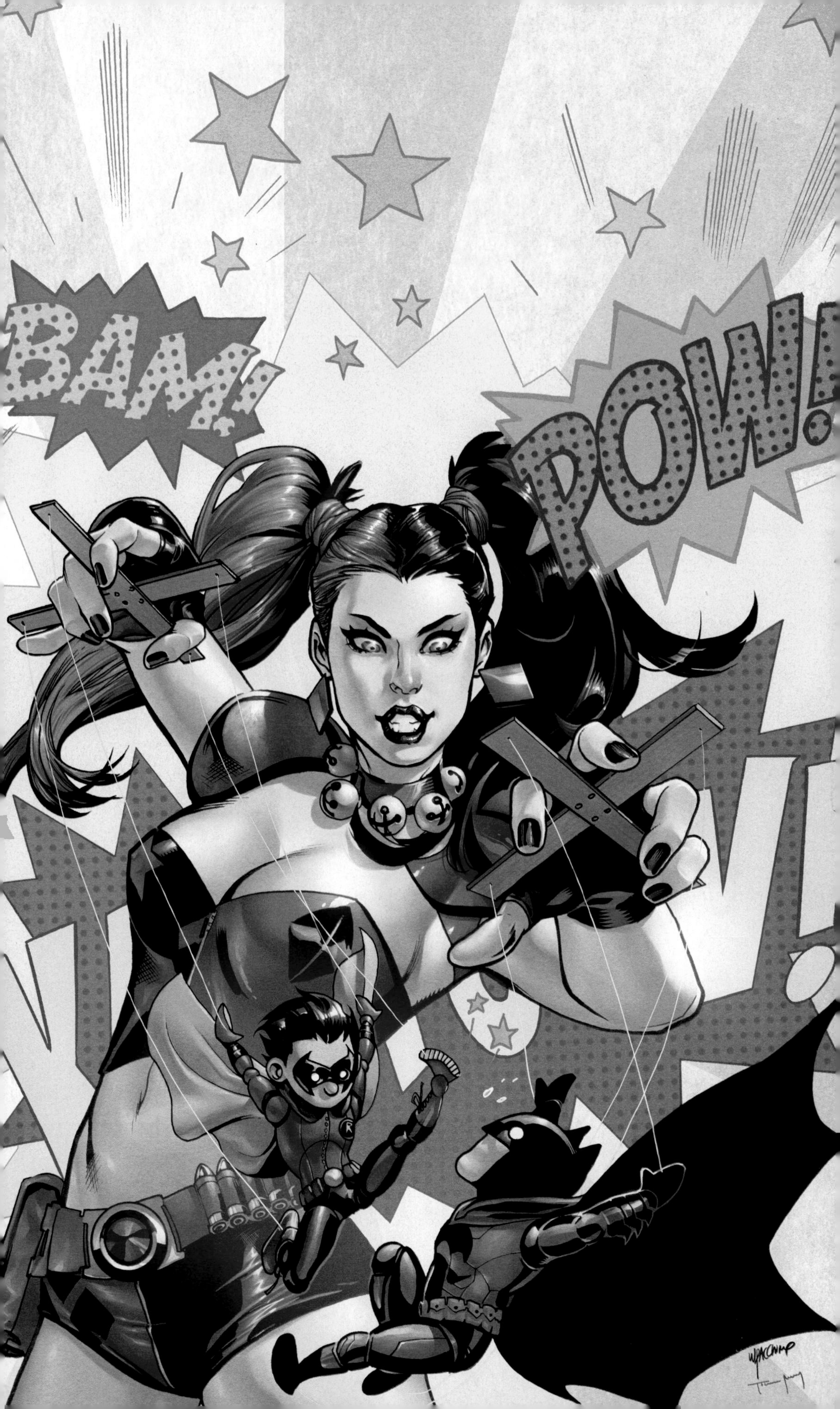
BAM!
POW!

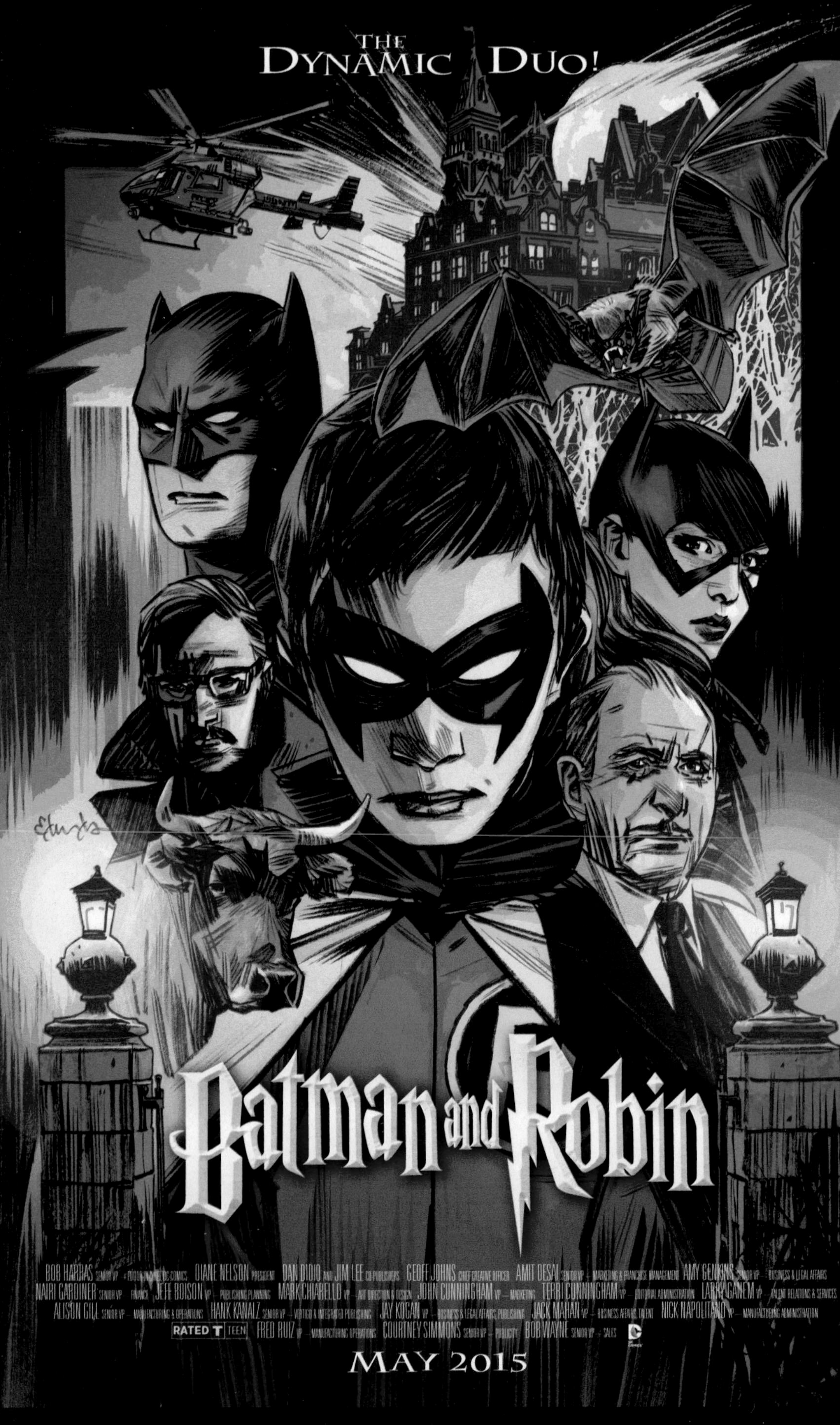
THE DYNAMIC DUO!
Batman and Robin
BOB HARRAS SENIOR VP – EDITOR-IN-CHIEF, DC COMICS DIANE NELSON PRESIDENT DAN DIDIO AND JIM LEE CO-PUBLISHERS GEOFF JOHNS CHIEF CREATIVE OFFICER AMIT DESAI SENIOR VP – MARKETING & FRANCHISE MANAGEMENT AMY GENKINS SENIOR VP – BUSINESS & LEGAL AFFAIRS
NAIRI GARDINER SENIOR VP – FINANCE JEFF BOISON VP – PUBLISHING PLANNING MARK CHIARELLO VP – ART DIRECTION & DESIGN JOHN CUNNINGHAM VP – MARKETING TERRI CUNNINGHAM VP – EDITORIAL ADMINISTRATION LARRY GANEM VP – TALENT RELATIONS & SERVICES
ALISON GILL SENIOR VP – MANUFACTURING & OPERATIONS HANK KANALZ SENIOR VP – VERTIGO & INTEGRATED PUBLISHING JAY KOGAN VP – BUSINESS & LEGAL AFFAIRS, PUBLISHING JACK MAHAN VP – BUSINESS AFFAIRS, TALENT NICK NAPOLITANO VP – MANUFACTURING ADMINISTRATION
RATED T TEEN
FRED RUIZ VP – MANUFACTURING OPERATIONS COURTNEY SIMMONS SENIOR VP – PUBLICITY BOB WAYNE SENIOR VP – SALES
MAY 2015

HELLBAT SKETCHES

CAPE & COWL
FUNCTIONS?

SMOKE SCREEN

BATARANGS
COME OUT OF
CAPE.

DEFENSIVE
SPIKES TO
PREVENT
GRAPPLING

SHIELD

OW!?

SMOKE SCREEN (BLACK)
CAPE, COWL MADE OF
BLACK METAL NANNO BOTS
ACTS LIKE BLACK LIQUID METAL

CAN CHANGE
SHAPE / FORM
SIMPLE WEAPONS
SMOKE SCREEN
ETC

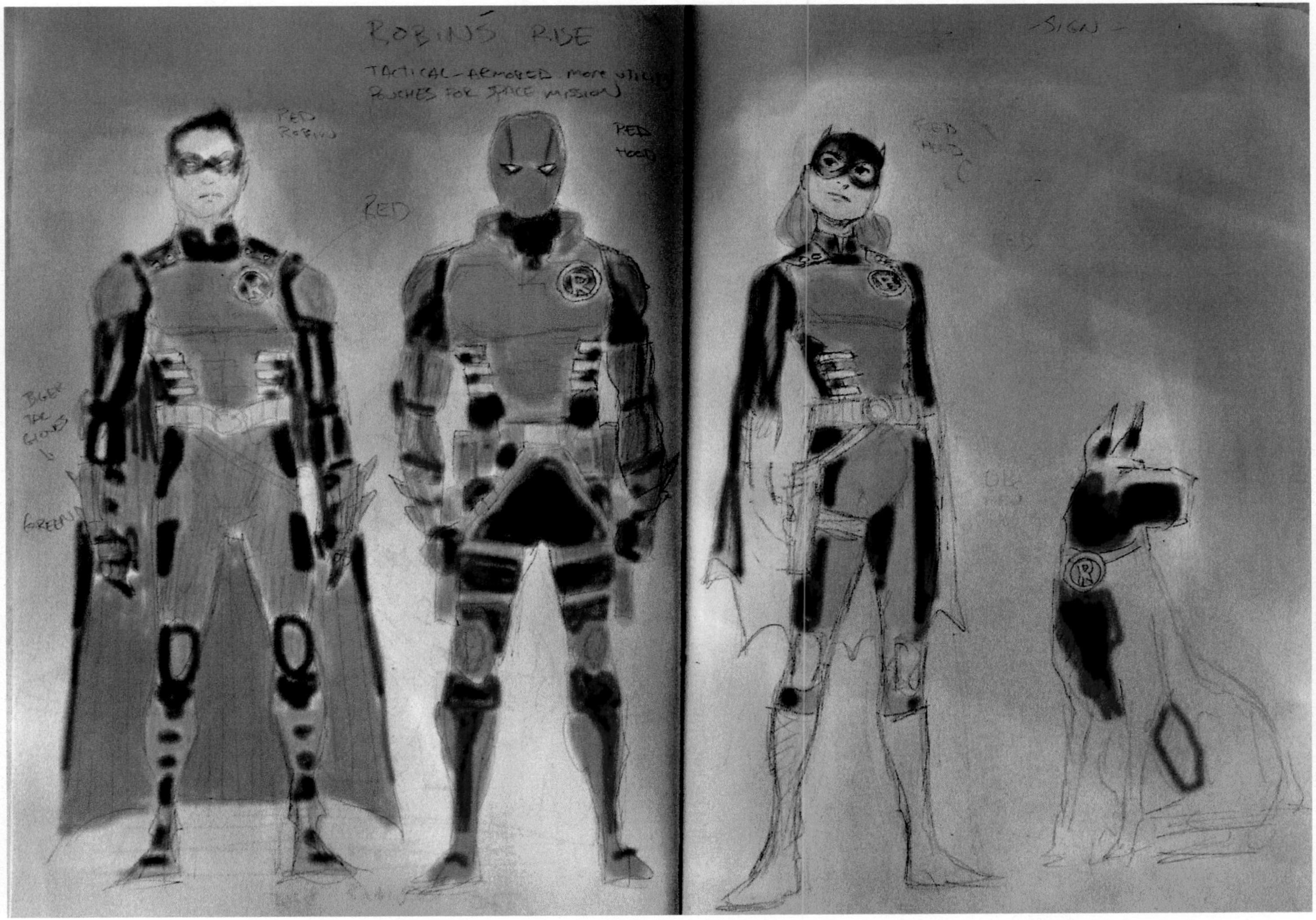
ROBINS RISE
TACTICAL-ARMORED more utility
POUCHES FOR SPACE MISSION
RED ROBIN
RED HOOD
RED
BIGER TAC GLOVES
GREEN
-SIGN-

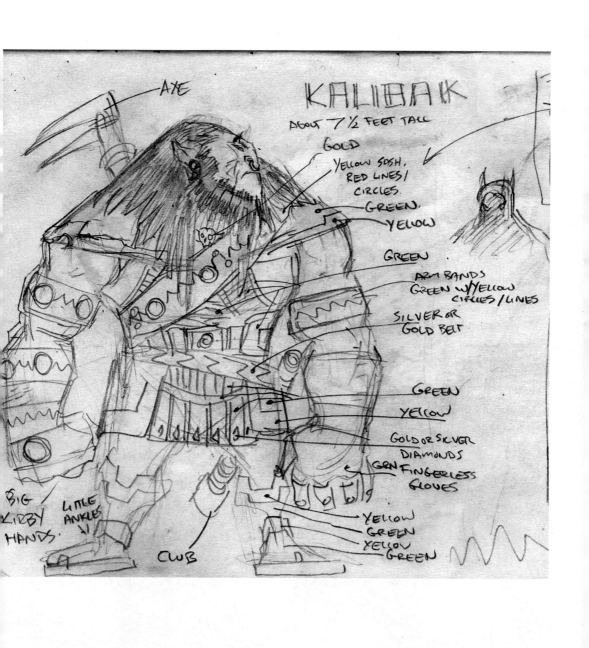

AXE

KALIBAK

ABOUT 7½ FEET TALL

GOLD

YELLOW SASH.
RED LINES/
CIRCLES.
GREEN.
YELLOW

GREEN

ARM BANDS
GREEN w/YELLOW
CIRCLES/LINES

SILVER OR
GOLD BELT

GREEN

YELLOW

GOLD OR SILVER
DIAMONDS

GRN FINGERLESS
GLOVES

YELLOW
GREEN
YELLOW
GREEN

BIG
KIRBY
HANDS.

LITTLE
ANKLES

CLUB

BATMAN AND ROBIN #36 COVER PENCILS

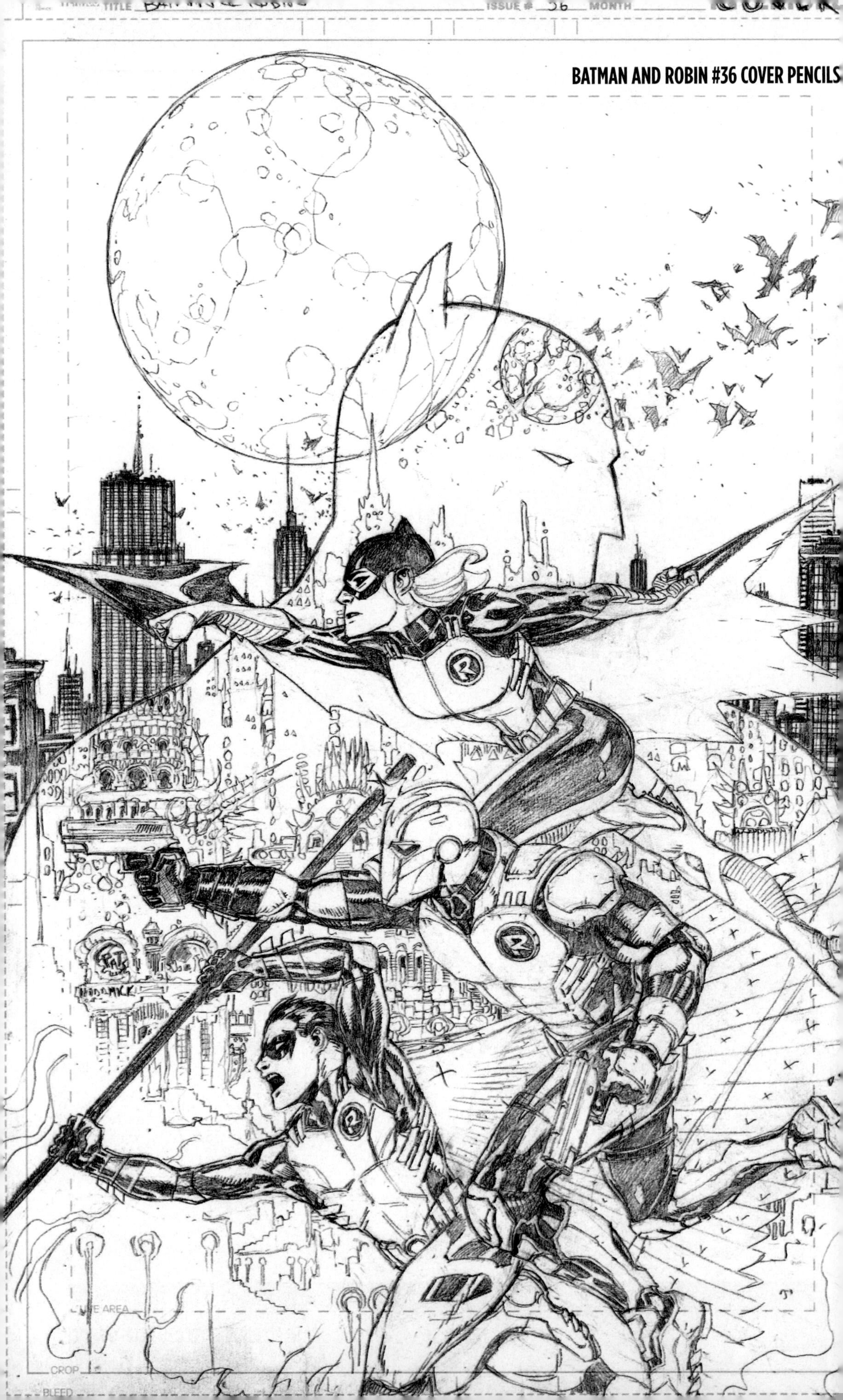
TITLE
ISSUE #
MONTH
CROP
BLEED

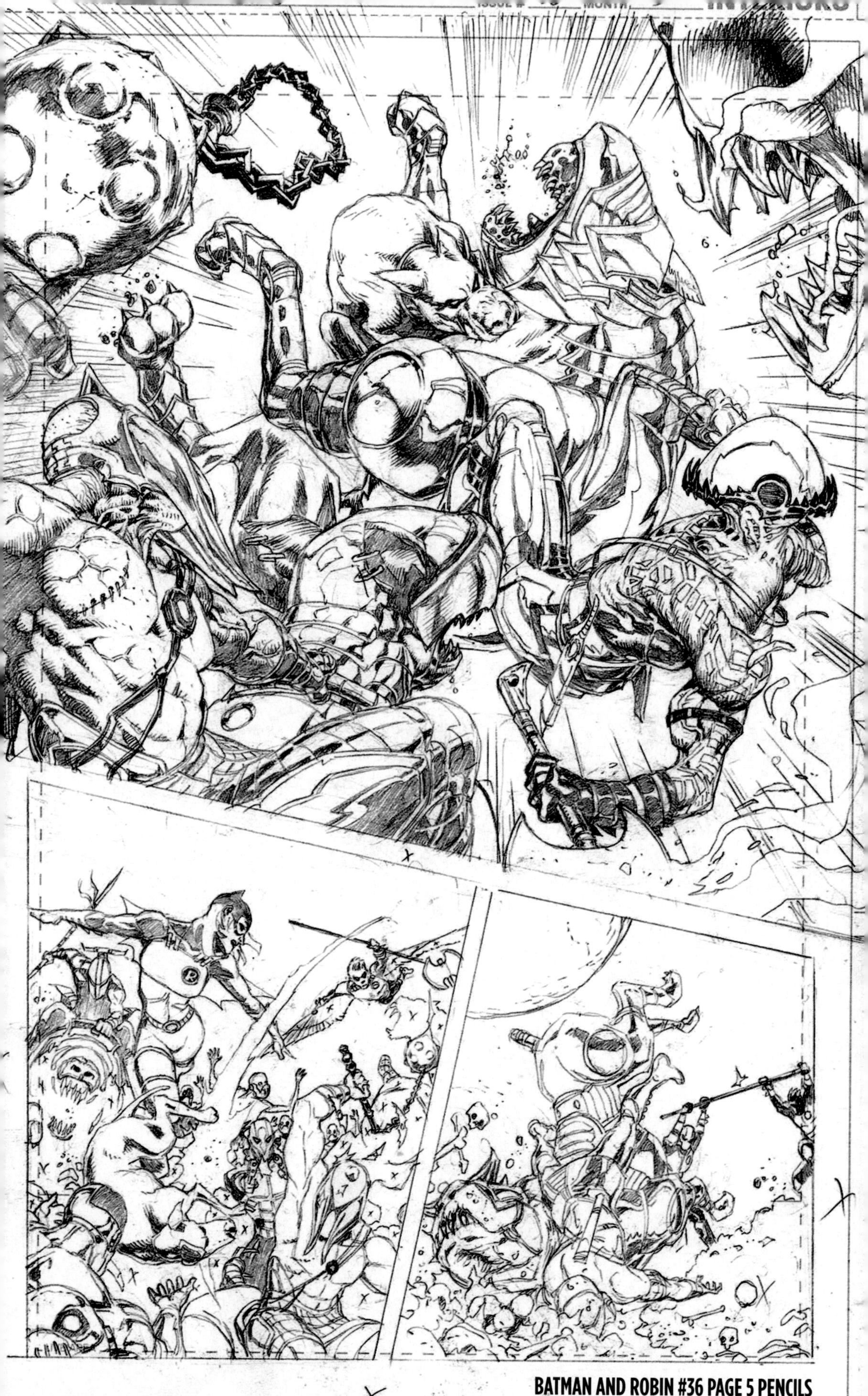

BATMAN AND ROBIN #36 PAGE 5 PENCILS

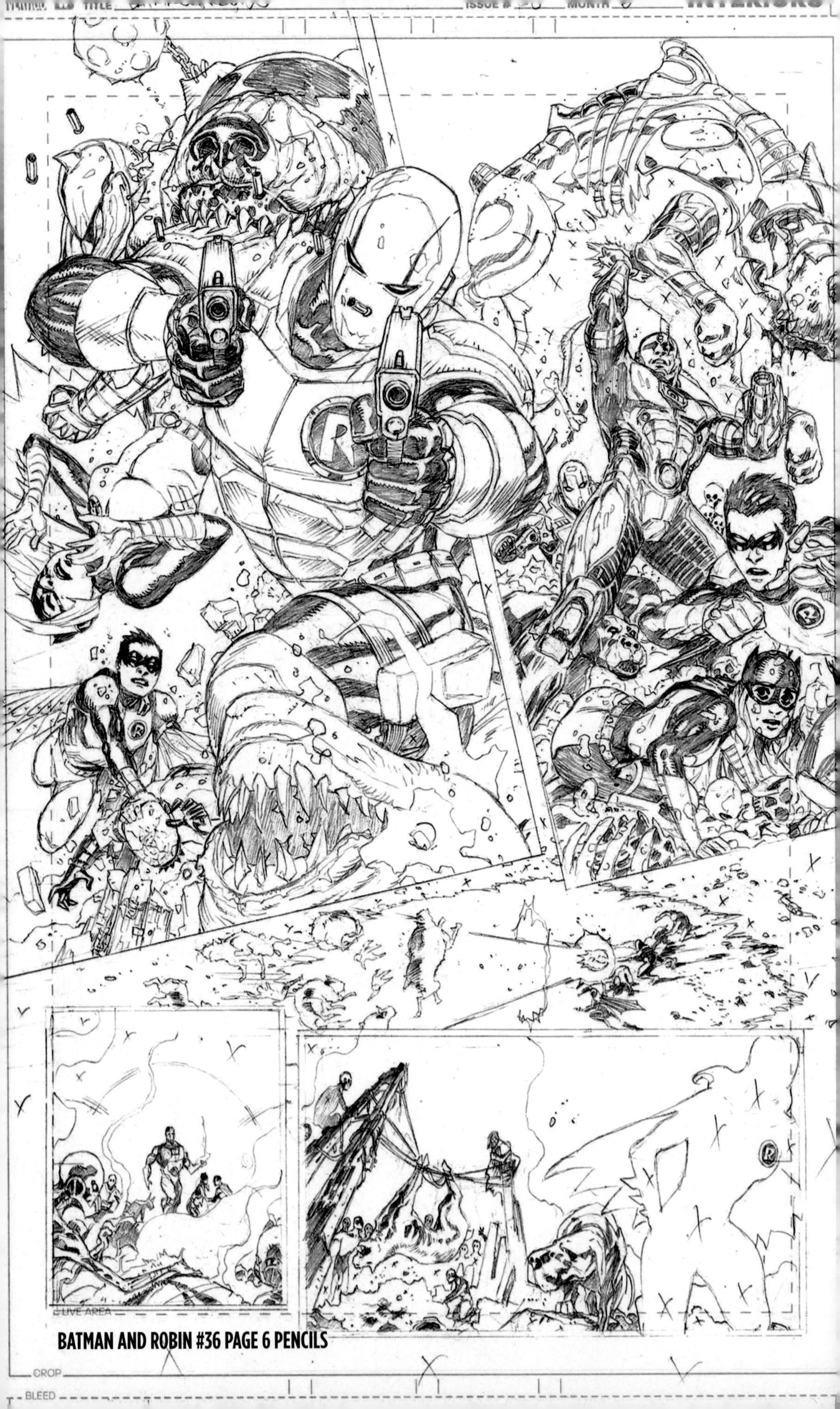
LIVE AREA
CROP
BLEED

BATMAN AND ROBIN #36 PAGE 6 PENCILS

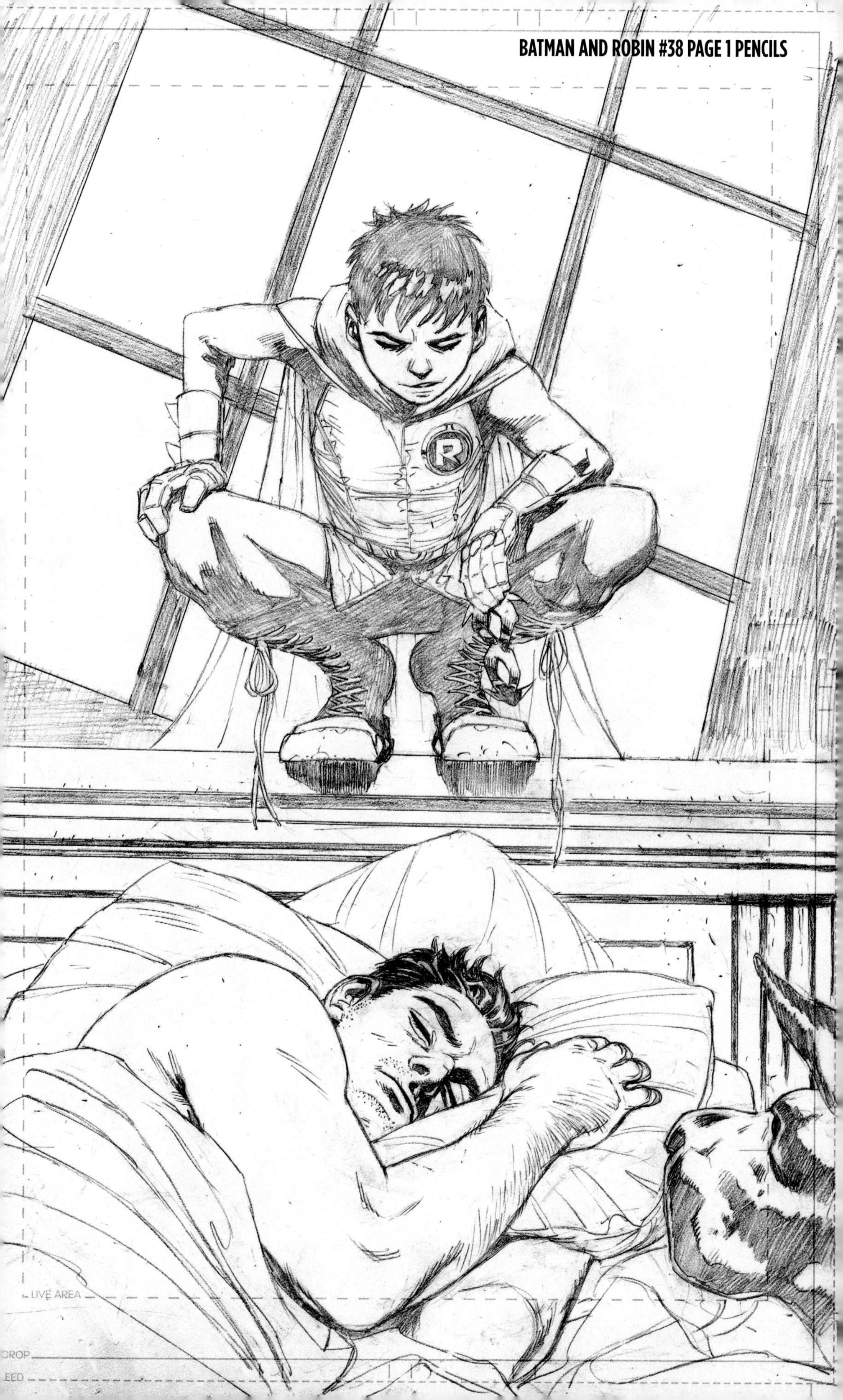

BATMAN AND ROBIN #38 PAGE 1 PENCILS

TITLE BATMAN + ROBIN ISSUE # 40 MONTH INTERIOR

BATMAN AND ROBIN #40 PAGE 20 PENCILS

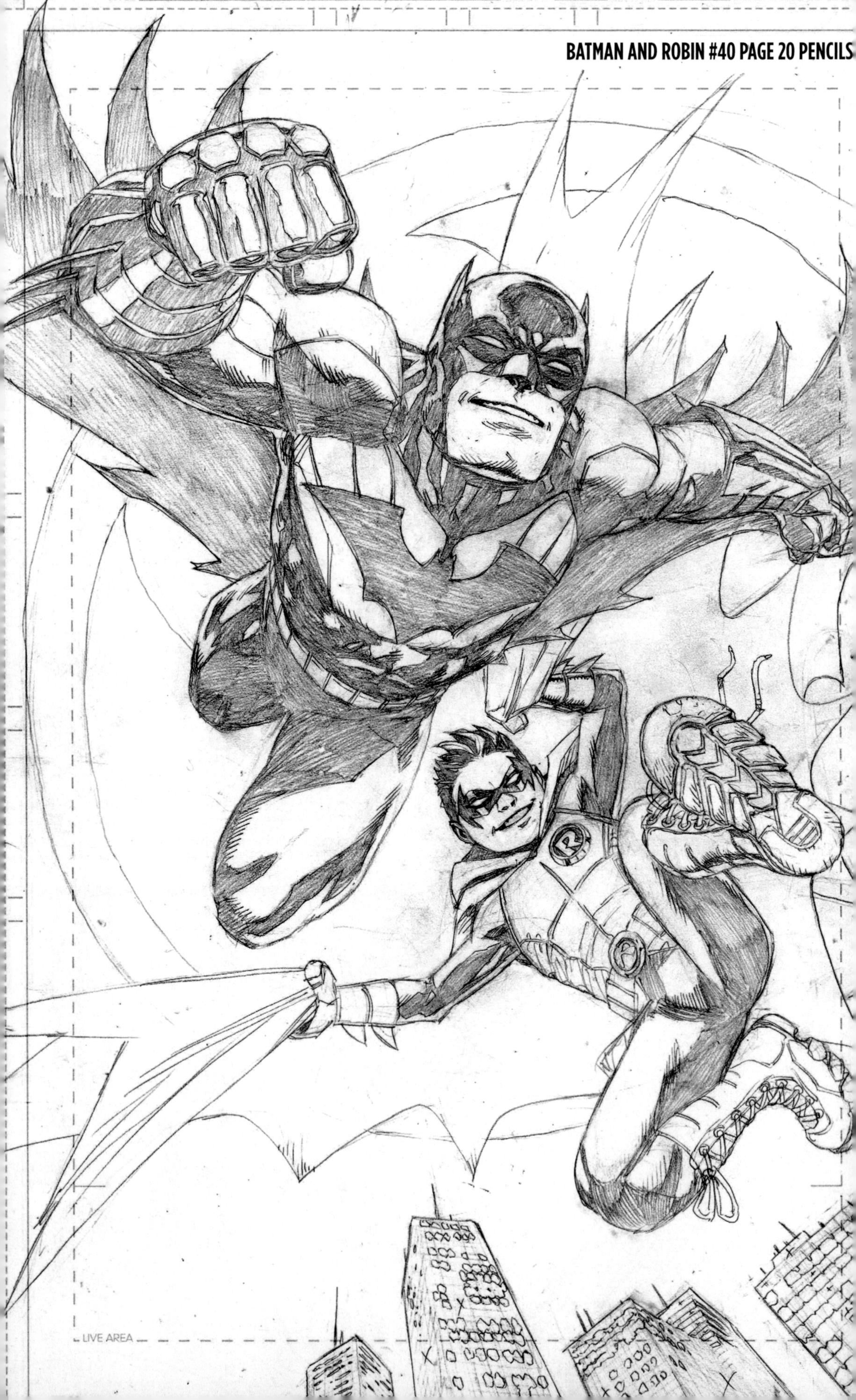
LIVE AREA